P9-CCB-557

Basic THEOLOGY

Basic THEOLOGY

CHARLES
CALDWELL
RYRIE

MOODY PRESS
CHICAGO

ISBN: 0-8024-2734-0

1 3 5 7 9 10 8 6 4 2

Printed in the United States of America

CONTENTS

SECTION V
OUR ADVERSARY THE DEVIL

SECTION VI
DEMONS: UNCLEAN SPIRITS

SECTION VII
MAN: THE IMAGE OF GOD

SECTION VIII
SIN

SECTION IX
JESUS CHRIST OUR LORD

SECTION X
SO GREAT A SALVATION

SECTION XI
THE HOLY SPIRIT

SECTION XII
"I WILL BUILD MY CHURCH"

SECTION XIII
THINGS TO COME

SECTION XIV
CENTRAL PASSAGES

SECTION XV
DEFINITIONS

WHO SHOULD READ THEOLOGY?

Theology is for everyone. Indeed, everyone needs to be a theologian. In reality, everyone *is* a theologian—of one sort or another.

And therein lies the problem. There is nothing wrong with being an amateur theologian or a professional theologian, but there is everything wrong about being an ignorant or a sloppy theologian. Therefore, every Christian should read theology.

Theology simply means thinking about God and expressing those thoughts in some way. There will be a more precise definition in the first chapter, but in this basic sense everyone is a theologian. Even an atheist has a theology. He thinks about God, rejects His existence, and expresses that sometimes in creed and always in lifestyle. The follower of a non-Christian religion has substituted his counterfeit deity for the true God and shows off that theology in various ways.

But almost all the readers of this book will be theists if not also believers in Jesus Christ. So your thoughts, however scattered or systematized, are about the living God, the only true God who exists. Because this is so, there is all the more reason for you to study theology, for all the time and energy you give to thinking about the true God will not only expand your mind but affect your life.

As an example of how theology can affect your life, think about the subject of accountability. All of us have various levels of accountability. We are accountable to ourselves; conscience sees to that. But conscience can be warped, seared, or ignored, thus reducing accountability on that level. We have accountability to society, but different societies have different standards for legality and morality, and an individual can sometimes violate standards and escape accountability. Other units of accountability include family, local church, employment, etc. But believers in the true God recognize that they also have to be accountable to Him. Sometimes we can seem to escape present accountability to God, but no one will escape future accountability, for we will all stand before the judgment seat of Christ. The theology of judgment forces us to think about a facet of God that should be expressed in a sober outlook on life now.

Good theologians come in many shapes. Some are, by the world's evaluation, ignorant; but nevertheless they do understand many truths about God. Others are studious but in a nontechnical way. Still others are highly skilled and widely read. Some are professional theologians; most are not.

This book is written for the most who are not. If I had been writing to professionals, I would have done a number of things differently. I would not have made a conscious effort to keep the language simple and the explanations uncomplicated, since the professional can understand complex language and technical explanations. I would not have used illustrations (though some technical books could well use them!). I would not have kept the footnotes to a minimum. Professionals want to be sure that an author has read everything on a subject (but who has?). At least they want to see proof of a wide range of reading by the quantity of a variety of footnotes, some of which must be very contemporary. I think I have demonstrated in other books that I can do this, but in this one I have chosen to keep footnotes to a minimum. I used them when it was necessary to document a statement the reader might think untrue or to make clear that I was not creating a straw man. But mostly I have used them to indicate books and articles I felt made a helpful contribution to the particular subject under discussion. In that way, it is possible for the reader to pursue a subject further if he desires to.

But if theology is thinking about God and expressing those thoughts, then judge this book on the basis of whether or not it reflects correct thoughts about God and expresses them accurately and plainly to you and in a manner that brings changes in your thinking and living.

The phrase "sound doctrine" that Paul used means healthy doctrine (e.g., 2 Tim. 4:3; Titus 1:9). Healthy doctrine or healthy theology is always expected to result in holy living. When Paul prayed for churches, he prayed for an increase in knowledge, for he realized that this would produce holy living (e.g., Phil. 1:9–11; Col. 1:9–10). Healthy theology is expressed not only in creed but in fruitful living, and holy living must be based on healthy theology.

How theology affects my life or your life is our personal and individual responsibility. But to conform our lives to the image of Christ is the ultimate goal in studying theology. Yet in the final analysis no book can do that. Only God and you can.

Section I
PROLEGOMENA

Chapter 1
CONCEPTS AND DEFINITIONS

Prolegomena, the title of this section, simply means prefatory or preliminary remarks. It furnishes the author with the opportunity to let his readers know something of the general plan he has in mind, both its extent and limitations, as well as some of the presuppositions of his thinking and the procedures he plans to use. Prolegomena serve to orient the readers to what the author has in mind for the book.

I. THE CONCEPT OF THEOLOGY

That a book is a work on theology says something at once about extent, focus, and limitations. The word "theology," from *theos* meaning God and *logos* meaning rational expression, means the rational interpretation of religious faith. Christian theology thus means the rational interpretation of the Christian faith.

At least three elements are included in that general concept of theology.

(1) Theology is intelligible. It can be comprehended by the human mind in an orderly, rational manner.

(2) Theology requires explanation. This, in turn, involves exegesis and systematization.

(3) The Christian faith finds its source in the Bible, so Christian theology will be a Bible-based study. Theology, then, is the discovery, systematizing, and presentation of the truths about God.

II. THE VARIETIES OF THEOLOGY

Theologies can be cataloged in various ways.

(1) By era: i.e., patristic theology, medieval theology, reformation theology, modern theology.

(2) By viewpoint: i.e., Arminian theology, Calvinistic theology, Catholic theology, Barthian theology, liberation theology, etc.

(3) By focus: i.e., historical theology, biblical theology, systematic theology, apologetic theology, exegetical theology, etc. Some of these distinctions are very important to anyone who studies theology.

A. Historical Theology

Historical theology focuses on what those who studied the Bible thought about its teachings either individually or collectively as in the pronouncements of church councils. It shows how the church has formulated both truth and error and serves to guide the theologian in his own understanding and statement of doctrine. A student can be more efficient in coming to his own understanding of truth by knowing the contributions and mistakes of church history. When it seems appropriate I shall include some history of doctrine in this book.

B. Biblical Theology

Though the term biblical theology has been used in various ways, it serves to label a specific focus on the study of theology. In a nontechnical sense it can refer to a pietistic theology (in contrast to a philosophical one), or to a Bible-based theology (in contrast to one that interacts with contemporary thinkers), or to exegetical theology (in contrast to speculative theology). Some contemporary biblical theologies from a liberal perspective fall under this latter category, exegetical, though the exegesis does not faithfully represent the biblical teaching. Often too their works consist of a running commentary through the Bible held together by some large category like kingdom or covenant or God (if Old Testament biblical theology), or categories like the teachings of Jesus, Paul, and primitive Christianity (if New Testament biblical theology).

Technically, biblical theology has a much sharper focus than that. It deals systematically with the historically conditioned progress of the self-revelation of God in the Bible. Four characteristics emerge from this definition.

(1) The results of the study of biblical theology must be presented in a systematic form. In this it is like other areas of biblical and theological studies. The system or scheme in which biblical theology is presented will not necessarily employ the same categories systematic theology uses. It does not have to use them, nor does it have to avoid them.

(2) Biblical theology pays attention to the soil of history in which God's revelation came. It investigates the lives of the writers of the Bible, the circumstances that compelled them to write, and the historic situation of the recipients of their writings.

(3) Biblical theology studies revelation in the progressive sequence in which it was given. It recognizes that revelation was not completed

in a single act on God's part but unfolded in a series of successive stages using a variety of people. The Bible is a record of the progress of revelation, and biblical theology focuses on that. By contrast, systematic theology views revelation as a completed whole.

(4) Biblical theology finds its source material in the Bible. Actually orthodox systematic theologies do too. This is not to say that biblical or systematic theologies could not or do not draw material from other sources, but the theology or doctrine itself does not come from anywhere but the Bible.

C. Systematic Theology

Systematic theology correlates the data of biblical revelation as a whole in order to exhibit systematically the total picture of God's self-revelation.

Systematic theology may include historical backgrounds, apologetics and defense, and exegetical work, but it focuses on the total structure of biblical doctrine.

To summarize: Theology is the discovery, systematizing, and presentation of the truths about God. Historical theology accomplishes this by focusing on what others throughout history have said about these truths. Biblical theology does this by surveying the progressive revelation of God's truth. Systematic theology presents the total structure.

Chapter 2
SOME PRESUPPOSITIONS

I. THE BASIC ONE

Consciously or unconsciously everyone operates on the basis of some presuppositions. The atheist who says there is no God has to believe that basic presupposition. And believing it, he then views the world, mankind, and the future in entirely different ways than the theist. The agnostic not only affirms we cannot know God, but he must believe that as basic to his entire outlook on the world and life. If we can know about the true God then his whole system is smashed. The theist believes there is a God. He mounts confirmatory evidence to support that belief, but basically he believes.

The trinitarian believes God is Triunity. That is a belief gleaned from the Bible. Therefore, he also believes the Bible to be true.

This stands as the watershed presupposition. If the Bible is not true, then trinitarianism is untrue and Jesus Christ is not who He claimed to be. We learn nothing about the Trinity or Christ from nature or from the human mind. And we cannot be certain that what we learn from the Bible about the Triune God is accurate unless we believe that our source itself is accurate. Thus the belief in the truthfulness of the Bible is the basic presupposition. This will be fully discussed under inspiration and inerrancy.

II. THE INTERPRETIVE ONES

If our source material is so crucial, then we must be concerned how we approach and use it. Accurate theology rests on sound exegesis. Exegetical studies must be made before theological systematization, just as bricks have to be made before a building can be built.

A. The Necessity of Normal, Plain Interpretation

Though a more thorough discussion of hermeneutics will appear in section III, we need to state here the importance of normal interpretation as the basis for proper exegesis. In giving us the revelation of

Himself, God desired to communicate, not obscure, the truth. So we approach the interpretation of the Bible presupposing the use of normal canons of interpretation. Remember that when symbols, parables, types, etc. are used they depend on an underlying literal sense for their very existence, and their interpretation must always be controlled by the concept that God communicates in a normal, plain, or literal manner. Ignoring this will result in the same kind of confused exegesis that characterized the patristic and medieval interpreters.

B. The Priority of the New Testament

All Scripture is inspired and profitable, but the New Testament has greater priority as the source of doctrine. Old Testament revelation was preparatory and partial, but New Testament revelation is climactic and complete. The doctrine of the Trinity, for instance, while allowed for in the Old Testament, was not revealed until the New Testament. Or, think how much difference exists between what is taught in the Old and New Testaments concerning atonement, justification, and resurrection. To say this is not to minimize what is taught in the Old Testament or to imply that it is any less inspired, but it is to say that in the progressive unfolding of God's revelation the Old Testament occupies a prior place chronologically and thus a preparatory and incomplete place theologically. Old Testament theology has its place, but it is incomplete without the contribution of New Testament truth.

C. The Legitimacy of Proof Texts

Liberals and Barthians have often criticized conservatives for using proof texts to substantiate their conclusions. Why do they complain? Simply because citing proof texts will lead to conservative, not liberal, conclusions. They charge it with being an illegitimate, unscholarly methodology, but it is no more illegitimate than footnotes are in a scholarly work!

To be sure, proof texts must be used properly, just as footnotes must be. They must actually be used to mean what they say; they must not be used out of context; they must not be used in part when the whole might change the meaning; and Old Testament proof texts particularly must not be forced to include truth that was only revealed later in the New Testament.

III. THE SYSTEMATIZING ONES

A. The Necessity of a System

The difference between exegesis and theology is the system used. Exegesis analyzes; theology correlates those analyses. Exegesis relates the meanings of texts; theology interrelates those meanings. The exegete strives to present the meaning of truth; the theologian, the system of truth. Theology's goal, whether biblical or systematic theology, is the systematization of the teachings under consideration.

B. The Limitations of a Theological System

In a word, the limitations of a theological system must coincide with the limitations of biblical revelation. In an effort to present a complete system, theologians are often tempted to fill in the gaps in the biblical evidence with logic or implications that may not be warranted.

Logic and implications do have their appropriate place. God's revelation is orderly and rational, so logic has a proper place in the scientific investigation of that revelation. When words are put together in sentences, those sentences take on implications that the theologian must try to understand.

However, when logic is used to create truth, as it were, then the theologian will be guilty of pushing his system beyond the limitations of biblical truth. Sometimes this is motivated by the desire to answer questions that the Scripture does not answer. In such cases (and there are a number of crucial ones in the Bible) the best answer is silence, not clever logic, or almost invisible implications, or wishful sentimentality. Examples of particularly tempting areas include sovereignty and responsibility, the extent of the Atonement, and the salvation of infants who die.

IV. THE PERSONAL ONES

One should also be able to presuppose certain matters about the student of theology.

A. He Must Believe

Of course unbelievers can write and study theology, but a believer has a dimension and perspective on the truth of God that no unbeliever can have. The deep things of God are taught by the Spirit, whom an unbeliever does not have (1 Cor. 2:10–16).

Believers need to have faith also, for some areas of God's revelation will not be fully understood by our finite minds.

B. He Must Think

Ultimately the believer must try to think theologically. This involves thinking exegetically (to understand the precise meaning), thinking systematically (in order to correlate facts thoroughly), thinking critically (to evaluate the priority of the related evidence), and thinking synthetically (to combine and present the teaching as a whole).

Theology and exegesis should always interact. Exegesis does not provide all the answers; when there can legitimately be more than one exegetical option, theology will decide which to prefer. Some passages, for example, could seem to teach eternal security or not; one's theological system will make the decision. On the other hand, no theological system should be so hardened that it is not open to change or refinement from the insights of exegesis.

C. He Must Depend

Intellect alone does not make a theologian. If we believe in the reality of the teaching ministry of the Holy Spirit, then certainly this must be a factor in studying theology (John 16:12–15). The content of the Spirit's curriculum encompasses all the truth, focusing especially on the revelation of Christ Himself which is, of course, found in the Scriptures. To experience this will require a conscious attitude of dependence on the Spirit, which will be reflected in humility of mind and a diligent study of what the Spirit has taught others throughout history. Inductive Bible study is a beneficial way to study, but to do it *only* is to ignore the results of the work of others, and to do it *always* can be an inefficient repetition of what others have already done.

D. He Must Worship

Studying theology is no mere academic exercise, though it is that. It is an experience that changes, convicts, broadens, challenges, and ultimately leads to a deep reverence for God. Worship means to recognize the worth of the object worshiped. How can any mortal put his mind to the study of God and fail to increase his recognition of His worth?

Chapter 3
THE QUESTION OF AUTHORITY

Authority constitutes the foundational principle in the study of theology. Presumably all who operate within the broadest concept of "Christian" theology would acknowledge the authority of God as the supreme norm for truth. However, how the authority of God is conceived and expressed varies considerably within the "Christian" spectrum.

I. AUTHORITY IN LIBERALISM

Subjectivism stands as the hallmark of liberalism, though the focus of that subjectivism may vary with different people. So one person could say, "The Word of God includes 'any act of God by which communication occurs between God and man.'"[1] That communication comes through human reason, feelings, or conscience.

A. Reason

Reason has always occupied a dominant place in liberal thought. Of course it is within the sphere of reason that concepts are formed that are the basis of communication from one person to another. Reason is a necessary channel for giving and receiving truth, and the evangelical recognizes that. But liberalism has certainly made human reason the judge of truth and often the creator of truth. Reason becomes autonomous, governed by no higher or outside authority, but also severely limited by its finitude and fallibility.

B. Feelings

As a reaction against rationalism, Schleiermacher (1768–1834) developed his theology of feeling. He emphasized the analysis of religious experience and based religion on feeling or awareness. In effect, theology became anthropology and psychology. Because of this, Karl Barth considered Schleiermacher to be the epitome of religious liberalism.

C. Conscience

This form of liberalism emphasizes conscience as the basis of authority. Our knowledge is unreliable and limited, so the basic moral instincts of the human soul become the basis for authority. Immanuel Kant (1724–1804) was the leader in this form of thought. Once again, theology had become anthropology.

In all forms of liberalism, human nature in one aspect or another is the source of religious truth. The Bible, then, is viewed as the product of human reasoning containing man's thoughts about God, himself, and this world. It records the historical development of man's religious experiences and beliefs, and is not, as conservatives believe, the record of a message from a transcendent God who broke into the course of history.

II. AUTHORITY IN NEO-ORTHODOXY

Neo-orthodoxy has sometimes been classed with liberalism and sometimes with conservatism. The reason for this confusion is that, on the one hand, it broke with liberalism by insisting that God, not man, must initiate revelation (and thus seemed to be conservative); while, on the other hand, it continued to teach liberal views concerning the Bible (and thus seemed to be liberal).

The basis of authority in neo-orthodoxy, at least as expressed by Karl Barth (1886–1968), is the Word. However, the Word is mainly Christ. The Bible witnesses to the Word, and does so fallibly, and Christian proclamation is a word about the Word.

The sovereign God took the initiative in revealing Himself, centering primarily in the revelation in Christ. The years of Christ's life exhibited the epitome of revelation, and His death was the climax of revelation. The Bible witnesses to the revelation of God, even though it is interpreted by all the canons of liberalism. The Bible, then, has no absolute authority, but only instrumental authority, since it serves as the fallible instrument by which we encounter Christ the Word. And it is that encounter of faith at the point of "crisis" in which God communicates Himself. That is absolute truth.

Though neo-orthodoxy seeks objectivity in God's sovereign initiative, it practices subjectivism in the experiences of faith's encounters. Even though the Bible is involved in those experiences, it is not allowed to be the ultimate judge of those experiences. Neo-orthodoxy lacks an external, objective standard of authority.

III. AUTHORITY IN CONSERVATISM

In conservatism the basis of authority is external to man and objective.

A. Conservative Catholicism

In Roman Catholicism authority ultimately rests in the church itself. To be sure, the Bible is believed, but it must be interpreted by the church. Furthermore, the traditions of the church are, along with the Bible, a source of divine revelation. Ecumenical councils and popes have from time to time made pronouncements that are considered infallible and therefore binding on church members.

The Eastern Church is similar as far as finding its authority in tradition, the church itself, and the Bible. Even though evangelicals reject tradition as authoritative, it should be recognized that Catholicism's authority is not found in man, as liberalism teaches.

B. Conservative Protestantism

"Conservative" eliminates liberalism's humanistic and subjective bases of authority, and "protestantism" removes the church as a base of authority. So one would agree that "orthodoxy is that branch of Christendom which limits the ground of religious authority to the Bible."[2] The Scriptures contain the objective revelation of God and are therefore the basis of authority for the conservative Protestant.

To be sure, understanding God's revelation in the Bible involves using the rational processes of a redeemed mind, a commitment of faith in matters not revealed or not understood, a dependence on the teaching ministry of the Holy Spirit, a conscience clear before God, and some insight into the lessons of history.

Sometimes in practice, though not in theory, conservatives can and do deny that the Bible is their sole basis of authority.

(1) In practice, some traditions or denominations give their creeds coordinate authority with the Bible. Creeds can provide helpful statements of truth, but creeds can never be the authoritative judge of truth. Creedal statements must always be considered fallible, in need of possible revision, and subservient to biblical authority.

(2) In practice, some groups give tradition and accepted practice coordinate authority with the Bible. A church has a divine mandate to set authoritative guidelines for its members (Heb. 13:7, 17), but these too are fallible, in need of periodic revision, and always subservient to biblical authority.

(3) In practice, some conservatives make religious experience authoritative. Healthy experience is the fruit of allegiance to biblical authority, but all experiences must be guided, governed, and guarded by

the Bible. To make experience normative and authoritative is to commit the same error as liberalism by replacing an objective criterion with subjective existentialism.

Observe the point of this chart: when objective authority is supplemented, compromised, or abandoned, theism will be weakened or even relinquished.

ORTHODOXY	NEO-ORTHODOXY	LIBERALISM	BELIEVES IN:
x			objective
x	x		transcendent
x	x	x	theism

Notes

1. L. Harold DeWolf, *The Case for Theology in Liberal Perspective* (Philadelphia: Westminster, 1959), 17.
2. Edward John Carnell, *The Case for Orthodox Theology* (Philadelphia: Westminster, 1969), 13.

Section II
THE LIVING AND TRUE GOD

Chapter 4
THE KNOWLEDGE OF GOD

I. THE POSSIBILITY OF THE KNOWLEDGE OF GOD

Unquestionably the knowledge of God is desirable; the religious yearnings of mankind testify to that. But is it possible?

The Scriptures attest to two facts: the incomprehensibility of God and the knowability of God. To say that He is incomprehensible is to assert that the mind cannot grasp the knowledge of Him. To say that He is knowable is to claim that He can be known. Both are true, though neither in an absolute sense. To say that God is incomprehensible is to assert that man cannot know everything about Him. To say that He is knowable is not to assert that man can know everything about Him.

Both truths are affirmed in the Scriptures: His incomprehensibility in verses like Job 11:7 and Isaiah 40:18, and His knowability in verses like John 14:7; 17:3; and 1 John 5:20.

II. CHARACTERISTICS OF THE KNOWLEDGE OF GOD

The knowledge of God may be characterized in relation to its source, its content, its progressiveness, and its purposes.

A. Its Source

God Himself is the Source of our knowledge of Him. To be sure, all truth is God's truth. But that cliché should be more carefully stated and used than it generally is. Only true truth comes from God, for since sin entered the stream of history man has created that which he calls truth but which is not. Furthermore, he has perverted, blunted, diluted, and corrupted that which was originally true truth that did come from God. For us today the only infallible canon for determining true truth is the written Word of God. Nature, though it does reveal some things about God, is limited and can be misread by mankind. The human mind, though often brilliant in what it can achieve, suffers limitations and darkening. Human experiences, even religious ones, lack reliability as sources of the true knowledge of God unless they conform to the Word of God.

Certainly the knowledge of what is true religion must come from God. In a past dispensation Judaism was revealed as God's true religion. Today Judaism is not the true religion; only Christianity is. And the true knowledge of Christianity has been revealed through Christ and the apostles. One of the purposes of our Lord's incarnation was to reveal God (John 1:18; 14:7). The promise of the coming of the Spirit after the ascension of Christ included further revelation concerning Him and the Father (John 16:13–15; Acts 1:8). The Holy Spirit opens the Scriptures for the believer so that he can know God more fully.

B. Its Content

A full knowledge of God is both factual and personal. To know facts about a person without knowing the person is limiting; to know a person without knowing facts about that one is shallow. God has revealed many facts about Himself, all of which are important in making our personal relationship with Him close, intelligent, and useful. Had He only revealed facts without making it possible to know Him personally, such factual knowledge would have little, certainly not eternal, usefulness. Just as with human relationships, a divine-human relationship cannot begin without knowledge of some minimal truths about the Person; then the personal relationship generates the desire to know more facts, which in turn deepens the relationship, and so on. This kind of cycle ought to be the experience of every student of theology; a knowledge about God should deepen our relationship with Him, which in turn increases our desire to know more about Him.

C. Its Progressiveness

The knowledge of God and His works was revealed progressively throughout history. The most obvious proof is to compare incomplete Jewish theology with the fuller revelation of Christian theology in respect, for example, to such doctrines as the Trinity, Christology, the Holy Spirit, Resurrection, and eschatology. To trace that progressiveness is the task of biblical theology.

D. Its Purposes

1. To lead people to the possession of eternal life (John 17:3; 1 Tim. 2:4).

2. To foster Christian growth (2 Pet. 3:18), with doctrinal knowledge (John 7:17; Rom. 6:9, 16; Eph. 1:18) and with a discerning lifestyle (Phil. 1:9–10; 2 Pet.1:5).

3. To warn of judgment to come (Hos. 4:6; Heb. 10:26–27).

4. To generate true worship of God (Rom. 11:33–36).

III. PREREQUISITES TO THE KNOWLEDGE OF GOD

A. God Initiated His Self-Revelation

The knowledge of God differs from all other knowledge in that man can have this knowledge only as far as God reveals it. If God did not initiate the revelation of Himself, there would be no way for man to know Him. Therefore, a human being must put himself under God who is the object of his knowledge. In other scholarly endeavors, the human being often places himself above the object of his investigation, but not so in the study of God.

B. God Gave Language for Communication

Certainly an essential part of God's revelation is a provision of means for communicating that revelation. Also the record of the personal revelation of God in Christ necessitates some means of recording and communicating that revelation. For this purpose God gave language. He devised it and gave it to the first man and woman in order that He might communicate His instructions to them (Gen. 1:28–30) and that they might communicate with Him (3:8–13). It also seemed to have a part in their subduing the unfallen creation and giving names to the animals. Even after the division of the one original language into many at Babel, languages served as the means of communication on all levels. We can certainly believe that the omniscient God made provision for languages that were sufficient to communicate His self-revelation to man.

C. He Created Man in His Image

When God created man in His image and likeness He made him, like Himself, a rational being with intelligence. To be sure, human intelligence is not the same as divine intelligence, but it is a real intelligence, not fictitious. Therefore, humans have the ability to understand the meaning of words and the logic of sentences and paragraphs. Sin has removed the guarantee that human understanding is always reliable, but it does not eradicate a human being's ability to understand.

D. He Gave the Holy Spirit

To believers God has given His Holy Spirit to reveal the things of God (John 16:13–15; 1 Cor. 2:10). This does not make the believer infallible, but it can give him the ability to distinguish truth from error (1 John 2:27).

These works of God make it possible for us to know and obey the many commands in Scripture to know Him (Rom. 6:16; 1 Cor. 3:16; 5:6; 6:19; James 4:4).

Chapter 5
THE REVELATION OF GOD

Historically, the two avenues through which God has taken the initiative to reveal Himself have been labeled general and special revelation. General revelation includes all that God has revealed in the world around us, including man, while special revelation includes various means He used to communicate His message in what was codified in the Bible. General revelation is sometimes called natural theology, and special revelation is called revealed theology. But, of course, what is revealed in nature is also revealed in theology. Some writers use the labels prelapsarian for general revelation and postlapsarian or soteric for special revelation. However, both general and special revelation are (a) from God and (b) about God.

In this chapter we shall discuss general revelation mostly, leaving other aspects of the doctrine of revelation to section III. General revelation provides evidences for the existence of God. Special revelation, on the other hand, generally assumes His existence.

I. CHARACTERISTICS OF GENERAL REVELATION

General revelation is exactly that—general. It is general in its scope; that is, it reaches to all people (Matt. 5:45; Acts 14:17). It is general in geography; that is, it encompasses the entire globe (Ps. 19:2). It is general in its methodology; that is, it employs universal means like the heat of the sun (vv. 4–6) and human conscience (Rom. 2:14–15). Simply because it is a revelation that affects all people wherever they are and whenever they have lived it can bring light and truth to all, or, if rejected, it brings condemnation.

II. AVENUES OF GENERAL REVELATION

General revelation comes to mankind in several ways.

A. Through Creation

1. Statement. Simply stated, this line of evidence (the cosmological argument for the existence of God) points out that the universe around us is an effect that requires an adequate cause.

2. *Presuppositions*. This line of evidence depends on three presuppositions: (a) every effect has a cause; (b) the effect caused depends on the cause for its existence; and (c) nature cannot originate itself.

3. *Development*. If something now exists (the cosmos) then either it came from nothing or it came from something that must be eternal. The something eternal in the second option could either be the cosmos itself, which would have to be eternal, or chance as an eternal principle, or God the eternal Being.

To say that the cosmos came from nothing means it was self-created. This is a logical contradiction, because for something to be self-created it must exist and not exist at the same time in the same way. Furthermore, self-creation has never been scientifically demonstrated and observed.

A variation of the view that holds to the eternality of matter is the Steady State Theory, which suggests that matter is constantly created near the center of the universe and destroyed at the outer perimeter of space. However, there is no evidence to support this theory, and if it were true it would violate the law of the conservation of mass and energy.

Does not the matter of cause and effect also apply to God? Is He not also an effect that required a cause? The answer is no, because God is not an effect (an effect being something that requires a cause) because He is eternal.

If the cosmos did not generate itself, then there must be something eternal that caused it. One option is that the cosmic process itself is eternal, an option scarcely held. Rather almost all hold that the universe had a beginning, however long ago it may have been.

Another option is that there is some eternal principle of chance or blind intelligence. To believe this option requires a large measure of faith. It can be demonstrated mathematically that random chance could not have produced what we observe today in the universe. But even if it could produce molecules and atoms, the "stuff" of the universe, could such a nonliving principle also produce the soul and spirit facets of life?

The third option is the theistic one; that is, the eternal Being that caused the cosmos is God. This does not mean that the universe reveals all the details of the character of that eternal Being, but it does mean that there is a living, powerful, intelligent Being who caused the universe. Living, because nonlife cannot produce life. Powerful, because of the very nature of what was formed. Intelligent, because of the order and arrangement of the cosmos, things that chance could not generate.

4. Scripture. Two key passages of Scripture show creation to be a channel of revelation.

a. Psalm 19:1–6. In this psalm David wrote of (1) the continuousness of the revelation through creation (vv. 1–2). The verbs express continuous action, indicating that the heavens, the expanse, day, and night continually tell of God's glory. He also wrote that (2) the center or arena of this revelation is the universe, the heavens and the earth (v. 4), (3) the character of this revelation is quite clear though nonverbal (v. 3), and (4) the coverage is everywhere and to everybody (vv. 4–6). It covers the entire earth, and every person can know it. Most can see the sun and the cycle of day and night, but even blind people can feel the heat of the sun (v. 6). This revelation ought to raise questions in people's minds. Where does the heat come from? Who made the sun? (5) Also, the content of this revelation is twofold. It tells something about the glory of God and the greatness of God.

b. Romans 1:18–32. In this key passage the emphasis is on the revelation of the wrath of God because mankind rejects what can be known of Him through the avenue of creation.

(1) The revelation of His wrath (v. 18). God's wrath is revealed against all who suppress truth and practice ungodliness. The particulars of how His wrath is revealed are listed in verses 24–32.

(2) The reasons for His wrath (vv. 19–23). The reasons are two: something can be known about God, but rather than receiving that truth, people rejected the revelation and, indeed, perverted it. "What has been made" (v. 20), the cosmos, clearly reveals (and has since the beginning of Creation) God's power and divine nature. In other words, all mankind should know from observing the universe around it that there exists a supreme Being. Instead mankind rejects that truth and makes idols over which people are supreme.

(3) The result of His wrath (vv. 24–32). Because man rejected general revelation, God gave him over (vv. 24, 26, 28). Some think this means a permissive giving over of people so that they suffer the retributive consequences of their sin. But the verb is active voice in verses 24, 26, and 28. Others take the verb in a privative sense; that is, God deprived man of His work of common grace. Still others feel this is a positive and judicial act on God's part, giving people over to judgment. This includes the privative sense but is more active than the permis-

sive viewpoint. It understands that at the same time people are responsible for their sinful actions (Eph. 4:19 uses the same verb). Man is justly condemned because he does not receive what God does tell him about Himself through the Creation.

Norman Geisler has restated the cosmological argument as follows:

(a) Some limited, changing being(s) exist. To deny this requires an affirmation from an existing being, so it is self-defeating.

(b) The present existence of every limited, changing being is caused by another. The potentiality for existence can only be actualized by some existence beyond it.

(c) There cannot be an infinite regress of causes of being.

(d) Therefore, there is a first Cause of the present existence of these beings.

(e) This first Cause must be infinite, necessary, eternal, simple, unchangeable, and one.

(f) By comparing the Being supported by this line of argumentation with the God of the Scriptures, we conclude they are identical.[1]

THE COSMOLOGICAL ARGUMENT

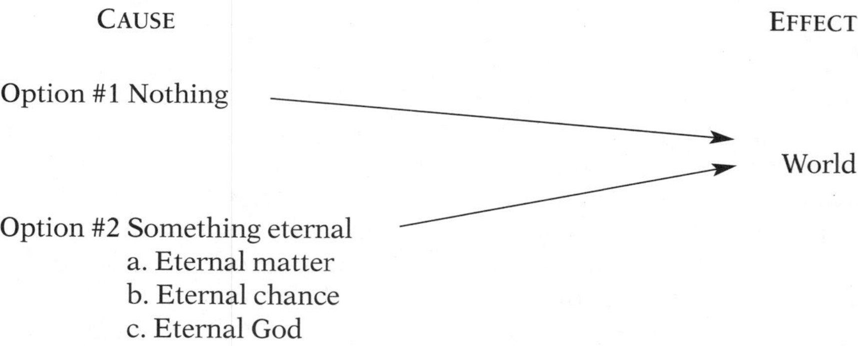

B. Through Organization

1. Statement. The purpose, order, and design we observe in the world calls for a designer. The most popular presentation of this teleological argument was in *William Paley's Natural Theology* (1802), including his illustration of the organization of a watch demanding a watchmaker. Likewise, the organization of the world requires someone who planned it.

2. Development. To be most effective the teleological argument should focus on the broader aspects of design in nature rather than details. To use one of J. Oliver Buswell's illustrations, the fact that no two snowflakes are alike is much less evidential of God's purpose and design for the world than is the important place snow occupies in the cycle of seasons and provision of moisture for the earth.[2] Furthermore, some of the specifics in nature do not make sense to us, often because of the working of evil. But the overall picture is one of order and design. Random action could never have produced the highly integrated organization that we observe in the world.

3. Scripture. Psalm 19:2 states that the world is evidence of the Creator's knowledge. When the people of Lystra were about to offer sacrifices to Paul and Barnabas because they thought the two were gods, Paul restrained them by using this teleological argument for the existence of the true God (Acts 14:15–18). The world shows the cycle of seasons and the gift of rain in order to give mankind food and gladness. This order in nature serves as a witness to the existence of the true and living God, Paul said.

C. Man

1. Statement. How can man, a moral, intelligent, and living being, be explained apart from a moral, intelligent, and living God?

2. Development. This so-called anthropological argument for the existence of God is sometimes split in several ways. Buswell, for example, separates the anthropological argument (God creating man in His image) and the moral argument (how did the ideas of right and wrong originate?).[3] Dale Moody separates this basic argument into four: the moral argument, the presence of mind, the total self (that is, the soul), and religious consciousness.[4] These divisions are, it seems to me, only aspects of the basic anthropological argument since they all focus on man. So whatever facet of man's being or experience is emphasized, whether morality, intelligence, emotions, or religious consciousness, it is still an aspect of man and properly belongs to the anthropological argument.

The several facets of man and all of them together demand some explanation as to their origin. They argue for the existence of a being who is moral and intelligent and living who could have produced man. Material, inanimate, or unconscious forces could hardly have produced man. Evolution cannot produce soul, conscience, or religious instincts. Lifeless idols do not generate living offspring.

3. Scripture. The psalmist declared: "He who planted the ear, does He not hear? He who formed the eye, does He not see?" (Ps. 94:9). In other words, a living, intelligent creature argues for a living, intelligent Creator.

At the Areopagus Paul argued the same way. If we are the offspring of God, he argued, then God cannot be like a gold or silver idol that the offspring formed (Acts 17:28–29). He, like His offspring, must be living and intelligent.

D. Being

The ontological argument (that is, an argument based on the study of "being") has been presented in various forms by Anselm, Descartes, and others, and has been accepted by some (Hegel) and rejected by others (Kant).

1. Statement. The argument goes like this: (a) we have an idea of a Most Perfect Being; (b) the idea of a Most Perfect Being includes existence, since a Being, otherwise perfect, who did not exist would not be so perfect as a Being who did exist; (c) therefore, since the idea of existence is contained in the idea of the Most Perfect Being, that Most Perfect Being must exist.

2. Discussion. While the argument is deductive, there is an inductive aspect to it. Where does the idea of God come from? Not every idea that people have corresponds to an ontological reality. But ideas do have causes and need to be accounted for. The idea of a tooth fairy exists but its existence does not prove the reality of a tooth fairy. Nevertheless, the idea can be accounted for. Similarly the idea of God exists. How is it to be accounted for? That is the inductive aspect of the argument. And the point is that this idea is inexplicable from nontheistic data.

III. CONTENT OF GENERAL REVELATION

The relevant biblical passages tell us authoritatively what can be learned from general revelation. This is not to say that everybody will understand all or even any of these things, but these are what God has communicated through the various avenues of general revelation.

(1) His glory (Ps. 19:1).
(2) His power to work in creating the universe (Ps. 19:1).
(3) His supremacy (Rom. 1:20).
(4) His divine nature (Rom. 1:20).
(5) His providential control of nature (Acts 14:17).

(6) His goodness (Matt. 5:45).
(7) His intelligence (Acts 17:29).
(8) His living existence (Acts 17:28).

IV. THE VALUE OF GENERAL REVELATION

In determining the value of general revelation, people run the risk of either overestimating it or underestimating it. Some give at least the impression that what is revealed through general revelation proves the existence of the true God of the Bible. This seems to overestimate its value. Others assign it no value, but this is wrong since the Bible does reflect the use of these arguments. What, then, is its proper value?

A. To Display God's Grace

That God did not withdraw His grace after the first or any subsequent rebellion is itself grace. That He did not cease to communicate with mankind after people turned away from Him is no small wonder. That He continued to provide the means through general revelation whereby people can know something about the true God displays His continuing grace. Some are affected positively by that common grace, showing evidence of morality and often of seeking more truth.

B. To Give Weight to the Case for Theism

It is an overstatement to say that these arguments for the existence of God prove the existence of the God of the Bible. Although a number of truths about God are revealed through general revelation, many important things will never be revealed through that means. But the questions general revelation raises and the answers it points to lend support for the claims of theism as opposed to, say, atheism, agnosticism, or evolutionism.

C. To Justly Condemn Rejecters

These lines of evidence do place unregenerate men and women under responsibility to give some response. God intends that people should be able to see that a mechanistic, atheistic, irrationalistic explanation is inadequate to account for the highly integrated world and the various facets of man. Mankind should respond by acknowledging that there has to be behind it all a living, powerful, intelligent, superhuman Being.

If men do not make that minimal but crucial acknowledgment, but rather turn away and offer some other explanation, then God is just if He rejects them and does not offer more truth. The rejection of what is revealed in general revelation is sufficient to condemn justly. But this does not imply that the acceptance of general revelation is sufficient to effect eternal salvation. It is not, simply because there is no revelation of the atoning death of God's Son.

If what I have said appears to erect a double standard, so be it. There is nothing inherently wrong with two standards as long as both are just. And in this case both are. It would not be just for general revelation to save if God provided before the foundation of the world a Lamb to be slain for sin. To give salvation apart from the Lamb would be an unjust provision. But not to condemn those who reject revelation at any point of their pilgrimage of rejection would also be unjust for a holy God. Thus the rejection of the truths of general revelation brings just condemnation at any and all times they are rejected.

If a concerned student goes to his fellow student who needs one thousand dollars for tuition and offers with genuine loving concern ten dollars (which is all he has), and if his ten dollar bill is thrown scornfully on the floor with a mocking "What good will that pittance do me?" what further obligation does the student have to provide additional help to his fellow student? If he should suddenly be able to give the entire one thousand dollars, would anyone charge him with injustice if he gave it to another needy student? Accepting a ten dollar gift will not "save" the person who needs one thousand dollars; but rejecting it will condemn him. We must not forget that the majority of people who have ever lived have rejected the revelation of God through nature, and that rejection has come with scorn and deliberate substitution of their own gods. They have condemned themselves, and when God rejects them, He does so justly.

NOTES

1. Norman Geisler, *Philosophy of Religion* (Grand Rapids: Zondervan, 1981), 190–208.
2. J. Oswald Buswell, *A Systematic Theology of the Christian Religion* (Grand Rapids: Zondervan, 1962), 87.
3. Ibid., 1:90–91.
4. Dale Moody, *The Word of Truth* (Grand Rapids: Eerdmans, 1981), 83–84.

Chapter 6
THE PERFECTIONS OF GOD

If the question of chapter 4 was, Can God be known? the question of this chapter is, Can God be defined? If a definition consists of "a word or phrase expressing the essential nature of a person or thing," then God cannot be defined, for no word or even phrase could express His essential nature. No one could put together such a definition of God.

But if the definition were descriptive, then it is possible to define God, though not exhaustively. Indeed, most definitions are descriptive. One of the most famous, that in the Westminster Shorter Catechism, illustrates this kind of definition when it describes God as "Spirit, infinite, eternal, and unchangeable, in His being, power, holiness, justice, goodness, and truth" (Question 4). The longer description in the Westminster Confession of Faith simply adds more attributes like love, mercy, and freedom. Thus those definitions simply list some of the attributes of God.

Attributes are qualities that are inherent to a subject. They identify, distinguish, or analyze the subject. Most theologies entitle this chapter "The Attributes of God." I prefer "Perfections" because all of the qualities or attributes of God are perfect. His attributes are His perfections.

I. CHARACTERISTICS OF THE PERFECTIONS OF GOD

The various perfections of God are not component parts of God. Each describes His total being. Love, for example, is not a part of God's nature; God in His total being is love. Although God may display one quality or another at a given time, no quality is independent of or preeminent over any of the others. Whenever God displays His wrath, He is still love. When He shows His love, He does not abandon His holiness.

God is more than the sum total of His perfections. When we have listed all the attributes we can glean from revelation, we have not fully described God. This stems from His incomprehensibility. Even if we could say we had a complete list of all God's perfections, we could not fathom their meaning, for finite man cannot comprehend the infinite God.

God's perfections are known to us through revelation. Man does not attribute them to God; God reveals them to man. To be sure, man can suggest attributes of God, but these cannot be assumed to be true unless they are revealed by God.

The perfections of God describe equally the Father, the Son, and the Holy Spirit. They describe the nature of the Triune God and therefore each person of the Trinity.

II. CATEGORIES OF THE PERFECTIONS OF GOD

Most theologies offer some classification of God's attributes.

A. Nonmoral (or Natural) and Moral Attributes

The former, like self-existence and infinity, belong to the constitution of God; the latter, like justice and holiness, to His will. But all of the so-called nonmoral qualities are qualities of the most moral Being in the universe, and all the moral attributes are from the nature of God.

B. Absolute and Relative Attributes

Absolute attributes include those that belong to the essence of God as considered in itself (eternity, infinity), and relative attributes belong to the essence of God as considered in relation to His Creation (like omniscience). Again, this is an artificial distinction, since we are unable to make such a determination when, in fact, all of His attributes relate to His Creation.

C. Incommunicable and Communicable Attributes

The former are those that belong only to God (eternity, infinity), whereas the latter are those that are found in a relative or limited degree in people (wisdom, justice). But the communicable attributes are found in people, albeit in a limited way, not because God somehow communicated them, but only because mankind was made in the image of God.

Categories may serve some purpose, but in my opinion, not much. Although some of the attributes may be classified into one or another of these suggested categories, some do not classify so easily. Although holiness is generally listed as communicable, God's holiness surely is not. Although omniscience is surely incommunicable, mankind does have limited knowledge. The classification often becomes more arbitrary than obvious. The important consideration is the study of the perfections themselves, not classifying them. And to that we now proceed.

III. CATALOG OF THE PERFECTIONS OF GOD

In alphabetical order, here are fourteen of the perfections of God considered under (a) meaning, (b) scriptural statement(s), and (c) application and/or any problem involved.

A. Eternity

1. Meaning. The attribute of eternity means that God exists endlessly. His existence extends endlessly backward and forward (from our viewpoint of time) without any interruption or limitation caused by succession of events. Putting these ideas together, Berkhof defines eternity as "that perfection of God whereby He is elevated above all temporal limits and all succession of moments, and possesses the whole of His existence in one indivisible present."[1]

God's eternity and self-existence are interrelated concepts. Some theologies use the word *aseity* to denote self-existence; i.e., God depends *a se,* on Himself. If God exists endlessly, then He never came into existence nor was He ever caused to come into existence. He is endlessly self-existent.

2. Scripture. God's eternality is reflected in Psalm 90:2, "from everlasting to everlasting," and in Genesis 21:33, where *El Olam,* the Everlasting God, comes from an original form that means "the God of eternity."

3. Question. What is God's relation to the succession of events? As an eternal Being He sees the past and the future as clearly as the present; further, He must see them as including succession of events, and yet He is in no way bound by that succession. An illustration of this is found in the heavenly scene in Revelation 6:9–11 where the Lord answered the question of the martyrs concerning how long it would be before they were avenged by telling them to wait until certain events had transpired on earth.

4. A ramification. A comforting ramification of God's eternity is the confidence that God has never, nor will He ever, cease to exist; therefore His sustaining, providential control of all things and events is assured.

B. Freedom

1. Meaning. Freedom in God means that He is independent of His creatures and His Creation.
2. Scripture. When Isaiah asked the people who had directed the Lord or taught Him anything or instructed Him, he expected the answer, "no one," because God is free, that is, independent of His creatures (Isa. 40:13–14).
3. Question. Is God restricted in any way if He is free? Usually the answer states that God is restricted only by His own nature; e.g., His holiness restricts Him from ever sinning. But how can we even use the word *restriction* in connection with perfection? There can be no restrictions in perfection.
4. An application. Being free, God is not obligated to us in any way unless He chooses to initiate an obligation. He does not have to do anything for us unless He chooses to do so. Consequently, we cannot put Him in our debt.

C. Holiness

1. Meaning. Usually defined negatively and in relation to a relative, not absolute, standard, holiness in the Bible means separation from all that is common or unclean. In respect to God, holiness means not only that He is separate from all that is unclean and evil but also that He is positively pure and thus distinct from all others.

An analogy may help in understanding this concept. What does it mean to be healthy? It is the absence of illness, but also a positive infusion of energy. Holiness is the absence of evil and the presence of positive right. In God, His holiness is a purity of being and nature as well as of will and act.
2. Scripture. Holiness is the attribute by which God wanted to be especially known in Old Testament times (Lev. 11:44; Josh. 24:19; Ps. 99:3, 5, 9; Isa. 40:25; Hab. 1:12). In the New Testament it appears in direct statements (John 17:11; 1 Pet. 1:15), in ascriptions of praise (Rev. 4:8), and in the figure of God being light (1 John 1:5).
3. Applications. The absolute, innate holiness of God means that sinners have to be separated from Him unless a way can be found to constitute them holy. And that way has been provided in the merits of Jesus Christ.

A proper view of the holiness of God should make the believer sensitive to his own sin (Isa. 6:3, 5; Luke 5:8).

The holiness of God becomes the standard for the believer's life and conduct (1 John 1:7). This should put to an end the often useless discussions over what is permitted and what is not in the Christian life. Proper conduct can be tested by the simple question, Is it holy? This is the believer's standard. Although he does not always measure up to it, he must never compromise it.

D. Immutability

1. Meaning. Immutability means that God is unchangeable and thus unchanging. This does not mean that He is immobile or inactive, but it does mean that He is never inconsistent or growing or developing.
2. Scripture. Malachi 3:6 and James 1:17 speak of immutability. Notice in the former verse immutability guarantees the preservation of Israel.
3. Problem. If God is immutable, how can it be said that He repents? (Gen. 6:6; Jon. 3:10). If there actually was a change in God Himself, then either He is not immutable or not sovereign or both. Most understand these verses as employing anthropomorphism; i.e., interpreting what is not human in human terms. In the unfolding revelation of God's plan there seems to be change. However, this can be said to be so only from the human viewpoint, for His eternal plan is unchanging, as is He.

However, the expression may simply mean that God was sorry or grieved, which eliminates any concept of change.
4. Ramifications in relation to God. "If self-existence should change, it would become dependent existence; eternity would become time; perfection imperfection; and therefore God would become not-God."[2] Immutability assures us that none of God's perfections change.
5. Ramifications in relation to us. Immutability offers comfort and assurance that God's promises will not fail (Mal. 3:6; 2 Tim. 2:13). Immutability reminds us that God's attitudes toward sin, for example, do not change. Therefore, God can never be coaxed or compromised into changing.

E. Infinity

1. Meaning. Infinity means that God has no bounds or limits. He is in no way limited by the universe or by time-space boundaries. But it does not mean that He is somehow spread out through the universe, one part here and another there. "The infinity of God must be conceived as intensive rather than extensive . . ."[3]
2. Scripture. Solomon acknowledged God's infinity at the dedication of

his temple (1 Kings 8:27), and Paul used this attribute of God to argue against the false deities of the Athenians (Acts 17:24–28).
3. Observation. Sometimes this attribute is labeled immensity. It differs from omnipresence in that it emphasizes the transcendence of God (because He is not bound by space), while omnipresence focuses on the immanence of God (because He is everywhere present).

F. Love

1. Meaning. Like many Christian terms, love is more often discussed than defined. Even the dictionary offers little help. Love consists of affection and also of correction. Babies are cuddled and corrected, and both are true expressions of parental love. Furthermore, both are done by parents in the belief that they are doing the best thing for the child at the time. Love seeks good for the object loved. What is good? In God it is the perfection of holiness and all that that concept implies. Love in God is seeking the highest good and glory of His perfections. This implies no selfishness in God as it would in human beings.
2. Scripture. The Bible directly states that "God is love" (1 John 4:8). The absence of the article before "love". (the verse does not say, God is the love) indicates that this is the very nature of God. The presence of the article before "God" (literally, the God is love) shows that the statement is not reversible; it cannot read, "Love is God" (as Christian Science asserts).
3. Applications. Since all the attributes are possessed by each person of the Trinity, there must be some loving interaction (inconceivable to humans, to be sure) within the Trinity.

God who is love allows Himself to love sinful people. That is grace (Eph. 2:4–8).

That love of God has been poured out into the believer's heart (Rom. 5:5).

In trials God shows His love toward His children (Heb. 12:6).
4. Some related words. Closely related to love are goodness, mercy, long-suffering, and grace. Although distinctions are made, they are not exact. Goodness may be defined as God's benevolent concern for His creatures (Acts 14:17). Mercy is that aspect of His goodness that causes God to show pity and compassion (Eph. 2:4; James 5:11). Long-suffering speaks of self-restraint in the face of provocation (1 Pet. 3:20; 2 Pet. 3:15). Grace is the unmerited favor of God shown to man primarily in the person and work of Jesus Christ. All of these concepts are related and stem from the love of God who is love.

5. A heresy. The heresy of universalism grows out of an unbalanced concept of the attributes of God. It teaches that since God is love He will ultimately save all people. But God's perfection of love does not operate apart from His other perfections, including holiness and justice. Therefore, love cannot overpower holiness and save those who reject Christ and die in their sins. Furthermore, universalism in reality does not have a proper definition of love, since it sees only the affection aspect of love and not the correcting aspect. Finally, universalism contradicts direct statements of Scripture (see Mark 9:45–48).

G. Omnipotence

1. Meaning. Omnipotence means that God is all-powerful and able to do anything consistent with His own nature. In actuality He has not chosen to do even all the things that would be consistent with Himself for reasons known ultimately only to Himself.

2. Scripture. The word "Almighty" is used only of God in the Bible, occurring fifty-six times, and is the basis for the concept of omnipotence. God revealed Himself as the Almighty One to Abraham (Gen. 17:1), to Moses (Exod. 6:3), to believers (2 Cor. 6:18), and to John several times in the Revelation (1:8; 19:6).

3. A question. Does omnipotence have any limitations? The answer is yes, and in two areas: natural limitations and self-imposed limitations. The natural limitations include the things God cannot do because they are contrary to His nature. He cannot lie (Titus 1:2), He cannot be tempted to sin (James 1:13), He cannot deny Himself (2 Tim. 2:13). Self-imposed limitations include those things He has not chosen to include in His plan that He might have included as long as they were not contrary to His nature. He did not choose to spare His Son; He did not choose to save all people; He did not choose all nations in Old Testament times; He did not choose Esau; He did not choose to spare James (Acts 12:2). Though He could have done any of these things without being inconsistent with omnipotence, He did not choose to do so in His plan.

Questions like "Can God make 2 + 2 = 6?" do not imply any deficiency in His omnipotence. That particular question is in the realm of arithmetic, not power. One might as well ask if a nuclear explosion could make 2 + 2 = 6. More important, God cannot ever make wrong right.

4. Ramifications. In the past, God's power was seen in Creation (Ps. 33:9), in preserving all things (Heb. 1:3), and in delivering Israel from

Egypt (Ps. 114). But the greatest display of His power was the resurrection of Christ from the dead (2 Cor. 13:4). For the believer, God's power relates to the Gospel (Rom. 1:16), to his security (1 Pet. 1:5), to his hope of bodily resurrection (1 Cor. 6:14), and to daily living (Eph. 1:19).

H. Omnipresence

1. Meaning. Omnipresence means that God is everywhere present with His whole being at all times.

2. Scripture. In Psalm 139:7–11 David asked the question if there is anyplace one can escape from the presence of God. His answer is no, for His omnipresence is unlimited by space (v. 8), undaunted by speed (v. 9), and unaffected by darkness (vv. 11–12).

3. Some distinctions. As stated in the definition, omnipresence does not mean that God's being is diffused throughout the universe as if part of Him is here and part of Him there. His whole being is in every place, and the presence of the Lord within every believer serves as a good illustration of this.

Omnipresence does not mean that the immediacy of His presence does not vary. It does. His presence on His throne (Rev. 4:2), in Solomon's temple (2 Chron. 7:2), or in the believer (Gal. 2:20) certainly differs in its immediacy from His presence in the lake of fire (Rev. 14:10). Though in the lake of fire people will be separated from the face-presence of God (2 Thess. 1:9, *prosopon*), they will never be separated from Him who is omnipresent (Rev. 14:10, *enopion*). There is obviously no presence of fellowship (for His face will be turned away from the wicked in the lake of fire) as exists when He indwells believers.

Omnipresence differs from pantheism, which identifies the universe with God. The term was first used by the English deist John Toland (1670–1722) in 1705 when he taught that "God is the mind or soul of the universe." This heresy fails to distinguish the Creator from the created, a distinction taught in the very first verse of the Bible.

Omnipresence also differs from pantheism as used by process theologians to mean that God's being penetrates the whole universe yet is not exhausted by the universe. Omnipresence does mean that God is everywhere present but not diffused throughout or penetrating the universe. Furthermore, God is not developing as process theology teaches.

4. Some ramifications. No person can escape the presence of God. This warns unbelievers and comforts believers who, because God is omnipresent, can practice the experience of His presence in every circumstance of life.

I. Omniscience

1. Meaning. Omniscience means that God knows everything, things actual and possible, effortlessly and equally well. A. W. Tozer wrote:

> God knows instantly and effortlessly all matter and all matters, all mind and every mind, all spirit and all spirits, all being and every being, all creaturehood and all creatures, every plurality and all pluralities, all law and every law, all relations, all causes, all thoughts, all mysteries, all enigmas, all feeling, all desires, every unuttered secret, all thrones and dominions, all personalities, all things visible and invisible in heaven and in earth, motion, space, time, life, death, good, evil, heaven, and hell.
>
> Because God knows all things perfectly, He knows no thing better than any other thing, but all things equally well. He never discovers anything, He is never surprised, never amazed. He never wonders about anything nor (except when drawing men out for their own good) does He seek information or ask questions.[4]

2. Scripture. God knows all His works from the beginning (Acts 15:18). He numbers and names the stars (Ps. 147:4). Our Lord displayed omniscience when He declared what might have happened in Tyre and Sidon (Matt. 11:21). God knows everything about our lives before we are born (Ps. 139:16).

3. Applications.

a. Omniscience and security. Nothing can ever come to light in the believer's life that would surprise God and cause Him to cast him out. "No talebearer can inform on us; no enemy can make an accusation stick; no forgotten skeleton can come tumbling out of some hidden closet to abash us and expose our past; no unsuspected weakness in our characters can come to light to turn God away from us, since He knew us utterly before we knew Him and called us to Himself in the full knowledge of everything that was against us."[5]

b. Omniscience and sensitivity. Every warning God gives comes from an omniscient Being, so we should be extremely sensitive to them. He does not warn us on the basis of only guessing what might happen. He knows.

c. Omniscience and solace. When faced with inexplicable circumstances in life, we invariably take refuge and find solace in the omniscience of God. Not only does He know what actually happened, but

He knows what might have happened. He always knows what ultimate good and glory will come from events we cannot understand.

d. Omniscience and sobriety. Sobriety ought to characterize all when they realize that they must stand before an all-knowing God (Heb. 4:13).

J. Righteousness

1. Meaning. Though related to holiness, righteousness is nevertheless a distinct attribute of God. Holiness relates to God's separateness; righteousness, to His justice. Righteousness has to do with law, morality, and justice. In relation to Himself, God is righteous; i.e., there is no law, either within His own being or of His own making, that is violated by anything in His nature. In relation to His creatures He is also righteous; i.e., there is no action He takes that violates any code of morality or justice. Sometimes these two aspects of righteousness are called absolute (in relation to Himself) and relative (in relation to His Creation).
2. Scripture. God's absolute righteousness is declared in Psalm 11:7, "For the Lord is righteous" (see also Dan. 9:7). David also declared His relative righteousness (Ps. 19:9; see also Acts 17:31).

K. Simplicity

1. Meaning. The attribute of simplicity means that God is not a composite or compounded being. This has to do with His essence, so that it in no way contradicts the revelation of the Trinity. But this attribute also reminds us that when we consider God as a Triune Being He is not divisible or composed of parts or multiple substances.
2. Scripture. "God is spirit" (John 4:24). By contrast, for example, human beings are spirit and matter. In the Incarnation, of course, our Lord became flesh, but the deity of the God-man was always and only Spirit.
3. Ramifications. The simplicity of God underscores His self-existence (for there was no prior cause to form a composite being), assures us that God will never be anything other than Spirit, and enables us to worship in spirit; i.e., not in material ways.

L. Sovereignty

1. Meaning. The word means principal, chief, supreme. It speaks first of position (God is the chief Being in the universe), then of power (God is supreme in power in the universe). How He exercises that power is revealed in the Scriptures. A sovereign could be a dictator

(God is not), or a sovereign could abdicate the use of his powers (God has not). Ultimately God is in complete control of all things, though He may choose to let certain events happen according to natural laws that He has ordained.

2. Scripture. God has a plan (Acts 15:18), which is all-inclusive (Eph. 1:11), which He controls (Ps. 135:6), which includes but does not involve Him in evil (Prov. 16:4), and which ultimately is for the praise of His glory (Eph. 1:14).

3. The problem. The sovereignty of God seems to contradict the freedom or actual responsibility of man. But even though it may seem to do so, the perfection of sovereignty is clearly taught in the Scriptures, so it must not be denied because of our inability to reconcile it with freedom or responsibility.

Also, if God is sovereign, how can the creation be so filled with evil? Man was created with genuine freedom, but the exercise of that freedom in rebellion against God introduced sin into the human race. Though God was the Designer of the plan, He was in no way involved in the commission of evil either on the part of Satan originally or of Adam subsequently. Even though God hates sin, for reasons not revealed to us, sin is present by His permission. Sin must be within God's eternal plan (or God would not be sovereign) in some way in which He is not the author of it (or God could not be holy).

Sovereignty/freedom forms an antinomy ("a contradiction between two apparently equally valid principles or between inferences correctly drawn from such principles"). Antinomies in the Bible, however, consist only of apparent contradictions, not ultimate ones. One can accept the truths of an antinomy and live with them, accepting by faith what cannot be reconciled; or one can try to harmonize the apparent contradictions in an antinomy, which inevitably leads to overemphasizing one truth to the neglect or even denial of the other. Sovereignty must not obliterate free will, and free will must never dilute sovereignty.

M. Truth

1. Meaning. Truth means "agreement to that which is represented" and includes the ideas of veracity, faithfulness, and consistency. To say that God is true is to say, in the most comprehensive sense, that He is consistent with Himself, that He is all that He should be, that He has revealed Himself as He really is, and that He and His revelation are completely reliable.

2. Scripture. God is the only true God (John 17:3), and thus cannot lie (Titus 1:2) and is always reliable (Rom. 3:4; Heb. 6:18).
3. Ramifications. Because God is true, He can do nothing inconsistent with Himself. His promises can never be broken or unfulfilled (see 2 Tim. 2:13), and the Bible, which is His Word, must also be inerrantly true.

N. Unity

1. Meaning. Unity means that there is but one God, who is indivisible.
2. Scripture. The unity of God was a major revelation in the Old Testament as epitomized in the celebrated Shema (from the first word, "Hear," in Deut. 6:4). The verse may be translated in several ways, including these: "The Lord is our God, the Lord is One," which emphasizes the unity of God; or "The Lord is our God, the Lord alone," which stresses the uniqueness of God in contrast to the gods of the heathen. The New Testament, even with its clear revelation of the Trinity, affirms the unity of God (Eph. 4:6; 1 Cor. 8:6; 1 Tim. 2:5). This means that the Persons of the Trinity are not separate essences within the one divine essence. God is One in number and uniqueness.

One important concluding thought about the perfections of God: they describe the only true God who exists. Man creates his own false gods whom he can manipulate and control. Christian people sometimes concoct a perverted or deficient concept of God for the same reason—to be able to manipulate Him or not to have to face up to the true and living God. But the only actual God who exists is the One who is revealed primarily in the Bible and revealed by these attributes or perfections of His being. To be able to know this living and true God requires a miracle of the gracious revelation of Himself. To walk in worship with that living and true God is the privilege of all who know Him.

Notes

1. L. Berkhof, *Systematic Theology* (Grand Rapids: Eerdmans, 1978), 60.
2. Gordon H. Clark, "Attributes, the Divine," in *Baker's Dictionary of Theology* (Grand Rapids: Baker, 1960), 78–79.
3. Berkhof, *Systematic Theology,* 59.
4. A. W. Tozer, *The Knowledge of the Holy* (New York: Harper, 1978), 62–63.
5. Ibid., 63.

Chapter 7
THE NAMES OF GOD

The many names of God in the Scripture provide additional revelation of His character. These are not mere titles assigned by people but, for the most part, His own descriptions of Himself. As such they reveal aspects of His character.

Even when no particular name is used, the occurrence of the phrase "the name of the Lord" reveals something of His character. To call on the name of the Lord was to worship Him (Gen. 21:33). To take His name in vain was to dishonor Him (Exod. 20:7). Not to follow the requirements of the Law involved profaning His name (Lev. 22:2, 32). Priests performed their service in the name of the Lord (Deut. 21:5). His name pledged the continuation of the nation (1 Sam. 12:22).

I. ELOHIM

A. Usage

The term *elohim* occurs in the general sense of deity about 2,570 times in the Old Testament. About 2,310 times it is a name for the true God. The first occurrence is in the first verse of the Bible. It is used in reference to false deities in Genesis 35:2, 4; Exodus 12:12; 18:11; 23:24.

B. Meaning

The meaning of *elohim* depends on its derivation. Some understand that it comes from a root that means fear and indicates that the deity is to be feared, reverenced, or worshiped. Others trace it to a root that means strong, indicating a deity of great power. Though not conclusive, the evidence seems to point to the latter derivation signifying, in the case of the true God, that He is the strong One, the mighty Leader, the supreme deity.

C. The Plural Form

Elohim, a plural form, is peculiar to the Old Testament and appears in no other Semitic language. Generally speaking there are three views as to the significance of this plural form.

1. It is a polytheistic plural; i.e., the word originally had a polytheistic sense and only later acquired a singular sense. However, the monotheism of the Old Testament was revealed and not developed from polytheism.

2. It is a trinitarian plural; i.e., the Triune Godhead is seen, or at least intimated, in the use of this plural form. However, as we shall see in the next chapter, to conclude this necessitates reading New Testament revelation back into the Old Testament. The plural may allow for the subsequent revelation of the Trinity, but that is quite different from saying that the plural indicates Triunity.

3. It is a majestic plural. The fact that the noun is consistently used with singular verb forms and with adjectives and pronouns in the singular affirms this. This plural of majesty denotes God's unlimited greatness and supremacy.

D. Relationships of This Name

If this name of God means the Strong One and occurs in a majestic plural, one would expect that it would be used in relation to His greatness and mighty acts.

1. In relation to His sovereignty. Elohim is used to describe Him as the "God of all the earth" (Isa. 54:5), the "God of all flesh" (Jer. 32:27), the "God of heaven" (Neh. 2:4), and the "God of gods and the Lord of lords" (Deut. 10:17).

2. In relation to His work of Creation. He is the *Elohim* who created all things (Gen. 1:1; Isa. 45:18; Jon. 1:9).

3. In relation to His judging (Pss. 50:6; 58:11).

4. In relation to His mighty works on behalf of Israel (Deut. 5:23; 8:15; Ps. 68:7).

E. Compound Names

1. El Shaddai. Though the derivation of this word is uncertain, the most accepted one is that *shaddai* is connected with an Akkadian word that means "mountain." Thus this name of God pictures Him as the Almighty One standing on a mountain. It was the name by which God appeared to the patriarchs to give comfort and confirmation of the covenant with Abraham (Gen. 17:1; 28:3; 35:11; Exod. 6:3; see also Ps. 91:1–2). This name is also often used in connection with the chastening of God's people (Ruth 1:20–21).

2. *El Elyon.* This name, "the Most High God" emphasized God's strength, sovereignty, and supremacy. It was first used by Melchizedek when he blessed Abraham (Gen. 14:19), though if Isaiah 14:14 records Satan's attempt to usurp the supremacy of God, this would be a prior use. After these early occurrences, its use recedes until about 1000 B.C., where it appears again in poetic and exilic literature (Ps. 9:2; Dan. 7:18, 22, 25, 27).
3. *El Olam.* This name means "the Everlasting God," from an original form meaning "the God of eternity" (Gen. 21:33). It emphasizes God's unchangeableness (Pss. 100:5; 103:17) and is connected with His inexhaustible strength (Isa. 40:28).
4. *El Roi,* "God who sees" (Gen. 16:13). Hagar gave this name to God when He spoke to her before Ishmael's birth.

II. YAHWEH

The second basic name for God is the personal one, *YHWH,* the Lord, or *Yahweh.* It is the most frequently used name, occurring about 5,321 times in the Old Testament.

A. Origin of the Word

The name apparently comes from the root *hawa,* which signifies either existence (as of a tree trunk where it falls, Eccles. 11:3) or development (as in Neh. 6:6). Perhaps both ideas can be combined in the significance of God's name by saying that it denotes Him as the active, self-existent One.

B. Revelation of the Name

This name was used by Eve (Gen. 4:1), people in the days of Seth (v. 26), Noah (9:26), and Abraham (12:8; 15:2, 8). But it was to Moses that the deep significance of the name was revealed. God said that even though He appeared to the patriarchs He was not known to them by His name *Yahweh* (Exod. 6:3). The meaning of the name was not known in its fullest and deepest sense. This revelation came to Moses at the burning bush when God identified Himself as "I AM WHO I AM" (3:14), the principal idea being that God was present with the people of Israel.

C. Sacredness of the Name

Since *Yahweh* was God's personal name by which He was known to Israel, in post-exilic times it began to be considered so sacred that it was not pronounced. Instead the term *Adonai* was usually substituted, and by the sixth to seventh centuries A.D. the vowels of *Adonai* were combined with the consonants *YHWH* to remind the synagogue reader to pronounce the sacred name as *Adonai.* From this came the artificial word *Jehovah.* But all of this underscores the awe in which the name was held.

D. Significance of the Name

Several facets seem to be included in the significance of the name *Yahweh.*

1. It emphasizes God's changeless self-existence. This may be supported by the etymology and from the Lord's use of Exodus 3:14 in John 8:58 to state His claim to absolute eternal existence.

2. It assures God's presence with His people. See Exodus 3:12.

3. It is connected with God's power to work on behalf of His people and to keep His covenant with them, which was illustrated and confirmed by His work in their deliverance from Egypt (Exod. 6:6).

E. Compounds with the Name

1. Yahweh Jireh, "the Lord Will Provide" (Gen. 22:14). After the Angel of the Lord pointed to a ram to use as a substitute for Isaac, Abraham named the place "the Lord Will Provide."

2. Yahweh Nissi, "the Lord is My Banner" (Exod. 17:15). After the defeat of the Amalekites, Moses erected an altar and called it *Yahweh Nissi.*

3. Yahweh Shalom, "the Lord is Peace" (Judg. 6:24).

4. Yahweh Sabbaoth, "the Lord of hosts" (1 Sam. 1:3). This is a military figure that pictures *Yahweh* as the Commander of the angelic armies of heaven as well as the armies of Israel (1 Sam. 17:45). The title reveals the sovereignty and omnipotence of God and was used often by the prophets (Isaiah and Jeremiah) to remind the people during times of national crisis that God was their Leader and Protector.

5. Yahweh Maccaddeshcem, "the Lord who sanctifies you" (Exod. 31:13).

6. Yahweh Roi, "the Lord is my shepherd" (Ps. 23:1).

7. Yahweh Tsidkenu, "the Lord our righteousness" (Jer. 23:6).

8. Yahweh Shammah, "the Lord is there" (Ezek. 48:35).

9. Yahweh Elohim Israel "the Lord, the God of Israel" (Judg. 5:3; Isa. 17:6).

Strictly speaking, these compounds are not additional names of God, but designations or titles that often grew out of commemorative events. However, they do reveal additional facets of the character of God.

III. ADONAI

Like *Elohim, Adonai* is a plural of majesty. The singular means lord, master, owner (Gen. 19:2; 40:1; 1 Sam. 1:15). It is used, as might be expected, of the relationship between men (like master and slave, Exod. 21:1–6). When used of God's relationship to men, it conveys the idea of His absolute authority. Joshua recognized the authority of the Captain of the Lord's hosts (Josh. 5:14), and Isaiah submitted to the authority of the Lord, his Master (Isa. 6:8–11). The New Testament equivalent is *kurios,* "lord."

IV. GOD (THEOS)

A. Usage

Theos is the most frequent designation of God in the New Testament and the most common translation in the Septuagint for *Elohim*. It almost always refers to the one true God, though sometimes it is used of the gods of paganism in the reported words of pagans or by Christians repudiating these false gods (Acts 12:22; 14:11; 17:23; 19:26–27; 1 Cor. 8:5; 2 Thess. 2:4). It also refers to the devil (2 Cor. 4:4) and sensuality (Phil. 3:19). Most importantly Jesus Christ is designated as *Theos* (though some of the passages are disputed). Notice Romans 9:5; John 1:1, 18; 20:28; and Titus 2:13.

B. Teaching

The uses of the word reveal a number of important truths about the true God.

1. He is the only one true God (Matt. 23:9; Rom. 3:30; 1 Cor. 8:4, 6; Gal. 3:20; 1 Tim. 2:5; James 2:19). This fundamental truth of Judaism, the unity of God, was affirmed by Christ and the early church.

2. He is unique. He is the only God (1 Tim. 1:17), the only true God (John 17:3), the only holy One (Rev. 15:4), and the only wise One (Rom. 16:27). Therefore, believers can have no other gods beside the one true God (Matt. 6:24).

3. He is transcendent. God is the Creator, Sustainer, and Lord of the universe and Planner of the ages (Acts 17:24; Heb. 3:4; Rev. 10:6).

4. He is Savior (1 Tim. 1:1; 2:3; 4:10; Titus 1:3; 2:13; 3:4). He sent His Son to be the Redeemer (John 3:16) and delivered Him to death for us (Rom. 8:32).

C. Christ as God

Christ, the Son of God, is called God in several New Testament texts.

1. In John. The Johannine teaching includes the following passages: John 1:1, 18, where some manuscripts read "the only begotten God," and that unusual reading may be regarded as grounds for accepting its authenticity; 20:28, where Thomas used both *kurios* and *theos* of Jesus; and 1 John 5:20.

2. In Paul. Titus 2:13 seems to be the clearest designation of Christ as God in Paul's writings since Romans 9:5 is questioned by some. However, it is linguistically proper and contextually preferable to ascribe the phrase "God blessed forever" to Christ.

V. LORD (KURIOS)

A. Usage

The majority of the 717 occurrences of *kurios* in the New Testament are by Luke (210) and Paul (275) since they wrote to people of Greek culture and language.

B. Meaning

The word emphasizes authority and supremacy. It can mean sir (John 4:11), owner (Luke 19:33), or master (Col. 3:22), or it can refer to idols (1 Cor. 8:5) or husbands (1 Pet. 3:6). When used of God as *kurios*, it "expresses particularly His creatorship, His power revealed in history, and His just dominion over the universe . . ."[1]

C. Christ as Kurios

During His earthly life Jesus was addressed as Lord, meaning Rabbi or Sir (Matt. 8:6). Thomas ascribed full deity to Him when he declared, "My Lord and my God" (John 20:28). Christ's resurrection and exaltation placed Him as Lord of the universe (Acts 2:36; Phil. 2:11). But "to an early Christian accustomed to reading the OT, the word 'Lord,' when used of Jesus, would suggest His identification with the God of the OT."[2] This means, in relation to a verse like Romans 10:9, that "any Jew who publicly confessed that Jesus of Nazareth was 'Lord,' would be understood to ascribe the divine nature and attributes to Him."[3] Thus the essence of the Christian faith was to acknowledge Jesus of Nazareth as the *Yahweh* of the Old Testament.

VI. MASTER (DESPOTES)

A. Meaning

This word connotes the idea of ownership, whereas *kurios* emphasizes authority and supremacy.

B. Usage

God is addressed in prayer as *Despot* by Simeon (Luke 2:29), Peter and those with him (Acts 4:24), and the martyrs in heaven (Rev. 6:10).

Twice Christ is called *Despot* (2 Pet. 2:1; Jude 4).

VII. FATHER

One of the distinctive New Testament revelations is that of God as Father of individuals. Whereas the word "Father" is used of God only fifteen times in the Old Testament, it occurs 245 times of God in the New. As Father, He gives His children grace and peace (a regular salutation in the Epistles; e.g., Eph. 1:2; 1 Thess. 1:1), good gifts (James 1:17), and even commandments (2 John 4). We also address Him as Father in prayer (Eph. 2:18; 1 Thess. 3:11).

To sum up: a name in Bible times was more than an identification; it was descriptive of its bearer, often revealing some characteristic of a person. "O Lord, our Lord, How majestic is Thy name in all the earth" (Ps. 8:1, 9).

Notes

1. H. Bietenhard, "Lord," in *The New International Dictionary of New Testament Theology*, ed. Cohn Brown, (Grand Rapids: Zondervan, 1976), 2:514.
2. S. E. Johnson, "Lord (Christ)," in *The Interpreter's Dictionary of the Bible* (New York: Abingdon, 1976), 3:151.
3. William G. T. Shedd, *Romans* (New York: Scribner, 1879), 318.

Chapter 8
The Triunity of God

Trinity is, of course, not a biblical word. Neither are triunity, trine, trinal, subsistence, nor essence. Yet we employ them, and often helpfully, in trying to express this doctrine that is so fraught with difficulties. Furthermore, this is a doctrine that is not explicit in the New Testament even though it is often said that it is implicit in the Old and explicit in the New. But explicit means "characterized by full, clear expression," an adjective hard to apply to this doctrine. Nevertheless, the doctrine grows out of the Scriptures, so it is a biblical teaching.

I. THE CONTRIBUTION OF THE OLD TESTAMENT

Unquestionably the Old Testament emphasizes the unity of God. However, there are clear suggestions that there are persons in the Godhead. Therefore, one might say that the Old Testament contains intimations that allow for the later revelation of the triunity of God. What are these intimations?

A. The Unity of God

The celebrated Shema in Deuteronomy 6:4, which became Judaism's basic confession of faith, teaches the unity of God. It may be translated "The Lord our God is one Lord," or "The Lord our God, the Lord is One," or "The Lord is our God, the Lord is One," or "the Lord is our God, the Lord alone." This last translation stresses the uniqueness of God more than unity, but it implies oneness by ruling out polytheism. Other passages like Exodus 20:3; Deuteronomy 4:35; 32:29; Isaiah 45:14; and 46:9 insist on Israel's loyalty to the one God.

B. Plural Words

We have already suggested that the plural name for God, *Elohim*, denotes God's unlimited greatness and supremacy. To conclude plurality of persons from the name itself is dubious. However, when God speaks of Himself with plural pronouns (Gen. 1:26; 3:22; 11:7; Isa. 6:8) and plural verbs (Gen. 1:26; 11:7), it does seem to indicate distinctions of persons, though only plurality, not specifically Trinity.

C. The Angel of Yahweh

Though this designation may refer to any of God's angels (1 Kings 19:7; cf. v. 5), sometimes that Angel is referred to as God, yet distinguished from Him (Gen. 16:7–13; 18:1–21; 19:1–28; Mal. 3:1). This points to personal distinctions within the Godhead. Since the Angel is called God, He could hardly be only a prophet, functioning in pre-prophetic times as the prophets did in later times (as Edmond Jacob suggests in *Theology of the Old Testament*).[1]

D. Distinction of Persons

Some passages apparently distinguish persons within the Godhead.

1. The Lord is distinguished from the Lord (Gen. 19:24; Hos. 1:7).
2. The Redeemer (who must be divine) is distinguished from the Lord (Isa. 59:20).
3. The Spirit is distinguished from the Lord (Isa. 48:16; 59:21; 63:9–10). In these verses the Spirit is personal and active.

E. The Wisdom of God (?)

Many theologies (Berkhof, Payne, Thiessen) see the personification of wisdom in Proverbs 8:12–31 as referring to Christ and thus an Old Testament indication of the existence of the Trinity. However, it seems better to understand the passage not as an adumbration of Christ but as describing the eternal character of wisdom as an attribute of God.[2]

How shall we evaluate the Old Testament contribution to this doctrine? Berkhof concludes that there is "clear anticipation"[3] of the fuller revelation in the New Testament, but its use of the word "clear" may push this into an overstatement. More accurate is Payne's conclusion that the Old Testament contains "genuine suggestions of the Persons that make up the Godhead."[4] We might also put it this way: the doctrine exists only in seminal form in the Old Testament. It is questionable whether, without the flowering of the doctrine in the New Testament, we would know solely from the Old Testament what those seeds were.

II. THE CONTRIBUTION OF THE NEW TESTAMENT

Though the New Testament contains no explicit statement of the doctrine of the triunity of God (since "these three are one" in 1 John 5:7 is apparently not a part of the genuine text of Scripture), it does contain a great deal of evidence. That evidence lies along two paths: One insists that there is only one true God, and the other presents a Man Jesus and the Holy Spirit who both claim to be God. To emphasize the oneness while disregarding the threeness ends in unitarianism. To emphasize the threeness while disregarding the oneness leads to tritheism (as in Mormonism). To accept both leads to the doctrine of the triunity of God.

A. Evidence for Oneness

Like the Old, the New Testament also insists that there is only one true God. Passages like 1 Corinthians 8:4–6; Ephesians 4:3–6; and James 2:19 are clear.

B. Evidence for Threeness

1. The Father is recognized as God. No debate exists here, and a number of passages teach this (John 6:27; 1 Pet. 1:2).

2. Jesus Christ is recognized as God. He Himself claimed attributes that only God possesses, like omniscience (Matt. 9:4), omnipotence (28:18), omnipresence (v. 20). He did things that only God can do (and the people of His day acknowledged this, though sometimes reluctantly), like forgiving sins (Mark 2:1–12) and raising the dead (John 12:9). Further, the New Testament assigns other works that only God can perform to Christ, like upholding all things (Col. 1:17), creation (John 1:3), and future judging of all (5:27).

The last phrase of John 1:1 correlates true and full deity with the Word (Christ). The phrase is best translated "the Word was God." Consistent exegesis forbids the Jehovah's Witnesses' translation "the Word was a god." The word "God" does not have an article, and if it is to be understood as indefinite ("a god") this would be the only time in John's Gospel that this form was used, making it highly improbable on grammatical grounds that it is indefinite here. John could not have chosen a more precise way of expressing the truths that the Word was God and yet was distinct from the Father.

3. The Holy Spirit is recognized as God. He is called God (Acts 5:3–4), He possesses attributes that only God has, like omniscience (1 Cor.

2:10) and omnipresence (6:19), and He regenerates people (John 3:5–6, 8), an exclusive work of God.

C. Evidence for Triunity

Matthew 28:19 best states both the oneness and threeness by associating equally the three Persons and uniting them in one singular name. Other passages like Matthew 3:16–17 and 2 Corinthians 13:14 associate equally the three persons but do not contain the strong emphasis on unity as does Matthew 28:19.

III. SOME CONSIDERATIONS FOR A DEFINITION

A definition of the Trinity is not easy to construct. Some are done by stating several propositions. Others err on the side either of oneness or threeness. One of the best is Warfield's: "There is one only and true God, but in the unity of the Godhead there are three coeternal and coequal Persons, the same in substance but distinct in subsistence."[5] The word "Persons" might be misleading as if there were three individuals in the Godhead, but what other word would suffice? The word "substance" might be too materialistic; some would prefer to use the word "essence." Many will not know the meaning of subsistence, but a dictionary can remedy that ("necessary existence").

Positively, the definition clearly asserts both oneness and threeness and is careful to maintain the equality and eternality of the Three. Even if the word "person" is not the best, it does guard against modalism, and, of course, the phrase "the same in substance" (or perhaps better, essence) protects against tritheism. The whole undivided essence of God belongs equally to each of the three persons.

John 10:30: "I and the Father are one," beautifully states this balance between the diversity of the persons and the unity of the essence. "I and the Father" clearly distinguishes two persons, and the verb, "We are," is also plural. "One" is neuter; that is, one in nature or essence, but not one person (which would require masculine form). Thus the Lord distinguished Himself from the Father and yet claimed unity and equality with the Father.

Traditionally the concept of the Trinity has been viewed from (a) an ontological perspective and (b) an economical or administrative one. The ontological Trinity focuses on the personal operations of the Persons or the *opera ad intra* (works within), or personal properties by which the Persons are distinguished. It has to do with generation (filiation or begetting) and procession, which attempts to indicate a logical order within the Trinity but does not imply in any way inequality, priority of time, or degrees of dignity. Generation and procession occur within the divine Being and carry with them no thought of subordination of essence. Thus, viewed ontologically, it may be said of the Persons of the Trinity: (1) The Father begets the Son and is He from whom the Holy Spirit proceeds, though the Father is neither begotten nor does He proceed. (2) The Son is begotten and is He from whom the Holy Spirit proceeds, but He neither begets nor proceeds. (3) The Holy Spirit proceeds from both the Father and the Son, but He neither begets nor is He the One from whom any proceed.

I agree with Buswell that generation is not an exegetically based doctrine.[6] The concept it tries to convey, however, is not unscriptural, and certainly the doctrine of sonship is scriptural. The phrase "eternal generation" is simply an attempt to describe the Father-Son relationship in the Trinity and, by using the word "eternal," protect it from any idea of inequality or temporality. But whether or not one chooses to use the idea of eternal generation, the personal and eternal and coequal relation of the Father and Son must be affirmed. Eternal generation should not be based on Psalm 2:7.

Procession seems to be more of a scriptural concept based on John 15:26. Berkhof defines it as "that eternal and necessary act of the First and Second Persons of the Trinity whereby They, within the divine Being, become the ground of the personal subsistence of the Holy Spirit, and put the Third Person in possession of the whole divine essence, without any division, alienation, or change."[7] The idea of *eternal* procession has to lean hard on the present tense of the word "proceeds" in John 15:26, an emphasis that is in my judgment misplaced. The verse does not really seem to relate anything about the mutual eternal relationships within the Trinity but rather what the Spirit would do to continue the work of the Lord Jesus after Christ's ascension.

The concept of the economical Trinity concerns administration, management, actions of the persons, or the *opera ad extra* ("works outside," that is, on the creation and its creatures). For the Father this includes the works of electing (1 Pet. 1:2), loving the world (John 3:16), and giving good gifts (James 1:17). For the Son it emphasizes His suffering (Mark 8:31), redeeming (1 Pet. 1:18), and upholding all things (Heb. 1:3). For the Spirit it focuses on His particular works of regenerating (Titus 3:5), energizing (Acts 1:8), and sanctifying (Gal. 5:22–23).

Even with all the discussion and delineation that we attempt in relation to the Trinity, we must acknowledge that it is in the final analysis a mystery. We accept all the data as truth even though they go beyond our understanding.

IV. ILLUSTRATION OF THE TRINITY

No illustration can possibly capture all that is involved in the biblical revelation of the Trinity. Most are at best only parallels of a "three-in-one" idea.

A common diagram attempts to picture the Godhead as one, yet showing each Person as God and also distinct.

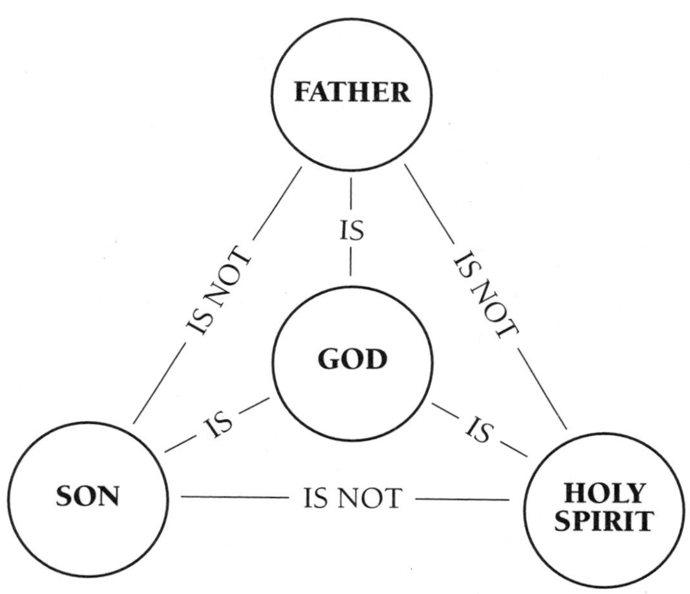

Water may serve as a "three-in-one" illustration since it retains its chemical activity whether in solid, gas, or liquid state. There is also a triple point for water, a condition under which ice, steam, and liquid water can coexist in equilibrium. All are water, yet distinct from each other.

The sun, its light, and its power may help illustrate the Trinity.[8] No one has actually seen the sun, just as no one has seen the Father. Yet we learn a great deal about the sun by studying the sunlight, just as we learn about the Father through Jesus Christ the Son who is the radiance of His glory (Heb. 1:3). We see the power of the sun as it is involved in the growth of seeds and trees and plants, and when asked what makes things grow, we say the sun does. The Holy Spirit is like the power of the sun, and He is God.

Whatever usefulness or limitations illustrations have, we say again that we are faced with a mystery.

V. A SURVEY OF THE HISTORY OF THE DOCTRINE

A. Monarchianism

The early church fathers did not formulate any clear statement concerning the Trinity. Some were unclear about the *Logos*, and most were unconcerned about giving attention to the Spirit except for His work in the lives of believers. In answer to Praxeus, Tertullian (ca. 165–220) asserted the threeness aspect of God, being the first to use the word Trinity. However, he did not have a full and accurate understanding of the Trinity, his views being tinged with subordinationism.

Tertullian was battling Monarchians who opted for the unity of God and denied trinitarianism. Monarchianism existed in two forms.
1. Dynamic Monarchianism (or adoptionism). This was first expounded by Theodotus of Byzantium about 210, and it viewed Jesus as a man who was given special power by the Holy Spirit at His baptism.
2. Modalistic Monarchianism. This was more influential, attempting not only to maintain the unity of God but also the full deity of Christ by asserting that the Father became incarnated in the Son. In the West it was known as Patripassianism since the incarnated Father also suffered in the Son; and in the East as Sabellianism after its most famous representative who taught that the Persons in the Godhead were modes in which God manifested Himself. Though Sabellius used the word "Person" he meant it as a role or manifestation of the one divine essence.

B. Arianism

Arius (ca. 250–336), an antitrinitarian presbyter of Alexandria, distinguished the one eternal God from the Son who was generated by the Father and who thus had a beginning. He also taught that the Holy Spirit was the first thing created by the Son, since all things were made by the Son. He found scriptural support for his views in passages that seem to picture the Son as inferior to the Father (Matt. 28:18; Mark 13:32; 1 Cor. 15:28).

Arius was opposed by Athanasius (ca. 296–373) who, while maintaining the unity of God, distinguished three essential natures in God and insisted that the Son was of the same substance as the Father. He taught that the Son was generated, but that this was an eternal and internal act of God, in contrast to Arius who rejected eternal generation.

When the Council of Nicaea convened to attempt to settle the dispute, Athanasius and his followers wanted it stated that the Son was of the same substance (*homoousios*) as the Father, while a large group of moderates suggested that the word *omoiousios* ("of similar substance") be substituted. Thorough-going Arians said that the Son was of a different substance (*heteroousios*). Emperor Constantine finally sided with the Athanasian party, resulting in the clear and unequivocal statement of the Nicene Creed that Christ was of the same substance with the Father (*homoousios*).

Concerning the Holy Spirit the Creed merely said, "I believe in the Holy Spirit." However, Athanasius in his own teaching maintained that the Spirit, like the Son, was of the same essence as the Father. In the aftermath of the Council of Nicaea, many documents were circulated in the fourth century, and the Arian party was popular partly because of the influence of Constantius, Constantine's successor, who was fond of Arius.

In the second half of the fourth century, three theologians from the province of Cappadocia in eastern Asia Minor gave definitive shape to the doctrine of the Trinity and defeated Arianism. They were Basil of Caesarea, his brother Gregory of Nyssa, and Basil's close friend Gregory of Nazianzus. They helped clarify the vocabulary concerning the Trinity by using *ousia* for the one essence of the Godhead and *hypostasis* for the Persons. Their emphasis on the three essential natures in the one God freed the Nicene Creed from suspicions of Sabellianism in the eyes of the moderates. They also vigorously maintained the *homoousios* of the Holy Spirit.

C. The Council of Constantinople (381)

In 373 a group led by Eustath called the Pneumatomachians ("fighters against the Spirit") regarded both the Son and the Spirit merely of like substance with the Father (some moderates did affirm the consubstantiality of the Son). The controversy grew to such proportions that Emperor Theodosius called a council at Constantinople consisting of 150 orthodox bishops who represented the Eastern church. Under the guidance of Gregory of Nazianzus the council formulated this statement concerning the Holy Spirit: "And we believe in the Holy Spirit, the Lord, the Life-giving, who proceeds from the Father, who is to be glorified with the Father and the Son, and who speaks through the prophets." Though the creed avoided the term "of the same substance" that had been used of Christ in the Nicene Creed, it described the work of the Spirit in terms that could not be predicated of any created being. Thus it settled the question of the deity of the Spirit, though it was less than a fully satisfactory statement since it did not use *omoousios* of the Spirit and did not define the relationship of the Spirit to the other two Persons.

D. Augustine (354–430)

1. De Trinitate. The statement of the Trinity in the Western church reached a final formulation in this work by Augustine. In this treatise he stated that each of the three Persons of the Trinity possesses the entire essence and that all are interdependent on the others. Though he was dissatisfied with the word "persons" to denote the three essential natures, he used it "in order not to be silent." He also taught that the Spirit proceeds from both the Father and the Son.

2. The Pelagian controversy (431). Augustine also laid great stress on efficacious grace as the work of the Spirit. This profoundly influenced not only his doctrine of man and of sin but also his doctrine of the Spirit.

E. The Synod of Toledo (589)

Although Western theologians generally held to the procession of the Holy Spirit from both the Father and Son, this was not formalized until the *filioque* ("and Son") clause was added to the Constantinople Creed at the Synod of Toledo. The Eastern church never accepted this, declaring it to be heresy, splitting the two groups even to today.

Photius, patriarch of Constantinople and adversary of Pope Nicholas of Rome, used the *filioque* clause as part of his effort to discredit Nicholas's claims as universal bishop. He charged the Western church with introducing doctrinal innovations, claiming that *filioque* had falsified the holy creed of Constantinople.

F. Reformation Teaching on the Trinity

The reformers and all Reformation Confessions express the doctrine of the Trinity in the orthodox fashion formulated in the early church (see Calvin *Institutes* 1.13, for example). Calvin seemed to find the idea of the eternal generation of the Son difficult, if not useless, though he did not deny it.

Luther accepted the orthodox doctrine of the Trinity because he felt it was taught in the Scriptures though he felt that faith alone could comprehend it. The Augsburg Confession (1530) clearly declares "that there is one divine essence which is called and is God . . . yet there are three Persons of the same essence and power, who also are coeternal, the Father, the Son, and the Holy Ghost" (111.7). Likewise the Westminster Confession (1647) states: "In the unity of the Godhead there be three Persons, of one substance, power, and eternity: God the Father, God the Son, and God the Holy Ghost: the Father is of none, neither begotten, nor proceeding; the Son is eternally begotten of the Father; the Holy Ghost eternally proceeding from the Father and the Son" (II. 3).

Socinianism in the sixteenth century denied the preexistence of the Son, considering Him only a man. It taught that there was only one divine essence containing only one Person. These views influenced English Unitarianism and English Deism. Many Unitarians were not Deists, but all Deists had a unitarian concept of God. The heretical lineage was Arianism to Socinianism to Unitarianism to Deism. American Unitarianism was a direct descendant of English Unitarianism.

G. Modern Views

The orthodox view of the Trinity was and is held by many in the modern period. However, there have been many impugners. Kant and Hegel opposed the orthodox teaching and held to adoptionism or impersonal pantheism. Swedenborg and Schleiermacher echoed Sabellianism. Many feel that Barth's concept was modalistic.[9] Others defend him as orthodox because he rejected Sabellianism and used his concept of "modes of being" in God in place of the concept of persons. Paul Tillich felt that the doctrine of the Trinity was produced by man to meet his own needs. Tillich in reality did not believe there was even one person in the Godhead, let alone three.

Jehovah's Witnesses espouse an Arian-like Christology by denying the eternality of the Son and the doctrine of the Trinity. They, like Arius, see the *Logos* as an intermediate being between the Creator and creation.

VI. SOME PRACTICAL RAMIFICATIONS

The richness of the concept of the Trinity overflows into several areas of theology.

The doctrine of redemption is an obvious example, for all persons of the Godhead are involved in that great work (John 3:6, 16; Rev. 13:8).

The doctrine of revelation serves as another example, the Son and Spirit both being involved in communicating God's truth (John 1:18; 16:13).

Fellowship and love within the Godhead is only possible in a trinitarian concept of God, and that fellowship is akin to the believer's fellowship with Christ (John 14:17).

Priority without inferiority as seen in the Trinity is the basis for proper relationships between men and women (1 Cor. 11:3).

Prayer is practiced in a trinitarian way. Though we may address any Person of the Trinity, ordinarily, according to the biblical precedent, we address the Father in the name of Christ as the Spirit directs us (John 14:14; Eph. 1:6; 2:18; 6:18).

NOTES

1. Edmund Jacob, *Theology of the Old Testament* (New York: Harper & Row, 1958), 75–77.
2. See Louis Goldberg, "Wisdom," in *Theological Wordbook of the Old Testament* (Chicago: Moody, 1980), 1:283.
3. L. Berkhof, *Systematic Theology* (Grand Rapids: Eerdmans, 1978), 86.
4. J. Barton Payne, in *The Theology of the Older Testament* (Grand Rapids: Zondervan, 1962), 166.
5. B. B. Warfield, "Trinity," *The International Standard Bible Encyclopaedia,* ed. James Orr (Grand Rapids: Eerdmans, 1930), 5:3012.
6. J. Oliver Buswell, *A Systematic Theology of the Christian Religion* (Grand Rapids: Zondervan, 1962), I:105–12.
7. Berkhof, *Systematic Theology,* 97.
8. *The Pilgrim Bible* (New York: Oxford, 1948), ix–x.
9. Leonard Hodgson, *The Doctrine of the Trinity* (London: Nisbet, 1955), 229.

Section III
THE BIBLE: GOD-BREATHED

Chapter 9
SPECIAL REVELATION

In the preceding section we examined the matter of general revelation—how God reveals Himself to all people in general. If the total revelation from God may be labeled The Book of Revelation, volume 1 contains general revelation. Volume 2, then, contains special revelation, which, by contrast, does not necessarily come to all people.

I. THE AVENUES OF SPECIAL REVELATION

A. The Lot

Although today we would not highly regard the use of the lot, it did serve sometimes to communicate the mind of God to man (Prov. 16:33; Acts 1:21–26).

B. The Urim and Thummim

The breastplate that the high priest wore in the Old Testament was a square piece of beautiful material that was folded in half and open at the top like a pouch. It was adorned with twelve precious stones, on which were engraved the names of the twelve tribes of Israel. The Urim and Thummim possibly were two precious stones placed inside the pouch that were used, like the lot, to determine God's will (Exod. 28:30; Num. 27:21; Deut. 33:8; 1 Sam. 28:6; Ezra 2:63).

C. Dreams

God apparently used dreams to communicate many times during the Old Testament period, and He will do so again at the time of the second coming of Christ (Gen. 20:3, 6; 31:11–13, 24; 40–41; Joel 2:28). Nonbelievers as well as believers experienced God-given dreams (Gen. 20:3; 31:24). Though a common experience, dreams were used by God in this special way to reveal truth.

D. Visions

In a vision the emphasis seems to be on what is heard, whereas in a dream, it is on what is seen. Also the human being involved seems to be more active in receiving a vision (Isa. 1:1; 6:1; Ezek. 1:3).

E. Theophanies

Before the Incarnation, theophanies were associated with the appearance of the Angel of the Lord, who communicated the divine message to people (Gen. 16:7–14; Exod. 3:2; 2 Sam. 24:16; Zech. 1:12).

F. Angels

God also uses created angels to carry His message to people (Dan. 9:20–21; Luke 2:10–11; Rev. 1:1). (Notice Rev. 19:17 where God will use an angel to communicate to birds!)

G. The Prophets

Old Testament prophets brought God's message to mankind (2 Sam. 23:2; Zech. 1:1), as did New Testament prophets (Eph. 3:5). They spoke with authority because they were communicating the Word of the Lord. A preacher or teacher today does not qualify as a prophet since he proclaims or explains God's Word, previously given and written.

H. Events

God's activity in history also constitutes a channel of revelation. Delivering the people of Israel from Egypt revealed the righteous acts of the Lord, according to Micah 6:5. Acts of judgment reveal who God is (Ezek. 25:7). And, of course, the incarnation of Christ exegeted God (John 1:14). It does not go without saying today that these events have to be historical and factual in order also to be communicative; for today some are putting existential faith before the historical. In other words, they are attempting to create revelation apart from historical facts, or finding meaning in historical facts while denying that the events actually happened. Such existential historiography was never a part of the framework of the biblical writers.

Not only must the events be historical, but they also need to be interpreted through divine inspiration if we are to understand accurately their meaning. For example, many people were crucified; how do we know that the crucifixion of one Jesus of Nazareth paid for the sins of the world? The Word of special revelation clarifies and correctly interprets the obscurity of the meaning of events.

I. Jesus Christ

Undebatably the incarnation of Jesus Christ was a major avenue of special revelation. He exegeted the Father (John 1:14), revealing the nature of God (14:9), the power of God (3:2), the wisdom of God (7:46), the glory of God (1:14), the life of God (1 John 1:1–3), and the love of God (Romans 5:8). Our Lord did all this by both His acts (John 2:11) and His words (Matt. 16:17).

J. The Bible

Actually the Bible serves as the most inclusive of all the avenues of special revelation, for it encompasses the record of many aspects of the other avenues. Though God undoubtedly gave other visions, dreams, and prophetic messages that were not recorded in the Bible, we know no details of them. Too, all that we know about the life of Christ appears in the Bible, though, of course, not all that He did or said was recorded in the Scriptures (John 21:25). But the Bible is not simply the record of these other revelations from God; it also contains additional truth not revealed, for example, through the prophets or even during the earthly life of Christ. So the Bible, then, is both the record of aspects of special revelation and revelation itself.

The revelation in the Bible is not only inclusive yet partial; it is also accurate (John 17:17), progressive (Heb. 1:1), and purposeful (2 Tim. 3:15–17).

Two approaches exist as to the credibility of the scriptural revelation. Fideists insist that the Scripture and the revelation it contains is self-authenticating, that is, autopistic. The infallibility of the Bible must be presupposed and can be because the Scripture says it is inspired and the Spirit accredits it. Empiricists, on the other hand, stress the intrinsic credibility of the revelation of the Bible as being worthy of belief, that is, axiopistic. The Bible's claim to authority is not in itself proof of its authority; rather there exist factual, historical evidences that constitute the Bible's credentials and validate the truth of its message. My feeling is that there is truth in both approaches; both can and should be used.

II. SOME CONTEMPORARY VIEWS OF REVELATION

All contemporary views concerning revelation hold several features in common. (1) They are subjective in orientation. Revelation is discovered in experience or in the interpreter's understanding of the experiences of others. (2) Without an objective standard or criteria they are unstable, for the understanding of revelation depends on the interpreter's concept. (3) Because of (1) and (2), contemporary views of revelation are sub-Christian, for they elevate the human mind over the material God has revealed.

A. Revelation as Divine Activity

This view maintains that revelation consists of the mighty acts of God in history. Of course, there is truth in this, for God did reveal Himself in historical acts. Conservatives believe that those acts were factual and, in some cases, miraculous. Liberals deny the actual historicity of those acts. However, both conservatives and liberals leave the interpretation of those acts to the genius of the interpreter. Those who deny the historical reality of these acts try to affirm that these were nevertheless the acts of God with significant meanings assigned to them by the interpreter. Revelation, then, may be little more than a psychological event in the mind of the interpreter.

B. Revelation as Personal Encounter

In this school of thought revelation does not consist of information that is communicated but in a person-to-person encounter. Therefore, God may only be known as subject, never as object, for the latter would necessitate propositions about Him. Revelation does not provide us with information about God, but with God Himself in a personal encounter. But revelation about God (propositions) are necessary for the revelation of God (encounter). Facts are essential to the encounter. Revelation as encounter cuts off revelation to some degree from history, and it certainly is existentially based. An example is this: "In the Bible, God's self-revelation is personal rather than propositional. That is to say, ultimately revelation is in relationship, 'confrontation,' communion, rather than by the communication of facts."[1]

Traditionally, revelation and the Bible have been inseparable. Contemporary views have driven a wedge between the Bible and revelation with devastating results. Now revelation need no longer be found only in the Bible, but in the mighty acts of God and in personal encounter. The existential experience has replaced objective truth as the Word of God.

To sum up: Special revelation as now recorded in the Bible furnishes the content of God's message to the world. Inspiration concerns the method God employed to actually record that content in the Scriptures. Inerrancy relates to the accuracy of that recording.

To these matters we now turn.

Note

1. C. F. D. Moule, "Revelation," in *The Interpreter's Dictionary of the Bible* (New York: Abingdon, 1976), 4:55.

Chapter 10
THE BIBLICAL DOCTRINE OF INSPIRATION

Although those holding many theological viewpoints would be willing to say the Bible is inspired, one finds little uniformity as to what is meant by inspiration. Some focus it on the writers; others, on the writings; still others, on the readers. Some relate it to the general message of the Bible; others, to the thoughts; still others, to the words. Some include inerrancy; many don't.

These differences call for precision in stating the biblical doctrine. Formerly all that was necessary to affirm one's belief in full inspiration was the statement, "I believe in the inspiration of the Bible." But when some did not extend inspiration to the words of the text it became necessary to say, "I believe in the verbal inspiration of the Bible." To counter the teaching that not all parts of the Bible were inspired, one had to say, "I believe in the verbal, plenary inspiration of the Bible." Then because some did not want to ascribe total accuracy to the Bible, it was necessary to say, "I believe in the verbal, plenary, infallible, inerrant inspiration of the Bible." But then "infallible" and "inerrant" began to be limited to matters of faith only rather than also embracing all that the Bible records (including historical facts, genealogies, accounts of Creation, etc.), so it became necessary to add the concept of "unlimited inerrancy." Each addition to the basic statement arose because of an erroneous teaching.

I. THE BIBLICAL DATA CONCERNING INSPIRATION

The doctrine of inspiration is not something theologians have forced on the Bible. Rather it is a teaching of the Bible itself, a conclusion derived from the data contained in it. And, whatever one may think of the Bible, it, like any other witness, has the right to testify on its own behalf. Some take exception to the validity of such evidence on the grounds that it is self-testimony and therefore may not be true. Granted, self-testimony may or may not be true, but it needs to be heard.

Here is the relevant data the Bible presents and confronts us with.

A. 2 Timothy 3:16

In this verse the apostle Paul declared that all Scripture is inspired of God and is profitable for a number of things. Notice three important claims in this statement.

1. All Scripture, the entire Bible, is inspired and profitable. This is the extent of inspiration. The New Testament uses this word "Scripture" fifty-one times and always in reference to some part of the Bible. Sometimes it refers to the entire Old Testament (Luke 24:45; John 10:35); sometimes, to a particular Old Testament passage (Luke 4:21); sometimes, to a particular New Testament passage (1 Tim. 5:18); and sometimes to a larger portion of the New Testament (2 Peter 3:16, referring to Paul's writings).

These last two references, 1 Timothy 5:18 and 2 Peter 3:16, carry a great deal of importance. In 1 Timothy 5:18 Paul combined an Old and a New Testament reference and designated them both as Scripture. The Old Testament quotation is from Deuteronomy 25:4, and the New Testament one is Luke 10:7 (although that sentiment is found in Lev. 19:13 and Deut. 24:15, Luke was clearly not quoting either verse; indeed, the emphasis in Lev. 19 and Deut. 24 is on not withholding wages overnight). To join a quotation from Luke to a canonical Old Testament quote is highly significant. Remember too that probably only five or six years had elapsed between the writing of Luke and the writing of 1 Timothy.

In 2 Peter 3:16 Peter labeled Paul's writings as Scripture, showing their early acceptance and recognized authority. Though it is true that not all of the New Testament was written when Paul wrote 2 Timothy 3:16 (2 Peter, Hebrews, Jude, and all of John's writings were not), nevertheless, because those books were eventually acknowledged as belonging to the canon of Scripture, we may conclude that 2 Timothy 3:16 includes all the sixty-six books as we know them today. Not any book nor any part is excluded; all Scripture is inspired of God.

Most do not deny that 2 Timothy 3:16 includes all of the canonical books. Those who wish to try to reduce the amount of Scripture included in the verse do so by translating it this way: "All Scripture inspired by God is also profitable" (instead of "All Scripture is inspired by God and is profitable"). In other words, whatever parts of Scripture that are inspired are profitable, but other uninspired parts are not profitable. That translation indicates that only part of the Bible is inspired.

Such a translation is possible, but not required. Actually either translation can claim to be accurate. Both translations have to supply the word *is* since it does not appear in the original. The matter becomes a question of whether to supply "is" only one time or two times ("Every Scripture inspired by God is also profitable" or "All Scripture is inspired by God and is profitable"). The preference goes to the latter translation for three reasons. First, by supplying "is" two times, both adjectives ("inspired" and "profitable") are understood the same way, as predicate adjectives, which is more natural. Second, the connective word, though it may be translated "also," much more frequently means "and." Third, a similar construction occurs in 1 Timothy 4:4 where both adjectives are clearly predicate adjectives. Thus the preferred translation makes it quite clear that all the Bible is inspired.

2. *The entire Bible is God breathed.* This expresses the means of inspiration. The form is passive, meaning that the Bible is the result of the breath of God. If, by contrast, the form were active, then it would mean that the Bible exudes or speaks of God. Of course, that is true, but it is not what Paul said in this verse. Our English word "inspire" carries the idea of breathing into something. But this word tells us that God breathed out something, namely, the Scripture. To be sure, human authors wrote the texts, but the Bible originated as an action of God who breathed it out.

3. *The entire Bible is profitable.* This expresses the purpose of inspiration. Its profit consists in teaching, reproving, correcting, restoring, and training in righteousness in order that the believer may be fitted, capable, or proficient, and furnished completely in every area of his being. The Bible is not to be put in a museum to be admired; rather, it is to be used in our lives.

To sum up: putting the three ideas of 2 Timothy 3:16 together, the verse teaches that the entire Bible came from God in order to show us how to live.

B. 2 Peter 1:21

This verse tells us as much as any single verse how God used the human writers to produce the Bible. The Holy Spirit moved or bore them along. The use of the same verb in Acts 27:15 illuminates our understanding of what is meant by "bearing" or "moving" the human writers. Just before the ship that was taking Paul to Rome was wrecked on the Island of Malta, it ran into a fierce storm. Though experienced men, the sailors could not guide it, so they finally had to let the wind take the ship wherever it blew. In the same manner as that ship was driven, directed, or carried about by the wind, God directed and moved the human writers He used to produce the books of the Bible. Though the wind was the strong force that moved the ship along, the sailors were not asleep and inactive. Similarly, the Holy Spirit was the guiding force that directed the writers who, nevertheless, played their own active roles in writing the Scriptures.

But this verse also makes another important point. It declares that the wills of the human authors did not direct the writing of the Bible. The same verb, "moved" or "bore," appears in the latter part of the verse as well. Thus prophecy was not borne by the will of man. The Spirit did it, not the will of man. This statement bears in an important way on the question of the inerrancy of the Bible. Man's will, including his will to make mistakes, did not bring the Scriptures; rather, the Holy Spirit, who cannot err, brought us the Scriptures. To be sure, the writers were active in writing, but what they wrote was directed, not by their own wills with the possibility of error, but by the Spirit who is true and infallible.

B. B. Warfield, commenting on 2 Peter 1:21, emphasized this point well:

> In this singularly precise and pregnant statement there are several things which require to be carefully observed. There is, first of all, the emphatic denial that prophecy—that is to say, on the hypothesis upon which we are working, Scripture—owes its origin to human initiative: "No prophecy ever was brought—'came' is the word used in the *English Version* text, with 'was brought' in the *Revised Version* margin—by the will of man." Then, there is the equally emphatic assertion that its source lies in God: It was spoken by men, indeed, but the men who spoke it "spake from God." And a remarkable clause is here inserted, and thrown forward in the sentence that stress may fall on it, which tells us how it could be that men, in speaking, should speak not from themselves, but from God: it was "as borne"—it is the same word which was rendered "was brought" above, and might possibly be rendered "brought" here—"by the Holy Spirit" that they spoke. Speaking thus under the determining influence of the Holy Spirit, the things they spoke were not from themselves, but from God.[1]

To sum up: 2 Peter 1:21 states that God used men and gave us a completely truthful Bible.

C. 1 Corinthians 2:13

Here Paul made the point that God's revelation came to us in words. This counters the contention of some that inspiration only relates to the thoughts that God wanted us to know, but not to the words in which those thoughts were expressed. Holding such a view relieves one of holding to the inerrancy of the text, for one could supposedly have truthful thoughts (God's) conveyed in erroneous words (man's). But Paul insisted that God's message came in the words of the text.

The fact that Paul says he spoke in words does not mean that he is not referring to his writings. Notice that Peter said that Paul "spoke" in his writings (2 Pet. 3:16). So "speaking in words" can certainly refer to Paul's written letters.

To sum up: this verse teaches that the actual words of the Bible are inspired.

D. A Group of Data

These data demonstrate some of the variety of material that God moved the human authors to include in the Bible.

1. Material that came directly from God. The two stones on which the Ten Commandments were written came directly from God (Deut. 9:10).

2. Researched material. Though some parts of the Bible were written straight off (like some of Paul's letters), some were researched before they were written. The Gospel of Luke is an example of this (Luke 1:1–4). Luke was not an eyewitness of the events of the life of Christ. So either God would have had to give him direct revelation of those events in order for Luke to write his Gospel, or Luke would have had to discover them through research. In his prologue, Luke told us that (a) he consulted eyewitnesses of Christ's life and ministry; (b) he used available written accounts of parts of His ministry; (c) he carefully investigated and sifted through all those sources; (d) he planned out the orderly arrangement of his material; and (e) the Holy Spirit moved and bore him along in the actual writing so that all he wrote was accurate and truthful.

3. Prophetic material. Approximately one fourth of the Bible was prophecy when it was written (though, of course, some of that material has been fulfilled). True prophecy can come only from the true, all-knowing God. No human writer could devise 100 percent true prophecy.

4. Historical material. Much of the Bible records history and does so accurately. Most of the historical portions were written by those who had personally lived through the events (e.g., Luke who was Paul's traveling companion on many of his travels, Acts 16:10–13; 20:5–21:18; 27:1–28:6, or Joshua who experienced and then wrote about the Conquest of Canaan in the Book of Joshua). Something like the history of Creation, of course, had to be revealed by God to Moses, since no human being was an eyewitness and Moses wrote about it long after it occurred.

5. Other material. The Bible does record things that are untrue, like the lies of Satan (Gen. 3:4–5), but it records them accurately. The Bible contains some quotations from the writings of unsaved people (Titus 1:12). It also has some passages that are strongly and vividly personal and emotional (Rom. 9:1–3). But this variety of material is accurately recorded.

To sum up: God sometimes revealed things supernaturally and directly; sometimes He allowed the human writers to compose His message using their freedom of expression. But He breathed out the total product, carrying along the authors in various ways, to give us His message in the words of the Bible.

II. A DEFINITION OF INSPIRATION

A proper definition must, of course, be formed on the basis of the data of Scripture on the subject as examined above. The "bare bones" of a definition is this: God carried men along so that they wrote His message in the Bible.

Putting some meat on those bones leads to a definition like this: God superintended the human authors of the Bible so that they composed and recorded without error His message to mankind in the words of their original writings.

Notice carefully some of the key words in that definition.

(1) The word "superintend" allows for the spectrum of relationships God had with the writers and the variety of material. His superintendence was sometimes very direct and sometimes less so, but always it included guarding the writers so that they wrote accurately.

(2) The word "composed" shows that the writers were not passive stenographers to whom God dictated the material, but active writers.

(3) "Without error" expresses the Bible's own claim to be truth (John 17:17).

(4) Inspiration can only be predicated of the original writings, not to copies or translations, however accurate they may be.

Observe: The procedure used in this chapter has been to examine the biblical data concerning inspiration and then to formulate a definition that incorporates that data. The definition, then, attempts to be a statement of the Bible's own claims for itself. We did not start with a definition and then impose it on the data, and in the process, force or select only the data that would fit it.

Finally, we should never lose sight of the incredible claims the Bible makes for itself in this matter of inspiration. No other book can compare with it. God breathed it; men wrote it; we possess it.

NOTE

1. B. B. Warfield, *The Inspiration and Authority of the Bible* (Philadelphia: Presbyterian and Reformed, 1948), 136.

Chapter 11
DEFECTIONS FROM THE BIBLICAL DOCTRINE OF INSPIRATION

Of course, not all understand the biblical doctrine of inspiration to be as expressed in the preceding chapter. Through the years, other understandings of the evidence have been proposed. Some are longstanding; others are newer. But all of them are, in my judgment, defective.

I. NATURAL INSPIRATION

This view understands the writers of the Bible to be men of great genius who did not need any supernatural help in writing the Bible. Some of the accompaniments of this view include the following: (1) The writers themselves conceived what they wrote; God did not breathe out the words. (2) This sort of inspiration can apply to books other than the Bible. "But the line of demarcation between it [the Bible] and other religious writings . . . is not so sharp and final as to establish a qualitative difference between *all* other writings and *every* part of the canonical Scriptures."[1] (3) If this be the true view of inspiration, then why cannot geniuses today write books that would be just as inspired as the books of the Bible? (4) Such a view of inspiration does not, of course, include infallibility of the product.

II. DYNAMIC OR MYSTICAL INSPIRATION

This viewpoint goes a step farther than natural inspiration, for it conceives of the writers as more than natural geniuses in that they were also Spirit-filled and guided. "The inspiration of the books of the Bible does not imply for us the view that they were produced or written in any manner generically different from that of the writing of other great Christian books. . . . There is a wide range of Christian literature from the fifth to the twentieth century which can with propriety be described as inspired by the Holy Spirit in precisely the same formal sense as were the books of the Bible."[2] Thus, (a) other Christian writings are as inspired as the Bible; (b) the Bible books are not infallible even though (c) they represent great religious literature that may even contain messages from God.

III. DEGREE INSPIRATION

Degree inspiration simply means that within the inspired Bible some parts are more inspired than other parts. All the Bible is inspired but not to the same degree. "Within this one great function of inspiration considerable variety exists. The inspiration of Isaiah or Paul is different from that of the compiler of Proverbs or the annalist who drew up Chronicles."[3] I incline to think this view has been replaced today by the idea of partial inspiration. Actually, degree inspiration confuses the illegitimate idea that there exist degrees of inspiration with the legitimate recognition of the variety of relevance of different parts of the totally inspired Bible.

IV. PARTIAL INSPIRATION

This concept teaches that while some parts of the Bible are inspired, other parts are not. Degree inspiration, by contrast, says that it is all inspired but some parts more so than others. Partial inspiration teaches that some portions are, in fact, not inspired at all. Usually the parts that are inspired are those that convey information otherwise unknowable (like the accounts of Creation or prophecies). Historical portions, on the other hand, that could be known from contemporary documents do not need to be inspired.

The contemporary expression of this view of inspiration teaches that the Bible is inspired in its purpose. That means we can trust the Bible when it tells us about salvation, but we may expect that errors have crept into other parts. In its parts that purpose to make us wise unto salvation the Bible is inspired, but in other parts that is not necessarily so. Here is an example: "I confess the infallibility and inerrancy of the Scriptures in accomplishing God's purpose for them—to give man the revelation of God in His redemptive love through Jesus Christ."[4] In other words, this view teaches that the Bible is inspired in its intent (to show men how to be saved) but not in its total content.

But is not the biblical teaching about salvation based on historical facts? Suppose those facts are inaccurate? Then our understanding about salvation might also be erroneous. You cannot separate history and doctrine, allow for errors (however few) in the historical records, and at the same time be certain that the doctrinal parts are true.

V. CONCEPT INSPIRATION

Some are willing to acknowledge that the concepts of the Bible are inspired but not the words. Supposedly this allows for an authoritative conceptual message to have been given, but using words that can in some instances be erroneous. The obvious fallacy in this view is this: How are concepts expressed? Through words. Change the words and you have changed the concepts. You cannot separate the two. In order for concepts to be inspired, it is imperative that the words that express them be also. Some seem to embrace concept inspiration as a reaction against the dictation caricature of verbal inspiration. To them if inspiration extends to the words, then God must have dictated those words. In order to avoid that conclusion, they embrace the idea that God inspired only the concepts; the writers chose the words, and not necessarily always accurately. But God's intended concepts somehow came through to us unscathed.

VI. BARTHIAN INSPIRATION

Karl Barth (1886–1968), though one of the most influential theologians in recent history, held a defective and dangerous view of inspiration, a view many continue to propagate. Barthians generally align themselves with the liberal school of biblical criticism. Yet they often preach like evangelicals. This makes Barthianism more dangerous than blatant liberalism.

For the Barthian, revelation centers in Jesus Christ. If He is the center of the circle of revelation, then the Bible stands on the periphery of that circle. Jesus Christ is the Word (and, of course, He is); but the Bible serves as a witness to the Word, Christ. The Bible's witness to the Word is uneven; that is, some parts of it are more important in their witness than other parts. The important parts are the ones that witness about Christ. Nevertheless, such parts, though important, are not necessarily accurate. Indeed, Barthians embrace the conclusions of liberalism regarding the Gospels, which teach that there are errors in those records.

Barthians charge evangelicals with holding a dictation view of inspiration. The biblical writers were typewriters on which God typed His message. Of course, this is not the orthodox view of inspiration.

In explaining the meaning of 2 Timothy 3:14–17 and 2 Peter 1:21, Barth stresses that in neither passage is there any occasion to think that the authors had special experiences. Inspiration, he says, is to be understood as "the act of revelation in which the prophets and apostles in their humanity became what they were, and in which alone they in their humanity can also become for us what they are."[5] Whatever such a statement means, clearly it does mean that the text is a human product full of errors, but which can become God's Word when it overpowers us.

That phrase "when it overpowers us" reminds us of the existential facet of the Barthian concept of inspiration. The Bible becomes God's Word when the Word of God, Christ, speaks to us through its pages. Inspiration, like revelation, emphasizes the subjective, existential encounter.[6]

Can such a Bible have any kind of authority? Yes, declares the Barthian. Its authority is in the encounter of faith with the Christ of Scripture. The Bible, because it points to Christ, has instrumental authority, not inherent authority. And those parts that do point to Christ have more authority than those that do not. Yet all the parts contain errors.

To sum up: Barthianism teaches that the Bible (B) points to Christ the Word (C). But in reality we do not know anything about C apart from B. It is not that we already have a clear concept of C by which we can test the accuracy of B, the pointer. Actually the Bible is the painter of C; that is, what we know about Christ comes from the Bible. So if the Bible has errors in it, the portrait of Christ is erroneous. And make no mistake about it, the Barthian Bible does have errors in it.

The subtleties of the various kinds of defections make it imperative to listen and read carefully to what people say and write about inspiration. The words may seem orthodox, but they may only be covering a very defective view of inspiration. The biblical data give us the correct doctrine. Everything must be tested against those data.

NOTES

1. Cecil J. Cadoux, *A Pilgrim's Further Progress* (London: Religious Book Club, 1945), 11.
2. Alan Richardson, *Christian Apologetics* (New York: Harper, 1948), 207.
3. Marcus Dods, *The Bible* (New York: Scribners, 1905), 127.
4. Ray Summers, "How God Said It," *The Baptist Standard,* 4 February 1970, 12.
5. Karl Barth, *Church Dogmatics,* I, 2, 563.
6. See Dewey M. Beegle, *The Inspiration of Scripture* (Philadelphia: Westminster, 1963), 126–31.

Chapter 12
The Inerrancy of the Bible

Attacks on the inerrancy of the Bible are not new and seem to be somewhat cyclical. However, the contemporary debate seems to be an intramural one; that is, it is among evangelicals, rather than between liberals and conservatives. Perhaps this makes it even more significant, for the debate has drawn lines among evangelicals that needed to be drawn. It has also served to sharpen distinctions that surround the concept of inerrancy.

I. THE IMPORTANCE OF INERRANCY

A. Its Importance Stated

Can one be an evangelical and deny the full concept of inerrancy? The answer is yes, simply because some evangelicals do. Strictly speaking, an evangelical is one who believes the Gospel. Can one be a Christian and not accept the concept of inerrancy? Of course, and undoubtedly many fall into that category. To be a Christian means being rightly related to Christ. Can one be a biblicist and deny inerrancy? Not if the Bible teaches its own inerrancy.

How important is this doctrine then? If it is a biblical teaching, then to deny it is to deny part of the truthfulness of the Bible. But consider this: If the Bible contains some errors, however few or many, how can one be sure that his understanding of Christ is correct? Perhaps one of those errors concerns something about the life of Christ. It would not be impossible that there might be an error about the crucial matter of His death and resurrection. What then would happen to one's Christology? It would be changed, perhaps even so drastically that there would be no Christian faith to embrace.

Or suppose the biblical teaching on the Holy Spirit were inaccurate. This could affect the cardinal doctrine of the Trinity, which in turn could also seriously affect Christology, soteriology, and sanctification. Even if the errors are supposedly in "minor" matters, any error opens the Bible to suspicion on other points that may not be so "minor." If inerrancy falls, other doctrines will fall too.

When inerrancy is denied one may expect some serious fallout in both doctrinal and practical areas.

Some doctrinal matters that may be affected by denying inerrancy include the following:

(1) A denial of the historical fall of Adam.

(2) A denial of the facts of the experiences of the prophet Jonah.

(3) An explaining away of some of the miracles of both the Old and New Testaments.

(4) A denial of the Mosaic authorship of the Pentateuch.

(5) A belief in two or more authors of the Book of Isaiah.

(6) A flirting with or embracing of liberation theology with its redefining of sin (as societal rather than individual) and salvation (as political and temporal rather than spiritual and eternal).

Some lifestyle errors that may follow a denial of inerrancy include the following:

(1) A loose view of the seriousness of adultery.

(2) A loose view of the seriousness of homosexuality.

(3) A loose view of divorce and remarriage.

(4) "Cultural" reinterpretation of some of the teachings of the Bible (e.g., teaching on women, teaching on civil obedience).

(5) A tendency to view the Bible through a modern psychological grid.

Inerrancy is an important doctrine, the denial or even diluting of which may result in serious doctrinal and life errors.

B. Its Importance Diluted

Still many insist that inerrancy is either unimportant, irrelevant, or unnecessary to the faith. Therefore, all the furor being stirred up over it is merely a tempest in a teapot, and those who insist on it are disturbing the peace of the church.

But that simply is not so. Inerrancy is a crucial issue, for if the Bible is not completely without error then it must have at least one error in it. Now if we could all agree on where that one error is then the problem might conceivably be tolerated. But if the current literature is any guideline, then there are about twenty candidates for that one error, and that means there might be as many as twenty errors. And if there could be as many as twenty errors, then the question becomes, How can I trust the Bible at all? So inerrancy is not a tempest in a teapot.

Several reasons are commonly offered for concluding that inerrancy is a nonessential doctrine.

Those who oppose or who want to diminish the importance of inerrancy often make this statement: "Since the Bible does not clearly teach inerrancy, neither can we." At the very least this places those who insist on the importance of inerrancy in the position of insisting on more than the Bible does. At the most, it implies or asserts that inerrancy is not a biblical doctrine.

But for the statement to be true requires (a) that we can show that the Bible does not clearly teach inerrancy, and (b) that if it does not (in the sense of providing proof texts), we cannot assert inerrancy on the basis of an inductive study of the evidence. Let's examine these statements. Does the Bible clearly teach inerrancy? The answer will depend on what is meant by "clearly." If by clearly one means proof texts such as are present in the Bible for substitutionary atonement, for example (Matt. 20:28), then admittedly there is not that type of "clear" evidence for inerrancy. But many doctrines are accepted by evangelicals as being clearly taught in the Scriptures for which there are no proof texts. The doctrine of the Trinity furnishes the best example of this. It is fair to say that the Bible does not clearly teach the doctrine of the Trinity, if by clearly one means there are proof texts for the doctrine. In fact, there is not even one proof text, if by proof text we mean a verse or passage that "clearly" states that there is one God who exists in three persons.

How then do we arrive at a clear doctrine of the Trinity? Simply by accepting two lines of evidence in the Bible: (a) clear statements that teach there is only one God; and (b) equally clear statements that there was Someone called Jesus and Someone designated the Holy Spirit who in addition to God the Father claimed to be God. Such evidence permits only one of two conclusions: either Jesus and the Holy Spirit are not divine, or God exists as a Triunity. Orthodox Christians have never shied away from the second conclusion even though evidence is of a different kind of clarity than that which proof texts provide.

Or to take another example, many deny that Jesus is God, because, they say, there is no "clear" evidence that He ever claimed to be divine. Robert S. Alley, then of the University of Richmond, stirred up a furor among Southern Baptists when he asserted that Jesus "never really claimed to be God or to be related to Him."[1] Even though he possessed the same evidence from the Bible as those who conclude that Jesus did claim to be God, he arrived at a completely different conclusion. Such heresy outrages orthodox believers, and rightly so.

Though I have not yet discussed the evidence for the clear teaching of the Bible as to its own inerrancy, let us assume for the moment that it does teach it clearly, though not necessarily by proof texts. If so, are errantists demanding of the Bible a higher standard of clarity to prove inerrancy than they require to prove the deity of Christ or the Trinity? In other words, do they not have one set of criteria for clearly proving the doctrine of the Trinity and another for inerrancy?

The above illustrations prove the fallacy of concluding that if something is not proof texted in the Bible we cannot clearly teach the results of an inductive study or reach logical conclusions drawn from the evidence that is there. If that were so, I could never teach the doctrines of the Trinity or the deity of Christ or the deity of the Holy Spirit or even forms of church government. Often I hear people say, "I will go only as far as the Bible does." That *can* be a good standard because we do not ever want to add to what the Bible teaches. But neither do we want to omit anything it teaches clearly whether by proof texts, deduction, induction, implication, logic, or principles. The claim for not wanting to go beyond what the Bible teaches can be merely an excuse for not wanting to face the implications of what it does teach. And I fear that for some that has been their excuse for not wanting to face what the Bible does say about its own inerrancy.

The second excuse for diluting the importance of inerrancy is that since we do not possess any original manuscripts of the Bible, and since inerrancy is related to those originals only, the doctrine of inerrancy is only a theoretical one and therefore nonessential. It is true we do not possess any of the original manuscripts of the Bible, and the doctrine of inerrancy, like inspiration, is predicated only on the original manuscripts, not on any of the copies. The two premises in the statement are correct, but those particular premises do not prove at all that inerrancy is a nonessential doctrine.

Obviously, inerrancy can be asserted only in relation to the original manuscripts because only they came directly from God under inspiration. The very first copy of a letter of Paul, for instance, was in reality only a copy, and not the original that Paul himself wrote or dictated. Both inspiration and inerrancy are predicated only on the originals. But would an errantist claim that inspiration is a nonessential doctrine on the basis of not having the originals and not attributing inspiration to the copies? I think not. Then why does he say that about inerrancy?

Another argument is that inerrancy is a recent teaching that the church formerly was not concerned about; therefore, we need not be concerned about it today.

The argument from church history seems to rear its head almost every time any doctrine is discussed. If the doctrine was taught in ancient times this supposedly makes it more reliable. If, on the other hand, it has not been taught until more recent years, then it is suspect.

Of course, the argument itself is invalid. The truth or untruth of any doctrine does not depend on whether or not it was ever taught in church history. Its truthfulness depends solely on whether or not it is taught in the Bible. Now, admittedly, a teaching that no one has ever before heard about might be suspect, but the Bible, not church history, is the standard against which all teachings must be measured.

Nevertheless, the history excuse persists with the doctrine of inerrancy. It is recent, they say, and therefore the debate should cease.

Some say inerrancy originated with B. B. Warfield at Princeton in the late 1800s. Others claim that Turretin, a Lutheran theologian, started it all just after the Reformation.

Actually neither man did. We believe that Christ taught inerrancy, as did the apostle Paul. Furthermore, Augustine, Aquinas, the Reformers, and other great men held to it throughout church history. Granted, such evidence from history does not validate the doctrine (Christ's and Paul's teaching do, and we shall examine that later), but it invalidates the claim that inerrancy is a recent invention.

For example, Augustine (354–430) clearly stated that "most disastrous consequences must follow upon our believing that anything false is found in the sacred books. That is to say that the men by whom the Scripture has been given to us and committed to writing put down in these books anything false. If you once admit into such a high sanctuary of authority one false statement, there will not be left a single sentence of those books, which, if appearing to anyone difficult in practice or hard to believe, may not by the same fatal rule be explained away as a statement, in which intentionally, the author declared what was not true" (*Epistula* p. 28). Here in ancient terms is the domino theory.

Again, Thomas Aquinas (1224–74) plainly said that "nothing false can underlie the literal sense of Scripture" (*Summa Theologica* I.1, 10, ad 3). Also, Luther declared, "The Scriptures have never erred" (*Works of Luther* XV.1481). John Wesley, the founder of Methodism, wrote, "Nay, if there be any mistakes in the Bible there may well be a thousand. If there is one falsehood in that Book it did not come from the God of truth" (*Journal* VI.117).

How can anyone say, then, that inerrancy is a recent invention? Even if it were, it could still be a true doctrine. Only the Bible, not history, can tell us.

II. THE MEANING OF INERRANCY

Definitions of inerrancy are not plentiful. Errantists equate inerrancy with infallibility and then limit its scope to matters of faith and practice or to revelational matters or to the message of salvation. An example of this: "The Bible is infallible, as I define that term, but not inerrant. That is, there are historical and scientific errors in the Bible, but I have found none on matters of faith and practice."[2] At least this is an honest distinction between infallibility and inerrancy.

The Lausanne Covenant declared the Bible to be "inerrant in all that it affirms." The phrase is admittedly flexible, since it may allow for errors in areas like Creation where, according to some interpreters, the Bible is not affirming historical facts. Both inerrantists and errantists could subscribe to that statement.

The International Council on Biblical Inerrancy in its Chicago statement affirmed inerrancy in a brief statement that the "Scripture is without error or fault in all its teaching. . . ." Then followed nineteen articles to further describe and explain inerrancy.

This brief statement would be unsatisfactory to errantists. If there were any doubt about that, certainly the nineteen-article elaboration would exclude errantists' agreeing with it.

The dictionary defines inerrancy as "being without error." Most definitions of inerrancy share this negative description. The question raised then by that definition is, what is error? Can the Bible use approximations and still be without error? Can a New Testament writer quote freely from the Old Testament and claim that the resultant quotation is without error? Can a biblical writer use the language of appearances without communicating error? Can there exist different accounts of the same event without involving error?

Admittedly, the data of Scripture often includes approximations, free quotations, language of appearances, different accounts of the same occurrence. Can that data support a definition of inerrancy as "being without error"? Obviously, the data and the definition must harmonize if that is a correct definition of what the Bible teaches about its own inerrancy.

Perhaps the tension would be erased if we defined inerrancy positively—the inerrancy of the Bible means simply that the Bible tells the truth. Truth can and does include approximations, free quotations, language of appearances, and different accounts of the same event as long as these do not contradict. For example, if you were to report to me that a mutual friend had a hundred-thousand dollar income last year, that would be an inerrant statement, even though his income for reporting to the IRS was $100,537. That approximation would tell the truth. Or if I said, "Sunrise over the Grand Canyon is one of the most spectacular sights I have ever seen," my statement with its own use of language of appearance would tell the truth, though the sun does not literally rise over the Grand Canyon.

Does the Bible say not to lie? Yes, it says don't lie. Is that a true statement? Of course, though it is also true (not more true) to say that the Bible says, "Lie not one to another." The free quotation is also true.

Or again, my wife told me that when she saw the changing of the guard at Buckingham Palace, a soldier fainted and fell on the ground. But the newspaper reported that on the same day *three* men fainted. That was also a true report. If my wife had said that *only* one man fainted, her report would have been wrong. Actually three did, but she focused only on the one nearest to where she was standing. She may even have noticed that the others also fainted, but she simply did not report that. Nevertheless, her statement was true.

If 1 Corinthians 10:8 says 23,000 died in one day and Numbers 25:9 records 24,000 but does not add the restriction "in one day," we understand both to be telling the truth (and probably both figures are approximations of the number that died in one day and the number of additional deaths later).

If a New Testament writer makes a free quotation from the Old Testament, since he was writing under the inspiration of the Spirit, that free quotation becomes part of the inspired, inerrant text. The Holy Spirit, the author of both Old and New Testaments, certainly has the right to quote Himself as He wishes and to use quotations with meanings we as uninspired interpreters might never have seen.

Using the language of appearances is a common way of communicating, sometimes even more vividly than scientific language could. We say that the sun rises and sets, which from the viewpoint of appearance is true. But if we were speaking scientifically we would have to explain that the earth moves, not the sun.

If Mark and Luke speak of one blind man given sight at Jericho, while Matthew reports two, both statements are true as long as Mark and Luke do not say only one man.

Most debates over truth and error get off track when they become philosophical and not down to earth. Most people understand clearly and easily that approximations, etc., tell the truth. The Bible is inerrant in that it tells the truth, and it does so without error in all parts and with all its words.

If it were not so, then how could the Lord affirm that man lives by every word that proceeds from the mouth of God (Matt. 4:4), especially if all Scripture is breathed out by God? (2 Tim. 3:16).

III. THE INCARNATION AND INERRANCY

The logic of some still insists that anything involving humanity has to allow for the possibility of sin. So as long as the Bible is both a divine and human Book the possibility and actuality of errors exist.

Let's examine that premise. Is it always inevitable that sin is involved where humanity is?

If you were tempted to respond affirmatively, an exception probably came to mind almost immediately. The title of this section could have put the clue in your mind. The exception is our Lord Jesus Christ. He was the God-man, and yet His humanity did not involve sin. So He serves as a clear example of an exception to the logic pressed by people who believe in errancy.

The true doctrine of the God-man states that He possessed the full and perfect divine nature and a perfect human nature and that these were united in one person forever. His deity was not in any detail diminished; His humanity was not in any way sinful or unreal, but sinless; and in His one Person His natures were without mixture, change, division, or separation.

Similarly, the Bible is a divine-human Book. Though it originated from God, it was actually written by man. It is God's Word, conveyed through the Holy Spirit. Sinful men wrote that Word but did so without error. Just as in the Incarnation, Christ took humanity but was not tainted in any way with sin, so the production of the Bible was not tainted with any errors.

Let me take the analogy further. In the humanity of Jesus Christ there were some features that were not optional. He had to be a Jew. He could not have been a Gentile. He had to be a man, not a woman. He had to be sinless, not sinful. But some features of sinless humanity might be termed optional. Jesus could have possessed perfect humanity within a variation of a few inches in height at maturity, though a dwarf or a giant would have been imperfect. He might have varied a little in weight at maturity and still have been perfect. Surely, within limits, the number of hairs on his scalp could have been a sinless option. However, the humanity He exhibited was, in fact, perfect humanity.

The writers of the Bible were not passive. They wrote as borne along by the Spirit, and in those writings some things could not have been said any other way. Paul insisted on the singular rather than the plural in Galatians 3:16. But conceivably there were some sinless options as in Paul's emotional statement in Romans 9:1–3. Yet the Bible we have is in fact the perfect record of God's message to us.

Everybody wrestles with the relationship between the divine and the human authors of Scriptures. The divine must not be so emphasized as to obliterate for all practical purposes the human, and the human must not be allowed to be so human as to permit errors in the text.

A similar thing happened with regard to the person of Christ in the early centuries of church history. Docetism, a first-century heresy, taught that Christ did not actually become flesh but only appeared as a man, thus robbing Him of genuine humanity. Docetism was, of course, a Christological error, but you can see the analogy with the question of the dual authorship of the Bible. Those who hold to errors in the Bible say that inerrancy overemphasizes the divine authorship to the neglect of its "humanness." Thus God's superintendence of the Bible to the extent of producing an errorless Bible is said to be a Docetic view of inspiration. Karl Barth made this charge, and more recently, so have Dutch theologian Berkhouwer and Fuller professor Paul Jewett.

But if it were true (which it is not) that those who hold to the total inerrancy of the Bible are espousing a heresy akin to Docetism, then it would be equally true that those who hold to any kind of errancy support a doctrine analogous to Ebionitism.

In the second century, the Ebionites denied the deity of Christ by denying His virgin birth and His preexistence. They regarded Jesus as the natural son of Joseph and Mary who was elected Son of God at His baptism, but not as the eternal Son of God. They thought Jesus was a great prophet and higher than the archangels, but not Divine.

If inerrancy is supposed to be a Docetic-like heresy, then errancy, albeit limited, is obviously an Ebionite-like heresy, since the humanity of the Bible has to permit errors in the Bible. According to the errancy view, since real men were involved, their writings cannot be guaranteed to be without error even though the Holy Spirit directed and inspired them. That's an Ebionite-like error.

There is an orthodox doctrine of the person of Christ, and there is an orthodox doctrine of the Bible. Both involve God and man, and each results in a sinless product.

NOTES

1. Robert S. Alley, "Some Theologians Question Factual Truth of Gospels," *The Richmond News Leader,* 17 July 1978, 1.
2. Stephen T. Davis, *The Debate About the Bible* (Philadelphia: Westminster, 1977), 115.

Chapter 13
INERRANCY AND THE TEACHINGS OF CHRIST

A deduction consists of a major premise, a minor premise, and a conclusion. The deductive evidence for inerrancy is this: God is true, God breathed out the Bible, therefore the Bible is true. Of course, any deduction is only as good as its premises. In this particular deduction, both premises are good and true simply because they are clearly stated in the Bible itself. So the deductive evidence for inerrancy is as strong and conclusive as the authority of the Bible itself.

But there is also another line of reasoning, the *inductive.* In an induction one reasons from parts to the whole, from particulars to the general. A conclusion is thus drawn from the evidence.

An induction is only as good as the completeness of the evidence studied. If the first five typewriters one saw were all electric, then one might conclude that all typewriters were electric. But, of course, the first nonelectric typewriter observed would invalidate the conclusion. Nevertheless, not all inductions run that high a risk of being invalid, for if one can examine as much evidence as possible, he can be assured of a very reliable conclusion.

We can examine all of the recorded teachings of Christ. We do not believe that there is any likelihood that some unrecorded teaching of Christ will turn up to invalidate the evidence we find from His teachings in the Gospels. If we can investigate all that He said concerning the reliability of the Bible, then we can draw a valid conclusion about Christ's view of the Bible.

I. THE EVIDENCE OF MATTHEW 4:1–11

The account of the temptation of our Lord reveals some important matters concerning His view of the Bible.

First, Jesus accepted the plenary inspiration of the Bible; when first approached by the devil to turn stones into bread, our Lord replied that man lives by *every word* that proceeds from the mouth of God (Matt. 4:4 quoting Deut. 8:3). He did not say "some words" but "every word." If Scripture is breathed out from God (2 Tim. 3:16), then

Scripture must be included in what sustains man, not only parts of Scripture but all of it.

The second temptation also illustrates the importance of plenary inspiration. Satan tried to entice the Lord to throw Himself off the pinnacle of the temple by assuring Him that He could claim the promise of Psalm 91:11–12 that God's angels would guard Him. But in quoting those verses Satan omitted part of verse 11: "To guard you in all your ways." The omission distorts the meaning of the promise, which is that God will keep the righteous on their journeys, not that He will preserve them when they take needless risks. Taking a needless risk is exactly what Satan proposed to Christ. The Lord replied that to bank on part of a verse would be to tempt God. Instead He would rely on *every* word that came from God, including every word of verses 11–12.

Second, Jesus accepted the truth of the propositions of the Bible. As has been said, a popular viewpoint today sees the Bible as containing only personal revelation, not propositional revelation. That is, the Bible reveals God and Christ accurately, but it does this in a person-to-person relationship rather than in statements. Therefore, although we can trust the message of the Bible, we really cannot (nor do we need to) trust the particular statements or propositions of the Bible. The Bible, they say, witnesses to the infallible truth, but it doesn't have to do so with inerrant statements. The pointer, the Bible, is fallible, but Christ, to whom it points, is infallible.

But Christ's response to Satan's attacks negates that viewpoint. He said, "It is written" (Matt. 4:4, 7, 10). He did not say, "It witnesses." He relied on propositional statements to convey truth in and of themselves and to convey it accurately.

II. THE EVIDENCE FROM CHRIST'S USE OF THE OLD TESTAMENT

Our Lord used historical incidents in the Old Testament in a manner that showed His total confidence in their factual historicity.

He acknowledged that Adam and Eve were created by God, that they were two living human beings, not merely symbols of man and woman, and that they acted in specific ways (Matt. 19:3–5; Mark 10:6–8).

He verified events connected with the flood of Noah's day; namely, that there was an ark and that the Flood destroyed everyone who was not in that ark (Matt. 24:38–39; Luke 17:26–27).

On two different occasions, He authenticated God's destruction of

Sodom and the historicity of Lot and his wife (Matt. 10:15; Luke 17:28–29).

He accepted as true the story of Jonah and the great fish (Matt. 12:40) and acknowledged the historicity of Isaiah (12:17), Elijah (17:11–12), Daniel (24:15), Abel (23:35), Zechariah (23:35), Abiathar (Mark 2:26), David (Matt. 22:45), Moses and his writings (8:4; John 5:46), Abraham, Isaac, and Jacob (Matt. 8:11; John 8:39).

Christ did not merely *allude* to these stories, but He *authenticated* the events in them as factual history to be completely trusted. These events include many of the controversial passages of the Old Testament, such as Creation, the Flood, and major miracles including Jonah and the fish.

Obviously, our Lord felt He had a reliable Bible, historically true, with every word trustworthy.

If we find that He only used or taught in a general way about the Bible, then we shall conclude that He believed in its reliability generally. If, on the other hand, we find that He relied on the minutiae of the Bible as accurate, then we must conclude that He believed it to be inerrant down to its details.

III. THE EVIDENCE OF MATTHEW 5:17–18

"Do not think that I came to abolish the Law or the Prophets; I did not come to abolish, but to fulfill. For truly I say to you, until heaven and earth pass away, not the smallest letter or stroke shall pass away from the Law, until all is accomplished."

First, what is the promise? It is that the Law and the Prophets will not be abolished, but fulfilled. Abolish means not to accomplish something, and fulfill means to accomplish the promises. Christ is guaranteeing something about promises not failing.

Second, what is encompassed in this promise? The "Law and the Prophets" included all of the Old Testament, our Lord's Bible. "Law" in verse 18 means the same thing (compare the use of "Law" in John 10:34, where it includes more than the Mosaic Law).

Third, in what detail will all the promises of the Old Testament be fulfilled? The Lord said you can count on the Old Testament promises being fulfilled down to the very jots and tittles (KJV).

The jot is the Hebrew letter *yodh.* It is the smallest of all the letters in the Hebrew alphabet. It would occupy proportionately about the same amount of space that an English apostrophe takes up in a line of English type. Actually, the Hebrew letter looks very much like an English apostrophe. Though it is the smallest of the Hebrew letters it is as important as any other letter, for letters spell words, and words compose sentences, and sentences make promises. If you spell a word one way, it is that word; if you spell it another way, even only a single letter differently, it is a different word. Tough means strong. One letter changed spells touch. One letter added spells though. Single letters change words. Our Lord promised that not one jot would fail. Every promise will be fulfilled just as it was spelled out.

Observe that Christ does not start with concepts and then allow for optional words to be used to convey those concepts (as concept inspiration teaches). He begins the other way around. The promises are based on the words as spelled, and those words can be relied on fully and in detail.

Neither did our Lord say that the promises would be fulfilled provided they were culturally relevant at the time of fulfillment. In some circles today, promises are culturally reinterpreted, thereby actually invalidating the original promises. But Christ taught that we could count on plain fulfillment of the original promises as spelled out in the Old Testament.

A tittle is even more minute than a jot. Whereas a jot is a whole letter, a tittle is only a part of a letter. The presence of a tittle forms a certain letter, but its absence causes that letter to become a different one. For example, the Hebrew letter *beth* looks like this ב. The letter *kaph* looks like this כ. Obviously they appear to be very similar. The only difference between the two letters is that the bottom horizontal line on the *beth* extends slightly to the right of the vertical line, whereas no extension appears on the *kaph.* That extension—not the entire bottom horizontal line but only the part of it that extends to the right of the vertical line—is a tittle. If it is present then the letter is a *beth;* if it is absent, it is a *kaph.* And whether you use a *beth* or a *kaph* will result in spelling different words.

Another example: The Hebrew letter *daleth* looks like this ד. The *resh* looks like this ר. Again the tittle is only that part of the horizontal line that extends to the right of the vertical line. But a word spelled with a *daleth* is different from one spelled with a *resh.*

The Lord's promise was that all of the promises of the Old Testament will be fulfilled precisely as they were spelled out.

In English we might illustrate a tittle this way. Suppose I invite you to my house to have some "Fun." You might rightly wonder what I consider fun. If I put a tittle or small stroke on the F, then you might conclude that I like to "Pun." Punning is fun to me. But you may not enjoy making puns, so I'll put another tittle on the letter. Now I have spelled "Run." To run is fun for some, but not to me. So I'll add another tittle, and now I am inviting you over to have a "Bun." The difference between Fun, Pun, Run, and Bun is just the addition of a tittle in each case. But four entirely different words result, and with them, four different invitations!

IV. THE EVIDENCE OF JOHN 10:31–38

Minutiae do make a difference. Toward the end of His earthly ministry the Lord again affirmed His total confidence in the minute reliability of the Scripture. At the temple celebration of the Feast of Dedication, or Hanukkah (instituted in 165 B.C. to commemorate the cleansing and reopening of the temple after its desecration by Antiochus Epiphanes three years earlier), the Jews asked Jesus to tell them plainly if He is the Messiah (John 10:24). His answer was, "I and the Father are one" (v. 30). The word "one" is neuter, "one thing," not "one person." In other words, He did not assert that He and the Father are identical but that He and the Father possess essential unity together, that He enjoys perfect unity of nature and of actions with His Father. The Jews had asked if He was the Messiah. His answer was more than they had bargained for, for in it He claimed also to be equal with God.

This was certainly the way they understood His claim, for immediately they prepared to stone the Lord for what they considered to be blasphemy. In order to restrain them the Lord appealed to Psalm 82. He called this portion of the Old Testament "the Law" (John 10:34), as He did on two other occasions (12:34 and 15:25). In that Law, He said, the judges of Israel, human beings, were called "gods" by virtue of their high and God-given office. Then, He concluded, if that psalm can apply the term "gods" to human beings, then certainly the term "Son of God" may be rightly applied to the One whom the Father sanctified and sent into the world. In other words, if *elohim* is applied to men, how much more appropriate it is to apply it to Himself, since He does possess essential unity with the Father.

Though the argument is highly sophisticated, certain claims Christ made about the Bible are crystal clear.

The Bible is *verbally* inspired. He pointed the Jews to what had been *written.* God's Word came in written propositional statements, not merely in concepts, thoughts, or oral tradition. It is the written record that was inspired and that can be relied on.

The Bible is *minutely* inspired. Psalm 82 is not what would be considered a major Old Testament passage. It is not a psalm of David or a messianic psalm. This is not said to demean the psalm in any way for, of course, it is equally inspired with all other parts of the Bible, but it is to emphasize that the Lord did not pick an outstanding passage on which to base His argument. Indeed one might say, without being disrespectful, that He chose a rather ordinary, run-of-the-mill passage. Of course, He would not have done so if He believed that such passages were not part of God's inerrant inspired Word. Furthermore, from that ordinary passage He focused on a single word, "gods." He could not have done so unless He believed in the minute inspiration of the Bible. He rightly assumed He could count on any part of the Bible and any word in any part.

The Bible is *authoritatively* inspired. In the midst of His sophisticated arguing the Lord threw in almost incidentally the statement: "and the Scripture cannot be broken." What does this mean? Simply that the Scripture cannot be emptied of its authority. The only way it could fail to have complete authority would be if it were erroneous, but Christ said here that it is both authoritative and inerrant. Some translations place this phrase in parentheses. It may be better to regard it as depending on the "if" that begins the sentence. That "if" introduces a first-class condition that means certainty, and is better translated "since." Thus the Lord was saying two things are certain: the psalm called them gods and the Scripture cannot be broken. Remember, Christ was here staking His life on the reliability, accuracy, and authority of just one word of Scripture, for His enemies were about to stone Him.

V. THE EVIDENCE OF MATTHEW 22:23–33

Picture the scene: The Lord on "Face the Jewish Nation" and "Meet the Pharisaic Press," all in the same day. The Herodians had tried to trap Him by asking if it was lawful to pay the poll tax to Caesar. Then the Sadducees took their turn (Matt. 22:23–33). In that dialogue we have more clear evidence of our Lord's faith in an inerrant and therefore minutely authoritative Scripture.

The Sadducees believed in the authority of the Pentateuch. They denied, however, the existence of angels and other spirits and belief in the resurrection of the dead because they could not find them taught in the Pentateuch. They immediately demonstrated their disbelief by asking Jesus a question about the resurrection. In addition they dreamed up an illustration based on the Pentateuch, to reinforce their question. It was the law of levirate marriage (from the Latin meaning "husband's brother's marriage," found in Deut. 25). The law required the brother-in-law of a childless widow to marry her if he was able to do so. If not, then the responsibility fell on his next of kin as in the story of Ruth and Boaz (Ruth 4:6).

It was on this basis that the Sadducees concocted a story about seven brothers, the first of whom married a woman and died. Each of the other six married her in turn after all of his older brothers died. Finally, the seventh husband died, and last of all the wife.

Then the Sadducees confronted the Lord with their question: "In the resurrection therefore whose wife of the seven shall she be? For they all had her."

His answer was scathing. He charged them with error, with ignorance of the Scripture, and with ignorance of the power of God (Matt. 22:29).

Then Christ evaluated the question and judged it irrelevant (v. 30) because in the resurrection people do not marry. They are similar to angels who do not marry because there is no need to procreate baby angels. The number of the angels was fixed at the time they were created. Similarly, in the afterlife human beings will not marry because there will be no need for infants to be born. Christ was not saying that people become angels after they die, but only that *like* angels they will not procreate. Since that is so, there was no need to answer the Sadducees' question. It was entirely irrelevant. The levirate marriage law was designed to ensure that children would be born to bear the family name of the first-dead husband, but in heaven there will be no need for such a provision; hence the irrelevance of the question.

As if it were not sufficient to charge the Sadducees with error, ignorance, and irrelevance, the Lord proceeded to teach them some sound doctrine from an Old Testament passage (Exod. 3:6) that they considered authoritative. The lesson was simply this: Contrary to your doctrine, your Bible teaches that there is life after death. Death does not end it all, as you teach.

Again our Lord used a very sophisticated argument. I expect that few of us would choose to use Exodus 3 to attempt to teach the doctrine of life after death. But our Lord did.

Notice too, just as in John 10:34, He based His argument on the written Word, not general concepts, but specific written words. Specifically, He based His case on how God identified Himself to Moses at the burning bush: "I am the God of Abraham, and the God of Isaac, and the God of Jacob" (Matt. 22:32). That proves, the Lord went on to say, that God is the God of the living, which means that Abraham, Isaac, and Jacob were still alive though they had died long before.

How does that identification prove the doctrine of life after death? Simply by the use of the present tense, "I am." Abraham, Isaac, and Jacob had died several hundred years before God spoke this way to Moses. Yet God said that He was still their God at the time He was speaking to Moses. This would not have been possible if when Abraham, Isaac, and Jacob died they ceased to exist. It was only possible if, contrary to the Sadducees' doctrine, death does not end it all.

Of course, the difference between *I am* and *I was* is a matter of verb tense. This argument was based on a present tense rather than a past tense. Christ used the present tense to support the doctrine of resurrection.

The force of what Christ was saying can be illustrated this way. Often as a visiting preacher, I am invited home to dinner after the church service by one of the members. I have discovered that usually one of the appropriate topics of conversation is to inquire about the children in that family. Suppose I should ask, "How many children do you have in your family?" and the father or mother replies, "We had four, but one died, so now we only have three." Faced with that kind of response, I cannot be very sure about the spiritual condition or maturity of those parents. But if, on the other hand, to the same question a parent replies, "We have four; one is in heaven and three are here with us," then I have a good deal of confidence about that family's beliefs. I can be almost certain that they do not believe that death ends it all but that there is a resurrection coming.

The difference is only in the tense of the verb used: we *had* or we *have* in the illustration, and I *was* their God or I *am* their God in the biblical text.

Observe carefully the ramifications of Christ's statement here.

(1) He assumed the historicity of God's appearance to Moses.

(2) He assumed that God's revelation came in a propositional statement.

(3) He assumed that every word of that statement could be trusted to be precisely accurate.

(4) He assumed that doctrinal truth has to be based on historical accuracy. The Bible cannot be inaccurate in matters of history and accurate in doctrine.

(5) He assumed that one could use even unlikely passages and trust their accuracy.

VI. THE EVIDENCE OF MATTHEW 22:41–46

Later that same day, when the Pharisees had joined the crowd of antagonists, the Lord became the aggressor, asking a straightforward question of them: "About the Christ, whose son is He?" (Matt. 22:42). Theirs was an immediate answer: "The Son of David." It was correct but incomplete. Christ is the son of David as far as His humanity is concerned, but He also is the Son of God, and the Lord wanted the Pharisees to acknowledge this as well. So He asked them, "Then how does David in the Spirit call Him 'Lord'?" To prove that David did, He quoted Psalm 110:1. In that psalm "the Lord [that is, the Father] says to my Lord [the Messiah who was David's Lord]: 'Sit at My right hand [the Father's] until I [the Father] make Thine [the Messiah's] enemies a footstool for Thy feet.'"

How could David call Messiah his Lord if Messiah were only David's son? The only answer is that Messiah was also David's God. In other words the Messiah had to be both God and man. As man He was David's son; as God, David's Lord. The pronoun "my" links David to his Messiah-Lord.

Perhaps an illustration will help. When Queen Elizabeth II dies or abdicates, the Prince of Wales will presumably become King Charles. Assume that Prince Philip, his father, is still living. I ask someone, "King Charles, whose son is he?" The answer would come back: "Prince Philip's." "But," I might reply, "I saw the coronation of King Charles on TV, and I saw Prince Philip bowing and swearing allegiance to him. Why does Philip call Charles 'lord'?" The answer is simple: King Charles is Philip's sovereign-king even though he is also Philip's natural son. He is both Philip's son and Philip's lord. So also Messiah was David's son and, because Messiah is equal with God, David's Lord.

Natural procreation links Messiah to David as David's descendant. The pronoun "my" in Psalm 110:1 links Messiah to David as David's Lord God. And the pronoun "my" is simply a *yodh,* that smallest of Hebrew letters, attached to the word Lord.

There is nothing more central to an orthodox Christology than the full deity and true humanity of Jesus Christ. If He were not the God-man then He could not have been an adequate Savior, High Priest, or Judge. Who of us would think of using Psalm 110 as our Lord did to emphasize the truth of who He is? But that is exactly what Jesus did, basing His argument with the Pharisees on the single Hebrew word "my." The seeming minutiae of Scripture can be trusted.

What have we learned from our Lord's attitude toward the Bible?

(1) The spelling of words can be trusted completely, and not one promise will be fulfilled in any way different from how it was spelled out.

(2) The only way the Scripture can lose its authority is if it contains errors, but Christ taught that the Scripture cannot be broken. Thus He must have believed it did not contain errors.

(3) The Lord built sophisticated arguments on single words and even the tense of a verb.

Who can say he fully follows the Lord without accepting His teaching concerning the inerrancy of the Scriptures?

Chapter 14
PROBLEM PASSAGES

I. SOME PROBLEMS IN THE OLD TESTAMENT

No one denies that there are passages in the Bible that contain problems of one kind or another. The inerrancy question does not involve interpretive problems or debates concerning the best text type. But problems of apparent discrepancies, conflicting numbers, differences in parallel accounts, or allegedly unscientific statements do concern the question of inerrancy.

Errantists and inerrantists both have access to the same facts concerning each of these problems. Both have capable minds to use in interacting with those facts. Both can read the conclusions of others. But they do not come to these problems with the same basic outlook. The errantist's outlook includes not only the possibility but the reality of errors in the Bible. Therefore, when he studies these problems one of his possible conclusions is that one or another of them is actually an error.

The inerrantist, on the other hand, has concluded that the Bible contains no errors. Therefore, he exercises no option to conclude that any of these same problems is an example of a genuine error in the Bible. His research may lead him to conclude that some problem is yet unexplainable. Nevertheless, he believes it is not an error and that either further research will demonstrate this, or he will understand the solution in heaven.

Consider this illustration: If a happily married man comes home unexpectedly one day to find his wife waving good-bye to a handsome man about to get into a car, what will he think? If his confidence and trust in his wife is total and unwavering because of their years of satisfying experiences together, he will assume she had a good reason for seeing that man. Though he may be curious, the husband will not doubt his wife's loyalty. Perhaps it will not be until later that he learns that the man he saw was delivering a special present his wife had ordered for him.

But if his confidence in his relationship with his wife is even a bit shaky, then his thoughts will wander into all kinds of paths including unfaithfulness on her part. Because of his insecurity, his wife will forever be branded an adulteress in his eyes.

The analogy is clear, isn't it? If I come to the Bible with confidence that its words were breathed out from God and are therefore without errors, and if that confidence has been buttressed by years of proving the Bible totally reliable, then I won't be shaken by a problem, and I certainly will not conclude that it is in error. But if I think there can be errors in the Bible, however few or many, then I will likely conclude that some of those problems are examples of errors. And even if there is only one, I have an errant Bible.

From the current literature on the inerrancy debate, it is difficult to present a definitive list of errors. It is probably not possible to list criteria by which to judge errors, only to list actual examples of errors. Though no two writers agree on a list of errors, when all the examples are put together there are about two dozen, more or less.

The lack of uniformity in these lists raises a serious question: Who and what determines the boundary line between the territory of permissible errancy and the territory of necessary inerrancy? If, for instance, some errancy can be expected and tolerated in historical matters, but not in doctrinal areas, how do I know *which* historical matters? After all, some important doctrines are built on historical matters. So where do I stop?

Admittedly, there are certain problem passages to examine. However, I maintain that reasonable suggestions can be found so that we need not conclude they are errors.

In a discussion like this I can only make suggestions, and there is not space to make those suggestions in great detail. Further information is readily available in other books and commentaries. But the point is that suggestions have been made that are compatible with the doctrine of inerrancy.

A. The "Two Accounts" of Creation

Although the allegation that there are two conflicting accounts of Creation has ramifications in a number of areas of interpretation, often in the inerrancy discussion the focus is on the supposed contradiction between Genesis 1:11–12, which records vegetation appearing on the third day and 2:5, which seems to say there was no vegetation until after Adam was created.

Two things are wrong about such a conclusion. First, chapter 2 adds details to the account of Creation in chapter 1, not in contradiction but in supplementation. For example, we are told that God created man (a generic term here) male and female (1:27), but this does not mean that the first creature was a male-female combination. The details of that creation of the male, Adam, and the female, Eve, are given in 2:18–23. Likewise, verse 5 adds details about the creation of vegetation on the third day.

Second, the words used in verse 5 refer to the kind of plants that require cultivation, not to all kinds of green plants. Plants that required such cultivation either did not appear until Adam was created and could then cultivate them, or they appeared but did not grow until Adam was created.

Leupold has summed up the matter well.

> Verse 4*b* takes us back into the time of the work of creation, more particularly to the time before the work of the third day began, and draws our attention to certain details, which, being details, could hardly have been inserted in chapter 1: The fact that certain forms of life, namely the kinds that require the attentive care of man in greater measure, had not sprung up. . . . When verdure covered the earth, the sprouting of these types of vegetation was retarded, so that they might appear after man was already in full possession of his domain and in a position to give them their needed care. . . . The fact that not the whole of vegetation is meant appears from the distinctive terms employed, neither of which had as yet appeared in the account. . . . From all this it appears sufficiently how absurd the claim is that in this account (2:4ff.) man is made first, then vegetation.[1]

Thus a contradiction and therefore an error appears in this account only for those who want it. Good exegesis requires no error.

B. Cain's Wife

Though by many inerrantists the question of where Cain got his wife would not be considered a problem at all, this question is often used by those who try to demonstrate that the Bible is unreliable in what it claims. How could it claim that Adam and Eve were the first human beings who had two sons, one of whom murdered the other, and yet who produced a large race of people? Clearly, the Bible does teach that Adam and Eve were the first created human beings. The Lord affirmed this in Matthew 19:3–9. The genealogy of Christ is traced back to Adam (Luke 3:38). Jude 14 identifies Enoch as the seventh from Adam. This could hardly mean the seventh from "mankind," an interpretation that would be necessary if Adam were not an individual as some claim. Clearly, Cain murdered Abel and yet many people were born. Where did Cain get his wife?

We know that Adam and Eve had other sons and daughters in addition to Abel, Cain, and Seth (Gen. 5:4), and if there was only one original family, then the first marriages had to be between brothers and sisters. Such marriages in the beginning were not harmful. Incest is dangerous because inherited mutant genes that produce deformed, sickly, or moronic children are more likely to find expression in children if those genes are carried by both parents. Certainly, Adam and Eve, coming from the creative hand of God, had no such mutant genes. Therefore, marriages between brothers and sisters, or cousins or other relatives, in the first and second generations following Adam and Eve would not have been dangerous.

C. Numbers 25:9

The plague that followed Israel's worship of Baal and Peor killed 24,000 people according to Moses. Yet Paul recorded only 23,000 deaths in 1 Corinthians 10:8. An obvious error? Not necessarily, for Paul limited his 23,000 figure to those killed on one day. The account in Numbers 25 records that the judges were involved in carrying out this judgment, and the number may include additional deaths that occurred on the following days. In other words, they may not have completed their awesome task in one day. The two accounts do not conflict because of Paul's additional phrase "in one day."

But no damage is done to inerrancy if we consider both numbers as round figures. If so, then the number killed was between 23,000 and 24,000. If either passage stated that "exactly" or "only" a certain number died and if they did not agree, this would constitute a clear error. But such is not the case.

D. Who Caused David to Number Israel? (2 Sam. 24:1; 1 Chron. 21:1)

One account says the Lord did, whereas the other says Satan did. But why does this have to be a conflict? Could not both the Lord and Satan have been involved? They have been in other matters. Paul said that the Lord sent a messenger from Satan to keep Paul from exalting himself (2 Cor. 12:7). Certainly the Lord and Satan are involved in activities that lead to Armageddon. Why not here also? Such a simple solution makes even the suggestion of a contradiction seem incredible.

Yet this is no straw man. One errantist emphatically stated that "both accounts cannot be accurate. But from the viewpoint of doctrinal integrity they both present exactly the same truth: What David did was wrong. . . ."[2]

E. Who Killed Goliath? (2 Sam. 21:19; 1 Sam. 17:50)

Did David kill Goliath or did someone else named Elhanan? Before assuming that the accounts are in conflict and therefore that one is in error, let's ask some other questions: (1) Could David have had two names, the other one being Elhanan? Solomon had two names (2 Sam. 12:24–25). (2) Could there have been two Goliaths? In the immediate context (21:20), another giant is mentioned at Gath. (3) Could some words like "the brother of" have been omitted from verse 19? Any of these solutions is equally plausible rather than concluding the presence of an error. And all of them are more plausible in light of the proven accuracy of the Bible elsewhere.

F. Certain Numbers in 2 Samuel 24 and 1 Chronicles 21

Other numbers in this parallel account seem not to harmonize, and errantists conclude that some things are in error. Second Samuel 24:9 reports 800,000 were numbered in Israel and 500,000 in Judah, whereas 1 Chronicles 21:5 gives a 1.1 million total for Israel and 470,000 for Judah. The difference in the total for Israel may be accounted for by assuming that the 800,000 figure did not include the 300,000 listed in 1 Chronicles 27, which if added would agree with the 1.1 million total in 1 Chronicles 21:5. Perhaps the 30,000 difference in the other figures involves the 30,000 specially mentioned in 2 Samuel 6:1.

When God gave David a choice of punishment, He offered as an option seven years of famine according to 2 Samuel 24:13 and three years of famine according to 1 Chronicles 21:12. The Septuagint translation says three years in both places, so likely the figure in 2 Samuel is a scribal error. (It has been changed to say three years in some versions, including the NIV.) Though copies were very carefully made, errors inevitably crept in. This seems to be one, but it is not an error in the original—that was inerrant when it was written, but inerrancy cannot be extended to the copies.

Finally, in these chapters the question of how much David paid for the property he bought from Araunah seems to be in conflict in the two accounts. Second Samuel 24:24 says 50 shekels of silver while 1 Chronicles 21:25 records 600 shekels as the price. The difference is too great even allowing for inflation! But is it too great if the 50 shekels were paid for the threshing floor alone (2 Sam. 24:24) while the larger amount included other property surrounding it?

G. The Laver in 2 Chronicles 4:2

In describing the measurements of this laver, the circumference is given as 30 cubits (or 540 inches if the cubit was 18 inches) while the diameter is 10 cubits. However, circumference is arrived at by multiplying the diameter by *pi* (3.14159), and that total is more than 565 inches, an apparent contradiction. One writer resolves it by saying that "in the culture of the day the measurement was not only accurate but also 'inerrant.'"[3] However, there is a better solution that does not include sleight of hand. The 10-cubit measurement was from brim to brim; that is, from one outside edge to the other. But verse 5 states that the width of the edge was a handbreadth, or about 4 inches. So the inside diameter was 10 cubits (180 inches) minus two handbreadths (8 inches). Multiplying 172 inches by pi, the total is 540 inches, the same circumference as given in verse 2.

These represent passages being currently used as illustrations of errors in the Old Testament. Without going into great detail, all I have tried to do is show that reasonable explanations are at hand. We need not conclude that errors are present in the text (with the exception of occasional copyists' errors). How one views these suggestions will be a reflection of his underlying confidence, or lack of it, in the Bible itself.

II. SOME PROBLEMS IN THE NEW TESTAMENT

Errantists also cite a number of passages from the New Testament that supposedly deny inerrancy or at least require a definition of inerrancy that contains so much latitude that it becomes errancy. One writer cited 2 Chronicles 4:2; Numbers 25:9; Mark 2:26; and Matthew 22:42 as examples of "a kind of inerrancy that falls short of perfect conformity to what was actually said" and of problems to which only "highly fanciful" explanations could be given.[4]

Another is troubled by Matthew 13:31–32 and problems in Acts 7 that he says cannot be solved compatibly with inerrancy.[5] Still another cited Matthew 27:9 as an error and said that there are "hundreds of examples like this one."[6] We obviously cannot discuss "hundreds" of unnamed examples, but we will look at the ones named in the writings of those who hold to something less than total inerrancy.

A. Taking a Staff (Matt. 10:9–10; Mark 6:8; Luke 9:3)

Mark records that Jesus allowed the disciples to take a staff while Matthew and Luke say He forbade it. This led an errantist to say: "I know of no way to reconcile this inconsistency. The proper conclusion, I think, is that the accounts are inconsistent and that at least one of the Gospels is in error."[7]

But resolution is not impossible. Putting the accounts together, the Lord permitted the disciples to take along any staffs they already had (Mark). However, they were not to take one if they did not have one or walked well without one (Luke). In no case were they to procure or buy a new staff (Matthew, who uses a different verb from Mark and Luke, one meaning to acquire or get). The principal idea of the Lord's instruction is clear: do not make any special provision for this mission.

B. The Mustard Seed (Matt. 13:32)

In His Parable of the Mustard Seed, the Lord said that the mustard seed was the smallest of all the seeds. Is this plainly an erroneous statement since the mustard seed is not the smallest? Before jumping to that conclusion, remember that it was stated by Jesus Christ, and if He spoke a lie then how could He have been sinless? This is not simply a small factual discrepancy; if the statement is an error, then it proves something about the One who made it, and that becomes a serious doctrinal matter. You cannot separate this history from its doctrinal ramification.

But how are we to understand the Lord's words? One suggestion stated well by Trench years ago is this: "This seed, when cast into the ground, is *'the least of all seeds'*—words which have often perplexed interpreters, many seeds, as of poppy or rue, being smaller. Yet difficulties of this kind are not worth making; it is sufficient to know that 'small as a grain of mustard seed' was a proverbial expression among the Jews for something exceedingly minute (see Luke 17:6). The Lord, in His popular teaching, adhered to the popular language."[8]

Another fact to note is that the word "smallest" is actually a comparative, not a superlative and should be translated (as in the NASB and NEB), "smaller" of all the seeds. In other words, the Lord did not state an absolute (the mustard seed is absolutely the smallest) but placed the mustard seed in the class of smallest seeds.

Perhaps the two suggestions should be combined. Technically, He placed the mustard seed among the smaller seeds and capitalized on the popular proverbial understanding of that seed as representing something exceedingly minute. But He did not make a technical or scientific error.

C. The Blind Men at Jericho (Matt. 20:29–34; Mark 10:46–52; Luke 18:35–43)

The accounts of the healing of the blind men at Jericho (one of them being Bartimaeus) contain some different details, which some have interpreted as irresolvable, leading to the conclusion that one or another of the accounts must contain errors. Matthew wrote that the Lord healed two blind men as He left Jericho. The other accounts mention only one blind man and record the miracle being performed as they entered Jericho. As to the number of blind men, if Mark or Luke said only one blind man, then there would be an error. But if Bartimaeus was the more forward of the two, then it would be natural for one writer to focus on him while another might mention both of them. The statement that there were two includes the focus on one. A statement that there were two would conflict if another Gospel contained a statement that there was only one. But such is not the case.

As to when the miracle happened, two plausible suggestions have been made. One is that the men pleaded with the Lord as He entered Jericho, but were not healed until He was leaving. The other is that since there were two Jerichos (old Jericho and the new city), the healing could have taken place after the group left old Jericho and as they were nearing new Jericho. Thus Matthew's "as they were going out" refers to old Jericho while Mark's and Luke's references to approaching Jericho refer to new Jericho.

Whichever suggestion is true it is clear that there is no need to see an insoluble contradiction in these accounts.

D. Zechariah's Father (Matt. 23:35)

In this verse Zechariah (not the prophet by the same name but a priest) is said to be the son of Berechiah, while in 2 Chronicles 24:20 he is said to be the son of Jehoiada. But "son of" does not have to mean the next immediate generation (as in Gen. 31:28 where Laban refers to his grandchildren as sons and daughters, or as in the case of Christ, the Son of David and Abraham, Matt. 1:1). Most likely, Jehoiada was Zechariah's grandfather and is named in the Chronicles account because of his fame.

E. Zechariah vs. Jeremiah (Matt. 27:9–10)

The main part of this quotation comes from Zechariah 11:12–13, whereas Matthew seems to ascribe it to Jeremiah. Is this not a clear mistake?

Before reaching such a conclusion, consider that Jeremiah was placed at the beginning of the Old Testament prophetic writings in the Babylonian Talmud. Matthew, then, may simply be using Jeremiah's name to designate the section of the Old Testament from which the Zechariah references come. It is much like saying, "In the book by Smith, Jones said. . . ." Jones wrote a chapter in a book which Smith edited. (This is not to suggest, however, that Jeremiah edited Zechariah's prophecy.) Note this same prominence given to Jeremiah in Matthew 16:14 where he is the only prophet named specifically though others are included in the statement.

Though this seems the most plausible explanation, some find a solution in the thought that Matthew had primarily in mind the events mentioned about the potter's house in Jeremiah 18 and 19.

F. Isaiah vs. Malachi (Mark 1:2–3)

These verses raise a problem since immediately after the words "as it is written in Isaiah the prophet," there follows a quotation from Malachi, then a quotation from Isaiah. Many regard this as an obvious error, though a harmless one. However, the structure of the chapter introduces the "beginning of the gospel" by focusing on the ministry of John the Baptist in the wilderness. So the quotation from Isaiah was in Mark's mind the principal one, since it predicted the figure in the wilderness. His attention being on the Isaiah prophecy explains why he only mentioned Isaiah in verse 2.

G. Abiathar vs. Ahimelech (Mark 2:26)

Mark, in referring to David eating the tabernacle bread, said Abiathar was the high priest, whereas the Old Testament record of this event states that Ahimelech was (1 Sam. 21:1–6). A solution recognizes that while the event actually happened during Ahimelech's priesthood, he soon was killed and Abiathar, who also would have been exercising priestly functions at that time, shortly became high priest and proved to be more prominent than Ahimelech. Mark was not saying that Abiathar was actually high priest when the event took place, but he was a ministering priest and soon became a very prominent high priest. Similarly one might speak of some event that occurred in the senatorial years of John F. Kennedy and refer to it as happening in the days of Kennedy, the president. He was not president when it happened, rather a senator, but he is identified as Kennedy the president because he (later) became president.

Again, these examples in Mark remind us that if one comes to the Bible expecting or allowing for error, he can make a case for an errant Scripture. But if he comes expecting the Bible to be inerrant, he can find plausible solutions, and even if he cannot honestly accept any of the suggested solutions, he still can believe that the Bible is inerrant and that we simply do not have enough facts to solve some of the seeming problems.

H. The Death of Judas

In Acts 1:18, Peter described Judas's death as "falling headlong, he burst open in the middle and all his bowels gushed out." Matthew said that Judas hanged himself (Matt. 27:5). Most likely both descriptions are true. He did hang himself, but something happened that caused his body to fall and break open. This is the simplest solution and has been suggested since the time of Augustine.

The same two accounts seem to contain another problem. Matthew stated that the priests bought the field of blood while Acts attributes it to Judas. Again the simple solution is that both accounts are correct. The priests could not take the money back, so they bought the field in Judas's name since they did not want to appear to have anything to do with his money.

I. Problems in Acts 7

Although it is well within the boundaries of the concept of inerrancy to permit Stephen in this speech to utter something erroneous and have Luke record it accurately, the serious interpreter will want to know as clearly as possible what Stephen was saying. One of the problems focuses on verse 6 where Stephen gives the length of the Egyptian captivity as 400 years whereas Exodus 12:40 says 430 years. Further, Paul in Galatians 3:17 wrote that the Law came 430 years after the Abrahamic promise. The problems in these figures are two: (a) The difference between 400 and 430; and (b) the apparently large error of Paul because the time between Abraham and the giving of the Law was considerably longer than 430 years. Many simply acknowledge that the 400/430 difference involves an approximation. Four hundred is 430 rounded off. The 430 years in Galatians does not use the termini from Abraham to the Law (Gen. 12 to Exod. 20). Rather, it refers to the period from the end of the Patriarchal Age (Gen. 35:11–12) to the giving of the Law in Exodus 20.

Others believe that 400 years was the duration of the Egyptian bondage and that both 430-year figures refer to the time between the last confirmation of the Abrahamic Covenant to Jacob and the giving of the Law. However, this illustrates a case where we simply do not have enough facts to be able to make a conclusive decision. So once again one's attitude comes into play: you can believe there are errors, or you can believe that there would be perfect resolution if all the facts were known.

Sometimes the apparent problem in verse 14 poses a question. There Jacob's family is said to be seventy-five persons while in Genesis 46:27 only seventy are included. Stephen in Acts follows the Septuagint number, which included five extra persons (the son and grandson of Manasseh and two sons and a grandson of Ephraim). Genesis does not include these. But in both numbers only a restricted group is included because the total number of the family of Jacob would have been much greater, including wives of Jacob's sons and grandsons and husbands of his daughters and granddaughters who are not listed. Anyone trying to list the number in an immediate family of this size would easily have come up with at least two ways of doing it and two different totals without contradiction.

These represent the New Testament problems being discussed. Some of them have been used throughout church history to try to prove that there are errors in the Bible. And reasonable solutions have been proposed throughout history to these problems. Some have come into focus more recently. Any of them might be used to conclude that the Bible contains errors, but all of them do have reasonable explanations.

It takes only one error to make an errant Bible. It may be a "small" error, an inconsequential one, a historical one, or a doctrinal one, but if there is one, then we do not have an inerrant Bible.

Notes

1. H. C. Leupold, *Exposition of Genesis* (Columbus: Wartburg, 1942), 112–13.
2. Ray Summers, "How God Said It," *The Baptist Standard,* 4 February 1970, 12.

3. Robert Mounce, "Clues to Understanding Biblical Accuracy," *Eternity,* June 1966, 18.
4. Ibid.
5. Daniel P. Fuller, "Evangelicalism and Biblical Inerrancy" (unpublished material, 1966), 18–19.
6. Berkeley Mickelsen, "The Bible's Own Approach to Authority," in *Biblical Authority,* ed. Jack B. Rogers (Waco, Tex.: Word, 1977), 86.
7. Stephen T. Davis, *The Debate About the Bible* (Philadelphia: Westminster, 1977), 106.
8. R. C. Trench, *Notes on the Parables of Our Lord* (New York: Revell, n.d.), 91.

Chapter 15
THE CANON

The subject of the canon involves the question of how many books belong in the Bible. Canon then refers to the authoritative list of the books of the Bible. Of course, the individual books were written over a long period of time by various writers. How then were they collected, and who decided which ones went into the canon of Scripture?

I. SOME BASIC CONSIDERATIONS

A. The Meaning of the Term *Canon*

1. Its derivation. The word comes from the Greek word *kanon,* which refers to a measuring instrument. It therefore came to mean a rule of action (Gal. 6:16; Phil. 3:16).

2. History of the use of the word. In the early church the word *canon* was used to refer to the creeds. In the middle of the fourth century it came to be used of the Bible; i.e., of the list of accepted books that were acknowledged to make up the Bible.

3. Its meaning. Actually the word *canon* has a twofold meaning. It refers to the list of books that met certain tests or rules and thus were considered authoritative and canonical. But it also means that the collection of canonical books becomes our rule of life.

B. Some Underlying Considerations in Investigating Canonicity

1. Self-authentication. It is essential to remember that the Bible is self-authenticating since its books were breathed out by God (2 Tim. 3:16). In other words, the books were canonical the moment they were written. It was not necessary to wait until various councils could examine the books to determine if they were acceptable or not. Their canonicity was inherent within them, since they came from God. People and councils only recognized and acknowledged what is true because of the intrinsic inspiration of the books as they were written. No Bible book became canonical by action of some church council.

2. Decisions of men. Nevertheless, men and councils did have to consider which books should be recognized as part of the canon, for some candidates were not inspired. Some decisions and choices had to be made, and God guided groups of people to make correct choices (not without guidelines) and to collect the various writings into the canons of the Old and New Testaments.

3. Debates over canonicity. In the process of deciding and collecting, it would not be unexpected that some disputes would arise about some of the books. And such was the case. However, these debates in no way weaken the authenticity of the truly canonical books, nor do they give status to those that were not inspired by God.

4. Completion of canon. Since A.D. 397 the Christian church has considered the canon of the Bible to be complete; if it is complete, then it must be closed. Therefore, we cannot expect any more books to be discovered or written that would open the canon again and add to its sixty-six books. Even if a letter of Paul were discovered, it would not be canonical. After all, Paul must have written many letters during his lifetime in addition to the ones that are in the New Testament; yet the church did not include them in the canon. Not everything an apostle wrote was inspired, for it was not the writer who was inspired but his writings, and not necessarily all of them.

The more recent books of the cults that are placed alongside the Bible are not inspired and have no claim to be part of the canon of Scripture. Certainly so-called prophetic utterances or visions that some claim to be from God today cannot be inspired and considered as part of God's revelation or as having any kind of authority like that of the canonical books.

II. THE CANON OF THE OLD TESTAMENT

A. The Evidence of the Old Testament Itself

1. From the Law. There are a number of references in the Old Testament to the Law of Moses as being authoritative. Here are some of those references: Joshua 1:7–8; 23:6; 1 Kings 2:3; 2 Kings 14:6; 21:8; 23:25; Ezra 6:18; Nehemiah 13:1; Daniel 9:11; Malachi 4:4. Such references validate the inspired nature of Moses' writings in the first five books of the Old Testament where he recorded the Law.

2. From the Prophets. The prophets claimed to be speaking the Word of God, and their prophecies were recognized as authoritative. Notice these references: Joshua 6:26 compared with 1 Kings 16:34; Joshua 24:29–33 compared with Judges 2:8–9; 2 Chronicles 36:22–23 com-

pared with Ezra 1:1–4; Daniel 9:2 compared with Jeremiah 25:11–12.
3. From Malachi 4:5. In Malachi 4:5 there is an indication that the prophetic witness would end with Malachi and not begin again until the coming of an Elijah-type prophet in the person of John the Baptist (Matt. 17:11–12).

B. The Evidence of the Dead Sea Scrolls

1. Their importance. The scrolls show us what books of the Old Testament were recognized as sacred in the period between the Old and New Testaments.
2. Their number. About 175 of the 500 Dead Sea Scrolls are biblical. There are several copies of many of the books of the Old Testament, and all the Old Testament books are represented among the scrolls, except Esther.
3. Their testimony. The existence of biblical books among the scrolls does not in itself prove their canonicity since some of the noncanonical books are also present. However, many of the Dead Sea Scrolls are commentaries, and so far all of those commentaries deal only with canonical books. That seems to show that a distinction between canonical and noncanonical books was recognized. Also twenty of the thirty-nine books of the Old Testament are quoted or referred to as Scripture. In summary, the scrolls give positive evidence for the canonicity of all but Chronicles, Esther, and the Song of Solomon.

C. Other Evidence

1. Prologue to Ecclesiasticus. This noncanonical book refers to a threefold division of books (namely, the Law, the Prophets, and hymns and precepts for human conduct), which was known by the writer's grandfather (which would be around 200 B.C.).
2. Philo. Philo (around A.D. 40) referred to the same threefold division.
3. Josephus. Josephus (A.D. 37–100) said that the Jews held as sacred only twenty-two books (which include exactly the same as our present thirty-nine books of the Old Testament. Josephus included five books for the Pentateuch, thirteen for the Prophets (Joshua, Judges with Ruth, Samuel, Kings, Chronicles, Ezra-Nehemiah, Esther, Job, Isaiah, Jeremiah with Lamentations, Ezekiel, the 12 minor prophets, Daniel), and four for "hymns to God and practical precepts to men" (Psalms, Song of Solomon, Proverbs, Ecclesiastes).
4. Jamnia. Jamnia (A.D. 90), was a teaching house of rabbis who discussed canonicity. Some questioned whether it was right to accept (as

was being done) Esther, Ecclesiastes, and the Song of Solomon. These discussions concerned an existing canon.

5. The church fathers. The church fathers accepted the thirty-nine books of the Old Testament. The only exception was Augustine (A.D. 400), who included the books of the Apocrypha (those "extra" books that some Bibles include between the books of the Old and New Testaments). However, he did acknowledge that they were not fully authoritative. The books of the Apocrypha were not officially recognized as part of the canon until the Council of Trent (A.D. 1546) and then only by the Roman Catholic Church.

D. The Evidence of the New Testament

1. The quotations of the Old Testament in the New. There are some 250 quotes from Old Testament books in the New Testament. None is from the Apocrypha. (Jude [v. 14] quotes from the noncanonical book of Enoch, but that book is classified as Pseudepigrapha, not Apocrypha.) All Old Testament books are quoted except Esther, Ecclesiastes, and the Song of Solomon.

2. Matthew 5:17. Here the Lord said that the Law and the Prophets were authoritative because they were sure to be fulfilled. This twofold division covers all of the Old Testament.

3. Luke 11:51. Here the Lord said something definitive about the extent of the canon of the Old Testament that He accepted. In condemning the leaders of the Jewish people for killing God's messengers throughout their history, He charged them with being guilty of shedding the blood of all the righteous from Abel to Zechariah. The murder of Abel is recorded in Genesis 4, and the murder of Zechariah in 2 Chronicles 24, which in the arrangement of the Hebrew canon was the last book in order (as Malachi is in our arrangement). So the Lord was saying, "From the first to the last murder recorded in the Old Testament." Now, of course, there were other murders of God's messengers recorded in the Apocrypha, but the Lord does not include them. Evidently He did not consider the books of the Apocrypha to be of equal authority with the books from Genesis to 2 Chronicles.

III. THE CANON OF THE NEW TESTAMENT

A. The Tests for Canonicity

1. The test of authority. In relation to Old Testament books, this meant having the authority of a lawgiver or a prophet or a leader in Israel behind them. In connection with New Testament books, this meant having the authority of an apostle behind the books that were accepted into the canon. This meant that the book either had to be written by an apostle or backed by one so that either way there was apostolic authority behind the book. For example, Peter was considered to be the apostle who stood behind the writings of Mark, and Paul the apostle behind the writings of Luke.

2. The test of uniqueness. To be taken into the canon a book had to show internal evidence of its uniqueness as an evidence of its inspiration.

3. The test of acceptance by the churches. As the books circulated they had to gain acceptance by the churches. Actually there was no book that was doubted by any large number of churches that eventually was accepted into the canon.

B. The Process of Acknowledgment of the New Testament Canon

Remember that the books were inspired when they were written and thus canonical. The church only attested to what was inherently true.

1. The witness of the apostolic period. The writers witnessed that their own writings were the Word of God (Col. 4:16; 1 Thess. 4:15). They also acknowledged that the writings of other New Testament books were Scripture. "Scripture" was a designation in Judaism for canonical books, so when it is used in the New Testament of other New Testament writings, it designates those writings as canonical. And it is so used in two significant places.

One is 1 Timothy 5:18 where a quotation from Deuteronomy 25:4 is linked with one from Luke 10:7, and both are called Scripture. To be sure the sentiment of Luke 10:7 is found in the Old Testament, but the form of quotation is found only in the Gospels. The other is 2 Peter 3:16 where Peter referred to the writings of Paul as Scripture. This is a significant attestation because of the relatively short span of time that had elapsed between the time Paul wrote some of his letters and the time when Peter acknowledged them as Scripture.

2. The witness of the period A.D. 70–170. During this period all the New Testament books were cited in other writings, and the church Fathers recognized as canonical all twenty-seven books. However, each Father does not include all twenty-seven. In addition, Marcion, a heretic (140), included in his canon only Luke and ten of Paul's epistles, which shows, at least, that a collection was being made this early of Paul's writings.

3. The witness of the period A.D. *170–350.* Three important pieces of evidence come from this period. First, the Muratorian canon (170) omitted Hebrews, James, and 1 and 2 Peter. However, there is a break in the manuscript, so we cannot be certain that these books were not included. This canon also rejects some other books like the Shepherd of Hermas, which did not become part of the canon.

Second, The Old Syriac Version (end of second century) lacked 2 Peter, 2 and 3 John, Jude, and Revelation. But no extra books were added to bring the total to twenty-seven.

Third, the Old Latin Version (200) lacked 2 Peter, James, and Hebrews, but added no extra books. So the unqualified candidates for books to be included in the canon were rejected during this period; most of the New Testament books were received; only a few were debated.

4. The Council of Carthage (397). It is generally agreed that this church council fixed the limits of the New Testament canon as including all twenty-seven books as we have them today.

5. A note on Luther's opinion of the Book of James. Sometimes it is claimed that Martin Luther rejected the book of James as being canonical. This is not so. Here's what he wrote in his preface to the New Testament in which he ascribes to the several books of the New Testament different degrees of doctrinal value. "St. John's Gospel and his first Epistle, St. Paul's Epistles, especially those to the Romans, Galatians, Ephesians, and St. Peter's Epistle—these are the books which show to thee Christ, and teach everything that is necessary and blessed for thee to know, even if you were never to see or hear any other book of doctrine. Therefore, St. James' Epistle is a perfect straw-epistle compared with them, for it has in it nothing of an evangelic kind." Thus Luther was comparing (in his opinion) doctrinal value, not canonical validity.

Chapter 16
THE INTERPRETATION OF THE BIBLE

I. THE PRINCIPLES OF HERMENEUTICS

A. A Definition of Hermeneutics

Hermeneutics is the study of the principles of interpretation. Exegesis consists of the actual interpretation of the Bible, the bringing out of its meaning, whereas hermeneutics establishes the principles by which exegesis is practiced.

In actuality every interpreter of the Bible has a system of hermeneutics, whether consciously so or not. As one practices his exegesis, he reveals his hermeneutics, though probably most interpreters do not ever systematize their hermeneutics. Few, if any, interpreters begin by working out their hermeneutics before proceeding to exegesis. Most seem to think about hermeneutics after they have been interpreting for years. But thinking about the subject of hermeneutics serves an important purpose, for it forces one to examine the basis of exegesis and the consistency of his interpretive practices.

B. Some Hermeneutical Systems

I believe (for reasons yet to be stated) that the correct system of hermeneutics is that which may be labeled normal, plain, or literal. However, examples of other systems that do not promote normal or plain interpretation (at least not consistently) can serve to sharpen what is meant by the normal interpretation and the hermeneutical principles on which it is based. It should be said that hardly anyone has a "pure" system of hermeneutics. Most combine elements of several systems.

1. Allegorical hermeneutics. An allegory is a symbolic representation. Allegorical hermeneutics stands in contrast to literal hermeneutics and is usually resorted to when the literal sense seems unacceptable to the interpreter. The actual words, then, are not understood in their normal sense but in a symbolic sense, which results in a different meaning of the text, a meaning that, in the strictest sense, the text never intended to convey.

If used consistently, allegorical hermeneutics would reduce the Bible to near-fiction, for the normal meaning of words would be irrelevant and would be replaced by whatever meaning the interpreter gives to the symbols. However, for the most part, allegorical hermeneutics is not practiced consistently or thoroughly. Evangelicals who use this system do so usually in the area of prophecy, while using normal or literal hermeneutics in other areas of biblical interpretation.

F. W. Farrar tells where this allegorical method originated. He says:

> Allegory by no means sprang from spontaneous piety, but was the child of rationalism which owed its birth to the heathen theories of Plato. It deserved its name, for it made Scripture say something else than it really meant. . . . Origen borrows from heathen Platonists and from Jewish philosophers a method which converts the whole of Scripture, alike the New and the Old Testament, into a series of clumsy, varying, and incredible enigmas. Allegory helped him to get rid of chiliasm and superstitious literalism and the "antitheses" of the Gnostics, but it opened the door for deadlier evils.[1]

2. Literal interpretation. At the opposite end of the spectrum from "pure" or consistent allegorical interpretation stands literal interpretation. Since the word "literal" has connotations that are either misunderstood or subjectively understood, labels like "plain" or "normal" serve more acceptably. "Literal" is assumed to preclude figures of speech, etc. (which is not the case).

Usually it is assumed that literal interpretation goes hand in hand with a belief in verbal, plenary inspiration. This is not necessarily so, for there are exegetes who practice literal hermeneutics but who do not hold to the highest view of inspiration.

More will be said about the principles of literal interpretation later. At this point I only want to present it as the opposite of allegorical interpretation.

3. Semiallegorical or semiliteral interpretation. Among evangelicals, at least, scarcely any are pure allegorists. Therefore, there exists a method of interpretation that may be labeled semiallegorical. Turning the coin over, it may also be called semiliteral, especially if there is a strong emphasis on literal interpretation in most of the areas of theology.

As I have said, usually literal interpretation is abandoned in the area of the interpretation of prophecy. Robert Mounce in his commentary *The Book of Revelation* exhibits a semiliteral exegesis. He states that Armageddon should be taken seriously but not literally. It "portrays the eschatological defeat of Antichrist . . . but does not require that we accept in a literal fashion the specific imagery with which the event is described."[2] Concerning the Millennium, he favors the idea that "John taught a literal millennium, but its essential meaning may be realized in something other than a temporal fulfillment."[3] "The millennium is not, for John, the Messianic Age foretold by the prophets of the O.T."[4]

Oswald T. Allis tried to develop legitimate reasons for semiallegorical hermeneutics. Arguing that no literalist takes everything literally, he proceeds to try to demonstrate why limitations must necessarily be placed on literal interpretation. The reasons he advances are: (a) the presence of figures of speech mean that we cannot take all the Bible literally; (b) the fact that the main theme of the Bible is spiritual requires a spiritual hermeneutic (he prefers "spiritual" to "allegorical"); and (c) the fact that the Old Testament is preliminary and preparatory to the New Testament in which we find deeper meanings.[5]

Now, of course, no one denies that the Bible uses figures of speech, but they convey literal truths and often more vividly and literally than if the figures were not used. They enhance rather than change the plain meaning behind the figures. The main theme of the Bible is spiritual (redemption), but content does not determine hermeneutical principles. Hermeneutics provide the principles on which the content is understood. Of course the Old Testament is preparatory to the fuller revelation of the New Testament, but that does not mean that the New is to be understood allegorically or spiritually. God communicated plainly in both Testaments.

But, granting Allis's limitations on literal hermeneutics (which I do not), the important question still remains: How do you know when to use literal and when to use allegorical interpretation? To this question Allis offers these guidelines: (1) Whether you should interpret a passage figuratively or literally depends solely on which gives the true meaning.[6] This, of course, is a circular argument. (2) The only way prophecy can be understood literally is when its literal meaning is clear and obvious. But since for Allis prophecy may be "indefinite," "enigmatical," and "deceptive," there are very few occasions when it can be understood literally.[7] (3) The interpretation of any prophecy hinges on the fulfillment of it. In other words, if it were clearly fulfilled literally (as the prophecies of the first advent of Christ), then of course those prophecies are interpreted literally. But Allis's theological system requires that prophecies about the Second Coming not be fulfilled literally, so on those he uses allegorical hermeneutics.

We must credit Allis with attempting to systematize his hermeneutics, though we may question with how much success. His discussion points out again that many evangelicals are consistent literalists in all areas of Bible doctrine except prophecy. To do so results in amillennialism; to be literalists in all areas results in premillennialism.

4. Theological interpretation. In a sense amillennialism, as illustrated by Allis's discussion, may be viewed not only as using semiallegorical hermeneutics but may also be viewed as an illustration of theological interpretation. The theological system does not permit an actual kingdom on this earth over which Christ reigns; therefore, certain passages cannot be interpreted literally.

Another illustration of theological interpretation is found in the writings of Daniel Fuller. In order to preserve the unity of the Bible, he says that we must use the principle of "theological interpretation," which means interpretation that does not result in two purposes of God in the Scripture (one for Israel and one for the church). The consistent use of the literal interpretation leads to a distinction between Israel and the church, while theological interpretation does not.[8]

C. Rationale for Literal Hermeneutics

1. The purpose of language. The purpose of language itself seems to require literal interpretation. That is, God gave man language for the purpose of being able to communicate with him. God created man in His image, which included the power of speech, in order that God might reveal His truth to man and that man might in turn offer worship and prayer to God.

Two ramifications flow from this idea. First, if God originated language for the purpose of communication, and if God is all-wise, then we may believe that He saw to it that the means (language) was sufficient to sustain the purpose (communication). Second, it follows that God would Himself use and expect man to use language in its normal sense. The Scriptures do not call for some special use of language, implying that they communicate on some "deeper" or special level unknown to other avenues of communication.

2. The need for objectivity. If one does not employ normal interpretation, then objectivity is lost to the extent that he does not use it consistently. Switching the hermeneutical base from literal to allegorical or to semiallegorical or to theological inevitably results in different, inconsistent, and often contradictory interpretations.

3. The example of the Bible. The prophecies of the first advent of Christ were all fulfilled literally. This obvious but extremely significant fact argues for the validity and use of the literal hermeneutics in all of biblical interpretation. It is said that more than three hundred such prophecies concerning the coming of Christ were literally fulfilled. Some examples include: Micah 5:2; Malachi 3:1; Isaiah 9:1–2; 42:1; 53:5; 61:1; Psalms 16:9–10; 22:1, 15–16, 18; 31:5; 34:20; 68:18; Zechariah 13:7. To be sure some prophecies of the Old Testament are given a typical fulfillment, but of the approximately twenty-four such prophecies only seven are cited as examples of a nonliteral hermeneutic (and, of course, not all agree that these seven prove this). The seven are Matthew 2:15, 18, 23; 11:10; Acts 2:17–21; Romans 9:24–26; and Galatians 4:21–31. Remember, however, that we are not just comparing seven out of a total of twenty-four, but seven out of a total of hundreds, for almost all Old Testament prophecies are clearly fulfilled literally in the New Testament. To be sure, the New Testament may use the Old Testament in ways other than fulfillment, but I am here speaking of prophecies and their fulfillments. This is a strong support for literal hermeneutics.

D. Principles of Normal Hermeneutics

1. Interpret grammatically. Since words are the vehicles of thoughts, and since the meaning of any passage must be determined by a study of the words therein and their relationships in the sentences, determining the grammatical sense of the text must be the starting point of normal interpretation.

2. Interpret contextually. Words and sentences do not stand in isolation; therefore, the context must be studied in order to see the relation that each verse sustains to that which precedes and to that which follows. Involved are the immediate context and the theme and scope of the whole book.

3. Compare Scripture with Scripture. The dual authorship of the Bible makes it necessary not only to know the human author's meaning but also God's. God's meaning may not be fully revealed in the original human author's writing but is revealed when Scripture is compared with Scripture. We must allow for a *sensus plenior,* which allows for a fuller (though directly related) meaning in the mind of the divine Author of Scripture. We cannot say that the human authors of Scripture always understood the full implications of their own words. When we compare Scripture with Scripture, we can discover the fuller intention of the divine Author.

S. Lewis Johnson summarizes this well.

> Thus the work of the biblical interpreter is not necessarily finished when he has come to the meaning intended by the original human author. . . . The total context of a passage is necessary for its correct understanding and, therefore, the intention of the secondary author must be subordinated to the intention of the primary Author, God Himself. The biblical principle of the *analogia Scripturae* should have taught us that *Scripture ex Scriptura explicanda est, or Scriptura sui ipsius interpres,* traditional expressions of the sense of the analogy, teach that our first and final task is to discern God's intention in the text of Scripture. After all, is not the Bible God's Word?[9]

4. Recognize the progressiveness of revelation. To be able to consistently interpret plainly, it is imperative to recognize that revelation was given progressively. This means that in the process of revealing His message to man, God may add or even change in one era what He gave in another. Obviously the New Testament adds much that was not revealed in the Old. What God revealed as obligatory at one time may be rescinded at another (as the prohibition of eating pork and other unclean meats, once binding on God's people, now rescinded, 1 Tim. 4:3).

To fail to recognize this progressiveness in revelation will raise unresolvable contradictions between passages if taken literally. Notice the following pairs of passages that will contradict if understood plainly unless one recognizes changes due to the progress of revelation: Matthew 10:5–7 and 28:18–20; Luke 9:3 and 22:36; Genesis 17:10 and Galatians 5:2; Exodus 20:8 and Acts 20:7. Notice too the crucial changes indicated in John 1:17; 16:24; 2 Corinthians 3:7–11. Those who will not consistently apply this principle of progressive revelation in interpretation are forced to resort to figurative interpretation or sometimes simply to ignore the evidence.

E. An Objection to Normal Hermeneutics

The most frequent objection by evangelicals to normal interpretation points out that since the New Testament uses the Old Testament in a nonliteral sense we also may interpret Old Testament prophecies (about the Millennium, for example) in a nonliteral sense. Or to put it more simply: since the New Testament spiritualizes the Old Testament, so can we.

This might seem at first glance to be a strong objection to the consistent use of normal hermeneutics. However, we must remember that most often the New Testament uses the Old Testament prophecies literally and does not spiritualize them. Instances cited where the New Testament uses a nonliteral hermeneutic in relation to Old Testament prophecies number only seven at most. Other uses of the Old Testament include using it (a) illustratively (Rom. 9:9–12); (b) analogically (1 Cor. 1:19); (c) applicationally (Rom. 12:19); (d) rhetorically (James 4:6); but (e) usually as fulfilled directly, eschatologically, or typically (Acts 2:25–29; John 13:18).

Hardly ever do New Testament writers not use the Old Testament in a historical-grammatical sense (which, of course, includes the use of figures of speech). The rule is that they interpreted the Old Testament plainly; exceptions are rare and typological (but in a sense all of the Old Testament is typical in relation to the fuller revelation of the New Testament).

However, the crux of the matter is this: Can we as interpreters follow the example of the biblical writers in these rare exceptional uses of the Old Testament that seem to be nonliteral? Of course, the answer is yes, if we want to. But if we do it, we do so without apostolic authority, only with personal authority; comparatively, that is not much authority. Any and all uses of the Old Testament that the New Testament writers made were made under divine inspiration and were therefore done properly and authoritatively. If we depart from the plain sense of the text, we do so improperly without such authority. What the biblical writers wrote was infallible; the work of all interpreters is fallible.

To sum up: It is God who desired to give man His Word. It is God who also gave the gift of language so He could fulfill that desire. He gave us His Word in order to communicate, not confound. We should seek to understand that communication plainly, for that is the normal way beings communicate.

II. THE DOCTRINES OF ILLUMINATION

A. Its Meaning

The verb *phōtizo* is used of a general enlightening that Christ brings to all people, especially through the Gospel (John 1:9; 2 Tim. 1:10); of the enlightening experience of conversion (Heb. 6:4); of the understanding of Christian truth (Eph. 1:18; 3:9); and of the searching character of future judgment (1 Cor. 4:5).

Theologically the word has been applied to several concepts. In the early church baptism was frequently described as illumination (e.g., Justin, *First Apology,* chap. 61). The illumination theory of inspiration regards inspiration as an intensifying and elevating of the perceptions of the biblical writers. But generally the concept of illumination relates to the ministry of the Holy Spirit helping the believer to understand the truth of the Bible.

B. The Means

Two principal passages describe this ministry of the Spirit (John 16:12–15 and 1 Cor. 2:9–3:2). They teach the following facts about illumination.

(1) The Spirit is the Teacher, and His presence in the believer guarantees the availability of this ministry to all believers.

(2) Unbelievers, therefore, cannot experience this ministry. Even though they may achieve a high level of understanding of the Bible, they consider what they know basically as foolishness.

(3) The Spirit's teaching encompasses "all the truth," including that of "what is to come," i.e. Christian doctrine including prophecy.

(4) Carnality in the believer can thwart this ministry.

(5) The purpose of the Spirit's ministry is to glorify Christ.

(6) The Spirit will use those who have the gift of teaching to carry out His ministry (Rom. 12:7; 1 John 2:27). This includes the writings of those who, now dead, have left the results of the Spirit's work in their lives in that written form.

The experience of illumination is not by "direct revelation." The canon is closed. The Spirit illumines the meaning of that closed canon, and He does so through study and meditation. Study employs all the proper tools for ascertaining the meaning of the text. Meditation thinks about the true facts of the text, putting them together into a harmonious whole and applying them to one's own life. The end result of the illumination ministry of the Spirit is to glorify Christ in the life, or to promote healthy doctrine—teaching that brings spiritual health and wholeness to the believer's life. Illumination is not concerned merely with understanding facts but with using those facts to promote Christlikeness.

HOW OUR BIBLE CAME TO US

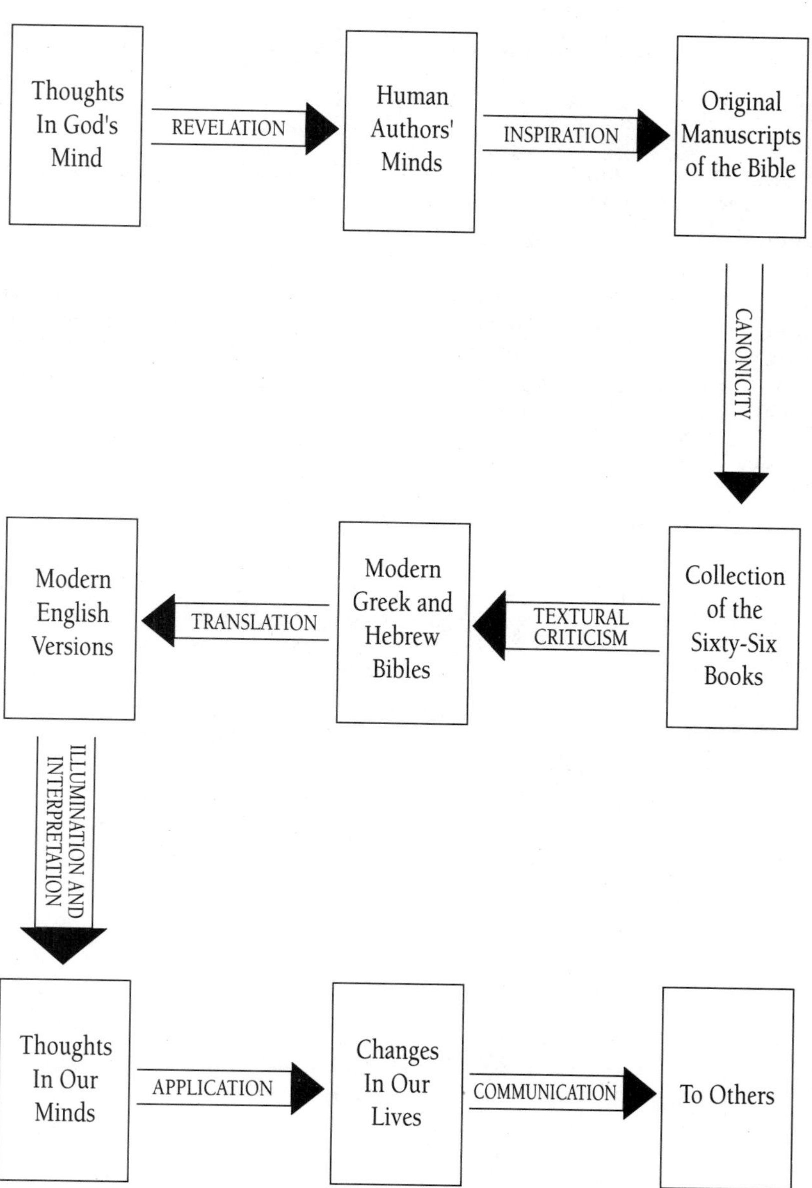

NOTES

1. F. W. Farrar, *History of Interpretation* (London: Macmillan, 1886), 193–94, 196.
2. Robert Mounce, *The Book of Revelation* (Grand Rapids: Eerdmans, 1977), 349.
3. Ibid., 359.
4. Ibid.
5. Oswald T. Allis, *Prophecy and the Church* (Philadelphia: Presbyterian and Reformed, 1945), 16–19.
6. Ibid., 18.
7. Ibid., 28–30.
8. Daniel P. Fuller, "The Hermeneutics of Dispensationalism," Th.D. dissertation, Northern Baptist Theological Seminary, 1957, especially 188; and *Gospel and Law: Contrast or Continuum?* (Grand Rapids: Eerdmans, 1980).
9. S. Lewis Johnson, *The Old Testament in the New* (Grand Rapids: Zondervan, 1980), 51.

Section IV
ANGELS: MINISTERING SPIRITS

Chapter 17
THE EXISTENCE OF ANGELS

When areas of theology are slighted, this will likely be one of them, at least in standard books of theology. One has only to note the amount of space devoted to angelology in standard theologies to demonstrate this. However, in the last years of the twentieth century there has been an increasing interest in the subject as well as in Satan and demons. Articles, books, and TV programs featuring angels, though more often "warm and fuzzy" than theologically accurate, have helped generate this interest in angelology. Nevertheless, only the Bible gives us totally accurate information about angels.

Even Calvin was cautious in discussing this subject.[1] Also, neo-orthodoxy's denial of the objective existence of angels has been countered by the widespread publicity given to demons and their activity. Although people may deny theologically the existence of an order of beings called angels (and demons), practically their reported activity seems to make it impossible to deny their existence. Thus on the one hand man's bias against anything supernatural rules out in his mind the existence of angels; while on the other hand activity that he cannot explain rationally makes their existence seem necessary.

I. HUMAN KNOWLEDGE

Man does not have the knowledge to judge what the makeup of the universe is. He has no *a priori* way to know if that makeup would or would not include an order of creatures like angels. Further, he has no predisposition to assume that it does include angels, for his natural predisposition is antisupernatural. In addition, his experience would not incline him to consider the possibility of angels, and his faith in his own intellect would compel him to seek other explanations for phenomena he cannot readily understand.

Ramm has fingered the limitations of human knowledge in this very clever way. "Mankind has no handbook titled *A Guide to All Possible Creations*. It has no information about creation, apart from the data afforded by this creation."[2] In other words, man's limited knowledge does not permit him to conclude there are no such beings as angels.

II. BIBLICAL REVELATION

If one accepts the biblical revelation, then there can be no question about the existence of angels. There are three significant characteristics about that revelation. First, it is extensive. The Old Testament speaks about angels just over 100 times, while the New Testament mentions them about 165 times. Of course, any truth has to be stated only one time in the Bible for us to acknowledge it as truth, but when a subject is mentioned as often as angels are, then it becomes that much more difficult to deny it.

Second, angels are mentioned throughout the Bible. The truth about them is not confined to one period of history or one part of the Scriptures or a few writers. They do not belong to some primitive era. Their existence is mentioned in thirty-four books of the Bible from the earliest (whether Genesis or Job) to the last.

Third, the teaching of our Lord includes a number of references to angels as real beings. So to deny their existence is to cast doubt on His veracity.

The actual details of the biblical revelation are, of course, important, but while surveying them, it is important to keep in mind these three characteristics of the nature of that revelation.

We shall examine first the amount and spread of the biblical facts, then the teachings of Christ.

A. In the Old Testament

The Old Testament always presents angels as real, objective, existing creatures. In no way are they considered illusions or figments of the imagination. In the thirty-four occurrences of the word in the Mosaic writings, angels always appear as real creatures who do specific things in character with their service as messengers (which is, of course, the meaning of both the Hebrew and Greek words for angels). For example, Abraham ate and conversed with angels (Gen. 18). Many of the references in the Pentateuch and in Judges are to the Angel of Yahweh, who seems to be Deity. An angel executed the judgment on Israel after David wrongly took a census of the people (2 Sam. 24:16—hardly an illusion). Isaiah refers to seraphim (6:2) and Ezekiel, to cherubim (10:1–3). Daniel mentions Gabriel (9:20–27) and Michael (10:13; 12:1). Zechariah mentions angels frequently as agents of God (chap. 1) and interpreters of visions (chaps. 1–6). In the psalms angels are depicted as God's servants who worship Him and who deliver God's people from harm (34:7; 91:11; 103:20).

B. In the New Testament

In addition to what our Lord taught about angels, the writers of the New Testament also affirmed their real existence. The Gospel writers relate their ministry to Christ's birth, life, resurrection, and ascension (Matt. 2:19; Mark 1:13; Luke 2:13; John 20:12; Acts 1:10–11).

In the record of the book of Acts angels were involved in helping God's servants, opening prison doors for the apostles (5:19; 12:5–11), directing Philip and Cornelius in ministry (8:26; 10:1–7), and encouraging Paul during the storm on his voyage to Rome (27:23–25).

Paul (Gal. 3:19; 1 Tim. 5:21), the writer of Hebrews (1:4), Peter (1 Pet. 1:12), and Jude (v. 6) all assumed the existence of angels in their writings. About sixty-five clear references to angels occur in the Revelation, more than in any other single book of the Bible. Clearly the New Testament furnishes clear, undebatable, and abundant evidence of the existence of angels.

C. In the Teachings of Christ

Angels ministered to Christ in the wilderness after His temptation by Satan (and, of course, no reporter was present at the Temptation, so His truthfulness is behind the account). He taught that the human state in the resurrection would be like the angels; i.e., non-procreative (Matt. 22:30). Angels will separate the righteous from the wicked at the end of the age (13:39) and will accompany the Lord at His second coming (25:31). Even without adding the references to Christ's activity in relation to demons, there is sufficient evidence that He believed in the reality of angels.

Usually the last thing critics of the Bible wish to abandon are the words of Christ. How, then, do they handle this evidence that Christ believed in the existence of angels?

Some say He was actually deceived. He believed they existed but actually they do not. Others affirm that He accommodated His teachings to the ignorant beliefs of the people of His day. In other words, since they believed in angels (and demons) He taught in that same vein, though actually He knew that angels did not really exist. But some of His references to angels cannot be explained in that way (see Matt. 18:10 and 26:53). Or it is sometimes claimed that the writers of the Gospels added these references to angels since they believed in them. There is nothing to prevent that sort of literary criticism from robbing us of other (perhaps even all) of the teachings of Christ.

Of course, there is another option, and it is the simplest and most obvious. Christ knew that angels exist and reflected that knowledge in His teaching.

NOTES

1. Calvin *Institutes* I.xiv, 3.
2. Bernard Ramm, "Angels," in *Basic Christian Doctrines,* ed. Carl F. H. Henry. (New York: Holt, Rinehart, and Winston, 1962), 64.

Chapter 18
The Creation of Angels

I. THE FACT OF THEIR CREATION

Angels are created beings (Ps. 148:5). This means they did not evolve from some lower or less complex form of life. This is reinforced by the fact that angels do not procreate (Matt. 22:30). When they were created, they were created as angels.

II. THE AGENT OF THEIR CREATION

All things were created by Christ (John 1:1–3). Specifically, angels were created by Him (Col. 1:16).

III. THE TIME OF THEIR CREATION

The Bible does not undebatably state the time of their creation. They were present when the earth was created (Job 38:6–7 NIV), so their creation had to be prior to the Creation of the earth.

IV. THE STATE OF THEIR CREATION

A. Holy

Originally all angelic creatures were created holy. God pronounced His Creation good (Gen. 1:31), and, of course, He could not create sin. Even after sin entered the world, God's good angels, who did not rebel against Him, are called holy (Mark 8:38). These are the elect angels (1 Tim. 5:21) in contrast to the evil angels who followed Satan in his rebellion against God (Matt. 25:41).

In addition to being created holy, all the angels were surrounded by holiness. Their Creator was absolute holiness. The atmosphere in which they lived and served was, until the sin of Satan, without the imperfections and taint of sin.

B. Creaturely

Angels are creatures, not the Creator. Yet they are a separate order of creatures, distinct, for example, from human beings (1 Cor. 6:3;

Heb. 1:14). As creatures they are limited in power, knowledge, and activity (1 Pet. 1:11–12; Rev. 7:1). Like all responsible creatures, angels will be subject to judgment (1 Cor. 6:3; Matt. 25:41).

Chapter 19
THE NATURE OF ANGELS

I. THEY ARE PERSONALITIES

Personality means to have personal existence; thus we mean that angels have personal existence and possess the quality or state of being persons. Commonly, the essential facets of personality are considered to involve intelligence, emotions, and will.

Angels then qualify as personalities because they have these aspects of intelligence, emotions, and will. This is true of both the good and evil angels. Good angels, Satan, and demons possess intelligence (Matt. 8:29; 2 Cor. 11:3; 1 Pet. 1:12). Good angels, Satan, and demons show emotions (Luke 2:13; James 2:19; Rev. 12:17). Good angels, Satan, and demons demonstrate that they have wills (Luke 8:28–31; 2 Tim. 2:26; Jude 6). Therefore, they can be said to be persons. The fact that they do not have human bodies does not affect their being personalities (any more than it does with God).

To be sure, the knowledge that angels possess is limited by their being creatures. This means they do not know all things as God does (Matt. 24:36); yet they seem to have greater knowledge than humans. This may be due to three causes. (1) Angels were created as a higher order of creatures in the universe than humans are. Therefore, innately they possess greater knowledge. (2) Angels know more about God than humans do (James 2:19; Rev. 12:12). (3) Angels gain knowledge through long observation of human activities. Unlike humans, angels do not have to study the past; they have experienced it. Therefore, they know how others have acted and reacted in situations and can predict with a greater degree of accuracy how we may act in similar circumstances. The experiences of longevity give them greater knowledge.

Though they have wills, the angels are, like all creatures, subject to the will of God. Good angels are sent by God to help believers (Heb. 1:14). Satan, though most powerful and cunning in carrying out his purposes in this world, is limited by the will of God (Job 2:6). Demons too have to be subject to the will of Christ (Luke 8:28–31).

The personality of angels means that they are not merely personifications of abstract good or evil, as some have considered them to be. This includes Satan, who also is a personality, not a personification of man's collective idea about evil.

II. THEY ARE SPIRIT BEINGS

Angels, demons (assuming they are fallen angels), and Satan belong to a class of beings that may be labeled spirit beings. Angels are said to be ministering spirits (Heb. 1:14). Demons are called evil and unclean spirits (Luke 8:2; 11:24, 26), and Satan is the spirit that now works in the sons of disobedience (Eph. 2:2).

As spirit beings they are immaterial and incorporeal. People have long wrestled with the meaning and ramifications of such a concept. Some Jews and early church fathers understood angels as having some kind of airy or fiery bodies, though in the Middle Ages it was concluded they were pure spirit beings. The tendency to ascribe to angels some sort of body grows out of the supposed impossibility of conceiving of a true creature without a body. Also it seems clear that angels are not omnipresent but have spatial limitations. Sometimes they were even seen by human beings. All of this seems to press for a conclusion that angels must have bodies. However, the Scriptures explicitly call angels and demons spirits (*pneumata*) in Matthew 8:16; Luke 7:21; 8:2; 11:26; Acts 19:12; Ephesians 6:12; and Hebrews 1:14. Though God is also a spirit Being, this does not mean that angels are infinite in nature as God is; rather they are finite spirit beings. Neither does their spirit nature forbid their appearing to human beings.

Usually they appear as males (though possibly the women of Zechariah 5:9 are angels). They have appeared in dreams and visions (Matt. 1:20; Isa. 6:1–8), in special unveiling of their presence (2 Kings 6:17), and to people in a normal, conscious, waking state (Gen. 19:1–8; Mark 16:5; Luke 2:13).

In heavenly visions they are described by superhuman characteristics that are quite different from other humanlike appearances (Dan. 10:5–7; Rev. 10:1–3; 15:6; 18:1). Some angels have wings (Isa. 6:2, 6; Ezek. 1:5–8).

III. THEY ARE IMMORTAL AND DO NOT PROPAGATE

The number of angels is and always will be the same. The Lord taught that angels do not propagate baby angels (Matt. 22:30) and that they do not die (Luke 20:36). However, the wicked angels will be punished in a place of separation from God (Matt. 25:41; Luke 8:31).

IV. THEY ARE HIGHER CREATURES THAN MEN

The writer to the Hebrews said that when our Lord became incarnate He became for a little while lower than the angels (2:7–9). Although there are problems connected with the writer's use of Psalm 8 in this passage, it does seem clear that Incarnation placed Christ in a position lower than the angels (though, of course, this was only temporarily true during the time of Christ's humiliation on earth). This is because man who was created in the image of God is lesser than God by nature. He is also lower than angels since they belong to a class of superhuman beings (*elohim*) who are stronger than man by nature and, unlike man, not subject to death.[1]

V. THEY WERE ORIGINALLY HOLY BEINGS

The Bible gives little specific evidence about the original state of the angels, though we know that when God finished His work of Creation He pronounced everything to be good (Gen. 1:31). Jude 6 also indicates that originally all the angels were holy creatures. Some were elect (1 Tim. 5:21) and others sinned (2 Pet. 2:4). Presumably all might have remained in that original state of holiness, and those who did not rebel were confirmed forever in their holy state. In other words, those who successfully passed the probationary test will always stay in that original holy state. Those who failed are now confirmed in their evil, rebellious state.

To sum up: though there are similarities between angels and Deity and between angels and men, angels are a distinct class of beings. Like Deity, but unlike men, they do not die. Like Deity, they are superior in strength to men though they are not omnipotent as God is (2 Peter 2:11). Like both Deity and men, they have personalities. Like Deity they are spirit beings, though not omnipresent as God is. Men, by contrast, are both spirit and material beings (James 2:26). Angels do not procreate as men do (Matt. 22:30). Man was made a little lower than the angels. And yet in his resurrected and glorified body, man will judge angels (1 Cor. 6:3).

NOTE

1. For a fuller discussion of the use of Psalm 8 in Hebrews 2 see C. Fred Dickason, *Angels, Elect and Evil* (Chicago: Moody, 1995), 55–57; and Donald R. Glenn, "Psalm 8 and Hebrews 2," in *Walvoord: A Tribute,* ed. by Donald K. Campbell (Chicago: Moody, 1982), 39–51.

Chapter 20
THE ORGANIZATION OF THE ANGELS

I. THE NUMBER OF ANGELS

Angels constitute an exceedingly large number that cannot be counted. That's the sense of *myriads,* which is used to describe the number of angels in Hebrews 12:22 and Revelation 5:11. Indeed that latter verse states that there are myriads of myriads of angels. How many this might be is left unspecified, though some have suggested that there are as many angels in the universe as the total number of all human beings throughout history (possibly implied in Matt. 18:10). There is no increase or decrease in their number, whatever it is.

II. THE FACT OF THEIR ORGANIZATION

The Scriptures speak of the "assembly" and "council" of the angels (Ps. 89:5, 7), of their organization for battle (Rev. 12:7), and of a king over the demon-locusts (9:11). They are also given governmental classifications, which indicate organization and ranking (Eph. 3:10, good angels; and 6:12, evil angels). Unquestionably God has organized the elect angels and Satan has organized the evil angels.

An important practical point emerges from this. Angels are organized; demons are organized; yet Christians, individually and in groups, often feel that it is unnecessary that they be organized. This is especially true when it comes to fighting evil. Believers sometimes feel that they can "go it alone" or expect victory without any prior, organized preparation and discipline. It is also true when it comes to promoting good. Believers sometimes miss the best because they do not plan and organize their good works.

III. THE RANKING OF ANGELS

A. The Archangel

Only Michael is designated as the archangel or high ranking angel (Jude 9; 1 Thess. 4:16). Although the Bible nowhere speaks of other archangels, there evidently are other high-ranking angels (Dan. 10:13).

When Paul says that the voice of the archangel will be heard at the translation of the church, he does not seem to feel the need to name that archangel, which supports the conclusion that there is only one.

In the Old Testament Michael appears as the guardian angel of Israel (Dan. 10:21; 12:1), who will particularly help Israel during its time of great trouble yet to come. He leads the angelic armies of heaven against Satan and his hosts of evil ones (Rev. 12:7). The reference in Jude 9 to Michael's disputing about the body of Moses indicates that Michael had something to do with the burial of Moses, that he had no power within himself to pronounce judgment on Satan, and that as a creature, even though a mighty one, he has to depend on the greater power of God.

B. Chief Princes

The phrase (Dan. 10:13), referring to a group of superior angels, underscores the fact of ranking among the angels. Of this group of chief princes, Michael apparently is the foremost one because he is the archangel. The apocryphal book of Enoch names Michael, Gabriel, Raphael, Jeremial and Uriel as the four principal angels who were privileged to stand around the throne of God (9:1; 40:9). It also numbers seven angels as archangels (20:1–7, cf. Tobit 12:15).

C. Governmental Rulers

1. Rulers or principalities. These words, used seven times by Paul, indicate an order of angels both good and evil involved in governing the universe (Rom. 8:38; Eph. 1:21; 3:10; 6:12; Col. 1:16; 2:10, 15).

2. Authorities or powers. This likely emphasizes the superhuman authority of angels and demons exercised in relation to the affairs of the world (Eph. 1:21; 2:2; 3:10; 6:12; Col. 1:16; 2:10, 15; 1 Pet. 3:22).

3. Powers. This word underscores the fact that angels and demons have greater power than humans (2 Pet. 2:11). See Ephesians 1:21 and 1 Peter 3:22.

4. Place of rule. In one place demons are designated as world rulers of this darkness (Eph. 6:12).

5. Thrones or dominions. This designation emphasizes the dignity and authority of angelic rulers in God's use of them in His government (Eph. 1:21; Col. 1:16; 2 Pet. 2:10; Jude 8).

D. Cherubim

Cherubim constitute another order of angels, evidently of high rank since Satan was a cherub (Ezek. 28:14, 16). They seem to function as guardians of the holiness of God, having guarded the way to the tree of life in the Garden of Eden (Gen. 3:24). The use of cherubim in the decoration of the tabernacle and temple may also indicate their guarding function (Exod. 26:1; 36:8; 1 Kings 6:23–29). They also bore the throne-chariot that Ezekiel saw (Ezek. 1:4–5; 10:15–20). Some identify the four living ones of Revelation 4:6 as cherubim, though others feel these represent the attributes of God. Representations of the cherubim will also be a part of the millennial temple (Ezek. 41:18–20).

E. Seraphim

All we know about this rank of angelic beings is found in Isaiah 6:2–7. Apparently the seraphim were an order similar to the cherubim. They acted as attendants at the throne of God and agents of cleansing. Their duty also was to praise God. Their description suggests a six-winged humanlike creature. The word may be derived from a root meaning "to burn" or possibly from a root which means "to be noble."

IV. PARTICULAR ANGELS

A. Gabriel

Mention has already been made of Michael because of his high rank. Gabriel also appears to be a high-ranking angel, though he is not designated as an archangel as Michael is. His name means "hero of God," and his function was to bring important messages from God to several individuals (Dan. 8:16; 9:21, to Daniel; Luke 1:19, to Zacharias; Luke 1:26, to Mary). In the Aramaic Targum, he is the angel to whom was ascribed the finding of Joseph's brothers, the burial of Moses, and the slaying of the armies of Sennacherib.

B. Angels with Special Responsibilities

Certain angels are designated in connection with a particular function they perform (Rev. 14:18, an angel who has power over fire; 16:5, the angel of the waters; 9:11, the angel of the abyss; 20:1–2, the angel who binds Satan).

C. Angels Associated with Future Judgments

Two of the three series of judgments of the Revelation are announced by angels. When angels sound the trumpets, the judgments of Revelation 8–9 begin, and the seven last plagues are poured out on the earth by angels (chap. 16).

D. Angels of the Seven Churches of Revelation 2–3

Each letter is addressed to the "angel" of the church, and those angels were seen in the right hand of the risen Christ in the vision of 1:16, 20. It is uncertain whether these are angelic beings or the human leaders of those churches.

Though the word "angel" clearly means messenger, it can refer to a superhuman being, that is, to the guardian angel for each church. Or it may refer to a human messenger, that is, to the human leader (pastor) of each church (see Mark 1:2; Luke 9:52; and James 2:25 for the use of "angel" as designating human beings).

E. Angel of Yahweh

As discussed in chapter 40, the Angel of Yahweh is a Christophany, a preincarnate appearance of Christ. The Angel spoke as God, identified Himself with God, and exercised the prerogatives of God (Gen. 16:7–12; 21:17–18; 22:11–18; Exod. 3:2; Judg. 2:1–4; 5:23; 6:11–24; 13:3–22; 2 Sam. 24:16; Zech. 1:12; 3:1; 12:8). Appearances of the Angel ceased after the incarnation of Christ, which supports conclusions that He was the preincarnate Christ.

Chapter 21
THE MINISTRY OF ANGELS

Basically and essentially good angels are servants (Heb. 1:14). God sends them for service or help (*diakonian*) of believers, and in so serving the angels function as priestly messengers (*leitourgika pneumata*) in the temple-universe of God.

I. IN RELATION TO GOD

In relation to God, angels' primary ministry is to worship and praise Him.

A. They Praise Him (Ps. 148:1–2; Isa. 6:3)

B. They Worship Him (Heb. 1:6; Rev. 5:8–13)

C. They Rejoice in What He Does (Job 38:6–7)

D. They Serve Him (Ps. 103:20; Rev. 22:9)

E. They Appear Before Him (Job 1:6; 2:1)

F. They Are Instruments of God's Judgments (Rev. 7:1; 8:2)

II. IN RELATION TO NEW EPOCHS

Angels appear to be unusually active when God institutes a new epoch in the sweep of history.

A. They Joined in Praise When the Earth Was Created (Job 38:6–7)

B. They Were Involved in the Giving of the Mosaic Law (Gal. 3:19; Heb. 2:2)

C. They Were Active at the First Advent of Christ (Matt. 1:20; 4:11)

D. They Were Active During the Early Years of the Church (Acts 8:26; 10:3, 7; 12:11)

E. They Will Be Involved in Events Surrounding the Second Advent of Christ (Matt. 25:31; 1 Thess. 4:16)

III. IN RELATION TO THE MINISTRY OF CHRIST

A. At His Birth

1. Prediction. Gabriel predicted His birth (Matt. 1:20; Luke 1:26–28).
2. Announcement. An angel announced His birth to the shepherds and was then accompanied in praise by a multitude of angels (Luke 2:8–15).

B. During His Life

1. Warning. An angel warned Joseph and Mary to flee to Egypt to escape Herod's wrath (Matt. 2:13–15).
2. Direction. An angel directed the family to return to Israel after Herod died (vv. 19–21).
3. Ministration. Angels ministered to Him after His temptation (4:11) and in His stress in Gethsemane (Luke 22:43).
4. Defense. He said that legions of angels stood ready to come to His defense if called on (Matt. 26:53).

C. After His Resurrection

1. Stone. An angel rolled away the stone from the tomb (Matt. 28:1–2).
2. Announcement. Angels announced His resurrection to the women on Easter morning (Matt. 28:5–6; Luke 24:5–7).
3. Ascension. Angels were present at His ascension (Acts 1:10–11).

D. At His Second Coming

1. Rapture. The voice of the archangel will be heard at the translation of the church (1 Thess. 4:16).
2. Second Coming. Angels will accompany Him at the Second Coming (Matt. 25:31; 2 Thess. 1:7).
3. Judgment. Angels will separate the wheat from the tares at His second coming (Matt. 13:39–40).

IV. IN RELATION TO NATIONS OF THE WORLD

A. In Relation to the Nation Israel

Michael, the archangel, especially guards Israel (Dan. 12:1).

B. In Relation to Other Nations

Angels watch over rulers and nations (Dan. 4:17) and seek to influence their human leaders (10:21; 11:1).

During the coming Tribulation years, angels will be involved in the administration of God's judgments (Rev. 8–9; 16).

V. IN RELATION TO THE UNRIGHTEOUS

A. Angels Announce Impending Judgments (Gen. 19:13; Rev. 14:6–7; 19:17–18)

B. Angels Inflict Judgments on the Unrighteous (Acts 12:23; Rev. 16:1)

C. Angels Will Separate the Righteous from the Unrighteous (Matt. 13:39–40)

VI. IN RELATION TO THE CHURCH

A. Basic Ministry

Basically angels help believers (Heb. 1:14).

B. Background Ministry

Angels have been involved in communicating and revealing the meaning of truth, which the church benefits from today (Dan. 7:15–27; 8:13–26; 9:20–27; Rev. 1:1; 22:6, 8).

C. Specific Ministries

1. Prayer requests. They bring answers to prayer (Acts 12:5–10).
2. Salvation. They aid in winning people to Christ (Acts 8:26; 10:3).
3. Observing. They observe Christian order, work, and suffering (1 Cor. 4:9; 11:10; Eph. 3:10; 1 Pet. 1:12).
4. Encouragement. They encourage in times of danger (Acts 27:23–24).
5. Present at death. They care for the righteous at the time of death (Luke 16:22).

Whether angels continue to function in all these ways throughout the present age is uncertain. But they did perform these ministries and may well continue to do so even though we are not aware of them. Of course, God is not obliged to use angels; He can do all these things directly. But seemingly He chooses to employ the intermediate ministry of angels on many occasions. Nevertheless, the believer recognizes that it is the Lord who does these things, whether directly or through using angels (notice Peter's testimony that the Lord delivered him from the prison though God actually used an angel to accomplish it, Acts 12:7–10 compared with vv. 11 and 17).

Perhaps an inscription I once saw in an old church in Scotland states the balance well.

> "Though God's Power Be Sufficient to Govern Us,
> Yet for Man's Infirmity He Appointed His Angels to Watch over Us."

Probably the statements about angels observing the conduct of redeemed people startle our thinking as much as any of these truths. The reason for their interest in us may stem from the fact that since angels do not personally experience salvation, the only way they can see the effects of salvation is to observe how it is manifest in saved human beings. We are indeed a theater in which the world, men, and angels make up the audience (1 Cor. 4:9). Let us put on a good performance for them as well as for the Lord before whom all things are naked and open.

Section V
OUR ADVERSARY THE DEVIL

Chapter 22
THE REALITY OF SATAN

The denial of Satan's reality usually takes the form of considering the idea of a satan as the personification of evil but not actually a being who has his own separate existence. The idea of "Satan" as a person developed more in New Testament times, and this necessitated, we are told, reinterpretations of the "legends" of the Old Testament, since, it is claimed, they do not contain the idea of a distinctive demonic figure. In addition, Iranian dualism, it is said, contributed to the Jewish idea of a personal Satan during the Greco-Roman period.[1]

I. EVIDENCE FROM THE TEXT

If one accepts the Scriptures as revelation from God, rather than merely a record of man's thoughts about God, then the reality of Satan cannot be denied. Satan did not evolve as a personal being; he existed and acted from the earliest to the last books of God's revelation. Seven books of the Old Testament teach his reality (Genesis, 1 Chronicles, Job, Psalms, Isaiah, Ezekiel, Zechariah). Every writer of the New Testament affirmed his reality and activity. Christ's teaching also assumes and affirms Satan's existence and activity. In twenty-five of the twenty-nine passages in the Gospels that speak of Satan, our Lord is speaking. In some of those passages there can be no question of Christ's accommodating His teaching to the crowd's supposed ignorances or faulty concepts of Satan due to Persian dualism. Notice especially passages like Matthew 13:39; Luke 10:18; and 11:18.

II. EVIDENCE OF PERSONALITY

A. The Traits of Personality

Like the angels, Satan is said to possess the traits of personality. He shows intelligence (2 Cor. 11:3); he exhibits emotions (Rev. 12:17, anger; Luke 22:31, desire); he demonstrates that he has a will (Isa. 14:12–14; 2 Tim. 2:26).

B. The Pronouns of Personality

Satan is referred to as a person in both Old and New Testaments (Job 1; Matt. 4:1–12). Notice that the information in this latter passage (the temptation of Christ) had to come from the Lord; thus He, by using personal pronouns, attributes personality to Satan.

C. The Moral Responsibility of Personality

If Satan were merely a personification that people have devised to express their ideas of evil, then such a personification could scarcely be held morally responsible for his actions, since, in reality, there is no being who can be held accountable. But Satan is held accountable by the Lord (Matt. 25:41), and this passage reminds us that to deny the reality of Satan requires denying the veracity of Christ's words.

III. HIS NATURE

A. He Is a Creature

Assuming that Ezekiel 28:11–19 refers to Satan (to be discussed later), that passage clearly states that Satan was created (v. 15). This means that he does not possess attributes that belong to God alone, like omnipresence, omnipotence, and omniscience. Though a mighty being, he has creaturely limitations. And as a creature he must be accountable to his Creator.

B. He Is a Spirit Being

Satan belongs to the order of angels called cherubim (Ezek. 28:14). Apparently he was the highest created angel (v. 12). Evidently this was the reason Michael, the archangel, did not dispute with Satan about the body of Moses (Jude 9). Satan may be called the archangel of all the evil angels. Even in his present, fallen state, he retains a great deal of power (though under the permission of God). Thus he is called the god of this world and the prince of the power of the air (2 Cor. 4:4; Eph. 2:2).

IV. HIS NAMES

The number and variety of names given to Satan further support the reality of his existence.

Satan (used about fifty-two times) from the Hebrew, *Satan,* means adversary or opposer (Zech. 3:1; Matt. 4:10; Rev. 12:9; 20:2).

Devil (used about thirty-five times) from the Greek, *diabolos*, means slanderer (Matt. 4:1; Eph. 4:27; Rev. 12:9; 20:2).

John records him as the evil one (John 17:15; 1 John 5:18–19). His evil character, indicated in this title, pervades the entire world, which is under his control. Yet the believer cannot ultimately be possessed by Satan.

A serpent was the way Satan first appeared to mankind (Gen. 3:1). This characterization sticks with Satan in the New Testament as well (2 Cor. 11:3; Rev. 12:9) and indicates his guile and craftiness.

Satan is also depicted as a great red dragon (Rev. 12:3, 7, 9). This emphasizes his fierce nature, especially in conflict. Note that the dragon has a tail; thus our Halloween caricatures of Satan are not far off! An illustration: an older student, when asked by a younger student what kind of a teacher so-and-so is, might reply, "Oh, he's a bear!" The meaning is clear: that teacher is hard. Satan is a dragon. The meaning is clear: he is ferocious in his attacks against believers.

One of Satan's activities is to be the accuser of the brethren (Rev. 12:10). He does this unceasingly—day and night. Of what does he accuse us? Of sins we commit. And, of course, he has an airtight case, for believers do sin, and any sin could undo our salvation. However, our Lord, our Advocate, defends us on the sole basis that all our sins were paid for by His death (1 John 2:1–2). Some, probably unconsciously, make a distinction between sins that could undo our salvation and those that would not do so—"little" sins. But any sin is enough to cause us to lose our salvation were it not for the constant intercession of our Lord that thwarts the constant accusations of our adversary, Satan.

One of my teachers years ago was H. A. Ironside. He always addressed us as "young gentlemen." When he came to this verse he would inevitably say, "Young gentlemen, Satan is the accuser of the brethren. Let's leave the dirty work to him."

Satan is also the tempter (Matt. 4:3; 1 Thess. 3:5). This has been his work from his first encounter with human beings (Gen. 3:1). His temptation to Eve was to accept the counterfeit plan he offered that did not involve the restriction of not eating the fruit of the tree of the knowledge of good and evil. His temptation of Christ was to have the glory that was due Him without the suffering of the Cross. He tempted Ananias to lie in not disclosing the full amount of money his sale of land had brought (Acts 5:3). He tempts believers with immorality (1 Cor. 7:5).

Satan's position over this world is seen in several titles given to him. He is the "ruler of this world" (John 12:31). He is the "god of this world" (2 Cor. 4:4). He is the "prince of the power of the air" (Eph. 2:2) and "the spirit that is now working in the sons of disobedience" (v. 2). He also deceives the whole world (Rev. 12:9; 20:3). He resides in the air (equivalent to "the heavenly places" in Eph. 6:12) and rules this cosmos as well as this age. The cosmos is that organized framework of things in which mankind lives and moves and that opposes God by eliminating and counterfeiting Him. The age (of which Satan is god) means "all that floating mass of thoughts, opinions, maxims, speculations, hopes, impulses, aims, aspirations, at anytime current in the world, which it may be impossible to seize and accurately define, but which constitute a most real and effective power, being the moral, or immoral, atmosphere which at every moment of our lives we inhale, again inevitable to exhale—all this is included in the aion, which is . . . the subtle informing spirit of the kosmos, or world of men who are living alienated apart from God."[2] That kind of rule over the world and atmosphere in which we live is awesome and fearful. Thankfully, greater is He who is in us than he who is in the world (1 John 4:4).

The name Beelzebul designates Satan as the chief of the demons (Luke 11:15). When Jesus' enemies alleged that He was possessed by Beelzebul, they made themselves guilty of the worst kind of blasphemy.

Paul uses Belial as a name for Satan in 2 Corinthians 6:15. The word means worthlessness or wickedness and aptly describes Satan's character.

The various names and designations for Satan not only affirm the reality of his existence but also reveal his many-faceted character and aspects of his work. A name often reveals something about the person's background ("Scotty") or looks ("Red") or characteristics ("Lover") or activities ("Gopher"). So with Satan: his background (adversary, accuser, tempter), looks (dragon, serpent), characteristics (liar, murderer, ruler), and activities (accuser, tempter). He is a powerful, intelligent, clever creature, and we must never forget or underestimate the reality of our enemy.

Notes

1. See T. H. Gaster, "Satan," in *The Interpreter's Dictionary of the Bible* (New York: Abingdon, 1976), 4:224–28.
2. R. C. Trench, *Synonyms of the New Testament* (London: Kegan Paul, 1886), 218.

Chapter 23
THE CREATION AND SIN OF SATAN

I. HIS CREATION

A. The Time of It

If Satan were not a created being then he must be eternal or self-existent, a dualism that is incompatible with monotheism. The Scriptures declare that all things were created by God through Christ, and there is nothing that was not made by Him (John 1:3; Col. 1:16–17). The time of his creation is not specified. If Ezekiel 28:13 refers to Satan and to the earthly garden in Eden, then, of course, he had to have been created before God planted the Garden in Eden (Gen. 2:8).

B. The Characteristics of It

Many debate whether or not Ezekiel 28:11–19 has Satan in view, but if it does, then it provides us with a number of descriptive details as to the characteristics of Satan's original condition at his creation. All agree that the subject of verses 1–19 is judgment on Tyre and its leader. But the question is, do verses 11–19 go beyond the human leader to reveal things about something or someone else? The candidates for that something or someone else called the king of Tyre are: (a) a symbol drawn from pagan mythology; (b) a primal being who lived in the Garden of Eden and was driven out through pride; (c) a mythological, unreal being presented in Phoenician mythology and incorporated and applied in this story to the king of Tyre; (d) an "ideal," though unreal, person; (e) the ideal man, the same as the historical first man, Adam, whose histories (initial privileges and subsequent sin) are analogous; (f) the sinister being Satan; (g) Satan's masterpiece, Antichrist.

Views (a) through (d) are incompatible with the principles of normal interpretation, for there is no justification for introducing such mythology into the text. View (e), though possible, seems to fall short of fulfilling the totality of the sinister nature of the figure behind the king of Tyre. Views (f) and (g) can be combined; i.e., Satan is the one behind it all, including being behind Antichrist who will be the climax of all people whom Satan has indwelt throughout history. The king of Tyre was one he indwelt in the past, as Antichrist will be the final one he will indwell in the future.

To understand the prophecy as including references to Satan does not mean that Ezekiel did not also have a historical leader of Tyre in mind in his denunciations. The question is, did he only have the historical human leader in view, or did he also have a greater being, Satan, in mind? The flowery and highly figurative language can argue for either conclusion. Those who feel that only the human leader is in view understand the language as a typical, exaggerated way an oriental ruler might be referred to. Those who also see Satan in the passage argue that such language includes too many superlatives and figures to be true of only an earthly king no matter how great he was. It would seem difficult to apply verses 14 and 15, for example, to any earthly king.[1]

It would, of course, not be unusual for a prophetic passage to refer both to a local personage and also to someone else who fully fulfills it. This is true of many passages that relate both to King David and Jesus Christ. It is also true of the reference to the prince of the kingdom of Persia in Daniel 10:13, a reference that must include a superhuman being related to the kingdom of Persia. So for Ezekiel 28 to refer both to the then-reigning king of Tyre as well as to Satan would not be a unique interpretive conclusion. Indeed, it seems the right conclusion: The historic king of Tyre was simply a tool of Satan, possibly indwelt by him. And in describing this king, Ezekiel also gives us glimpses of the superhuman creature, Satan, who was using, if not indwelling, him.

Assuming, then, that Satan is in the picture in these verses, what do we learn about his original characteristics at his creation? Whatever specifics these verses teach, they convey the clear idea that Satan was highly privileged, the epitome of God's Creation, who had an unparalleled position in the universe.

1. Satan had unparalleled wisdom and beauty (Ezekiel 28:12). Satan stood at the zenith of God's creatures, filled with wisdom and perfect in beauty.

2. Satan had an unparalleled habitation (v. 13). This may refer to a heavenly Eden or to the earthly Eden. In either case, it was, before sin entered, a unique place.

3. Satan had an unparalleled covering (v. 13). The dazzling description of his dress or robe indicates something of the glory bestowed on him.

4. Satan had an unparalleled function (v. 14). He belonged to the order of angelic creature designated cherubim. They are associated with guarding the holiness of God (Gen. 3:24), with the throne of God (Ezek. 1:5), and here apparently with the actual presence of God. Satan was on the holy mountain of God, and he walked in the midst of the stones of fire, likely references to the presence of God Himself. Apparently Satan was the chief guardian of God's holiness and majesty.
5. Satan had unparalleled perfection (Ezek. 28:15). He was perfect in the sense of being completely sound and of having total moral integrity. Here, as well as in verse 13, we are reminded that Satan was created, and as a creature, he must someday answer to his Creator.

In every way Satan was the epitome of God's Creation.

> He awoke in the first moment of his existence in the full-orbed beauty and power of his exalted position; surrounded by all the magnificence which God gave him. He saw himself as above all the hosts in power, wisdom, and beauty. Only at the throne of God itself did he see more than he himself possessed, and it is possible that even that was in some sense not fully visible to the eyes of the creature. . . . Before his fall he may be said to have occupied the role of prime minister for God, ruling possibly over the universe but certainly over this world.[2]

II. HIS SIN

A. The Origin of Satan's Sin

Sin was found in him (Ezek. 28:15). This is really the only verse in the Bible that states exactly the origin of sin. The details of Satan's sin are specified elsewhere, but the origin is only expressed here. Barnhouse terms it as "spontaneous generation in the heart of this being in whom such magnificence of power and beauty had been combined and to whom such authority and privilege had been given."[3]

This sin must have been included in the eternal plan of God. Yet God never assumes the responsibility for the commission of any sin, including Satan's. J. O. Buswell steers a careful course in this matter.

> According to the Bible, then, sin originated in an act of free will in which the creature deliberately, responsibly, and with adequate understanding of the issues chose to corrupt the holy character of godliness with which God had endowed His creation. . . . Satan sinned necessarily. God is rightly angry with all sin. . . . The denial of free will seems to be purely arbitrary philosophical dogmatism,

> contrary to the biblical view. If God is rightly angry with sin, then it follows that the sinner is blameworthy—cosmically, ultimately, absolutely. . . . Sin must be within God's eternal decrees in some sense in which He is not the author of it. . . . Within the decrees of God, there are decrees of the permission of those things of which God Himself is not the author. This is not mere permission of the unavoidable.[4]

Sin was found in Satan; yet he was created perfect. God is not the blameworthy cause of Satan's sin; yet it was included in His plan.

B. The Nature of Satan's Sin

The New Testament pinpoints Satan's particular sin as arrogance, conceit, or being puffed up (1 Tim. 3:6). It is likened to the conceit a new convert may have when he is either pushed forward or asserts himself too quickly and begins to take to himself the glory that belongs to God. Ezekiel 28:16 assigns the cause of Satan's downfall to the abundance of his trade. In other words, Satan used his position for personal profit—to traffic in his own self-promotion.

Isaiah gives more detail of Satan's sin (14:12–17). Like the Ezekiel 28:11–19 passage there is a question as to whether or not this refers at all to Satan. (1) Some regard the Isaiah passage as referring only to the fall of the king of Babylon mentioned in verse 4. (2) Others understand the passage to relate only to the fall of Satan. (3) Those who hold views (1) or (2) may also see the king of Babylon or Satan as prefiguring the fall of the coming Antichrist. (4) Likely the truth includes all of these references; i.e., the fall of the king of Babylon is an antitype of the previous fall of Satan and a type of the future fall of Antichrist. Delitzsch says it concisely: "A retrospective glance is now cast at the self-deification of the king of Babylon, in which he was the antitype of the devil and the type of Antichrist."[5] The passage transcends anything that can be said of an earthly king and has been understood from earliest times to also refer to Satan's fall as described in Luke 10:18.

Satan is called the morning star in Isaiah 14:12. The Latin equivalent is Lucifer, which, on the basis of this passage, became a name for Satan. However, the use of morning star with reference to Satan gives us an indication of the basic character of his plot against God. Since the same title is used in Revelation 22:16 of Christ, we are alerted to the fact that Satan's plan was to counterfeit the plan of God, and indeed it was and is. How he initiated that plan is detailed in the five "I will" phrases in Isaiah 14:13–14.

1. I will ascend to heaven. As guardian of God's holiness Satan had access to heaven, but this expresses his desire to occupy and settle in heaven on an equality with God.
2. I will raise my throne above the stars of God. The meaning of this depends on the understanding of "stars." If they refer to angels (Job 38:7; Jude 13; Rev. 12:3–4), then Satan wished to rule over all the angels. If they refer to the luminous heavenly bodies, then he wished to rule in the heavens.
3. I will sit on the mount of assembly in the recesses of the north. This bespeaks Satan's ambition to govern the universe as the assembly of Babylonian gods supposedly did.
4. I will ascend above the heights of the clouds. He wanted the glory that belonged to God (clouds are often associated with God's presence, see Exod. 16:10; Isa. 19:1).
5. I will make myself like the Most High. Here his counterfeit is crystal clear. Satan wanted to be like, not unlike, God. The name Elyon for God stresses God's strength and sovereignty (Gen. 14:18). Satan wanted to be as powerful as God. He wanted to exercise the authority and control in this world that rightfully belongs only to God. His sin was a direct challenge to the power and authority of God.

Satan's sin was all the more heinous because of the great privileges, intelligence, and position he had. His sin was also more damaging because of the widespread effects of it. It affected other angels (Rev. 12:7); it affects all people (Eph. 2:2); it positioned him as the ruler of this world, which he uses to promote his kingdom and to counterfeit God's (John 16:11); it affects all the nations of the world, for he works to deceive them (Rev. 20:3).

All sin is serious, and all sin affects others. But sin in high places is more serious and its ramifications more widespread. The sin of Satan should serve as a constant reminder and warning to us.

Notes

1. See a full discussion in Charles L. Feinberg, *The Prophecy of Ezekiel* (Chicago: Moody, 1969), 158–63.
2. Donald Grey Barnhouse, *The Invisible War* (Grand Rapids: Zondervan, 1965), 26–27.
3. Ibid., 30.
4. J. Oliver Buswell, "The Origin and Nature of Sin," *Basic Christian Doctrines*, Carl F. H. Henry, ed. (New York: Holt, Rinehart and Winston, 1962), 107–9.
5. Franz Delitzsch, *Biblical Commentary on the Prophecies of Isaiah* (Edinburgh: T. & T. Clark, 1875), 1:312.

Chapter 24
THE ACTIVITIES OF SATAN

The variety of names that Satan has alerts us to the fact that he can attack his opponents in a variety of ways. From the fierceness of a dragon (Rev. 12:3) to the attractiveness of an angel of light (2 Cor. 11:14), Satan can adapt himself and his tactics to suit the person and the occasion. Although he may prefer to operate in a certain manner, he will meet people where they are and use whatever might defeat them in particular circumstances. Though not all-knowing, Satan has observed many others in situations in which we may find ourselves, and he can predict with a high degree of accuracy what will best defeat us.

I. IN RELATION TO CHRIST

The animosity between Satan and Christ was first predicted after the sin of Adam and Eve (Gen. 3:15). The enmity between spiritual descendants of Satan and the family of God was predicted here. Also an individual (Christ) from among the woman's seed would deal a fatal blow to Satan's head, while Satan would bruise Christ's heel (a nonfatal blow, but one that caused Him great suffering). This exchange of blows took place at the cross.

When our Lord did actually appear on this earth, Satan made concerted attempts to thwart His mission to die for the sins of the world. Undoubtedly Herod's killing of the children under two was Satan-inspired (Matt. 2:16). Christ clearly said that Peter aligned himself with Satan's plan when Peter wanted to dismiss the idea that Christ would have to die in Jerusalem (16:21–23). The sharpness of Christ's rebuke underscores the fact that His central purpose in coming to earth was to die. When Judas was about to betray the Lord, Satan entered into him (John 13:27).

But the principal and most direct attack of Satan on our Lord was at His temptation (Matt. 4:1–11). The word "test" or "tempt" includes two ideas: proving and soliciting to evil. Satan's testing of Christ involved both facets. In the process of Satan's soliciting Him to commit evil, God would prove through the test that Christ was sinless. God and Satan were both involved in His test. The Spirit led Jesus into the wilderness place in order that He might be tempted by the devil. For forty days Satan tempted Him with many temptations (Luke 4:2), and during that period our Lord fasted. This served to sensitize Him against all the tests, but especially against the three attacks that came at the end of those forty days. These three were the epitome of the areas in which a person can be tested: the lusts of the flesh, the lusts of the eyes, and the boastful pride of life (1 John 2:16).

These were tests particularly suited to the God-man. Only He (not we) could turn stones to bread. Only He (not we) could jump off the pinnacle of the temple and land unharmed in the area below. Only He (not we) could expect to have all the kingdoms of this world.

The basic purpose of Christ's temptation was to prove His competence to be the sinless Savior. Satan was trying to cause our Lord to deviate from the path and purpose for which He came into the world and to make Himself independent from God and His plan by offering Him glory without suffering. This, then, would have made His substitutionary death unnecessary. Specifically, Satan tempted Christ to independence (Matt. 4:3–4), to indulgence (vv. 5–7), and to idolatry (vv. 8–10).

There was no doubt in Satan's mind that Christ was the promised Deliverer. But he wanted the Lord to assert His independence from the Father by turning the stones to bread. Just as the manna given to Israel in the wilderness came from God, so Christ's food should come in the Father's time and way. To turn stones to bread would be to assert His independence of the will of the Father. "Though He was hungry, and it was right to eat, yet He would not eat independently of the Father's will. Satan had tempted Him not away from spiritual bread but away from the Father and toward literal bread, gained independently of the Father's will."[1] Satan still tempts Christ's followers to take things into their own hands rather than yielding to the Father's will.

To have cast Himself off the pinnacle or wing or projection of the temple to the valley 450 to 600 feet below and to have landed unharmed would certainly have been a spectacular sign of the Messiah. But to have done so would have been to take a shortcut and show a lack of faith. Rashness, signs, or presumption never substitute for the constancy of faith, though Satan still tempts us to indulge in these.

Satan has temporarily been given authority over this world (cosmos), but ultimately Christ will rule it. Thus Satan had the right to offer the Lord the kingdoms of this world, but had Christ taken them He would have shortcut the plan of God and bypassed the atoning work of His death. Satan still tempts us with the immediate and visible.

Since Satan was unsuccessful in preventing the Cross, he attacks the Gospel, the followers of Christ, and what yet remains of the plan of God for this world.

II. IN RELATION TO GOD

The principal tactic Satan uses to attack God and His program in general is to offer a counterfeit kingdom and program. This was evident when he originally sinned by wanting to be like, not unlike, God. The counterfeit was first attempted on mankind when Satan offered Eve the chance to be like God, knowing good and evil (Gen. 3:5).

The temptation of Christ was also an attempt at counterfeit. A counterfeit is as like the genuine as possible, only without some vital feature. Satan's offer to our Lord was to have the glory due Him without the essential feature of His death.

Today Satan promotes a form of godliness while denying its power (2 Tim. 3:5). To do this, Satan disguises his servants as servants of righteousness (2 Cor 11:15). He promotes a doctrinal system through the demons who in turn use people who advocate a false asceticism or unbridled license (1 Tim. 4:1–3; Rev. 2:24). The ultimate counterfeit will be the coming Antichrist, whose activities will be in accord with Satan and who will pawn off on mankind "the lie" (2 Thess. 2:9–11 NIV).

III. IN RELATION TO NATIONS

His principal activity in this arena is to deceive the nations (Rev. 20:3). Deceive them how? Apparently into thinking they can govern righteously and bring peace in the world apart from the presence and rule of Christ. Again, his tactic is to counterfeit.

He apparently employs demons in carrying out his deception (Dan. 10:13, 20), and he uses governments to hinder the progress of the Gospel (1 Thess. 2:18).

During the coming days of Great Tribulation Satan will deceive the nations into receiving the Antichrist as their savior. Satan, the dragon, will give Antichrist his power, and the world will give allegiance to him (Rev. 13:2–4). At the conclusion of the Tribulation Satan and his demons will influence the armies of the nations to march to their doom at the war of Armageddon (16:13–16 NIV).

During the millennial kingdom Satan will be bound, but at the close of that period he will be released and will attempt to lead the world in a final revolt against Christ's kingdom. After this unsuccessful attempt, Satan will be cast forever into the lake of fire (Rev. 20:7–10).

IV. IN RELATION TO UNBELIEVERS

In relation to unbelievers Satan blinds their minds so that they will not accept the Gospel (2 Cor. 4:4). He often does this by making them think that any way to heaven is as acceptable as the only way. Again, a counterfeit. This blindness attacks the minds of people, and while unbelievers may think and reason, a power greater than Satan must remove that blindness. Human reasoning and convincing arguments have a ministry, but only the power of God can remove satanic blindness. Sometimes the devil comes and takes away the Word that people have heard in order to prevent their believing (Luke 8:12).

In promoting blindness Satan uses counterfeit religion as detailed in the preceding section. This may include everything from asceticism to license, from theism (for being a theist does not necessarily mean being saved) to occultism. In other words, Satan will use any aspect of the world system that he heads in order to keep people from thinking about or doing that which will bring them into the kingdom of God (Col. 1:13; 1 John 2:15–17).

V. IN RELATION TO BELIEVERS

A. Satan, the Tempter

Just as Satan tried the Lord, he also tries believers. His aim is to get us to commit evil. God may sometimes use Satan in testing us to prove us in resisting his tests. Tests can have three beneficial purposes in the life of the believer: (1) to prove us (1 Pet. 1:6–7); (2) to teach us (4:12–13; see also Heb. 5:8); and (3) to increase our love for God (James 1:12). But Satan's only purpose is to tempt the believer to commit evil.

There are at least three areas in which Satan tempts believers. The first is in the area of conforming to the pressures and structures of society (1 Thess. 3:5). Paul, you remember, had been forced to leave Thessalonica after probably only one month's ministry in that city (Acts 17:5–10). Further, Satan had used some governmental ban to keep him from returning (1 Thess. 2:18). So he sent Timothy, who was not under that ban, back to Thessalonica to see if they had succumbed to Satan's temptations. What temptations? It was too early in the first century for Paul to be referring to official persecution from the Roman Empire. These temptations must have been more of an unofficial, societal, personal nature. Perhaps Satan tempted them to continue to conform to the lifestyles they experienced before they were saved. Also many of the converts were Gentiles, and Satan may have tempted them with the pride of intellect.

Second, Satan tempts believers to cover up selfishness. The story of Ananias and Sapphira serves as the classic illustration. This couple wanted to retain some of the money they received from the sale of their property, while at the same time receiving praise for their contribution. Peter discerned that it was Satan who had filled their hearts to lie (Acts 5:1–11). They had the right to own and sell property. They had no necessary obligation to give all the proceeds to the church. But they were obliged not to feign generosity and at the same time cater to their selfishness by keeping part of the money received.

Third, Satan tempts believers to immorality (1 Cor. 7:5). God provided marriage for proper expression of physical needs and relationships, and He expects husbands and wives to assume their respective and mutual responsibilities. When this is not done, Satan has opportunity to tempt believers to illicit or perverted sexual sins.

B. Satan, the Adversary

As adversary, Satan accuses and opposes believers in various areas of their lives. First, he opposes our witness to the Gospel. He does this by confusing us when he plants tares among the wheat (Matt. 13:38–39), by snatching away the Word that has been sown (Mark 4:15), by aligning governmental authorities against believers (1 Thess. 2:18), or by imprisoning believers, believing this will keep their testimony from spreading or make them fearful of witnessing (Rev. 2:10).

Second, Satan spotlights our sins (12:10). He accuses us before God when we sin, thinking he can cause us to lose our salvation. But Christ, our Advocate, takes our case and reminds the Father again and again that He paid for all our sins when He died on the cross (1 John 2:1–2).

Third, Satan opposes the believer by bringing pressure on him that he may not be able to bear. There are two examples of this in the New Testament. One concerned the man disciplined in 1 Corinthians 5. Apparently the discipline had had its desired effect, and he had confessed his sin of incest. Now the church should have received him back into fellowship. Seemingly, some wanted to do this and some did not. So Paul urged them to do so, not only to heal any division that might develop but also lest the brother involved be overwhelmed by excessive sorrow. He needed to know the forgiveness of his brothers and sisters (2 Cor. 2:5–11). Not to restore him would give Satan an advantage.

The second example concerns women who are widowed at a young age (1 Tim. 5:14–15). Paul urged them to marry again and bear children and lead useful lives. Some, idle and gossiping, were following Satan.

In general we may say that Satan the adversary wants passionately to squelch the believer's testimony. To accomplish this he prowls the earth like a roaring lion seeking someone to devour (1 Pet. 5:8). The word "devour" is the same word used to describe the way the Red Sea swallowed up the Egyptians when they were pursuing the Hebrews (Heb. 11:29). It paints a vivid picture of Satan's ultimate goal—to completely drown the believer's testimony and usefulness.

As I mentioned earlier, Satan may prefer to do some things over others. But he will do whatever he has to in order to promote his plans and programs successfully. Remember too that he is powerful, he is experienced, and he has a host of demons to help him. Therefore, the believer can successfully fight him only in the strength and power of God who dwells within him. Other aspects of the believer's defense will be discussed in another chapter.

Note

1. S. Craig Glickman, *Knowing Christ* (Chicago: Moody, 1980), 41.

Chapter 25
SATAN'S WORLD

We have already noticed that Satan is called both "the god of this age" (*aion,* 2 Cor. 4:4 NIV) and "the prince of this world" (*cosmos,* John 12:31 NIV). It is the relation of Satan and the Christian to the cosmos that is the subject of this chapter.

I. THE MEANING OF THE COSMOS

The word *cosmos* is used 185 times in the New Testament, 105 of which occur in the writings of John. Basically the word denotes an ornament or order, cosmos being the opposite of chaos. That concept is found in its use in 1 Peter 3:3 and in our modern word "cosmetic." The universe (that is, heaven and earth) is called the cosmos because it is an ornament of harmonious relationships (Acts 17:24). The inhabited earth is also designated by the word *cosmos* (Rom. 1:8), as are the people who live on the earth (John 3:16; 12:19). It is the people of the world whom God loves and for whom Christ died (John 3:16; 1 John 2:2).

But usually the New Testament views the cosmos as an orderly system that functions apart from God. This concept of the world as opposed to Christ is a new use that the word acquires in the New Testament in contrast to its usual use in Greek writings as referring to something attractive. B. F. Westcott summed it up this way: "It is easy to see how the thought of an ordered whole relative to man and considered *apart* from man passes into that of the ordered whole *separated* from God. Man fallen impresses his character on the order which is the sphere of his activity. . . . The world, instead of remaining the true expression of God's will under the conditions of its creation, becomes His rival."[1] The only feature missing from Westcott's statement is the position of Satan as the head of the world system. Thus there must be three facets to any definition of the world: the idea of an ordered system, the relation of Satan to it, and the concept of its hostility to God. Here is a suggested definition: the cosmos world is that system organized by Satan, headed by Satan, and run by Satan, which leaves God out and is a rival to Him.

II. SATAN AND THE COSMOS

A. His Authority over the Cosmos

Clearly the Scriptures teach that Satan does have supreme authority over the cosmos. Of course, this is within the sovereign purpose of God and with His permission. Nevertheless, Satan's usurped authority over the cosmos is supreme. Our Lord recognized this when He called him the ruler of the world (John 12:31; 16:11) and when He did not dispute Satan's prerogative in offering Him the kingdoms of the world in the temptation (Matt. 4:8–9). The apostle John acknowledged the same truth when he wrote that the whole cosmos lies in the power of the evil one (1 John 5:19).

B. His Aim in the Cosmos

Satan's aim is to create a system that rivals God's kingdom but that leaves Him out. It is to promote a counterfeit order. Basically, the cosmos is evil because it is independent of God. It may contain good aspects as well as overtly evil aspects, but its inherent evil lies in its being independent of God and a rival to Him. This sharp rivalry surfaces in such verses as James 1:27, where the believer is told to keep himself unstained from the world; in 4:4, where friendship with the world is said to be hostility toward God; and in 1 John 2:16, where John declares that all that is in the world is not from the Father.

To achieve his aim, Satan must try to make the values of his godless system seem attractive. Thus he works to make people give top priority to self as number one and to the here and now as most important. When John wrote that all that is in the world is not of the Father, he explained what he meant by "all" by three epexegetical statements that follow in 1 John 2:16. All of them emphasize self as number one. Satisfy the lusts of the flesh, Satan counsels. Try to get what the inordinate desires of the eyes make you covet. And build a self-sufficient, arrogant attitude that arises from boasting about the possessions one has in life. This selfishness is, of course, the prevailing philosophy of the world, and it comes from Satan who promoted himself from the beginning.

Satan also seeks to focus people's attention on the present rather than on eternity. That is why John reminds us in 1 John 2:17 that the world passes away but the one that does the will of God abides forever. Thus Satan seeks to achieve his purposes by trying to change our priorities (self first) and our perspective (here and now more important). In reality the truth is that God is first and eternity most important.

III. GOD AND THE COSMOS

A. Planned Termination

God has already announced that the cosmos will be judged and terminated. Satan's rebellious system will come to an end. Nebuchadnezzar saw it in the dream Daniel interpreted when the stone (Christ's kingdom) struck the statue and filled the whole earth (Dan. 2:34–35, 44). That event is described in Revelation 17–19 and summarized in 1 John 2:17.

When our Lord returns, the cosmos kingdom of Satan will be replaced by the kingdom of Christ who will rule on this earth. It is important to observe that the arena of Christ's victory will be the same as that of Satan's kingdom, the earth. In the same arena where Satan has reigned, Christ will be victorious.

B. Permissive Toleration

In the meantime God permits the rebellion to continue and the cosmos to flourish. His plan permits evil to run its course, and His long-suffering permits many to come to the truth (Rom. 2:4).

IV. THE CHRISTIAN AND THE COSMOS

A. Separated from It

Pure religion, James wrote, is to keep oneself unstained from the cosmos (James 1:27). The same word "unstained" or "unspotted" is used of Christ in 1 Peter 1:19. Thus the believer's separation from the cosmos means Christlikeness in this cosmos. This includes having His perspectives, His standards, His goal (to do the will of the Father), His activities while living here. It means being able to say that we always do those things that are pleasing to the Father (John 8:29). This is true biblical separation.

B. Situated in It

But, of course, the believer, though separated from the cosmos, has to live his life in the cosmos. Thus we have to have contact with evil things and evil people. The only way to avoid such contact would be to "go out of the world" (1 Cor. 5:10). Such "separation by suicide" Paul did not recommend!

How, then, can we be properly related to the cosmos in which we are situated? Here are two guidelines.

(1) Use it but do not abuse it (1 Cor. 7:31). This summary statement is in a context where Paul mentioned marriage and singleness, weeping and rejoicing, having and not having things. It is proper to use all of these but not to abuse or overuse them. Do not let marriage have top priority; do not weep too long; do not be so happy you cannot be serious; do not put your trust in things you may properly buy. To do so is to abuse the cosmos. To have a "take-it-or-leave it" attitude while using these things is proper use.

(2) Enjoy but do not love the things of this cosmos (1 Tim. 6:17; 1 John 2:15). Though these may seem to be opposing principles, they cannot be, since both are clearly stated. What God gives us in this world we can legitimately enjoy, as long as we realize that all things are uncertain and that our dependence is on God whether He gives us little or much (Phil. 4:12; 1 Tim. 6:17).

When does proper enjoyment become improper loving? That is impossible to say in generalities. Each believer will have to examine his or her own particular circumstances. Undoubtedly if we make an idol of something we are loving it improperly. And an idol is anything at any time that comes between a believer and his love for God.

C. Sufficient for It

The believer can live victoriously in Satan's world through faith in Christ who Himself has become the victor over Satan (1 John 5:4–5). No contingency is attached to the promise in these verses. Every believer, whether new or mature, has victory simply because he is a believer.

> John's terminology guards against several errors. The initial clause in 1 John 5:4 shows that this overcoming is not something that is subsequent to salvation, for it is "everyone who is begotten [*gegennemenon,* a perfect form indicating an existing condition based on a completed act] of God" who "is overcoming [*nika,* a present form referring to an ongoing pattern of life] the world" (author's translation). The second clause, by the use of the aorist form *nikēsasa* (has overcome), shows that today's victory is based on yesterday's; that is, our victory is based on His. Finally, John counters the error that abstract faith (i.e., faith without the appropriate object) is efficacious. . . . Faith that overcomes involves trust in Jesus (the man), who is God's Son.[2]

Effecting that victory will involve habits, defenses, activities, but it is our faith in Jesus that makes us believers and thus overcomers, sufficient to live Christlike lives in the satanic cosmos.

NOTES

1. B. F. Westcott, *The Gospel According to St. John* (London: John Murray, 1908), 1:64–65.
2. W. Robert Cook, *The Theology of John* (Chicago: Moody, 1979), 115n.

Section VI
DEMONS: UNCLEAN SPIRITS

Chapter 26
THE REALITY OF DEMONS

The twentieth century has witnessed an almost complete turnaround in attitudes toward the reality of demons. In the first part of the century, their reality was commonly denied; in the latter part, it is much more readily and universally affirmed. Undoubtedly the increase in the number of witches and astrologers as well as booming sales of accompanying paraphernalia (including trade journals) has contributed to this change. Movies and books on the extraterrestrial have created a more favorable climate for the acceptance of demons.

I. THE TESTIMONY OF SCRIPTURE

Scripture unequivocally affirms the reality of demons, though not all who profess Christianity admit the validity of this evidence. Note this way of evading the force of some of the scriptural teaching: "Demons often survive as figures of speech (e.g., 'gremlins') long after they have ceased to be figures of belief. Accordingly, the mention of a demon's name in a scriptural text is no automatic testimony to living belief in him."[1]

A. The Testimony of Christ

A number of times during His earthly ministry our Lord cast out demons from various people. These instances, of course, affirmed His belief in their real existence (Matt. 12:22–29; 15:22–28; 17:14–20; Mark 5:1–16). He also gave the disciples authority to cast out demons in a context that did not require, as some allege, accommodation to their ignorant belief in demons (Matt. 10:1). Never did our Lord correct anyone for their acceptance of the reality of demons (Luke 10:17), yet He was willing on many other points to correct false theology.

If we cannot accept the Lord's testimony, then we would have to conclude that either (a) He was lying, or (b) He was accommodating His teaching to the ignorances of His audience (which in effect makes Him guilty of propagating falsehood), or (c) the early church redactors of the text added the parts about His teachings on demons.

B. The Testimony of Other Parts of the New Testament

All the writers of the New Testament (except the writer of Hebrews) mention demons for a total of more than 100 references. See, for example, 1 Corinthians 10:20–21; James 2:19; Revelation 9:20. These references all use the word *daimonion.* Other references to demons use the words "angel" and "spirit." Note too that demons are mentioned in the first (James) and last (Revelation) books written.

C. The Testimony of the Old Testament

Much less frequently does the Old Testament refer to demons. The *shedhim* of Deuteronomy 32:17 and Psalm 106:37 were lord-idols whom the Hebrews regarded as visible symbols of demons. The *seirim* of Leviticus 17:7; 2 Chronicles 11:15; Isaiah 13:21; and 34:14 were also demonic conceptions.

To deny the reality of demons requires ignoring or denying the truth of many passages in Scripture.

II. THE ORIGIN OF DEMONS

Various suggestions have been made as to the origin of demons.

A. They Are the Spirits of Wicked, Deceased People

This view seems to come from the ancient Greek belief about demons as being the disembodied spirits of deceased people, especially those who were evil in life. It has no support whatsoever in Scripture, since the Bible always places the unsaved dead as confined in a place of torment, unable to return to roam on the earth (Ps. 9:17; Luke 16:23; Rev. 20:13).

B. They Are the Disembodied Spirits of a Pre-Adamic Race

This view understands Satan as originally ruling over a perfect earth and a pre-Adamic race of people. When Satan sinned against God, this race of people were somehow involved in his rebellion. They lost their bodies and became disembodied spirits or demons.[2] This concept distinguishes between all angels, both good and bad, and demons. It offers as support the idea that demons seek embodiment, thus indicating that they are disembodied spirits. But against the view is the plain fact that nowhere does the Bible even hint at the existence of a pre-Adamic race. Indeed, the Lord declared that Adam was the first man (Matt. 19:4). Also, the Scriptures nowhere indicate that deceased people are free to return to earth.

C. They Are the Offspring of the Union Described in Genesis 6:1–4

To validate this suggestion requires at least two assumptions: (a) the sons of God are angels, and (b) the offspring were not human. That the sons of God were angels is a possible view, but that the offspring were demons is most unlikely. This would have to mean that the offspring were mongrels, part human and part angelic (either the Nephilim or the mighty men of renown of v. 4), who were destroyed in the Flood and whose disembodied spirits then became the demons.

D. They Are Fallen Angels

This view states that the demons are the angels who rebelled with Satan. In support of this are the following considerations.

Satan is designated the prince of the demons (Matt. 12:24 NIV), indicating that since their leader, Satan, is an angel, the demons must also be angels, but fallen as Satan is.

We know that Satan has well-organized ranks of angels who further his purposes. Two of these ranks are labeled rulers and authorities, which are the same designations for two of the ranks of good angels (Eph. 3:10; 6:12). This seems to indicate that the same kinds of beings make up the personnel of these ranks, and therefore that the evil beings are fallen angels.

In several places demons are called spirits (though unclean spirits), which associates them with the spirit world of angels, not humans. For example, the demon referred to in Matthew 17:18 is called an unclean spirit in the parallel account in Mark 9:25. The same equation of demons and spirits is found in Luke 10:17–20. Also, according to Matthew 8:16, the Lord healed many demon-possessed people by casting out the unclean spirits from them.

We must acknowledge that nowhere in the Scriptures are demons directly said to be fallen angels, but the evidence just cited seems to point to the conclusion that they are.

III. THE CONFINEMENT OF SOME FALLEN ANGELS

The Scriptures clearly indicate two groups of fallen angels, one consisting of those who have some freedom to carry out Satan's plans and the other who are confined. Of those who are confined, some are temporarily so, while others are permanently confined in Tartarus (2 Pet.

2:4 and Jude 6). The Greeks thought of Tartarus as a place of punishment lower than hades. Those temporarily confined are in the abyss (Luke 8:31; Rev. 9:1–3, 11), some apparently consigned there to await final judgment while others will be loosed to be active on the earth (Rev. 9:1–3, 11, 14; 16:14).

Why are some in Tartarus? If it is a result of their original sin of rebellion with Satan, then why are not all fallen angels there? And why not Satan himself as well? Confinement in Tartarus for some of the fallen angels must be punishment for some sin other than the original one, and a unique sin at that. Some suggest the unnatural sin of Genesis 6:2–4 committed by some of the fallen angels (called "sons of God" in the passage) caused their confinement in Tartarus.

Though angels do not reproduce after their kind (that is, do not produce baby angels), they may have been permitted to cohabit with human women on this one occasion to produce human offspring. However, the exceptional nature of this permission, which is contrary to all we know about angels and marriage, constitutes the weakness in this view. But if it was permitted on this single occasion, it only emphasizes the uniqueness of this incredibly monstrous sin that resulted in the permanent confinement of the angel participants in the prison of Tartarus. The human partners in the sin, of course, perished in the Flood. Other views of the "sons of God" in this passage include (a) the godly line of Seth, which cohabited with the ungodly women of the line of Cain, and (b) rulers from the line of Cain. The weakness of (a) lies in the need to believe that the godly and ungodly lines were kept distinct through all the years before the event of Genesis 6 occurred. The weakness in (b) (a view suggested in the Aramaic Targums) is the lack of evidence that a monarchical system of rulers had been established in the line of Cain by this time. Though I personally incline to the fallen-angel view, this is an interpretive problem we cannot solve.

What was the specific sin involved by whomever committed it? Three answers are possible. (1) If angels were involved then the sin was angelic cohabitation with human beings. (2) If the sons of God were humans, it was the sin of marrying indiscriminately without regard to spiritual condition (if Sethites) or royal status (if kings were involved). (3) It was the sin of polygamy because verse 2 may be understood to mean that they (whoever they were) took all the wives they chose (cf. 4:19). The offspring were men of strength and military prowess (the Nephilim probably lived on the earth before these marriages and were not the result of them).

To sum up these matters of the existence, origin, and confinement of some of the fallen angels, one might chart the concepts like this:

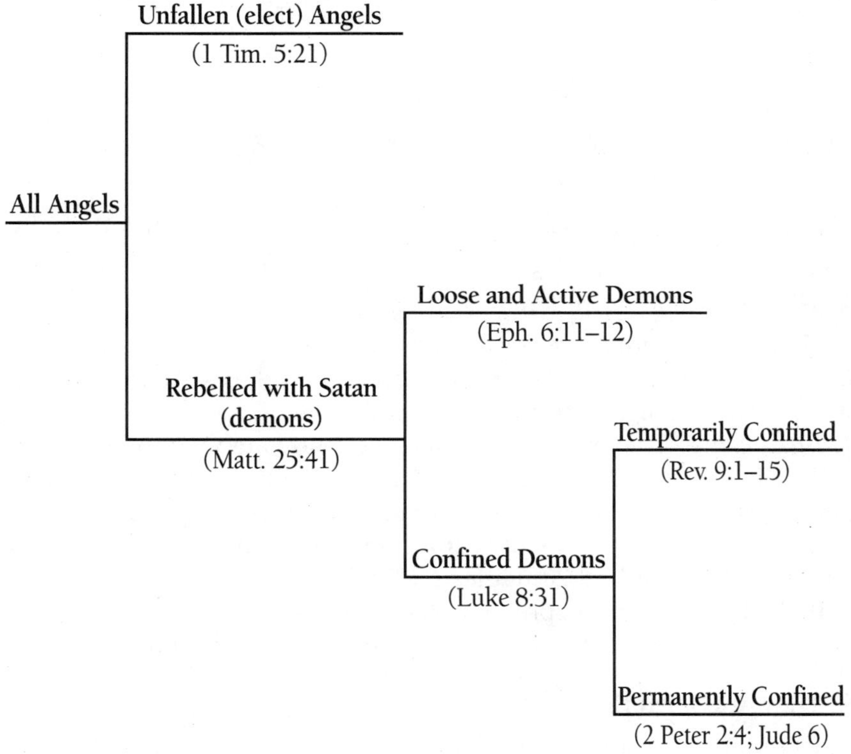

Notes

1. T. H. Gaster, "Demon," in *The Interpreter's Dictionary of the Bible* (New York: Abingdon, 1976), 1:818.
2. G. H. Pember, *Earth's Earliest Ages* (New York: Revell, ca. 1900), 72–73.

Chapter 27
What Are Demons Like?

Since demons belong to the same class of beings as angels and Satan, all these creatures have much in common.

I. THEIR PERSONAL NATURE

A. They Are Genuine Persons

Demons are not forces or concepts that merely exist in our minds. Demons exist; their reality does not depend on the existence and ability of human beings to conceive of them.

1. Intelligence. They possess intelligence, knowing who the Lord was while He was on earth (Mark 1:24) and knowing their own eventual doom (Matt. 8:29). They also believe in monotheism (James 2:19).

2. Emotions. They can exhibit emotion, especially when confronted with judgment (Luke 8:28; James 2:19).

3. Wills. They can give expression to their wills (Luke 8:32).

4. Personality. They are described by personal pronouns (Luke 8:27–30).

B. They Are Spirit Beings

In contrast to flesh and blood beings, demons are spirit beings (Eph. 6:12). Nevertheless, they are localized, since, as creatures, they are limited and not infinite as God is. Generally they are invisible to human beings, though on occasion their presence is apparent through various means (Acts 19:15; Rev. 9:1–12; 16:13).

II. THEIR INTELLECTUAL NATURE

Demons show great intelligence, as would be expected from such a high order of beings. They knew who Jesus is (Mark 1:24). They realized their own eventual doom (Matt. 8:29). They know there is only one God (James 2:19). They develop and promote systems of doctrine (1 Tim. 4:1–3), an activity that will apparently increase as the end of the age approaches.

Intelligence can be enhanced by experience. Every demon, of course, has existed throughout all the span of human history. Though each one has not observed everything that has transpired throughout history, their longevity gives an added dimension to their native intelligence. They have observed human beings in almost every conceivable situation; therefore, they can accurately predict what individuals will do in most circumstances.

III. THEIR IMMORAL NATURE

A. In Their Beings

Demons are designated as "unclean spirits" (Matt. 10:1), as "evil spirits" (Luke 7:21), as "the spirit of an unclean demon" (Luke 4:33), and "spiritual forces of wickedness" (Eph. 6:12). All of these terms clearly indicate the immoral nature of demons.

B. In Their Goals

Immorality is whatever is inconsistent with good, but good must ultimately be defined in relation to the will of God. Therefore, the immoral activities of demons may include anything that opposes the will of God.

Here are some observations of one who was deeply involved in spiritism.

> The spirits I encountered at seances were, for the most part, very moralistic. They encouraged us not to smoke or drink or do anything else that would harm our minds and bodies. Ministers were told to preach morality, good manners, and civic pride. I knew ministers who actually had spirit messages taken down by their secretaries and then used them from the pulpit! The spirits often talked about an ethical Jesus, but never about the Savior who died a sacrificial death for sin.
>
> In contrast to the high moral and ethical tone of the seances in our home, I attended some where the spirits were blasphemous and sensual.[1]

The immoral goals of demons must include both the promotion of evil immorality and good immorality. This is completely in line with Satan's goals and his desire to counterfeit what is right.

IV. THEIR POWERS

A. Their Strength

At times demons can exhibit superhuman strength as they work through human beings. The demon-possessed maniac of the Gerasenes was able to break all shackles and chains (Mark 5:3). The sons of Sceva were overpowered by the demon-possessed man in Acts 19:16.

B. Their Intelligence

I have already mentioned their superior intelligence. But the question always arises, do demons know the future? Certainly they can understand the plan of God for the future as they find it in the Bible. Does Acts 16:16 indicate they can predict the future? Evidently not, for the word "fortunetelling," used only here in the New Testament, must be understood in a bad sense; that is, "pretending to foretell the future." When it is used in the Septuagint, it invariably refers to the words of lying prophets or those who practiced evil arts that were forbidden by the Law.

C. Their Presence

Demons are not infinite; they are limited and they are creatures, albeit superhuman ones. Apparently they are not present everywhere; yet they are not so restricted as humans are by the normal barriers of space (Luke 8:30—a legion of demons dwelt in one man). The very fact that demons can enter human or animal bodies shows they can pass through barriers that would restrict human beings.

The very large number of demons may make them seem to be everywhere present, though that is not so. Yet Satan working with them can use their number to attempt to promote his plans everywhere.

To sum up: Demons are not humans; neither are they God. But they are superhuman with superior intelligence and experience and powers. To deny the existence of demons is not skepticism; it only displays ignorance. To be unrealistic about their power is foolhardy.

NOTE

1. Victor H. Ernest, *I Talked with Spirits* (Wheaton: Tyndale, 1970), 38.

Chapter 28
WHAT DO DEMONS DO?

I. IN RELATION TO SATAN

In general demons act as Satan's emissaries to promote his purpose to thwart the plan of God. Though Satan experiences creaturely limitations, demons extend his power and activities greatly. In fact, at times it may seem that Satan enjoys omniscience and omnipresence, though in actuality he does not. It is just that the demons extend Satan's activities so much that one might think Satan himself is doing it all (Eph. 6:11–12).

II. IN RELATION TO GOD

A. They Oppose the Plan of God

Having chosen to rebel against God and side with Satan, demons continue to oppose the purposes of God in this world (Dan. 10:10–14; Rev. 16:13–16).

B. They May Be Used by God to Carry Out His Purposes

On occasion God may use demons to further His purposes. He sent an evil spirit to stir up the people of Shechem against Abimelech (Judg. 9:23). He used an evil spirit to punish Saul with a mental disturbance that bordered on madness (1 Sam. 16:14). He sent a deceiving spirit to control the prophets and to give Ahab the wrong advice (1 Kings 22:22). He used one to afflict Paul so that he would not become overly proud (2 Cor. 12:7). Because they are creatures, demons are accountable to God and thus can be used by Him as He may desire.

III. IN RELATION TO RELIGION

A. They Promote Idolatry

In carrying out their opposition to God, demons actively try to turn men to the worship of idols. This was true in Old Testament times (Lev. 17:7; Deut. 32:17; Ps. 106:36–38). It is true now (1 Cor. 10:20), and demon worship will apparently be widespread during the coming Tribulation days (Rev. 9:20).

B. They Promote False Religion

1. They teach a worthless savior. John warned his readers to test the spirits, for demons influence false (human) prophets (1 John 4:1–4). A major test of orthodoxy (though not the only one) was the affirmation of the reality of the Incarnation; for if Christ had not taken on Himself a human body He could not have died and been our Savior.

Paul also warned of this attack on the Incarnation in the teachings of demons (1 Tim. 3:16–4:3). If 3:16 is a summary of truth contained in what was likely part of an early Christian hymn, then we may assume that demons attack not only the Incarnation, but also the historical resurrection and ascension of the Lord.

2. They teach a works salvation. This seems to be the point of 1 Timothy 4:3–4. By promoting asceticism as a good work, they replace the grace of God with a works program for salvation.

3. They teach a libertine ethic. The "deep things of Satan," undoubtedly promoted by his demons, attempt to teach people that wrong is right (Rev. 2:20–24).

IV. IN RELATION TO NATIONS

Daniel 10:13 relates that the prince of the kingdom of Persia resisted the coming of a good angel to bring Daniel a message. That prince was in turn resisted by Michael the archangel, indicating that the prince must have been a powerful demon. Just before Armageddon demons will be involved in moving the leaders of the nations to prepare for that military campaign (Rev. 16:13–16). Apparently there is warfare between the angels and demons that involves the affairs of nations of this earth. To deceive the nations is part of Satan's master plan, and he uses demons in carrying it out. What this may mean in international politics staggers the imagination, for there is no reason not to believe that it is still going on today.

V. IN RELATION TO PEOPLE

A. Affliction

Demons are able to inflict physical diseases (Matt. 9:33, muteness; 12:22, blindness and muteness; 17:15–18, seizures). They can also cause mental disorders (Mark 5:4–5; 9:22; Luke 8:27–29; 9:37–42).

They can be involved in bringing death to people (Rev. 9:14–19). Of course, not all physical or mental problems result from demonic activity; actually the Bible distinguishes natural illnesses from demonic ones (Matt. 4:24; Mark 1:32, 34; Luke 7:21; 9:1).

B. Perversion

The fact that demons are also called unclean spirits shows that whatever they do perverts what is clean, noble, and right. Demons want to pervert people by having them turn aside from the plan of God to Satan's plan. Sometimes they do this by promoting a perverted system of doctrine and lifestyle that may seem good to human beings (1 Tim. 4:1–3). Sometimes they do this by promoting evil and unclean activities (Deut. 32:17; Ps. 106:37–39). The immorality of the Canaanites seems to be traceable to demon activity (Lev. 18:6–30; Deut. 18:9–14).

C. Possession

1. Definition. Demon possession is the direct control by demon(s) of an individual by residing in him. All people, believers and unbelievers, are influenced and affected by demon activity, but not all are possessed. To draw an analogy, demon influence is to demon possession as general providence is to special miracles. Possessed individuals are not capable of severing themselves from the control of the demon(s).

The term "to be possessed by a demon" or "to be demonized" occurs thirteen times in the New Testament, all in the Gospels (e.g., Matt. 4:24; 12:22; Mark 5:15–18; Luke 8:36; John 10:21). The same phenomenon is described by terms like "cast out" or "come out" (Mark 1:25–26; 9:25). After the Day of Pentecost demon possession and exorcism are mentioned only in Acts 5:16; 8:7; 16:16–18; 19:12. The spiritual gift of discerning spirits (1 Cor. 12:10) most likely refers to the ability to distinguish between true and false sources of supernatural revelation when that revelation was being given in oral form, and not to the ability to cast out demons from people.

2. Characteristics. The characteristics of demon possession can be as varied as the activities of demons, ranging from mild to severe and even bizarre. Not too many specific symptoms of demon possession are described in the accounts, but they include the following: physical abnormalities like muteness, blindness, and convulsions (Matt. 9:32; 12:22; Luke 9:39); tendencies to self-destruction (Mark 5:5; Luke 9:42); insanity (at least the people believed demons could produce this, John 10:20); superhuman strength (Mark 5:3–4); and occult powers (Acts 16:16–18). Though demons can do these things in people, this does not mean that all illness, for example, comes from demon activity. Dr. Luke clearly distinguished demon-induced diseases from illnesses due to other, more natural, causes (Acts 5:16).

Here is a description of voodoo possession in the country of Haiti:

> The subject enters a trancelike state (usually after undergoing convulsions), during which one of the loas enters his or her body and "rides" it. The human personality is displaced by the superhuman, the human features take on the characteristics of the spirit's (masculine or feminine, good or evil, old or young, crafty or honest), and the human throat utters the loa's words, some of them in wholly unintelligible "tongues." The possession may last minutes or hours or sometimes days, during which time the person invaded by the spirit is fed the spirit's favorite food and drink (often quite impossible for unpossessed humans to consume) and offered his favorite diversions. Afterward, the human remembers nothing of his behavior as a god.[1]

3. *Responsibility.* The Scripture says very little explicitly on this point. The warnings to be on guard against and to resist the attacks of the devil imply that failure to do so exposes one to the possibility of control by Satan and his demons. Thus an individual may bear the responsibility for what eventuates in demon possession by giving in to preceding satanic attacks.

Yet the case of the lad who was demonized from childhood seems to indicate this was a condition over which he had no control (Mark 9:21). And certainly Paul's thorn in the flesh was not something he brought on himself, but was God using a demon to inflict the problem (2 Cor. 12:7).

4. *Extent.* Is demon possession restricted to unbelievers, or can it extend also to believers? In other words, can a Christian be demon possessed today? The argument against a believer's being able to be demon possessed is often based on the fact of the indwelling of the Holy Spirit in the believer's heart. In other words, since the Spirit indwells the believer, it is impossible for Satan or demons also to indwell and thus possess the believer at the same time. But do not the Spirit and the flesh war within the believer? (Gal. 5:16–17). If it be argued that the old man has been judged (Rom. 6:6), it may also be pointed out that Satan has been judged too (John 12:31). So if Spirit and flesh, the new and the old, can be present within the believer at the same time, why cannot the Spirit and Satan (or demons)?

Verses cited to support the view that believers can be possessed by demons are usually these: 1 Samuel 16:14; Luke 13:11–16; Acts 5:3; 1 Corinthians 5:5; 2 Corinthians 11:4; and 12:7. But when these verses are examined, they do not prove that believers can be demon possessed. Perhaps the question should be restated. Instead of asking whether a believer can be demon possessed, we should ask whether or not Satan or demons can work from within a believer as well as from outside. In other words, can the base of operation for Satan or demons be inside as well as outside a believer?

The reference in 1 Samuel says that an evil spirit tormented Saul, but the base of operation is not stated. Nor do we know definitely Saul's spiritual condition before God. Luke attributes the woman's deformity to a demon, and the Lord calls her "a daughter of Abraham." Some understand this to be a clear case of a demon working within a believer. However, it is unclear whether "daughter of Abraham" indicated a believer or only that she was one of God's chosen people, Israel. Clearly she was not a Christian in the post-Pentecost sense of the word.

The punishment on the sinning brother in 1 Corinthians 5 involved delivering him over to Satan (see also 1 Tim. 1:20). But whether this meant that Satan and or demons would work from within his life or simply that he was now being put out of the fellowship and protection of the church into the domain of Satan, the world, is debatable. The "different spirit" of 2 Corinthians 11:4 is not a demon any more than "another Jesus" in the verse is. It is another gospel that brings bondage. The base of operation of the messenger of Satan (a demon) that God sent to afflict Paul is unstated in 12:7. Though the result was a thorn in the flesh, this did not mean that the demon had to reside in Paul.

Acts 5:3 clearly states that Satan filled the heart of Ananias to cause him to lie to the Spirit. The word "fill" is the same as used in Ephesians 5:18 of the filling of the Spirit. Since there is no reason not to believe that Ananias was a believer, here is a clear statement that Satan did fill the heart of a believer. Nothing is said about demons here, though presumably if Satan filled his heart, demons could have also.

How can this evidence be evaluated? Here are two suggestions. First, we should discard phrases like "demon possession" and "demon indwelling" when referring these concepts to believers, because we tend to read into these terms the same idea we have about Spirit indwelling (i.e., a permanent residence in the believer). Neither Satan nor demons can permanently indwell a believer or ultimately have victory over him, even though they may dominate or control a believer's life for some time. A believer may be delivered to Satan for the destruction of the flesh, but the spirit will be saved in the Day of the Lord Jesus (1 Cor. 5:5). Whatever Satan or demons can do to a believer, and whether from without or within as their base of operation, their control cannot be permanent and eternal. John clearly declares that the evil one cannot "touch" the one who is born of God (1 John 5:18). The word "touch" here involves the purpose of harming—Satan cannot harm the believer. John uses the word in only one other place, John 20:17 (KJV), and it means not a superficial touching but a grasping, clinging to, or holding on to someone. Satan can never hang on to the believer with the purpose of harming him, for that believer belongs eternally and irrevocably to God. Satan (or demons) may afflict and even control for a time, but never permanently or eternally.

Second, the indefiniteness of the New Testament concerning the base of operation of demons in relation to Christians coupled with the lack of direct commands (after Pentecost) to exorcise demons may give us a clue as to how to fight the enemy. Normally one should not look to exorcism as the way to attack demons, but rather one must use the normal weapons of our warfare against Satan and his demons. The Christian should treat demon molestation as he would resist temptation or fight against the activities of his flesh. He should examine himself to see if there are any areas of rebellion against the law or will of God, confess any and all known sin, rely on the power of the indwelling Spirit who is greater than Satan (1 John 4:4), and use all the armor of God (Eph. 6:13–18).

Even if exorcism may be called for in some extreme instances, the exorcist cannot prevent demons from attacking the same person again, for no human being can guarantee to bind demons or send them into the abyss. Paul reminds us that we struggle against the powers of darkness all our lives. Therefore, the Christian must be alert (1 Pet. 5:8), be clothed in God's armor, and use all the things that contribute to healthy spirituality (Rom. 12:2; 2 Cor. 10:5; Phil. 4:8). A note of caution: Not all problems are initiated by demons, not all physical illnesses, not all emotional problems, not all sins. Some arise from natural causes, some from the flesh. Casting out demons would do no good in such instances, but fighting the good fight of faith will benefit in all things.

NOTE

1. Carter Harman, "The West Indies," *Life World Library* (New York: Time, Inc., 1963), 53–54.

Section VII
MAN:
THE IMAGE OF GOD

Chapter 29
EVOLUTION AND ORIGINS

Possibly no subject is more widely debated in various forums today than this question of how man originated. The night before I wrote these words our local TV news gave several minutes of coverage to two creationists who were seeking to show that the discovery of some human bones made naturalistic evolution impossible. Court cases concerning the teaching of "scientific creationism" in the public schools have given nationwide publicity to this subject. The debate over inerrancy has rightly included discussion concerning the historicity of the Genesis account of Creation. A number of views vie for acceptance even among evangelicals.

I. VIEWS CONCERNING ORIGINS

A. Evolution

Evolution simply means change in any direction. There is, of course, a completely legitimate use of the word, as, for example, in the sentence, "There has been considerable evolution in the field of communications in this century." But when the word evolution is used in relation to origins it means much more than change or development. It includes the idea of origin by natural processes, both the origin of the first living substance and the origin of new species. It theorizes that several billion years ago chemicals in the sea, acted on by sunlight and cosmic energy, formed themselves by chance into one or more single-celled organisms, which have since developed through beneficial mutations and natural selection into all living plants, animals, and people.

That there has been change and development in many areas of creation no one denies. However, for the evolutionist this development has also included the production of new species of more complex and intricate forms from less complicated substances. None of this requires the idea or activity of God. Charles Darwin said, "I will give absolutely nothing for the theory of natural selection if it requires miraculous additions at any one stage of descent."[1] Julian Huxley also affirmed that "to postulate a Divine interference with these exchanges of matter and energy at a particular moment in the earth's history is both unnecessary and illogical."[2]

In relation to the origin of man, evolution teaches that he evolved over long periods of time through the action of mutations and natural selection from simpler, brute forms, which in turn had evolved from other forms, which ultimately came from an original single-celled creature.

Obviously the bases of naturalistic evolution are science and faith.

B. Theistic Evolution

Theistic evolution holds that God directed, used, and controlled the processes of naturalistic evolution to "create" the world and all that is in it. Usually this view includes the idea that the days of Genesis 1 were ages, that evolutionary processes were involved in the "creation" of Adam, and that the earth and prehuman forms are of great antiquity.

Darwin declared that the supernatural was unnecessary in his theory. The creationist insists that naturalistic evolution is excluded in this view. Thus theistic evolution tries to ride two horses (evolution and Creation), which are going in opposite directions.

The creation of Eve poses a special problem for some who teach theistic evolution. Adam, it is claimed, emerged from a preexisting form into which God breathed the breath of life, but Eve did not come from some preexisting form of life. She was a special act of creation. And if she was, why not Adam also?

Pierre Teilhard de Chardin (1881–1955), a Roman Catholic Jesuit priest and paleontologist, advocated a synthesis between evolution and traditional Christian theology. Evolution stands as his central theme, though his ideas also resemble aspects of process philosophy.

Strictly speaking, all that theistic evolution needs to postulate to be theistic is that there was a supernatural Being who was the invisible force that started the long process of evolution. Typically one would find this position among Roman Catholic, liberal Christian, and neoorthodox thinkers. But many who fall into the general category of theistic evolutionists perceive God as being involved not only at the beginning of the process but at various points along the way. God stepped in to create at the major stages of life throughout geologic history (e.g., the vertebrates, the birds, the mammals, and man). But He also permitted and used naturalistic evolution processes throughout the long periods of geologic time. This view is known as progressive creationism or threshold evolution and often is linked with the day-age view of Genesis 1. Although I would place progressive creationism under the general category of theistic evolution, some evangelicals who favor progressive creationism would object, claiming that it really belongs under creationism. However, the kind of evolution involved in progressive creationism is naturalistic, and the extent to which it occurred was large; so the view is in my judgment misnamed, and it is a form of theistic evolution.

The bases on which theistic evolution rest are the Bible and science.

C. Creation

Though there are variations within the broad category of creationism, the principal characteristic of this view is that the Bible is its sole basis. Science may contribute to our understanding, but it must never control or change our interpretation of the Scriptures in order to accommodate its findings. As far as man is concerned, Creation teaches that God created the first man in His image from the dust of the ground and His own breath of life (Gen. 1:27 and 2:7). No subhuman creature was involved, nor was any process of evolution.

Creationists hold to different views regarding the days of Creation, but to be a creationist one must believe that the biblical record is factually historical and that Adam was the first man.

One view teaches that the biblical account of the creation of Adam and Eve relates only to what occurred in the Garden of Eden rather recently and does not tell us anything about what was happening in the rest of the earth. Therefore, while Adam was the result of special creation by God, in other parts of the earth creatures were evolving over long periods of time. In other words, Adam was an island of creation in the midst of a sea of evolution. I would not consider this view as belonging under the general category of creationism, for Adam is not understood to be the first man from whom all mankind descended.

II. THE PROPOSAL OF EVOLUTION

We need to consider in more detail evolution's proposal to answer the question of origins and some of the problems of that proposal. Many good books have been written on this subject to which one may refer for greater detail. Some I would recommend include the writings of Henry M. Morris, Bolton Davidheiser, and A. E. Wilder Smith, and recent books by Phillip E. Johnson and Michael J. Behe.[3]

A. The Principles of Evolution

Evolution rests on several basic principles. Theories vary, but these are some common premises.

(1) The planets and stars resulted from a big-bang explosion of compressed, rotating protons and neutrons. This dense, compressed mass continues to expand away from the original nucleus at fantastic speeds. An alternate to this principle is the so-called steady-state theory that teaches that matter is continually being created in outer space and that this process has been going on for an infinite period of time.

(2) Life began completely by chance when a single cell appeared from nonliving matter.

(3) Having thus begun by chance, all other living organisms have developed from that first and subsequent simpler forms of life, which gradually increased in complexity. This development also produced man.

B. The Process of Evolution

If one were to reduce the process to a formula it would look like this: M(utations) + N(atural) S(election) x T(ime) = Evolution. This formula expresses the mechanism of evolution.

Mutations constitute *the* explanation for evolution. Mutations are sudden, small changes in the DNA code of the genes, which are passed on to the offspring, causing them to differ from their parents in well-marked characteristics. In other words a small change in an organism is passed on to the offspring. Eventually another small change appears by chance, etc. If enough of these occur and are preserved, then the organism will become more complex and evolve into a different organism, etc. This is the way all existing forms of life were produced from the simple, single-cell original. The importance of mutations as the explanation for how evolution occurred cannot be overemphasized. Julian Huxley wrote: "Not only is it an effective agency of evolution, but it is *the* only effective agency of evolution."[4]

Natural selection is the mechanism that preserves the changes caused by mutations. When a change occurs that is beneficial to the organism, then natural selection will preserve that change simply because it is beneficial. Any harmful changes would not be preserved because natural selection would breed them out of the line as useless. (A beneficial mutation is one that increases the complexity of the organism.) It is important to remember that natural selection is just that—natural. It is not laboratory selection or hothouse selection; it means that selection process in raw nature that allegedly eliminates harmful mutations and keeps helpful ones. By this process the strain of organisms is gradually improved, given enough time.

Time, and long periods of it, are therefore necessary to evolution. Since mutations do not occur frequently, there will have to be a lot of time in order for enough of the beneficial mutations to occur, then to be preserved by natural selection, thereby effectively changing the organisms to increasingly complex ones. In order to decrease the time required, some evolutionists posit "bursts" of mutations having occurred at about the same time, which effected a number of beneficial changes in an organism almost immediately, thus foreshortening the time required for the necessary changes to take place.

III. PROBLEMS OF EVOLUTION

A. Problems in Mutations

Can mutations really do all they are alleged to do? Consider the following.

1. Mutations are rare and almost always harmful. In the fruit fly experiment where mutations were produced by artificial means, it is estimated that only one fruit fly out of one million will develop a mutation. Furthermore, Theodosius Dobzhansky, who conducted many fruit fly experiments, acknowledged that "most mutants . . . are more or less disadvantageous" and that "the deleterious character of most mutations seems to be a very serious difficulty."[5]

2. Where do new genes come from? No mutation has ever produced a new species or even a new organ or system in an existing species. Yet this had to occur if evolution is valid. Protozoa, for instance, do not have teeth. Where, then, did the genes come from that produced teeth if we have evolved from protozoa? Mutations concern changes in existing organisms; they do not produce new ones. Yet somewhere and somehow along the line new species had to be produced, and even new systems (like the circulatory system or the hearing system) had to be produced within existing species.

Here is a sample of how evolution wrestles with this question.

> If mutation, which is the only form of hereditary change of which we have definite evidence is always change in genes already

> present, it would at first sight seem that we have here no basis at all for understanding the evolution of novelties in the organization of the body. For their evolution we surely need new hereditary factors, not change in those already present. But we must remember that conditions in the body and in the hereditary material are extremely complex. Possibly changes in the distribution of enzymes in the body, if they were somehow brought about, might cause new differences in rate of growth of parts, as for instance, in a part of the frontal bones of the skull resulting in the early evolution of horns. It is hard to see how redistribution of its enzyme could be brought about by mutation of a gene, but, in view of the complexity of the conditions in the body, it may perhaps be possible. Also, it is not impossible that new genes may be evolved. We know that genes may be reduplicated within the chromosomes and when that has happened, one member of such a pair might become so altered by mutation as to give us what is functionally a new gene.
>
> These suggestions are purely hypothetical. For the present we cannot say more than that novelties of organization undoubtedly occur in evolution; that they are essential to the increase in complexity which is associated with progress in evolution; that we have no accurate knowledge of the details of their evolution.[6]

This appears to be more an exercise in faith than fact!

B. Problems in Natural Selection

1. Does natural selection really guarantee improvement? Of course it must do so; otherwise, if a weak substrain developed, it would soon die out and there could be no evolution at all. But the problem is, will *natural* selection bring improvements? Laboratory selection may, but will natural? An evolutionist acknowledges this problem: "In fact, natural selection with evolutionary consequences has only been observed where men have created drastically new conditions which impose a heavy selection pressure."[7]

2. Single mutations. Would natural selection recognize the worth of a single mutation while waiting for other mutations to happen that would be necessary for the production of a new system in the organism? In the evolution of the eye, for example, if the mutation that made the tear duct occurred first, would natural selection keep it in the organism until other mutations happened that produced the lashes, slit, cornea, lens, etc.? Or would natural selection breed out the organism that had a tear duct but no other components of a seeing system simply because it was not useful alone?

3. Circular argument. The interreaction of mutations and natural selection to explain evolution is a circular argument. Julian Huxley admitted it clearly: "On the basis of our present knowledge, natural selection is bound to produce genetic adaptations; and genetic adaptations are thus presumptive evidence for the efficacy of natural selection."[8]

C. Problems in the Length of Time Required

Even though mutations are rare and usually harmful, and even though natural selection would most likely breed out a mutant from the strain, it seems quite plausible to laymen that given enough time anything, even evolution, can happen. Huxley explains: "All living things are equally old—they can all trace their ancestry back some 2,000 million years. With that length of time available, little adjustments can easily be made to add up to miraculous adaptations; and the slight shifts of gene frequency between one generation and the next can be multiplied to produce radical improvements and totally new kinds of creatures."[9]

But such a claim can be challenged by putting it to the test.

> The odds are 10^{161} to 1 that not one usable protein would have been produced by chance in all the history of the earth, using all the appropriate atoms on earth at the fantastic rate described. This is a figure containing 161 zeroes. It might be well to recall that even if one molecule *were* obtained, it would not help at all in arranging the second protein molecule unless there existed an accurate duplication process. Even if there were such a process, there are many other *kinds* of proteins needed before there can be a living organism. In Morowitz's minimal cell, the 239 protein molecules required include *at least 124 different protein species.* (italics in original).[10]

Others have arrived at similar conclusions about the probability of forming one protein molecule by chance. French scientist Lecomte du Nouy said it is 1 chance out of 10^{243}. Swiss mathematician Charles E. Guye calculated it as 1 chance out of 10^{160}. Murray Eden of MIT and Marcel Schutzenberger of the University of Paris both concluded that their digital computers showed that evolution was impossible.[11]

While probability is expressed by a fraction (e.g., one in five million times), and when the fraction is as small as these are for the chance production of a protein molecule, then the mathematician would declare the probability of its happening as zero. The evolutionist would likely point out that there still exists a chance, however infinitesimal, of evolution happening because of the billions of years involved. However, even billions of years will not reduce the probability enough to put it in the range of reasonable possibility. Davidheiser tested the well-known statement that if a million monkeys were permitted to strike the keys of a million typewriters for a million years, they might by chance type a copy of a Shakespearean play. Setting up a controlled experiment with only capital letters, continuous typing at a uniform rate of speed, and requiring only the first verse of Genesis, he shows that a million monkeys would never type Genesis 1:1, let alone a Shakespearean play in billions of years.[12] Even to type the first line of Hamlet ("Ber: Who's There?") would require on the average of a number of repeated experiments 284 trillion years, a period considerably longer than it took evolution to do all it supposedly did.

The obvious conclusion of this is simply that it requires an incredible amount of faith to believe that evolution could have caused by chance all life that ever did or does now exist.

Could life have evolved by chance? The probability of forming one protein molecule by chance is one in 10^{243}, which is a figure of 1 followed by 243 zeros. This fraction is so small that one may say that the probability is zero.

1 Chance out of 1,000,000,000,000,000,000,000,000,000,000,000,
000,000,000,000,000,000,000,000,000,000,000,
000,000,000,000,000,000,000,000,000,000,000,
000,000,000,000,000,000,000,000,000,000,000,
000,000,000,000,000,000,000,000,000,000,000,
000,000,000,000,000,000,000,000,000,000,000,
000,000,000,000,000,000,000,000,000,000,000,
000,000,000,000.

D. Problem with the Second Law of Thermodynamics

This second law of thermodynamics states that though energy in the cosmos remains constant, the amount available to do useful work is always decreasing (and entropy, the measure of unavailable energy, is increasing). Everything, then, is moving toward less orderliness or greater chaos. This, of course, runs directly contrary to what evolution teaches. In fact, in a debate in which I was participating, I heard an evolutionist glibly remark that evolution was "the grand exception to the second law."

How do evolutionists react to the seemingly insoluble problem the second law poses?

Some say the long time since Creation allows for anything, particularly evolution, to happen. But remember, during those billions of years entropy was increasing; the law was not suspended.

Some point out that there seem to be exceptions to the law. This may be true, but they can only be temporary and at the expense of an increase in entropy somewhere else in the environment.

Some claim the earth is an open system and draws energy from the sun. But the infusion of solar energy is useless unless there exists some sort of motor within the elements on which it shines that can convert that energy to reverse the second law. For example, the sun may beat on concrete blocks for thousands of years without ever producing additional or mutated concrete blocks because there is no mechanism within concrete blocks to convert that energy. There must be an appropriate energy conversion process along with a preprogrammed template to work from before solar energy can reverse the second law. Or as one evolutionist asked: "How, when no life existed, did substances come into being, which today are absolutely essential to living systems, yet which can only be formed by those systems?"[13]

IV. THE PICTURE OF EVOLUTION

The fossil record, it is claimed, provides evidence of the process of evolution. Fossils do not explain how it occurred; they picture what did occur through mutations and natural selection over long periods of time. Evolutionists claim that because the simpler forms of life are found in lower layers of rocks and more complex forms in upper layers, this proves that the more complex forms arose from the simpler ones.

Strictly speaking, the fossil argument is a circular one. The strata are dated by the fossils they contain and the fossils are dated by the strata in which they are found. The evolutionist states that this circle is broken by outside dating methods. However, dating methods are predicated on a uniform rate of decay of the element. A candle will burn at a uniform rate unless a window is open and a breeze causes it to burn more rapidly for a time. The disappearance of a vapor canopy over the earth or the extreme pressures of a flood could have been like an open window to change that rate during the earth's history. If so, then the dates arrived at would be very wrong. Carbon-14 dating would be significantly affected by those events. The potassium-argon method of dating assumes that rock samples tested contained no argon-40 when they were formed, which is a questionable assumption. Some submarine pillow basalt from Kilauea volcano in Hawaii that is known to be only a few thousand years old at most was dated by this method as from 100,000 to 40 million years old, indicating that age may be simulated by hydrostatic pressure among other factors.[14]

A major problem in the fossil picture is the lack of transitional forms, none of which have ever been found among the millions of fossils that exist. Surely there would be one discovered somewhere. Actually the earliest fossils of each group exhibit all the features of that group without any suggestion of graduation from one form to another. Some evolutionists claim that the Archaeornis (or Archaeopteryx) is an example of a missing link because it looks like part bird and part reptile. But it may be considered all bird, albeit unusual. In any case it appeared suddenly and therefore without any transitional ancestry.

Another problem is that many simple forms of life are found in strata of rocks above the more complex forms. Hundreds of such cases are known, and of course they all are contrary to the picture evolution should give.

Obviously much more could be written on this subject. I have tried only to focus on the principal arguments of evolution and suggest their main weaknesses. No one can keep all the arguments in mind. So I suggest knowing and exposing the gaps in the theory—rare and harmful mutations, natural selection that will eliminate those harmful changes, not nearly enough time for everything to happen by chance, opposition to the second law of thermodynamics, embarrassing gaps in the fossil record.

Finally, we need to underscore the bottom line of evolution, namely faith. In the final analysis one must believe evolution, just as one must believe Creation. Two scientists stated this fairly when they wrote:

> Actually biologists are still as far away as they ever were in their attempts to explain how the first protoplasm originated. The evidence of those who would explain life's origin on the basis of the accidental combination of suitable chemical elements is no more tangible than that of those people who place their faith in Divine Creation as the explanation of the development of life. Obviously, the latter have as much justification for their belief as do the former.[15]

NOTES

1. R. E. D. Clark, *Darwin: Before and After* (London: Paternoster Press, 1948), 86.
2. Julian Huxley, *Evolution in Action* (New York: New American Library, 1964), 20.

3. Henry M. Morris (several books); Bolton Davidheiser, *Evolution and Christian Faith* (Philadelphia: Presbyterian and Reformed, 1969); A. E. Wilder Smith, *Man's Origin, Man's Destiny* (Wheaton, Ill.: Harold Shaw, 1968); Phillip E. Johnson (e.g., *Darwin on Trial* and *Reason in the Balance* [Downers Grove, Ill.: InterVarsity, 1991 and 1995]); and Michael J. Behe, *Darwin's Black Box* (New York: Free Press, 1996).
4. Huxley, *Evolution in Action,* 35.
5. Theodosius Dobzhansky, *Evolution, Genetics, and Man* (New York: John Wiley and Sons, 1955), 150.
6. G. S. Carter, *A Hundred Years of Evolution* (New York: Macmillan, 1958), 184–85.
7. J. B. S. Haldane, *Nature,* 14 March 1959, 51.
8. Huxley, *Evolution in Action,* 43.
9. Ibid., 41.
10. James F. Coppedge, *Evolution: Possible or Impossible?* (Grand Rapids: Zondervan, 1973), 109–10.
11. *Mathematical Challenges to the Neo-Darwinian Interpretation of Evolution,* eds. P. S. Moorhead and M. M. Kaplan (Philadelphia: Wistar Institute Press, 1967); and Lecomte du Nouy, *Human Destiny* (London: Longmans, Green and Co., 1947), 34.
12. Davidheiser, *Evolution and Christian Faith,* 362–63.
13. Harold F. Blum, *Time's Arrow and Evolution* (Princeton: Princeton University Press, 1968), 170.
14. *Science,* 1968, 161:1132, cf. *Journal of Geophysical Research,* 1968, 73:4603.
15. Harry J. Fuller and Oswald Tippo, *College Botany* (New York: Holt, Rinehart & Winston, 1961), 25.

Chapter 30
THE BIBLE AND ORIGINS

Although it is true that the Bible is not a textbook on science, this does not mean it is inaccurate when it reveals truths that belong to the arena of science. Indeed, whatever it reveals in whatever area of knowledge is true, accurate, and reliable. The Bible does not answer every question we might like to have answered in the area of origins, but what it does reveal must be acknowledged as truth. And it says more on this subject than some may realize.

I. SOME NECESSARY PRESUPPOSITIONS

A. Faith

The writer to the Hebrews reminds us that it is by faith that we understand that the ages were framed by the Word of God and that what is seen was not made out of visible things (Heb. 11:3). The ages refers to all the periods of time as well as all that they contain. Since obviously there were no human spectators to Creation, and since the first man was placed in an already existing universe, we must accept by faith whatever God has revealed about Creation. Otherwise we will know nothing with certainty about Creation.

By contrast evolutionists would have to change Hebrews 11:3 to this: "By faith, we evolutionists understand that the worlds were *not* framed by the word of any god, so that what is seen has indeed been made out of previously existing and less complex visible things, by purely natural processes, through billions of years."[1]

B. Facts

Truth about Creation is found only in the Bible. Whatever truths science may uncover can never be accepted as absolute truth. The facts God has revealed in the Bible are reliable facts, including those in the opening chapters of Genesis. That means the events actually took place in time and space once they had been created. In other words, the sequential acts of Creation and the events of the temptation and sin of Adam and Eve transpired in time and space; that is, they could have been marked on a calendar and a map. Genesis records facts, not myths or legends. Other biblical passages confirm this (e.g., Exod. 20:9–11; Matt. 19:4–6).

These facts were written by Moses. Whatever sources he may have used in connection with the superintending work and revelatory power of God in his writing, he was a man trained and educated. Some imply that revelation of events in an early period cannot be factual because they come through "savages." This makes *primitive* and *savage* synonymous and deprecates the operative power of inspiration. If Moses' words do not mean what they say, even though they speak of an early period of history, then how may we trust Christ's words (John 5:47)?[2]

II. THE GOD OF CREATION

Genesis 1:1 identifies *Elohim* as the Creator. *Elohim* is a generic word for Deity as well as a proper name for the true God. It means the strong One, mighty Leader, supreme Deity. The plural form of the word indicates His plentitude of power and majesty. This identification of Elohim as Creator refutes several serious heresies. (1) It refutes atheism. (2) It refutes polytheism, for the verb that follows is singular. (3) It denies pantheism, for God is presented as separate from His creation.

III. CREATIO EX NIHILO

This phrase means that God did not use any preexisting materials in creating. Hebrews 11:3 indicates this, as does the thrust of the record in Genesis 1. Prior to the creative fiat, there was no other kind of phenomenological existence. This rules out the idea that matter is eternal, and it counters the concept of dualism.

The verb *bara* used in Genesis 1:1, 21, and 27 does not in itself preclude the use of preexisting material (see Isa. 65:18), though none is stated or implied in the account. It means essentially the same as *asa,* "to do or make" (Gen. 1:25; Exod. 20:11; Neh. 9:6). A third word for God's creative activity, *yatsar,* formed, occurs in Genesis 2:7.

Creatio ex nihilo is a helpful concept "if we understand it to mean that *physical* entities were created out of the nonphysical resources of God's omnipotence. Technically, the expression is applicable only to the creation of inorganic substances, for God did employ previously created inorganic materials in forming the bodies of living things."[3]

IV. THE TIME OF CREATION

The "beginning" of Genesis 1:1 apparently refers to the beginning of the Creation of the world. The first verse is an absolute statement, not a dependent clause related to verse 2.[4] Even so the statement does not set the time of God's creative activity. Ussher fixed the time as 4004 B.C., while evolutionists suggest 4,500,000,000 B.C.

(1) Some creationists hold to a recent Creation, both of the earth and of man.

(2) Some agree that man was a recent creation but the earth is not. The gap theory and the day-age idea often go along with this view.

(3) Some make a distinction between men represented by the fossils who were very old and lived and died before Adam, and Adam himself who was a recent creation.

(4) Some understand Adam to be an island of creation in the sea of contemporary evolution including subhuman forms.

(5) Theistic evolutionists regard man as ancient and the result of evolutionary processes by which the pre- and subhuman eventually produced humans.

(6) A few understand Genesis 1:1 not as describing "the primeval Creation ex nihilo, celebrated by the angels (Job. 38:7; Isa. 45:18), but the much later refashioning of a judgment-ridden earth in preparation for a new order of creation-man."[5] The original Creation took place, according to this view, before Genesis 1:1.

Obviously there is no agreement as to the time of Creation. However, it seems clear that the recent appearance of man is well established in the scriptural account. Even assuming day-ages, Adam was created on the sixth day-age, which would be relatively recent. The genealogical tables in Genesis 5 and 11 (even with some gaps within them) also argue for the recent creation of Adam. In order to come to some decisions about the scriptural evidence, we need to consider some relevant interpretations and considerations.

V. THE GAP CONCEPT

A. Its Description

The gap concept (also called the ruin-reconstruction theory and the restitution theory) proposes a way to harmonize the Genesis record with the long periods of time seemingly demanded by geology (which as a science came into being at the first of the nineteenth cen-

tury). First popularized by Thomas Chalmers of Scotland in 1814, it was elaborated by George H. Pember,[6] incorporated in the notes of the *Scofield Reference Bible* (1909), and defended by, among others, Eric Sauer[7] and Arthur C. Custance.[8]

According to this concept the original Creation of Genesis 1:1 was not only perfect and beautiful but was populated with plants and animals (some also say perhaps with pre-Adamic men). Then in the gap between verses 1 and 2 Satan rebelled against God, thus bringing sin into the universe. God's judgment involved a global flood followed by darkness and an Ice Age in which all plant, animal, and human (if it existed) life was destroyed. Thus the fossils found today came from this judgment on the original Creation because of the sin of Satan. Verse 2 pictures the state of things that resulted from this judgment. The six days of Creation, then, describe a re-creation, restoration, or restitution, not the original Creation.

B. Its Support

(1) The phrase in Genesis 1:2 should be translated "the earth became without form and void." That is, it became that way because of the catastrophic judgment on Satan.

(2) "Without form, and void," (KJV), describe an evil condition that could not have been part of the original Creation by God because He did not make the earth without form (Isa. 45:18).

(3) Darkness cannot be good; therefore, Genesis 1:2 cannot describe the original Creation by God.

(4) God's command to Adam to "replenish the earth" (Gen. 1:28 KJV) indicates the earth must have been previously inhabited.

(5) The use of *bara* in verse 1 indicates a different creation from what follows.

C. Its Weaknesses

(1) Verse 2 begins with what is technically called a disjunctive *waw* ("now" rather than "and") and which introduces a circumstantial clause, with the imperfect sense of the verb, translated "now the earth was. . . ." To translate "the earth had become formless and void," a *waw* consecutive (which would indicate a sequential clause and be translated "and") with the pluperfect sense of the verb would be expected. To be sure, grammar allows the pluperfect sense "had become" and usage shows that the verb "to be" can be understood as "to become" (as in Gen. 19:26; Judg. 11:39; 2 Kings 17:3). But the verb

normally serves as a linking verb ("to be" not "to become"), as in Genesis 2:25 and 3:1 where it could not be understood as "to become." Also the disjunctive use of the *waw* seems required because the author apparently is calling the reader's attention to something about the earth —"now as to the earth it was. . . ." Furthermore, parallel constructions to Genesis 1:2 are found in Jonah 3:3 and Zechariah 3:1–3 where the *waw* is disjunctive (translated "now") and the verb cannot be translated "to become."[9]

Actually this grammatical and translation choice is the principal support for the gap concept; and since it is at best weak, we must conclude that the theory lacks solid exegetical basis in the text.

A logical problem also exists with the construction the gap theory places on this verse. If the verb means "had become" (a pluperfect sense), then Genesis 1:2 is saying that the earth had become formless and void prior to the Creation of verse 1. But the gap concept requires the becoming to happen after the creating.

(2) "Formless and void" do not necessarily imply judgment and an evil condition. *Tohu* (formless) appears in the Old Testament referring to space (Job 26:7) and the wilderness (Deut. 32:10) without any evil connotations. However, according to the gap proponents, the formless condition of the earth could not have been its original state, since Isaiah 45:18 says God did not create it formless. Therefore, they conclude, the earth became that way after the original Creation. But this argument is not at all conclusive, for Isaiah 45:18 says that it was not God's ultimate intention that the earth be formless and void. In other words, God did originally create the world formless and void, but since this was not His ultimate wish for it, He proceeded to fill it with living things, including man.

(3) Although it is true that darkness is used as a symbol of judgment and evil, does it follow that darkness is inherently evil? I think not. It was made for creation's good just as light was (Ps. 104:19–24). Although it is true that God called the light good but does not say anything about the darkness (Gen. 1:4), does it follow that the darkness was not good? I think not. If so, then we would have to conclude that the expanse that He created but did not specifically call good was not good (vv. 6–8).

(4) God's command to Adam to replenish the earth (v. 28 KJV), implying that it had previously been inhabited in the original Creation was literally a command to fill, not refill, the earth. Replenish and refill are faulty translations of the Hebrew word.

(5) No argument can be built on the use of *bara* in verse 1, as previously discussed under III.

(6) One additional weakness should be mentioned. There exists no biblical proof that Satan's fall resulted in judgment on the earth. Adam's fall did (Gen. 3:17–19).

To sum up: The gap concept does not rest on solid exegetical grounds. The fact that it became popular about the same time as geology came on the scene makes one suspect that it gained acceptance because it easily accommodates the findings of uniformitarian geology.

VI. SOLAR DAYS OR AGES?

Actually there are four views that fall within this discussion. (1) The literal solar-day view in which the days of Creation are understood to be solar days (which we now calibrate as twenty-four hours). (2) The day-age view that understands the days to be long ages. This view, of course, accommodates the geologic ages easily. (3) Solar days with long gaps between. The days in Genesis 1 are solar days, but they did not follow each other immediately; rather they were separated by long periods of time. This view, too, will accommodate uniformitarian geology. (4) The revelatory-day view says that the days have nothing to do with God's work of creating but with His revealing these matters to Moses. In other words, they were the days on which certain things were revealed, not performed.[10]

Even though there are these various views, the principal discussion centers on whether the days are solar or age-long.

A. Arguments for Solar Days

(1) The word "day" when used with a numerical adjective in the Pentateuch always indicates a solar day. Why would Genesis 1 be an exception? Indeed this is true for all the uses of "day" with a numeral or ordinal in the entire Old Testament. The only possible exceptions to this might be 2 Chronicles 21:19 and Hosea 6:2, though both passages may well be interpreted as understanding solar days. To be sure, the word "day" is used in several senses, but with the numeral or ordinal it only means a solar day (Gen. 1:5, 8, 13, 19, 23, 31). In verses 5, 14, 16, 18, it refers to the period of daylight as contrasted with night. Of course, this latter usage of day as the time of daylight relates to a solar day. It makes no sense to talk about the day of an age as contrasted with the night of an age.

(2) The qualifying phrase "evening and morning" attached to each of the six days of Creation supports the meaning of the days as twenty-four-hour periods. Proponents of the day-age idea reply that evening and morning is a figure of speech for beginning and ending. Each "evening" saw the completion of the work of that age, which was followed by the "morning" of renewed activity. But evening and morning, each occurring more than 100 times in the Old Testament, are never used to mean anything other than a literal evening and literal morning, ending or beginning a solar day. Notice the phrase in Daniel 8:26 referring to solar days.

(3) Exodus 20:11 and 31:17 state that God made everything in six days, that He rested on the seventh, and this pattern serves as the basis for man's weekly cycle. In both these passages, these are the words God spoke directly to Moses. If God meant ages instead of days, why did He not use *dor* or *olam,* which mean age, or attach an adjective like *rab,* which means "long," to the word "day"?

B. Arguments for Age-Days

(1) The word "day" sometimes refers to a longer, indefinite period of time. In Genesis 2:4 it refers to the entire creative period, in Job 20:28 to the time of God's wrath, and in Psalm 20:1 to a day or time of trouble. The plural is sometimes used in the sense of "the time of" (Gen. 26:18). The argument focuses especially on Genesis 2:4, which seems to indicate that God did His work of creating in an unspecified but long period of time, certainly longer than six solar days. "Since the previous chapter has indicated that there were at least six days involved in creating the heavens and the earth, it is abundantly evident that *yom* in verse 4 cannot possibly be meant as a twenty-four-hour day—unless perchance the Scripture contradicts itself!"[11] But this fails to recognize that "in the day that" is simply a vivid Hebrew idiom for "at the time when." There is no article before the word *day*—in a day, at the time.

(2) Since the sun was not created till the fourth day, we may assume that the first three days were of indefinite length of time. Is this an admission that the last four were solar days? Solar-day advocates reply that God must have created some source of light on the first day simply because the text says there was light; and the rotation of the earth in relation to that light source brought the day/night, evening/morning cycle mentioned in relation to those first three days.

(3) The seventh day on which God rested was longer than twenty-four hours; therefore, the first six days were also. The use of God's rest in Hebrews 4 reinforces this conclusion. Also, Peter says that with the Lord a day is as a thousand years (2 Pet. 3:8).

Before accepting the conclusion, observe the following. Though the rest of the Christian life in Hebrews 4 is likened to the satisfying rest God enjoyed on the seventh day of the Creation week, nowhere does the writer of Hebrews suggest that that seventh day for God was other than the same length of day as the other six days of the Creation week. If they were ages, they were all ages; if days, all were days. But strictly speaking, Hebrews does not say other than God rested on the seventh day. It does say He rest*ed,* not He rest*s*. Of course, Peter does not say that a day *is* a thousand years any more than he says that a thousand years *is* a day.

To sum up: Exegetically, the burden of proof rests on those who want to understand the days of Genesis 1 as ages. Normal interpretation of that passage, the use of the word day with numbers, the accompanying phrase "evening and morning," and the two passages in Exodus constitute strong evidence from the biblical text itself that the days were solar days. If God wished to convey the idea of solar days, how could He have said it more clearly?

VII. APPEARANCE OF HISTORY

Any act of creation will of necessity carry with it the appearance of history. Even if God originally created only the simplest forms they would have necessarily had the appearance of some history. The first light source, the waters, the first vegetation (even if only the seeds), the sun and moon, the creatures, and Adam and Eve all had the appearance of history when they first appeared.

Indeed, this is normal for miracles. Several of our Lord's miracles involved apparent history. The wine made from water at Cana had the appearance of having gone through the natural processes involved in making wine, but, in fact, it had not (John 2:1–11). The food that fed five thousand men on one occasion as well as that which fed four thousand later had the appearance of having been grown and harvested, whereas in actuality it had no such chronological history.

That God has created with the appearance of history in the past seems irrefutable. The only question is, how much of this did He do? No more than was necessary and not anything that would tend to deceive us. God's own evaluation of His creative work was that it was good. Christ's miracles were done to show forth His glory (John 2:11). Goodness and glory leave no room for deception.

VIII. SOME CONCLUDING OBSERVATIONS

(1) There was an actual, factual, historical, supernatural Creation of the heavens, earth, and man by God. To deny, adjust, or compromise this by casting doubt on the reliability of Genesis does not do away with this truth, for the original creative activity of God is mentioned elsewhere in the Bible (Exod. 20:11; 31:17; 1 Chron. 1:1; Job 38:4–7; Matt. 19:4–5; 1 Cor. 11:7–8). If Genesis is untrustworthy, so must other parts of the Bible be.

(2) A worldwide flood in the time of Noah did actually occur. That it was worldwide is attested to about a dozen times in Genesis 6–11 as well as in 2 Peter 2:5 and 3:6. The Lord confirmed the actuality of the Flood in Matthew 24:38–39 and Luke 17:26–27. So again, if the truth of the Flood is rejected or the extent of it shrunk to something local, then one will also have to reject the Lord's testimony and Peter's (see also Heb. 11:7). The record of the Flood, like that of Creation, cannot be said to be an exaggeration or falsification due to the "primitive" revelation of Genesis.

Ramifications of the truth of a universal Flood include these. The water involved may indicate the existence of a vapor canopy that condensed at the time of the Flood, producing the forty days of heavy rainfall (Gen. 1:6–8; cf. 7:11–12). This would have caused a drastic change in the climate of the world after the Flood and certain other results.[12] Of course, the uniformitarianism on which dating methods are based would have been affected by this.

The Flood destroyed all life that was not in the ark Noah built, accounting for the fossil remains in the earth.

(3) An original Creation prior to 1:1 may be possible, but to me seems unlikely. If there were such, and if it contained plant and animal life, then fossils may have come from that period.

(4) The gap concept between verses 1 and 2 does not have good exegetical support.

(5) Neither do age-days in chapter 1 have sufficient evidence to be accepted. Solar days are indicated. Verse 3 records the beginning of events on day one (because of the phrase "Then God said, 'Let . . .'" which also appears at the beginning of the succeeding days). This means that we do not know how long the unformed and unfilled condition of the earth of verse 2 lasted before the days began. But, how-

ever long or short, that condition did not involve plant, animal, or pre-Adamic human life (Matt. 19:4; 1 Cor. 15:45). Thus the original unfashioned earth might have been old, but the fashioned earth, vegetation, animals, and man, all of which were created during the six days of Creation, cannot be older than solar days and genealogical tables allow.

To sum up: Ultimately we have to believe what God has revealed about Creation. No human being was present when it happened. But the revelation of it was given by God, who is true, to Moses, who was an educated and reliable writer. Though not all details are included in the record, many facts are, and they should be exegeted in the same way as other Scriptures are. Furthermore, the truths revealed in Genesis are attested to in other parts of the Bible and by our Lord.

Notes

1. John C. Whitcomb, *The Early Earth* (Grand Rapids: Baker, 1972), 42.
2. See W. H. Griffith Thomas, *The Principles of Theology* (London: Church Book Room Press, 1945), xix.
3. Whitcomb, *The Early Earth,* 21.
4. See discussion in John J. Davis, *Paradise to Prison* (Grand Rapids: Baker, 1975), 39–40.
5. Merrill F. Unger, "Rethinking the Genesis Account of Creation," *Bibliotheca Sacra (*January 1958) :28.
6. George H. Pember, *Earth's Earliest Ages* (Grand Rapids: Kregel, 1975).
7. Eric Sauer, *The King of the Earth* (London: Paternoster Press, 1962).
8. Arthur C. Custance, *Without Form and Void* (Brockville, Canada: Author, 1970).
9. For detailed support of this see Weston W. Fields, *Unformed and Unfilled* (Nutley, N.J.: Presbyterian and Reformed, 1976), 81–86.
10. See Bernard Ramm, *The Christian View of Science and Scripture* (Grand Rapids: Eerdmans, 1954), 214ff.
11. Gleason L. Archer, *Encyclopedia of Bible Difficulties* (Grand Rapids: Zondervan, 1982), 63.
12. See Joseph C. Dillow, *The Waters Above* (Chicago: Moody, 1980).

Chapter 31
THE CREATION OF MAN

I. THE CHARACTERISTICS OF MAN'S CREATION

The biblical record alone gives us accurate information about the origin of mankind. Certain characteristics of this act stand out in the text.

A. It Was Planned by God (Gen. 1:26)

The act of creating man was based on the deliberate counsel of God. Though all that God had done in Creation up to that point He pronounced as good, Creation was incomplete without man. Man was no afterthought, but the result of deliberate forethought on the part of the Godhead. And after God created man, He then said that everything He had made was "very good" (v. 31).

B. It Was Direct, Special, and Immediate (Gen. 1:27; 2:7)

It did not involve any evolutionary processes that relate man to some sub-, non-, or prehuman brute forms.[1] That would mean that as far as his physical nature was concerned man was derived from some nonhuman animal form into which God breathed the breath of life. Genesis 2:7 does not support this theory at all. Indeed, it reinforces the fact of special creation from materials that were inorganic; it does not lend support to the idea of a derived creation from some previously living form.

If one could sustain the theory that Adam was created from some preorganic form, Eve certainly was not. Her body was clearly a direct, special, and immediate act of creation. To acknowledge this in the case of Eve while denying it in the case of Adam is, to say the least, illogical.

Furthermore, the dust of the ground out of which man's body was made cannot be an allegorical reference to some animal form because God said man will return to dust when he dies, and man does not return to an animal state at death (3:19).

C. It Involved Two Facets

God used the dust from the ground into which He breathed the breath of life. This caused man to become animate. The same phrase ("a living creature") is also used of animals (1:21, 24; 2:19), but since animals were not created in the image of God, as was man, there exists a clear distinction between animals and man.

In the case of Eve, God first took a rib with its surrounding flesh from Adam's side and then fashioned or built it into a woman (Gen. 2:21–23). God constructed Eve after taking the parts from Adam's side. "Build applies to the fashioning of a structure of some importance; it involves constructive effort."[2]

II. THE PATTERN FOR MAN'S CREATION

God created man in His image and according to His likeness (Gen. 1:26–27). Other relevant Scriptures to this doctrine include 5:1, 3, which speak of the transmission of the image from Adam to his descendants; 9:6, which relates the concept to capital punishment; 1 Corinthians 11:7, which correlates the doctrine to headship; Colossians 3:10, which exhorts the believer to put on the new man that is according to the image of his Creator; and James 3:9, which relates the concept to proper speech. Psalm 8, though not containing the phrase "image of God," deals in poetic form with the creation of man and his dominion.

A. The Meaning of the Words "Image" and "Likeness"

The Hebrew words in Genesis 1:26–27 are *tselem* and *demuth* (translated in the Vulgate by *imago* and *similitudo*). The equivalent New Testament words are *eikon* and *homoiosis.* Though some have attempted to make a distinction between the two words to teach two aspects of the image of God, no sharp distinction between them can be sustained linguistically. *Tselem* means a fashioned image, a shaped and representative figure, an image in some concrete sense (2 Kings 11:18; Ezek. 23:14; Amos 5:26). *Demuth* refers also to the idea of similarity, but more in the abstract or ideal. By using the two words together, the biblical author "seems to be attempting to express a very difficult idea in which he wants to make clear that man is in some way the concrete reflection of God, but at the same time he wants to spiritualize this toward abstraction."[3]

The Greek and Latin fathers distinguished between image and

likeness, referring the former to the physical and the latter to the ethical part of God's image. Irenaeus understood the image to refer to man's freedom and reason and likeness to the gift of supernatural communion with God that was lost in the Fall. But such distinctions cannot be substantiated on the basis of the words. Note also that the prepositions are used interchangeably in Genesis 1:26–27 and 5:1–3.

B. The Meaning of the Concept

Much has been written attempting to explain what is meant by man's being created in the image of God. Here are some of the explanations.

1. The corporeal view. This relates the image of God to man's total being, including his corporeality. Strictly speaking, it includes both the material and immaterial aspects of man. But since it includes the material body of man as part of the image of God, it may be labeled the corporeal view.

> Man is a representative by his entire being, for Israelite thought always views man in his totality, by his physical being as well as by his spiritual functions, and if choice had to be made between the two we would say that the external appearance is perhaps even more important than spiritual resemblance. According to L. Koehler the image of God could consist in man's upright position . . . [but] the solemnity with which the priestly writer speaks of the imago Dei seems to prove that he did not restrict it to this single aspect. . . . It is also to a rather physical sense that we are directed by the passage in Genesis which refers to the image of God over the matter of blood vengeance (9:6).[4]

Two obstacles appear to stand in the way of accepting this view. (1) Since God is spirit and has no body, how could the image of God in which man was created be corporeal? (2) Animals have bodies but are not said to have been created in the image of God, so corporeality does not necessarily have to be related to the image of God.

2. The noncorporeal view. This view connects the image of God to facets of personality. Many writers emphasize moral likeness, dominion, the exercise of will, and intellectual faculties (ability to speak, organize, etc.) as specifics of the noncorporeal image of God.

3. A combination view. I would suggest a combination of the two previous views, as follows. Genesis 1:27 states that mankind, male and female, was created in the image of God. No one attributes gender to God because of this statement; yet male and female indicate gender.

Similarly, just because man, created in the image of God, has a body, does not necessitate attributing a body to God. But obviously man was created a total being, material and immaterial, and that total being was created in the image of God.

Therefore, (1) man's body is included in the image of God.

> While God is not physical in any way, there is a sense in which even a man's body is included in the image of God, for man is a unitary being composed of both body and soul. His body is a fit instrument for the self-expression of a soul made for fellowship with the Creator and is suited eschatologically to become a "spiritual body" (1 Cor. 15:44). . . . [His body] was not something apart from the real self of Adam, but was essentially one with it.[5]

(2) To be created in the image of God also means to be a living being. This was Paul's emphasis on Areopagus (Acts 17:28–29). Refuting the belief that inanimate idols could represent the living God, he argues that since mankind is the offspring of God, and since human beings are living beings, God must also be a living Being.

(3) Man is not only a living being, but a being like God with both intelligence and will that give him the ability to make decisions that enable him to have dominion over the world (Gen. 1:28).

(4) Adam was not only a unitary, living, intelligent, determining being, but also one who was able to have unhindered fellowship with God. How can we express Adam's original condition? Some use the word *innocent,* but Adam was more than innocent, which seems to connote only the absence of wrong. Adam's original holiness was positive; yet it was not equal with God's—it was creaturely. Because it was subject to testing, it was unconfirmed. It provided immortality, for until Adam failed the test, he was not subject to the inevitable law of death due to sin.

To sum up: the image of God in which man was created included the totality of his being as living, intelligent, determining, and moral.

4. The Roman Catholic view. This distinguishes image and likeness. Image is the natural image that belongs to man as created and includes spirituality, freedom, and immortality. Likeness indicates that moral image that did not belong to man as originally created but was rapidly and very early superadded to him. It needed to be added because of concupiscence, which is a natural bent toward the lower appetites, though not in and of itself sinful. Likeness adds original righteousness and holiness.

When man sinned he lost the likeness but kept the image. That original righteousness that was lost in the Fall can be added through the sacraments of the Roman church.

5. *The neo-orthodox view.* Among neo-orthodox writers Brunner's concept is somewhat similar to that of the Roman Catholic church. He taught that there was a formal image that could not be lost in the Fall because it constituted man as man. He also saw a material image that was lost through the Fall.

Barth rejected the idea of a formal image because of his belief that man was utterly corrupted by sin.

C. Ramifications of the Concept

When sin entered the human race, the image of God in which man was created was not lost. One may say it was defaced though not erased. If the image concept was described correctly, then if man lost it he would no longer be a living, rational being.

Further evidence that the image was not lost is found in the use the Scripture makes of it after the Fall. The fact that man was created in the image of God is the basis for the institution of capital punishment (Gen. 9:6). Headship of the man is also based on his being in the image of God (1 Cor. 11:7). James cautions us about cursing a fellow human being on the ground that mankind was made in the likeness of God (James 3:9). These passages would have no basis if the image had been erased in the Fall.

Regeneration and sanctification serve to renew the believer according to the image of Christ, to whose image we shall someday be perfectly conformed (Rom. 8:29; 2 Cor. 3:18). Only grace can do this.

III. THE TRANSMISSION OF MAN'S BEING

When Adam begat Seth, he became the father of a son in his own likeness, according to his image (Gen. 5:3). Though Adam was made directly in the image of God, his children were generated in Adam's image, which, of course, still bore God's image even after the Fall (cf. 1 Cor. 11:7). Thus the transmission of man's being was and is through natural generation.

No one questions this as far as the material aspect of man's being is concerned. Our bodies come from our parents, and theirs from theirs, etc. But how is the immaterial aspect of man passed from generation to generation? To this question several answers have traditionally been proposed.

A. Preexistence

This view states that at the beginning God created all human souls, which were confined in physical bodies as punishment. Souls go through various incarnations throughout history and in the process incur sinfulness. Plato and the Greeks taught this transmigration of souls, and in the early church Origen held a similar view (ca. 185–ca. 254). In modern times it is taught by theosophy, Hinduism, and philosopher F. R. Tennant. Orthodox Christianity has never held this view, for it has no biblical basis. Furthermore, the reincarnation aspect of the teaching stands in direct conflict with the biblical teaching on eternal life or eternal punishment for every individual born into this world.

B. Creationism

As defended by Charles Hodge, creationism teaches that God creates the soul at the moment of conception or birth and immediately unites it with the body.[6] The soul is sinful not because its creation was somehow defective, but because of its contact with inherited guilt through the body. Hodge offers three arguments in support of creationism. (1) It is more in accord with Scriptures like Numbers 16:22 and Hebrews 12:9, which say the soul comes from God (while, in contrast, the body comes from earthly parents). (2) Since the nature of the soul is immaterial it could not be transmitted by natural generation. (3) Christ's sinlessness could only be true if His soul were created (and of course it would not have been united with a sinful body—hence His Person would be sinless). Roman Catholics and many Reformed theologians prefer creationism.

C. Traducianism

This view holds that the soul is transmitted along with the body through the processes of natural generation. William G. T. Shedd cited three kinds of support for this view.[7] (1) Scriptural: Hebrews 7:10 indicates a rational and moral act on the part of unborn Levi; Genesis 2:1–3 states that God rested on the seventh day of Creation because His work of Creation was finished. No fresh acts, like creating new souls, are indicated; and verse 7 does not allow for the breath of life to be breathed into anyone else other than Adam. (2) Theological: creationism places God in the position of creating a perfect soul (He could not create a sinful one), then having it fall in the case of each newborn infant. The case of the sinless Christ is in every respect an exception and not the pattern for deciding this question. (3) Physiological: man is always seen as a union of soul and body; therefore, it is more natural to consider both the psychical and physical as developing together.

It seems to me that traducianism provides a more natural explanation than creationism does. I agree with J. O. Buswell's observation:

> As between these two views, it does seem to me that there is a certain obvious fact which has been neglected in the historical discussion, and that is the perfect uniformity and regularity of the arrival of a soul whenever a human life begins to be. In our ordinary thinking when we observe such perfect uniformity and regularity in other matters, we usually ascribe the results to the secondary forces which God has created and which He maintains by His divine providence. For this reason, and for this reason only, I am inclined toward the traducian view, but I do not feel that it can be firmly established on the grounds of any explicit scriptural teaching.[8]

NOTES

1. Contrast A. H. Strong, *Systematic Theology* (Philadelphia: Judson, 1907), 465–76.
2. H. C. Leupold, *Exposition of Genesis* (Columbus: Wartburg, 1942), 135.
3. Addison H. Leitch, "Image of God," in *The Zondervan Pictorial Encyclopedia of the Bible* (Grand Rapids: Zondervan, 1975), 3:256.
4. Edmond Jacob, *Theology of the Old Testament* (New York: Harper & Row, 1958), 168–69.
5. Ralph E. Powell, "Image of God," in *Wycliffe Bible Encyclopedia* (Chicago: Moody, 1975), 1:832.
6. Charles Hodge, *Systematic Theology* (Grand Rapids: Eerdmans, 1940), 2:70ff.
7. William G. T. Shedd, *Dogmatic Theology* (New York: Scribner, 1891), 2:7ff.
8. J. Oliver Buswell, *A Systematic Theology of the Christian Religion* (Grand Rapids: Zondervan, 1962) :252.

Chapter 32
THE FACETS OF MAN

I. THE NATURE OF MAN

A. Bipartite Unity

When God created Adam, He took the dust of the earth and breathed into it the breath of life to make a living person (Gen. 2:7). Although there were two steps to the act of creating, the result was a single, unitary living person. To be sure, the particles of the earth provided the material, while God's breath effected life. Material and immaterial combined to produce a single entity. Within the material exists a variety of features—arteries, brain, muscles, hair, etc., and within the immaterial we also find a variety—soul, spirit, heart, will, conscience, etc. But without the unity of man's being, this diversity could not function. "The biblical view of man shows him to us in an impressive diversity, but it never loses sight of the unity of the whole man, but rather brings it out and accentuates it."[1]

That man is bipartite in nature is undebatable. Man is a material and nonmaterial entity, the two aspects being distinguishable. Physical death is described as the separation of body and spirit (James 2:26). Biblical dichotomy differs from Plato's teaching that the body was perishable but the soul existed in the heavenly world of pure form or idea before its incarnation in the human body and was therefore uncreated and immortal, a part of Deity. Biblical dichotomy certainly does not teach that the body is the prison house of the soul, which is released at death to return to the heavenly world or to be reincarnated in another body. Biblical dichotomy is radically different from Platonic dualism.

B. Not Trichotomy ("cut in three parts")

Aristotle further developed Plato's twofold division by dividing the soul into (a) an animal soul (the breathing aspect) and (b) the rational soul (the intellectual aspect). This distinction was further developed in Roman Catholic doctrine through Thomas Aquinas. Early Christian writers, influenced by the Greeks, thought they found support for trichotomy in certain New Testament passages, as do some modern writers.

Popular trichotomy (man is composed of body, soul, and spirit) makes the spirit superior to the soul, and the spirit and soul superior to the body. Body relates to self, soul to the world, but spirit to God. Spirit and the spiritual are to be cultivated, while soulishness and body are deprecated. This prioritizing is incompatible with popular trichotomy's attempt to draw an analogy between the tripartite nature of God and man. Certainly the persons of the Trinity are equal, though the parts of man are not. To which person of the Trinity would the body correspond? Trichotomy, popular or formal, cannot be substantiated logically, analogically, or scripturally.

But what about the passages commonly cited to support trichotomy?

Hebrews 4:12 seems to separate soul from spirit, thus supporting the trichotomy view. However, the verse does not say that the Word severs soul from spirit but that it pierces through *to divide* soul and spirit, thus exposing the innermost aspects of man. The point is simply that the Word of God leaves nothing hidden.

First Thessalonians 5:23 seems to indicate that the immaterial aspect of man is composed of soul and spirit. Trichotomists understand spirit, soul, and body in this verse as defining the parts of man; dichotomists say they represent the whole man. If these three terms are inclusive of all the aspects of man, then what place do heart, mind, will, and conscience have? Why did not Paul also include them in the list? The emphasis of the verse is on the completeness of sanctification.

First Corinthians 15:44 appears to teach a difference between the present body (a soul body) and the resurrection body (a spiritual body). But that does not mean that the spirit is superior to the soul. Also John saw people in heaven as "souls" (Rev. 6:9; 20:4).

The spirit can partake of pollution along with the flesh (2 Cor. 7:1). Trichotomy ought to have pollution affecting the flesh and soul, not the spirit. Fleshly lusts war against the soul (1 Pet. 2:11). Trichotomy ought to have flesh warring against the spirit, or soul against spirit. How can the Lord command us to love Him with all our souls if the soul is world-conscious, not God-conscious? (Mark 12:30). Trichotomy ought to have the command read "with all your spirit," but spirit is not mentioned at all in the command. In Hebrews 10:38 soul is used of God.

Man is made up of two substances, material and immaterial. Each consists of a variety within. The many facets of the material and the many facets of the immaterial join together to make up the whole of each person. Man is rich diversity in unity.

II. THE FACETS OF THE IMMATERIAL ASPECT OF MAN

Man is like a diamond with its many facets. Those facets are not separate entities, yet they reflect various aspects of the whole. They may serve similar or overlapping functions, yet they are distinguishable. They are not parts; they are aspects, facets, faces of the whole.

A. Soul

In its most basic sense, the Hebrew word, *nephesh,* means "life." It designates man originally created as a living being (soul) (Gen. 2:7) as well as other forms of life (1:20–21, 24, 30; Lev. 17:11). Notice also Exodus 21:23 and Joshua 2:13. This is the sense in which English would speak of an individual as a soul.

That life principle departs at the time of physical death (Gen. 35:18; Jer. 15:2). Yet the corpse is called soul (Lev. 21:1–3; Num. 6:6; 9:6). In the Old Testament "soul" does not exist apart from the body, emphasizing again the unity of man's being. "Rich and abundant though this use of *n.* (nephesh, soul) for life is, we must not fail to observe that the n. is never given the meaning of an indestructible core of being, in contradistinction to the physical life, and even capable of living when cut off from that life."[2]

Soul also is the center of various spiritual and emotional experiences of mankind. These include sympathy (Job 30:25), despair (Ps. 43:5), bitterness (2 Kings 4:27), hate (2 Sam. 5:8), love (Song of Sol. 1:7; 3:1–4), and grief (Jer. 13:17).

The New Testament reveals some similarities and differences in its use of the word "soul" (*psyche*). It denotes the whole individual person (Acts 2:41; 27:37 KJV). But it can refer to the immaterial part of man only (Matt. 10:28). It also designates people in the intermediate state between death and the resurrection of the body (Rev. 6:9).

Soul seems to be a principal focus of redemption (though of course, the physical body also experiences the effects of redemption). Notice passages like Hebrews 10:39; 13:17; James 1:21; 1 Peter 1:9, 22; 2:11, 25.

To sum up: soul can mean the whole person, alive or after death; it can designate the immaterial part of a person with its many feelings and emotions; and it is an important focus of spiritual redemption and growth.

B. Spirit

Spirit (*ruach* and *pneuma*) refers only to the immaterial part of man, unlike soul, which can denote the whole man, material and immaterial. Man is a soul, but man is not said to be a spirit—he has a spirit.

The spirit originates from God, and all people have spirits (Num. 16:22; Heb. 12:9). It is simply not biblical to talk of man not having a spirit until he receives the Holy Spirit at salvation (cf. 1 Cor. 2:11; Heb. 4:12; James 2:26).

As a facet of the immaterial part of man, one's spirit is the center of various traits, emotions, and activities. Some of these include thinking (Isa. 29:24), remembering (Ps. 77:6), humility (Matt. 5:3), grief (Gen. 26:35), vexation (John 13:21), jealousy (Num. 5:14), haughtiness (Prov. 16:18), and contriteness (Ps. 34:18). Because it may evince undesirable emotions, the spirit needs attention in the spiritual life (Ps. 51:10; 2 Cor. 7:1).

Though soul and spirit can relate to the same activities or emotions, there does seem to be a distinction and contrast between soul and spirit in Pauline thought. This accounts for his emphasis on the spiritual (1 Cor. 2:14; 3:1; 15:45; Eph. 1:3; 5:19; Col. 1:9; 3:16). Why?

> When Paul became a Christian, the experience of God in Christ became the determining factor, not only in his view of God, but in everything. Because Paul was a Jew, his attitude to God affected and determined all his thoughts. In Christian experience, *psyche,* the term for purely human vitality, became unimportant. *Pneuma,* the term that began with God but proceeded into man, became central. The infrequency of the use of *psyche* in Paul is the key to the understanding of it. . . . Paul's knowledge of the Holy Spirit set the basis of his anthropology and *pneuma* took the leading role.[3]

To sum up: spirit does not indicate the whole person, but the immaterial part with its various functions and feelings. In Pauline thought it assumes prominence in relation to the spiritual life.

C. Heart

Heart is a very comprehensive concept in both Old and New Testaments. Used about 955 times it stands for the center and seat of life, both physical and psychical. Only a relatively few occurrences refer to the physical organ (2 Sam. 18:14; 2 Kings 9:24). The greater number use heart to denote the inner man, the essence of the many facets of his personality. Some of these include the following.

1. Heart is the seat of intellectual life. It considers (Deut. 8:5); it obtains a knowledge of the Word (Ps. 119:11); it is the source of evil thoughts and actions (Matt. 15:19–20); it has thoughts and intentions (Heb. 4:12); it can be deceitful (Jer. 17:9).

2. Heart is the seat of the emotional life. It loves (Deut. 6:5); it produces self-reproach (Job 27:6); it rejoices and is glad (Ps. 104:15; Isa. 30:29); it can be sorrowful (Neh. 2:2; Rom. 9:2); it has desires (Ps. 37:4); it can be bitter (73:21).

3. It is the seat of the volitional life. It seeks (Deut. 4:29); it can be turned aside (Exod. 14:5); it can be hardened (8:15; Heb. 4:7); it is capable of choice (Exod. 7:22–23); it can be uncircumcised (Jer. 9:26; Acts 7:51).

4. It is the seat of spiritual life. With the heart man believes resulting in righteousness (Rom. 10:9–10). For the believer the heart is the abode of the Father (1 Pet. 3:15), the Son (Eph. 3:17), and the Holy Spirit (2 Cor. 1:22). The believer's heart should be pure (1 Tim. 1:5; Heb. 10:22) and circumcised (Rom. 2:29).

D. Conscience

The conscience is a witness within man that tells him he ought to do what he believes to be right and not to do what he believes to be wrong. Conscience does not teach us what is right or wrong but prods us to do what we have been taught to be right. One can do what is wrong in good conscience because he has been misinformed as to what is right and wrong (Acts 23:1).

Conscience appears only in the New Testament. Those functions of conscience are assigned to the heart in the Old Testament (e.g., 1 Sam. 24:5; Job 27:6). In the New Testament conscience occurs most often in Paul's writings (John used the word heart, as in 1 John 3:19–21). The unsaved person's conscience may be a good guide (John 8:9; Rom. 2:15), or it may not be even though it may seem to guide correctly (Acts 23:1; 1 Tim. 4:2; Titus 1:15; Heb. 10:22). Conscience may be likened to unreliable brakes on an automobile. They may do their job at times, but they cannot be counted on. The Christian's conscience operates to prod him to do what is right in various relationships of life. (1) It prods him to obey the government under which he lives

(Rom. 13:5). (2) It tells him to bear up under an unjust employer (1 Pet. 2:18–19). (3) The conscience of a weaker brother that does not permit him to eat meat sacrificed to idols should be respected by the stronger brother (1 Cor. 8:7, 10, 12). (4) Conscience may be called to witness to the depth and reality of a spiritual commitment (Rom. 9:2; 2 Cor. 1:12; 4:2).

E. Mind

Like conscience, mind is more specifically a New Testament concept. In the Old Testament heart is usually the word behind the translation mind. Mind includes both the faculties of perceiving and understanding as well as those of feeling, judging, and determining. *Phroneo, nous,* and *sunesis* are the principal New Testament words for this concept.

The unsaved man's mind is said to be reprobate (Rom. 1:28 KJV), vain (Eph. 4:17 KJV), defiled (Titus 1:15), blinded (2 Cor. 4:4), and darkened (Eph. 4:18). Further, he is without that critical faculty represented by *sunesis* (Rom. 3:11).

The believer's mind occupies a central place in his spiritual development. God uses it in his understanding of truth (Luke 24:45; 1 Cor. 14:14–15). The dedicated life must include a renewed mind (Rom. 12:2). The mind is involved in deciding doubtful things (14:5), in pursuing holiness (1 Pet. 1:13), in understanding the Lord's will (Eph. 5:17), and in loving the Lord (Matt. 22:37). Every thought must be captive to the obedience of Christ (2 Cor. 10:5).

F. Flesh

Though flesh sometimes refers to tissue (Luke 24:39) or to the whole material part of man (1 Cor. 15:39; Heb. 5:7), when used of a facet of the immaterial nature it refers to that disposition to sin and to oppose God (Rom. 7:18; 1 Cor. 3:3; 2 Cor. 1:12; Gal. 5:17; Col. 2:18; 2 Pet. 2:10; 1 John 2:16). Both the believer and unbeliever possess this capacity.

G. Will

Actually the Bible says much more about the will of God than man's will, and what it does say is unsystematic. A believer can will to do what is right or what is wrong (Rom. 7:15–25; 1 Tim. 6:9; James 4:4). Will may be more of an expression of oneself through the other facets of his personality, rather than a distinct faculty in and of itself.

These are the facets of the immaterial part of man through which he may glorify himself or glorify and serve his Lord.

NOTES

1. G. C. Berkouwer, *Man—The Image of God* (Grand Rapids: Eerdmans, 1952), 200.
2. Hans Walter Wolff, *Anthropology of the Old Testament* (Philadelphia: Fortress, 1974), 20.
3. W. David Stacey, *The Pauline View of Man* (London: Macmillan, 1956), 126–27.

Chapter 33
THE FALL OF MAN

Views concerning the validity of the account of the Fall of man in Genesis 3 may be classified into three categories.

(1) Some say it is legend, which means that the facts are not true. "That such sketches cannot possess the value of historical accounts is evident from the whole style of the narrative. It is a general picture of religion and morals in the light of a later period. But for giving a knowledge of those primitive days it is not by any means, on that account, wholly valueless."[1]

(2) Others want to preserve the "truth" of the story without having to accept its historical trustworthiness. Thus A. M. Hunter calls it a "true myth." "Unless we are invincible fundamentalists we know that Genesis 3 is properly to be regarded as 'a true myth'—that, though Eden is on no map and Adam's fall fits no historical calendar, that chapter witnesses to a dimension of human experience as present now as at the dawn of history—in plain terms, we are fallen creatures, and the story of Adam and Eve is the story of you and me."[2]

(3) Many regard the account as factual, historical truth. "The account of the creation, its commencement, progress, and completion, bears the marks, both in form and substance, of a historical document in which it is intended that we should accept as actual truth, not only the assertion that God created the heavens and the earth, and all that lives and moves in the world, but also the description of the Creation itself in all its stages."[3]

Other Scriptures validate the historicity of the Fall. Notice 1 Corinthians 15:21–22 and 1 Timothy 2:14. But especially observe how Paul pressed the historicity of Adam's sin in Romans 5:12–21. He repeatedly compared it with what Christ did on the cross. Many who understand Genesis 3 to be legend, poem, true myth, or whatever, do not deny the factuality of Christ's death (though they may not agree on its significance). But Paul's comparison and contrast in the passage demands either that both Adam's and Christ's actions be true or that both be legend or myth. To accept Christ's death as factual and Adam's sin as not is, to say the least, straining the passage to the breaking point. This is exactly what Barthians try to do. They not only accept the historicity of Christ's death but for them it is the highest point of revelation. Yet they do not accept the account of Genesis 3 as factual, though they acknowledge the truth and reality of sin. But if, according to that passage, Christ and what He did stand in the realm of fact, then also do Adam and his actions.

I. THE TEMPTED

What was Adam's nature and his relation to God before he sinned?

A. His Endowments

We know that Adam possessed powers of understanding and reason that enabled him to name the animals and to reason about the relationship of Eve to himself (Gen. 2:19–23). God also endowed him with the ability to use language so that communication was possible between God and himself (vv. 16, 20, 23).

B. His Moral Nature

However we describe Adam's moral nature before the Fall, it is clear that he was without sin. Some say this means a kind of passive holiness in that Adam was innocent of wrong. His holiness was such as to enable him to enjoy complete fellowship with God. Perhaps it is too strong to speak of a positive holiness since Adam was able to choose to sin. I prefer a description like this: Adam possessed unconfirmed (because he had neither passed nor failed the test) creature (because his holiness was not the same as the Creator's) holiness (because he was more than "innocent").

Adam had a free will and a mind capable of weighing choices.

> Adam, therefore, could have stood if he would, since he fell merely by his own will; but because his will was flexible to either side, and he was not endued with constancy to persevere, therefore he so easily fell. Yet his choice of good and evil was free; and not only so, but his mind and will were possessed of consummate rectitude, and all his organic parts were rightly disposed to obedience, till, destroying himself, he corrupted all his excellencies.[4]

C. His Responsibilities

1. To exercise dominion over the earth (Gen. 1:26, 28). Theonomists understand this so-called "cultural mandate" as authorizing man to bring all the world's structures under the lordship of Christ, demolishing every kind of opposition to God. Reformed writers understand it similarly except that they do not emphasize the establishment of Old Testament law in all its aspects on society today. However, observe that the phrase "subdue the earth" is not part of the mandate given to Noah and his descendants (including us) after the Flood (9:1). Further observe that the word "subdue" in 1:28 comes from a root that means "to knead" or "to tread" and refers to bringing the earth under cultivation so that the race could multiply. Adam was to administer the earth and its creatures so that it would sustain the people who would fill it. This was the context in which Adam was commanded to cultivate and keep the Garden of Eden (2:15). Presumably it could have grown in exuberant disorder if Adam had not attended to it.

2. *To enjoy the fruits of his care of the Garden* (Gen. 2:16–17).

II. THE TEST

Ultimately the test was whether Adam and Eve would obey God or not. The particular way they could prove that was by not eating the fruit of one of the trees in the Garden, the tree of the knowledge of good and evil. In one sense it was a minor prohibition in comparison with the many trees in the Garden from which they could eat the fruits. In another sense it was a major matter, since this was the specific way they could show their obedience or disobedience to God. By way of contrast, how many ways can we show our obedience or disobedience to God in the course of a single day?

In setting a test at all, God showed that He wanted men to voluntarily choose to obey Him and to serve Him. He did not want automatons.

III. THE TEMPTER

Satan wisely used a creature Eve was acquainted with instead of appearing himself, something that would likely have alerted her to the unusual and put her on guard. Satan used an actual serpent, since the serpent as well as Satan were cursed after the Fall. For some reason, Eve was not alarmed that the serpent spoke with her. "The tempter addresses himself to the woman, probably [because] . . . the woman had not personally received the prohibition from God, as Adam had; cf. verses 16–17."[5]

IV. THE TEMPTATION

A. Satan's Counterfeit

A counterfeit, of course, attempts to come as close to the genuine article as possible, while leaving something costly out. A master counterfeiter, Satan had previously aspired to be like God, not unlike God (Isa. 14:14). Now he approached Eve with the suggestion that his plan was like God's but without the restriction of total obedience. When approached with the question whether God had placed any tree in the Garden off limits, Eve quickly affirmed that she and Adam could eat of all the trees of the Garden except one. And that exception seemed to come to her mind almost as an afterthought. Satan had hinted at the possibility that God had placed too-sweeping restrictions on them, and Eve began to entertain that thought.

Then Satan proceeded to offer his own plan, which did not have that restriction. "The woman acts on the supposition that God's intent is unfriendly, whilst Satan is animated with the desire to promote her well-being."[6] Satan was attempting to counterfeit the goodness of God.

Satan's temptation may be viewed in the form of a syllogism. The major premise was that restrictions were not good. The minor premise was that God's plan included a restriction. The conclusion then was that God's plan was not good. On the other hand, Satan's plan did not include any restrictions; therefore, it was good. The validity of the conclusion depends on the truth of the major premise, which in this case is not true. Restrictions are not necessarily wrong or undesirable. Indeed, the restriction placed on Adam and Eve in the Garden was good in that it provided the principal way they could show their obedience to the will of God. Satan's counterfeit plan did away with that restriction and offered the false hope that if Eve ate the forbidden fruit she could be like God.

B. Eve's Rationalizations

Eve's rationalization of what she was about to do may have been along these lines. As she examined Satan's proposition, she reasoned that the fruit would be good to eat, and providing good things for Adam was one of her wifely responsibilities. Further, why would God withhold the fruit that was beautiful to the eyes, since He made so many other beautiful things for them to enjoy? And, of course, God would certainly want them to be wise. Therefore, it would be desirable, even necessary, to eat this fruit. Gone from her mind was God's express command not to eat it. Quickly forgotten were all the blessings He had provided. Eve's mind seemed only to be filled with her rationalizations—the fruit would give physical sustenance, it would cultivate their aesthetic tastes, and it would add to their wisdom. Having justified what she was about to do, she took fruit from the tree and ate it.

V. THE PENALTIES

A. On the Race (Gen. 3:7–13)

1. A sense of guilt as evidenced by making a covering (v. 7).
2. A loss of fellowship as evidenced by hiding from God (v. 8). This also brought both spiritual and physical death to the race. Death is always separation; immediately Adam and Eve experienced spiritual separation, and immediately they began to experience the decaying process in their bodies, which ultimately resulted in physical death (Rom. 5:12).

B. On the Serpent (Gen. 3:14)

The serpent was condemned to crawl, perhaps as a sign of degradation and/or perhaps indicating that it was an upright creature before this penalty was imposed. Even in the Millennium this posture will continue (Isa. 65:25). Actually the entire animal kingdom was affected by the Fall in order that man in his fallen condition could still exercise a measure of dominion over it (Rom. 8:20).

C. On Satan (Gen. 3:15)

1. Satan's seed and woman's seed. Enmity will exist between Satan's seed (all the lost, John 8:44; Eph. 2:2) and the woman's seed (all the family of God).
2. Death for Satan; bruise for Christ. An individual from the woman's seed (Jesus Christ) will deal a death blow to Satan's head at the cross (Heb. 2:14; 1 John 3:8) while Satan will cause Christ to suffer ("bruise his heel" KJV). Pre-Christian Jews showed a "veiled acceptance of messianic idea in Genesis 3:15."[7]

D. On Eve and Women (Gen. 3:16)

1. Conception. God would multiply women's sorrow in conception (not "thy sorrow and thy conception" KJV—two things). Childbirth would now be accompanied by pain.

2. *Woman's desire would be to her husband.* Some understand this to indicate a compensating factor to the sorrow and pain of childbirth; i.e., in spite of the pain, she would experience a deep, sexual attraction to her husband and thus desire to bear children. Others understand it to mean she shall have a desire to rule her husband contrary to God's established order. The same word for desire is used with this sense in Genesis 4:7.[8]

3. *Hierarchy of rule.* Women will be ruled by men, a necessary hierarchical arrangement for a sinful world. The New Testament does not abrogate this arrangement (1 Cor. 11:3; 14:34; Eph. 5:24–25; Titus 2:3–5; 1 Pet. 3:1, 5–6).

E. On Adam and Men (Gen. 3:17–24)

1. *Curse on ground.* The ground was cursed because of Adam's sin so that it would grow thorns and thistles, increasing his work to make it produce. Before this, Adam's labor was enjoyable and satisfying; now it would be difficult and empty.

2. *Death.* Adam and mankind would return to the dust of the ground at death.

3. *Expulsion.* Adam was driven from the Garden, which was both a geographic and spiritual act symbolizing the break in fellowship.

VI. THE RAMIFICATIONS

In addition to these specific penalties, two important ramifications of Adam's and Eve's sin must be pointed out.

First, all sin affects others. Eve's sin affected Adam, and Adam's sin affects the entire race. No one sins totally in private without ramifications in relation to others. All that we do or fail to do affects few or many in one way or another.

Second, sin, once committed, can never be undone. Forgiveness can be experienced and fellowship restored, but history cannot be changed or erased. Adam and Eve, once expelled, could not return to the Garden of Eden. Esau could not retrieve the birthright he sold (Heb. 12:16–17). Moses could not personally enter the Promised Land but could only see it from a distance because of his sin (Num. 20:12; Deut. 3:27). The kingdom was taken from Saul and his descendants because he did not wait for Samuel to come and offer the sacrifices (1 Sam. 13:13–14). These are sobering examples of the ramifications of sin.

Yet there is another side to both ramifications. Sin affects others, but so do grace and goodness. History cannot be erased, but the future can be different (better) because we learn the lessons of history. Paul thought John Mark's conduct on the first missionary journey disqualified him from going with him on the second trip (Acts 15:38). But Mark must have learned some lesson from this, for later Paul wanted the ministry of Mark (2 Tim. 4:11). The Fall affected all human beings, bringing depravity and death, and it will always be the darkest hour of all human history; yet where sin abounded, grace superabounds, and the one who does the will of God abides forever (Rom. 5:20; 1 John 2:17).

NOTES

1. Hermann Schultz, *Old Testament Theology* (Edinburgh: T. & T. Clark, 1895), 1:89.
2. A. M. Hunter, *Interpreting Paul's Gospel* (London: SCM, 1954), 77.
3. C. F. Keil and F. Delitzsch, *The Pentateuch* (Edinburgh: T. & T. Clark, n.d.), 1:137.
4. John Calvin, *Institutes,* I, XV, 215.
5. Geerhardus Vos, *Biblical Theology* (Grand Rapids: Eerdmans, 1948), 45.
6. Ibid., 47.
7. David Baron, *Rays of Messiah's Glory* (Winona Lake, Ind.: BMH Books, 1979), 44–45.
8. See Susan T. Foh, *Women and the Word of God* (Nutley, N.J. : Presbyterian & Reformed, 1980), 67–69.

Section VIII
SIN

Chapter 34
The Biblical Concept of Sin

The biblical concept of sin comes from a study of words used in both Testaments for sin. The terms are numerous, compared to the words for grace in the Bible. Only three words are needed to express grace (*chen* and *chesed* in the Old Testament and *charis* in the New). By contrast, there are at least eight basic words for sin in the Old Testament and a dozen in the New. Together they furnish the basic concepts involved in the doctrine.

I. IN THE OLD TESTAMENT

A. Chata

In all of its forms this basic word for sin occurs about 522 times in the Old Testament. Its basic meaning is to miss the mark. It is equivalent to the Greek word *hamartano.* But missing the mark also involves hitting some other mark; i.e., when one misses the right mark and thus sins, he also hits the wrong mark. The idea is not merely a passive one of missing, but also an active one of hitting. It is used of moral evil, idolatry, and ceremonial sins. Some important references include Exodus 20:20; Judges 20:16; Proverbs 8:36; and 19:2.

B. Ra

Used about 444 times in the Old Testament, this word, equivalent to *kakos* or *poneros,* carries the basic meaning of breaking up or ruin. It often means calamities and is translated by the word "wicked" many times. It may indicate something injurious as well as something morally wrong (Gen. 3:5; 38:7; Judg. 11:27). In Isaiah 45:7 God is said to create light and darkness, well-being and *ra.* Some understand this to mean calamities and others, evil. If the latter, then it can only indicate that all things, including evil, are included in the plan of God, though the responsibility for committing sin rests on the creature, not the Creator.

C. Pasha

The basic idea in this word is to rebel, though it is usually translated by the word *transgression.* Notice 1 Kings 12:19; 2 Kings 3:5; Proverbs 28:21; and Isaiah 1:2.

D. Awon

The word includes both the ideas of iniquity and guilt, which in Hebrew thought were closely allied (1 Sam. 3:13). Note its use in connection with the Suffering Servant (Isa. 53:6), and in connection with a defiant sin (Num. 15:30–31).

E. Shagag

The word means to err or go astray as a sheep or a drunkard might do (Isa. 28:7). It refers to error for which the one committing it was responsible. Thus in the Law it implies that the one who goes astray was responsible for knowing what the Law commanded (Lev. 4:2; Num. 15:22).

F. Asham

Almost all the uses of this word are found in connection with the ritual of the tabernacle and the temple in Leviticus, Numbers, and Ezekiel. Guilt before God is its principal idea. It designates the guilt and sin offerings and therefore includes both intentional and unintentional guilt (Lev. 4:13; 5:2–3).

G. Rasha

Rarely used before the Exile, it occurs frequently in the Psalms, Ezekiel, and the Wisdom literature. It means wicked, the opposite of righteous (Exod. 2:13; Ps. 9:16; Prov. 15:9; Ezek. 18:23).

H. Taah

This word means to wander away, to go astray. The sin is deliberate, not accidental, even though the person may not realize the scope of his sin. Notice Numbers 15:22; Psalms 58:3; 119:21; Isaiah 53:6; and Ezekiel 44:10, 15.

From the word study we may draw certain conclusions about the Old Testament teaching on sin.

(1) Sin may take many forms, and because of the variety of words used, an Israelite could be aware of the particular form his sin took.

(2) Sin is that which is contrary to a norm, and ultimately it is disobedience to God.

(3) Although disobedience involved both positive and negative ideas, the emphasis is on the positive commission of wrong and not merely on the negative omission of good. Sin was not only missing the mark, but hitting the wrong mark.

II. IN THE NEW TESTAMENT

The New Testament employs at least a dozen basic words to describe sin.

A. Kakos

Meaning bad, the adverb is sometimes used of physical badness, that is, disease (Mark 1:32), but the adjective usually indicates moral badness (Matt. 21:41; 24:48; Mark 7:21; Acts 9:13; Rom. 12:17; 13:3–4, 10; 16:19; 1 Tim. 6:10).

B. Poneros

This is a basic term for evil and almost always indicates moral evil (Matt. 7:11; 12:39; 15:19; Acts 17:5; Rom. 12:9; 1 Thess. 5:22; Heb. 3:12; 2 John 11). It also is used of Satan (Matt. 13:19, 38; 1 John 2:13–14; 5:18; and possibly Matt. 6:13 and John 17:15) and of demons who are called evil spirits (Luke 11:26; Acts 19:12).

C. Asebes

Meaning godless, this word appears mostly in 2 Peter and Jude, meaning godless apostates. The unsaved are designated as ungodly (Rom. 4:5; 5:6). Occasionally it appears with other words for sin (1:18; 1 Tim. 1:9; 1 Pet. 4:18).

D. Enochos

The word means guilty and usually denotes someone whose crime is worthy of death (Matt. 5:21–22; Mark 14:64; 1 Cor. 11:27; James 2:10).

E. Hamartia

This is the most frequently used word for sin, occurring in its various forms about 227 times. When a writer wanted one inclusive word for sin, he used this one. The metaphor behind the word is missing the mark, but, as in the Old Testament, this is not only a negative idea but includes the positive idea of hitting some wrong mark. When it is used in the Gospels, it almost always occurs in a context that speaks of forgiveness or salvation (Matt. 1:21; John 1:29). Other instructive references include Acts 2:38; Romans 5:12; 6:1; 1 Corinthians 15:3; 2 Corinthians 5:21; James 1:15; 1 Peter 2:22; 1 John 1:7; 2:2; and Revelation 1:5.

F. Adikia

This refers to any unrighteous conduct in the broadest sense. It is used of unsaved people (Rom. 1:18), of money (Luke 16:9), of parts of the human body (Rom. 6:13; James 3:6), and of actions (2 Thess. 2:10).

G. Anomos

Often translated "iniquity," the word means lawless. It concerns breaking the law in the broadest sense (Matt. 13:41; 24:12; 1 Tim. 1:9). Eschatologically, it refers to the Antichrist, the lawless one (2 Thess. 2:8).

H. Parabates

Meaning transgressor, this word usually relates to specific violations of law (Rom. 2:23; 5:14; Gal. 3:19; Heb. 9:15).

I. Agnoein

This may refer to the ignorant worship of other than the true God (Acts 17:23; Rom. 2:4), but such ignorance makes one guilty and in need of atonement (Heb. 9:7).

J. Planao

To go astray in a culpable sense is the meaning of this word (1 Pet. 2:25). People can deceive others (lead them astray) (Matt. 24:5–6); people can deceive themselves (1 John 1:8); and Satan leads the whole world astray (Rev. 12:9; 20:3, 8).

K. Paraptōma

The idea in this word is falling away, and in most occurrences it is deliberate. Paul uses the word six times in Romans 5:15–20. See also Matthew 6:14; 2 Corinthians 5:19; Galatians 6:1; Ephesians 2:1; and James 5:16.

L. Hypocrisis

The word incorporates three ideas: to interpret falsely as an oracle might do, to pretend as an actor does, and to follow an interpretation known to be false. These ideas seem to blend in the account of Peter's defection in Galatians 2:11–21. False teachers of the end times will interpret falsely and pretend to be what they are not, and many will follow their teaching (1 Tim. 4:2). Hypocrites first deceive themselves into making wrong right; then they deceive others. This is the terrible nature of this sin.

Several conclusions may be drawn from the New Testament word study.

(1) There is always a clear standard against which sin is committed.

(2) Ultimately all sin is a positive rebellion against God and a transgression of His standards.

(3) Evil may assume a variety of forms.

(4) Man's responsibility is definite and clearly understood.

III. IN A DEFINITION

Sin may properly be defined by using all these descriptive words for its various forms as recorded in the Old and New Testaments. Such a definition would be accurate though lengthy. Indeed, it might be a good idea to define it thus: sin is missing the mark, badness, rebellion, iniquity, going astray, wickedness, wandering, ungodliness, crime, lawlessness, transgression, ignorance, and a falling away.

More briefly sin has generally been defined as lawlessness (from 1 John 3:4). This is an accurate definition as long as law is conceived of in its broadest sense, that is, defection from any of God's standards. Strong furnishes an example when he defines sin as "lack of conformity to the moral law of God, either in act, disposition, or state."[1]

Sin may also be defined as against the character of God (from Rom. 3:23, where the glory of God is the reflection of His character). Buswell defines sin in this way: "Sin may be defined ultimately as anything in the creature which does not express, or which is contrary to, the holy character of the Creator."[2]

Certainly the chief characteristic of sin is that it is directed against God. (This may be expressed in relation to God's Law as well.) Any definition that fails to reflect this is not a biblical one. The cliché that categorizes sins as against self, against others, or against God fails to emphasize the truth that all sin is ultimately against God (Ps. 51:4; Rom. 8:7).

Let not our word and definition study sidetrack us from remembering how terrible sin is in the sight of a holy God. Habakkuk said it succinctly: "Thine eyes are too pure to approve evil, and Thou canst not look on wickedness with favor" (Hab. 1:13). And sin is so damaging that only the death of God's Son can take it away (John 1:29).

NOTES

1. A. H. Strong, *Systematic Theology* (Philadelphia: Judson, 1907), 269.
2. J. Oliver Buswell, *A Systematic Theology of the Christian Religion* (Grand Rapids: Zondervan, 1962), 1:264.

Chapter 35
CHRIST'S TEACHING CONCERNING SIN

When one surveys the teaching of our Lord concerning sin, at least two things stand out. One is the sheer number of references He made to the subject, both in His direct teaching as well as in His parables. In spite of this, we usually do not think of sin as one of Christ's principal emphases. Yet it was. Second, His teaching on sin was very specific, as will be seen as the teaching is developed. In other words, on this subject of sin Christ had a lot to say, and He said it in specific detail.

I. SOME SPECIFIC SINS

Our Lord used all the major words for sin, and in so doing He specified a number of sins. The following is a list of the individual sins He mentioned in His teaching.

A. Sacrilege (Mark 11:15–18)

In cleansing the temple of the money changers, He condemned their sin of sacrilege (that is, violating the temple that was consecrated to God and showing irreverence toward hallowed things). Christ cleansed the temple at the beginning and end of His ministry (see also John 2:12–16).

B. Hypocrisy (Matt. 23:1–36)

In His scathing condemnation of the hypocrisy of the Sadducees, scribes, and Pharisees, our Lord pointed out several specific ways they showed that hypocrisy.

(1) They did not practice what they preached (vv. 1–4).

(2) They sought to exalt themselves by encouraging the adulations of the people (vv. 5–12).

(3) They escaped performing their oaths by trying to make a difference between swearing by the temple and swearing by the gold of the temple (vv. 16–22).

(4) They scrupulously tithed but neglected to promote justice (v. 23).

(5) Outwardly they appeared to be righteous, but inwardly they were hypocrites (v. 25).

C. Covetousness (Luke 12:15)

Sensing this was the root problem of the man who wanted the Lord to settle a dispute he had with his brother, the Lord warned the crowd against the sin of greed.

D. Blasphemy (Matt. 12:22–37)

By ascribing the miracles of Christ to the power of Satan, the Pharisees were blaspheming. However, they could right the situation by a correct confession of Christ (vv. 33–37; see pp. 405–7 for a fuller discussion of this).

E. Transgressing the Law (Matt. 15:3–6)

To avoid having to care for aged parents, the scribes devised a way to dedicate the money that would have been used for that purpose to the temple, eventually to receive it back. This, the Lord said, was a direct violation of the commandment to honor parents.

F. Pride (Matt. 20:20–28; Luke 14:7–11)

Pride of position or seeking places of honor has no place in the life of the true servant.

G. Being a Stumbling Block (Matt. 18:6)

Doing something that might cause others to sin is itself a sin.

H. Disloyalty (Matt. 8:19–22)

Putting comforts or even proper duties before loyalty to Christ is sin.

I. Immorality (Matt. 5:27–32)

This sin can be committed in the body, in the heart, or in marriage.

J. Fruitlessness (John 15:16)

Because believers have been chosen to bear fruit, not to do so would be contrary to God's purpose.

K. Anger (Matt. 5:22)

Anger, the Lord cautioned, can lead to murder.

L. Sins of Speech (Matt. 5:33–37; 12:36)

The Lord warned against perjuring oneself by failing to keep a promise made under oath. He also said that we shall be accountable for all our useless words.

M. Showing Off (Matt. 6:1–18)

Parading one's supposed piety is sin. This may be done in doing good things like almsgiving, prayer, and fasting, but doing them with a view to attracting praise from men rather than approval from God.

N. Lack of Faith (Matt. 6:25)

Having anxiety concerning one's needs shows lack of faith in God's provision.

O. Irresponsible Stewardship (Matt. 25:14–30; Luke 19:11–27)

Both parables illustrate the need for responsible stewardship on the part of Christ's followers. The talents represent different abilities given to different people, whereas the minas that were distributed equally represent the equal opportunity of life itself. The servants who did not use their abilities and opportunities were condemned for their irresponsible conduct.

P. Prayerlessness (Luke 18:1–8)

We ought to pray at all times and never lose heart.

I am sure this list could be lengthened, but it certainly demonstrates how many particular sins the Lord spoke of.

II. SOME CATEGORIES OF SIN

These many specific sins may be grouped under certain categories.

A. Violations of the Mosaic Law

"Corban" illustrates this category well (Mark 7:9–13). Corban is the transliteration of a Hebrew word meaning a "gift." If a son declared that the amount needed to support his parents was Corban, the scribes said he was exempt from his duty to care for his parents, a duty that the Law commanded. Apparently he was not really obligated to devote that sum to the temple but could use it himself.

B. Open Sins

Although all sins are sinful, not all sins are of equal magnitude. Some sins are truly more sinful than others. The Lord affirmed this in His teaching on the speck and log (Matt. 7:1–5) and when He said that Caiaphas's sin of delivering Christ to the authorities was greater than Pilate's (John 19:11).

Some examples of open sins that are often of greater magnitude include sins of speech, especially those that show defiance of Christ's claims (Matt. 12:22–37) and open opposition and rejection of God's messengers (21:33–46).

C. Wrong Inward Attitudes

Outward actions bespeak inner attitudes and character, and the Lord often put His finger on the inward root of sin. Notice Luke 12:13–15 and Matthew 20:20–22.

D. Leaven

Everywhere in the Bible, leaven typifies the presence of impurity or evil (though some understand Matthew 13:33 to be an exception, where leaven indicates the growth of the kingdom through the power of the Gospel). However, unquestionably when Christ warned of the leaven of the Pharisees or Sadducees or Herodians, He was referring to something sinful.

1. Of the Pharisees. The leaven of the Pharisees was externalism. Though outwardly they were righteous (Matt. 5:20), knowledgeable about the Scriptures (23:2), tithers (Luke 18:12), those who fasted (Matt. 9:14) and prayed (Luke 18:11), inwardly they were unclean, and our Lord denounced their leaven of hypocrisy (Matt. 23:14, 26, 29; Mark 8:15; Luke 12:1).

2. Of the Sadducees. Their leaven was spreading false doctrine. Their beliefs were rooted in the senses; therefore, they did not believe in the existence of angels or in resurrection. Our Lord did not denounce this as often, for false teaching is in itself something more apparent because it is more difficult to hide (Matt. 16:6).

3. Of the Herodians. Their leaven was secularism and worldliness. As a party they supported Herod and the Roman rule that gave him his power. Thus they sought to use worldly power to promote "spiritual" ends, and Christ warned against this (Mark 8:15).

These same sins—externalism, false doctrine, and worldly methods

—are all too apparent in some groups today. And our Lord's warning against them is relevant.

III. SOME SOURCES OF SIN

A. Satan

Christ was acutely aware of the power, program, and procedures of Satan. Some have tried to suggest that the Lord really did not believe in the reality of Satan but was accommodating the ignorances of the people when He taught about Satan. However, He spoke of Satan on occasions when there was no need to do so unless He believed Satan actually existed (e.g., Luke 10:18). Our Lord acknowledged Satan as the ruler of this world (John 12:31), the head of his own kingdom (Matt. 12:26), the father of rebellious people (John 8:44), the father of lies (v. 44), the evil one who opposes the reception of the Gospel (Matt. 13:19), the enemy who sows tares among the good seed (v. 39), and thus the one who causes people to do these things he promotes.

B. The World

Satan's world stands in opposition to God's people and promotes Satan's purposes. So the world system is a source of sin when anyone conforms to it (John 15:18–19).

C. The Heart

Often the Lord emphasized that what a person does externally is a reflection of what is in his heart (Matt. 15:19).

IV. THE UNIVERSALITY OF SIN

In a direct statement the Lord said that only God is good and no human is (Matt. 19:17). He stated that His chosen disciples were evil (Luke 11:13), even though He recognized that they could do good things. Sin alienates people from God, and all are sinners.

V. SOME CONSEQUENCES OF SIN

A. It Affects Destiny

Sin causes people to be lost (Matt. 18:11; Luke 15:4, 8, 24). If unforgiven it causes them to perish (John 3:16). It brings people into judgment (Luke 12:20).

B. It Affects the Will

The Lord made it clear that the Pharisees were slaves to the desires of the devil (John 8:44). When He announced His mission in the synagogue in Nazareth, He indicated that one thing He came to do was to free the captives (Luke 4:18), apparently a reference to those who were spiritually captive, since the Lord did not effect the release of those who were jailed. (He could have done so with John the Baptist.)

C. It Affects the Body

Of course not all sickness is the result of sin (John 9:3), but some evidently is. The Lord indicates this in the case of the man who was healed at the Pool of Bethesda (5:14). Notice also Matthew 8:17.

D. It Affects Others

The sins of the scribes affected widows and others who followed their traditions (Luke 20:46–47). Clearly the sin of the prodigal son affected his father (15:20). Additionally, the sins warned against in the Sermon on the Mount all have their effect on others. No one can sin in total isolation.

VI. THE FORGIVENESS OF SIN

A. The Basis for Forgiveness

At the beginning of Christ's ministry John the Baptist announced the purpose of it when he pointed to Jesus as the Lamb of God who takes away the sin of the world (John 1:29). The Lord Himself made it clear that His death was the basis for forgiveness (Matt. 20:28; 26:28).

B. The Ramification of Forgiveness

Forgiven people should forgive others. This is a recurring theme in the Lord's teaching (Matt. 6:14–15; 18:21–35; Luke 17:3–4).

VII. THE ESCHATOLOGY OF SIN

In His great eschatological discourse, the Lord detailed the future outworking of sin in the coming period of Tribulation on this earth (Matt. 24:1–28).

A. In International Affairs

Sin will be the cause of wars during the Tribulation days (vv. 6–7).

B. In Personal Affairs

Sin will cause people to betray one another and to hate one another (vv. 10, 12).

C. In Spiritual Affairs

The Tribulation period will be a time of intense spiritual deception. Many false religious leaders will deceive people with miraculous signs that they will be empowered to perform (vv. 5, 11, 24), and the Antichrist will bring false religion to its zenith when he sits in the temple in Jerusalem demanding to be worshiped (vv. 15–21). During this time, evil will be more open and more damaging than at any other time in history.

To sum up: Our Lord's teaching covered many aspects of sin emphasizing both the variety and specifics of sin. He always underscored man's personal responsibility for sin, and His teaching was laced with the practical ramifications of sin.

Chapter 36
THE INHERITANCE OF SIN

I. A DEFINITION

Inherited sin is that sinful state into which all people are born.

Theologians have used several labels to describe this concept. (1) Some call it, as the title of this chapter, inherited sin. This emphasizes the truth that all people inherit this sinful state from their parents, and their parents from their parents, all the way back to Adam and Eve. (2) Others call it the sin nature, which focuses on the fact that sin has corrupted our entire nature. The term "sin nature" provides a clear contrast between that root nature and its fruits (which are particular acts of sin). (3) Still others prefer the term "original sin" because Adam's original sin produced that moral corruption of nature that was transmitted by inheritance to each succeeding generation.

II. SCRIPTURAL EVIDENCE

The Bible clearly states that all aspects of man's being are corrupt. "By nature" we are children of wrath—that is, objects of wrath (Eph. 2:3). By actions we are also objects of God's wrath, but this verse refers to something innate. Psalm 51:5 indicates that this is something we have from conception, not something acquired by actions during our lifetimes.

Every facet of man's being is affected by this sin nature. (1) His intellect is blinded (2 Cor. 4:4). His mind is reprobate or disapproved (Rom. 1:28). His understanding is darkened, separated from the life of God (Eph. 4:18). (2) His emotions are degraded and defiled (Rom. 1:21, 24, 26; Titus 1:15). (3) His will is enslaved to sin and therefore stands in opposition to God (Rom. 6:20; 7:20).

III. TOTAL DEPRAVITY

The scriptural evidence provides the basis for what has been commonly called total depravity. The English word "depravity" means perverted or crooked. It is not used in the translation of the King James Version, but some modern translations do use it to translate *adokimos* in Romans 1:28. This word means "not standing the test" and gives us a clue as to how to define the concept of depravity. Depravity means that man fails the test of pleasing God. He denotes his unmeritoriousness in God's sight. This failure is total in that (a) it affects all aspects of man's being and (b) it affects all people.

Negatively, the concept of total depravity does not mean (a) that every person has exhibited his depravity as thoroughly as he or she could; (b) that sinners do not have a conscience or a "native induction" concerning God; (c) that sinners will indulge in every form of sin; or (d) that depraved people do not perform actions that are good in the sight of others and even in the sight of God.

Positively, total depravity means (a) that corruption extends to every facet of man's nature and faculties; and (b) that there is nothing in anyone that can commend him to a righteous God.

Total depravity must always be measured against God's holiness. Relative goodness exists in people. They can do good works, which are appreciated by others. But nothing that anyone can do will gain salvational merit or favor in the sight of a holy God.

IV. THE PENALTY CONNECTED WITH INHERITED SIN

The penalty that is particularly related to inherited sin is spiritual death. Death always indicates a separation of some kind, so spiritual death means a separation from the life of God in this present life (Eph. 2:1–3). If this condition continues unchanged throughout life, then eternal death or the second death follows (Rev. 20:11–15).

Cut flowers well illustrate living human beings who do good things but who nevertheless are spiritually dead. Is the blossom that has been cut from the plant alive or dead? At first it is beautiful and fragrant, and in combination with other cut flowers, it may grace the finest home, church, or occasion. It looks alive; it is useful; but it is in reality dead, for it has been severed from the life of the plant that produced it. At this point the illustration breaks down, for it is not possible to give the flower new and eternal life, something God can do for the one who believes in the Lord Jesus.

V. THE TRANSMISSION OF INHERITED SIN

The label itself indicates how original sin is transmitted from one generation to the next and the next and the next. We inherit it from our parents as they did from theirs, and so on back to the first parents, Adam and Eve. After they sinned they could only propagate after their kind; that is, their children were sinners by birth (Gen. 4:1; Ps. 51:5; Rom. 5:12). This means that everyone born into this world is a sinner. No one is born good, nor is anyone born partly good and partly sinful. All are equally sinful in God's sight. If this were not so, then those who were, say, only 50 percent sinful would need only 50 percent of God's salvation.

VI. THE REMEDY FOR INHERITED SIN

The remedy is twofold. (1) Redemption includes a judgment on the sin nature so that the believer is no longer bound to serve sin (Rom. 6:18; 8:1; Gal. 5:24). All that which belongs to the old life has been crucified with Christ. Death always means separation; therefore, His death separated us from the dominion of original sin. (2) However, the old is not eradicated until the resurrection; therefore, God has given us His Holy Spirit to give us victory over sin in daily life.

We are separated from the dominion of sin by Christ's death, and we are free from its domination by the power of the Spirit.

VII. SOME ATTACKS AGAINST THIS DOCTRINE

A. Pelagianism

Pelagius, a monk from Britain who preached in Rome around A.D. 400, believed that since God would not command anything that was not possible, and that since He has commanded men to be holy, everyone therefore can live a life that is free from sin. He taught that man was created neutral—neither sinful nor holy—and with the capacity and will to choose freely either to sin or to do good. Everyone is born in the same condition as Adam before the Fall; only now man has before him Adam's bad example. But Adam in no way transmitted a sin nature or the guilt of his sin to his posterity. Man has a will that is free, and sin comes from the separate acts of man's will. Man is also free to do good works, and all of his good deeds come from the unassisted capabilities of his human nature. Thus Pelagianism exaggerates the merit of works and their efficacy in salvation.

B. Semi-Pelagianism

Pelagius's teaching was opposed by his contemporary, Augustine, who emphasized man's total inability to achieve righteousness and therefore his need for sovereign grace alone. Semi-Pelagianism is a mediating position between Augustinianism (with its strong emphasis on predestination and man's inability) and Pelagianism (with its insistence on man's complete ability). Semi-Pelagians teach that man retains a measure of freedom by which he can cooperate with the grace of God. Man's will has been weakened and his nature affected by the Fall, but he is not totally depraved. In regeneration man chooses God, who then adds His grace. Semi-Pelagianism is the teaching of the Roman Catholic church as well as some Protestant groups. Original sin is eliminated in water baptism.

C. Socinianism

This movement, named after Lelio Socinus (1525–62) and his nephew Faustus (1539–1604), was the forerunner of Unitarianism. Its teachings include a denial of the deity of Christ, a denial of predestination, original sin, total inability, and penal substitution.

D. Arminianism

Though the views of Jacobus Arminius (1560–1609) were not so divergent from traditional Reformed theology, those of his successors were increasingly so. Arminianism teaches that Adam was created in innocency, not holiness, that sin consists in acts of the will, that we inherit pollution from Adam but not guilt or a sin nature, that man is not totally depraved, that man has the ability to will to do good and to conform to God's will in this life so as to be perfect, and that the human will is one of the causes of regeneration. Wesleyan theology, sometimes called evangelical Arminianism, holds similar views on the subjects of Adam's sin and man's ability, though it differs in other points.

E. Neo-orthodoxy

In general, neo-orthodoxy takes sin very seriously. It is defined as self-centeredness, rather than God-centeredness. However, the account of Adam's sin in Genesis 3 is not seen as historical in that it was an actual event that happened at a certain time and in a particular place. Adam was not a real individual who actually lived on this earth, yet Adam represents man at every stage of his development. The story of Adam's fall is the story of all of us. With such a view of biblical history, there can be no connection between the sin of Adam and his posterity.

Chapter 37
The Imputation of Sin

I. THE MEANING OF IMPUTATION

To impute means to attribute or reckon or ascribe something to someone. It is not mere influence but involvement that is at the heart of the concept.

The Old Testament provides several examples of imputation. Leviticus 7:18 and 17:4 indicate that lack of blessing and guilt were ascribed to the Israelite who did not follow the prescribed ritual in the offerings. In 1 Samuel 22:15 and 2 Samuel 19:19 (KJV), are pleas not to impute something to certain individuals. In Psalm 32:2 David expresses the happiness of the person to whom the Lord does not impute iniquity. In all these cases imputation includes some kind of involvement, not mere influencing.

The New Testament refers several times to imputation in the Old Testament. Paul stated that sin is not imputed as a specific violation of a legal code when there is no law (Rom. 5:13). He referred to the righteousness God imputed to Abraham when he believed and to the righteousness David knew when he confessed his sin (Rom. 4). James also referred to Abraham's imputed righteousness (James 2:23). The death of Christ enabled God not to impute man's sins against him (2 Cor. 5:19).

The letter to Philemon contains what is probably the most beautiful illustration of imputation. Paul told Philemon that if his slave Onesimus owed anything to reckon it to Paul's account. In other words, any debt Onesimus might have incurred would be charged against Paul's account and Paul would pay it. Similarly, our sins were attributed, ascribed, reckoned to Christ, and He paid our debt fully.

II. THREE BASIC IMPUTATIONS

Theologians have generally recognized three basic imputations.

A. The Imputation of Adam's Sin to the Race (Rom. 5:12–21)

This is the one that concerns us in this section on sin, and we shall return to a full discussion of it.

B. The Imputation of Man's Sin to Christ (2 Cor. 5:19; 1 Pet. 2:24)

C. The Imputation of Christ's Righteousness to Believers (2 Cor. 5:21)

III. THE IMPUTATION OF ADAM'S SIN

A. The Central Passage (Rom. 5:12)

The concept of imputed sin arises from interpreting the meaning of "all sinned" at the end of verse 12.

Some understand it to mean that each individual sins personally, and because of these sins people die. "Sinned refers to actual sins (cf. 3:23) viewed as an individual expression and endorsement of Adam's representative act."[1] However, babies die even though they have not committed sins personally. Also, "all sinned" is connected with the one man, Adam, through whom sin entered the world. The verse does not say that Adam sinned and others sin also. Five times in 5:15–19 Paul stated that condemnation and death reign over all because of the one sin of Adam, not because of the various sins of all of us.

Some understand the meaning as "all are sinners" or "all are sinful." However, the word is an active voice verb (all did something), not a noun or adjective (all are something). Of course, it is true that all are sinners, but that is not the meaning of "all sinned" in this verse. Shedd's objections to the meaning "all are sinful" are much to the point. He observes that such an interpretation would be contrary to the invariable usage of the active voice of the verb, and it would require the addition of the verb "to be."[2]

Barthians understand this to mean that sin is part of the experience of all people, but since they do not believe Adam was an actual person or that his sin was an actual time-space event, there can be no connection between Adam and the race. To them, this verse says nothing about original sin or about imputed sin.

Another interpretation is that all sinned when Adam sinned. This seems to be the only meaning that does justice to the verb and its relationship to the preceding part of the verse. "The tense of the verb indicates a distinct historic entrance. . . . Physical death came to all men but not because they were all in the process of individually sinning. All men did sin (except for infants dying in infancy) experientially. But Paul is not talking about that here. The sin of all is centered in that of the one man Adam."[3]

B. The Relation Between Adam and the Race

Though Paul clearly states the fact that all men sinned when Adam sinned, the question remains, how did they do so? What is the relation between Adam and the race?

Historically, two answers have been given. They are commonly labeled as (a) the federal or representative view and (b) the seminal or realistic or Augustinian view.

1. The representative view. This views Adam as the representative of the whole human race so that when Adam sinned his sin became the ground of condemnation of his race. No one but Adam actually committed that first sin, but since Adam represented all people, God viewed all as involved and thus condemned. The word "federal" means covenant and indicates that Adam was appointed to represent the race in the so-called Covenant of Works. Because the covenant head sinned, the guilt of his sin was imputed to each of his posterity. Hosea 6:7 is cited as a reference to this covenant.

2. The seminal view. The seminal, realistic, or Augustinian view sees Adam as containing the seed of all his posterity so that when he sinned, all actually sinned. Mankind was not merely represented by Adam but was actually organically joined to Adam. "Paul's concept of racial solidarity seems to be a universalizing of the Hebrew concept of family solidarity. A tragic picture of family solidarity is seen in Joshua 7:16–26, where Achan is discovered as the cause of Israel's defeat at Ai. . . . Achan blamed no one else. . . . But in the administration of the punishment . . . everything connected with Achan was blotted out of Israel."[4] Hebrews 7:9–10 furnishes another example of the seminal or germinal concept in the human race. The writer plainly stated that Levi, though not born until almost two hundred years later, actually paid tithes in his great-grandfather Abraham. The ancestor, Abraham, contained his descendant, Levi. Similarly, our ancestor, Adam, contained all of us, his descendants. Therefore, just as Levi did something in paying the tithe, so we did something in sinning in Adam.

Thus Adam's sin was imputed to each member of the human race because each member of the human race actually sinned in Adam when Adam sinned.

I came across an illustration of imputation in a sad experience a former student had. This man, Bill, shared the expenses of a ride home at Christmastime in Joe's car. On the way another car went through a stop sign and hit Joe's car broadside. At the time of the accident, Joe was driving and Bill was asleep in the car. Because Bill was seriously and permanently injured, he sued to collect damages from the owner of the other car. But that owner (or his insurance company) tried to prove negligence on Joe's part. Bill's attorney wrote to him in part as follows: ". . . and if the jury finds that he [Joe] was negligent, it will undoubtedly be imputed to you, and you cannot recover. I don't think that there is anything that we can do to change that situation now."

What linked Bill to Joe and to Joe's possible negligence? It was the fact that Bill had shared expenses. Money joined Bill to Joe and to Joe's actions. Humanity joined all of us to Adam and to Adam's sin. We all share in Adam's sin and Adam's guilt. We are all equally guilty and in need of a remedy for our sin.

IV. THE TRANSMISSION OF IMPUTED SIN

Imputed sin is transmitted directly from Adam to each individual in every generation. Since I was in Adam, Adam's sin was imputed to me directly, not through my parents and their parents. Imputed sin is an immediate imputation (that is, directly, not through mediators between Adam and me).

This contrasts with how the inherited sin nature is transmitted. It comes to me from my parents, and theirs from their parents, and so on back to Adam. Inherited sin is a mediate transmission since it comes through all the mediators of generations between Adam and me. Charted, the contrast looks like this:

A COMPARISON OF HOW INHERITED AND IMPUTED SIN ARE TRANSMITTED

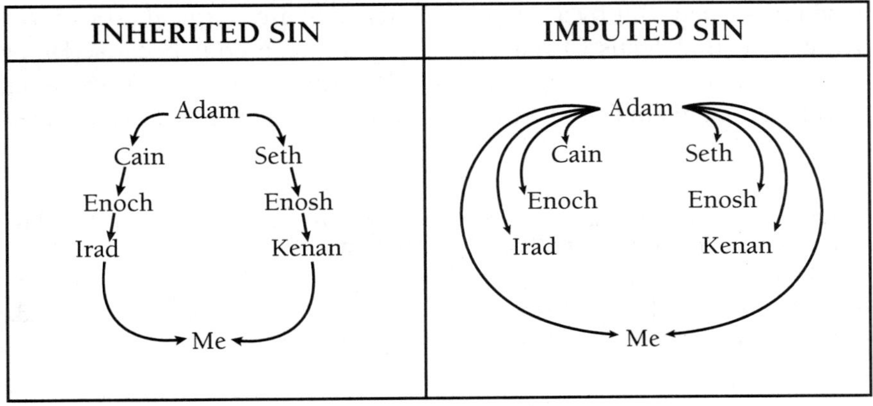

V. THE PENALTY OF IMPUTED SIN

Physical death is the particular penalty connected with imputed sin (Rom. 5:13–14). The particular penalty connected with inherited sin, you remember, is spiritual death.

VI. THE REMEDY FOR IMPUTED SIN

The remedy for imputed sin is the imputed righteousness of Christ. The moment anyone believes, Christ's righteousness is reckoned or imputed to that individual. As all are in Adam, so all believers are in Christ, and being in Him means that His righteousness is ours.

A vivid illustration of this came to me in my student days. A criminal in the state penitentiary was soon to be executed for murder. His story received an uncommon amount of publicity because he had willed that the cornea of one of his eyes should be used in what was then the very new procedure of corneal transplant. Further, the recipient was designated prior to the criminal's execution, and indeed the two men met before the execution was carried out. This made great human interest copy for the media.

In due time the murderer was put to death. His cornea was taken from his body, and by the miracle of medicine it was transplanted into the eye of a blind man who then could see. Now suppose some policeman should have tried to arrest that man who received the cornea and have him executed because he had the cornea of a murderer. Any judge would say, "But that cornea that formerly was in the body of a murderer is now in the body of a man who is righteous before the law. Therefore, the cornea is as righteous as the man is." And that illustrates my point. I was in Adam and justly condemned to die because I sinned when he sinned. But by a miracle greater than any surgical procedure, I was placed in Jesus Christ. And now I am righteous because He is righteous and can stand before a holy God uncondemned. From being in Adam to being in Christ—that's my story by the miracle of His grace.

NOTES

1. Leslie C. Allen, "Romans," in *A New Testament Commentary,* ed. Howley, Bruce, and Ellison (Grand Rapids: Zondervan, 1969), 352.
2. William G. T. Shedd, *Dogmatic Theology* (New York: Scribner, 1891), 2:183–85.
3. A. Berkeley Mickelsen, "Romans,"in *The Wycliffe Bible Commentary,* ed. Pfeiffer and Harrison (Chicago: Moody, 1962), 1197.
4. Ibid., 1197–98.

Chapter 38
PERSONAL SINS

The area of personal sin is likely the first one most people would think about when they think about sin. Of course, they say, sin is real because people sin. But sin is also a reality because we have inherited a sin nature and Adam's sin was imputed to us. Yet it is true that our personal sins bring home the reality of sin.

I. SOME SCRIPTURAL EVIDENCES

In Romans 3:9–18 Paul demonstrated the condemnation of all people on the basis of their committing sins personally. The condemnation is universal and based on evil acts of both word and deed. People are corrupting, deceitful, uncharitable, blasphemous, murderous, oppressive, quarrelsome, and impious.

Many passages name specific sins. Notice lying in 1 John 1:6, partiality in James 2:4, carnality in 1 Corinthians 3:1–4, and the list in Galatians 5:19–21 that includes sorcery, immorality, factions, and envy.

II. SOME CHARACTERISTICS OF PERSONAL SINS

A. Their Universality

All commit sins personally except infants. James makes that very clear when he states that we all stumble in many ways (James 3:2). Before Paul lists those sins in Romans 3 he says that all, both Jews and Gentiles, are under sin (v. 9). After the list he repeats that fact, declaring that all are coming short of the glory of God (v. 23).

B. Their Overtness

Personal sins are not only those that are committed overtly but also those that are committed in our thoughts. Immorality, envy, greed, and idolatry are examples of sins that occur in our thought lives (and also may erupt in specific actions). See Matthew 5:27–28; 2 Corinthians 10:5; and Colossians 3:5–6.

Furthermore, sins of omission, which are not overt, are as sinful as sins that are actually committed (James 4:17).

C. Their Classification

The Lord ranked Caiaphas's sin in delivering Him to Pilate as greater than Pilate's sin. But this did not excuse Pilate, for if there is greater sin (Caiaphas's) there must also be lesser sin (Pilate's). As a governmental agent, Pilate could only do what God allowed his government to do. Caiaphas as high priest had greater light and thus greater responsibility.

The Old Testament distinguished sins of ignorance from defiant sins. Defiant sins were, literally, sins with a high hand; that is, sins with a raised, clenched fist in defiance of God and His commands. For such sins there was no acceptable offering (Num. 15:30–31). An example of a defiant sin follows in the account of a man gathering wood on the Sabbath in defiance of God's clear command. By contrast, the sin offering atoned for sins of ignorance; that is, sins done unintentionally out of weakness or waywardness (Lev. 4:2). Some examples included withholding evidence when called on to testify, accidental ceremonial defilement because of contact with an unclean animal or person, and inability to fulfill a rash vow (5:1–4).

The New Testament counterpart to this Old Testament classification contrasts sins committed against much light as compared to sins against little light (Luke 12:47–48).

Other classifications include the unpardonable sin (Matt. 12:31–32) and a sin unto death (1 John 5:16).

The Roman Catholic church distinguishes venial sins (pardonable sins) and mortal sins (death-bringing sins). A person commits a venial sin when he transgresses the law of God in an unimportant matter. Such a sin is forgiven easily, even without confession. Only the sacrament of penance can forgive a mortal sin. This teaching is not a scriptural one.

In an analogous fashion, those who believe that a child of God can lose his salvation also make distinctions between sins that are not so bad and that most believers commit sometime but that do not cause the loss of salvation and sins that are bad enough to cause the loss of salvation. What sins belong to each of those categories is usually determined very subjectively.

III. THE TRANSMISSION OF PERSONAL SINS

Strictly speaking, personal sins are not transmitted from one individual or generation to another. Each person commits his own sins. Affects of personal sins are transmitted in the sense that our sins do affect others, but each must suffer consequences for his own sins.

IV. THE RESULT OF PERSONAL SINS

If we need one idea to describe the result of all personal sins, it would be the loss of fellowship. The unbeliever has no fellowship with God because of his sins, and the believer who has been brought into the fellowship of God's family loses the enjoyment of that fellowship when he sins. He is not expelled from the family, though he may lose some of the privileges of being in the family. When he confesses and is forgiven, he is restored to fellowship.

V. THE REMEDY FOR PERSONAL SINS

The remedy is forgiveness. For the unbeliever who receives Christ, that forgiveness covers all the guilt of his sins (Eph. 1:7). For the believer, that forgiveness restores the enjoyment of fellowship in the family of God (1 John 1:9). Or to put it another way, judicial forgiveness brings the unbeliever into the family of God, while family forgiveness restores the temporarily broken relationship within the family.

A COMPARISON OF THE SEVERAL ASPECTS OF SIN

ASPECT	SCRIPTURE	TRANSMISSION	PRINCIPAL CONSEQUENCE	REMEDY
INHERITED SIN	Ephesians 2:3	Generation to generation	Spiritual death	Redemption and the gift of the Holy Spirit
IMPUTED SIN	Romans 5:12	Direct from Adam to me	Physical death	Imputed righteousness
PERSONAL SINS	Romans 3:23; 1 John 1:9	None	Loss of fellowship	Forgiveness

Chapter 39 THE CHRISTIAN AND SIN

I. THE STANDARD FOR THE BELIEVER

Becoming a Christian does not exempt one from sinning or free him from obedience to the law of Christ. To say it does is to fall into one or both of the common errors concerning the Christian and sin. The one is a false perfectionism and the other antinomianism.

Unbiblical perfectionism teaches that the believer does not sin at all because he has rooted out the principle of sin. No believer can experience this kind of sinless perfection until the resurrection when he will be free from the sin principle within. A modified form of sinless perfection does not include eradication of the sin nature but teaches that a Christian can live without practicing sin for some period of time. But not practicing sin not only means not committing sin but also practicing and conforming to the will of God. Sinless perfection involves more than the absence of sin. In reality, the biblical doctrine of perfection means ripeness, maturity, fullness, completeness. Biblical perfection does not stand in contrast with sinfulness but with immaturity, and biblical perfection is something expected of a believer here on earth.[1]

Antinomianism teaches that the Christian is not bound by the law. Antinomianism's concept of freedom from law often leads to license. Antinomianism is sometimes equated with Christian liberty, a wrong equation. The opposite of liberty is slavery, and the believer has been brought from slavery to sin to a position of freedom in Christ. The opposite of antinomianism is obedience to law. Which law, for there have been several throughout biblical history? For the believer today it is the law of Christ (Gal. 6:2).

What is the biblical standard for the Christian? It is neither sinless perfection nor antinomianism. It is to walk in the light (1 John 1:7). God is light or holy. This absolute standard is always before the believer. Yet no believer can be without sin, as God is, in this life. Does God then mock us? Not at all. Rather, He tailors His requirement for each of us to our stage of spiritual development. And that tailored requirement is to walk in the light of His holiness. If we say we have no sin principle (as sinless perfectionism claims), we lie (v. 8). Likewise, if we say we have not sinned for whatever period of time (as modified perfectionism teaches), we make God a liar (v. 10). If we walk in the light, we will not fall into the error of antinomianism, for we will keep His commandments (2:4, 6; 3:24).

Each believer can meet the requirement to walk in the light. The amount of light each has will be different, but the requirement to respond to that amount is the same for all. As we grow, the circle of light will expand. And as we respond to increasing light, we will receive more light, and so on. But at each stage the requirement is the same—walk in the light.

To sum up: The standard is God's holiness. The requirement is to walk in the light. Our experience should always be a growing one, growing to maturity. That is true biblical perfectionism.

II. THE ENEMIES OF THE BELIEVER

The believer is continually opposed by the world, the flesh, and the devil.

A. The World

We have already discussed in detail the concept of this world system under satanology. Suffice it to review and add only a few details at this point.

1. Its description. Satan stands as its head and controlling force. Its chief characteristic is counterfeiting, though Satan will use any tactic he can in order to defeat the believer. Often borderline issues are the most difficult to discern and decide.

2. Our defense. A number of things serve as the believer's defense against the counterfeit of the world—the armor (Eph. 6:13–18), knowledge of Satan's strategies (2 Cor. 2:11), sobriety, vigilance (1 Pet. 5:8). Perhaps faith should be placed at or near the top of the list. Our faith is the victory that overcomes the world (1 John 5:4–5), the faith that identified us with Christ's work on the cross. Since every believer has such faith, he has an adequate defense against the world. Yet such faith needs to be constantly exercised to realize victory (1 Tim. 6:12).

B. The Flesh

1. The concept. The flesh is that principle of sin within all of us. Some equate the sin nature and flesh. The flesh produces works (Gal. 5:19),

is characterized by lusts and passions (v. 24; 1 John 2:16), and can enslave the believer (Rom. 7:25). In it is nothing good (v. 18), for the presence of the new life in Christ makes all that is associated with the flesh old and useless. This includes blatantly evil things as well as amoral things and sometimes things that might be good in themselves but that bring no pleasure to God because they are works of the flesh.
2. *The control.* The flesh can only be controlled by actualizing our co-crucifixion with Christ. We have crucified the flesh; that is, we have been separated from its domination by our association with Christ's dying unto sin (Gal. 5:24). We can experience victory not by eradication of the flesh but by walking in dependence on the Spirit to control it (v. 16).

C. The Devil

Having already discussed Satan, we mention here only a few reminders of his work in attacking believers.
1. *His strategy is planned.* Satan devises methods, uses strategies, and employs all the craftiness of a superhuman creature to trap the believer (2 Cor. 2:11; Eph. 6:11).
2. *His strategy is persistent.* He continually stalks the believer, waiting for the right moment to attack (1 Pet. 5:8).
3. *His strategy is powerful.* The believer must wrestle in hand-to-hand combat against Satan, never underestimating his power (Eph. 6:12; 1 John 4:4; Jude 9).

III. THE PENALTIES FOR SINS

A. For the Unbeliever

The unbeliever who dies without the forgiveness of his sins must suffer eternal torment in the lake of fire (Rev. 20:15).

B. For the Sinning Believer

1. *Loss of fellowship.* Sin brings an interruption of fellowship in the area of the sin (1 John 1:3, 6–7).
2. *Loss of joy.* Sin causes a loss of joy (John 15:11; Gal. 5:22).
3. *Darkened walk.* Sin causes the believer to walk in darkness (1 John 1:6; 2:10).
4. *Weak prayer.* Sin brings a lack of confidence in prayer (1 John 3:19–22).

C. For the Persistently Sinning Believer

If a believer persists in some sin, then other consequences may follow.

1. *Punishment.* Chastisement of some form may come (Heb. 12:5–11). Sickness may be one form of punishment (1 Cor. 11:30).
2. *Excommunication.* Excommunication from the local church may be necessary (Matt. 18:17; 1 Cor. 5).
3. *Physical death.* In some cases physical death may be a punishment for persistent sin (1 Cor. 11:30; 1 John 5:16).

Our merciful heavenly Father is often very patient with our sinning, not bringing severe penalties on us. But we must never forget that sin does take its toll in many ways, internal and external, even if no obvious punishment comes. And at the Judgment Seat of Christ, all our deeds will be examined by our Lord (2 Cor. 5:10).

IV. THE PREVENTIVES FOR SIN

Always it is better to prevent than to cure, and God has provided for us ways to prevent sin in our lives. These serve like vaccinations to prevent our succumbing to the disease.

A. The Word of God

God's Word in our hearts will serve to prevent sin, for it will warn, remind, encourage, strengthen, and guide us when we are tempted to sin (Ps. 119:11).

B. The Intercession of Christ

Our Lord ever lives to pray for us (Heb. 7:25). One thing He prays for is that we might not sin. See the illustration of this in Peter's case in Luke 22:32 as well as the direct statement in John 17:15. Doubtless we will never know what this has involved until we arrive in heaven, and even then we might not be told all.

C. The Indwelling of the Spirit

Many of the ministries of the Spirit in the believer today relate to preventing sin in our lives, but several seem to stand out.

1. *Actualizing aspects of our position in Christ.* For example, we have put to death the flesh with its affections and lusts, yet we need to walk in the Spirit to actualize this in our experience (Gal. 5:16–24).
2. *Teaching.* Teaching us the deep things of the Word helps us to dis-

cern good and evil (1 Cor. 2:10; Heb. 5:14). Superficial knowledge may prevent obvious sins, but deeper knowledge can prevent more sins.
3. Leading in prayer. Leading us in our prayers, the Spirit can guide us to think about ways sin can be prevented in our lives (Matt. 6:13; Rom. 8:34; Eph. 6:18).
4. Enabling for service. Enabling us to serve (John 7:37–39) may keep us from using the time, money, and energies to sin (Rev. 12:11).

V. THE REMEDY FOR SINS

The remedy for believers' sins may be stated in one word: confess (1 John 1:9). This does not mean to merely mouth or recite the sins. It means to see those sins as God sees them. That will surely bring repentance and the earnest desire to change. But if the same sins reoccur, the remedy remains the same.

VI. A CONCLUDING THOUGHT

When we contemplate sins of unbelievers, it does not seem so difficult to comprehend the enormity of sin, for we know the punishment will be eternal separation from God. But somehow when we consider sins in believers, we lighten their seriousness. But make no mistake about it. All sin grieves God. Christ had to die for the sins we committed before and after we were saved. His death was the punishment for all sins. The fact that we are members of the family of God may bring more sorrow to our heavenly Father when we sin. We ought to know better. We ought to use the power He has provided. We ought to want to please Him. We ought to struggle and fight harder and use every weapon He has given us. But above all, we ought to be making progress and showing growth in our lives.

> We may take comfort about our souls if we know anything of an inward fight and conflict. It is the invariable companion of genuine Christian holiness. . . . Do we find in our heart of hearts a spiritual struggle? Do we feel anything of the flesh lusting against the Spirit and the Spirit against the flesh, so that we cannot do the things that we would? Are we conscious of two principles within us, contending for the master? Do we feel anything of war in our inward man? Well, let us thank God for it! It is a good sign. It is strongly probable evidence of the great work of sanctification. . . . Anything is better than apathy, stagnation, deadness, and indifference.[2]

Fellow members of God's family: press on to maturity (Heb. 6:1).

NOTES

1. An excellent discussion of the biblical doctrine was written by W. H. Griffith Thomas, "The Biblical Teaching Concerning Perfection," *The Sunday School Times,* 22 July 1944, 515–16.
2. J. C. Ryle, *Holiness* (London: Hunt, 1839), 82.

Section IX
JESUS CHRIST OUR LORD

Chapter 40
THE PREINCARNATE CHRIST

The doctrine of Christ may include both a study of His person and His work. However, since His principal work was the Atonement, soteriology is usually separated from Christology. His other works are normally considered under Christology.

The doctrine can be organized more or less chronologically. A study of the preincarnate Christ comes first. This would be followed by a section on Christ in His humiliation, i.e., during His earthly life. (It would be erroneous to call this section Christ Incarnate, since the Incarnation continues beyond His earthly life.) Then would come a study of His present and future ministries. The major theological problems appear in the period of Christ's humiliation while in an earthly body, problems like the meaning of *kenosis,* the relation of His two natures, and impeccability.

The doctrine of the person of Christ is crucial to the Christian faith. It is basic to soteriology, for if our Lord was not what He claimed to be, then His atonement was a deficient, not sufficient, payment for sin.

I. THE PREEXISTENCE OF THE PREINCARNATE CHRIST

A. The Meaning of Preexistence

Preexistence of Christ means that He existed before His birth. For some writers it means that He existed before Creation and before time. But strictly speaking, preexistence is not synonymous with eternality. Practically speaking, they stand for a similar concept, for a denial of preexistence almost always includes a denial of eternality and vice versa.

B. The Importance of Preexistence

1. At birth. If Christ came into existence at His birth, then no eternal Trinity exists.

2. Not God. If Christ was not preexistent then He could not be God, because, among other attributes, God is eternal.
3. Liar. If Christ was not preexistent then He lied, because He claimed to be. Then the question arises, what else did He lie about?

C. The Evidence for Preexistence

1. His heavenly origin. Verses that claim heavenly origin for Christ attest to preexistence before birth. Note especially John 3:13 and 31.
2. His work as Creator. If Christ was involved in creating, then, of course, He had to exist before Creation. See John 1:3; Colossians 1:16; and Hebrews 1:2.
3. His relationship with God. He claimed equality of nature with God (John 10:30). He claimed equal glory with the Father before the world began (17:5). Paul also claimed Christ had the same nature as God (Phil. 2:6). These passages are evidences for eternality as well.
4. His attributes. He claimed full Deity, and others attested to it. These claims will be examined later, but for now Colossians 2:9 will suffice—in Christ dwells all the fullness of Deity.
5. His relation to John the Baptist. Though John was born before Jesus, John acknowledged that Jesus existed before him (John 1:15, 30, literally "first of me" but referring to preexistence as the basis for Christ's superiority over John).

II. THE ETERNALITY OF THE PREINCARNATE CHRIST

A. The Meaning of Eternality

Eternality means not only that Christ existed before His birth or even before Creation but that He existed always, eternally. Usually eternality and preexistence stand or fall together, though Arius taught preexistence of the Son but not His eternality. He insisted that if Christ was the Only Begotten He must have had a beginning. Jehovah's Witnesses today have an Arian-like Christology, which denies the eternality of the Logos.

B. The Importance of Eternality

If eternality is denied then (a) there is no Trinity, (b) Christ does not possess full Deity, and (c) He lied.

C. The Evidence for Eternality

His relationship with God as of the same essence demonstrates eternality, since God is eternal. Notice the word *charakter* in Hebrews 1:3, which indicates that Christ is the exact representation of God's nature or essence.

Possession of divine attributes includes the attribute of eternality.

The Old Testament prophets claimed eternality for Messiah. Micah said that His goings forth are from the days of eternity (5:2; see Hab. 1:12). Though the words can mean "from the days of old," that is, from earliest times, they can also mean from eternity. Isaiah 9:6, "Eternal Father," likely refers to Christ as a Father to His people always (thus it only looks forward, not backward to eternity past).

Christ claimed eternality when He declared, "Before Abraham was, I am" (John 8:58 KJV). This is more than limited existence before Abraham was born because He said "I am." "I was" might indicate that He existed for several centuries before Abraham, but I am (*eimi*) states eternality.

John's plain statement was that Christ is God (John 1:1). "The Word was God." Not the Word was divine (as in Moffatt and Goodspeed) since that would require *theios* (as in Acts 17:29 and 2 Pet. 1:3). Nor does John say that the Word was a god (as Jehovah's Witnesses translate it). Definite nouns that precede the verb, as here, regularly lack the definite article.[1]

III. THE ACTIVITY OF THE PREINCARNATE CHRIST

A. His Activity as Creator

1. The extent of it. He was involved in the Creation of all things (John 1:3; Col. 1:16; Heb. 1:2). This demonstrates His power (to be able to create all things).

2. The purpose of it. All things were created for Him (Col. 1:16), meaning for the purpose of achieving His ends in the creation. This demonstrates His prerogative (to have creation serve His purposes).

3. The continuation of it. He also now sustains His creation, for in Him all things hold together (Col. 1:17). This demonstrates His presence (continuing to sustain creation).

B. His Activity as Angel

1. His identity as Angel of Yahweh. Clearly the Angel of Yahweh is a self-manifestation of Yahweh, for He speaks as God, identifies Himself with God, and claims to exercise the prerogatives of God (Gen. 16:7–14; 21:17–18; 22:11–18; 31:11–13; Exod. 3:2; Judg. 2:1–4; 5:23;

6:11–22; 13:3–22; 2 Sam. 24:16; Zech. 1:12; 3:1; 12:8). Yet He is distinguished from Yahweh (Gen. 24:7; Zech. 1:12–13). That He is a Member of the Trinity is indicated by the fact that the appearances of the Angel of Yahweh cease after the Incarnation. This is confirmed by the Old Testament statement that the Angel of God accompanied Israel when they left Egypt (Exod. 14:19; cf. 23:20) and the New Testament statement that the Rock who followed Israel was Christ (1 Cor. 10:4).

2. His ministries as Angel of Yahweh. (1) He often acted as messenger to various people (Gen. 16:7–14; 22:11–18; 31:11–13). (2) He guided and protected Israel (Exod. 14:19; 23:20; 2 Kings 19:35). (3) He was the instrument of judgment on Israel when God sent a pestilence on the people (1 Chron. 21:1–27). (4) He was the agent of refreshment to Elijah (1 Kings 19:5–7).

C. His Other Activities

No other historical activities of Christ are revealed as happening in His preincarnate state. His work as Messiah required the Incarnation, though it was predicted in the Old Testament. Likewise His work as Savior necessitated the Incarnation. The Old Testament does not give specific revelation of the second person as Savior, only God as Savior. To have done so would also have required an Old Testament revelation of the Trinity. Rather that period is called "the times of ignorance" (Acts 17:30).

Though our Lord was not inactive in His preincarnate state, His greatest works necessitated the Incarnation. Nevertheless, He stands magnificent in His person as the eternal God, but, as it were, in the shadows, waiting the spotlight of the Incarnation to reveal His glory and grace (John 1:17; Titus 2:11).

NOTE

1. See Leon Morris, *Commentary on the Gospel of John* (Grand Rapids: Eerdmans, 1971), 77n.

Chapter 41
THE INCARNATION OF CHRIST

I. THE MEANING OF INCARNATION

Though the word itself does not appear in Scripture, its components ("in" and "flesh") do. John wrote that the Word became flesh (John 1:14). He also wrote of Jesus coming in the flesh (1 John 4:2; 2 John 7). By this he meant that the eternal second person of the Trinity took on Himself humanity. He did not possess humanity until the birth, since the Lord became flesh (*egeneto,* John 1:14, in contrast to the four occurrences of *en* in vv. 1–2). However, His humanity was sinless, a fact Paul guards by writing that He came "in the likeness of sinful flesh" (Rom. 8:3).

II. THE PREDICTIONS OF INCARNATION

A. Prediction of the God-Man

In this prophecy concerning Messiah in Isaiah 9:6; Isaiah foretold the union of Deity and humanity in Him. He said that a child would be born (a reference to humanity) and that His character would be such that He may be designated as the Mighty God (*el gibbor,* a reference to Deity). Isaiah uses *el* only in reference to God (see 31:3); *gibbor* means hero. Thus the phrase means a hero whose chief characteristic is that He is God. Thus in this single verse both the humanity and deity of our Lord are predicted.[1]

The name Immanuel reveals the same truth about the Lord (Isa. 7:14). This means more than God's presence with His people in His providential dealings. It means in this text that the very presence of the virgin-born Child brings God to His people.[2]

B. Prediction of the Virgin Birth (Isa. 7:14)

In this prophecy Isaiah foretold the means of the Incarnation as being a virgin birth. Liberals have challenged the translation "virgin" for the Hebrew word *almah,* stating that *bethulah* should have been used if Isaiah unmistakably meant virgin. It is true that *almah* means a sexually mature, marriageable maiden, and *bethulah* means a separated woman, usually a virgin, but not always (Esther 2:17; Ezek. 23:3; Joel 1:8). Thus it is not true to say, as the critics do, that *bethulah* would have been a more precise word to use if Isaiah clearly meant virgin.

Apparently *almah* is not a technical term for virgin but refers to a young woman, one of whose characteristics is virginity (Gen. 24:43). There is no instance where it can be proved that *almah* designates a young woman who is not a virgin. The Septuagint translates it by *parthenos* in two of its seven occurrences, as does Matthew 1:23. Thus the word means a young woman of marriageable age, one of whose characteristics was virginity, and necessarily so in the case of the fulfillment of this prophecy in Christ's birth.

Who is *the* virgin referred to in the prophecy? The interpretations fall into three basic categories. (1) The nonmessianic interpretation that understands the prophecy fulfilled by some unknown woman in the past who may or may not have been a virgin. How then can verse 23 be explained? (2) The strictly messianic interpretation that sees the prophecy referring only to Mary with no reference to any maiden of Isaiah's time. Unquestionably it does refer to Mary (v. 23), but whether to her only is the question. Without a reference to someone in Isaiah's time what value would the sign have been to Ahaz? (3) The prophecy refers both to someone in Isaiah's day and to Mary in the future.

According to this third interpretation, who would be the maiden in Isaiah's day? Again there are three answers: (a) Ahaz's wife; (b) some unknown maiden in Israel; or (c) Isaiah's second wife to whom he was not yet married when the prophecy was given. If (a) is true then the son was Hezekiah. If (b) is true, then the son is unknown. If (c) is true the son was either Maher-shalal-hash-baz (Isa. 8:3) or another unmentioned son of Isaiah. In this view Isaiah's first wife, the mother of Shear-jashub (7:3) had already died.

Matthew unambiguously sees Christ as the fulfillment of Isaiah's prophecy. Of this there can be no question. And both the strictly messianic and the double-reference views acknowledge that.

III. THE MEANS OF INCARNATION

A. The Evidence

The Virgin Birth was the means of the Incarnation. The Incarnation, once accomplished, is a lasting state for our Lord. It began at His birth and continues (albeit in a resurrection body now) forever. In contrast to the Incarnation, the Virgin Birth was an event that lasted only a matter of hours.

When Gabriel announced to Mary that she would bear the Messiah, she protested that she would need a husband. The angel's response was, in essence, you won't need a husband, because the Spirit will come upon you and the power of the Most High will overshadow you (Luke 1:35). The statement emphasizes more the fact of divine generation of the Child than the method.

Matthew carefully guarded the fact of the Virgin Birth in the genealogical table of our Lord (Matt. 1:16). He recorded that Joseph was the husband of Mary, but that it was by Mary only that Jesus was born. The pronoun "by whom" is feminine singular, indicating clearly that Jesus was born of Mary only and not of Mary and Joseph.

Whether Galatians 4:4, "born of a woman," indicates the Virgin Birth or not is unclear. It may simply mean that Christ assumed humanity just like He assumed a position under the Law, as the next phrase says. Or it might refer to the Virgin Birth since the verb is not the regular verb for "be born" but the same verb as in John 1:14 that refers to the Incarnation, though not to the Virgin Birth as such. However, the passages in Isaiah, Matthew, and Luke are clear.

What was the purpose of the Virgin Birth? It need not be the necessary means of preserving Christ sinless, since God could have overshadowed two parents so as to protect the baby's sinlessness had He so desired. It served as a sign of the uniqueness of the person who was born. How early and how widely the fact was known among the contemporaries of Christ we cannot say. Of course, when Matthew and Luke were written it was known, and from that time on the early church regarded it as a crucial doctrine, and by the early second century an established doctrine.[3]

B. The Genealogies

Matthew and Luke both trace the genealogy of the virgin-born Son. Matthew contains forty-one selected names, whereas Luke includes seventy-seven. Matthew traces the King back to Abraham; Luke goes back to Adam. Matthew's list is commonly regarded as Joseph's line and Luke's, Mary's.

There has been much discussion particularly over the question of whether Luke's genealogy is that of Jesus through Mary His mother. Alfred Plummer raised this objection to that view: "It is probable that so obvious a solution, as that one was the pedigree of Joseph and the other the pedigree of Mary, would have been very soon advocated, if there had been any reason (excepting the difficulty) for adopting it. But this solution is not suggested by anyone until Amnnius of Viterbo propounded it, ca. A.D. 1490."[4]

On the other side, F. Godet argued effectively for Mary's lineage in Luke on the basis of the absence of the article before Joseph (3:23), which links Jesus directly with Eli and seemingly puts Joseph out of the genealogical line altogether.[5]

Various explanations are given for both genealogies being Joseph's line. One is that Matthan and Matthat are the same person, making Jacob and Eli brothers and making Joseph the son of Eli and the nephew of Jacob. If Jacob died without heirs his nephew Joseph would have become the heir, or possibly Joseph became the heir of Jacob because Eli (assuming that his wife had died) married Jacob's widow according to the custom of levirate marriage.[6]

A strong argument for the Lucan genealogy being Mary's relates to the curse placed on Jehoiachin (Jeconiah or Coniah) in Jeremiah 22:30. He was pronounced "childless," which is explained in the verse as meaning no physical descendant of his would prosperously reign on the throne of David. (He apparently did have seven sons, though perhaps adopted, 1 Chron. 3:17–18.) Thus Jesus could not expect to be a ruling king (though He had the legal right) if He were a blood descendant of Joseph, who was a descendant of Coniah. Therefore the virgin birth was necessary to free Him from the line of the curse.[7] However, this could also be accomplished if Jesus is linked to Joseph (not as His natural father, of course) through Nathan rather than Solomon (as Luke might be indicating).

It has also been suggested that the curse on Coniah was ended by God's choosing and exalting Zerubbabel (Hag. 2:23 KJV). Making him "as a signet" elevated him to a place of authority, and choosing him transferred to Zerubbabel and his family among David's descendants the messianic promise. Zerubbabel's name does appear in both the Matthew and Luke genealogies.

In any case Luke carefully avoided the impression that Jesus might be the natural son of Joseph; yet he preserved His kingly claims by not linking Him solely to His mother (since the claim passed through the male members). Never in His lifetime did anyone dispute Jesus' claim to the throne of David.

IV. THE PURPOSES OF THE INCARNATION

Why did God send His Son in the likeness of sinful flesh? The Scriptures give several answers to that question.

A. To Reveal God to Us

Though God reveals Himself in various ways, including the magnificences of nature around us, only the Incarnation revealed the essence of God, though veiled (John 1:18; 14:7–11). The only way man can see the Father is to know about the Son, and the only way we can do that today is through studying the record of His life in the Scriptures. Because He became a man, the revelation of God was personalized; because He is God, that revelation is completely truthful.

B. To Provide an Example for Our Lives

The earthly life of our Lord is held up to us as a pattern for our living today (1 Pet. 2:21; 1 John 2:6). Without the Incarnation we would not have that example. As man He experienced the vicissitudes of life and furnishes for us an experienced example; as God He offers us the power to follow His example.

C. To Provide an Effective Sacrifice for Sin

Without the Incarnation we would have no Savior. Sin requires death for its payment. God does not die. So the Savior must be human in order to be able to die. But the death of an ordinary man would not pay for sin eternally, so the Savior must also be God. We must have a God-man Savior, and we do in our Lord (Heb. 10:1–10).

D. To Be Able to Fulfill the Davidic Covenant

Gabriel announced to Mary that her Son would be given the throne of David (Luke 1:31–33). This is not fulfilled by the invisible God reigning over the affairs of men (which He does, to be sure). To have an occupant of David's throne requires a human being. Therefore, Messiah had to be a human being. But to occupy that throne forever requires that the occupant never die. And only God qualifies. So the One who ultimately fulfills the Davidic promise has to be a God-man.

E. To Destroy the Works of the Devil (1 John 3:8)

Notice that this was done by Christ's appearing. The focus is on His coming, not on His resurrection as might be expected. Why was the Incarnation necessary to defeat Satan? Because Satan must be defeated in the arena he dominates, this world. So Christ was sent into this world to destroy Satan's works.

F. To Be Able to Be a Sympathetic High Priest (Heb. 4:14–16)

Our High Priest can feel our weaknesses because He was tested as we are. But God is never tested, so it was necessary that God become man so that He could be tested in order to be a sympathetic Priest.

G. To Be Able to Be a Qualified Judge

Though most people think of God the Father as the Judge before whom all will appear, the truth is that Jesus will be that Judge (John 5:22, 27). All judgment will be executed by our Lord "because He is the Son of Man." This is the title that links Him to the earth and to His earthly mission. Why is it necessary for the Judge to be human and to have lived on earth? So that He may put down all excuses people might try to make. Why must the Judge also be God? So that His judgment will be true and just.

Thus the Incarnation has ramifications in relation to our knowledge of God, to our salvation, to our daily living, to our pressing needs, and to the future. It truly is the central fact of history.

NOTES

1. See Edward J. Young, *The Book of Isaiah* (Grand Rapids: Eerdmans, 1964), 1:335–38.
2. Ibid., 1:289–91.
3. Ignatius *Smyrna* I.1, for example; see also Hans von Campenhausen, *The Virgin Birth in the Theology of the Ancient Church, Studies in Historical Theology* (Naperville: Allenson, 1964), 2:10–20.
4. Alfred Plummer, *A Critical and Exegetical Commentary on the Gospel According to Luke* (ICC, Edinburgh: T. & T. Clark, 1910), 103.
5. F. Godet, *A Commentary on the Gospel of St. Luke* (Edinburgh: T. &. T. Clark, 1910), 1:195–204.
6. See J. G. Machen, *The Virgin Birth of Christ* (New York: Harper, 1930), 207–9.
7. See Robert Gromacki, *The Virgin Birth of Christ* (Grand Rapids: Baker, 1981), 150–59.

MINISTRIES OF THE GOD-MAN

TITLE	REFERENCE	MAN	GOD
SAVIOR	ROMANS 1:3–4	TO DIE	TO GIVE DEATH MEANING
HIGH PRIEST	HEBREWS 4:14–16	TO REPRESENT MAN AS A SACRIFICE FOR SIN	TO REPRESENT HIS PEOPLE BEFORE GOD
JUDGE	JOHN 5:22	TO JUDGE AS A PEER	TO JUDGE RIGHTEOUSLY
SOURCE OF CHRISTIAN LIVING	1 JOHN 2:6	TO BE OUR EXAMPLE	TO EMPOWER OUR LIVES

Chapter 42
THE PERSON OF CHRIST INCARNATE

The statement on the person of Christ incarnate formulated at the Council at Chalcedon (A.D. 451) has been considered definitive by orthodox Christianity. It reads as follows:

> Therefore, following the holy fathers, we all with one accord teach men to acknowledge one and the same Son, our Lord Jesus Christ, at once complete in Godhead and complete in manhood, truly God and truly man, consisting also of a reasonable soul and body; of one substance with the Father as regards His Godhead, and at the same time of one substance with us as regards His manhood; like us in all respects apart from sin; as regards His Godhead, begotten of the Father before the ages, but yet as regards His manhood begotten, for us men and for our salvation, of Mary the virgin, the God-bearer; one and the same Christ, Son, Lord, Only-Begotten, recognized in two natures, without confusion, without change, without division, without separation; the distinction of natures being in no way annulled by the union, but rather the characteristics of each nature being preserved and coming together to form one Person and subsistence, not as parted or separated into two Persons, but one and the same Son and only-begotten God the Word, Lord Jesus Christ; even as the prophets from earliest times spoke of Him, and our Lord Jesus Christ Himself taught us, and the creed of the fathers has been handed down to us.

More concisely one may describe the person of Christ incarnate as being full Deity and perfect humanity united without mixture, change, division, or separation in one person forever. The key components of the description include "full Deity" (no diminution of any attribute of Deity), "perfect humanity" ("perfect" rather than "full" in order to emphasize His sinlessness), "one Person" (not two), and "forever" (for He continues to have a body, though resurrected, Acts 1:11; Rev. 5:6).

I. THE FULL DEITY OF CHRIST INCARNATE

A. He Possesses Attributes That Only God Has

1. Eternality. He claimed to exist from eternity past (John 8:58; 17:5).

2. Omnipresence. He claimed to be everywhere present (Matt. 18:20; 28:20).
3. Omniscience. He showed knowledge of things that could only be known if He were omniscient (Matt. 16:21; Luke 6:8; 11:17; John 4:29).
4. Omnipotence. He demonstrated and claimed the power of an omnipotent person (Matt. 28:18; Mark 5:11–15; John 11:38–44).

Other attributes of Deity are claimed for Him by others (e.g., immutability, Heb. 13:8), but these cited are claims He made for Himself.

B. He Performs Works That Only God Can Do

1. Forgiveness. He forgives sins eternally. Men may do that temporarily, but Christ grants eternal forgiveness (Mark 2:1–12).
2. Life. He gives spiritual life to whomever He wishes (John 5:21).
3. Resurrection. He will raise the dead (John 11:43).
4. Judgment. He will judge all people (John 5:22, 27).

Again, all of these examples are things He did or claims He made, not claims others made of Him.

C. He Was Given the Names and Titles of Deity

1. Son of God. Our Lord used this designation of Himself (though rarely, John 10:36), and He acknowledged its truthfulness when it was used by others of Him (Matt. 26:63–64). What does it mean? Though the phrase "son of" can mean "offspring of," it also carries the meaning "of the order of." Thus in the Old Testament "sons of the prophets" meant of the order of prophets (1 Kings 20:35), and "sons of the singers" meant of the order of the singers (Neh. 12:28). The designation "Son of God" when used of our Lord means of the order of God and is a strong and clear claim to full Deity.

> In Jewish usage the term Son of . . . did not generally imply any subordination, but rather equality and identity of nature. Thus Bar Kokba, who led the Jewish revolt 135–132 B.C. in the reign of Hadrian, was called by a name which means "Son of the Star." It was supposed that he took this name to identify himself as the very Star predicted in Numbers 24:17. The name "Son of Encouragement" (Acts 4:36) doubtless means, "The Encourager." "Sons of Thunder" (Mark 3:17) probably means "Thunderous Men." "Son of man," especially as applied to Christ in Daniel 7:13 and constantly in the New Testament, essentially means "The Representative Man." Thus for Christ to say, "I am the Son of God" (John 10:36) was understood by His contemporaries as identifying Himself as God, equal with the Father, in an unqualified sense.[1]

2. *Lord and God.* Jesus is called Yahweh in the New Testament, a clear indication of His full Deity (cf. Luke 1:76 with Mal. 3:1 and Rom. 10:13 with Joel 2:32). He is also called God (John 1:1; 20:28; Heb. 1:8), Lord (Matt. 22:43–45), and King of kings and Lord of lords (Rev. 19:16).

D. He Claimed to Be God

Perhaps the strongest and clearest occasion of such a claim was at the Feast of Dedication when He said, "I and the Father are one" (John 10:30). The neuter form of "one" rules out the meaning that He and the Father were one person. It means that they are in perfect unity in natures and actions, a fact that could only be true if He were as much Deity as the Father. The people who heard this claim understood it that way, for they immediately tried to stone Him for blasphemy because He made Himself out to be God (v. 33).

How can anyone say that Jesus of Nazareth Himself never claimed to be God, but rather that His followers made the claim for Him? Most of the passages cited above are from Christ's own words. Therefore, one must face the only options: either His claims were true or He was a liar. And these claims are for full and complete Deity—nothing missing or removed during His life on earth.

II. THE PERFECT HUMANITY OF CHRIST INCARNATE

Denials of the humanity of Christ are less common than denials of His deity. Why? Because as long as you do not inject the Deity factor into the person of Christ, He is only a man, however fine or exalted, and as merely a man He cannot disturb people with His claims so much as if He is the God-man. However, those who may readily affirm His humanity may not so readily affirm His perfect humanity. They may acknowledge Him as a good man (how so if He lied?) or a great man (how so if He misled others?) but not as a perfect man (for then they might feel more obligated to listen to Him even though they may not acknowledge Him as God).

A. He Had a Human Body

Though Christ's conception was supernatural, He was born with a human body that grew and developed (Luke 2:52). He called Himself a man (John 8:40).

B. He Had a Human Soul and Spirit

The perfect humanity of our Lord included a perfect immaterial nature as well as a material one. It was not that the human nature provided Christ's body while the divine nature consisted of soul and spirit. The humanity was complete and included both material and immaterial aspects (Matt. 26:38; Luke 23:46).

C. He Exhibited the Characteristics of a Human Being

Our Lord was hungry (Matt. 4:2). He was thirsty (John 19:28). He grew weary (4:6). He experienced love and compassion (Matt. 9:36). He wept (John 11:35). He was tested (Heb. 4:15). These are characteristics of true humanity.

D. He Was Called by Human Names

His favorite designation of Himself was "Son of Man" (more than eighty times). This name linked Him to the earth and to His mission on earth. It focused on His lowliness and humanity (Matt. 8:20); on His suffering and death (Luke 19:10); and on His future reign as King (Matt. 24:27).

He was also the Son of David, a title that linked Him to His ancestor David and to the royal promises to be fulfilled ultimately by Messiah.

Paul called Him a man in 1 Timothy 2:5.

III. THE UNION OF DEITY AND HUMANITY IN CHRIST INCARNATE

This concept of the hypostatic or one-person union of the divine and human natures in one person is probably one of the most difficult concepts to comprehend in theology. Not one of us has ever seen Deity except as the Scriptures reveal God, and not one of us has ever seen perfect humanity except as the Scriptures reveal prefallen Adam and our Lord. To try to relate these two concepts to the person of Christ adds complexities to ideas that are in themselves difficult to comprehend.

A. The Meaning of "Nature"

Though the English words "nature" and "substance" can be synonymous, meaning essence, we need to make a distinction between the two words for theological purposes. If nature is conceived of as a substantive entity, then nature and substance would be the same, and the incarnate Christ would consist of two substances, and would be essentially two persons, as Nestorianism held. But if "nature" is viewed as a "complex of attributes"[2] this error is more apt to be avoided. The single person of the incarnate Christ retained the total complex of divine attributes and possessed all the complex of human attributes essential to a perfect human being.

B. The Character of the Union

The Chalcedonian Creed stated that the two "natures" were united without mixture, without change, without division, and without separation. This means that the entire complex of the attributes of Deity and those of perfect humanity were maintained in Jesus Christ at all times since His Incarnation. There is no mixture of divine and human attributes (as Eutychians taught), no change in either complex (as Apollinarians taught), no dividing of them, and no separating them so as to have two persons (as Nestorianism taught). Orthodoxy says Jesus has two natures comprising one person or hypostasis forever. It is correct to characterize Christ as a theoanthropic person, but not accurate to speak of theoanthropic natures (since that would mix the divine and human attributes).

Calvinism has held that the union involves no transfer of attributes from one nature to the other. Lutheranism teaches the ubiquity of Christ's body, which does involve a transfer of the attribute of omnipresence to the humanity of Christ. In other words, ubiquitarianism holds that Christ is present in His human nature everywhere and at all times. Luther developed this doctrine in 1527–28 to support his belief in the Real Presence in the Lord's Supper.

C. The Communion of Attributes

This simply means that the attributes of both natures belong to the one person without mixing the natures or dividing the person. Practically speaking, it is the basis for Christ being seen to be weak, yet omnipotent; ignorant, yet omniscient; limited, yet infinite.

I have said that attributes cannot be transferred from one nature to the other. To do so would change the mix of the complex of attributes and thus the nature. If infinity can be transferred to humanity, then Deity loses infinity and is no longer full Deity. However, attributes of both natures must be expressed through the one person. Thus the person can seem to "transfer" back and forth from the expression of one or the other natures, though the attributes themselves must remain as part of whichever nature they properly belong to. Thus theologians have developed a system to classify the actions of the person of Christ with respect to origination of the action. Hodge has four categories, and Walvoord has seven.[3] Some examples include (a) actions predicated on the whole person, like redemption (both natures being involved); (b) actions predicated on the divine nature (though the whole person is the subject), like preexistence (true only of the divine nature); and (c) actions predicated on the human nature, like being thirsty.

Whatever help such a classification may give, it seems more important to remember that the person does whatever He does, revealing whatever attribute of whichever nature He reveals. The person thirsted; the person knew all things; the person does not know the day or the hour; and (probably the hardest one) the person died. Of course, Deity does not die or thirst, but the person, Jesus Christ, the God-man, did both.

D. The Self-Consciousness of Christ

Another question is whether Christ in His own self-consciousness was aware of His deity and humanity at all times. The answer is that the person was always aware in Himself with respect to His deity and that the person grew in self-consciousness with respect to His humanity (Luke 2:52; John 8:56–58).

E. The Will(s) of Christ

Did Christ have one or two wills? Chalcedon said one Christ in two natures united in one person, implying two wills. In the seventh century the Monothelites insisted that Christ had but one will, but this view was declared heresy by the Council at Constantinople in 680. If will is defined as a "behavior complex" as Buswell does, then our Lord may be said to have had a divine behavior pattern and a perfect human one as well; hence two wills. If will is defined as the resulting moral decision as Walvoord does, then the person of Christ always made only one moral decision; hence one will. However, it seems to me that every single decision stemmed from either the "will" of His divine nature or the "will" of His human nature or a blending of both, making it proper to think of two "wills."

IV. EARLY HISTORY OF THIS DOCTRINE

A. Docetism

In the late first century Marcion and the Gnostics taught that Christ only appeared to be a man (*dokeo,* to seem or to appear). The apostle John referred to this false teaching in 1 John 4:1–3. This heresy undermines not only the reality of the Incarnation but also the validity of the Atonement and bodily resurrection.

B. Ebionism

In the second century this heresy denied the deity of Christ, considering Jesus to be the natural son of Joseph and Mary but elected to be Son of God at His baptism when He was united with the eternal Christ.

C. Arianism

A heresy that denied the eternality of Jesus as the Logos. Arius reasoned that since Jesus was begotten, He must have had a beginning. Arians held that the divine nature of Christ was similar to God, *homoousian,* but not the same, *homoousian.* The Council of Nicaea condemned this teaching in A.D. 325, affirming that Jesus had the same nature as God.

D. Apollinarianism

Apollinarius, the younger (died about 390), sought to avoid undue separation of the natures of Christ. He taught that Christ had a human body and a human soul, but that He had the divine Logos instead of a human spirit (this assumes a trichotomous view of man). This Logos dominated the passive human body and soul. This was an error affecting the humanity of Christ.

E. Nestorianism

Nestorianism divided Christ into two persons (though it is disputed whether or not Nestorius himself clearly taught this). He explained that Jesus Christ was the *prosopon* (form or appearance) of the union of two natures. The humanity had the form of Godhead bestowed on it, and the Deity took upon itself the form of a servant, the result being the appearance of Jesus of Nazareth. Thus in this view the two natures were separated, resulting in two persons. The teaching was condemned by the Council of Ephesus in 431.

F. Eutychianism

Eutyches (ca. 378–454) reacted against Nestorianism and taught that there was only one nature in Christ. This error is also known as monophysitism. The divine nature was not fully divine, nor was the human nature genuinely human, and the result was a mixed single nature. This was condemned at the Council of Chalcedon in 451.

A similar error developed after Chalcedon that taught that Christ had only one will though conceding verbally that He had two natures. It is called monothelitism. This was condemned at the third council of Constantinople in 680.

A study of errors should help clarify the truth and make us more careful how we express it. Semantics are very important in the statements of theology.

GROUP	TIME	HUMAN NATURE	DIVINE NATURE	CHURCH COUNCIL
Docetists	1st century	Denied–only an appearance of humanity	Affirmed	
Ebionites	2nd century	Affirmed	Denied–Jesus was natural son of Joseph and Mary	
Arians	4th century	Affirmed	Denied–Jesus not eternal; similar to, but not same as God	Condemned by Nicea, 325
Apollinarians	4th century	Divine Logos replaced human spirit	Affirmed	Condemned by Constantinople, 680
Nestorians	5th century	Christ was two Persons		Condemned by Ephesus, 431
Eutychians	5th century	Not fully human Christ was a single mixed nature	Not fully divine	Condemned by Chalcedon, 451
Orthodoxy		Perfect humanity Christ is one Person	Full deity	Defined by Chalcedon, 451

NOTES

1. J. Oliver Buswell, *A Systematic Theology of the Christian Religion* (Grand Rapids: Zondervan, 1962), 1:105.
2. Ibid., 1:54.
3. Charles Hodge, *Systematic Theology* (Grand Rapids: Eerdmans, 1960), 2:78ff; John F. Walvoord, *Jesus Christ Our Lord* (Chicago: Moody, 1974), 116–17.

Chapter 43
CHRIST: PROPHET, PRIEST, AND KING

Sometimes the work of Christ is considered under this threefold division of the offices of Christ as Prophet, Priest, and King. Eusebius (ca. 260–340) used these categories, so they have great antiquity.[1] Furthermore, a connection can be made between Messiah, the Anointed One, and the fact that prophets (1 Kings 19:16; Isa. 61:1), priests (Exod. 30:30; 40:13) and kings (1 Sam. 10:1; 15:1; 1 Kings 19:15–16) were all inaugurated by anointing.

I. CHRIST AS PROPHET

A. The Designation of Christ as Prophet

Moses predicted that God would raise up a prophet like himself (Deut. 18:15). Whatever other fulfillments this may have had in the succession of Old Testament prophets, its ultimate fulfillment was by Jesus Christ, who is identified as that Prophet (Acts 3:22–24). The ordinary people of Christ's day acknowledged Him as a prophet so enthusiastically that the chief priests and Pharisees feared reprisals if they took any strong action against the Lord (Matt. 21:11, 46; John 7:40–53). Further, the people called Him Rabbi (John 1:38; 3:2), not because He had been trained formally, but because they recognized the quality of His teaching.

Our Lord also claimed to be a Prophet (Matt. 13:57; Mark 6:4; Luke 4:24; 13:33; John 4:44) who came to do what prophets did, that is, deliver God's message to man (John 8:26; 12:49–50; 15:15; 17:8).

B. The Manner of Christ as Prophet

One of our Lord's principal activities while on earth was proclaiming God's message through preaching (Matt. 4:17) and teaching (7:29). The manner of His preaching and teaching included these interesting characteristics.

1. It was an occasional thing. This does not mean He taught infrequently, but rather as the occasion arose. He was always open to opportunities and the variety of situations that presented themselves. He used the synagogue services when possible (Mark 1:21). He preached outdoors if an indoor situation was unavailable (4:1). He seized every opportunity.

2. It was unsystematic. This was due to the fact that He took opportunities as they arose, rather than waiting until a planned curriculum could be followed. Think, for example, of where you will find the Lord's teaching on sin; and the answer is in various passages of various types—some didactic, some parabolic. The interpreter of Scripture has to systematize Christ's teachings.

3. It was profusely illustrated. Those illustrations were themselves varied and appropriately chosen for the audience (notice an illustration for women and men in Matthew 24:40–41 and Luke 15:4, 8).

4. It made use of questions. This was true especially in situations of controversy (Matt. 22).

5. It was authoritative. This was probably the outstanding feature of Christ's ministry as a Prophet. His authority stood in sharp contrast to the teaching of the scribes and Pharisees (Mark 1:22) because it probed the depths of the reality of the truth.

C. The Material of Christ as Prophet

Though much of His prophetic material is scattered throughout the Gospels, four major messages are preserved for us: the Sermon on the Mount (Matt. 5–7), the parables of the mysteries of the kingdom (Matt. 13), the conversation with four of His disciples on the Mount of Olives on Tuesday of Holy Week (Matt. 24–25), and the message to the disciples in the Upper Room on Thursday evening (John 13–16).

The teachings of Christ are possibly the most difficult part of the entire Bible to interpret accurately. Why is this so? Because our Lord lived under the Mosaic Law and perfectly kept it; but He also presented Himself to Israel as their King; and when He was rejected as King, He introduced the new part of God's program, the church, and gave some teaching about it. In other words, He lived and taught in relation to three different aspects of God's program for this world—the Law, the church, and the kingdom. To keep those strands of teaching distinct and without confusion is not always easy.

1. The Sermon on the Mount. Some view this discourse as an exposition of the way of salvation. The problem with such an interpretation is simply that the great salvation words like redemption or justification do not occur at all in these chapters. Also, if this is the correct interpretation, then salvation is surely through good works.

Others consider the sermon a blueprint for Christian living today. To use it this way would require deliteralizing much of what is taught in order to be able to obey it in this unrighteous world. Further, if this is truth for the church, then why did our Lord not mention the Holy Spirit, so important for Christian living, or even the church itself?

Still others understand its primary purpose to relate to Christ's kingdom message. The forerunner, John, had announced the kingdom (Matt. 3:2); Christ Himself began to preach that message (Matt. 4:17); now He explained what was involved in true repentance. The kingdom they preached and the kingdom the people expected was that messianic, Davidic, millennial kingdom promised in the Old Testament. Christ gave no indication that they should have understood otherwise by changing the meaning of the kingdom He was talking about. But the people had placed their hopes so much on a political kingdom that they forgot there were spiritual requirements for even that political kingdom. So the Lord explained what was involved in spiritual preparation for the Davidic kingdom.

Preached in relation to the kingdom, this discourse seems mainly to emphasize getting ready for the kingdom. Some of the requirements to be practiced totally would necessitate the establishment of the kingdom with its righteous government (Matt. 5:38–42) though the general principle may be followed anytime.

So the sermon is a call to repentance for those who had disassociated inner change from the requirements for establishing the kingdom. Therefore, it has relevance for any time that the kingdom is imminent—which includes the time Christ preached it, and the future time of the Tribulation. It also pictures conditions as they will be in the kingdom when it is established. But, like all Scripture, it is profitable for disciples in any age since it is one of the most detailed ethical codes in the Bible.

2. Parabolic mysteries about the kingdom. Later on the same day as the blasphemous accusation of the scribes and Pharisees (Matt. 12:22–37), the Lord turned to His disciples to instruct them about the characteristics of the kingdom in this time between His death and return. These are called "mysteries" since they were unknown in the Old Testament but are now revealed to those rightly related to Him (Matt. 13:11). These characteristics of God's kingdom are different from those of the Davidic kingdom, past and future, and they cover a period yet future from the time when Christ spoke these words (v. 24 "is like" [NIV] is an aorist used proleptically, that is, in anticipation of something future) and terminating with events at His Second Coming (vv. 39–50).

Among other things, these parables relate different people's responses to the message, the presence of Satan's counterfeits in the kingdom, the rapid growth of the kingdom, evil in the kingdom, the value of the kingdom, and the presence of wicked people in the kingdom. This form of the kingdom is temporary—until He returns.

3. The message on the Mount of Olives. By the time this message was given at the end of Christ's earthly life, it was quite clear that the Jewish leaders had rejected the kingdom, and Christ Himself had introduced the church as the coming thing in God's program (Matt. 16:18). Did this mean that the kingdom was scratched from God's program forever? Not at all, and this message details some future events leading up to the return of Christ to establish that messianic, Davidic, millennial kingdom. Matthew 24:4–14 lists details that will happen during the first part of the coming Tribulation period. Verses 15–28 do the same for the second half of that period. Then Christ will return to earth and take the throne of His kingdom (v. 30; 25:31, 34). That this did not occur in the disciples' lifetimes as they expected in no way abrogates the assurance that one day Christ will rule in His kingdom (Acts 1:6).

4. The message in the Upper Room. The night before His crucifixion the Lord revealed in capsule form a number of things about the new Church Age soon to be inaugurated. He repeated these things in capsule form because the disciples could not yet understand what was really happening (John 16:12). What were some of those new revelations? (1) He gave a new command—to love each other in the same way He loves us (13:34). (2) He opened up a new hope—a place that He would prepare and take believers (14:1–3). (3) He promised another Paraclete who would minister in a number of new ways: advising, exhorting, comforting, interceding, convicting, teaching, etc. (v. 16). (4) He unveiled new relationships—the Holy Spirit in them, not just with them, believers in Christ, and Christ in believers (vv. 17, 20). (5) He established a new basis for prayer in His name (16:24, 26). All of these reveal tremendous differences between the economy then operative and the coming new dispensation of the church.

D. The Authentication of Christ as Prophet

The Law commanded that false prophets be stoned (Deut. 13:5,

10). Of course if a prophet lived to the time when his prophecy was either fulfilled or not, you could easily tell if he were a true or false prophet. If he did not, then it was more difficult. Our Lord's prophetic ministry was authenticated in two ways: by the fact that some of His prophecies came true in His lifetime and by the miracles that verified to the people of His day that He was a true Prophet.

The test case is His detailed prediction of His death. He prophesied that someone close to Him would betray Him (Matt. 26:21), that His death would be instigated by the Jewish leaders (16:21), that He would die by crucifixion and that three days later He would come back to life (20:19). For anyone to be able to give this kind of detail about His death and for these details to come true authenticates Him as a true Prophet.

In addition, some of Christ's miracles were directly linked as attesting to His being a true Prophet (Luke 7:16; John 4:19; 9:17). Truly in these last days God has spoken to us by His Son (Heb. 1:1–2).

II. CHRIST AS PRIEST

The prophet spoke to men from God; the priest speaks to God for men. Being of the tribe of Judah disqualified Christ from being an Aaronic priest; therefore, God arranged ahead of His coming for another order of priests, the order of Melchizedek, and Christ is a priest of that order with respect to His person and His work. Yet there are similarities between Aaronic priests and Christ as Priest both in His person and His work.

A. As Aaronic Priest

An Aaronic priest had to be a man chosen by God and qualified for His work (Lev. 21; Heb. 5:1–7). Our Lord, chosen, incarnate, and tested, qualified in His person to be a ministering Priest.

Aaronic priests served by representing the people to God and especially in offering sacrifices. Their sacrifices were many, repeated, and not in themselves eternally efficacious. They did make atonement for sin in the context of the theocracy, but the writer to the Hebrews makes it clear that had they been able to effect eternal satisfaction for sin there would have been no need for their repetition year after year (10:2–3). In contrast, our Lord's sacrifice of Himself for our sins was a single sacrifice, once for all, and for all mankind. In this, His great work of redemption, He did a work that was foreshadowed by the work of the Aaronic priests, even though He was not a priest after the order of Aaron.

B. As Melchizedekan Priest

The portrait of Melchizedek in Genesis 14:18–20 and Hebrews 7:1–3 seems deliberately limited to those features that liken him to Christ. The form of "made like" in 7:3 is not an adjective that would indicate that Melchizedek was like Christ in his being (lending weight to the interpretation that he was a theophany), but a participle, meaning that the likeness is being made by the biblical writer's statement. The features of the portrait are limited so that the resemblance may be more extensive.

Features of the Melchizedekan priesthood include these:

(1) It was a royal priesthood. Melchizedek was a king as well as a priest. The uniting of these two functions was unknown among Aaronic priests, though predicted of Christ in Zechariah 6:13.

(2) It was unrelated to ancestry. "Without father, without mother" (Heb. 7:3) does not mean that Melchizedek did not have parents, nor that he was not born or did not die, but only that the Scriptures contain no record of these events so that he might be more perfectly likened to Christ. Aaronic priests depended on their ancestry to qualify.

(3) It was timeless, having no recorded beginning or ending so Melchizedek might again be more like the Lord who is a Priest forever after the order of Melchizedek.

(4) It was superior to the Aaronic order. Abraham, out of whom came the Aaronic order, acknowledged the superiority of Melchizedek when he gave tithes of the spoils of the war to him (Gen. 14:20). Levi, though unborn, and all the priests that came from him, were involved in this act that demonstrated the superiority of Melchizedek.

In what ways does Christ function as a Melchizedekan priest? Like Melchizedek He is a ruler. He receives our obeisance. He blesses us. And as Melchizedek offered bread and wine to Abraham to refresh and sustain him after the battle, so our Lord as Priest refreshes and sustains His people. He did this, for example, to Stephen at the time of his martyrdom. Our Lord was standing to sustain Stephen (Acts 7:55). He does the same today with respect to local churches as He walks among the golden lampstands (Rev. 2:1). His work of redemption is finished, so He is seen seated, indicating He will never have to rise again to do it over or to add to it in any way (Heb. 1:3). But His ministry of helping and sustaining goes on, so He is seen standing to do this. We have a great High Priest standing and ready to come to the aid of those who are tested (2:18) and anxious to give grace to help in time of need (4:16).

III. CHRIST AS KING

The concept of king includes a wide range of prerogatives. A king in Israel had legislative, executive, judicial, economic, and military powers. The concept of Christ as King may be surveyed around five words: promised, predicted, proffered, rejected, and realized. God's gracious covenant with David promised that the right to rule would always remain with David's dynasty. It did not promise uninterrupted rule, for, in fact, the Babylonian Captivity did interrupt it (2 Sam. 7:12–16). Isaiah predicted that the Child who would be born would establish and reign on the throne of David (Isa. 9:7).

Gabriel announced to Mary that her Baby would have the throne of David and reign over the house of Jacob (Luke 1:32–33). Throughout His earthly ministry Jesus' Davidic kingship was proffered to Israel (Matt. 2:2; 27:11; John 12:13), but He was rejected.

The Gadarenes repudiated His claims (Matt. 8:34). The scribes rejected His claim to be able to forgive sins (9:3). Many people in various cities rejected His credentials (11:20–30; 13:53–58). The Pharisees rejected Him (12; 15:1–20; 22:15–23). Herod, Pontius Pilate, Gentiles, and Jews all rejected Him with finality at the Crucifixion (John 1:11; Acts 4:27).

Because the King was rejected, the messianic, Davidic kingdom was (from a human viewpoint) postponed. Though He never ceases to be King and, of course, is King today as always, Christ is never designated as King of the church (Acts 17:7 and 1 Timothy 1:17 are no exceptions, and Revelation 15:3, "King of saints," KJV, is "King of the nations" in the critical and majority texts). Though Christ is a King today, He does not rule as King. This awaits His second coming. Then the Davidic kingdom will be realized (Matt. 25:31; Rev. 19:15; 20). Then the Priest will sit on His throne, bringing to this earth the long-awaited Golden Age (Ps. 110).

NOTE

1. Eusebius *Ecclesiastical History* I.iii, 8, 9.

Chapter 44
THE SELF-EMPTYING OF CHRIST

I. THE ORIGIN OF THE CONCEPT

The question of Christ's self-emptying or *kenosis* (from the verb in Phil. 2:7) has been discussed throughout church history. The Synod of Antioch in 341 said that Christ emptied Himself of "the being equal with God" while clearly defending the full deity of Christ. During the Reformation the discussion centered on the possibility of Christ emptying Himself of the attributes of omnipotence, omniscience, and omnipresence without affecting essential Deity. In the seventeenth century some boldly asserted that Christ was actually less than divine. But the nineteenth century brought an almost new form of Christology with the appearance and spread of many false ideas of the *kenosis.* This was due to the fact that that century saw the rise of many new scientific theories like evolution and radical criticism. It also brought an emphasis on the rediscovery of the "real" humanity of Jesus and with it the magnitude of His self-denial and self-emptying.

Of course, there is a true statement of *kenosis* since it is taught in Philippians 2:7, and that statement does not contradict other truths that the Scriptures reveal about the Lord. Actually the Bible does not elaborate a doctrine of *kenosis,* though basic elements usable in forming a true statement are revealed. To put this all together and to avoid heresy is the task of this chapter.

II. THE TRUE MEANING OF THE CONCEPT

A. The Central Passage

The central passage on the *kenosis,* Philippians 2:5–11, begins with an exhortation to humility of mind, following the example of Christ who left glory to suffer on the cross. Then follows this concise statement about the preincarnate and incarnate Christ.

1. The eternal existence of Christ (v. 6). This is clearly stated by the form *hyparchon,* which in this present participle (especially as contrasted with the following aorists) declares Christ's indefinite continuance of being. There is in the choice of this word (in contrast to *eimi*) a suggestion of being already (as in Acts 7:55), thus underscoring the eternality of His existence. That indefinite existence was in the *morphe* of God, the essential form including the whole nature and essence of Deity. If "form of God" implies anything less than fully God, then "form of a bond-servant" in Philippians 2:7 would have to mean that on earth Christ was something less than a servant. But the full reality of His being a Servant is the point of the passage. Likewise, the full reality of His deity is the point of "form of God" in verse 6.

J. B. Lightfoot, after a detailed study of *morphē* in Greek philosophy, in Philo, and in the New Testament, concluded that it connotes that which is intrinsic and essential to the thing. Thus here it means that our Lord in His preincarnate state possessed essential Deity.[1]

Paul then reinforced Christ's deity by asserting that coequality with God was not something to be grasped, simply because He always had it. He did not covet it; He had no need to, for it was His eternally. Nor did He exploit it; rather, He willingly emptied Himself.

2. The self-emptying (vv. 7–8). Notice that whatever the emptying involved, it was self-imposed. No one forced Christ to come into this world and eventually die on a cross as our Sin-bearer. Other uses of the verb *empty* are found in Romans 4:14 (void); 1 Corinthians 1:17 (void); 9:15; 2 Corinthians 9:3: but they do not really contribute to the understanding of this passage.

Of what did this consist? Of all that was involved in His eventual death on the cross. This included taking the form (*morphē*) of a slave. Yet in this form He was no less at the same time in the form of God though His glory was veiled to most (but see John 1:14). To take the form of a slave He had to be human, something the next two phrases in Philippians 2:7–8 describe. He was made "in the likeness of men." "Likeness" indicates two things: first that He was really like men, and second that He was different from men. His humanity subjected Him to trials and limitations; yet the word "likeness" guards against concluding that He was identical with men. He was different because He was sinless (see Rom. 8:3). Further, He was found in the appearance (*schema*) of a man. This word refers to that which is outward; i.e., in actions, dress, manners, and all appearances He was a man. Thus He humbled Himself and became obedient to death on a cross, the epitome of shame.

The movement of the passage starts with Christ's preincarnate glory and proceeds to His shameful death on the cross. Obviously, in order to die, He had to become man. In order to do that He had to empty Himself of His preincarnate position, yet without diminishing the Person. There was no way He could become a man and remain in the position He had in His preincarnate state. But He could and did become a man while retaining the complete attributes of His preincarnate Person, that is, of full Deity.

The self-emptying permitted the addition of humanity and did not involve in any way the subtraction of Deity or canceling the use of the attributes of Deity. There was a change of form but not of content of the Divine Being. He did not give up Deity or the use of those attributes; He added humanity. And this in order to be able to die. Isaiah put it this way: "He poured out Himself to death" (53:12).

It seems to me that even evangelicals blunt the point of the passage by missing its principal emphasis as suggested above and focusing on trying to delineate what limitations Christ experienced in His earthly state. To be sure, the God-*man* experienced limitations; but equally sure the *God*-man evidenced the prerogatives of Deity. Therefore, conservatives suggest that the *kenosis* means the veiling of Christ's preincarnate glory, which is true only in a relative sense (see Matt. 17:1–8; John 1:14; 17:5). Or they suggest it means the voluntary nonuse of some of His attributes of Deity. This was true on occasion but certainly not always throughout His life (see John 1:48; 2:24; 16:30). Neither did He only do His miracles always in the power of the Spirit, but sometimes in His own power (Luke 22:51; John 18:6). So if our understanding of *kenosis* comes from Philippians 2, we should get our definition of the concept there. And that passage does not discuss at all the question of how or how much Christ's glory was veiled. Nor does it say anything about the use or restriction of divine attributes. It does say that the emptying concerned becoming a man to be able to die. Thus the *kenosis* means leaving His preincarnate position and taking on a servant-humanity.

B. A Definition

In the *kenosis* Christ emptied Himself of retaining and exploiting His status in the Godhead and took on humanity in order to die.

III. THE FALSE MEANINGS OF THE CONCEPT

A. Christ Surrendered Some or All of His Attributes

This misconception states that *kenosis* means our Lord actually gave up His attributes of deity or at least the relative attributes of omnipresence, omnipotence, and omniscience. Biblically this is false, and theologically it is impossible. If He surrendered any attribute then He ceased to be God during His earthly life. There would then be no way He could have said what He did in John 10:30 that He and the Father were One in essence. Christ did not denude Himself of any aspect of His deity.

B. Christ Appeared as a Man by Disguising His Deity

This is less blatantly heretical, but essentially also denies the full deity of Christ, because the disguise involved a change in the mode of Christ's existence. It denies that Christ was God at the same time He was man. And if this is true then how could He say that whoever saw Him saw the Father (John 14:9)?

This entire discussion is clarified if we remember that the relation and activity of the two natures in our Lord concern the doctrine of the hypostatic union. The doctrine of *kenosis* focuses more on the fact of His Incarnation as necessary to His death.

NOTE

1. J. B. Lightfoot, *St. Paul's Epistle to the Philippians* (London: Macmillan, 1913), 127–33.

Chapter 45
THE SINLESSNESS OF CHRIST

I. THE MEANING OF CHRIST'S SINLESSNESS

Sinlessness in our Lord means that He never did anything that displeased God, violated the Mosaic Law under which He lived on earth, or in any way failed to show in His life at all times the glory of God (John 8:29). It does not exclude His experiencing sinless limitations that accompany humanity. For example, He was weary (4:6); He was hungry (Matt. 4:2; 21:18); He was thirsty (John 19:28); He slept (Matt. 8:24). But at every stage of His life, infancy, boyhood, adolescence, manhood, He was holy and sinless.

II. THE TESTIMONY TO CHRIST'S SINLESSNESS

A. The Evidence

The Scriptures definitely assert the sinlessness of Christ.

Our Lord was announced as a holy Child (Luke 1:35). He challenged His enemies to show that He was a sinner, which they could not do (John 8:46). They failed in their attempts to trap Him by using something He said (Matt. 22:15). He claimed to do always those things that pleased the Father (John 8:29). He said that He kept the Father's commandments (John 15:10). During the trials and Crucifixion, He was acknowledged as innocent eleven times (by Judas, Matt. 27:4; by Pilate six times, 27:24, Luke 23:14, 22; John 18:38; 19:4, 6; by Herod Antipas, Luke 23:15; by Pilate's wife, Matt. 27:19; by the repentant thief, Luke 23:41; and by the Roman centurion, Matt. 27:54). Furthermore, there is no record of our Lord ever offering a single sacrifice, though He frequented the temple. This silence speaks of the fact that He did not need to do so since He was without sin.

Paul said of our Lord that He "knew no sin" (2 Cor. 5:21).

Peter also declared that Christ did not commit any sin, nor was deceit ever found in His mouth (1 Pet. 2:22). He was a Lamb without blemish and without spot (1:19).

John affirmed the same truth when he said that in Christ was no sin (1 John 3:5).

The writer of Hebrews attested to our Lord's sinlessness by several phrases: He was without sin (4:15); He was holy, innocent, undefiled, separated from sinners (7:26), and without any need of offering sacrifices for Himself (v. 27).

Thus Christ's own testimony and that of the writers of the New Testament are uniform—He was sinless.

B. The Debate

Though conservatives agree that Christ was sinless, they do not agree on the question of whether or not He could have sinned. That He did not is affirmed; whether He could have is debated.

The concept that He could not have sinned is called impeccability (*non posse peccare*). The concept that He could have, whether He did or not, is peccability (*posse non peccare*). Liberals, of course, think that not only could He have sinned but that He also did sin. That is peccability combined with sinfulness. The concept of peccability does not need to include sinfulness, and conservatives do not include it.

III. THE TESTING OF CHRIST'S SINLESSNESS

A. The Relation of Testing to Peccability/Impeccability

The debate as to whether Christ was peccable or impeccable is closely linked to the temptation of Christ. Those who support peccability reason that if He could not have sinned then His temptations were not real and He cannot serve as a truly sympathetic High Priest. In other words, peccability requires a constitutional susceptibility to sin. Those who support impeccability point out that it relates to the union of the divine and human natures in the one person so that even though the human nature was peccable, the person was impeccable. It could not be otherwise with a person who has all power and a divine will.

Hodge represents the peccability viewpoint. "Temptation implies the possibility of sin. If from the constitution of His person it was impossible for Christ to sin, then His temptation was unreal and without effect, and He cannot sympathize with His people."[1]

On the other side Shedd wrote:

> It is objected to the doctrine of Christ's impeccability that it is inconsistent with His temptability. A person who cannot sin, it is said,

> cannot be tempted to sin. This is not correct; any more than it would be correct to say that because an army cannot be conquered, it cannot be attacked. Temptability depends on the constitutional *susceptibility,* while impeccability depends on the *will.* . . . Those temptations were very strong, but if the self-determination of His holy will was stronger than they, then they could not induce Him to sin, and He would be impeccable. And yet plainly He would be temptable.[2]

B. The Nature of Christ's Testings

That His tests were real goes without saying. They happened, so they were obviously real. Actually the particular tests Christ experienced were suited to a God-man. No ordinary man would ever be tempted to try to turn stones into bread, but the God-man could have done that. No sane man would be seriously tempted to prove his messiahship by jumping off a high place expecting to land unharmed. No man would take seriously an offer from Satan to give him *all* the kingdoms of this world—perhaps a corner of some kingdom, but not all. So these were tests designed to test a God-man in a way no other has ever been tested.

Though the particular tests were out of the ordinary experience of human beings, the areas of testing that they represented were common to all people. All sinful desires can be classified as either lusts of the flesh, lusts of the eyes, or the boasting about possessions (or a combination thereof, 1 John 2:16). The tests that Satan put the Lord through fall into those three categories (Matt. 4:1–11).

When the writer to the Hebrews said that our Lord was tested in all (*kata panta*), he couldn't mean that He experienced every test that people experience (Heb. 4:15). He was, for example, never tested to misuse television. But He did experience tests tailor-made for a God-man that fell into the same categories into which all tests fall, including ours. And the reason He could be tested at all was that He had a human nature, for God is not tempted with evil (James 1:13). He was tested, the writer continued, "according to likeness." In other words, the fact that He was made in the likeness of sinful flesh allowed Him to be tested. Yet there was a major difference between His humanity and ours. He was "without sin." He had no sin nature and He never committed a single sin. Still that does not mean that His humanity was impeccable. It was peccable, though it never knew sin. But the person of the God-man was impeccable.

Shedd correctly observed: "Consequently, Christ while having a peccable human *nature* in His constitution, was an impeccable *Person.* Impeccability characterizes the God-Man as a totality, while peccability is a property of His humanity."[3]

C. The Results of Christ's Testings

1. Sensitivity. He became sensitive to the pressure of testing. He experienced it with emotions and powers we cannot understand.
2. Example. He furnishes us an example of victory over the severest kinds of tests.
3. Understanding. He can offer sympathetic understanding to us when we are tested.
4. Grace and power. He can also provide the grace and power we need in times of testing. People who have experienced the same problems we might have are sensitized and sympathetic, but often they can do little or nothing about our problems. He can do something and offers us grace to help in time of need (Heb. 4:16). Only a God-man High Priest can do both—sympathize because He was genuinely tested and empower because He is God.

D. An Illustration

When I first began to teach at the seminary level, I was appalled at the number of misspellings I found in students' tests. Early in my career I gave an exam to a class of probably no more than twenty students that expected the word *Gethsemane* in one of the answers. Believe it or not, that class misspelled that word eight different ways! That is not easy to do even deliberately. *Deity* and *millennium* were other words commonly misspelled. Remember, these students were college and university graduates.

When I visited my family home the first Christmas vacation, I found myself one evening socializing with a group of public school teachers. They were members of a Bible class my father had taught for years, and many of them had been my teachers in my early years. Of course they were interested in how I liked teaching. When I complained about misspellings, I struck sympathetic chords in almost all of them. I complained about *Gethsemane.* They complained about *neither* or *cat* or other much simpler words that seminary students are never tempted to misspell. My students' temptations to misspell were particularly related to theological words. The particular words were suited to the different levels of students. But the area was the same—misspelling words each group should have known. Because we shared a common problem area, we could sympathize genuinely with each other.

It would be true to say that every student in my class was truly tested with respect to the correct spelling of Gethsemane. Those who knew it passed the test, but the test was there for all to take. We have a High Priest who can genuinely sympathize because He was really tested with tests peculiar to a God-man. He did not sin and He could not have sinned. He was and is holy, innocent, and undefiled, God's spotless Lamb.

NOTES

1. Charles Hodge, *Systematic Theology* (Grand Rapids: Eerdmans, 1960), 2:457.
2. William G. T. Shedd, *Dogmatic Theology* (New York: Scribner, 1891), 2:336.
3. Ibid., 2:333.

Chapter 46
The Resurrection and Ascension of Christ

I. THE RESURRECTION

A. The Importance of Christ's Resurrection

1. To His person. If Christ did not rise from the dead then He was a liar, for He predicted that He would (Matt. 20:19). To the women who came to His tomb wondering where He was, the angel said, "He is not here, for He has risen, just as He said" (28:6). The Resurrection authenticates our Lord as a true Prophet. Without that, all that He said would be subject to doubt.

2. To His work. If Christ did not rise from the dead then, of course, He would not be alive to do all His post-resurrection ministries. His ministry would have ended at His death. We would not, therefore, have a High Priest now, an Intercessor, Advocate, or a Head of the church. Furthermore, there would be no living Person to indwell and empower us (Rom. 6:1–10; Gal. 2:20).

3. To the Gospel. In the classic passage, 1 Corinthians 15:3–8, Christ's death and resurrection are said to be "of first importance." The Gospel is based on two essential facts: a Savior died and He lives. The burial proves the reality of His death. He did not merely faint only to be revived later. He died. The list of witnesses proves the reality of His resurrection. He died and was buried; He rose and was seen. Paul wrote of that same twofold emphasis in Romans 4:25: He was delivered for our offenses and raised for our justification. Without the Resurrection there is no Gospel.

4. To us. If Christ did not rise then our witness is false, our faith is without meaningful content, and our prospects for the future are hopeless (1 Cor. 15:13–19). If Christ is not risen then believers who have died would be dead in the absolute sense without any hope of resurrection. And we who live could only be pitied for being deluded into thinking there is a future resurrection for them.

B. The Evidences for Christ's Resurrection

1. His appearances after the Resurrection. The number and variety of people in a variety of circumstances who saw the Lord after His resurrection give overwhelming proof of the fact that He did rise from the dead. When, for example, on the Day of Pentecost Peter offered as proof of his message the fact that they were witnesses of the resurrected Christ, he did so in the city where the Resurrection had occurred less than two months before and to an audience who could ask around to check on Peter's claim (Acts 2:32).

The order of appearances between Christ's resurrection and ascension seems to be as follows: (a) to Mary Magdalene and the other women (Matt. 28:8–10; Mark 16:9–10; John 20:11–18); (b) to Peter, probably in the afternoon (Luke 24:34; 1 Cor. 15:5); (c) to the disciples on the Emmaus road toward evening (Mark 16:12; Luke 24:13–32); (d) to the disciples, except Thomas, in the Upper Room (Luke 24:36–43; John 20:19–25); (e) to the disciples, including Thomas, on the next Sunday night (Mark 16:14; John 20:26–29); (f) to seven disciples beside the Sea of Galilee (John 21:1–24); (g) to the apostles and more than 500 brethren and James, the Lord's half brother (1 Cor. 15:6–7); (h) to those who witnessed the Ascension (Matt. 28:18–20; Mark 16:19; Luke 24:44–53; Acts 1:3–12).

2. Effects that must have a cause (the Resurrection). Some astounding facts must be explained. It is inconceivable to think they could have a satisfactory explanation other than being caused by the resurrection of Christ.

What caused the tomb to be empty? The disciples saw that it was empty. The guards reported to the chief priests that it was empty and took a bribe to keep quiet about it (Matt. 28:11–15). If the story they were ordered to tell (that the disciples came and stole the body) were true, then, of course, they should have been punished or executed for allowing that to happen while they were on guard duty. Some have suggested that the disciples went to the wrong tomb, but again the presence of the guard makes this inconceivable. The tomb was empty (the effect) because Christ had risen (the cause).

What caused the events of the Day of Pentecost? Pentecost came and went every year, but the year that Christ rose it saw the descent of the Holy Spirit as He had promised (Acts 1:5). In his sermon Peter attributed the coming of the Spirit to the fact that the risen Christ sent the Spirit (2:33). The coming of the Spirit (the effect) had to have a sufficient cause (the risen Christ).

What caused the day of worship to change? All the first Christians were Jewish, accustomed to worshiping on the Sabbath. Yet suddenly and uniformly they began to worship on Sunday though it was an ordinary workday (Acts 20:7). Why? Because they wanted to commemorate the resurrection of their Lord, which took place on Sunday, they changed their day of worship. Sunday worship, the effect; Christ's resurrection, the cause.

C. The Results of Christ's Resurrection

1. A new, prototype body. With the resurrection of Christ there appeared for the first time in history a new kind of resurrection body, for He rose with an eternal body, never to die again. Before that event, all resurrections were restorations to the former earthly bodies.

Christ's resurrection body had links with His unresurrected earthly body. People recognized Him (John 20:20), the wounds inflicted by crucifixion were retained (20:25–29; Rev. 5:6), He had the capacity (though not the need) to eat (Luke 24:30–33, 41–43), He breathed on the disciples (John 20:22), and that body had flesh and bones proving that He was not merely a spirit showing itself (Luke 24:39–40).

But His resurrection body was different. He could enter closed rooms without opening doors (Luke 24:36; John 20:19), He could appear and disappear at will (Luke 24:15; John 20:19), and apparently He was never limited by physical needs such as sleep or food.

The most detailed description of Christ risen and ascended is found in Revelation 1:12–16. Here John recorded his vision of the glorified Christ. He was like a son of man, which links Him to His former earthly appearance, but He also radiated glory from His eyes, feet, voice, and face. This is the way we shall see Him someday.

His resurrection also serves as a prototype of the resurrection of believers. Twice Christ is referred to as the firstborn from the dead (Col. 1:18; Rev. 1:5). This means that He was the first to have an eternally resurrected body. Our resurrection bodies, like His, will be different from our earthly bodies. When answering the question, What will believers' resurrection bodies be like? Paul said that they will not be the same bodies that were laid in the grave simply reconstituted; but they will be new yet related to the former ones (1 Cor. 15:35–41).

Believers in the eternal state will be "like Him" (1 John 3:2). What does this mean? John explained in the following verses. To be like Him means to be pure (v. 3), to be without sin (v. 5), and to be righteous (v. 7). Our entire beings, including our bodies, will be characterized these ways.

2. A proof of His claims. We have already mentioned that His resurrection proved His truthfulness as a Prophet (Matt. 28:6). It also validated His claim to be Lord and Messiah, a point Peter drove home in his Pentecost sermon (Acts 2:36). Paul states that the Resurrection proved Him to be the Son of God (Rom. 1:4).

3. A prerequisite to all His subsequent ministries. If Christ did not rise then His life and ministry ended on the cross, and He does nothing from that time on. Through the Resurrection and Ascension our Lord entered into His present and future ministries, which will be discussed in the next chapter.

The resurrection of Christ has always been the joyous, captivating, and motivating truth for the church. One of the simplest prayers and earliest creeds of the church was "Maranatha," "our Lord, come" (1 Cor. 16:22). No one could say that who denied the resurrection of his Lord. It affirmed in the clearest way that Jesus is the living and coming Lord.

Maranatha!

II. THE ASCENSION

A. Statements About the Ascension

1. In the Old Testament. Two references foretell the ascension of Messiah (Ps. 68:18, quoted in Eph. 4:8 and Ps. 110:1, quoted in Acts 2:34–35).

2. In the sayings of Christ. Our Lord spoke of going to His Father (John 7:33; 14:12, 28; 16:5, 10, 28) and specifically of the Ascension (6:62; 20:17).

3. In the writings of the New Testament. The debated ending of Mark records the Ascension (16:19); Luke speaks of it twice (Luke 9:51; 24:51); but the principal description is in Acts 1:6–11. Other New Testament passages refer to it (Eph. 4:10; 1 Tim. 3:16; Heb. 4:14; 1 Pet. 3:22), and others that tell of the present exaltation of Christ presuppose it (e.g., Col. 3:1).

B. Description of the Ascension

1. The place. It occurred in "the vicinity of Bethany" (Luke 24:50 NIV), that is, on the Bethany side of the Mount of Olives (Acts 1:12).

2. The procedure. Christ actually traveled up as if supported by the cloud (v. 9). The ascent was not a sudden disappearance but a gradual, though not long, movement upward.
3. The promise. As the disciples watched, two angels appeared and promised that He who had just been taken from them would return again "in just the same way" (v. 11).

C. Problems Raised with Regard to the Ascension

1. It was contrary to the laws of nature. Yes it was, but Christ's resurrection body was not necessarily subject to the laws of nature and Christ, as God, could supersede the laws He made.
2. Did He ascend to heaven before the public ascension? Some think that John 20:17 indicates one or more ascensions before the one detailed in Acts 1. However, the verb "I ascend" is most likely a futuristic present referring to the coming public ascension of Acts 1 and referring to it with certainty. It is as if the Lord were saying to Mary, "Stop clinging to Me. There is no need for this, as I am not yet at the point of permanent ascension. You will still have the opportunity to see Me. However, there is no question but that I certainly will ascend to My Father."[1]

D. Significance of the Ascension

The Ascension marked the end of the period of Christ's humiliation and His entrance into the state of exaltation. Even the forty days between His resurrection and His ascension involved some limitation as, for example, with respect to showing His glory. Notice that His post-resurrection, preascension appearances did not startle the disciples as far as the appearance of His resurrection body was concerned. But the post-ascension appearance of Christ to John described in Revelation 1 must have shown His glory much more vividly.

The Ascension having taken place, Christ then was ready to begin other ministries in behalf of His own and of the world.

NOTE

1. See Leon Morris, *Commentary on the Gospel of John* (Grand Rapids: Eerdmans, 1971), 840–41.

Chapter 47
THE POST-ASCENSION MINISTRIES OF CHRIST

The resurrection and ascension of our Lord provided His entrance into heaven and the beginning of additional ministries for Him. One, at least, He has already done; others He is doing throughout the entire period between His ascension and His second coming; others are yet to begin in the future. In this chapter we shall look at these ministries briefly (since many overlap other areas of theology).

I. PAST MINISTRY

Before His death our Lord promised not to leave the disciples orphans but to send another Paraclete (John 14:16–18, 26; 15:26; 16:7). That last verse plainly says that the coming of the Spirit depended on Christ's going to the Father.

Peter reiterated this on the Day of Pentecost, claiming that it was the risen and ascended Christ who sent the Holy Spirit and accompanying proofs that they witnessed on that day (Acts 2:33). Both the Resurrection (v. 32) and Ascension (v. 34) are specifically mentioned by Peter as prerequisite to the sending of the Spirit.

II. PRESENT MINISTRY

A. As Head of His Body

By His resurrection and ascension our Lord was positioned in the place of honor at the right hand of the Father to be Head over the church, His body (Eph. 1:20–23). This involves a number of specific ministries He performs in relation to the body.

1. He formed the body. He formed the body by sending the Spirit on the Day of Pentecost to baptize believers into the body (Acts 1:5; 2:33; 1 Cor. 12:13). Though the Spirit's work of baptizing is the immediate agent that effects placing people in the body, the ascended Christ is the ultimate Agent because He sent the Spirit. The practical effect of this new position should be disassociation from the old life and demonstration of newness of life (Rom. 6:4–5).

2. He cares for His body in a number of ways. He sanctifies it (Eph. 5:26), a reference to the entire process of sanctification that begins at conversion and continues until we are presented perfect in His presence in heaven. Conversion in this passage is signified by the reference to "washing" and "with the word," the former apparently referring to baptism and the latter to the public confession by the one being baptized at that time.

His work of sanctifying includes nourishing and cherishing His body (Eph. 5:29). To nourish means to bring to maturity (as in 6:4). To cherish means literally to keep warm, thus to love and care for His children (the only other occurrence of the word is in 1 Thess. 2:7).

3. Our ascended Lord also gives gifts to the body (Eph. 4:7–13). First He descended into "the lower parts [i.e.] the earth" ("earth" in v. 9 is an appositive genitive that names the lower parts). Then He ascended on high. And when He ascended, He led captive a host of captives. Here Paul uses an illustration from Psalm 68:18 in which the triumphant warrior is exalted when he returns with captured prisoners. He receives gifts from the conquered people and gives gifts to his own people. Christ conquered sin and death during His ministry on earth; now He gives gifts to His followers during His ministry in heaven. In 1 Corinthians 12:5 the giving of gifts is also related to the Lord.

4. The ascended Lord also empowers the body (John 15:1–10). This well-known illustration of the Vine and branches makes clear that without the power of the living Christ flowing through us we can do nothing. Clearly that power is resurrection power dependent on a relationship of our being in Him and His being in us (14:17). And that relationship did not exist before He went to the Father. On His part this ministry involves discipline or encouragement (depending on the meaning of "takes away" [15:2], as in 11:39, but which can also mean "lifts up," as in 8:59), and cleansing (15:3). On our part it requires abiding, which means keeping His commandments (v. 10; 1 John 3:24).

B. As Priest for His People

As a faithful Priest our ascended Lord sympathizes, succors, and gives grace to His people (Heb. 2:18; 4:14–16). In the latter passage the writer predicates this ministry on the Ascension—He "passed through the heavens."

As a faithful Priest our Lord intercedes for His people (Heb. 7:25). The writer linked this ministry to the fact that this Priest, unlike Old Testament priests, is not subject to death anymore but abides a Priest forever and lives forever to intercede for His people. As to the exact form this ministry may take in communicating or mentioning our needs we cannot fully know; but it apparently focuses both on the positive aspect of asking that things be prevented from happening in our lives (Luke 22:32) and the negative aspect of cleansing us from evil things that do happen (1 John 2:1–2). We will not know until we are in heaven all that this ministry of our High Priest has meant in our lives, both in its positive and negative facets.

As High Priest our Lord also serves as a Forerunner, assuring us that we will eventually have an entrance into heaven as He already has had (Heb. 6:19–20). The word "forerunner" is used of a scout reconnoitering, or of a herald announcing the coming of a king; in other words, it implies that others are to follow. Christ is now in heaven as our Priest; this assures us that we will follow Him there someday.

C. As Preparer of a Place for Us

Just before His death, the Lord informed the disciples that He was shortly going to prepare a place for them, after which He would return to take them there (John 14:1–3). The "Father's house" refers to heaven, and in heaven are many abiding places. The word occurs only in verses 2 and 23 and indicates permanent residences. Part of His present work today is preparing these residences for His own. To be able to begin to do this He must go to the Father through the way (v. 6) of death and resurrection.

III. FUTURE MINISTRY

Though detailed discussion of what will happen in the future belongs to eschatology, I think it appropriate to mention here at least three aspects of our Lord's ministry in the future.

A. He Will Raise the Dead

In the future all people will hear the voice of Christ raising them from the dead (5:28–29). Some will be called to eternal life and others to condemnation. Though we know from other Scriptures that both groups will not be raised at the same time, His voice calling them will be the cause of the resurrection of all. Believers of the Church Age will be raised at the Rapture of the church (1 Thess. 4:13–18). Old Testament saints will apparently be raised at the Second Coming (Dan. 12:2). The unbelieving dead of all time will not be raised until after the Millennium (Rev. 20:5).

B. He Will Reward All People

Though the average person thinks of God (the Father) as the Judge of all people, the Lord said that all judgment has been delegated to Him (John 5:22, 27). As with resurrection, judgment for all will not take place at the same time, but Christ will judge all.

Believers will be judged by Him at the Judgment Seat of Christ (1 Cor. 3:11–15; 2 Cor. 5:10) after the Rapture of the church. The outcome of this judgment for all will be heaven, though with a varying number of rewards. All will receive some praise from God (1 Cor. 4:5).

Unbelievers will be judged at the Great White Throne at the conclusion of the millennial kingdom (Rev. 20:11–15). All will be rewarded for their deeds by being cast into the lake of fire. None will be shown to be deserving of heaven. But regardless of the time, all will be judged by our Lord.

C. He Will Rule This World

When our Lord returns He will take the reins of government and rule the nations of this world as a benevolent dictator (Rev. 19:15). Then and only then will the world experience a time of righteousness, justice, social welfare, economic prosperity, and spiritual knowledge. He will show Himself to be King of kings and Lord of lords in the same arena where man's rebellion against God took place.

Section X
SO GREAT A SALVATION

Chapter 48
SOME INTRODUCTORY CONSIDERATIONS

I. THE SCOPE OF THE SUBJECT

Soteriology, the doctrine of salvation, is one of the grandest themes in the Scriptures. It embraces all of time as well as eternity past and future. It relates in one way or another to all of mankind, without exception. It even has ramifications in the sphere of the angels. It is the theme of both the Old and New Testaments. It is personal, national, and cosmic. And it centers on the greatest Person, our Lord Jesus Christ.

From God's perspective, salvation includes the total work of God in bringing people from condemnation to justification, from death to eternal life, from alienation to filiation. From the human perspective, it incorporates all of the blessings that being in Christ brings both in this life and the life to come.

The inclusive sweep of salvation is underscored by observing the three tenses of salvation. (1) The moment one believed he was saved from the condemnation of sin (Eph. 2:8; Titus 3:5). (2) That believer is also being saved from the dominion of sin and is being sanctified and preserved (Heb. 7:25). (3) And he will be saved from the very presence of sin in heaven forever (Rom. 5:9–10).

II. THE MOTIVES FOR SALVATION

Why should God want to save sinners? Why should He bear the pain of giving His only begotten Son to die for people who had rebelled against His goodness? What could it possibly mean to God to have a family of human beings?

The Bible indicates at least three reasons that God wanted to save sinners.

(1) This was the greatest and most concrete demonstration of the love of God. His good gifts in nature and through His providential care (great as they are) do not hold a candle to the gift of His Son to be our Savior. John 3:16 reminds us that His love was shown in His gift, and Romans 5:8 says that God proved conclusively that He loved us by the death of Christ.

(2) Salvation also gives God a display of His grace throughout all eternity (Eph. 2:7). Each saved person will be a special trophy of God's grace forever. Only redeemed human beings can provide this display.

(3) God also wanted a people who would do good works in this life and thus give the world a glimpse, albeit imperfect, of God who is good (v. 10).

Without the salvation Christ provided, these things would not be possible.

III. THE IMPORTANCE OF SALVATION

In only two instances does the New Testament pronounce a curse on Christians for failure to do something. One is not loving the Lord (1 Cor. 16:22), and the other is preaching a gospel other than the Gospel of grace of God (Gal. 1:6–9). Not comprehending clearly the doctrine of salvation can lead to proclaiming a false or perverted Gospel, and many statements of the Gospel one hears today may well come under this curse. Yet the grace of God overpowers our unclear presentations, and people are saved in spite of, though not as a result of, an unclear or misstated Gospel.

Positively, this doctrine is crucial simply because a Gospel witness is the responsibility of all believers. For the preacher it is even more important, for he is the link between God and the unregenerated person, and his message must be clear (Rom. 10:14–15). Chafer, whose ministry began in evangelism, still thought near the end of his life that "in a well-balanced ministry, Gospel preaching should account for no less than 75 percent of the pulpit testimony. The remainder may be for the edification of those who are saved."[1] This certainly underscores the importance of studying and understanding this great theme of soteriology.

NOTE

1. Lewis Sperry Chafer, *Systematic Theology* (Grand Rapids: Zondervan, 1981), 3:9.

Chapter 49
THE BIBLICAL TERMINOLOGY

I. THE OLD TESTAMENT USAGE

The most important Hebrew root word related to salvation in the Old Testament is *yasha'*. Originally it meant to be roomy or broad in contrast to narrowness or oppression. Thus it signifies freedom from what binds or restricts, and it came to mean deliverance, liberation, or giving width and breadth to something. Sometimes this deliverance came through the agency of man (e.g., through judges, Judg. 2:18; 6:14; 8:22; 12:2; or kings, 1 Sam. 23:2), and sometimes through the agency of Yahweh (Pss. 20:6; 34:6; Isa. 61:10; Ezek. 37:23; Zech. 3:4). Sometimes salvation is individual (Ps. 86:1–2) and sometimes corporate, that is, of the nation (Isa. 12:2, though all the world will share in it, 45:22; 49:6). In the Old Testament salvation was not only a deliverance from some trouble but also a deliverance to the Lord for His special purpose (43:11–12; 49:6).

Faith was the necessary condition for salvation in the Old Testament as well as in the New. Abraham believed in the Lord, and the Lord counted it to him for righteousness (Gen. 15:6). The Hebrew prefix *beth* indicates that Abraham confidently rested his faith on God (cf. Exod. 14:31; Jon. 3:5). The covenant relationship established by the Mosaic Law also implied that an Israelite had to have faith in the God of that covenant if he were to be pleasing to Him and not be cut off.

The object of faith was always the true God (Num. 14:11; 20:12; 2 Kings 17:14, Ps. 78:22, Jon. 3:5). This Savior God was the sole origin of salvation (Ps. 3:8, Jon. 2:9). To trust in idols was not only ineffective but ludicrous, for salvation was of the Lord.

II. THE NEW TESTAMENT USAGE

In both the Septuagint and the New Testament the Greek verb *sōzō* and its cognates *sōtēr* and *sōtēria* usually translate *yasha'* and its respective nouns. However, a number of times the *sōzō* group translates *shalom,* peace or wholeness, and its cognates. Thus salvation can mean cure, recovery, remedy, rescue, redemption, or welfare. This can be related to preservation from danger, disease, or death (Matt. 9:22; Acts 27:20, 31, 34; Heb. 5:7). But the full Christian usage means saving from eternal death and endowing a person with everlasting life (Rom. 5:9; Heb. 7:25).

As in the Old Testament, the initiative of salvation is entirely with God (John 3:16). The Lord Jesus Christ's death on the cross is the sole basis for that salvation (Acts 4:12; Heb. 5:9). As stated before, this salvation has a past aspect that occurred when we believed, a present aspect, and a future consummation.

But word usage does not begin to fathom all that the biblical revelation declares about salvation. Other concepts like sacrifice, redemption, reconciliation, propitiation, and justification are vital to a full understanding of the doctrine. These will be considered later, but I mention them now lest anyone think that the doctrine is built only on the words related to saving.

Salvation affects the whole person. Nevertheless, the removal of man's fallen nature and the receiving of a resurrection body awaits a future day. But this is also a part of our salvation (Rom. 8:23). In addition, the curse that has been on the world will be removed (vv. 18–23), and the entire universe will feel the effects of Christ's work of reconciliation (Col. 1:20).

Chapter 50
THE PASSION OF CHRIST

The basis of all the facets, accomplishments, and benefits of the death of Christ is, of course, the historical event of His death on the cross. "Passion" means suffering, and particularly the sufferings of Christ between the night of the Last Supper and the Crucifixion.

I. THE NEED FOR HIS PASSION

Because of man's sinfulness and helplessness, someone else had to step in and aid him if he was to find acceptance and fellowship with a holy God. Sin brought and brings estrangement from God, and depravity means that nothing man can do will merit any favor or consideration from God as far as salvation is concerned.

Without repeating the material under the doctrine of sin, the salient points need to be reviewed. Everyone born into this world stands condemned because of (a) his relation to Adam's sin (Rom. 5:12) and (b) because of the sin nature with which everyone is born (Eph. 2:3). In addition, (c) all commit sin, which is the inevitable fruit of the sin nature (Rom. 3:9–23). This not only means universal condemnation but also establishes a universal need that all have to be saved from sin's penalty.

Everyone born into this world is helpless to do anything to gain soteriological favor with God. Depravity, you remember, does not mean that people cannot or do not perform actions that are good in man's and God's sight; nor does it mean that sinful man has no conscience to judge between good and evil for himself; nor that people indulge in every form of sin or even in any particular sin to the greatest extent possible. But depravity does mean that because man's entire being has been corrupted he can never do anything that would merit saving favor with God. In relation to salvation this means that help will have to come from someone who has not been affected with that corruption, someone who is sinless.

II. THE PERSON OF THE PASSION

The person involved in that atoning sacrifice was the God-man. Only this kind of Being could have effected our salvation. Again, without repeating material under Christology, let me review some of the salient features of His person that bear on His atoning work.

Though a number of reasons are stated in Scripture for the Incarnation, the principal one was that He might save His people from their sins (Matt. 1:21). To do this required Incarnation; that is, God in flesh. God has declared that the penalty for sin has to be death. Since God cannot die, there had to be an Incarnation in order that there be a human nature to experience death and thus pay the penalty for sin.

The God-ordained means of accomplishing the Incarnation was the Virgin Birth. Whether He could have done it some other way and still preserve the sinlessness of Jesus Christ can only be a matter of conjecture. The fact of the matter is that He did do it through the Virgin Birth. The feminine singular relative pronoun "by whom" in Matthew 1:16 undebatably links Christ to one human parent, His mother. It was a Virgin Birth.

The result of the Virgin Birth was a God-man. God always was. The total human nature was conceived by the Spirit in the womb of Mary, and the Baby born was fully God and a perfect human being, united in one person forever. This is called the hypostatic union.

This God-man, unique in all history, alone qualifies to be an adequate Savior. The Savior had to be human in order to be able to die, for God does not die, and the Savior had to be God in order to make that death an effective payment for sin. When a sinful person dies, he or she dies for his or her own sins. A sinless person can atone for the sins of others.

Notice this truth in the opening verses of Romans 1. When Paul described the Gospel (v. 1), he said that it concerns God's Son (v. 3); and that Son was human (from the seed of David, v. 3) and divine (designated to be the Son of God, v. 4). In other words, we have a Gospel simply because we have a God-man Savior-man who as man is able to die, and as God can make that death a satisfactory payment for the sins of the world. No other kind of savior can save.

III. THE SUFFERINGS IN THE PASSION

The sufferings of Christ in His death have been labeled His passive obedience in classical Protestant theology. This passive obedience stands in contrast to Christ's active obedience, which refers to the obedience exhibited during His lifetime. His life was, of course, one of obedience, beginning with His willing acceptance of the Incarnation (Heb. 10:5–10) and continuing throughout His entire life on earth (Luke 2:52; John 8:29). Through suffering He learned obedience (Heb. 5:8).

The sufferings of Christ's life, though real, were not atoning. Nevertheless, the merit of His atoning death is inseparable from the sinlessness and perfection of His life, which was attested to by His life of obedience. Thus while theologians have made this distinction between life and death sufferings (active and passive obedience), it fails to be very significant, since only the sufferings of His death and His obedience in being the sacrificial Lamb were atoning.

Strictly speaking, then, only the sufferings on the cross were atoning. It was during the three hours of darkness when God laid on Christ the sins of the world that Atonement was being made. The abuse and scourgings that preceded His time on the cross were part of the sufferings of His life.

IV. THE OUTLINE OF THE PASSION

As we noted at the beginning of this chapter, the Passion usually includes the events from the Last Supper to the Crucifixion. Here is an outline of these events and the nature of the things involved in those last hours of Christ's life.

A. The Trials

The traditional site of the Passover is in an Upper Room in the southwest corner of the city of Jerusalem.

From there the group made their way across the city to the Garden of Gethsemane (on the slope of the Mount of Olives to the east of Jerusalem) where the Lord was betrayed and arrested, and where He also restored Malchus's ear. This happened perhaps around 3 A.M.

Back again through the city the Lord was taken to the house of Annas for a hearing. Both Annas's and Caiaphas's houses were in the southwestern part of the city, not far from the Upper Room where the Lord and His disciples had been earlier.

Then they moved to the court of Caiaphas's house where at least a quorum of the Sanhedrin gathered and passed sentence on the Lord.

When morning came the full Sanhedrin confirmed the sentence passed a few hours before.

The Lord was then taken before Pilate since the Jews did not have the authority to carry out a sentence of death. Pilate's judgment hall was near the northwest corner of the temple area, across the city from Caiaphas's house.

An examination by Herod followed. His palace stood at the western wall of the city. So once again the Lord traversed the city.

Across the city and back to Pilate, the Lord was condemned to be crucified.

The site of the Crucifixion is debated. The two candidates are the Church of the Holy Sepulchre, west of Pilate's judgment hall, and Gordon's Calvary, northwest of Pilate's judgment hall. Either location required another trip across a major portion of Jerusalem. The total distance covered by our Lord in His enfeebled condition was about two and one-half miles.

B. The Day

The traditional view of a Friday crucifixion has everything to commend it and nothing to contradict it. All the Gospels state that the day following the Crucifixion was Sabbath (Matt. 27:62; 28:1; Mark 15:42; Luke 23:56; John 19:31). All the Gospels state that the women visited the tomb of Jesus on the day after the Sabbath, that is, on the first day of the week, Sunday (Matt. 28:1; Mark 16:2; Luke 24:1; John 20:1). It was a common practice of the Jews to refer to a part of a day or night as the whole day (Gen. 42:17–18; 1 Sam. 30:12–13; 1 Kings 20:29; 2 Chron. 10:5, 12; Esther 4:16; 5:1). Therefore, to fulfill the "three days and three nights" of Matthew 12:40 required that the Lord be in the tomb the part of Friday before sundown (day #1), all of Saturday (day #2), and the part of Sunday after sundown on Saturday and until the Resurrection occurred (day #3). And, of course, the Scriptures say He rose "on the third day" (1 Cor. 15:4).

C. The Method

Crucifixion was Eastern in origin. The Persians practiced it, and Alexander the Great seemed to have learned of it from them. Phoenicia, famed for its barbaric practices, frequently employed crucifixion. Rome apparently borrowed it from Carthage and perfected it as a means of capital punishment. The extent to which Rome used it staggers the imagination.

After being sentenced, the condemned person was flogged with a leather whip loaded with metal or bone. He was then required to shoulder the cross beam and carry it to the place of execution. This beam was approximately six feet long and weighed about thirty pounds. This was affixed to the upright stake, which was already in place at the execution site. Nails about seven inches long with a head (to keep the body from sliding off) were driven through the hands and feet of the victim. Sometimes ropes were also used to keep the body on the cross.

The Romans had learned to push the feet upward when they nailed them to the cross so that the victim could lean on the nail and push himself upward momentarily in order to breathe easier. This kept the victim alive longer. Death rarely came in less than thirty-six hours, and most people survived two or three days before they died. Insatiable thirst, pain from the scourging, cramps, dizziness, public shame, and the horror of knowing what lay ahead before the release of death all combined to make crucifixion a horrible means of dying.

This is what men did to our Lord. And God laid on Him the iniquity of us all. He died to pay the penalty of sin, and He died for you and for me.

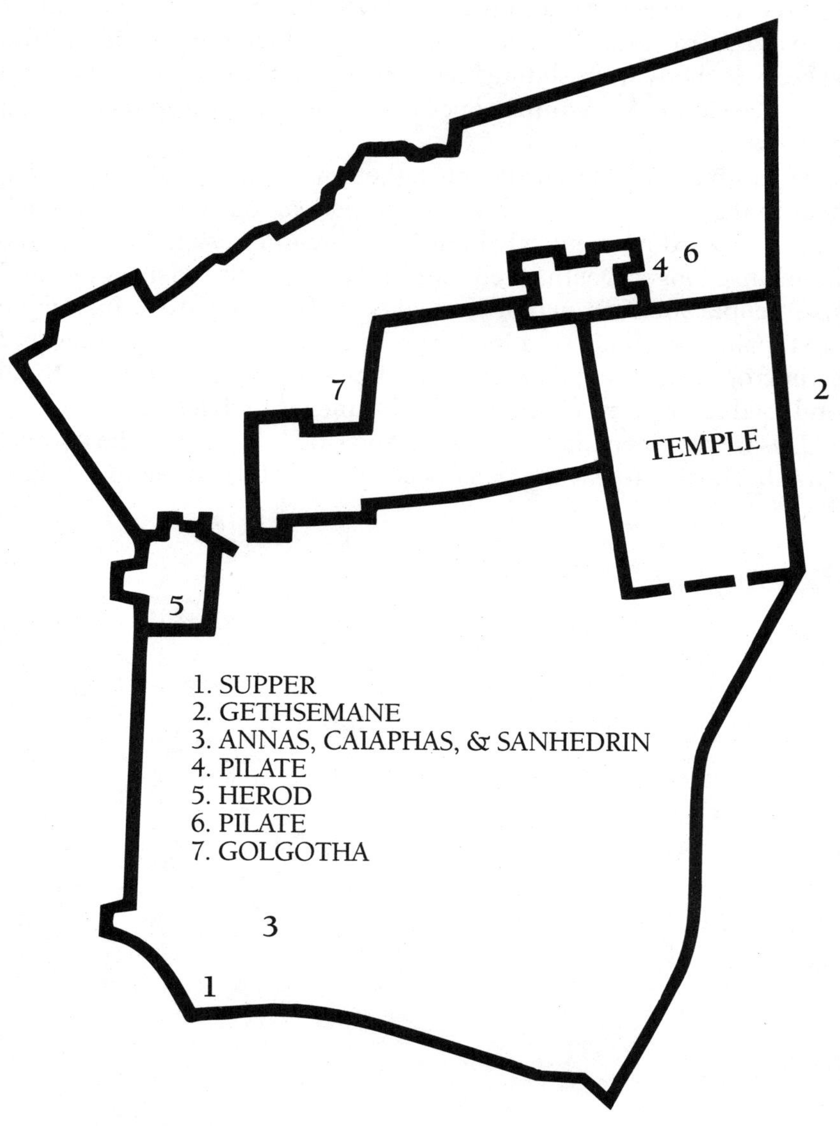
4
6
7
2
TEMPLE
5
1. SUPPER
2. GETHSEMANE
3. ANNAS, CAIAPHAS, & SANHEDRIN
4. PILATE
5. HEROD
6. PILATE
7. GOLGOTHA
3
1

Chapter 51
THE MEANING OF THE DEATH OF CHRIST

Although it is true that the full meaning of the death of Christ cannot be captured in one or two slogan-like statements, it is also true that its central meaning can and must be focused on several very basic ideas. There are four such basic doctrines: Christ's death was a substitution for sinners, a redemption in relation to sin, a reconciliation in relation to man, and a propitiation in relation to God. Not to emphasize these four or not to insist on their basic importance to a proper understanding of the meaning of the death of Christ is to beggar or even pervert the biblical concept. For example, it is proper and biblical to view the death of Christ as a great display of the love of God or to see it as an example for us to be self-sacrificing (these are biblical truths, John 15:13; Rom. 5:8), but if these comprised the only meaning of the death of Christ, there would be no eternal value in it. It must provide a substitution and a payment for sin, or the example means relatively little. So we must understand these basic facts first, for they form the saving and eternal meaning of the death of our Lord.

I. A SUBSTITUTION FOR SINNERS

A. The Concept of Substitutionary Atonement

1. The meaning of substitutionary atonement. Substitutionary or vicarious atonement simply means that Christ suffered as a substitute for us, that is, instead of us, resulting in the advantage to us of paying for our sins.

Man could atone for his sins personally only if he could suffer eternally the penalty that sin incurred. Man, of course, could never do this, so in His love and compassion, God stepped into a hopeless situation and provided a Vicar in Jesus Christ who did provide an eternal satisfaction for sin.

PERSONAL ATONEMENT	VICARIOUS ATONEMENT
Provided by the offending party	Provided by the offended party
A matter of strict justice	A combination of justice and love
Never finished	A completed sacrifice

2. Objections to substitutionary atonement. Certain objections have been raised against this concept.

a. The idea of substitutionary atonement makes God unjust since He condemned His Son to bear the sins of mankind. This might be a valid objection except for the fact that the Triune God was involved in planning redemption, and the Son voluntarily took upon Himself the work of substitution. In other words, although this might be a valid objection on a finite level, it cannot be on the infinite level, since at that level there are not three separate parties involved.

b. Vicarious atonement makes the innocent Christ suffer for the wicked. This is absolutely true, and is essential to atonement. It is also plainly scriptural (1 Pet. 3:18). Therefore, to raise this as an objection is to question the plan and purpose of God.

c. A moral agent cannot be responsible for sin unless he commits it personally. This simply is not so in human government; so it need not be so in divine government. Guilt can come on members of a board of directors for the wrongdoings of their executives. Negligence on the part of school employees opens its officials to lawsuits.

B. The Evidence for Substitutionary Atonement

Clearly the Bible teaches that Christ's sacrifice was not a matter of sympathy but of substitution.

1. In the Old Testament. The arrangements of the sacrificial system of the Old Testament included the necessity of the offerer laying his hands on the animal being offered as a sacrifice.

> This meant transmission and delegation, and implied representation; so that it really pointed to the substitution of the sacrifice for the sacrificer. . . . If the sacrifice was brought by more than one, each had to lay on his hands. It is not quite a settled point whether one or both hands were laid on; but all are agreed that it was to be done "with one's whole force"—as it were, to lay one's whole weight upon the substitute.[1]

The animal's death took the place of the death due the one offering that animal. The system clearly taught substitution.

2. *In the use of the preposition* anti. The root meaning of this preposition, which occurs twenty-two times in the New Testament, is face-to-face, opposite, as two objects placed over against each other and one being taken instead of the other as in an exchange. Critics of substitutionary atonement label this "crude transactionalism." Nevertheless, the preposition *anti* does support substitution.

a. In classical Greek. Anti uniformly means "in the place of," and it has no broader meaning as, for instance, "for the sake of."[2]

b. In Greek of the New Testament Period. Moulton and Milligan give no examples of *anti* meaning "on behalf of" or "for the sake of." The common meaning is "instead of." The same and only meaning is found in Polybius (ca. 200–ca. 118 B.C.), Philo, and Josephus.

c. In the Septuagint. Among the 318 occurrences of *anti* there is no example of the broader meaning "on behalf of." Uniformly it means "in place of" and translates *tachath* (Gen. 44:33).

d. In the New Testament. Examples of the clear meaning "instead or in place of" are found in Matthew 2:22 and Luke 11:11. Instances where the idea of exchange is prominent occur in John 1:16; Romans 12:17; 1 Thessalonians 5:15; Hebrews 12:16; and 1 Peter 3:9. Matthew 17:27 (the incident concerning paying the temple tax) seems to bear a clear substitutionary sense. The tax was redemption money (Exod. 30:11–16). The idea of equivalence appears in Matthew 5:38 and 1 Corinthians 11:15, though some understand the use of *anti* in the latter reference to mean that a woman's hair serves in place of a covering. However, this would seem to contradict Paul's teaching in the preceding verses, so likely it has the idea of equivalence. That is, hair in the natural realm is equivalent to what the covering stands for in the spiritual realm.[3] Clearly none of these verses support the meaning "on behalf of" or "for the benefit of."

The crucial verse is Mark 10:45 (KJV): "For even the Son of man came . . . to give his life a ransom for many" (see also Matt. 20:28). *Anti* demands the interpretation that our Lord came to die in our place and as our substitute. It cannot be understood otherwise, and this, of course, was Christ's own interpretation of the meaning of His sacrifice. *Anti* also appears as the prefix on the compound word *antilutron* in 1 Timothy 2:6. Christ was our substitution ransom.

3. *In the use of the preposition* huper. The original meaning of this preposition was over, upper, and for one's benefit. The idea included

standing over someone to protect him and to receive the blows on his behalf and in his place. Thus the basic ideas in the word include both benefit and substitution, simply because to act on behalf of or for the benefit of someone often includes acting in his place. Both these ideas occur in the New Testament usage, as we shall see.

a. In classical Greek. Both ideas of benefit and substitution occur in classical writings.[4]

b. In the Greek of the New Testament period. Again both ideas are found. Often *huper* is used of someone writing a letter for someone else who was illiterate. Clearly this is a substitutionary idea.

c. In the Septuagint. Again both ideas are found, but it is especially important to soteriology to note that the substitutionary meaning is clearly the meaning in such verses as Deuteronomy 24:16 and Isaiah 43:3–4.

d. In the New Testament. No one debates that *huper* means "for the benefit of." The debate centers on whether or not it can mean "in the place of." Those who deny substitutionary atonement naturally want to eliminate the latter meaning and insist that Christ's death was not in any sense a substitutionary payment but only a benefit to mankind. Those who affirm substitutionary atonement can rest their case on the meaning of *anti,* but they can also point to the substitutionary meaning in *huper.* The case is further strengthened by the fact that *huper* clearly has a substitutionary meaning in passages that are not concerned with the Atonement. There are three clear ones.

(1) In Romans 9:3 Paul wishes he could be accursed in the place of his fellow Jews. He wanted to take their place under God's curse.

(2) First Corinthians 15:29 most likely refers to those who by being baptized showed that they had joined the Christian ranks to take the place of those who had died, and therefore could be said to have been baptized for (in the place of) those who had died. This understanding of the verse requires a substitutionary meaning of *huper.*

(3) Even if there were any question about the two preceding examples, there certainly can be no question about the substitutionary meaning of *huper* in Philemon 13. Onesimus, the converted slave, was in Rome with Paul, and he was about to return to his master Philemon in Colossae. In this wonderful letter of intercession on Onesimus's behalf, Paul told Philemon that he would like to keep Onesimus with him in Rome to help him on Philemon's behalf (*huper sou*). That can only mean that someone had to be in Rome with Paul—either Philemon himself or his slave Onesimus as his substitute. Of course, the

idea of benefit is present as well, but the only way there could have been any benefit to Paul was to have Philemon's substitute, Onesimus, with him in Rome. If *huper* has both ideas, benefit and substitution in nonatonement passages, then it may also carry both meanings in atonement passages, and indeed it does. Some important examples where the substitutionary idea is present are John 11:50–51; Romans 5:6–8; 2 Corinthians 5:21; Galatians 3:13; Titus 2:14; and 1 Peter 3:18.

To summarize: *anti* always has the idea of equivalence, exchange, or substitution. It never has the broader idea of "for the sake of" or "on behalf of." *Huper* has both ideas, including the idea of substitution in atonement passages in the New Testament.

C. The Denial of Substitutionary Atonement

Attempts to deny the force of this evidence are usually made in one of two ways. Some claim that even though substitution may be in the picture, it must not be made the controlling meaning of Christ's death. Thus substitution is submerged in and among the other meanings of His death until it becomes such a minor part of the concept that it has disappeared for all practical purposes. Here is an example: "The death of Jesus is bigger than any definition, deeper and more profound than any rationale. . . . By a rich variety of terms and analogies it is set forth, but it is never completely captured in any verbal net. . . . Even though no final rationale of the cross is to be achieved, we must seek its meaning again and again."[5]

Others simply attempt to reinterpret substitution as always meaning "for the sake of." Here is an example:

> The fact is that he [Paul] intends what we may call a "representative" view of Christ's death. When Paul writes that Christ died "for" me, he usually means not "instead of me" but "for my benefit." . . . Thus it cannot be a matter of substitution or of a scapegoat. In another context, it is true, the analogy of the ransom of a captive or (very rarely) that of a sacrificial offering is brought in play by Paul and suggests substitution. But this motif . . . is dominated by the ruling conception of our participation with Christ in His death to sin and the Law.[6]

This writer fails to examine any of the evidence of the prepositions or verses I have cited.

Clearly, according to His own teaching and that of the rest of the New Testament, Christ's death was a substitution for sinners.

II. A REDEMPTION IN RELATION TO SIN

Redemption means liberation because of a payment made. To believers the concept has a special significance since the payment was the death of the Lord Himself.

A. The Old Testament Doctrine

Three Hebrew words form the lexical basis for the Old Testament doctrine: *g'l, pdh,* and *kopher.* The primary idea in *g'l* is family obligation related to payment of a price. The kinsman-redeemer had the responsibilities of (a) redeeming family property that had changed ownership and (b) marrying a childless widow to raise up children in her dead husband's name. When there was no brother available, the responsibility was extended to the next of kin (Ruth 3:9).

The meaning of the root *pdh* is that of ransom by payment of a price, as in a commercial transaction, without any obligation arising from kinship (Exod. 13:12; Num. 18:15–17). This word may have more overtones of grace than *g'l* simply because the one who redeems has no obligation to do so.

The meaning of *kopher* refers to the sum paid to redeem a forfeited life (Exod. 21:28; 30:12). All these words consistently signify deliverance by payment of a price. The circumstances may vary from redeeming a prisoner of war, a slave, a pawned article, or the nation Israel, but always because of the payment of a price.

Little direct association is evident in the Old Testament between redemption and sin (but see Ps. 130:8; Isa. 59:20). The lack of formal statements making the association is doubtless due to the ever-present and obvious link between redemption and sin seen in the sacrificial system. Because it was continually seen, it did not have to be said so frequently.

B. The New Testament Words

1. Agorazō. The basic idea in this word is to frequent the forum. Then it took the meaning of buying or acquiring in the forum. The New Testament uses it twenty-four times in this usual meaning of buying (e.g., Matt. 13:44; Luke 9:13). The Septuagint uses it with the same basic meaning of buying, a simple commercial transaction (e.g., Gen. 41:57; 42:5, 7).

The soteriological use of *agorazō* in the New Testament includes three basic ideas. (1) In His work of redeeming, Christ paid the purchase price for all mankind (2 Pet. 2:1). (2) The price itself is clearly stated to be the blood of Christ (Rev. 5:9–10). (3) Because we have been bought with that purchase price, we are to serve Him (1 Cor. 6:19–20; 7:22–23).

2. *Exagorazō.* The compound simply adds the idea of purchasing out of the forum. Two passages in which this word is used are especially significant. In Galatians 3:13 the substitutionary nature of Christ's death stands out clearly. We were under a curse. He bore that curse. We have been removed from the curse. In 4:5 Paul declared that believers have been completely removed from being under the Law.

In passing, we might note an interesting use of this compound in a nonatonement passage, Ephesians 5:16. Here believers are exhorted to redeem the time, that is, to buy it up and remove it from useless activities.

3. *Peripoioumai.* This word occurs only one time with reference to the Atonement, in Acts 20:28. It means to keep safe or to preserve. In the middle voice as used in this verse, it means to keep or save for oneself or to acquire or gain possession of. Thus the idea is that God acquired the church through the blood of His own Son for His personal possession. Again the idea of a price paid is prominent, and that price clearly was the death of Christ.

4. *Lutroō.* From the root *luo,* to loose, this word was used for loosing clothes or animals or prisoners. It was usually connected with a ransom being paid as a condition of release. Thus its meaning is to release on receipt of a ransom.

a. In the Septuagint. The half-shekel atonement money levied before the tabernacle was constructed was a ransom payment for each Israelite twenty years and older (Exod. 30:11–16). The Year of Jubilee involved redemption of property (Lev. 25:31–32). The difference between the greater number of firstborn and the lesser number of Levites was compensated for by a five-shekel ransom per extra person (Num. 3:46–51). In all these instances the idea was freedom because of a price paid.

b. In classical Greek. Again the meaning is uniformly release on receipt of ransom paid. The word was often used in relation to the redemption of slaves and prisoners of war.

c. In the New Testament. The verb *lutroō* appears in Luke 24:21 (of the national deliverance of Israel); Titus 2:14; and 1 Peter 1:18–19 (of individual redemption). Note especially in the latter reference that the price paid is the blood of the Lamb. The noun *lutron* occurs only in

Matthew 20:28 and Mark 10:45. As previously discussed under the meaning of *anti* this verse clearly affirms substitution, and the price to be paid is the death of Christ. *Lutrōsis* is used in connection with the national deliverance of Israel in Luke 1:68 and 2:38. In Hebrews 9:12 the sacrificial system of the Old Testament serves as the background for the once-for-all sacrifice of Christ. Again the price is clearly "His own blood."

Apolutrōsis appears ten times in the New Testament: once referring to non-Christian release (Heb. 11:35), once in the general sense of Christian redemption (1 Cor. 1:30), three times with reference to eschatology (Luke 21:28; Rom. 8:23; Eph. 4:30), and five times of the unbeliever's release (Rom. 3:24; Eph. 1:7, 14; Col. 1:14; Heb. 9:14). Clearly the price paid is the death of Christ. We have already discussed *antilutron* in 1 Timothy 2:6 under substitution. His death was a substitute ransom payment for all.

C. The Doctrine Summarized

Redemption may be summarized around three basic ideas. (1) People are redeemed from something; namely, from the marketplace or slavery of sin. (2) People are redeemed by something; namely, by the payment of a price, the blood of Christ. (3) People are redeemed to something; namely, to a state of freedom; and then they are called to renounce that freedom for slavery to the Lord who redeemed them.

III. A RECONCILIATION IN RELATION TO THE WORLD

Reconciliation means a change of relationship from hostility to harmony and peace between two parties. People can be reconciled to each other (Matt. 5:24, *diallasso;* 1 Cor. 7:11, *katallasso*), and people have been reconciled to God (Rom. 5:1–11; 2 Cor. 5:18–21, *katallasso;* Eph. 2:16; Col. 1:20, *apokatallasso*).

A. The Need for Reconciliation—Why?

Because of sin God and man are in a relationship of hostility and enmity. Though this is not mentioned in 2 Corinthians 5, it is clear in Romans 5. We were enemies of God (v. 10). Does this refer to mankind's enmity toward God or to God's enmity toward man? The latter seems to be the sense; that is, God reckoned us to be His enemies. This is the sense of the same word in Romans 11:28, where God is said to reckon the people of Israel His enemies. Paul's mention of God's wrath in 5:9 supports the interpretation that the enemies were the object of His wrath. Our state of estrangement could not have been more serious, nor the need for a change, a reconciliation, more urgent.

B. The Cause of Reconciliation—How?

Clearly the testimony of the New Testament is that reconciliation comes about through the death of the Lord Jesus (Rom. 5:10). God made Him to be sin for us that we might be made the righteousness of God in Him. The death of Christ completely changed man's former state of enmity into one of righteousness and complete harmony with a righteous God.

C. The Object of Reconciliation—Who?

There are three main answers to this question: God is reconciled to man, man is reconciled to God, both are reconciled to each other.

Shedd taught that God is reconciled to man. He explained verse 10, which says man is reconciled to God this way: "Yet this does not mean the subjective reconciliation of the sinner toward God, but the objective reconciliation of God toward the sinner."[7] His reasoning for the statement is that since it is God's wrath that is removed, then God must be reconciled. However, effecting a change in God would seem to conflict with His immutability.

Walvoord[8] and others are equally certain that reconciliation affects only man. Second Corinthians 5:19 seems clear: God in Christ reconciled the world to Himself. The world of mankind is clearly the object of reconciliation. Romans 5:10 agrees by stating that we were reconciled to God. "God is the One who is active in reconciliation (2 Cor. 5:18–19), and men are said to be reconciled (Rom. 5:10; 2 Cor. 5:20); i.e., they are acted upon by God. Thus believers are said to receive reconciliation. They are recipients of a relationship of peace and harmony brought about by God."[9]

Still others see reconciliation as involving both God and man. Berkhof taught that the Atonement reconciled God to the sinner. "This is undoubtedly the primary idea, but does not imply that we cannot also speak of the sinner's being reconciled to God. . . . And even when we speak of the sinner as being reconciled, this must be understood as something that is secondary. The reconciled God justifies the sinner who accepts the reconciliation. . . ."[10]

Leon Morris, who also holds that both man and God are reconciled, carefully notes that

> When we say that God can be thought of as reconciled to man, that does not mean that, with various imperfections, He alters completely His attitude to man. Rather it is our groping way of expressing our conviction that He reacts in the strongest possible way against sin in every shape and form, and that man comes under His condemnation accordingly; but that when reconciliation is effected, when peace is made between man and God, then that condemnation is removed and God looks on man no longer as the object of His holy and righteous wrath, but as the object of His love and His blessing.[11]

The central passages clearly state that man is reconciled to God. Man is the object of reconciliation. Yet there remains a sense in which, after man has received personally the reconciliation, both parties, man and God, may be said to be reconciled in that they have come together. Still the grievance against man and the initiative to effect a change were God's; He acted on man to reconcile him to Himself.

D. The Provision and Application of Reconciliation

God's provision of reconciliation is universal. Because of the death of Christ the position of the world was changed—people were now able to be saved. But that alone saves no one, for the ministry of reconciliation must be faithfully discharged by proclaiming the Gospel message. When an individual believes, then he receives the reconciliation God provided in Christ's death (2 Cor. 5:18–21). The world has been reconciled, but people need to be reconciled. The universal reconciliation changes the position of the world from an unsalvable condition to a salvable one. Individual reconciliation through faith actually brings that reconciliation in the individual's life and changes the position of the individual from unsaved to saved. Then, and only then, are his sins forgiven, though they were paid for on the cross.

> [Man] has been reconciled with God because the reconciliation by God of sinful men to Himself, effected once and for all *in Christ,* has lasting effects. It is not applicable merely to one period or to one group of people, but to all the world. Whenever the *word of reconciliation* is proclaimed by those to whom God has committed it, and whenever it is appropriated by an individual sinner, whoever and wherever he may happen to be, that person is reconciled by God to Himself, and his reconciliation means that God no longer *imputes* to him his *trespasses;* i.e., He no longer counts his sins against him.[12]

To summarize: The need for reconciliation lies in God's enmity against sinful mankind. God took the initiative and reconciled the world to Himself. This was done by the death of Christ, and that provision changed the world into a savable position before God. Yet though the world has been reconciled, man needs to be reconciled by changing his position about Christ. Then, and only then, is his condition before God changed.

IV. A PROPITIATION IN RELATION TO GOD

Propitiation means the turning away of wrath by an offering. In relation to soteriology, propitiation means placating or satisfying the wrath of God by the atoning sacrifice of Christ.

A. The Need for Propitiation: The Wrath of God

The reality of the wrath of God raises the need for appeasing that wrath or for propitiation. Though to the liberal such an idea is pagan, the truth is that the wrath of God is a clear teaching of both the Old and New Testaments.

1. In the Old Testament. More than twenty different words occurring about 580 times express the wrath of God in the Old Testament (2 Kings 13:3; 23:26; Job 21:20; Jer. 21:12; Ezek. 8:18; 16:38; 23:25; 24:13). Everywhere sin constitutes the reason for God's wrath. Idolatry especially aroused His wrath (Deut. 6:14; Josh. 23:16; Ps. 78:21; Isa. 66:15–17). The effects of God's wrath included general affliction (Ps. 88:7), pestilence (Ezek. 14:19), slaughter (9:8), destruction (5:15), being delivered to enemies (2 Chron. 28:9), drought (Deut. 11:17), plagues (2 Sam. 24:1), leprosy (Num. 12:10), and exile (2 Kings 23:26–27; Ezek. 19:12).

Ways of averting God's wrath included purging sin (Deut. 13:15–17), repentance (Jon. 3:7, 10); intercession (Ps. 106:23; Jer. 18:20), and God's own action in removing it (Ps. 78:38; Isa. 48:9).

At the same time the Old Testament also portrays God as loving His people and yearning for their fellowship. So the Old Testament concept is not a pagan one of an unreasonable God who demands to be placated, but of a righteous God who cannot overlook sin but whose love also provides avenues for fellowship with Himself.

2. In the New Testament. Though not mentioned so frequently as in the Old Testament, wrath in the New Testament is a basic concept to show the need for propitiation. The New Testament uses two principal words. *Orge* conveys a more settled anger (John 3:36; Rom. 1:18; Eph. 2:3;

1 Thess. 2:16; Rev. 6:16), while *thumos* indicates a more passionate anger (Rev. 14:10, 19; 15:1, 7; 16:1; 19:15). Together they clearly convey the divine hostility against sin in a personal way. His wrath is not simply the inevitable, impersonal result of the working of cause and effect, but a personal matter. To appease that wrath was not a matter of vengeance but of justice, and it required the sacrificial gift of God's Son.

B. The Provision of Propitiation: The Sacrifice of Christ

Paul undebatably linked propitiation with the death of Christ in Romans 3:25. His blood (that is, His death) made Him the propitiation. An interpretive question exists as to the shade of meaning in *hilasterion* in the verse. Since it is the same form as is used in Hebrews 9:5, many understand this to refer to Christ as the place where propitiation was made. He was the mercy seat. Others understand the reference to mean that Christ was the propitiatory offering as supported in Hebrews 2:17; 1 John 2:2; and 4:10. Perhaps we are to include both shades of meaning in this passage; that is, our Lord was the satisfactory sacrifice for sin and therefore the place where propitiation was made. Notice the interconnection of sin, sacrifice, blood, and propitiation in these passages.

The references in 1 John 2:2 and 4:10 both stress the fact that Christ Himself is the offering that turns away the wrath of God. He is not called the propitiator (note that He is named Savior in 4:14) as if to allow for the possibility that He might have used some other means of propitiation outside of Himself. He is the offering.

C. The Negation of Propitiation: The Teaching of C. H. Dodd

1. His background. C. H. Dodd (1884–1973) was a British Congregational minister and New Testament scholar. He held professorships at Manchester and Cambridge, and after his retirement he served as general director of the *New English Bible* translation. He is primarily known for his work in "realized eschatology" and in the apostolic *kērygma.*

2. His view on propitiation. Dodd's view was first stated in an article in the *Journal of Theological Studies* (1931, 32:352–60) entitled "*Hilaskesthai,* Its Cognates, Derivatives, and Synonyms." In essence his view is this: "The rendering propitiation is . . . misleading, for it suggests the placating of an angry God, and although this would be in accord with pagan usage, it is foreign to biblical usage."[13] Though he cited elaborate philological and exegetical evidence, his principal reason for this conclusion appears to be theological. To him it is sub-Christian to think that God can be angry and therefore needs to be appeased; therefore, propitiation must be defined in some other way. He proposed expiation as the substitute word and concept for propitiation.

3. *His evidence.* Dodd cites the following. (1) At least two pagan contexts furnish examples of the meaning expiate and show that in pagan usage the meanings of expiate and propitiate were ambiguous. (2) The Old Testament word *kipper* is translated in the Septuagint by sanctify, purify, cancel, purge, forgive, and not by propitiate. Therefore, *hilaskesthai* will have those other meanings also. (3) *Hilaskesthai* is used to translate other Hebrew words as cleanse and forgive. (4) When the word is used to translate *kipper,* it does not mean appeasement but to remove guilt.

4. *The response.* Roger Nicole has offered the most comprehensive and persuasive reply to Dodd's arguments.[14] He points out (a) that Dodd's choice of evidence is selective, since he omits consideration of a number of relevant words; (b) that he fails to include evidence from Philo and Josephus, both of whom understand propitiation as appeasement; (c) that he often ignores the contexts of passages that if considered would not support his conclusions; and (d) that basically his logic is faulty when he assumes that the root meaning of a word is changed or lost just because it is used to translate words other than the most directly equivalent ones.

Basically, the stumbling block to Dodd's way of thinking is the idea of the wrath of God. He must eliminate that and goes to great philological lengths to try to accomplish it. However, he does not succeed either philologically or biblically. Romans 1:18; 2:5; Colossians 3:6; 1 Thessalonians 1:10; 2 Thessalonians 1:7–9; and Revelation 6:16 cannot be explained away by Dodd or anyone else. Yet his influence has been widespread (T. W. Manson, D. M. Baillie, Vincent Taylor, C. K. Barrett, and the *Revised Standard Version*).

D. The Distinction between Propitiation and Expiation

Propitiation, as we have seen, means the placating of the personal wrath of God. Expiation is the removal of impersonal wrath, sin, or guilt. Expiation has to do with reparation for a wrong; propitiation carries the added idea of appeasing an offended person and thus brings into the picture the question of why the offended person was offended. In other words, propitiation brings the wrath of God into the picture while expiation can leave it out. If one wanted to use both words correctly in connection with each other, then he would say that Christ propitiated the wrath of God by becoming an expiation for our sins.

E. An Important Practical Point

If because of the death of Christ God is satisfied, then what can the sinner do to try to satisfy God? The answer is nothing. Everything has been done by God Himself. The sinner can and need only receive the gift of righteousness God offers.

Before Christ died, it was perfectly proper to pray, as did the tax-gatherer in Luke 18:13, "God, be merciful [lit., be propitiated] to me, the sinner." Though provision for fellowship with God was provided under the Law, this man could not rely on a finished and eternal sacrifice for sin that would appease God once and for all. So that was an entirely appropriate prayer for him to pray. But now Christ has died and God is satisfied, and there is no need to ask Him to be propitiated. He is appeased, placated, and satisfied eternally. This is the message we bring to a lost world: Receive the Savior who through His death satisfied the wrath of God.

Notes

1. Alfred Edersheim, *The Temple, Its Ministry and Service* (Grand Rapids: Eerdmans, 1950), 113–14.
2. See the detailed analysis by R. E. Davies, "Christ in Our Place—The Contribution of the Prepositions," *Tyndale Bulletin* 21 (1970): 71–91.
3. See Colin Brown, ed., *The New International Dictionary of New Testament Theology* (Grand Rapids: Zondervan, 1971), 3:1179.
4. Compare Davies, "Christ in Our Place," 82.
5. Frank Stagg, *New Testament Theology* (Nashville: Broadman, 1962), 135–36.
6. Amos N. Wilder, *New Testament Faith for Today* (New York: Harper, 1955), 134.
7. William G. T. Shedd, *Dogmatic Theology* (New York: Scribners, 1891), 2:396.
8. John F. Walvoord, *Jesus Christ Our Lord* (Chicago: Moody, 1974), 179–86.
9. A. Berkeley Mickelsen, "Romans,"in *Wycliffe Bible Commentary* (Chicago: Moody, 1962), 1197.
10. L. Berkhof, *Systematic Theology* (Grand Rapids: Eerdmans, 1941), 373.
11. Leon Morris, *The Apostolic Preaching of the Cross* (Grand Rapids: Eerdmans, 1956), 221.
12. R. V. G. Tasker, *The Second Epistle of Paul to the Corinthians* (Grand Rapids: Eerdmans, 1958), 89.
13. C. H. Dodd, *The Epistle of Paul to the Romans* (London: Hodder and Stoughton, 1935), 55.
14. Roger Nicole, "C. H. Dodd and the Doctrine of Propitiation," *Westminster Theological Journal*, May 1955, 17:127–48.

Chapter 52
SOME RESULTS OF SALVATION

A list of results or benefits of salvation could conceivably include hundreds of items. I only intend to discuss in this chapter some of the principal things God has done, is doing, or will do on the basis of the completed sacrifice of Christ.

I. JUSTIFICATION

Justification is not only one of the great benefits of the death of Christ but is also a cardinal doctrine of Christianity because it distinguishes it as a religion of grace and faith. And grace and faith are the cornerstones of the doctrine of justification.

A. The Meaning of Justification

To justify means to declare righteous. Both the Hebrew (*sadaq*) and the Greek (*dikaioo*) words mean to announce or pronounce a favorable verdict, to declare righteous. The concept does not mean to make righteous, but to announce righteousness. It is a courtroom concept, so that to justify is to give a verdict of righteous. Notice the contrast between to justify and to condemn in Deuteronomy 25:1; 1 Kings 8:32; and Proverbs 17:15. Just as announcing condemnation does not make a person wicked, neither does justification make a person righteous. Condemning or justifying announces the true and actual state of the person. The wicked person is already wicked when the verdict of condemnation is pronounced. Likewise, the righteous person is already righteous when the verdict of justification is announced.

B. The Problem in Justification

Since this is a forensic idea, justification is related to the concept of God as Judge. This theme is found throughout the Bible. Abraham acknowledged God as the Judge of all the earth who had to do what was right (Gen. 18:25). In the song of Moses, God's justice and righteousness were rehearsed (Deut. 32:4). Paul called God the righteous Judge (2 Tim. 4:8). The writer of Hebrews called God the Judge of all, and James reminded his readers that the Judge stood at the door (James 5:9).

If God, the Judge, is without injustice and completely righteous in all His decisions, then how can He announce a sinner righteous? And sinners we all are. There are only three options open to God as sinners stand in His courtroom. He must condemn them, compromise His own righteousness to receive them as they are, or change them into righteous people. If He can exercise the third option, then He can announce them righteous, which is justification. But any righteousness the sinner has must be actual, not fictitious; real, not imagined; acceptable by God's standards, and not a whit short. If this could be accomplished, then, and only then, can He justify.

Job stated the problem accurately when he asked, "How can a man be in the right before God?" (Job 9:2).

C. The Procedure in Justification (Rom. 3:21–26)

God does put into effect that third option: He changes sinners into righteous people. How? By making us the righteousness of God in Christ (2 Cor. 5:21), by making many righteous (Rom. 5:19), by giving believers the gift of righteousness (v. 17). Five steps were involved in the outworking of this procedure as detailed in the central passage on justification, Romans 3:21–26.

1. The plan (Rom. 3:21). God's plan for providing the needed righteousness centered in Jesus Christ. It was apart from Law. The construction is without an article, indicating it was apart from not only the Mosaic Law, which could not provide that righteousness (Acts 13:39) but also from all legal complications. It was manifested (a perfect passive form) at the Incarnation of Christ, and the effects of that great intervention in history continue. It is constantly witnessed by the Law and the Prophets, who testified of the coming of Messiah (1 Pet. 1:11). Thus the plan centers in a person.

2. The prerequisite (Rom. 3:22). Righteousness comes through faith in the now-revealed Jesus Christ. The New Testament never says we are saved because of faith (that would require *dia* with the accusative). It always makes faith the channel through which we receive salvation (*dia* with the genitive). But, of course, faith must have the right object to be effective, and the object of saving faith is Jesus Christ.

3. The price (Rom. 3:24–25). Quite clearly the price paid was the blood of Christ. The cost to Him was the greatest. To us the benefit comes freely (the same word is translated "without a cause" in John 15:25), that is, without any cause in us, and so by His grace.

4. *The position.* When the individual receives Christ, he is placed in Christ. This is what makes him righteous. We are made the righteousness of God in Him. This righteousness alone overcomes our desperate, sinful condition and measures up to all the demands of God's holiness.

5. *The pronouncement* (Rom. 3:26). Not only does Christ's righteousness, which we have, meet God's demands, but it also demands that God justify us. We are in fact, not fiction, righteous; therefore, the holy God can remain just and justify the one who believes in the Lord Jesus.

Therefore, no one can lay anything to the charge of God's elect, for we are in Christ righteous in God's sight. And this is why God can justify us.

D. The Proof of Justification

Justification is proved by personal purity. "He who has died is freed [lit., justified] from sin" (Rom. 6:7). We stand acquitted from sin so that it no longer has dominion over us. Justification before the bar of God is demonstrated by holiness of life here on earth before the bar of men. This was the perspective of James when he wrote that we are justified by works (James 2:24). Unproductive faith is not genuine faith; therefore, what we are in Christ will be seen in what we are before men. Faith and works are like a two-coupon ticket to heaven. The coupon of works is not good for passage, and the coupon of faith is not valid if detached from works.

One final thought: justification assures us of peace with God (Rom. 5:1). Our relationship with Him is right, legal, and eternal. This forms a sure foundation for peace with God.

II. THE JUDGMENT OF THE SIN NATURE

A second very important benefit of the death of Christ relates His death to the judgment of the believer's sin nature (Rom. 6:1–14). Justification, we saw, will be seen in a life of holiness; and the basis for that life of holiness, like the basis for justification, is the death of Christ.

In the preceding chapter Paul used that startling phrase "the gift of righteousness" (5:17). This raises the question of 6:1. If righteousness is a gift, then would it not be better to continue in sin in order that grace may increasingly be seen? If salvation were by works, this question would never be raised, since one would have to keep on doing good works in order to merit salvation. But if salvation is by grace, then cannot one sin as much as he pleases and will this not actually display grace all the more? Paul answers the question with an emphatic no. He gives two reasons that the justified person will not continue in sin.

A. The Judgment Frees Us from the Domain of Sin (Rom. 6:2–10)

1. Its accomplishment (Rom. 6:2–4). Being joined to the death and resurrection of Christ is that which actually accomplishes our transference from the domain of the old life to that of the new life. Death to sin becomes, then, not a hope, but a reality, because Christ died to sin once and we were joined to Him in that death by baptism.

Death means separation, not extinction. So death to sin in this paragraph means separation from its domain or realm, but not the extinction of its presence. Baptism means association or identification with someone or something. Here it refers to our identification with Christ in His death so that we have been separated from the power of sin. Baptism cannot refer here to a ceremony or even a sacrament, but rather to a relational union to the Lord (similar to the Israelites being relationally united to Moses in the crossing of the Red Sea, 1 Cor. 10:2). Ritual or water baptism illustrates this union but cannot accomplish it. Thus this baptism unites us to Christ's death unto sin (separation from its domain), to His burial (to demonstrate conclusively that His death was actual), and to His resurrection (to give us newness of life).

2. Its accompaniments (Rom. 6:5–10). Identification with Christ in His death unto sin brings (a) a uniting with Him in resurrection life (v. 5), (b) an annulling of the old self (v. 6), and (c) a freeing from the mastery of sin (v. 7). The future tense in verse 5 indicates what must inevitably occur (as in Gal. 6:5). Thus it refers to our resurrection to new spiritual living, not our future physical resurrection. The old man in Romans 6:6 relates to our place in the old creation under the sway of sin and death. Though removed from its domain, the old order still seeks to dominate through the old man (Eph. 4:22) as it tries to express itself, using the body as a vehicle of sin (which is likely the meaning of "body of sin"). For a similar and instructive use of "destroyed" or "done away with" in Romans 6:6, see Hebrews 2:14, which relates the death of Christ to destroying Satan's power.

B. The Judgment Frees Us from the Dominion of Sin (Rom. 6:11–14)

Now Paul appeals to believers to be free from the dominion of sin on the basis of Christ's death unto sin. The appeal involves reckoning (v. 11), refusing (v. 12), and presenting (v. 13). Reckoning or considering means to calculate, to add up the truth of the facts presented in verses 1–10 and then act accordingly. In addition we must refuse to obey the evil desires of sin, and present ourselves, including all the members of our bodies, to God for His use. These phrases all appeal for a decisive and urgent break with the old life.

Godet put all these ideas together well when he wrote:

> The Christian's breaking with sin is undoubtedly gradual in its realization, but absolute and conclusive in its principle. As, in order to break really with an old friend whose evil influence is felt, half measures are insufficient, and the only efficacious means is a frank explanation, followed by a complete rupture which remains like a barrier raised beforehand against every new solicitation; so to break with sin there is needed a decisive and radical act, a divine deed taking possession of the soul, and interposing henceforth between the will of the believer and sin (Gal. 6:14). This divine deed necessarily works through the action of faith in the sacrifice of Christ.[1]

III. THE BASIS FOR THE BELIEVER'S FAMILY FELLOWSHIP

No passage is more basic for understanding the believer's family fellowship than 1 John 1:5–10. In it John lays down vital principles for daily Christian living, and this fellowship is based on the death of Christ (v. 7). Thus another benefit of His death is that it provides for enjoyment of fellowship within the family of God.

That this passage refers to family fellowship, not initial justification, seems clear from the reoccurrence of the pronouns "we" and "us" eighteen times in the six verses. Also 2:1 continues the subject and addresses it clearly to believers. Salvation, of course, brings a perfect, complete, and eternal forgiveness (Eph. 1:7), but Christians sin and therefore need continual forgiveness in order to enjoy fellowship within the family relationships. Some have denied that this is necessary, claiming that since Christians are already forgiven, they need not ask for what they already have.[2] But believers do need to forgive and to ask for forgiveness (see Luke 11:4; 2 Cor. 2:10; Eph. 4:32; Col. 3:13).

What are the conditions for enjoying family fellowship? They are two: conforming to the standard of light and confessing sin. God is light—an impossible standard for anyone in a mortal body to meet, so it is good that that is not the requirement. The requirement is that we walk in the light. This places us in the same moral realm as the Father so we can share fellowship. The requirement is tailored to every believer, for no matter what his or her state of maturity, he receives some light from the Word to which he must respond. As he responds, then more light comes and with it more response. So fellowship grows as that circle of light expands.

Of course, response does not always follow. Sin enters and confession is needed to restore fellowship. What is confession? It is saying the same thing about sin as God does. It is having the same perspective on that sin as God does. This must include more than simply rehearsing the sin, for God's perspective would also include forsaking that sin. Therefore, to confess includes an attitude of forsaking that sin.

Private confession to God is always necessary to restore fellowship. What about public confession as well? That depends. There are scriptural examples of public confession (James 5:16 gives a general exhortation and Acts 19:18 a specific example). Public sin would normally require public confession. Years ago I was discussing this matter of public confession with an elderly saint. He gave me two worthwhile guidelines to govern public confession. (1) Be sure God is prompting you to confess publicly. Satan, emotions, or public pressure can also urge you to do something that might not be of the Lord. (2) Before you say anything, ask whether or not it will edify those who hear, for all things in the public assembly should be done to edify.

When we confess to the Father, He is reliable and righteous to forgive and to restore us to family fellowship. This is true whether or not we feel it to be so. And notice that He does this because of the death of Christ who was the propitiation for our sins (1 John 2:1–2).

IV. THE END OF THE LAW

Another important benefit of the death of Christ was the inauguration of the faith-righteousness principle to replace the law-works principle. However, Paul's statement in Romans 10:4 that Christ is the end of the Law might be understood as either signifying termination or purpose. In other words, either Christ terminated the Law, or the purpose of Christ's coming was to fulfill the Law (Matt. 5:17). However, termination seems clearly to be the meaning in this context because of the contrast (beginning in Rom. 9:30) between the Law and God's righteousness. Paul's argument that follows is not that the Jew was incomplete and needed the coming of Christ to perfect his position before God, but that his position under the law-works principle was absolutely wrong because it sought to establish righteousness by human effort rather than by accepting God's gift of righteousness. Though it is true that our Lord fulfilled the Law, this passage is not teaching that, but rather that He terminated the Law and provided a new and living way to God.

A. The Nature of the Law

The Law that our Lord terminated was, of course, the Mosaic Law according to the contrast in the passage itself. In order to develop the importance of this benefit of the work of Christ, it is first necessary to observe some features of the Mosaic Law.

1. The Mosaic Law was a unit. Generally the Law is divided into three parts: the moral, the ceremonial, and the judicial. The Ten Commandments comprise the moral part (Exod. 34:28). The judgments begin at 21:2 and include a list of various responsibilities with attendant judgments on offenders. The ceremonial part begins at 25:1 and regulated the worship life of Israel. Though this threefold division is almost universally accepted in Christian theology, the Jewish people either did not acknowledge it or at least did not insist on it. Rather they divided the 613 commandments of the Law into twelve families of commandments, which were then subdivided into twelve families of positive and twelve families of negative commands. Specific commands that fell into these various categories were drawn from many places within the Law simply because the Law was viewed as a unit.

Noticing the penalties attached to certain commands further emphasizes the unitized character of the Law. When the command to keep the Sabbath (one of the "commandments") was violated by a man who gathered sticks on that day, the penalty was death by stoning (Num. 15:32–36). When the people of Israel violated the command concerning the Sabbatical Year for the land (one of the "judgments"), God sent them into Captivity, where many died (Jer. 25:11). When Nadab and Abihu offered strange fire before the Lord (one of the "ordinances"), they immediately died (Lev. 10:1–7). Clearly these commands from various parts of the Law were equally binding and the punishment equally severe. The Law was a unit.

James approached the Law as a unit. He decried partiality because it violated the law to love one's neighbor as oneself, and this single violation, he said, made the people guilty of the whole Law (James 2:8). He could scarcely arrive at such a conclusion unless the Law were a unit.

2. The Law was given to Israel. Both the Old and New Testaments are unanimous in this (Lev. 26:46; Rom. 9:4). Further, Paul contrasted the Jews who received the Law with the Gentiles who did not (2:14).

B. The End of the Law

The Jerusalem Council settled this matter early and clearly (Acts 15). Debating the question of whether or not circumcision was necessary for salvation, the council said an emphatic no. Peter described the Law as an unbearable yoke. When the leaders wrote to the Gentile believers to curb their liberty in matters that were offensive to Jewish believers, they did not try to place the believers under the Law (which would have settled the problem quickly), for they realized the Law had come to an end.

In 2 Corinthians 3:7–11 Paul even specified that the part of the Law that was written on stones (the Ten Commandments) was done away. He dared to label the moral part of the Law as a ministry of death and condemnation, but, thank God, this has been replaced by the New Covenant, which brings life and justification.

In Hebrews 7:11–12 the writer demonstrated the superiority of the priesthood of Melchizedek over that of Aaron. He concluded that if the Aaronic or levitical priesthood could have brought perfection to the people, there would have been no need for another priesthood based on Melchizedek. And that change of priesthood necessitated a change in the Law. In other words, if the Law has not been done away, then neither has the levitical priesthood, and Christ is not our High Priest today. But if Christ is our High Priest, then the Law can no longer be operative and binding on us.

C. The Problem Raised

If Christ ended the Law, then why does the New Testament include some laws from the Mosaic Law in its ethic? How could the unit end and yet have specifics in it still binding on the Christian? If the New Testament included all the Ten Commandments the answer would be simple: the moral Law continues while the rest has been concluded. But the New Testament only includes nine of the ten, and it further complicates any simple solution by including some laws from parts other than the moral section of the Law (Rom. 13:9; James 2:8).

D. Suggested Solutions to the Problem

1. Calvin's. Calvin taught that the abrogation of the Law had reference to liberating the conscience from fear and to discontinuing the ancient Jewish ceremonies. He distinguished between the moral Law, which he said was abrogated only in its effect of condemning people, and the ceremonial Law, which he said was abrogated both in its effects and in its use. In discussing 2 Corinthians 3 he only distinguished in a general way the difference between death and life in the Old and New Covenants. He presented a very fine exposition of the Ten Commandments, but he did not consider Sunday to be a continuation of the Sabbath (as the Westminster Confession did). In other words, Calvin, as many who have followed him, considered part but not all of the Law as ended and the Ten Commandments as binding on believers today, except the Sabbath one, which he took nonliterally (*Institutes* II, XI, 4 and II, VIII, 33). Obviously this does not really solve the problem.

2. Murray's. John Murray plainly stated the Commandments were abolished, but he saw them as applicable in some deeper sense, whatever that means. He wrote: "Hence the abolition of these regulations is coincident with the deeper understanding of the sanctity of the Commandments. It is this same line of thought that must also be applied to the fourth commandment. Abolition of certain Mosaic regulations? Yes! But this in no way affects the sanctity of the commandment nor the strictness of observance that is the complement of that sanctity."[3]

3. Mine. The only solution (which I have never seen proposed by anyone else) that seems to do full justice to the plain sense of these various Scriptures distinguishes between a code and the commandments contained therein. The Mosaic Law was one of several codes of ethical conduct that God has given throughout human history. That particular code contained 613 commandments. There have also been other codes. Adam lived under laws, the sum of which may be called the code of Adam or the code of Eden. Noah was expected to obey the laws of God, so there was a Noahic code. We know that God revealed many commands and laws to Abraham (Gen. 26:5). They may be called the Abrahamic code. The Mosaic code contained all the laws of the Law. And today we live under the law of Christ (Gal. 6:2) or the law of the Spirit of life in Christ (Rom. 8:2). This code contains the hundreds of specific commandments recorded in the New Testament.

The Mosaic Law was done away in its entirety as a code. It has been replaced by the law of Christ. The law of Christ contains some new commands (1 Tim. 4:4), some old ones (Rom. 13:9), and some revised ones (Rom. 13:4, with reference to capital punishment). All the laws of the Mosaic code have been abolished because the code has. Specific Mosaic commands that are part of the Christian code appear there not as a continuation of part of the Mosaic Law, or in order to be observed in some deeper sense, but as specifically incorporated into that code, and as such they are binding on believers today. A particular law that was part of the Mosaic code is done away; that same law, if part of the law of Christ, is binding. It is necessary to say both truths in order not to have to resort to a nonliteral interpretation of 2 Corinthians 3 or Hebrews 7 and in order not to have to resort to some sort of theological contortions to retain part of the Mosaic Law.

An illustration of this idea: As children mature, different codes are instituted by their parents. Some of the same commandments may appear in those different codes. But when the new code becomes operative, the old one is done away. So it was with the Mosaic Law when our Lord became the end of the Law for righteousness to all who believe.

V. ADOPTION

Our adoption into the family of God is another benefit of the death of Christ.

A. The Meaning of Adoption

Adoption is the act of God that places the believer in His family as an adult. In contrast, being born again emphasizes the idea of coming into God's family as a babe with the attendant need for growth and development (John 1:12; 3:3). But adoption teaches the ideas of adulthood and full privileges in the family of God. Concomitant with adoption is the divesting of all relationships and responsibilities of the previous family relationship. Both being adopted and being born occur at the moment of saving faith, but they indicate different aspects of our relation to the family of God.

B. The Background of Adoption

Most cultures had some practice akin to adoption. Moses, a slave, was adopted by Pharaoh's daughter in Egypt. The Nuzu tablets reveal a custom whereby a childless couple could adopt a son who would serve them in life and be their heir in death. Hebrew laws did not include one that concerned adoption, and the Greek word for adoption does not occur in the Septuagint. This was probably due to the law of levirate marriage, which provided a way for a family to have heirs to inherit the family property. Polygamy may also have been another way to overcome the problems of childlessness.

Adoption was a very common aspect of Greco-Roman life, and this is the background of the New Testament concept. Childless couples would often adopt a son, who then became their heir. Even if the adopted son had living biological parents, they had no more claim over him after the adoption had taken place. Often parents were willing to let their sons be adopted by another family if it meant a better lot in life.

C. The Pauline Doctrine of Adoption

The doctrine is exclusively Pauline, and he used the term five times (Rom. 8:15, 23; 9:4; Gal. 4:5; Eph. 1:5).

1. The adoption of Israel as a nation (Rom 9:4). See also Exodus 4:22.

2. The adoption of believers as individuals. This act of God was predestined (Eph. 1:5) so that it may be said that God's predetermined plan included our destiny as adopted sons. It was made possible by the death of Christ (Gal. 4:5). It happened when we believed and became part of the family of God (Rom. 8:15), yet it awaits its full realization until we receive resurrection bodies (Rom. 8:23).

D. The Ramifications of Adoption

1. Adoption means placing us in a family to which we did not naturally belong (cf. Eph. 2:3). Children of wrath become sons of God.

2. Adoption means complete freedom from former relationships, particularly to the Law (Gal. 4:5). In other words, the other side of adoption is freedom from the Law.

3. Adoption is possible only because of a voluntary act of the One doing the adopting. Before the foundation of the world God's plan included our adoption (Eph. 1:5).

4. Adoption means we have full rights to all the privileges of being in God's family (Rom. 8:15). Spiritual growth may be involved in the enjoyment of those privileges, but every believer has the right to them from the moment of salvation on.

And this is all true because of Christ's redemption (Gal. 4:5).

Notes

1. F. Godet, *Commentary on Romans* (Edinburgh: T. & T. Clark, n.d.), 1:404.
2. For an excellent critique of this concept see Zane Hodges, "Fellowship and Confession in 1 John 1:5–10," *Bibliotheca Sacra,* 129 (January 1972): 48–60.
3. John Murray, *Collected Writings* (Carlisle, Pa.: Banner of Truth Trust, 1976), 1:212.

Chapter 53
THEORIES OF THE ATONEMENT

As one would expect, various views of the Atonement, both true and false, have been propagated throughout church history. A study of these, even in a summary manner, should do two things: it should help prevent one falling into the same errors others have made, and it should help one to state the truth more precisely because of errors that have been made.

LABEL	SOURCE	TEACHING
Ransom to Satan	Origen (185–254)	The death of Christ was a ransom paid to Satan to satisfy any claims Satan had against man. Ultimately Satan was deceived. The Bible does not say anything about to whom a ransom was paid.
Recapitulation	Iranaeus (130–202)	Christ recapitulated in Himself all the stages of life, including what belongs to us as sinners. His obedience substituted for Adam's disobedience, and this should effect a transformation in our lives.
Satisfaction	Anselm (1033–1109) *Cur Deus Homo*	Sinful man robbed God of His honor. God rewarded the death of Christ by viewing it as a work of supererogation so that He can pass on its stored-up merits to us. Faith is necessary to appropriate this.

LABEL	SOURCE	TEACHING
Moral Influence	Abelard (1079–1142) Also Schleiermacher, Ritschl, Bushnell	Death of Christ was not an expiation for sin but a suffering with His creatures to manifest God's love. This suffering love should awaken a responsive love in the sinner and bring an ethical change in him. This, then, liberates from the power of sin.
Example	Socinus (1539–1604)	Christ's death did not atone for sin, but revealed faith and obedience as the way to eternal life and inspiring people to lead a similar life.
Governmental	Grotius (1583–1645) Also Wardlaw, Miley	God's government demanded the death of Christ to show His displeasure with sin. Christ also did not suffer the penalty of the Law, but God accepted His suffering as a substitute for that penalty.
Dramatic	Aulen (1879–1978)	Christ in His death gained victory over the powers of evil.
Barthian	Barth (1886–1968)	Christ's death was principally a revelation of God's love and His hatred of sin.
Penal Substitution	Calvin (1509–1564)	Christ the sinless One took on Himself the penalty that should have been borne by man and others.

All of these viewpoints may perhaps be cataloged under three basic categories. (1) Views that related the death of Christ to Satan (Origen, Aulen). (2) Views that consider His death as a powerful example to influence people (Abelard, Socinus, Grotius, Barth). (3) Views that emphasize punishment due to the justice of God and substitution (perhaps Anselm—though deficient—and the Reformers). Although there may be truth in views that do not include penal substitution, it is important to remember that such truth, if there be some, cannot save eternally. Only the substitutionary death of Christ can provide that which God's justice demands and thereby become the basis for the gift of eternal life to those who believe.

Chapter 54
The Doctrine of Election

The doctrine of election forms one of the bases of salvation, though it is not the only one. Other doctrines such as the death of Christ, faith, efficacious grace, and regeneration may also properly be termed bases as well. All are necessary in bringing to fruition the plan of God for the salvation of people.

I. THE MAJOR VIEWPOINTS ON ELECTION

A. Foresight Election

This view holds that God elects on the basis of foreseen faith. "By election we mean that sovereign act of God in grace whereby He chose in Christ Jesus for salvation all those whom He foreknew would accept Him."[1] It is probably true to say that a great majority of evangelicals consciously or unconsciously hold this concept of election. God looked down the corridor of time and in His foreknowledge saw who would accept Christ and then elected them to salvation. This makes foreknowledge foresight without any pretemporal elective action on God's part.

B. Corporate Election

A form of this view was held by Karl Barth. He taught that election is primarily election of Christ, then the election of the community, and finally the election of individuals. Actually all are elect in Christ, though unbelievers do not yet know that. This is why Barth's doctrine of election caused him to be accused of universalism.

An evangelical form of this same concept (perhaps in some cases influenced by Barth and in some cases not) views election as the choosing of the group, the church, in Christ, but not of individuals until after they become members of the group by faith. In the evangelical form there is no suggestion of universalism, though the idea of corporate election is common to both. We cannot speak of individuals being elected before the foundation of the world but only of the church being so elected in Christ (Eph. 1:4). When an individual believes in Christ, he is placed in that elect group, and then he can be said to be elect. "What did God choose before the foundation of the world? The church. Not individuals, but the body of Christ."[2]

C. Individual, Pretemporal Election

In this viewpoint election is "that eternal act of God whereby He, in His sovereign good pleasure, and on account of no foreseen merit in them, chooses a certain number of men to be the recipients of special grace and of eternal salvation."[3] Thus election is unconditional (i.e., there is nothing in the creature that conditions God's choice), pretemporal (before the foundation of the world), unmerited (i.e., of grace), and the basis of salvation. Those who hold this view also acknowledge that election is in Christ, but they mean that He is the ground and cause and guarantee of the election of individuals. They reject the corporate election concept, insisting rather that God elected individuals (and not on the basis of foresight), and those elect individuals form the group, the church.

II. THE TERMINOLOGY OF ELECTION

A proper understanding of a number of terms that are directly and indirectly related to election will help to formulate the concept more biblically. Often the chief problem in understanding this doctrine is not including enough facets of it. No human mind will ever harmonize sovereignty and free will, but ignoring or downplaying one or the other in the interests of a supposed harmony will solve nothing.

A. Background Terminology

Certain terms and concepts form the backdrop against which election must be viewed.

1. Omniscience. This means that God has innate knowledge of all things actual and possible. Thus God's choices were made with the greatest knowledge possible.

2. Decree, design, drawing. The decree of God is His plan for everything. The decree contains many decrees. Decreeing and foreordaining are synonymous theological concepts, but they obviously emphasize the sovereignty facet rather than the free will aspect. The word "design" is less weighted toward sovereignty, while the word "drawing" seems almost neutral.

Scripture teaches clearly that God's plan includes all things (Eph. 1:11), but it also reveals that the degree and directness of God's relationship to specific events is varied. Sometimes He directly ordains something (Deut. 32:39; Acts 5:1–11). Almost always He works through the natural laws He has ordained and does not lift them to make exceptions even for believers (Phil. 2:30). Sometimes He decides to allow people to give full expression to their sinful natures almost without restraint (Rom. 1:24, 26, 28). Sometimes He expects us simply to make choices on the basis of what seems right or what we desire to do (1 Cor. 10:27).

In the light of this variety, I personally think a word other than decree could better express all these aspects. Design may be satisfactory. Drawing may be too neutral, as if God did the initial work and then gave up control. And yet design brings the word "architect" into view, which does serve as a helpful concept in this doctrine. God is the Architect of a plan, which does include all things but includes them in a variety of relationships. Architects' plans are detailed. So is God's plan. In the process of constructing a building, experts can predict that so many workers will be injured and in some cases that some will lose their lives. Such grim statistics are included in the planning of the building, and yet we would not hold the architect responsible for the injuries and deaths (assuming proper safety measures). Carelessness, indifference to rules, even violation of safety restrictions are usually the causes of accidents. But whose fault are they? The individuals who are careless or indifferent. So God's plan has been designed so that the responsibility for sin lies with the individual, even though God knowingly included sin in His plan.

3. Sovereign, free. These synonymous words can only refer to God in the absolute sense. He alone is sovereign and free. Exactly how He exercises that sovereignty and freedom we know only through the revelation of His plan as discussed in the preceding paragraph. Of course when He chooses to restrict Himself, that in no way makes Him less sovereign or free. Sovereign means supreme, and God always was, is, and will be the Sovereign who freely chose the plan He did.

B. Direct Terminology

1. Election. Election emphasizes God's free choice of individuals to salvation (the election of Christ, Israel, or angels are not under consideration here). When Paul uses the verb, he uses it in the middle voice, indicating that God's choice was made freely and for His own purposes (1 Cor. 1:27–28; Eph. 1:4). Individual Thessalonians were chosen (2 Thess. 2:13); as many as were set (previous to their believing) in the group of those who would have eternal life did believe (Acts 13:48); Paul was a chosen instrument (for salvation and service, Acts 9:15; Gal. 1:15); and some individuals' names were not written in the Book of Life from the foundation of the world (Rev. 13:8; 17:8), which must mean some were. Election is unconditional and individual.

God's elect in this age have not been chosen from the spectacular people of this world (1 Cor. 1:27–28; James 2:5). They were chosen before the foundation of the world (Eph. 1:4), and because they are elect they are to live godly lives (Col. 3:12; 2 Pet. 1:10).

2. Predestination. To predestine is to preplan a destiny. The word *proorizō* means to mark off beforehand. The death of Christ and its meaning were predestined by God (Acts 4:28; 1 Cor. 2:7). God's elect are predestined to adoption (Eph. 1:5), to an inheritance (v. 11), and to ultimate conformity to Christ (Rom. 8:28–29).

Biblically, predestination is limited to the elect people and assures their present position and future destiny. Theologically, the term has been used to include all things, that is, as a synonym for the total plan of God. From this theological definition it is an easy step for some forms of Calvinism to use predestination in relation to the destiny of the nonelect. Thus there arises a doctrine of double predestination. However, this is a logical assumption, not based on biblical texts. The Bible is clear that the elect are predestined, but it never suggests that there is a similar decree to elect some to damnation. The Scriptures seem content to leave that matter as a mystery, and so should we.

3. Foreknowledge. The word *proginoskō* is used (a) of prior, temporal knowledge (Acts 26:5; 2 Pet. 3:17); (b) of God's relation to Israel (Rom. 11:2); (c) of Christ's sacrifice (Acts 2:23; 1 Pet. 1:20); and (d) of God's people today (Rom. 8:29; 1 Pet. 1:2).

The debate centers around the question of how much relationship exists in the word "foreknowledge." Does it mean merely that God foreknows in the sense of foreseeing without any relationship? Or, a variation of this, does it mean He foresaw faith and not people? Or, as Calvinism holds, does it mean that He related Himself to people before time in some way so that there is a causative connection that makes *foreknow* practically equivalent to *predestine* or *foreordain?* Clearly people are foreknown, not their faith (Rom. 8:28–29). Clearly too foreknowledge as mere perception is not the basis of election, for 1 Peter 1:2 includes a decision on God's part. Election is in harmony (*kata*) with foreknowledge, and that foreknowledge included the procedure used in working out the choice. Therefore, there is some relationship and/or decision inherent in the meaning of foreknow. Certainly verse 20 includes those ideas or it would assure nothing about the sacrifice of Christ. Likewise there is decisiveness and certainty in Acts 2:23 and Romans 11:2. An apocryphal use of the word also includes certainty: "And Thy judgments are in Thy foreknowledge" (Judith 9:6). To be sure, the word does not say "elect," but neither can it be reduced to a neutral concept of perception only. It does include decision that in turn has to involve an assurance that comes from certainty.

C. Opposite Terminology

By this I mean the ideas involved in retribution and preterition. Retribution means deserved punishment, while preterition is the passing over of those not elected to salvation. Both terms avoid the concept involved in double predestination or reprobation, which means foreordination to damnation. None of these terms appear in the Scripture, though the idea is clearly taught in Romans 9:18, 21; 1 Peter 2:8; and Revelation 17:8. Therefore, the Scriptures do contain a doctrine of preterition, though there is not a decree to condemn in the same sense that there is a decree to elect. Obviously the very idea of election has to include the idea of the greater number out of which they were chosen, and those who were not chosen were certainly passed by.

This in no sense implies that God delights in the destiny of the wicked, or that they are driven against their wills, or that the doctrine of election nullifies a "whosoever" Gospel, or that any individual can know he is not elect and thereby try to excuse himself for rejecting Christ. All are accountable to God for their attitude toward Christ.

III. THE DOCTRINE SUMMARIZED

A. God's Election Is Grounded in His Own Being

Therefore, the act of electing a people has to be compatible with all of His attributes. It is based on His omniscience, so that we may be assured that when He elected He did so knowing full well all of the alternative possibilities. It is related to the exercise of His sovereign will, so that He was in no way forced to do what He did. It was done by the God who is love, so that predestination was done in love (Eph. 1:4–5). It expressed His mercy; otherwise how could God have loved Jacob? (Rom. 9:15). It demonstrates His matchless grace (Eph. 2:7–8). And the ultimate purpose of election is to display His glory (1:6, 12, 14). Usually we put the emphasis on the fact that God *elects*. We need to remember that it is *God* who elects, and He can do nothing unloving or unjust.

B. God's Election Was of Individuals

This has already been discussed. He chose individuals, who then together make up the people of God.

C. God's Election Was Not Based on Foreknowledge (Meaning Foresight)

To foreknow is not a neutral concept but involves some sort of relationship.

D. God's Election Was Before the Foundation of the World

He did not choose us only after we chose Him (Eph. 1:4).

E. Election Alone Does Not Result in the Salvation of People

To be sure, election assures that those chosen will be saved, but it alone does not save them. People are saved through faith in the substitutionary death of Christ. And, of course, they must learn about the death of Christ somehow in order to have content to their faith. Thus election, the death of Christ, testimony of His death, and personal faith are all necessary in the salvation of an individual. Election alone does not save.

F. Election Is Purposeful, Not Capricious

Its purpose for us is service and good works (John 15:16; Gal. 1:15–16; Eph. 2:10; 1 Thess. 1:4–10).

Its purpose for God is to manifest His glory (Eph. 1:6, 12, 14).

Therefore, the doctrine of election is highly motivating and should never be deadening to one's spiritual life (Col. 3:12).

IV. OBJECTIONS TO THE DOCTRINE OF ELECTION

Of course election is only a part of the broader consideration of the entire decree or plan or sovereignty of God. These objections are the ones usually raised against that doctrine.

A. It Equals Fatalism

Popularly, this objection is expressed like this: "What's going to be is going to be anyway, and I cannot do anything about it." There are two very important differences between the biblical doctrine of the decree of God and the false teaching of fatalism. (1) Behind the decree is an intelligent, loving Being. Behind fatalism lies only impersonal blind chance. (2) Fatalism has no place for the importance of means. It only emphasizes ends. The decree of God includes all the means essential to arriving at the ends. And those means are as essential as the ends. Thus, the biblical doctrine gives proper place to human responsibility. What's going to be is going to be through certain means and procedures and responsible human actions. Ephesians 1:11 spotlights all things, not solely ends.

B. It Is Inconsistent with Human Freedom

This is the same objection raised in Romans 9:19: Why can God fault anyone, since no one really resists His will if everything is part of His plan? Though it is true that God has the right to do anything consistent with His nature, it is equally true that He has chosen to exercise His rights by including the responsible and relatively free actions of people (Philemon 14; Rev. 17:13 linked with v. 17). I say relatively free simply because no one has absolute freedom, if for no other reason than the limitations of being fallen human creatures. He has made us responsible, and when we fail to act responsibly we are justly blamed.

An illustration: Does God know the day you are going to die? The answer is yes, He does. Question: Could you die a day sooner? The answer is no. Question: Then why do you eat? Answer: to live. The means of eating is essential to the end of living to the preordained day of death. From this point on the illustration can easily and uselessly get into the realm of the hypothetical. Suppose I do not eat? Then I will die. Would that be the day God planned that I should die? These are questions that do not need to be asked or answered. Just eat.

Or to change the illustration: Has God planned the answers to my prayers? Yes. Then why pray? Because those answers come when I pray.

Or again: Does God know who are elect? Of course, He elected them. Can any of them be lost? No. Then why pray and witness? Because that is how they will be saved. Will any of them fail to believe? No. Then why do they have to believe? Because that is the only way they can be saved, and unless they do believe they will not be saved. Do not let your mind ask the theoretical and useless questions. Let your mind and your life concentrate on doing what is God's will and making sure you act responsibly.

C. It Makes God the Author of Sin

I think we must acknowledge that God did construct a plan that included sin, and its inclusion did not come as a surprise. Yet we must guard the clear teaching of Scripture that God hates sin (Ps. 5:5), that He is never responsible for our committing sin (James 1:13), and that including sin in His plan does not make it somehow less sinful and us less culpable.

All that the Bible says about the concrete appearance of sin in creatures is that it was found in Satan (Ezek. 28:15). Isaiah 45:7 may refer to God's including evil in His plan; some understand the verse to refer to the results of sin, such as calamity. Proverbs 16:4 teaches also that all things are included in God's plan. We must seek a balance in this truth and live with the unresolved tensions.

Finally, face the ramification of all things not being included in one way or another in God's plan. This would mean that there were things outside of His control, and that is a frightening idea.

Listen to these words of Calvin:

> Herein appears the immeasurable felicity of the godly mind. Innumerable are the evils that beset human life; innumerable too the deaths that threaten it. We need not go beyond ourselves: since our body is the receptacle of a thousand diseases—in fact holds within itself and fosters the causes of diseases—a man cannot go about unburdened by many forms of his own destruction, and without drawing out a life enveloped, as it were, with death. For what else would you call it, when he neither freezes nor sweats without danger? Now, wherever you turn, all things around you not only are hardly to be trusted but almost openly menace, and seem to threaten immediate death. Embark on a ship; you are one step away from death. Mount a horse; if one foot slips, your life is imperiled. Go through the city streets; you are subject to as many dangers as there are tiles on the roofs. If there is a weapon in your hand or a friend's, harm awaits. All the fierce animals you see are armed for your destruction. But if you try to shut yourself up in a walled garden, seemingly delightful, there a serpent sometimes lies hidden. Your house, continually in danger of fire, threatens in the daytime to impoverish you, at night even to collapse upon you. Your field, since it is exposed to hail, frost, drought, and other calamities, threatens you with barrenness, and hence, famine. I pass over poisonings, ambushes, robberies, open violence, which in part besiege us at home, in part dog us abroad. Amid these tribulations must not man be most miserable, since, but half alive in life, he weakly draws

> his anxious and languid breath, as if he had a sword perpetually hanging over his neck?
>
> You will say: these events rarely happen, or at least not all the time, nor to all men, and never all at once. I agree; but since we are warned by the examples of others that these can also happen to ourselves, and that our life ought not to be excepted any more than theirs, we cannot but be frightened and terrified as if such events were about to happen to us. What, therefore, more calamitous can you imagine than such trepidation? Besides, it is an insult to God to say that He has exposed man, the noblest of His creatures, to the blindness and temerity of fortune.[4]

Then join with Paul in his magnificent doxology that comes at the conclusion of his lengthy and detailed section on election when he wrote: "Oh, the depth of the riches both of the wisdom and knowledge of God! How unsearchable are His judgments and unfathomable His ways! For who has known the mind of the Lord, or who became His counselor? Or who has first given to Him that it might be paid back to him again? For from Him and through Him and to Him are all things. To Him be the glory forever. Amen" (Rom. 11:33–36).

NOTES

1. Henry C. Thiessen, *Introductory Lectures in Systematic Theology* (Grand Rapids: Eerdmans, 1959), 344; though this definition was not allowed to stand in Doerksen's revision, 1981, 258.
2. Dan Esterline, "The Doctrine of Predestination," *Moody Monthly,* February 1979, 86; for the same view see also Roger T. Forster and V. Paul Marston, *God's Strategy in Human History* (Wheaton, Ill.: Tyndale, 1975); and Robert Shank, *Elect in the Son* (Springfield, Mo.: Westcott, 1970), 48–49.
3. L. Berkhof, *Systematic Theology* (Grand Rapids: Eerdmans, 1941), 114.
4. *Institutes of the Christian Religion,* I, XVII, 10.

Chapter 55
THE EXTENT OF THE ATONEMENT

I. THE QUESTION

Limited atonement or particular redemption can scarcely be termed a cornerstone doctrine. Nevertheless, it obviously is sometimes a hotly debated one. Berkhof is typical of those who hold the view and who express the issue this way: "Did the Father in sending Christ, and did Christ in coming into the world, to make atonement for sin, *do this with the design or for the purpose of saving only the elect or all men?* That is the question, and that only is the question."[1] If indeed the question is properly expressed this way, then the answer is clear: The Atonement was limited, for Christ did not come into the world to save all men. Our understanding of election makes that answer certain.

But is Berkhof's question the correct question? The answer is no. It is false to say that "that is the question, and that only is the question." Rather, the actual question is: Did Christ purpose by coming into the world to make provision for the salvation of all people, realizing that the Father would mysteriously draw the elect to Himself and allow others to reject the provision made? Because some reject does not invalidate the provision or mean that the provision was not made for them. If we say that a father provides sufficient food for his family, we do not exclude the possibility that some members of that family may refuse to eat what has been provided. But their refusal does not mean that the provision was made only for those who actually do eat the food. Likewise, the death of Christ provided the payment for the sins of all people—those who accept that payment and those who do not. Refusal to accept does not limit the provision made. Providing and possessing are not the same.

II. THE VIEWS

Arminians accept universal redemption or unlimited atonement (along with the idea that sufficient grace is supplied to all so that they may believe). Among Calvinists there are some who hold to universal redemption (so-called four-point Calvinists or Amyraldians, after Moses Amyraldus, 1596–1664), and some who teach particular redemption (so-called ultra or five-point Calvinists). The latter group holds that Christ died to secure salvation for the elect; thus His death was limited in its extent to the elect. Moderate Calvinists see the purpose of Christ's death as providing a substitution for all; therefore, it was unlimited in its extent.

These views relate to the question of the order of the decrees of God. This discussion concerns logic more than revelation, and it only serves to highlight the different perspectives by attempting to place an order on the parts of the single decree of God, especially focusing on the relation of election to the Fall (*lapse*—fall). Supralapsarianism places election first (*supra*—above) followed by the decrees to create, allow the Fall, and then provide for the salvation of the elect. Infralapsarianism (*infra*—later) lists Creation, Fall, election, and then provision for the salvation of the elect. Sublapsarianism (*sub*—beneath) sees this order: Creation, Fall, provision of salvation for all, election of some to be saved. Some theologians do not recognize the distinction between *infra* and *sub,* and I must say that none of these schemes really confirms anything. The issue under discussion concerns the extent of the Atonement, and it will not be settled or even enlightened much by deciding the supposed order of the decrees.

III. SOME IMPORTANT AFFIRMATIONS

When discussing this question, it is essential to keep certain truths clearly in mind.

(1) Unlimited redemptionists are not universalists. They do not believe that all will ultimately be saved. Nor does their view require or logically lead to such a heretical conclusion. To assert this is to create a straw man.

(2) All people are lost, including the elect. The fact that an individual is elect does not in some way make him less lost than a nonelect person.

(3) Anyone who will be saved must believe. The Father will draw the person, yet he must come (John 6:37, 44).

(4) Some Scriptures do relate the Atonement particularly to the elect. See John 10:15 and Ephesians 5:25 for clear examples. Unlimited people readily acknowledge this. But this is not the issue. The question is: Are there Scriptures that broaden the extent of the Atonement beyond the elect? Limited advocates say no and attempt to explain

those passages that seem to broaden the Atonement in ways that do not broaden it. In other words, unlimited advocates acknowledge that the Atonement is both limited and unlimited; limited advocates insist that it is strictly limited and do not recognize any unlimited passages as teaching unlimited atonement.

IV. EXEGETICAL CONSIDERATIONS

A. 2 Peter 2:1

It is generally acknowledged that the verse most difficult to harmonize with the limited atonement view is 2 Peter 2:1. Apparently it says that the false teachers (who are not among the elect) had the price of redemption paid for them by the Lord, for in their teaching they deny the Lord who bought (*agorazō*) them. In other words, Peter seems to be saying that the Lord in His sacrifice paid the price of redemption for these nonelect people.

Some particular redemptionists say that Peter was only recording what the false teachers claimed. They said that the Lord bought them, but in reality He did not because He died only for the elect. Thus Peter simply acknowledged what they were saying without affirming the truth of it, and indeed, it is not a true statement from the limited viewpoint. But, of course, even if this is an expression of what the false teachers were saying, it still can be a true statement, so it cannot be assumed to be false simply because it comes from their mouths. But more likely Peter was emphasizing the depth of their defection by pointing out that they denied the Lord who bought them. This is sometimes called the "Christian Charity" view.

Others understand this to mean that the Lord (as Creator) "purchased" these nonelect people in the sense that He as Creator possessed them. Thus *agorazō* (buy, redeem) comes to mean *ktizō* (create). The Lord possessed them as He did Israel when He effected a temporal deliverance from Egypt (Deut. 32:6).

In attempting to reinforce this interpretation, particular redemptionists cite three lines of alleged support. (1) The word for Lord (*despotes*) when used in the New Testament refers to God, not Christ, and it should refer to Christ if this verse teaches a soteriological ransom (see, for example, Acts 4:24; Rev. 6:10). While the word does usually refer to the Father when it refers to Deity, does not Jude 4 use it in reference to Christ? It seems so, and if so there, then there is no reason that it does not also refer to Christ in 2 Peter 2:1.

(2) They also point out that in other occurrences of *agorazō* where it refers to soteriological redemption in the New Testament, the price paid is mentioned in the context. Therefore, since no price is mentioned in 2 Peter 2:1, this must not refer to an actual soteriological redemption, but rather a Creator-creature "possession." However, in Revelation 14:4 no price is mentioned in the context of relating the soteriological redemption of the 144,000. Likewise, 2 Peter 2:1 could also refer to a soteriological redemption without mentioning the specific price.

(3) Further it is alleged that *agorazō* is always used in contexts where there is a real, take-possession kind of buying. Because the false teachers in 2 Peter 2:1 were not actually saved, *agorazō* cannot refer to a salvation purchase since no real possession took place. But notice Luke 14:18–19 where a real, actual purchase was made of a piece of property and yet the purchaser had not even seen it. Likewise, the unlimited redemptionist argues, the false teachers were actually purchased (that is, Christ did die for them) even though they were never possessed (that is, they were not saved).[2]

B. 1 John 2:2

This verse also seems to say rather clearly that the death of Christ was for the whole world, since He is the propitiation not only for our sins but also for the sins of the whole world. "Our" seems to refer to those who are (or will be) saved while "the whole world" includes those who are not saved. How do limited redemptionists explain this verse so as to be compatible with their viewpoint?

Actually three suggestions are made. In all three, "ours" and "the whole world" add up to the sum total of all the elect; therefore, "ours" refers to some of the elect and "the whole world" to others of the elect. (1) Some understand "ours" to mean the elect living in Asia Minor where the apostle John was; "the whole world" then refers to the elect living outside Asia Minor. This is a geographical distinction. (2) Others see a racial distinction; that is, "ours" means the elect from among Jewish people, and "the whole world" designates the elect from among Gentiles. (3) Still others make a chronological distinction. "Ours" designates the elect living in the first century, while "the whole world" focuses on the elect in subsequent centuries. In other words, limited atonement sees the Atonement from this verse as geographically, ethnically, or chronologically universal, but only in relation to the elect, not all people.[3]

To be sure, the word "world" does not always mean all people (see John 12:19), but no dictionary gives it the meaning of only the elect.

Furthermore, the only other occurrence of the phrase "the whole world" in John's writings is in 1 John 5:19, and there it undebatably includes everybody. So the presumption is that it also means everyone in 2:2. And this means that Christ died for all people even though all are not ultimately saved.

C. 1 Timothy 2:4–6; 4:10

Generally, limited redemptionists understand the "all" in 1 Timothy 2 to refer to all kinds of people. That is, Christ died for all kinds of sinners (among the elect), and God wishes all kinds of people (among the elect) to be saved. In 4:10, however, some understand Savior to mean that Christ provides the general benefits of providence to all and especially to believers. "Savior" then has no soteriological connotation, according to this interpretation. The logic behind these interpretations is that if Christ is the Savior of all people absolutely, then all must be saved, and since all are not saved, then He cannot be the Savior of all in any soteriological sense. But is not God the Father of all people absolutely (Acts 17:29), and yet not all people are in the redeemed family? (Gal. 3:26). Similarly, Christ can be said to be the Savior of all without all being saved.[4]

D. Hebrews 2:9

Again it seems clear that the Atonement was universal. How else could the writer say that He tasted death for every man? Notice that the preceding verses use the word "man" also and the meaning is clearly all people, not just the elect.

E. John 3:16

Limited redemptionists are forced to say that this verse means God loved only the world of the elect. One advocate of limited redemption understands the verse to emphasize the intensity of God's love; that is, God loved the world of sinners. But it is still restricted to the elect sinners. Now if John 3:16 is so restricted, then no limited redemptionist could tell his young children, for example, that God loves them, since he could not know at that age whether or not they belonged to the elect. The Lord, however, expressed His love *agapaō* for an unsaved (and evidently a nonelect) man (Mark 10:21).

F. Acts 17:30

This verse states the matter as broadly as it could be said. God commands all men everywhere to repent. To read it to say all men without distinction of race or rank everywhere in the earth but only among the elect (which is the way it would have to be understood to support limited atonement) does not appear to be the most secure exegesis!

Exegesis clearly supports the unlimited position.

V. THEOLOGICAL CONSIDERATIONS

A. Universal Gospel Preaching

Unlimited advocates claim that in order for one to preach the Gospel to all, Christ had to die for all. It does seem to make more sense to say that unlimited redemption is more compatible with universal Gospel preaching. However, it must be recognized that believing in limited atonement does not necessarily dampen one's evangelistic efforts. Some great evangelists, like Spurgeon, held to limited atonement. And some who hold to unlimited atonement fail in their responsibility to witness.

B. The Value of Christ's Death

Is some of the value of Christ's death lost if all for whom He died are not actually saved? The limited person says yes; therefore, he concludes, Christ only died for the elect. But if God designed that there be value in a universal sacrifice in that it made the whole world savable, in addition to the saving value for those who do believe, then all the value is realized, though in different ways.

C. Do the Nonelect Have Their Sins Paid for Twice?

Some limited advocates argue that if Christ died for all, then the sins of the nonelect were paid for at the cross by the death of Christ and will be paid for again at the judgment by the condemnation of the nonelect to the lake of fire. So in effect their sins are paid for twice. Logically, then, either the death of Christ should not include the nonelect, or the nonelect should not be condemned to the lake of fire.

An analogous question might be asked. Did the Israelite who refused to apply the Passover blood to the door of his house have his sins paid for twice? When the Passover Lamb was killed, his sins were covered. But if he did not put the blood on the door, he died. Was this a second payment for his sins? Of course not. The first and sufficient payment was simply not applied to that particular house. Death after failure to apply the blood was just retribution for not appropriating the sufficient sacrifice. The Atonement of Christ paid for the sins of the whole world, but the individual must appropriate that payment through faith. The world was reconciled to God (2 Cor. 5:19), but those reconciled people need to be reconciled to God (v. 20).

An illustration: In one school where I have taught, the student aid was handled in this way. People made gifts to the student aid fund. Needy students applied for help from that fund. A committee decided who would receive aid and how much. But when the actual money was distributed, it was done by issuing a check to the student, who then was expected to endorse it back to the school, which would then place the credit on his account. The money was not moved directly from the aid fund to the individual student's account. The student had to receive it personally and place it on his account. Let us suppose you gave a gift to cover one student's tuition for one year. You could properly say that his tuition was fully paid. But until the selection is made by the committee, and until the student receives the gift and places it on his account, his tuition is not paid. If he fails to endorse the check, it will never be paid even though it has been paid!

The death of Christ pays for all the sins of all people. But not one individual has his own account settled until he believes. If he never believes, then even though the price has been fully paid, his sins will not be forgiven. The death of Christ is like some benefactor paying the tuitions of all students in all schools everywhere. If that could be true, what should we be telling students? The good news that their tuitions are paid.

Christ died for all. What should we be telling the world?

NOTES

1. L. Berkhof, *Systematic Theology* (Grand Rapids: Eerdmans, 1941), 394.
2. See John Owen, *The Death of Death in the Death of Christ* (London: Banner of Truth Trust, 1959), 250–52; and Gary Long, *Definite Atonement* (Nutley, N.J.: Presbyterian and Reformed, 1976), 67–82.
3. See John Murray, *Redemption—Accomplished and Applied* (Grand Rapids: Eerdmans, 1961), 82–85.
4. See Owen, *Death of Death,* 235.

Chapter 56
The Application of Salvation

In this chapter we shall consider the ministries involved in the application of salvation. Historically, this consideration has been labeled the *ordo salutis,* or way of salvation, and it attempts to arrange in logical order (not temporal order) these activities involved in applying salvation to the individual. But like the question of the order of the decrees in lapsarianism, the *ordo salutis* in reality contributes little of substance. The most argued point is the relation between regeneration and faith, which we shall discuss later. Rather than trying to establish an order, it is more useful to note which ministries are solely of God (calling, regeneration) and which involve man as well (conviction, conversion).

I. CONVICTION

A. What Is Conviction?

As recorded in John 16:8–11, the Lord promised that after Pentecost the Holy Spirit would convict the world of sin, righteousness, and judgment. What is conviction? It is not the same as conversion. It is convincing or refuting an opponent so that he has the matter set before him in a clear light whether he accepts or rejects the evidence.

> The idea of "conviction" is complex. It involves the conceptions of authoritative examination, of unquestionable proof, of decisive judgment, of punitive power. Whatever the final issue may be, he who "convicts" another places the truth of the case in dispute in a clear light before him, so that it must be seen and acknowledged as truth. He who then rejects the conclusion which the exposition involves, rejects it with his eyes open and at his peril. Truth seen as truth carries with it condemnation to all who refuse to welcome it.[1]

Notice the use of the word in Matthew 18:15. The man reproved or convicted may accept the evidence and repent, or he may not, which would then result in a further confrontation. Conviction, then, offers proof, but does not guarantee the truth will be accepted, which is necessary for conversion.

B. Who Are Convicted?

The world. Does this refer only to the elect? No, since the ministry of conviction expects that some will not accept the truth. Does it mean everyone in the world? Likely not, since this involves the specifics of sin, righteousness, and judgment, not just general conviction that comes from natural revelation. It must mean a large number of people, more than the elect, but not everybody (cf. John 12:19).

C. Of What Are They Convicted?

Conviction comes in the specific areas of sin, righteousness, and judgment. The *hotis* may mean because or namely or a mixture in the three clauses. For example, if because, then the world is convicted of sin because of unbelief. If namely, then the world is convicted of the sin of unbelief. The righteousness is that which Christ provided on the cross, vindicated by His ascension to the Father. The judgment may be the sinner's future judgment, assured by the already completed judgment of Satan, or it may refer to Satan's judgment on the cross (John 12:31).

The order is a logical one. Man needs to see his state of sin, have proof of the righteousness that the Savior provides, and be reminded that if he refuses to receive that Savior he faces certain condemnation.

D. How Is Conviction Accomplished?

Most likely several ways are involved. The Spirit may speak directly to man's conscience, which, though able to be seared, can still convict. He may speak through the written Word. He may also use the spoken testimony or preached word. But whether or not people are involved in effecting this ministry of conviction, if conviction comes to an individual the Spirit must do it. We readily acknowledge that regeneration is the work of the Spirit, but we sometimes let ourselves think that our clever or convincing presentations can convict. Not so. God must do even that.

II. CALLING

A. The General Call

Only one or two references in the New Testament use the word "call" to convey the idea of a general call to elect and nonelect alike.

Matthew 22:14 clearly supports the concept, while 9:13 may also. However, the idea is clearly expressed in passages like Luke 14:16–24 and John 7:37. This is God's general invitation to men to come to Him.

B. The Effective Call

This is the call that only the elect respond to through faith and that results in their salvation (Rom. 8:30; 1 Cor. 1:2). This is God's work, though He uses the proclamation of the Word of God (Rom. 10:17). The call is unto fellowship (1 Cor. 1:9), light (1 Pet. 2:9), liberty (Gal. 5:13), holiness (1 Thess. 4:7), and His kingdom (2:12).

III. REGENERATION

A. The Meaning of Regeneration

The word, used only twice in the New Testament (Matt. 19:28; Titus 3:5), means to be born again. To be born from above (*anothen*) occurs in John 3:3 and probably includes the idea of being born again also (see the use of *anothen* in Gal. 4:9). It is the work of God that gives new life to the one who believes.

B. The Means of Regeneration

God regenerates (John 1:13) according to His will (James 1:18) through the Holy Spirit (John 3:5) when a person believes (1:12) the Gospel as revealed in the Word (1 Pet. 1:23).

C. The Relation of Regeneration and Faith

In the Reformed statement of the *ordo salutis,* regeneration precedes faith, for, it is argued, a sinner must be given new life in order to be able to believe. Although this is admittedly stated only as a logical order, it is not wise to insist even on that; for it may as well be argued that if a sinner has the new life through regeneration, why does he need to believe? Of course, there can be no chronological order; both regeneration and faith have to occur at the same moment. To be sure, faith is also part of the total package of salvation that is the gift of God (Eph. 2:9); yet faith is commanded in order to be saved (Acts 16:31). Both are true.

D. The Fruit of Regeneration

The new life will bear new fruit. In 1 John 2:29; 3:9; 4:7; 5:1, 4, and 18, some of the results of the new life include righteousness, not committing sin, loving one another, and overcoming the world.

IV. FAITH

A. The Meaning of Faith

Faith means confidence, trust, to hold something as true. Of course, faith must have content; there must be confidence or trust about something. To have faith in Christ unto salvation means to have confidence that He can remove the guilt of sin and grant eternal life.

B. The Necessity of Faith

Salvation is always through faith, not because of faith (Eph. 2:8). Faith is the channel through which we receive God's gift of eternal life; it is not the cause. This is so man can never boast, even of his faith. But faith is the necessary and only channel (John 5:24; 17:3).

Normally the New Testament word for believe (*pisteuō*) is used with the preposition *eis* (John 3:16), indicating reliance or confident trust in the object. Sometimes it is followed by *epi,* emphasizing the trust as laying hold on the object of faith (Rom. 9:33; 10:11). Sometimes it is followed by a clause that introduces the content of the faith (10:9). The verb is used with a dative in Romans 4:3. But whatever the form, it indicates reliance on something or someone.

C. The Kinds of Faith

The Scriptures seem to distinguish four kinds of faith.

1. Intellectual or historical faith. This apprehends the truth intellectually as a result of education, tradition, rearing, etc. It is human and does not save (Matt. 7:26; Acts 26:27–28; James 2:19).

2. Miracle faith. This is faith to perform or receive a miracle, and it may or may not be accompanied by salvation (Matt. 8:10–13; 17:20; Acts 14:9).

3. Temporary faith. Luke 8:13 illustrates this kind of faith. It seems similar to intellectual faith, except that there seems to be more personal interest involved.

4. Saving faith. This is a reliance on the truth of the Gospel as revealed in the Word of God.

D. The Facets of Faith

1. The intellectual facet. This involves a factual and positive recognition of the truth of the Gospel and the person of Christ.

2. *The emotional facet.* The truth and the person of Christ are now seen in an interested and absorbing way.
3. *The volitional facet.* Now the individual appropriates personally the truth and the Person and places his reliance on Him.

Although these three facets may be distinguished, they must be integrated when saving faith takes place. The person believes in Christ with all his being, not just his intellect or emotions or will.

Perhaps one of the clearest statements of the necessary content to saving faith is found in the words of the Lord to the sinful Samaritan woman. He said, "If you knew the gift of God, and who it is who says to you, 'Give Me a drink,' you would have asked Him, and He would have given you living water" (John 4:10). Know about the gift and the Person, then ask and receive eternal life.

NOTE

1. B. F. Westcott, *The Gospel According to St. John* (London: Murray, 1908), 2:219.

Chapter 57
THE SECURITY OF THE BELIEVER

I. DEFINITIONS AND DISTINCTIONS

The title of this chapter was not chosen indiscriminately. In some theologies or dictionaries it would have been entitled Assurance; in others, Perseverance; in a few, Preservation. What are the differences, and why choose Security?

Eternal security is the work of God that guarantees that the gift of salvation, once received, is forever and cannot be lost. The concept of eternal security emphasizes God's activity in guaranteeing the eternal possession of the gift of eternal life. It relates to those the Holy Spirit regenerates, and its veracity does not rest on feelings or experiences.

Preservation is quite similar to eternal security in emphasizing the work of God in preserving the believer in his salvation.

Perseverance, the term generally used in Calvinism, labels the fifth point in Calvin's theology, the "final perseverance" of the saints. It means that believers "can neither totally nor finally fall away from the state of grace, but shall certainly persevere therein to the end, and be eternally saved" (Westminster Confession, XVII, I). It seems to focus on the believer—it is the believer who perseveres (albeit through the decree and power of God). Security focuses on God—it is God who secures our salvation. It does not deny that there may be times of backsliding, but it stresses the need for demonstrable fruit throughout the Christian life. Sometimes those who approach this doctrine from the viewpoint of perseverance deny the possibility of a Christian's being carnal.

Though eternal security, preservation, and perseverance in reality all teach the same bottom-line conclusion (namely, that the true believer will not lose his salvation), assurance is a different doctrine. It is the realization of the truth of eternal security or perseverance. A secure salvation is a true fact whether one realizes it or not. Thus a believer has security whether or not he has assurance.

II. THE DOCTRINE OF ASSURANCE

Assurance is the realization that one possesses eternal life. Lack of assurance often brings unnecessary but terrible trauma to a person's life. Why do people lack assurance?

Four reasons may be suggested. (1) Some doubt the reality of their committal to Christ. Sometimes this may be connected with the inability to pinpoint a time when one received Christ. Regeneration occurs at a specific point in time. People are either saved or lost at any given moment. No one grows into conversion. But we all do grow in our comprehension of conversion. So, although in God's sight and in our experience there was a point in time when we were saved, in our recollection or understanding we may not be able to specify it.

Sometimes this doubt is more basic than just the matter of time. Did I *really* trust Christ? Such doubt may be dispelled by calling on the name of the Lord again (and again and again, if necessary). No one can be born again more than one time, but one may honestly tell the Lord his doubt and call on Him for salvation again.

(2) Some lack assurance because they question the correctness of the procedure they went through when they expressed faith in Christ. *I did not go forward. Am I really saved? Did I pray the proper prayer? I received Christ privately. Is this sufficient, or do I need to make some kind of public demonstration?* This problem, which is very real to more people than it should be, has been aggravated by elevating some method of invitation to the place where it almost becomes the means of salvation.

(3) If one does not believe in the security of the believer, then he will undoubtedly lack assurance more than once in his lifetime.

(4) When sin, especially a serious sin, enters the believer's life, then doubt sometimes accompanies such an experience. Security does not grant a license to sin, but to have assurance we need to realize that Christians will sin, and that sin does not cause us to lose our salvation. The normal Christian experience never includes sinlessness, for "we all stumble in many ways" (James 3:2). This never excuses sin, for the Christian will also grow in holiness. But the experience of sin does not forfeit salvation.

III. THE ARMINIAN VIEW OF SECURITY

James Arminius (1560–1609) received his training in strict Reformed theology. When asked to defend supralapsarianism against sublapsarianism, he found himself guardedly defending the sublapsarian position. His writings, collected in three volumes, consist mostly of occasional treatises that grew out of the controversies he found himself in. The system known as Arminianism took his views much further and was forged by Simon Episcopius (1583–1643).

Among the principal teachings of Arminianism are the following.

1. Foreknowledge. God's decrees are based on His foreknowledge (meaning foresight). Election was due to foreseen faith and reprobation to foreseen resistance to grace. Though Arminius also viewed foreknowledge as foresight, he did say that "God decreed to save some and damn certain particular persons."[1]

2. Pollution, not guilt. Man inherited pollution from Adam but not imputed guilt. Depravity is not total, for man can incline his will toward good deeds.

3. Perfection. It is possible for a believer to live in such conformity to God's will so as to be called perfect.

4. Loss of salvation. Arminianism clearly teaches that a believer may lose his salvation. Arminius said: "I never taught that a true believer can either totally or finally fall away from the faith and perish; yet I will not conceal that there are passages of Scripture which seem to me to wear this aspect."[2]

On a more popular level, Arminians sometimes equate the position of eternal security with a license to sin. Of course, Calvinists do sin and excuse it, but so do Arminians. Our life should adorn our doctrine, but our life, good or bad, neither makes doctrine true or untrue.

As a practical matter, the Arminian view of the possibility and reality of losing one's salvation sometimes leads to a cataloging of sins. In one category are sins that will cause you to lose your salvation; in another, those that do not. Of course, some sins are worse than others (Matt. 7:1–5; John 19:11), but if one sin can cause the loss of salvation, then any sin can. Resistance to this conclusion may account for the perfectionism teaching in Arminianism.

IV. THE REASONS FOR ETERNAL SECURITY

Basically security is based on the grace of God and the fact that eternal life is a gift and it is eternal. When a person believes in Christ, he is brought into a relationship with the Godhead that assures his salvation is secure. Of course, this is true only of born again people. There are those who profess but do not possess life. Sometimes we can make a reasonably sure judgment as to whether an individual only professes or actually possesses eternal life. Sometimes we cannot. But the regenerated person's salvation is secure because of that relationship to God that he has through faith.

A. Reasons Related to the Father

1. His purpose. God purposed to glorify the same group He predestined, called, and justified (Rom. 8:30). This daring statement could not be made if any one of that group could lose his salvation. If so, then the ones whom He justified would not be the same number as the ones He glorified. But the text says they will be the same.
2. His power. Most would agree that God's power is able to keep the believer (and it is, Jude 24), but some would argue that it can be thwarted by a person renouncing his faith. But the Lord said that we are secure in His hand and the Father's hand and that no one can seize the believer from the safe position (John 10:28–29). "No one" means no one, including the individual himself. The promise does not say that no one, except yourself, can seize the believer out of God's hand. It says no one.

B. Reasons Related to the Son

1. His death. Paul asks two questions in Romans 8:33: Who will bring a charge against God's elect, and who condemns them? His answer that no one can is based on the death, resurrection, intercession, and advocacy of Christ (v. 34). If any sin can undo a believer's salvation, and if in fact, he can lose that salvation, then Christ's death did not pay for that sin. But it did, Paul asserts. Our Lord Himself also declared that He would lose nothing of what the Father gave Him (John 6:39–40)—everyone who believes in Him will be raised at the last day, not everyone who believes and perseveres.
2. His prayers. Christ's present ministry in heaven of praying for His own consists of two aspects: a preventive ministry (intercession) and a curative ministry (advocacy). His prayer in John 17 illustrates the preventive aspect. There He prayed that we might be kept from the evil one (v. 15), that we would be sanctified (v. 17), that we would be united (v. 21), that we would be in heaven with Him (v. 24), and that we might behold His glory (v. 24). Because of His unceasing intercession for us He is able to save us completely and eternally (Heb. 7:25).

Advocacy comes into action when we sin (1 John 2:1). Again, if any sin can undo salvation (and any can), then Satan has an airtight case against any believer whenever he sins (Rev. 12:10). He can justly demand the Christian's eternal damnation, and were it not for our Advocate, we would be condemned. But the Lord points to His work on Calvary that removes the guilt of all our sins, those committed before and after salvation, and this suffices to answer Satan's charge.

> I sinned. And straightway, posthaste, Satan flew
> before the presence of the Most High God,
> And made a railing accusation there.
> He said, "This soul, this thing of clay and sod,
> Has sinned. 'Tis true that he has named Thy name,
> But I demand his death, for Thou hast said,
> 'The soul that sinneth, it shall die.' Shall not
> Thy sentence be fulfilled? Is justice dead?
> Send now this wretched sinner to his doom.
> What other thing can righteous Ruler do?"
> And thus he did accuse me day and night,
> And every word he spoke, O God, was true!
> Then quickly One rose up from God's right hand,
> Before whose glory angels veiled their eyes,
> He spoke, "Each jot and tittle of the Law
> Must be fulfilled; the guilty sinner dies!
> But wait—suppose his guilt were all transferred
> To Me, and that I paid his penalty!
> Behold My hands, My side, My feet! One day
> I was made sin for him, and died that he
> Might be presented faultless, at Thy throne!"
> And Satan fled away. Full well he knew
> That he could not prevail against such love,
> For every word my dear Lord spoke was true!
> —Martha Snell Nicholson

C. Reasons Related to the Spirit

1. He regenerates. If we are born again by the Spirit when we believe, then if we can renounce our faith to lose our salvation, we would have to have the new birth taken away as well.

2. He indwells. If salvation can be lost, then the presence of the Spirit within the life of the believer would have to be removed. The Christian would become disindwelt.

3. He baptizes. The Spirit joins the believer to the body of Christ when he believes (1 Cor. 12:13); therefore, if salvation can be lost, the Christian would have to be detached from the body of Christ.

4. He seals. The Spirit seals the believer until the day of redemption (Eph. 4:30). If salvation can be lost, then His sealing would not be until the day of redemption but only until the day of sinning, or apostasy, or disbelief.

Of course, Scripture gives no hint that a Christian can lose the new birth, or that he can be disindwelt, or that he can be removed from the body of Christ (thus maiming His body) or be unsealed. Salvation is eternal and completely secured to all who believe.

To be sure, believers sin and are warned against false profession and Christian immaturity, but God never takes back the gift of His salvation once it is received. Believers will not always persevere in godliness. Peter did not (Gal. 2:11). Many Ephesian believers did not (Acts 19:18). Lot did not (2 Pet. 2:7). At the Judgment Seat of Christ there will be some whose works will be burned and who will be saved as through fire (1 Cor. 3:15). Even though every believer will bear some fruit (4:5), it is difficult if not impossible to quantify how much or what kind each one will bear and thus to make judgments as to the spiritual condition of an individual.

V. SOME "PROBLEM" PASSAGES

Certain passages are sometimes understood as invalidating the doctrine of eternal security. We shall examine some of these to show that at least there is a reasonable interpretation that does not contradict the doctrine of security.

A. Passages That Warn Against Substituting Law for Grace

Two passages severely warn against trying to replace the way of grace with the old way of the Law. In Galatians 5:4 Paul clearly declared that those who attempt to be justified by the Law have "fallen from grace." That is, to try to use the Law as the ground for justification is to fall away from grace, which provides the only way to be justified.

The same kind of warning appears in Hebrews 10:26–31. Here the writer warned that if a person rejects the truth of Christ's death for sin, there is no other sacrifice for sin available and no other way to come to God. Such unbelief brings the threefold indictment detailed in verse 29.

B. Passages That Warn Against Losing Rewards (but Not Salvation)

Quite clearly Paul spoke to this possibility in the "race" passage, 1 Corinthians 9:24–27. Races are run for rewards, and Paul himself felt the need to live a disciplined life so that at the end he would not be disapproved, not eliminated from the race, not lose his crowns.

The Lord's illustration of the Vine and the branches teaches the same basic truth (John 15:1–17). These branches are in Him, thus referring to believers. Believers, then, are exhorted to abide in Him in order to be fruitful. Abiding means to keep Christ's commandments (v. 10 and 1 John 3:24). The believer who does not abide, though still in Christ and thus saved, loses his opportunities and rewards, both in life and at the Judgment Seat of Christ. The casting forth, withering, and burning refer not to loss of salvation but to loss of present witness and future reward.

C. Hebrews 6:1–8

This much-debated passage has been variously interpreted.

(1) The Arminian viewpoint sees the people described as believers who actually can lose their salvation ("fall away"). But if the passage teaches that, it also teaches that such a person who has lost his salvation can never be saved a second time, for "it is impossible to renew them again to repentance."

(2) Others see this as a reference to professing believers who only fall away from knowledge of the truth to which they have been exposed but which they never personally accepted. In this view security is not an issue since professors are not saved.

(3) I personally understand the passage to be describing born again people. The phrases in verses 4 and 5 clearly refer to a conversion experience (cf. "enlightened" in 10:32, "taste" in 2:9, and "partakers" in 12:8). But they are willfully immature believers (cf. 5:11–14). Now, the writer warned, since it is impossible to go back in the Christian life to start it over (but if one could it would be necessary to fall away first in order to go back to the beginning), there are only two remaining options: stay where you are in this state of immaturity, or move forward to maturity (6:1). Since their present state was undesirable, this passage was a strong warning to go on in the Christian life. This warning is similar to that which a teacher might give a class: "It is impossible for you students, once enrolled in this course, turning the clock back (which cannot be done, but which would have to be done if one could go back to the beginning) to start this course over. Therefore, go on to further knowledge."

The warnings against immaturity and fruitlessness are severe and the consequences significant. But those consequences do not include hell because of losing eternal life. Paul exulted in the confidence that nothing, including any other created thing (which has to include yourself), can separate us from the love of God which is in Christ (Rom. 8:38–39). And again he declared: "If we are faithless, He remains faithful; for He cannot deny Himself" (2 Tim. 2:13). The consistency of God's character guarantees a secure salvation.

Notes

1. *The Works of James Arminius,* trans. James Nichols (Auburn: Derby and Miller, 1853), 1:248.
2. Ibid. 1:254.

Chapter 58
WHAT IS THE GOSPEL?

Confusion abounds with respect both to the content and presentation of the Gospel of the grace of God. Some do not present it purely; some do not present it clearly; some do not present it sincerely. But because God is gracious, He often gives light and faith in spite of our imprecise witness.

I. SOME FALLACIES IN THE PRESENTATION OF THE GOSPEL

A. The Fallacy That the Gospel Primarily Concerns Other Than Sin

There can be no Good News for the person who does not sense that he needs Good News. And there can be no sense of need without some realization of sin. Of course, sin has many symptoms that can alert an individual to the basic problem, sin. Therefore, a Gospel presentation can focus on lack of joy or peace or the need to have help in solving problems, but those are symptoms of the sin that alienates from God. Nevertheless, one does not need to be saved in order to have joy or peace or the solution to problems. He needs to be saved in order to have sins forgiven. Lack of joy is not what bars people from heaven. Sin is. The Gospel believed solves the sin problem.

B. The Fallacy That There Are Different Gospels for Different Age-Groups

There is not one Gospel for children, another for young people, yet another for adults, one for unchurched people, while another for those with a church background. There is one Gospel. There may be different ways of explaining the Gospel to different groups, but unless the content is the same, those different explanations may create different gospels. Different vocabulary may be indicated, but those different words must convey the same Gospel.

C. The Fallacy That the Truth Is in Other Than the Word of God

Experience can confirm or deny truth, but it does not create infallible truth. Neither does archaeology. Neither does fulfilled prophecy, for the prophecies of the Bible were true before they were ever fulfilled. Neither does apologetics. These approaches have their place, but only in the Word do we have absolute truth. Like the apostles, we must preach the Word (Acts 13:5) and reason out of the Scriptures (17:2).

D. The Fallacy That Cleverness Will Convict

If the convicting ministry of the Spirit is to set the truth of the Gospel before the unsaved person in such a light that he must acknowledge it as truth (whether he believes it or not), then this must be done by the Spirit, not by my cleverness. Of course, our presentation should be well prepared and well presented, but these in themselves do not guarantee that anyone will be convinced. God must do that.

E. The Fallacy That Charm Will Assure Results

Insofar as we can exercise control, we should not be offensive as to dress, speech, or culture, but the moment we announce the Gospel we take on the offense of the Cross (Gal. 5:11). The message is a stumbling block; the messenger should not be. But even though he is not, this will not guarantee results. Charm does not convert people.

F. The Fallacy That Procedures Produce Conversions

Procedures do produce results, but results are not always the same as conversions. Pressure can produce results; music can hypnotize; settings can intoxicate; and stories can move; but none of these necessarily bring conversions. A good test for any Gospel message is this: Did the speaker give his listeners something to believe, not did he give them something to do.

II. SOME FALLACIES IN STATING THE CONTENT OF THE GOSPEL

A. The Fallacy of Adding Baptism

Though an important Christian ordinance, baptism is not a part of the Gospel. To include it in the Gospel is to add a work to the grace of God. However, some feel certain verses do make baptism a requirement to be saved.

1. Mark 16:16. The original ending of Mark's Gospel is the subject of much debate. It is doubtful that what we designate as verse 16 was part of the genuine close of the Gospel. At best, it would be unwise to base any doctrine on the content of verses 9–20. However, it is also possible that if verse 16 is a part of the inspired text that the reference is to baptism of the Spirit. After all, the Lord would have spoken Mark 16:16 at almost the same time as He spoke Acts 1:5 concerning the imminent baptizing ministry of the Spirit.

2. *Acts 2:38.* Baptismal regenerationists understand this verse to teach that repentance and baptism lead to the forgiveness of sins. Unquestionably baptism was a clear proof in New Testament times of conversion, whether it be conversion to Judaism, to John the Baptist's message, or to Christianity. To refuse to be baptized raised a legitimate doubt as to the sincerity of the profession. Therefore, when the Jewish crowd asked Peter what they must do, he quite naturally said to repent (change their minds about Jesus of Nazareth) and be baptized (give clear proof of that change).

Though it is true that exegetically the text may be understood to say that baptism is unto (*eis*) the forgiveness of sins, it is equally true that it may say that baptism is not *for* the purpose of the forgiveness of sins but *because* of forgiveness (that had already taken place at repentance). *Eis* is clearly used with this meaning in Matthew 12:41—they repented at (on the basis of, or because of) the preaching of Jonah. It certainly cannot mean in that verse that they repented with a view to the preaching of Jonah. So Acts 2:38 may be understood that the people should repent and then be baptized because their sins were forgiven.[1]

3. *Acts 22:16.* The verse contains four segments: (a) arise (which is a participle, arising); (b) be baptized (an imperative); (c) wash away your sins (another imperative); and (d) calling on the name of the Lord (another participle). To make the verse teach baptism as necessary for salvation necessitates connecting parts b and c, be baptized and wash away. But rather than being connected to each other, each of those two commands is actually connected with a participle. Arising is necessary before baptism, and calling before sins can be washed away. Thus the verse should be read this way: arising, be baptized; wash away your sins, calling on the Lord. The verse correctly understood does not teach baptismal regeneration.

B. The Fallacy of Misunderstanding Repentance

Repentance means a genuine change of mind that affects the life in some way. Like other significant theological terms it must be defined specifically by asking a further question, namely, Change the mind about what? Unsaved people can truly repent but without being saved, as, for example, to change the mind about a bad habit and to break that habit as a result. Christians can repent of specific sins and stop doing them (Rev. 2:5; 2 Cor. 7:9—notice that in this verse sorrow leads to repentance, but it is not necessarily the same as repentance). And unsaved people can repent unto salvation. This saving repentance has to involve a change of mind about Jesus Christ so that whatever a person thought of Him before, he changes his mind and trusts Him to be his Savior. That is the only kind or content of repentance that saves (Acts 2:38; 17:30; 2 Pet. 3:9). However, saving repentance may be preceded by a repentance concerning sin (which activates an individual's sense of need for forgiveness) or a repentance toward God (which alerts him to the fact that he has offended a holy God and therefore needs a way to appease Him). This aspect of repentance (like John 16:8–11) is still not saving unless it is accompanied by faith in Christ (Acts 20:21).

C. The Fallacy of Making Surrender of Life a Part of the Gospel

1. The question. The question is simply this: Does one have to make Christ Lord of his life or be willing to do so in order to be saved? One yes answer puts it this way.

> The lordship view expressly states the necessity of acknowledging Christ as the Lord and Master of one's life in the act of receiving Him as Savior. These are not two different, sequential acts (or successive steps), but rather one act of pure, trusting faith. It takes little theological acumen to discern the base differences between the lordship and nonlordship views of the presentation of the Gospel.[2]

In the same vein, Arthur W. Pink wrote:

> Something more than "believing" is necessary to salvation. A heart that is steeled in rebellion against God cannot savingly believe: it must first be broken. . . . No one can receive Christ as his Saviour while he *rejects Him as Lord!* It is true the preacher adds that the one who accepts Christ should also surrender to Him as Lord, but he once spoils it by assertion that though the convert fails to do so nevertheless heaven is sure to him. That is one of the devil's lies.[3]

Simply stated the question is: Does the lack of commitment to the lordship of Christ over the years of one's life mean a lack of saving faith? Or, as Boice asked, "Is 'faith' minus commitment a true biblical faith?"[4] Boice says no, it is not.

Notice that the question is not whether believers will sin, or if they will bear fruit. All believers will bear some fruit in their Christian lives. Nor is it a question of whether believers should decide who will direct their lives. That is an essential question for spiritual growth, and some apparently decide that issue when they believe and some do not. The question is: Is commitment of life a necessary part of faith and thus of the Gospel?

2. Some examples. The Bible furnishes some clear examples of people who were saved but who lacked commitment. These are not examples only of sins committed after salvation (though they include such), but they demonstrate saving faith without commitment.

Remember the life of Lot. It scarcely qualifies as an example of commitment at any point, yet the New Testament declares that he was a righteous person (2 Pet. 2:7). If we only had the Old Testament record, we might seriously question that he was righteous before God.

Observe also the condition of the believers at Ephesus. Paul ministered in that city more than two years. Some believed at the beginning of his ministry; others, later on. They were converted from a lifestyle that included devotion to magical arts based on the gibberish written on the statue of Diana in the temple at Ephesus. After believing in the Lord, many, if not most, of those believers (and Acts 19:18 undebatably states they were believers) still continued their superstitious practices. It would be wishful thinking to imagine they did not know such practices were wrong when they accepted Christ and during the two years that many continued to do them. But not until the end of Paul's ministry in Ephesus did the believers finally become convicted about this and confess their sins and burn their books of magic. Theologically, then, this says that there were people at Ephesus who became believers in Christ knowing they should give up their use of magic but who did not (some for as long as two years), but who nevertheless were born again. Their salvation did not depend on faith plus submission to the lordship of Christ over their use of magic.

3. Some observations. This lordship teaching fails to distinguish salvation from discipleship and makes requirements for discipleship prerequisites for salvation. Our Lord distinguished the two (Luke 14:16–33). This teaching elevates one of the many aspects of the person of Christ (Master over life) in making it a part of the Gospel. Why not require faith in His kingship? Or in the fact that He is Judge of all, or that He was the Creator? Though my view has been dubbed "easy believism," it is not easy to believe, because what we ask the unsaved person to believe is not easy. We ask that he trust a person who lived two thousand years ago, whom he can only know through the Bible, to forgive his sins. We are asking that he stake his eternal destiny on this. Remember the example of Evangelist Jesus. He did not require the Samaritan woman to set her sinful life in order, or even be willing to, so that she could be saved. He did not set out before her what would be expected by way of changes in her life if she believed. He simply said she needed to know who He is and to ask for the gift of eternal life (John 4:10).[5]

Notes

1. See A. T. Robertson, *Word Pictures in the New Testament* (New York: Harper, 1930), 3:35–36.
2. K. L. Gentry, "The Great Option: A Study of the Lordship Controversy," *Baptist Reformation Review* 5 (Spring 1976) 5: 52.
3. Arthur W. Pink, *Present-Day Evangelism* (Swengel, Pa.: Bible Truth Depot, n.d.), 14–15.
4. James M. Boice, "The Lord Christ," *Tenth,* October 1980, 10:8, and "The Meaning of Discipleship," *Moody Monthly,* February 1986, 34–37.
5. See Charles Ryrie, *Balancing the Christian Life* (Chicago: Moody, 1969), 169–81 and *So Great Salvation* (Chicago: Moody, 1997).

Section XI
THE HOLY SPIRIT

Chapter 59
WHO IS THE HOLY SPIRIT?

Many people have labeled the twentieth century as the century of the Holy Spirit. The rise and spread of Pentecostalism, with its major emphasis on the ministries of the Spirit, and the blossoming of dispensationalism's emphasis on works of the Spirit are distinctive to this age. The century's concern for the evangelization of the world also highlighted a need to know the power of the Spirit to accomplish this. Though this attention on the work of the Spirit has been a good thing, it has not always been scripturally guided; thus there exists an even greater need today for careful attention to the biblical teaching on this subject.

I. HE IS A PERSON

Denial that the Spirit is a person often takes the form of substituting the concept that He is a personification of, say, power—much like claiming that Satan is a personification of evil. This denial of His personality has occurred throughout church history, first by the Monarchians, the Arians, the Socinians, and today by Unitarians, liberals, and some neo-orthodox theologians. But there is a great deal of evidence that He is a person.

A. He Possesses and Exhibits the Attributes of a Person

1. He has intelligence. He knows and searches the things of God (1 Cor. 2:10–11); He possesses a mind (Rom. 8:27); and He is able to teach people (1 Cor. 2:13).

2. He shows feelings. He can be grieved by the sinful actions of believers (Eph. 4:30—an influence cannot be grieved).

3. He has a will. He uses this in distributing gifts to the body of Christ (1 Cor. 12:11). He also directs the activities of Christians (Acts 16:6–11).

Since genuine personality possesses intelligence, feelings, and will, and since the Spirit has these attributes, He must be a person.

B. He Exhibits the Actions of a Person

1. He guides us into truth by hearing, speaking, and showing (John 16:13).
2. He convicts of sin (John 16:8).
3. He performs miracles (Acts 8:39).
4. He intercedes (Rom. 8:26).

These are activities that an influence or personification could not do but that Scripture shows the Holy Spirit can do.

C. He Receives Ascriptions That Would Be Given Only to a Person

1. He is One to be obeyed (Acts 10:19–21).
2. He can be lied to (Acts 5:3).
3. He can be resisted (Acts 7:51).
4. He can be grieved (Eph. 4:30).
5. He can be blasphemed (Matt. 12:31).
6. He can be insulted (Heb. 10:29).

To think of acting and reacting to an influence in these ways is incongruous.

D. He Relates as a Person to Other Persons

1. To the apostles. He related to the apostles in a manner that shows His own distinct personality (Acts 15:28). He is a person as they are persons; yet He is a distinct and identifiable person.
2. To Jesus. He relates to the Lord Jesus in such a way that if the Lord has personality one must conclude that the Spirit does also. Yet He is distinct from Christ (John 16:14).
3. To other Trinity members. He relates to the other persons of the Trinity as an equal person (Matt. 28:19; 2 Cor. 13:14).
4. To His own power. The Spirit is related to His own power yet distinguished from it so that we may not conclude that He is merely a personification of power (Luke 4:14; Acts 10:38; 1 Cor. 2:4).

E. A Grammatical Consideration

Several times the writers of the New Testament use a masculine pronoun to refer to the Spirit (which is a neuter). The clearest example of this exception to normal grammatical usage is John 16:13–14 where the masculine demonstrative pronoun is used twice to refer to the Spirit mentioned in verse 13. Other references are less clear since the masculine pronouns used may refer to the word "Paraclete" (which is masculine, 15:26; 16:7–8) or to the word “earnest” (which is also masculine, Eph. 1:14–15 KJV). Nevertheless, the clear exception to normal accidence in John 16:13–14 does support the true personality of the Spirit.

Each of these lines of scriptural evidence leads to the conclusion that the Holy Spirit, even though a spirit being, is as real a person as the Father, or the Son, or as we are.

II. HE IS GOD

Not only is the Spirit a person, but He is a unique person, for He is God. Proofs of personality are not necessarily proofs of Deity; but proofs of Deity are also proofs of His personality. If God is a person, and if the Spirit is also God, then He is a person also.

A. His Appellations Show Deity

The divine names of the Spirit reveal His Deity. Sixteen times He is related by name to the other two persons of the Trinity (Acts 16:7—“the Spirit of Jesus” and 1 Cor. 6:11—“the Spirit of our God”).

Further, promise of our Lord to send “another Helper” (John 14:16) uses the word for “another” that means another of the same kind. In other words, if Christ is God, then the Spirit, the other Helper of the same kind, is also God.

B. His Attributes Are Those That Belong to God Alone

As we have seen, the Spirit has attributes that show that He is a genuine person, but He also possesses attributes that only God has, which shows, therefore, that He is Deity. These attributes are omniscience (Isa. 40:13; 1 Cor. 2:12), omnipresence (Ps. 139:7), and omnipotence by virtue of His work in Creation (Job 33:4; Ps. 104:30).

He is also truth, love, life-giver, but man can be these things in a relative sense as well.

C. His Actions Are Those That Only God Can Perform

1. *He was the cause of the Virgin Birth* (Luke 1:35).
2. *He was the Agent in giving the inspired Scriptures* (2 Pet. 1:21).
3. *He was involved in the Creation of the world* (Gen. 1:2). Here as with other uses of the “Spirit of God” in the Old Testament we may ask if the references clearly are to the third person of the Trinity or to God as spirit (which He is). Leupold, commenting on verse 2, gives a thoughtful answer to the question.

> Absolutely none other than the Holy Spirit is here under consideration. . . . It may require the full light of New Testament revelation to enable us to discern that the Spirit of God here is the same as He who in the New Testament is seen to be the Holy Spirit; but having that light, we need not hesitate to believe that it sheds clear light back on the Old Testament usage of the expression. . . . Does it not seem reasonable that the Spirit of inspiration should have so worded the words that bear upon His activity that, when the full New Testament revelation has come, all statements concerning the Spirit are in perfect harmony with this later revelation?[1]

D. His Associations with the Other Persons of the Godhead Demonstrate Deity

1. Spirit as Yahweh. The New Testament identifies the Spirit as Yahweh of the Old Testament, particularly when quoting an Old Testament passage that God spoke and attributing it to the Spirit (cf. Acts 28:25–27 with Isa. 6:8–10 and Heb. 10:15–17 with Jer. 31:31–34). This is strong evidence that the New Testament writers considered the Spirit to be God.

2. Spirit and God. Blasphemy of and lying to the Spirit are the same as doing these things to God (Matt. 12:31–32; Acts 5:3–4).

3. Equality. The Spirit is associated on an equal basis with the Father and Son (Matt. 28:19; 2 Cor. 13:14). In the Matthew reference the use of the singular "name" strengthens the proof.

He is a person and He is God.

NOTE

1. H. C. Leupold, *Exposition of Genesis* (Columbus: Wartburg, 1942), 49–50.

Chapter 60
THE HOLY SPIRIT IN OLD TESTAMENT TIMES

The approximately 100 references to the Spirit of God in the Old Testament give evidence of His working during that period. Not all, however, see these references as indicating the third person of the Trinity. P. K. Jewett, for example, believes that in the Old Testament the Holy Spirit is never used to indicate "a Person distinct from the Father and the Son," but rather "the divine nature viewed as vital energy."[1] Although it is true that the Old Testament does not reveal the doctrine of the Trinity, still it seems to convey the idea that the Spirit is a person, not simply vital energy (Ps. 104:30). Leon Wood correctly observed that "it is also important to recognize that the matter of the identity of the Holy Spirit in the Old Testament is not so much a question of what people thought regarding this member of the Godhead as it is what the intention was of God Himself who inspired the writers."[2] And we do know from the New Testament that it was the Holy Spirit who was at work in Old Testament times (Acts 7:51; 2 Pet. 1:21).

I. THE SPIRIT'S WORK IN CREATION

A. The Evidence

Seven verses speak of various aspects of the Spirit's work in Creation. They are Genesis 1:2; Job 26:13 (?); 27:3; 33:4; Psalms 33:6; 104:30; and Isaiah 40:12–14. Although some feel these are not clear references to the Spirit, there really are no good reasons for not considering them to be (even though in some of these verses translations will use "breath" instead of Spirit).

B. His Activity

The Spirit was involved in the general planning of the universe (Isa. 40:12–14).

He was also active in relation to the creation of the stars of heaven (Ps. 33:6).

The Spirit participated in the Creation of the earth (Gen. 1:2). The word "moved" (KJV) (found elsewhere only in Deut. 32:11, "hovers" [NASB] or "fluttereth" [KJV] and Jer. 23:9, "shake"[KJV]) means that the Spirit hovered over and cared for the yet unfashioned and uninhabited earth.

The Spirit worked in creating the animals (Ps. 104:30) and in the creation of man (Job 27:3; 33:4). Thus the range of His activity included all the basic facets of Creation.

II. THE SPIRIT'S WORK IN REVELATION AND INSPIRATION

That the Holy Spirit was the Agent of revealing and recording God's message to man in Old Testament times is clearly taught in both the Old and New Testaments.

Peter provides the most inclusive statement on the subject in 2 Peter 1:21. Prophecies were not borne by man's will, but the writers were borne or carried along by the Spirit. The same verb appears in both parts of the verse, indicating that the will of man was not the carrier but rather the Spirit of God was. The men who wrote acted as agents, but their wills did not control or interfere with what God wished to communicate; the Spirit was the One who carried them along.

Specific Old Testament verses like 2 Samuel 23:2 and Micah 3:8 indicate that the prophets spoke by means of the Spirit.

Furthermore, the New Testament assigns certain Old Testament quotations to the Spirit as their author. When debating the Pharisees, Christ quoted from Psalm 110, which He acknowledged was written by David but given by the Spirit (Matt. 22:43–44). Peter quoted from Psalm 41 in connection with the replacement for Judas and said that the Holy Spirit foretold this concerning Judas by the mouth of David (Acts 1:16–17). Later Peter also stated that Psalm 2 was given "by the Holy Spirit, through the mouth of our father David" (Acts 4:25). Paul also quoted from the Old Testament and assigned the authorship to the Holy Spirit (28:25–27 from Isa. 6:9–10), and the writer to the Hebrews did the same in two places in that epistle (Heb. 3:7–11; 10:15–16). Clearly, then, these New Testament references indicate that the Spirit acted in giving God's truth in Old Testament times.

III. THE SPIRIT'S WORK IN RELATION TO PEOPLE

The Spirit's ministry to people in Old Testament times was not the same as it has been since the Day of Pentecost. Whatever it was, the Lord made it quite clear it would be different after Pentecost. Notice how repeatedly the Lord spoke of the "coming" of the Spirit (who was already present) in His conversation with the disciples in the Upper

Room (John 15:26; 16:7–8, 13). This indicates both that the Spirit was at work then and that His work would take on a different character after Pentecost. When the Lord summarized that contrast, He said the Spirit "abides [present tense] with [*para*] you, and will be [future tense] in [*en*] you" (14:17). Although there is an alternative reading of the present tense in the second clause (i.e., is in you), most commentators prefer the future tense.

This, of course, delineates the contrast between the ministry of the Spirit at the time the Lord spoke these words and the future ministry after Pentecost. Buswell, wishing to blunt that contrast, translates the *en* as "among," making the promise mean that the Spirit would be among the company of disciples. He does acknowledge that it might be construed to mean "in you individually."[3] Many commentators simply seem to be unaware of any distinction being made here. F. Godet's comment is to the point.

> The preparatory operation of the Spirit upon the disciples is expressed by the words: *"He dwelleth with you";* and the closer relation into which He would enter with them at Pentecost by: *"He shall be in you."* Hence we must be careful neither to read with the Vulgate, *menei* in the future, *He shall dwell* in the first proposition, nor with some Alexandrines, *esti, is,* in the second. The whole meaning of the phrase consists in the antithesis of the present *dwelleth* (comp. *menon* in v. 25) and the future *shall be.* The contrast of the two regimens *with you* (comp. *par' humin* of v. 25) and *in you* corresponds exactly with that of the tenses.[4]

With this contrast in mind, we need to try to delineate and systematize what the Spirit did for people in Old Testament times.

A. The Nature of His Work

Three words seem to explain the Spirit's ministry to people in the Old Testament.

1. He was in certain ones. Pharaoh recognized that the Spirit was in Joseph (Gen. 41:38). Likely Pharaoh did not understand this was the Holy Spirit, but later revelation seems to make this clear. The Spirit was in Joshua, which is why God chose him (Num. 27:18). The Spirit was in Daniel (Dan. 4:8; 5:11–14; 6:3). In these instances the preposition used is *beth,* "in."

2. The Spirit came upon some. The preposition used to depict this is *al.* A number of people experienced this ministry of the Spirit (Num. 24:2;

Judg. 3:10; 6:34; 11:29; 13:25; 1 Sam. 10:10; 16:13; 2 Chron. 15:1). These included judges, Saul, and the prophets Balaam and Azariah.
3. *The Spirit filled Bezalel* (Exod. 31:3; 35:31). This seemed to be a special enablement to lead the craftsmen as they worked on the tabernacle.

B. The Extent of His Work

1. *Limited as to people.* After God chose Israel to be His people, the Spirit's work was with that group primarily if not exclusively. Israel, of course, was a spiritually mixed nation with unbelievers as well as believers. Yet the Spirit ministered to the entire nation by being present and guiding the people (Neh. 9:20; Isa. 63:10–11, 14). This seemed to be a general relationship. There were apparently closer relationships He had with some within the nation (see above and Num. 11:29).

However, we do not have clear revelation of the Spirit's ministry outside Israel. Genesis 6:3 may be an exception if the verse means that the Spirit judged mankind for its wickedness in the days of Noah. But the verse may be a warning that the human spirit God placed in human beings would not always abide because mankind would be wiped out in the Flood. Certainly there was no indication that the Spirit convicted the world of sin in Old Testament times (as He does now, John 16:8), and no other nations enjoyed His general presence among them as Israel did. As far as the record is concerned, His ministry was to Israel and individuals in Israel.
2. *Limited as to kinds of ministry.* As stated above, we find no ministry of general conviction, no indwelling and empowering as after Pentecost (John 7:37–39), no sealing, and certainly no baptizing (it is still future in Acts 1:5). Regeneration of the Spirit is not mentioned specifically, though some feel that the Spirit was regenerating in the Old Testament because believers give evidence of a struggle within their beings brought on by the presence of both the old and new.
3. *Limited as to eternality.* The Spirit empowered Samson; later the Lord left him (Judg. 13:25; 16:20). The Spirit came on Saul and later left him (1 Sam. 10:10; 16:14). Apparently there was no guarantee of permanent presence of the Spirit in Old Testament times.

Perhaps I could draw an analogy between the Spirit's ministry in the Old Testament and grace in the Old Testament. Both were present during that period, but the Spirit who worked in the Old Testament would "come" in new and fuller ministries after Pentecost, just as the displays of grace in the Old Testament were dim compared with grace that flooded the world when Christ came (John 1:17; Titus 2:11).

NOTES

1. P. K. Jewett, "Holy Spirit," in *The Zondervan Pictorial Encyclopedia of the Bible* (Grand Rapids: Zondervan, 1975), 3:184.
2. Leon Wood, *The Holy Spirit in the Old Testament* (Grand Rapids: Zondervan, 1976), 19.
3. J. Oliver Buswell, *A Systematic Theology of the Chrisian Religion* (Grand Rapids: Zondervan, 1962), 1:115.
4. F. Godet, *Commentary on the Gospel of St. John* (Edinburgh: T. & T. Clark, 1881), 3:141.

Chapter 61
THE HOLY SPIRIT IN THE LIFE OF OUR LORD

I. THE BIRTH OF CHRIST

The Holy Spirit was involved in the conception of our Lord in the womb of the virgin Mary. The result was His Incarnation (Luke 1:35).

II. THE LIFE OF CHRIST

A. The Aspects of the Ministry of the Spirit

1. Christ was filled with the Spirit (Luke 4:1). The word here indicates that this was the characteristic of His life (as in Acts 6:3, 5). It was not a momentary thing, but a relationship He had all of His life.
2. Christ was anointed with the Spirit (Luke 4:18; Acts 4:27; 10:38; Heb. 1:9). This signified that He is the Messiah (Anointed One) and empowered Him for His prophetic ministry.
3. Christ rejoiced in the Spirit (Luke 10:21). This was perhaps an evidence of His being full of the Spirit.
4. Christ was empowered by the Spirit throughout His life. This was predicted by Isaiah (Isa. 42:1–4; 61:1–2) and experienced by Jesus of Nazareth in His ministries of preaching (Luke 4:18) and doing miracles (Matt. 12:28).

B. The Areas of the Ministry of the Spirit

1. The Spirit's ministry in the life of our Lord was related to Christ's office as a Prophet. At the beginning of His public ministry, He declared that the Spirit of the Lord was upon Him to proclaim the favorable year of the Lord (Luke 4:18).
2. The Spirit's ministry also enabled Him to perform some of His miracles. Some of the Lord's miracles were undebatably done in the power of the Spirit. This claim was what evoked the incident concerning the unpardonable sin (Matt. 12:28, 31). He also gave sight to the blind because the Spirit was upon Him (Luke 4:18). In the Old Testament giving sight to the blind was a prerogative of God (Exod. 4:11; Ps. 146:8) and something Messiah would do (Isa. 29:18; 35:5; 42:7). Thus when

the Lord restored sight to blind people He was making a clear claim to be Israel's long-awaited Messiah. One would expect the ministry of the Spirit (anointing and empowering) to be connected with this kind of miracle, which demonstrated that Jesus was the anointed Messiah.

In all the Old Testament there is no account of any blind person receiving sight. None of the Lord's disciples was involved in restoring sight to any blind person. Only Ananias's involvement in Paul's regaining his sight is somewhat relevant, though this was different from what our Lord did when He gave sight to those who had never seen. Thus when Christ came on the scene of history and gave sight to so many blind people, this was a strong claim to His messiahship.

More miracles of Christ in this category are recorded than in any other. Matthew records the healing of two particular blind people (9:27–31), the general healing of the blind (11:5), the healing of blind people that provoked the unpardonable sin (12:22), additional unspecified numbers of blind cured (15:30), and the healing of blind people in the temple on Palm Sunday (21:14). Mark records the opening of a blind man's eyes at Bethsaida (Mark 8:22–26) and the restoration of sight to Bartimaeus and his friend at Jericho (10:46–52, also recorded in Matthew and Luke). John records the healing of the man who was born blind (John 9). And all of these were done in the power of the Spirit.

But some of our Lord's miracles were evidently done in His own inherent God-man power. The woman with the continual hemorrhage was healed through His own power (Mark 5:30). The healing of the paralytic who was let down through the roof by his friends is attributed to the power of the Lord (Luke 5:17). The mass healing of the multitude after the choosing of the disciples was the result of His own power (6:19). Those who came to arrest Him in the Garden of Gethsemane were thrown back for the moment by a display of the power of His own deity when He said, "I am" (John 18:6).

Some would say that these miracles were attributed to Christ but actually empowered by the Spirit within Him. Although that could be true, it does not seem to be the normal way to read the texts. So it is better to acknowledge that He did some of His miracles in the power of the Spirit (particularly those that gave evidence of His claim to be Messiah by restoring sight to the blind) and some in His own power.

C. The Conflict over the Ministry of the Spirit

Matthew 12:22–37 and Mark 3:22–30 record the conflict over the power of the Spirit that occurred in Galilee, while Luke records a similar incident in Judea about a year later (11:14–23).

The conflict recorded in Matthew and Mark arose because the Lord healed a man who was blind and mute (which probably meant that he was also deaf). However, the real cause of his problems was demon possession. Although Jewish exorcists could cast out demons, they would have a very difficult time with this case, because how do you communicate with a person who is blind and mute and likely also deaf? When the Lord healed all the maladies at once, the people were astonished and began to suggest that Jesus was really their Messiah. This provoked the Pharisees' blasphemous accusation that Satan was obliging his friend Jesus by withdrawing demons from people to make it look like Christ Himself had that power. So, they said, who would want to follow a person who was a friend of Satan as Jesus obviously was?

The Lord's reply consisted of three statements:

(1) A kingdom or house that is divided against itself cannot stand. In other words, Satan would not destroy his own kingdom by aligning himself with Jesus' kingdom. True, Satan might allow Jewish exorcists to cast out demons, but that would not create the kind of basic rift in Satan's kingdom that Jesus' doing it would, if indeed He were doing it by Satan's power.

(2) The Lord then pointed out that the charge was absurd since the Pharisees recognized that the Jewish exorcists did not cast out demons by the power of Satan. So why should they accuse Him of doing it that way?

(3) The only logical conclusion to be reached from these facts is that the kingdom of God had come, since Christ was defeating Satan by taking his victims from him and doing so in the power of the Spirit of God.

Now, by accusing Jesus of being in league with Satan, the Pharisees were putting themselves on the side of Satan. Furthermore, they were accusing the Holy Spirit in whose power Christ cast out demons. What did the Lord mean when He said that a sin against the Son of man was forgivable but not against the Spirit? He meant that though they might misunderstand His claims, such ignorance, though deplorable, was forgivable. But to misunderstand the power of the Spirit was unforgivable since the Spirit's power and ministry was well known from Old Testament times.

Speaking against the Spirit was not merely a sin of the tongue. The Pharisees had not sinned only with their words. It was a sin of the heart expressed in words. Furthermore, theirs was a sin committed to

His face. To commit this particular sin required the personal and visible presence of Christ on earth; to commit it today, therefore, would be impossible. But to show wickedness of heart is unpardonable in any day if one dies persisting in his or her rejection of Christ. A person's eternal destiny is determined in this life, but no sin is unpardonable as long as a person has breath. As a matter of fact, the Lord urged the Pharisees to side with Him rather than against Him (Matt. 12:30), to show repentance of heart (vv. 33–35), and to speak words that would demonstrate a righteous heart and not those which would result in their condemnation (vv. 36–37). Paul himself is evidence that blasphemy is forgivable (1 Tim. 1:13).

D. The Significance of the Ministry of the Spirit

1. Development of humanity. We may reasonably assume that the Spirit played a role in the development of the humanity of Christ (Luke 2:52; Heb. 5:8). His growth must have been related to the Spirit who filled and anointed Him.

2. Christ's dependence. He did depend on the Spirit for leading and for power, in some of the miracles at least.

If the sinless Son of God used these ministries of the Holy Spirit, how can we expect to live independently of His power?

III. THE DEATH OF CHRIST

Usually Hebrews 9:14 is cited as evidence that our Lord offered Himself in His death through the Spirit. The evidence as to whether or not this is a reference to the Holy Spirit is fairly equally divided, making a definite conclusion difficult.

The evidence that this is a reference to the Spirit is as follows. The lack of the article (literally, through eternal spirit) points to the Holy Spirit just as the lack of the article in Hebrews 1:1 points more clearly to Christ.

Theologically it is reasonable to expect that if the Spirit played a role in Christ's birth and life He would also be involved in His death.

The evidence that this is not a reference to the Holy Spirit but to Christ's own eternal spirit that His deity had is as follows. The lack of the article would more naturally refer to other than the Holy Spirit since the designation Holy Spirit usually includes the article.

If this refers to Christ's eternal spirit, then it is not a reference to the divine nature offering up the human nature, but to the entire person offering up Himself by the action of the highest spirit-power within Him. His own divine spirit was involved in the offering of the God-man.

Another verse, 1 Peter 3:18, may refer to an action of the Spirit with respect to the death of Christ. Usually, however, it is thought that this verse relates the Spirit's work to the resurrection of Christ. Two major problems emerge in the exegesis of it. One concerns the identification of "spirit" whether it refers to the Holy Spirit or to Christ's own eternal spirit. If the former, then the form is instrumental, "by the [Holy] Spirit" (KJV); if the latter, then it is locative, "in the [Christ's] spirit." The parallel with "flesh" may give preference to the idea of Christ's spirit. If so, then we have no record of the Holy Spirit's ministry in relation to Christ's death (unless Heb. 9:14 applies) or to His resurrection.

But even if the reference is to the Holy Spirit, another problem still exists. It concerns the use of an aorist participle, "quickened by the spirit" (KJV). Normally, the aorist participle indicates activity simultaneous or antecedent to that of the main verb, but not subsequent. (Acts 25:13 [KJV] is not an exception since their "coming" may be a period of time in which the saluting was a part, or since greetings were often sent ahead of arrival.) If the main verb is "died," then the action of quickening cannot refer to the Resurrection, which was subsequent to His death. It would refer to some quickening at the time of the Crucifixion (simultaneous action). However, if the main verb is "bring" in the clause, then conceivably the quickening could refer to the Resurrection, which was antecedent to our being brought to heaven. In this case, the reference is to the resurrection of Christ. In the first option it refers to some kind of quickening or empowering on the cross. But in either case it is not clear that the Holy Spirit was involved, rather than Christ's spirit.

Finally, some cite Romans 1:4 to show that the Holy Spirit had a part in the resurrection of Christ. Again two exegetical problems exist. One concerns the identification of "spirit of holiness." The parallelism with "according to the flesh" (v. 3) argues that it refers to Christ's own spirit, rather than the Holy Spirit. The second problem concerns identifying what resurrection(s) is in view. Literally, the text says "a resurrection of dead [pl.]." This could refer (a) to Christ's resurrection from among dead persons, or (b) to the resurrections He did while on earth, or (c) to all of them, including His own. But in any case it is far from certain that the Spirit was directly involved.

Actually no clear evidence exists for the Spirit's direct working in the death or resurrection of our Lord. Of course, in the sense that these activities relate to the second person of the Godhead, all the persons are involved.

Chapter 62
THE SPIRIT INDWELLING

As we noted in the preceding chapter in discussing John 14:17, the Spirit does certain new and special things since His "coming" on the Day of Pentecost. At the heart of these distinctive ministries lies the ministry of dwelling in believers, for it is foundational to all His ministries to Christians in this age.

I. THE PEOPLE INDWELT

To express indwelling Paul not only used the preposition *en* but also the verb *oikeō,* to dwell (Rom. 8:9; 1 Cor. 3:16; though, of course, sometimes he used only the preposition as in 6:19). He related this ministry of the Spirit to all believers.

A. The Indwelling Spirit Is a Gift from God to All Believers

A number of passages clearly teach that the Spirit is given to all believers rather than selectively to some (John 7:37–39; Acts 11:16–17; Rom. 5:5; 1 Cor. 2:12; 2 Cor. 5:5). One would expect this to be so since a gift is not a reward and no merit is involved in receiving this gift.

B. Not to Possess the Indwelling Spirit Indicates an Unsaved Condition

Not to have the Spirit is the same as not belonging to Christ, Paul declared (Rom. 8:9). Jude also described apostates as those who did not have the Spirit (Jude 19) and who were "natural" (NIV). This is the same word used in 1 Corinthians 2:14, another verse that describes an unsaved individual. To be natural is to be unsaved and not to have the Spirit. Therefore having the Spirit characterizes all born again people.

C. Sinning Believers Are Indwelt by the Spirit

The acid test of whether or not the Spirit indwells all believers is whether or not He lives in sinning Christians. Clearly He does. First Corinthians 6:19 was written to a very spiritually mixed group, some fine, spiritual believers, but many who were carnal and worldly; yet Paul did not say that only the spiritual group were indwelt by the Spirit. One brother, who in Paul's judgment was a believer (5:5) was living in gross sin. Others were at legal swords' points with each other (chap. 6). Still Paul said that the Spirit was "in" all of them (1 Cor. 6:19). Not only did he make no exceptions to his statement, but he made the indwelling of the Spirit the ground for his exhortation to holy living. Clearly then, all believers, but *only* believers, have the Spirit living in them.

II. THE PERMANENCE OF INDWELLING

Some who agree that the Spirit is given to all believers feel that He may withdraw from those who commit certain sins. Thus they acknowledge His indwelling but deny its permanence.

Whatever sins could cause His departure would have to be more grievous than the fornication of chapter 5 or the legal disputes of chapter 6, for Paul did not exclude these believers from his statement that the Spirit dwelt in them (v. 19).

Furthermore, if the Spirit leaves sinning Christians, then they are no longer Christians according to Romans 8:9. The Spirit cannot leave a believer without throwing that believer back into a lost, unsaved condition. Disindwelling has to mean loss of salvation, and loss of salvation must include disindwelling. The security of the believer and the permanent indwelling of the Spirit are inseparable doctrines.

But we also have the positive promise of the Savior that He would pray to the Father who would give another Helper in order "that He may be with you forever" (John 14:16). To be sure, sin affects the effectiveness of the Spirit in the believer's life, but it does not remove His presence from believers.

III. SOME PROBLEMS CONCERNING THE INDWELLING OF THE SPIRIT

A. Is Not Obedience a Condition for Indwelling?

Peter spoke of the Holy Spirit "whom God has given to those who obey Him" (Acts 5:32). Does this mean that obedience is a condition for the giving of the Spirit and thus only certain (i.e., obedient) believers have the Spirit? Yes, if obedience is understood in the way Peter used it. He was addressing the unbelieving Sanhedrin and concluded by pressing the matter of their obedience. Obedience to what? Certainly the obedience of the Sanhedrin had nothing to do with obedience to matters in the Christian life, for they were not Christians. The obedience Peter called them to was to obey (believe) the truth that Jesus was their Messiah. Shortly after, some of the priests in Jerusalem did believe and Luke said "a great many of the priests were becoming obedient to the faith" (Acts 6:7).

Two other references use obedience as a synonym for receiving Christ's salvation. Paul described the purpose of his mission as "for obedience to the faith among all nations for his name" (Rom. 1:5 KJV). The writer to the Hebrews said that Christ became the Source of eternal salvation to all who obey Him (Heb. 5:9). Therefore, if obedience is understood correctly (as obeying the Gospel), it is a condition for receiving the gift of the Spirit.

B. Are There Not Illustrations of the Temporariness of Indwelling?

Yes, there are, but they are all before the Day of Pentecost (1 Sam. 16:14; perhaps Ps. 51:11; Luke 11:13; John 20:22). But there are no such examples after the coming of the Spirit on the Day of Pentecost. Since those before Pentecost relate to a different economy of the Spirit, they cannot be used to prove that the same thing happens after Pentecost when the Holy Spirit came to indwell believers permanently.

C. Does Not the Delay in Giving the Spirit to the Samaritans Show That It Is Subsequent to Salvation and Thus Selective?

That there was a delay in giving the Spirit to the Samaritans is clear; the question is, Why? Some say it shows that indwelling comes subsequent to salvation and not necessarily to all believers. Others equate this giving of the Spirit with the filling of the Spirit. Still others say the procedure was different in this instance because the Samaritans were the first non-Jewish group to be taken into the church. The latter is partly true: Samaritans were part Jewish and part Gentile. The purely Gentile pattern for the giving of the Spirit is found in Acts 10:44, where the Spirit was given to the Gentiles in Cornelius's house at the moment they believed.

The best explanation of this delay in the case of the Samaritans lies in the schismatic nature of Samaritan religion. Their worship rivaled Jewish worship in Jerusalem; therefore, God needed to prove to them that their new Christian faith was not also to rival the Christian church in Jerusalem. The best way to show beyond doubt that the Samaritan Christians belonged to the same group as the Jerusalem Christians (and vice versa, to show the Jerusalem leaders that Samaritans were genuinely saved) was to delay the giving of the Spirit until

Peter and John came from Jerusalem to Samaria. This delay and God's use of Peter and John in conveying the gift of the Spirit saved the early church from having two rival mother churches.

D. Does Not Acts 19:1–6 Show That Indwelling Is Subsequent to Salvation?

To answer yes to this question requires understanding that the twelve disciples of John the Baptist were already Christian believers before they met Paul at Ephesus. But this is not the correct understanding. They did not become believers in Jesus by believing John's message and receiving his baptism; they became Christian believers only after Paul explained to them the difference between John and Jesus. In fact, it does not appear from the text that they even understood much about John's message. But when they understood and believed what Paul explained to them, they immediately received the Spirit through Paul's laying on of hands. There was no delay.

The normal Gentile pattern for receiving the Spirit was established in the house of Cornelius, where the Spirit was given when the people believed, which was while Peter was preaching and before they were baptized in water (10:44, 47).

E. What Is the Relation of Indwelling to Anointing?

Anointing in the Old Testament, a very solemn matter, made a person or thing holy and sacrosanct (Exod. 40:9–15). It was associated with the Holy Spirit and with equipping for service (1 Sam. 10:1, 9; Zech. 4:1–14). In the New Testament Christ was anointed (Luke 4:18; Acts 4:27; 10:38; Heb. 1:9) and all believers are anointed (2 Cor. 1:21; 1 John 2:20, 27). As far as the anointing of believers is concerned, these passages teach that it is not something repeated but something that abides. Although Old Testament anointing was related more to service (as also was Christ's anointing), New Testament believers' anointing concerns a relationship that enables us to understand truth. Old Testament anointing seems closer to the idea of the filling of the Spirit, whereas believers' anointing is akin to the indwelling of the Spirit. Not every believer experienced it in the Old Testament; all do today. It may have been repeated in the Old Testament; it abides on all believers today.

The New Testament clearly teaches that all believers are permanently indwelt. Let not our familiarity with this blunt the significance of it. This universal and permanent ministry to believers stands in sharp contrast with the indwelling ministry of the Spirit in the Old Testament (John 14:17). It means that whether or not we feel it, God the Holy Spirit lives within our beings constantly. This ought to give us (a) a sense of security in our relationship with God, (b) a motivation to practice that presence of God, and (c) a sensitivity to sins against God.

Chapter 63
THE SPIRIT SEALING

Three New Testament passages speak of this particular ministry of the Spirit. The first, 2 Corinthians 1:22, says that God has sealed us and given us the earnest of the Spirit. Ephesians 1:13 adds that we were sealed with the Spirit (*tō pneumati*) when we believed, and again, that the Spirit is the earnest of our inheritance. Ephesians 4:30 states we were sealed by or with (*en*) the Spirit until the day of redemption.

This specific ministry of the Spirit constitutes something nowhere mentioned in the Old Testament. Leon Wood tries to build a case for its occurring during that period by arguing that since sealing is related to security of the believer and also to indwelling, and since Old Testament saints were both secure and indwelt, they must also have been sealed.[1] If this be true it can only be inferred; it is nowhere specifically stated. It appears, rather, to be something God has done for believers only since the Day of Pentecost.

I. THE PEOPLE WHO ARE SEALED

As with indwelling, sealing belongs to believers only and to all believers. In 2 Corinthians 1:22 Paul makes no exceptions in writing to a group in which exceptions could easily be justified. All are sealed. If this were not true, then how could Paul make it the basis for the exhortation not to grieve the Spirit in Ephesians 4:30? He would have to be saying that only that group of believers who are sealed should not grieve the Spirit.

II. THE TIME OF SEALING

Like indwelling, sealing takes place at the time of our conversion. The "and" in 2 Corinthians 1:22 links sealing with the gift of the Spirit as the earnest. And the Spirit is given when we believe (Acts 2:38).

Ephesians 1:13 can legitimately be exegeted two ways, which result in two different answers to the question of when are people sealed. The principal verb is "you were sealed." The aorist participle that accompanies it is "believing." The participle may express an action that preceded that of the principal verb. If so, then the believing occurred before being sealed; i.e., there was an interval of time between believing and being sealed. Or the participle may indicate action that occurred at the same time as that of the principal verb. If so, then the believing and the sealing happened at the same time. Exegetically either could be correct. But theologically, believing and sealing must be simultaneous. Otherwise it would be possible to have unsealed believers.

III. THE AGENT(S) OF SEALING

Clearly God does the sealing of believers (2 Cor. 1:22). Less clear is the question of whether the Holy Spirit is also an agent. Ephesians 4:30 seems to indicate that He is, because it uses the phrase "by whom." However, this could mean "in whom." Ephesians 1:13 is ambiguous; no preposition is expressed. The Spirit may be the Agent or the sphere of the sealing, or both. We are sealed by the Spirit and in the Spirit.

If both, it might be like saying, "I went to the store in my car." You could mean "by means of my car" viewing the car as the agent that took you to the store. Or you could mean "by sitting within (the sphere of) my car," viewing the car as the enclosure in which you were taken. Actually you did both. The car served both as the agent that took you and the enclosure in which you were located. Similarly, the Spirit did the sealing as the agent, and as a result we are enclosed in Him.

IV. THE DURATION OF SEALING

Sealing is to the day of redemption (Eph. 4:30). This refers to that future day when our redemption shall be fully accomplished, including receiving our resurrection bodies (cf. Rom. 8:23). Thus the sealing guarantees the complete fulfillment of God's promises to us. And no believer can become unsealed on his way to heaven.

V. THE RAMIFICATIONS OF SEALING

A. Security

The concept of sealing includes the ideas of ownership, authority, responsibility, and, above all, security. Sealing assures us of the security of God's promises to us, especially our salvation. We can be certain (a) that He possesses us, (b) that we have a secure salvation sealed by and with the Spirit, and (c) that He purposes to keep us to the day of our full redemption.

Registered mail furnishes a good example of the security concept in sealing. When registering a piece of mail, it not only has to be sealed carefully, but then the post office stamps it a number of times across the edges of the seal to be able to detect any tampering with that seal. Only two people can legitimately break the seal, the recipient or the sender (if it is delivered back to him). In the case of believers, God is the Sender, and God is the Recipient, and God is the One who does the sealing. So only God can break the seal, and He has promised not to do so until the day of redemption.

Both 2 Corinthians 1:22 and Ephesians 1:13–14 mention the gift of the Spirit as an earnest along with sealing. The association is quite logical. Sealing guarantees that we shall receive all that God has promised us, some of which awaits our future redemption. The presence of the Spirit in our lives serves as an earnest or pledge that all will be fulfilled. In human affairs, once earnest money has been given and received, both the purchaser and the seller are pledged to complete the transaction. Similarly, the gift of the Spirit serves as God's pledge that He will not go back on any of His promises to us.

B. Purity

The thought of the day of our full redemption when we shall be perfect should shame us about sin in our lives now. Furthermore, the fact that we have a relationship with the *Holy* Spirit who is grieved when we sin should motivate us to purity.

What sins grieve Him? Any and all sins. But in the immediate context (the two verses that surround Eph. 4:30), sins of the tongue are highlighted. Of course, what comes from our mouths is indicative of what is in our hearts. The thought of being sealed by and in the Holy Spirit should guard our lips.

NOTE

1. Leon Wood, *The Holy Spirit in the Old Testament* (Grand Rapids: Zondervan, 1976), 70–71.

Chapter 64
THE SPIRIT BAPTIZING

Another ministry of the Spirit that is distinctive to this post-Pentecost Age is that of baptizing those who believe into the body of Christ. It was first predicted not in any Old Testament passage but by John the Baptist (Matt. 3:11 and parallels). But this ministry was never experienced by anyone during the earthly lifetime of our Lord, for after His resurrection and just prior to His ascension He said it was to happen "not many days hence" on the Day of Pentecost (Acts 1:5 KJV). This distinctive ministry served a particular purpose—adding people to the body of Christ—and since the body of Christ is distinctive to this age, then the baptizing work of the Spirit also would be.

I. CONFUSION CONCERNING THE SPIRIT'S BAPTIZING

Confusion surrounds this area of pneumatology, causing divisions among believers and obscuring of this great truth. Why is this so?

One reason for the confusion relates to an unclear conception of the body of Christ. If one believes that the church began with Abraham or with John the Baptist then it will likely be more difficult to see the distinctiveness of the baptizing ministry of the Spirit in this age. So baptism is usually made a synonym for the conversion experience.[1] But if one recognizes the body as a work of God that began at Pentecost, then the necessity of the Spirit's baptizing people into that body will be clear.

Overemphasis on water baptism, particularly by immersion, often obscures or even obliterates the doctrine of Spirit baptism. If the two truths are not distinguished, usually the truth of Spirit baptism gets lost, for it is regarded simply as another way of talking about water baptism. E. Y. Mullins, Baptist theologian of a previous generation, understood the baptism of the Spirit as the baptism into the (local) church, implying that literal (water) baptism is a Spirit-guided activity according to 1 Corinthians 12:13.[2] Dale Moody, a Baptist theologian of this generation, states that "God imparts the Spirit in baptism."[3]

The contemporary Pentecostal association of baptism of the Spirit with a second blessing and/or with the experience of tongues as the evidence of having been baptized adds to the confusion.

Sometimes baptism of the Spirit and filling of the Spirit are not distinguished, with the resulting idea that the "filling-baptism" happens subsequent to conversion and not to all believers. This view does not necessarily involve speaking in tongues. It considers baptism an infilling for special power. The lack of clarity is compounded by the fact that great men like R. A. Torrey and D. L. Moody were unclear in this area. Torrey taught that a person could or could not be baptized with the Spirit at the moment of salvation.[4] In his biography of Moody, Torrey recounts Moody's baptism as something that occurred subsequent to salvation.[5]

Admittedly, sometimes this lack of clarity is innocent; but regrettably sometimes these misconceptions are deliberately promoted. In either case believers are robbed of an important truth that involves our union with Christ and a solid basis for holy living.

II. CHARACTERISTICS OF THE SPIRIT'S BAPTIZING

A. It Is Operative Only in This Dispensation

As already pointed out, no Old Testament prediction of the baptism exists, and our Lord said it would happen for the first time when the Spirit came on the Day of Pentecost (Acts 1:5). Later Peter called this "the beginning" (11:15–16). Also the purpose of the baptism, to join believers to the body of Christ, and the distinctiveness of the body to this dispensation, support the conclusion that this is a ministry operative only in this dispensation.

B. It Is Experienced by All Believers in This Dispensation

Three facts support this conclusion. The central text, 1 Corinthians 12:13, clearly states that all have been baptized, just as all have been made to drink of the Spirit (through His indwelling). That this was said of the church people of Corinth, which included such a variety of spiritual conditions, indicates that carnality does not cause one to miss this ministry.

Nowhere in the Scriptures is there a single exhortation for anyone to be baptized with the Spirit. This indicates that all believers have experienced this ministry.

If "one baptism" in Ephesians 4:5 refers to the baptism of the Spirit (which is most likely), then it is something true of the same group who have "one Lord" and "one faith," that is, all believers.

C. It Occurs at Salvation and Is Not Repeated Thereafter

If it did not occur at salvation then there would exist believers who were truly saved but who, because they had not been baptized with the Spirit, did not belong to the body of Christ. Baptism is what joins a believer to the body, so if one could be saved and not baptized, he could be an out-of-the-body believer.

If baptism needs to be repeated, then it could only be if the believer were detached from the body of Christ and needed to be rejoined. Since the first baptism at conversion joins one to the body, then if a second baptism is needed, there would have to have been a removal from the body between the two baptisms.

III. CONSEQUENCES OF THE SPIRIT'S BAPTISM

A. It Joins Us to the Body of Christ

This involves the following great and often convicting truths. Being in His body means we are risen with Him to newness of life (Rom. 6:4), and we should exercise our gifts to keep that body functioning properly (the context of 1 Cor. 12:13).

Experiencing the one baptism serves as the basis for and exhortation to keep the unity of the body (the context of Eph. 4:5).

The nonnecessity for a second baptism assures us of the security of our position in His body.

B. It Actualizes Our Cocrucifixion with Christ

Being associated with Christ in His death, burial, and resurrection establishes the basis for realizing our separation from the power of indwelling sin and our walk in newness of life (Rom. 6:1–10; Col. 2:12).

IV. CONTEMPORARY DOCTRINE OF TWO SPIRIT BAPTISMS

Because 1 Corinthians 12:13 is so clear about all believers being baptized, and because some contemporary teachers want to justify the concept of a special baptism for power (a second blessing), a doctrine of two Spirit baptisms has arisen that is, as far as I know, a new teaching. Whereas old Pentecostalism uniformly taught that the baptism of the Spirit was an endowment for power, tongues being the evidence of the experience, newer Pentecostalism sees two baptisms. One is that of verse 13, which all believers experience and which is accomplished *by* the Spirit and places people in the body of Christ. The other is the baptism seen in the book of Acts and is accomplished *by* Christ to place people in the Spirit for experiences of power. The first happens at conversion and results in a position; the second occurs later and can be repeated and is for power. The first does not require speaking in tongues; the second ideally does.

The New Testament uses the phrase "to baptize with, in, or by the Spirit" only seven times (Matt. 3:11; Mark 1:8; Luke 3:16; John 1:33; Acts 1:5; 11:16; 1 Cor. 12:13). Actually these seven occurrences can be placed in three categories: the predictions in the Gospels, the pointing ahead and pointing back to Pentecost in the two Acts references, and the doctrinal explanation in 1 Corinthians. In the Gospels it appears more natural to understand Christ as the Baptizer and the Spirit as the sphere into which people are baptized. In Acts and Corinthians it seems to be more natural to understand the Spirit as the Agent of baptism and the body of Christ as the sphere into which people are baptized. However, those distinctions are not hard and fast. Both Christ and the Spirit are Agents, and both the Spirit and the body are spheres. Christ is the ultimate Agent, for He sent the Spirit who is, so to speak, the intermediate Agent (Acts 2:33). Clearly the body is one sphere, and the Spirit is another. This is similar to the Spirit's work in sealing—He is both the Agent who seals and the sphere in which we are sealed.

However, neo-Pentecostalism needs to make sharp distinctions. The references in the Gospels and in Acts, they say, are references to Christ as Agent and the Spirit as sphere, which bring power to the believer. This is the baptism *in* the Spirit. The reference in 1 Corinthians reveals the Spirit as the Agent and the body as the sphere and is the baptism *by* the Spirit. All believers have been baptized *by* the Spirit, but not all believers have experienced the baptism *in* the Spirit.

Interestingly, ultradispensationalism uses the same argument for two baptisms to support their teaching of two churches within the Acts period. The Petrine church, or Jewish church, existed from Pentecost to Paul, and the body church from Paul on. The Jewish church received power by the baptism *in* the Spirit, and the Pauline, or body, church is formed by the baptism *by* the Spirit.[6]

Such an infrequently used and seemingly technical phrase would more likely refer to the same activity in all its occurrences. To establish two separate and quite distinct baptisms is tenuous at best. To see two agents is biblical because of Acts 2:33 and quite normal because different persons of the Trinity are often involved in the same work. Besides, Ephesians 4:5 says there is only one baptism. It is Christ's work through the agency of the Spirit's ministry to join those who believe to the church, the body of Christ, with all the privileges and responsibilities that come with that position.

NOTES

1. Donald Guthrie, *New Testament Theology* (Downers Grove: InterVarsity, 1981), 564.
2. E. Y. Mullins, *International Standard Bible Encyclopedia* (Grand Rapids: Eerdmans, 1943), 1:399–401.
3. Dale Moody, *The Word of Truth* (Grand Rapids: Eerdmans, 1981), 447.
4. R. A. Torrey, *The Baptism with the Holy Spirit* (Minneapolis: Bethany House, 1972), 13–14.
5. R. A. Torrey, *Why God Used D. L. Moody* (New York: Revell, 1923), 51–55.
6. Charles F. Baker, *A Dispensational Theology* (Grand Rapids: Grace Bible College Publications, 1971), 503.

THE BAPTISM IN OR BY THE HOLY SPIRIT

(baptizein en pneumati)

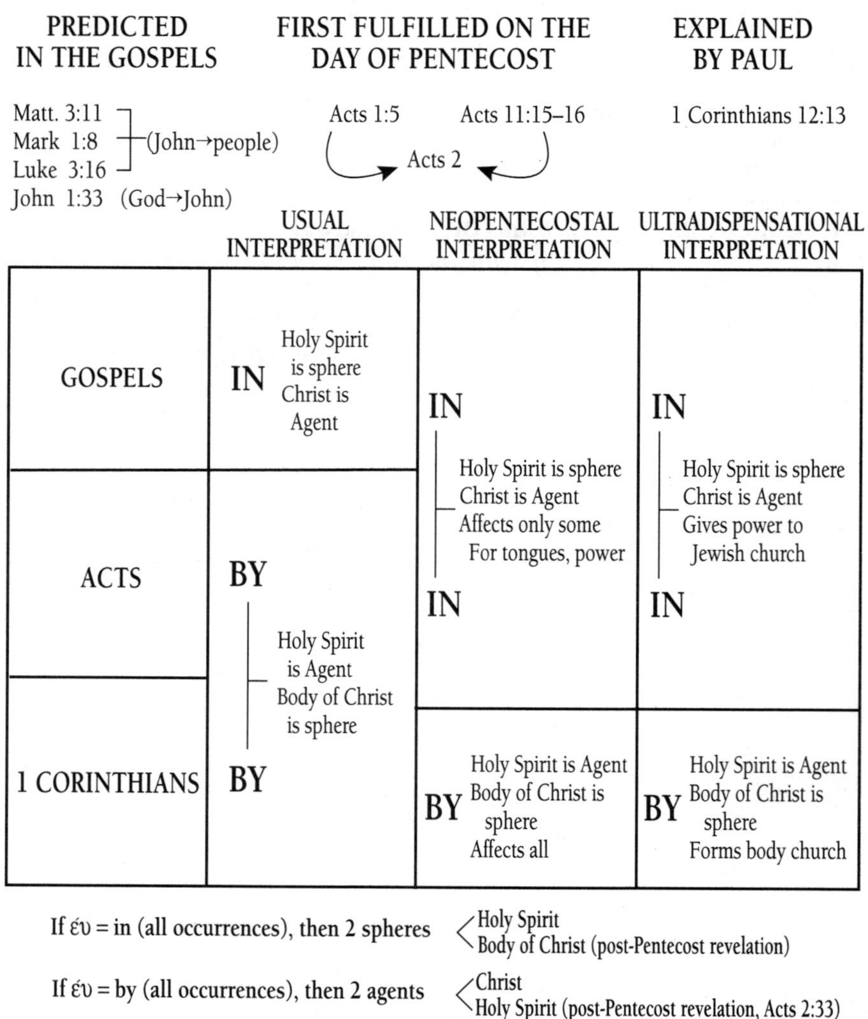

If ἐν = in (all occurrences), then 2 spheres ⟨ Holy Spirit / Body of Christ (post-Pentecost revelation)

If ἐν = by (all occurrences), then 2 agents ⟨ Christ / Holy Spirit (post-Pentecost revelation, Acts 2:33)

BUT . . . only 1 baptism (Ephesians 4:5)

Chapter 65
THE SPIRIT GIFTING

The doctrine of spiritual gifts is almost exclusively a Pauline doctrine, the only use of the word outside of Paul being in 1 Peter 4:10. The major passage in Ephesians 4 attributes the giving of gifts to the risen and ascended Christ. The major passage in 1 Corinthians 12 emphasizes the Spirit's work as the One who gives gifts. The other principal passage, Romans 12, leaves the Agent unspecified. Since we only mentioned briefly the ministry of Christ in relation to giving gifts to His body under Christology, we will look at the doctrine in detail here.

I. THE DEFINITION OF SPIRITUAL GIFTS

A. What Is Meant

The word for spiritual gifts (*charisma*), obviously related to the word for grace, means something that is due to the grace of God. The use of the word in the New Testament ranges from the gift of salvation (Rom. 6:23), to the gift of God's providential care (2 Cor. 1:11), to the most frequent use in relation to gifts of grace to the believer. When used in this latter relationship I suggest that a spiritual gift is a God-given ability for service.

In this proposed definition the synonym for gift is ability. A spiritual gift is an ability. "God-given" reminds us that Christ and the Spirit are the givers of gifts, and "for service" seeks to capture the emphasis in the central passages that gifts are to be used in serving the body of Christ. Though there exists a close analogy between spiritual gifts and talents (certainly both are God-given, 1 Cor. 4:7), talents may or may not be used for serving the body.

B. What Is Not Meant

1. A spiritual gift is not a place of service. The gift is the ability, not where that ability is used. Teaching can be done in or out of a formal classroom situation and in any country of the world. Helping can be done in the church or in the neighborhood.

2. A spiritual gift is not an office. The gift is the ability and can be exercised whether one holds an office in a local church or not. In this regard much confusion exists over the gift of pastor. The gift is the ability to shepherd people. This can be done by the person who occupies what we call, in our modern ecclesiology, the office of the pastorate. Or it can be done, say, by a dean of men or a dean of women in a school. Or it can be done by the wife and mother in a home.
3. A spiritual gift is not a particular age group ministry. There is no gift of youth work or children's work. All ages need to be served by pastors, teachers, administrators, helpers, etc.
4. A spiritual gift is not a specialty technique. There is no spiritual gift of writing or Christian education or music. These are techniques through which spiritual gifts may be channeled.
5. A spiritual gift is different from a natural talent. I have already mentioned that a talent may or may not serve the body of Christ, while a spiritual gift does. Let's notice some further contrasts between spiritual gifts and natural talents.

NATURAL TALENTS	SPIRITUAL GIFTS
Given by God through our parents	Given by God independent of parents
Given at birth	Evidently given at conversion
To benefit mankind generally	To benefit the body particularly

Thus a spiritual gift is a God-given ability to serve the body of Christ wherever and however He may direct.

II. THE DISTRIBUTION OF SPIRITUAL GIFTS

A. They Are Distributed by the Risen, Ascended Christ (Eph. 4:11)

The fact that the Head of the body gives gifts to His body raises the use of gifts to a high and holy level. These are His gifts, entrusted to us because He needs us to use them in order to build up His body. What dignity this gives even to what may seem to be the lowliest kind of service!

B. They Are Distributed by the Holy Spirit at Will (1 Cor. 12:11, 18)

Why does He give a believer a specific gift? Because He knows best what is needed by the body and what best fits each believer for service. If we would believe that, it would keep us from complaining that we are not like someone else, and it ought to motivate us to use to the fullest what God has given us.

When does the Spirit give us our gifts? Most likely at conversion. If these are gifts of the Spirit, and if we do not possess the Spirit until conversion, then it seems that His gifts would be given at that time. We may not discover all the gifts given at salvation, but I am inclined to believe that we have them all at that time. As we grow, other gifts may come to light to use at different times in our life, but likely we possess them all from conversion. Probably we cannot say what particular combination of gifts we have until we can look back over our lives and see what ones God used through all of our days.

C. They Are Distributed to All Believers

No believer is without at least one spiritual gift. Peter made it clear that all have at least one (1 Pet. 4:10). Every believer is either single or married, and both states are said to be spiritual gifts (1 Cor. 7:7). Possibly many believers also have the gift of helps or serving.

But no believer has all the gifts. If they did, then the metaphor in 1 Cor. 12:12–27 would be meaningless. If any believer possessed all the gifts then he or she would have no need for other believers. He would be the hand and foot and eye and ear—the whole body—which is impossible. Believers need other believers simply because no believer possesses all the gifts.

D. They Are Distributed to the Body of Christ as a Whole

By this I mean to emphasize that not every congregation need expect that it will have all the gifts represented in it. The state of growth and maturity may not require this. God knows what each group needs and will see that it is supplied accordingly.

I mean too that not every generation may necessarily expect to have all the gifts. A gift given once is a gift given to the whole body of Christ. God gave the foundation gifts of apostles and prophets at the beginning (Eph. 2:20). After the foundation was laid by those who used those gifts, other gifts were needed. But in the twentieth century we are still benefiting from and building on those foundational gifts. They were given in the first century to the whole body in all centuries. No generation has been slighted. The Spirit endows the church as He wills, and He knows exactly what each believer, each congregation, and each generation needs.[1]

III. THE DISCOVERY AND DEVELOPMENT OF SPIRITUAL GIFTS

The "peril of the pendulum" operates in relation to spiritual gifts. On the one swing of the pendulum is the idea that spiritual gifts are essentially irrelevant to Christian service today because the gifts were given to the early church only and the important matter today is maturity, not gifts. On the opposite swing is the emphasis that you cannot even begin to serve unless you are sure of your spiritual gift(s). If spiritual gifts were given to the early church only or are irrelevant to service today, then why do they appear in New Testament books written to the second generation of believers and to those who lived throughout the Roman Empire (Ephesians and 1 Peter)? Furthermore, since gifts are necessary for the proper functioning of the body of Christ, how could they not be given today and yet have the church maintain that proper functioning?

On the other hand, if a believer must know his or her spiritual gift(s) before serving, then why are there no commands to discover one's spiritual gifts? We are all commanded to use our gift (1 Pet. 4:10—"employ it"). No text says we must know what gift we have before we can be expected to serve. Yet I will risk using the word discovery in this heading in order to encourage the reader to use his or her gifts.

A. Inform Yourself About the Total Package of Gifts in Your Life

There exist three categories of gifts in every Christian's life.

1. Natural abilities. God-given at birth, they include things like IQ, a measure of health and strength, musical talents, linguistic abilities, mechanical aptitudes, etc.

2. Acquired abilities. These include things like cooking, sewing, driving a car, learning a language, learning to play an instrument, etc. Although we may tend to take such skills for granted, many people in the world have few opportunities to acquire skills in these areas.

3. Spiritual gifts. A believer should inform himself of the total package of these various abilities that God has placed in his life. In other words, he should take inventory to know what stock he has available for the Lord's use. Just going through the process of taking inventory periodically may help the believer ascertain what areas of service he ought to explore.

B. Prepare Yourself by Taking Every Opportunity Available

This principle applies to all three categories of abilities. Sharpen talents, acquire skills, and work on the development of spiritual gifts. If one thinks he may have the gift of teaching, then it will be necessary to study. The ability to communicate may be more directly given (though even that skill can be sharpened by education), but certainly the content must be learned.

If one suspects he has the gift of giving, then he will work on being a good steward in all areas of life (1 Cor. 4:2). The ability to be generous is God-given, but to have the wherewithal with which to be generous requires discipline in financial affairs.

The gift of evangelism in the early church not only involved the preaching of the Good News but also itinerating with the message. To be able to do this may involve paying special attention to one's health in order to have the stamina to travel in spreading the Gospel.

If one has the gift of exhortation, it certainly should be based on biblical knowledge. The only valid and worthwhile exhortation must be rooted in biblical truths. And, of course, to have biblical knowledge requires study.

C. Be Active in the Lord's Work

Gifts are both discovered and developed by activity. Practice brings perception of one's total package of abilities, and practice develops those abilities. If you are seeking to discover your gift(s), then do not turn down opportunities to serve, even if you think they do not fall within the range of your abilities. God may be trying to tell you that you have abilities you do not recognize.

If you are active in doing what you can, then other opportunities may arise that will bring to light additional spiritual gifts. For example, when we first meet Philip in the book of Acts we see him helping distribute the relief money to needy (and bickering) widows (6:5). It is doubtful that before he undertook this ministry he sat down to decide whether or not he had that spiritual gift! Here was an opportunity to serve, and he took it. He proved faithful in performing this menial task. The Lord then entrusted him with another ministry, that of evangelizing the Samaritans (8:5), and, later, the Ethiopian eunuch. As he used that gift he became known as Philip the evangelist (21:8). But first he was Philip the helper of widows.

The same principle was true in Stephen's life. He first served along with Philip in ministering to the widows. But he also was full of faith (6:5), and he was a great witness (7:1–53). Faithfulness in one opportunity leads to other opportunities.

Let me show you an interesting comparison between some of the spiritual gifts and some of the commands that are given to all believers. The bottom line of this comparison simply says that we are commanded to minister in many areas whether or not we think we have the corresponding spiritual gift.

GIFTS GIVEN TO SOME	COMMANDS GIVEN TO ALL
1. Ministering	1. Serve one another (Gal. 5:13)
2. Exhortation	2. Exhort one another (Heb. 10:25)
3. Giving	3. All give (2 Cor. 9:7)
4. Teaching	4. Great Commission (Matt. 28:19)
5. Showing mercy	5. Be kind (Eph. 4:32)
6. Faith	6. Walk by faith (2 Cor. 5:7)
7. Evangelism	7. All witness (Acts 1:8)

Thus all are commanded to do various ministries whether or not they possess the corresponding spiritual gift. If we faithfully obey these commands, we may discover our particular spiritual gifts.

D. Be a Good Steward of the Single or Married State

If either state is a spiritual gift (1 Cor. 7:7), then being faithful in the stewardship that goes with either state is essential. Being single or being married are spiritual gifts that need to be developed. Both categories of people need to be faithful stewards (4:2). Both need to be growing in sanctification (1 Thess. 4:3). Both need to redeem the time (Eph. 5:16).

The single person needs to pay particular attention to purity, to financial discipline, to using free time to study the Word, and to seeking opportunities to serve, say, in a foreign land for a short term. The single person must be concerned for the things of the Lord and how he or she may please Him (1 Cor. 7:32). The married person must give attention to the family and yet put the Lord's work above all (vv. 29, 33). The proper exercise and development of these gifts may be an important factor in the use of other gifts throughout life.

E. Be Willing to Do Anything for God

Actually, dedication or willingness to do anything is more important than discovering your spiritual gift(s). The passage on gifts in Ephesians 4 begins with an exhortation to a worthy life and lowly walk (vv. 1–2). The extended discussion on gifts in 1 Corinthians 12 is preceded in that letter by several exhortations to dedication (3:16; 6:19–20; 10:31). And the passage in Romans 12 begins with that great call to dedication of life in verses 1 and 2. One who is not dedicated will never discover all the abilities God has given him, nor will he fully develop those that he does discover.

IV. THE DESCRIPTION OF SPIRITUAL GIFTS

A. Apostleship (1 Cor. 12:28; Eph. 4:11)

In a general sense the word means one who is sent (as used of Epaphroditus in Phil. 2:25). But the technical sense of apostleship refers to the Twelve and possibly a few others like Paul and Barnabas (Acts 14:14). The gift was given for the founding of the church and was accredited by special signs (2 Cor. 12:12; Eph. 2:20). This is not a gift that God gives today.

B. Prophecy (Rom. 12:6; 1 Cor. 12:10; 14:1–40; Eph. 4:11)

Like apostleship, prophecy is also used in both a general sense and a technical sense. In the general sense it refers to proclaiming and thus to preaching. But technically a prophet was not only able to proclaim God's message but he also was able to predict the future. All of his messages, whether proclaiming or predicting, came from God directly through special revelation.

The gift must have been rather widely given in New Testament times, though only a few prophets are mentioned specifically (Agabus, Acts 11:27–28; prophets in the church at Antioch, 13:1; Philip's four daughters, 21:9; and the prophets in the Corinthian church, 1 Cor. 14). This, too, was a gift for the founding of the church, unnecessary after that period and after Revelation was written in the New Testament.

C. Miracles (1 Cor. 12:28) and Healings (vv. 9, 28, 30)

This is the ability to perform special signs, including physical healing. Paul exercised this gift at Ephesus (Acts 19:11–12); yet he did not or could not use this gift in the cases of Epaphroditus (Phil. 2:27), Timothy (1 Tim. 5:23), or Trophimus (2 Tim. 4:20). The gift of healing might be viewed as a category within the larger gift of miracles. For example, Paul's calling down blindness on Elymas the sorcerer (Acts

13:11) was the exercise of his gift of miracles, but it certainly was not a healing. We recognize that a miracle or healing may be done by God apart from anyone's exercising a spiritual gift (as the physical sign that accompanied the filling of the Spirit in 4:31).

If this is so, then it does not follow that if one considers the gifts of miracles and healings temporary, he is also saying that God does not perform miracles or healings today. He is simply saying that the gifts are no longer operative because the need for them has ceased; i.e., to authenticate the Gospel message.

A believer today cannot necessarily expect to be healed. It is not God's will to give everyone good health. Though Paul prayed earnestly and repeatedly, and though he himself possessed the gift of healing, it was not God's will to heal Paul of his thorn in the flesh (2 Cor. 12:8–9). If it were God's will to heal every believer, then no believer would die, for even the last illness would be healed. Healers recognize their limitations, for they do not claim to heal decayed teeth or to instantaneously mend broken bones.

To disregard human means available for healing and to simply pray for a miraculous cure is like praying for a harvest and then sitting in a rocking chair, refusing to plant or cultivate the ground.

D. Tongues and Interpretation of Tongues (1 Cor. 12:10)

Tongues is the God-given ability to speak in a language of earth that is unknown to the speaker. Interpretation of tongues is the ability to interpret that message in a language understood by the hearers. Unquestionably the first occurrence of tongues in Acts 2 was languages (note the word "language" in vv. 6 and 8). The presumption is that the tongues in Corinthians were no different.

The purposes of interpreted tongues were two: to communicate truth from God and to authenticate the truth of the Christian message, especially to Jewish people (1 Cor. 14:5, 21–22). Because the Corinthians were abusing this gift, Paul laid down strict regulations for its use: Only two or three were to speak in any meeting; no one was to speak in tongues unless the message could be interpreted; prophecy was always preferred; and women were to keep silent (vv. 27–34).

Uninterpreted tongues, especially a private prayer language, is unfruitful (v. 14) simply because even the one praying does not know what he or she is asking for. Therefore, it is better to pray with understanding, which means using a language that the person understands.

Whether one believes the biblical gift of tongues is given today or not, the Pentecostal teaching that tongues are the necessary sign of having been baptized by the Spirit is wrong. Paul said that all the believers in Corinth were baptized (12:13) but not all spoke in tongues (v. 30).

E. Evangelism (Eph. 4:11)

This ability to proclaim the Gospel message with exceptional clarity also included the idea that the ministry of an evangelist was itinerant. He was sent out by the church, but his ministry was done outside it. It might also be done publicly or privately. Whether or not one has the gift of evangelism, all believers are to be witnesses.

F. Pastor (Eph. 4:11)

This is the ability to shepherd, provide for, care for, and protect God's people. In verse 11 teaching is linked to pastoring, and in Acts 20:28 ruling is.

G. Serving (Rom. 12:7; 1 Cor. 12:28; Eph. 4:12)

This is the ability to help or serve in the broadest sense of the word.

H. Teaching (Rom. 12:7; 1 Cor. 12:28; Eph. 4:11)

This is the ability to explain God's truth to people. Apparently the gift is sometimes given alone and sometimes in connection with that of pastor.

I. Faith (1 Cor. 12:9)

This is the ability to believe God for the supply of specific needs. Every believer should walk by faith, and each has a measure of faith, but not all have the gift of faith.

J. Exhortation (Rom. 12:8)

This involves the ability to encourage, comfort, and admonish people.

K. Distinguishing Spirits (1 Cor. 12:10)

This was the ability to distinguish between true and false sources of supernatural revelation when it was being given in oral form before the completion of the canon.

L. Showing Mercy (Rom. 12:8)

Like the gift of serving, this involves succoring, particularly those who are sick and afflicted.

M. Giving (Rom. 12:8)

This seems to be the ability to be very generous with what means one has. It should be exercised with simplicity, that is, with no thought of return or self-gain.

N. Administration (Rom. 12:8; 1 Cor. 12:28)

This is the ability to rule in the church.

O. Wisdom and Knowledge (1 Cor. 12:8)

Like other early-church gifts, these involved the ability to understand and communicate God's truth to people.

The list numbers eighteen separate gifts (though I have linked several together). Is this all? Nowhere is there any suggestion that there are other gifts, and these that are listed would seem to be sufficient for the building of the body of Christ.

NOTE

1. One of the most balanced and concise treatments of this entire doctrine is William J. McRae, *The Dynamics of Spiritual Gifts* (Grand Rapids: Zondervan, 1976).

Chapter 66
THE SPIRIT FILLING

The concept of the Spirit filling people appears fifteen times in the New Testament, four of them before Pentecost. If seems to have a twofold thrust, and its ramifications are very significant in relation to the Christian's life and activity.

I. THE RELATION OF SPIRIT FILLING TO SPIRITUALITY

A. A Definition of Spirituality

In 1 Corinthians 2:15 we have the nearest thing to a definition of spirituality, and that is actually only a description. If the spiritual believer judges or examines or discerns all things, yet himself is not understood by others, then spirituality means a mature, yet maturing, relationship to God.

This requires at least three things: (a) regeneration; (b) the ministries of God in the believer's life; and (c) time to grow in maturity.

B. The Role of the Spirit in Producing Spirituality

If maturity is a key facet in spirituality, then the Holy Spirit must play a major role in producing it. To be able to discern involves knowledge of God's will and perspective. This the Spirit produces through His ministry of teaching (John 16:12–15). It will also include praying according to the will of God, which is directed by the Spirit (Rom. 8:26; Eph. 6:18). The spiritual believer will surely be exercising the spiritual gifts that the Spirit gives and empowers (1 Cor. 12:7). He or she will learn to war victoriously against the flesh by the power of the Spirit (Rom. 8:13; Gal. 5:16–17). In short, the fullness of the Spirit is key to producing spirituality in the believer.

C. Some Ramifications of the Concept

If spirituality is related to maturity, then there can be degrees of spirituality, since there are stages of maturity. Paul apparently expected the believers at Corinth to have reached a level of maturity whereby they could be called spiritual in five or six years. The Gospel was first preached in Corinth on his second missionary journey (about A.D. 50), and his first letter to the church, in which he chided the Christians because he could not treat them as spiritually mature people, was written about A.D. 55.

Seemingly a person could backslide in an area of spirituality without losing all that he or she had gained through the years. Some sins would affect more areas of life and fellowship than others.

If Spirit filling relates to the control of the Spirit in a life, then a new believer can certainly be controlled in whatever areas he knows about. But that does not mean he is spiritual, since not enough time has elapsed for him to mature. As maturity comes, more areas of needed control come to light. As we respond positively and allow the Spirit to expand His control, then we mature more. And so on.

Being a Christian for some time does not guarantee spirituality, since the person may not have allowed the Spirit control of his life during some of those years.

There are stages of maturity. Even though one may reach maturity, there is always more maturity to be achieved. Spirituality is a mature, yet maturing, relationship to God.

II. THE FILLING OF THE SPIRIT

There seem to be two facets to Spirit filling. The first may be described as a sovereign act of God whereby He possesses someone for special activity. This is expressed by the Greek phrase *pimplēmi pneumatos agiou,* and it highlights the event of being filled rather than the resultant state of fullness. It occurs in Luke 1:15 (John the Baptist), 41 (Elizabeth), 67 (Zacharias); Acts 2:4 (the group on the Day of Pentecost); 4:8 (Peter), 31 (the believers); 9:17 (Paul); and 13:9 (Paul).

Observe that this facet of filling was experienced by some of the same people more than once and without sin between that might necessitate a repeated filling. The repetition was caused by a new need for special service, not intervening sin (2:4; 4:8, 31). God did this as His sovereign act without imposing conditions on those to be filled.

The second facet of Spirit filling may be described as the extensive influence and control of the Spirit in a believer's life. It evidences an abiding state of fullness rather than the specific event. It produces a certain character of life and seems to be a close synonym to spirituality. It is indicated by the Greek phrase *plere* or *pleroo pneumatos agiou.* It occurs in Luke 4:1 (Christ); Acts 6:3, 5 (the first helpers of the apostles); 7:55 (Stephen); 11:24 (Barnabas); 13:52 (the disciples); and Ephesians 5:18 (believers).

This facet of the Spirit's filling is the finest character reference one could have. It seems to be something every believer can experience (Acts 13:52) but not something every believer does experience (6:3). Though specific conditions are not mentioned in these contexts, the normal requirements for Christian growth would be implied conditions for attaining this kind of character.

The only time Paul wrote of filling (Eph. 5:18), he emphasized this aspect of being filled. Since he commanded it, apparently he did not think all his readers had experienced it. Two questions arise in the interpretation of this verse.

The first is what is the meaning of "spirit"? Does it refer to the Holy Spirit or to the human spirit? If the latter, then the verse means to make use of the human spirit in corporate worship (though there is no other New Testament reference to filling of the human spirit). Indeed, the other occurrences of *en pneumati* in Ephesians (2:22; 3:5; 6:18) and Colossians (1:8) all clearly refer to the Holy Spirit. So one would assume Paul meant the Holy Spirit also in Ephesians 5:18. Note that the verb *pleroō* is used in relation to God (3:19) and to the Son (4:10). Why would Paul switch to the human spirit in 5:18?[1]

The second question concerns the use of *en*. Does it mean with the Spirit or by the Spirit? In other words, is the Spirit the content of our filling or the Agent? The case can mean either or both. (For the idea of "content" see Rom. 1:29 and 2 Cor. 7:4.) Perhaps both ideas are to be understood here. The Spirit is the Agent who fills us with Himself.[2]

To sum up: Spirit filling is both God's sovereign empowering us by the Spirit for special activity and the Spirit's filling us with His own character.

III. THE CHARACTERISTICS OF SPIRIT FILLING

A. Christlike Character (Gal. 5:22–23)

When the Spirit controls a life, His fruit will be produced in that life. And, of course, the description of the fruit of the Spirit is a description of Christlikeness. However, each of these characteristics must be viewed in all their aspects, not just as a facet that is compatible with our ideas of Christlikeness.

Many undoubtedly conceive of Christlikeness as a reflection of their own personalities. An introvert will probably think of our Lord as shy and retiring, whereas an extrovert will see Him as an aggressive Leader. When the nine words that comprise the fruit of the Spirit are fully defined, we will have a well-rounded picture of true Christlikeness.

For example, love consists not only of tenderness but sometimes sternness. When Christ dealt with children, He showed tenderness. When He drove out the money changers, He showed sternness. But both acts were displays of love because He is God and God is love.

Joy is not only displayed in happiness but also in heaviness (1 Pet. 1:6). Peace involves tranquillity but may include problems in human relationships (Matt. 10:34). Longsuffering means evenness and patience but does not exclude prodding (as the Lord did with Philip, John 14:9). Gentleness and goodness mean beneficient thoughts and actions, which could include casting pigs into the Sea of Galilee as a kindness to the people who were engaged in that illegal business (Matt. 8:28–34). Faithfulness certainly includes serving with regularity and dependability, but it may include an irregular action. Meekness is gentleness but does not mean weakness. Self-control affects all areas of life (1 Cor. 9:27).

B. Evangelistic Involvement

When the filling of the Spirit is mentioned in the book of Acts, conversions are recorded. Spirit filling on the Day of Pentecost (2:4) resulted in the conversion of three thousand people (v. 41). The filling of the disciples in 4:31 resulted in multitudes of men and women turning to the Lord (5:14). One of the qualifications for the choosing of the first helpers was that they be Spirit filled (6:3). This was followed by the conversion of a number of priests (v. 7). Paul was filled with the Spirit after his conversion, and the fruit of his life is well known. When Barnabas, who was filled with the Spirit, went to Antioch, many were converted (11:24). Certainly those who prayed (4:24) and those who gave (v. 34) were as involved as those who gave the direct witness that resulted in these conversions.

C. Praise, Worship, Thanksgiving, Submissiveness (Eph. 5:19–21)

Paul listed these four evidences of Spirit filling after writing the command to be filled in verse 18. Praise is expressed outwardly by speaking to one another in psalms and hymns and spiritual songs. Singing and making melody in the heart is evidence of the inner attitude of worship. Giving thanks should be viewed as inclusively as possible, and it was written by a man who was at the time under house arrest in Rome, awaiting trial. Submissiveness in the relationships of life (husband/wife, parents/children, masters/slaves) also characterizes the Spirit-filled life. Note that all of these are very ordinary things that affect the routines of life, not extraordinary feats of spiritual strength.

IV. HOW CAN I BE SPIRIT FILLED?

No example of praying for the filling of the Spirit exists in the post-Pentecost material of the New Testament. So praying, however earnest, is apparently not the way to be filled.

If filling relates to the control of the Spirit in one's life (whether in the sense of God's sovereign seizing of a person or of a sustained control that results in character), then filling is related to yieldedness. When I am willing to allow the Spirit to do what He wishes, it is up to Him to do or not to do with me whatever is His pleasure. I can check my willingness, but I cannot manipulate His activities.

As one matures, his knowledge and perspectives will deepen and broaden. New areas that need to be yielded will come to light. Therefore, filled people need to be filled as they continue to mature in the Lord. But no believer can afford not to be filled at every stage of his or her spiritual growth.

Notes

1. For a statement of the human spirit view see S. D. F. Salmond, "The Epistle to the Ephesians," in *The Expositor's Greek Testament* (Grand Rapids: Eerdmans, 1952), 3:362.
2. This is the view of C. J. Ellicott, *St. Paul's Epistle to the Ephesians* (London: Longmans, 1868), 124.

BAPTISM	**FILLING**
OCCURS ONLY ONCE IN EACH BELIEVER'S LIFE	IS A REPEATED EXPERIENCE
NEVER HAPPENED BEFORE DAY OF PENTECOST	OCCURED IN THE OLD TESTAMENT
TRUE OF ALL BELIEVERS	NOT NECESSARILY EXPERIENCED BY ALL
CANNOT BE UNDONE	CAN BE LOST
RESULTS IN A *POSITION*	RESULTS IN *POWER*
OCCURS WHEN WE BELIEVE IN CHRIST	OCCURS THROUGHOUT THE CHRISTIAN LIFE
NO PREREQUISITE (EXCEPT FAITH IN CHRIST)	DEPENDS ON YIELDEDNESS

Chapter 67
OTHER MINISTRIES OF THE SPIRIT

I. TEACHING

The teaching ministry of the Spirit was one of Christ's last promises before His crucifixion. He said,

> I have many more things to say to you, but you cannot bear them now. But when He, the Spirit of truth, comes, He will guide you into all the truth; for He will not speak on His own initiative, but whatever He hears, He will speak; and He will disclose to you what is to come. He shall glorify Me; for He shall take of Mine, and shall disclose it to you. All things that the Father has are Mine; therefore I said, that He takes of Mine, and will disclose it to you. (John 16:12–15)

A. Time

This particular ministry of the Spirit was yet future when our Lord spoke these words. It began on the Day of Pentecost and continues throughout this age. Peter's clear comprehension as revealed in his Pentecostal sermon is evidence of the beginning of this ministry.

B. Content

In general the content of the Spirit's ministry encompasses "all the truth" (the definite article appears in the text). This, of course, means revelation concerning Christ Himself, but on the basis of the written Word (for we have no other information about Him except through the Bible). Therefore, He teaches the believer the content of the Scripture, which leads him to an understanding of prophecy ("things to come"). This particularizing of the general promise concerning teaching ought to encourage every believer to study prophecy. Notice too that the Spirit does not originate His message—it comes from the Lord.

C. Result

The result of the teaching ministry of the Spirit is that Christ is glorified. If He is not glorified, then the Spirit has not been ministering. Note also that it is not the Spirit who is glorified or who is supposed to be glorified in a religious service, but Christ. Further, if Christ is known only through the written Word, then He will be glorified when the Word of God is expounded in the power of the Spirit.

D. Procedure

How does the Spirit teach the believer? John declares: "The anointing which you received from Him abides in you, and you have no need for anyone to teach you; but as His anointing teaches you about all things, and is true and is not a lie, and just as it has taught you, you abide in Him" (1 John 2:27). This could not mean that human teachers are unnecessary in explaining the Word of God. If it could, then what would be the use of the gift of teaching? (Rom. 12:7). John wrote concerning the presence of antichrists in the group. Having stated his own conviction concerning their heresies, he simply declared that no man really had to tell them the truth, for the Holy Spirit would confirm it to them. Human teachers are a necessary link in the procedure of instructing believers, though the ultimate authentication of the teaching comes from the Spirit.

II. GUIDING

"For all who are being led by the Spirit of God, these are sons of God" (Rom. 8:14). Leading is a confirmation of sonship, for sons are led. This work of guidance is particularly the work of the Spirit. Romans 8:14 states it and the book of Acts amply illustrates it (8:29; 10:19–20; 13:2, 4; 16:6–7; 20:22–23). This ministry of the Spirit is one of the most assuring ones for the Christian. The child of God never needs to walk in the dark; he is always free to ask and receive directions from the Spirit Himself.

III. ASSURING

The Spirit is also the One who assures the Christian that he is a child of God. "The Spirit Himself bears witness with our spirit that we are children of God" (Rom. 8:16). The word for children here is *tekna* (in contrast to *huioi,* sons) and emphasizes the fact that the believer shares in the life of the Father. Because of this, he also shares as an heir in the possessions of the Father. Assurance of all this is the work of the Spirit to the heart of each Christian.

Undoubtedly assurance is also brought to the heart of the believer by an increased understanding of some of the things that the Spirit has done for him. For instance, assurance will deepen when one understands what it means to be sealed with the Spirit and to have been given the earnest of the Spirit as a guarantee of the completion of redemption (Eph. 1:13–14). The comprehension of what is involved in the Spirit's joining the believer to the risen, undying body of Christ will also nurture assurance. Of course, the comprehension of these great accomplishments is part of the teaching ministry of the Spirit, so in many ways the Holy Spirit is connected with and concerned about the assurance of the child of God.

IV. PRAYING

A. The Statement

Though we may not fully understand the ramifications of the Spirit's praying in the believer, the fact that He does is perfectly clear: "And in the same way the Spirit also helps our weakness; for we do not know how to pray as we should, but the Spirit Himself intercedes for us with groanings too deep for words" (Rom. 8:26).

B. The Need

The stated reason that we need help is because of our infirmity (the word is singular). He helps our entire weakness, but especially as it manifests itself in relation to our prayer life, and particularly in relation to knowing what to pray for at the present moment. While we wait for our full redemption, we need guidance in the particulars of prayer.

C. The Method

The way the Spirit helps meet our needs is described in general by the word "helps," which literally means "puts His hand to the work in cooperation with us."[1] Specifically this help is given in the form of "groanings too deep for words." These groanings, the meaning of which cannot be grasped, find no adequate or formulated expression. One thing we do know—they are according to the will of God.

In another passage we are told that the Spirit guides and directs our prayers (Eph. 6:18). This is more the guidance of the believer's heart and mind as he prays than the unutterable groanings of the Spirit Himself.

D. The Result

The result of such a prayer life is assurance to the believer of the certainty of his future and full redemption (Rom. 8:23). This ministry of the Spirit is a kind of earnestlike guarantee of that redemption. Such a satisfying prayer life will help keep us content in this present world as we wait for the consummation. The ministry of the Spirit, then, is not only connected with answered prayer, but it cultivates our assurance and contentment in this life.

V. SANCTIFYING

A. The Concept of Sanctification

The word *sanctify* basically means to set apart. It has the same root as the words *saint* and *holy*. For the Christian, sanctification includes three aspects. The first is called positional or definitive sanctification, which relates to the position every believer enjoys by virtue of being set apart as a member of God's family through faith in Christ. This is true for all believers regardless of different degrees of spiritual growth. Paul addressed the carnal Christians with all of their sinful practices as sanctified (and thus as saints, 1 Cor. 1:2; see also 6:11 where the verbs indicate accomplished facts, not something to be attained).

The second aspect of sanctification concerns the present experiential or progressive work of continuing to be set apart during the whole of our Christian lives. Every command and exhortation to holy living concerns progressive sanctification (1 Pet. 1:16).

The third aspect is usually called ultimate sanctification, which we will attain in heaven when we shall be completely and eternally set apart to our God (Eph. 5:26–27; Jude 24–25).

B. The Agents in Sanctification

All persons of the Trinity are involved in sanctification, and believers are too. In positional sanctification, which comes when we are saved, the Holy Spirit sanctifies us, our responsibility being to believe the truth (2 Thess. 2:13). Christ's death is the basis for our position in sanctification (Heb. 10:10). In ultimate sanctification God is the one who will present us blameless.

In the process of progressive sanctification several agents are involved. It was to the Father that our Lord prayed that He would sanctify us through the truth (John 17:17 and 1 Thess. 5:23). Thus the Bible becomes an indispensable foundation for our sanctification. How else could we know for sure what pleases a holy God except through His Word? Christ's death (to which He sanctified or set Himself apart) serves as the basis for our being able to progress in sanctification (John 17:19; Rom. 6:1–13). However, the Holy Spirit is the prominent agent in the outworking of our progressive sanctification. It is by the Spirit that we put to death the deeds of the body (Rom. 8:13). The Spirit ignites love in our hearts (Rom. 5:5). By the Spirit we are changed from glory to glory to become more and more like Christ (2 Cor. 3:18). And it is the fruit of the Spirit that produces in us Christlikeness, which is the goal of sanctification (Gal. 5:22–23).

Yet the believer must faithfully discharge his or her responsibilities in sanctification. When we present ourselves as slaves to righteousness, sanctification results (Rom. 6:19; see also Rom. 6:13; 2 Cor. 7:1; 1 Pet. 2:11). We must obey the commands and exhortations of the Christian life in order to progress in holiness.

To withhold or withdraw areas of our lives from God's desired sanctification for us will result in our being controlled by the flesh rather than by the Spirit. This will result in the believer's being carnal in those unyielded or rebellious areas (1 Cor. 3:1–5). Carnality exhibits the characteristics of the unsaved life because of being controlled by the flesh (Gal. 5:16–21). Thus yieldedness, Spirit filling, and the sanctifying process are involved in setting us apart more and more to the image of Christ.

NOTE

1. R. St. John Parry, "Romans," in *Cambridge Greek Testament* (New York: Cambridge University Press, 1912), 120.

Chapter 68
HISTORY OF THE DOCTRINE OF THE SPIRIT

I. TO THE COUNCIL OF NICAEA

A. Orthodox Witness

Doctrinal formulation of the Christian faith did not occur all at once at some point in the history of the church. Nor did a definition of all Christian doctrines take place at any equal rate. Sometimes one doctrine came in for attention; at other times the spotlight would focus on a different doctrine.

The doctrine of the Holy Spirit did not receive much attention in the early centuries as far as formal definition was concerned. What we have come to know as the orthodox expression of the doctrine of the Spirit was witnessed to by the early church in the baptismal formula, in the Apostles' Creed, and in the castigating of error when it did appear. The use of the threefold name of Father, Son, and Spirit shows that implicitly and in practice the deity and personality of the Spirit were acknowledged by the early church.

As far as the Spirit was concerned, the principal emphasis in the Subapostolic Age was on the experience of the Spirit rather than on the doctrine. This emphasis is particularly notable in *The Shepherd of Hermas*. In the era of the apologists the Spirit is very much in the background of the literature, since the emphasis was on the Logos. At the same time there seemed to be no erroneous experience of the Spirit in spite of the lack of doctrinal definition.

B. Montanism (170)

It was in Montanism that the subject of the Holy Spirit came into more prominence. The original impetus for this movement grew out of a reaction against the increasing rigidity and frigidity of the organized church. Montanism (also called the Phrygian heresy) appeared in Phrygia about 170 through the ministry of Montanus and two women, Prisca and Maximilla. They announced themselves as prophets and announced the period as the Age of the Paraclete in which new revelations from God were to be given. They emphasized the nearness of the end of the world and insisted on very high and strict moral standards in their followers. It was this high morality that attracted Tertullian and others to the movement.

Montanism was also a reaction against gnosticism with its intellectualism, which seemingly raised a barrier against the soul's personal communication with God. For many, Montanism stood for the active presence and ministry of the Spirit in the church and for a more spiritual type of church life. However, Montanism was officially rejected because of its insistence on additional revelation, and in so doing, the church affirmed the belief that the Spirit does not give new revelations apart from the Scriptures. Still, with all this emphasis on the experience of the Spirit, the doctrine remained for the most part without formulation at that time.

C. Sabellianism (215)

Monarchianism was the predecessor of Sabellianism. In its modalistic form, Monarchianism taught that the Son was merely another mode of expression of the Father. Noetus and Praxeas were leaders in this movement, and they also taught patripassianism (i.e., the Father was crucified). Since the Monarchians taught that the Son was another mode of expression of God, it was inevitable that the church was forced to consider the relation of the Spirit to the Son and to the Father. Sabellius taught that God is a unity but that He revealed Himself in three different modes or forms. These three forms were not three hypostases but three roles or parts played by the one God. Sabellianism was the first major error concerning the Trinity that gained a large following in the church.

D. Arianism (325)

The Arian controversy is thus called because it was occasioned by the anti-Trinitarian views of Arius, a presbyter of Alexandria. The monotheistic principle of Monarchianism was a dominant concept in his view. However, he distinguished the one eternal God from the Son who was generated by the Father and who had a beginning. He also believed that the Holy Spirit was the first thing created by the Son, for all things were made by the Son. Arius was opposed by Athanasius, and the Council of Nicaea was called to discuss the dispute.

The principal statement of the council concerned the deity of the second person, and the conclusion was that Christ was "of the same substance" as the Father. The attention of the council was focused on the Son rather than on the Spirit, and the Nicene Creed merely mentions the Spirit: "I believe in the Holy Spirit." The statement can be said only to infer the deity and personality of the Holy Spirit because of its connection with the specific declaration concerning the Son. Why the council was not equally specific concerning the Spirit is only a matter of conjecture. Possibly the church was content not to anticipate heresy or to go beyond what the occasion demanded. Athanasius, however, was much more definite in his own teaching, vigorously maintaining that the Spirit, like the Son, was of the same essence as the Father.

II. FROM NICAEA TO THE PROTESTANT REFORMATION

A. The Council of Constantinople (381)

Not all was settled by the Nicene Council. Though Athanasius's own teaching was clearly orthodox and detailed, the Nicene Creed had been indefinite concerning the Spirit. A new controversy soon arose, and people began to assert their unbelief in the deity of the Spirit. As a result, there arose the Macedonians, whose founder, Macedonius, bishop of Constantinople, maintained that the Spirit was a creature subordinate to the Son. His party was nicknamed Pneumatomachians ("evil speakers against the Spirit"). The mainstream of orthodox teaching was that the Holy Spirit was divine or else the Son was not divine either. Basil of Caesarea, Gregory of Nazianzus, and Gregory of Nyssa were leaders in propagating the orthodox view and preparing the way for the Council of Constantinople.

The controversy grew to such proportions that Emperor Theodosius had to call a council at Constantinople consisting of 150 orthodox bishops representing the Eastern church only. In 381 the council met and under the guidance of Gregory of Nazianzus formulated the following statement concerning the Holy Spirit: "And we believe in the Holy Spirit, the Lord, the Life-giving, who proceeds from the Father, who is to be glorified with the Father and the Son, and who speaks through the prophets." It has been pointed out that the creed used remarkable moderation in avoiding the term "of the same substance" (which was used of Christ in the Nicene Creed) to express the Spirit's oneness with the Father and the Son. Actually the Spirit is not even called God in the creed, though the terms in which His work is described cannot possibly be predicated of any created being. Nevertheless, the statement did counter the Macedonians, even though it did not assert the consubstantiality of the Spirit with the Father or define the relation of the Spirit to the Father and the Son; and it settled the question of the deity of the Spirit just as the Nicene Council had settled the question of the deity of Christ.

B. Augustine (354–430)

1. De Trinitate. The concept of the Trinity in the Western church reached a final formulation in this work by Augustine. His interest in the doctrine of grace would naturally lead to a consideration of the Spirit, for his own experiences taught him how necessary the power of the Spirit is to the believer. In this treatise he stated that each of the three persons of the Trinity possesses the entire essence and that all are interdependent on the others. He declared that he was not satisfied with the word "persons" to express the three hypostases, but he used it "in order not to be silent." In his conception of the Trinity, the Spirit proceeds from both the Father and the Son.

2. The Pelagian controversy (431). Augustine also laid great stress on efficacious grace as the work of the Spirit. This profoundly influenced not only his doctrine of man and of sin but also his doctrine of the Spirit. Pelagius, his opponent in the controversy, advocated a practical denial of original sin and emphasized the ability of man to do good apart from the enablement of the Spirit. The Council of Ephesus dealt with the controversy in 431 and condemned Pelagius and his views and upheld Augustine and his. Though Pelagianism was condemned officially, it was not eradicated from the church, for Pelagianism and semi-Pelagianism (as well as Augustinianism) have come down to this present day.

C. The Council of Chalcedon (451)

In 451 the Council of Chalcedon, representing the sees of Rome, Constantinople, Antioch, and Jerusalem, confirmed the decisions of Nicaea and Constantinople. The council explicitly stated that the Nicene Creed was sufficient as a proper statement of the doctrine of the Trinity and that the clauses added by the Council of Constantinople in 381 were only intended to clarify, not change, the Nicene Creed. This firmly established the doctrine of the deity of the Holy Spirit.

D. The Synod of Toledo (589)

Though the question of the deity of the Spirit had been settled at

Constantinople and Chalcedon, there still remained the important and mysterious question of the Spirit's precise relation to the Father and the Son. This was a problem that developed in the West (the matter of the deity of the Spirit was Eastern). The term "generation" was used to describe the relation of the Son to the Father, while the term "procession" was employed to denote the relation of the Spirit. The question was: Did the Spirit proceed from the Father only, or from the Father and the Son? Though the Council of Constantinople did not declare that the Spirit proceeded from the Son as well as from the Father, this was the belief of many church leaders. It was felt necessary to believe that, lest procession from the Father only look like a denial of the essential oneness of the Son with the Father. However, there was not unanimity on this point, for others felt that to say that the Spirit proceeded from the Father and the Son would mean that the Spirit was dependent on the Son and would thus infringe on His deity.

The Western theologians held to the procession from the Father and the Son, and they added the famous "filioque" ("and Son") clause to the Constantinopolitan Creed at the Synod of Toledo. The clause stated that the Spirit "proceedeth from the Father and the Son." How the *filioque* clause came into the creed is a matter of discussion. Some think it was the "blunder" of a copyist. In any case, the clause never caused suspicion but was repeated synod after synod as orthodox doctrine. Leaders in the Eastern church felt that the Western church was tampering with the creed set at Constantinople and never adopted the *filioque* addition, declaring it heresy to this day.

Thus three things concerning the Trinity were settled beyond all question, at least in the Western church. The deity of the Son was settled at the Council of Nicaea; the deity of the Spirit at Constantinople; and the procession of the Spirit from the Father and the Son at the Synod of Toledo. The presence of heresy had forced the church to settle these great doctrinal matters.

E. Abelard (1079–1142)

Abelard spoke of the Trinity in ways that caused him to be charged with Sabellianism. The name of the Father, he said, stands for power; the Son, for wisdom; the Spirit, for goodness. Sometimes he seemed to indicate real personal distinctions in the Godhead, but his illustrations and expressions at other times were modalistic.

F. Thomas Aquinas (1225–74)

In Thomas there was the usual orthodox understanding of the Trinity. Generally speaking, however, the centuries preceding the Protestant Reformation added little to the doctrine of the Spirit beyond what was so well systematized by Augustine. In the West, while the influence of Augustine was still at work, the church became semi-Pelagian (de-emphasizing original sin and emphasizing the freedom of man's will). This together with the increasing sacerdotalism and its consequences (which promoted special powers of the clergy) tended to keep the minds of many away from any further study of the Holy Spirit. Though there were tendencies toward mysticism on the part of some, no real fresh study of the doctrine of the Spirit was made until the time of the Reformation.

III. FROM THE REFORMATION TO THE PRESENT

A. The Protestant Reformation (1517)

Up to the time of the Reformation the church's attention had been directed only toward the person of the Spirit. In the Reformation, attention was given to His work. As far as the Spirit's person was concerned, all the Reformed confessions express the orthodox doctrine of the Spirit in relation to the other persons of the Trinity. As far as His work is concerned, there was renewed emphasis on the necessity of His work in regenerating man because there was a return to the Augustinian emphasis on the total depravity of man.

Another important contribution of the Reformers was their emphasis on the need of illumination by the Spirit. The Roman church taught that only the priest could interpret the Word of God, whereas the Reformers advocated openly the study of the Bible, asserting that all believers could be taught its truths by the teaching ministry of the Holy Spirit.

Luther's emphasis on justification by faith caused him to say much about the Spirit's work in this connection. Calvin emphasized those aspects of the work of the Spirit that are associated with the Trinity and the ministry of the Spirit in the hearts and lives of believers.

The various documents and creeds growing out of the Reformation are uniform in their orthodoxy. The Augsburg Confession, the Anglican Articles, the Formula Concordiae, the Helvetic Confession, and the Westminster Confession all asserted the deity of the Spirit following the Council of Chalcedon, including the *filioque* clause as well as the particular emphases brought to light by the Reformation itself. Indeed, it may be said that it was not until the time of the Reformation that there was a developed doctrine of the Holy Spirit.

B. The Socinians and Arminians

Almost every religious movement is followed by excesses and reactions. The Reformation was no exception. Some went to an extreme of unbalanced enthusiasm and mysticism. Others tended toward a rationalism that almost completely ignored the work of the Spirit in the life. In the sixteenth century the Socinians declared that it was erroneous to believe that the persons of the Trinity possessed a single essence. In this teaching they echoed the Arians, but they went beyond them in denying the preexistence of the Son and defining the Holy Spirit as "a virtue or energy flowing from God to man."

From the Reformed church itself there arose the serious trouble in connection with what is known as Arminian theology (Arminius, 1560–1609). The entire tendency of this teaching was to emphasize human effort and will and to make salvation a work of man rather than a work of God, with the human will replacing the work of the Spirit in regeneration.

The Synod of Dort (1618–19) met to deal with the matter, and it condemned Arminian theology, emphasizing in the strongest possible way the need of the working and power of the Holy Spirit. However, the synod did not erase Arminian theology, which flourishes to this day. The Puritan movement in England did much to counter Arminianism by its emphasis on the doctrine of grace.

C. John Owen (1616–83)

One of the most important contributions of the Puritans was Owen's book *Discourse Concerning the Holy Spirit.* Many think his work has never been superseded. It is a development of the great Reformation principles in relation to the Holy Spirit and the Christian life.

D. Abraham Kuyper (1837–1920)

The work of Kuyper is also a classic in its field, particularly in view of the rationalism that had swept over Europe. Swedenborg (1688–1772) denied the Trinity. Schleiermacher (1768–1834), though he countered the prevalent rationalism by emphasizing the need and reality of personal religion, denied the objective realities of the Incarnation, the Cross, and the coming of the Spirit. His doctrine of the Trinity was Sabellian—the persons of the Godhead were only modes of manifestation. The distinct personality of the Spirit was denied, and the Spirit's work was defined as "the collective Spirit of the new corporate life that was initiated by Christ." Ritschl (1822–89) revived the Monarchianism of Paul of Samosata. His was a theology without metaphysics, which necessarily affected his view of the Spirit.

E. The Plymouth Brethren (1825)

It is to the Brethren that we owe a proper understanding of the baptizing ministry of the Spirit and the distinct nature of the New Testament church. The church owes much to the Brethrens' testimony to the importance of the Word of God, the illumination of the Spirit, and the position that the believer has in Christ by the work of the Spirit. There were deplorable schisms within their group, but the Brethren had an important witness to the presence, power, and guidance of the Spirit in the church.

F. Neo-orthodoxy

Neo-orthodoxy is a twentieth-century movement arising out of the theology of Karl Barth (1886–1968). It was a reaction to the liberalism that held sway until the horrors of a world war forced men to think more seriously about sin and their lack of competency to solve their own problems. The neo-orthodox movement claimed to be a new reformation that called men back to the Bible. It did this, but not to the Bible of the Reformers, for neo-orthodox theologians have willingly embraced the teachings of liberalism concerning the accuracy and truth of the Bible, while at the same time trying to preach the message of the Bible.

Though neo-orthodoxy has about as many exponents as there are neo-orthodox theologians, it may be said that in general its view of the Holy Spirit leaves much to be desired. Most neo-orthodox writers deny the distinct personality of the Spirit and affirm His deity only in that He is represented as a divine manifestation of God. The Holy Spirit is regarded as more of an activity of God than a person of the Godhead.

Barth's own view of the Trinity has been called modalistic, though he would reject the term. He rejected what is commonly conceived of as modalism of divine manifestation of God in three ways as saying too little in rightly expressing the doctrine of the Trinity. On the other hand, he rejected the term "person" in regard to the Trinity as teaching too much; i.e., tritheism or three Gods. His view seemed to be that the Trinity is a threefold mode of manifestation and less than three persons. Barth, in contrast to most neo-orthodox teachers, did believe in the deity of the Spirit.

G. Neoliberalism

The rise and wide acceptance of neo-orthodox theology has caused liberalism to examine its own tenets. The result has been the new liberalism, which is the old liberalism with a tendency to take sin more seriously and to be less optimistic. Its approach to world problems may be different, but its teachings differ little from the older liberalism. The new liberal dispenses quickly and completely with the orthodox doctrine of the Spirit simply because he does not believe in the deity of the second person of the Trinity. Hence there is in reality no Trinity, and of course no divine third person. The Spirit is merely a function of God without possessing any distinct quality of personality.

H. Pentecostalism

Undoubtedly modern Pentecostalism is a reaction to the sterility that began to characterize the established churches in the modern era. It emphasizes the baptism of the Spirit as a second work of grace for endowment with power, and it promotes a return of experiencing all the gifts that were given and used in New Testament times. The orthodox doctrine concerning the person of the Spirit is assumed; it is the reality of the work of the Spirit in the lives of Christians that is promoted and not always correctly.

Thus in the sweep of church history one sees first the formulation of what has come to be known as the orthodox doctrine of the Spirit, then the definition of it in the early councils, and the development of it during the Reformation. With every surge toward defining or developing the truth, there have been movements away from it, either in the form of rationalistic coldness or unbalanced enthusiasm and mysticism. History should teach us that orthodox doctrine is not only important to faith but equally vital to life. Perhaps in no doctrine is this wedding of truth and life more important than in the doctrine concerning the Holy Spirit.

Section XII
"I WILL BUILD MY CHURCH"

Chapter 69
What Is the Church?

The importance of the church can scarcely be overstated. It is that which God purchased with the blood of His own Son (Acts 20:28). It is that which Christ loves, nourishes, and cherishes (Eph. 5:25, 29), and which He shall present to Himself blameless in all her glory one day (v. 27). Building His church constitutes Christ's principal work in the world today (Matt. 16:18) through His giving of spiritual gifts (Eph. 4:12). Thus the exercise of those gifts by believers aligns us with what Christ is doing today.

I. THE MEANING OF THE WORD CHURCH

A. The English Word

The English word *church* (and the cognate form *kirk*) are derived from the Greek word *kyriakon,* which means "belonging to the Lord." The only two uses of that word in the New Testament occur in 1 Corinthians 11:20 (referring to the Lord's Supper) and Revelation 1:10 (referring to the Lord's Day). The word came to be used to refer to other things such as the place or people or denomination or country related to the group that belong to the Lord.

B. The Hebrew Word

The Hebrew word *qahal* means simply an assembly and is usually translated in the Septuagint by *ekklesia.* However, it does not necessarily refer to a religious assembly (Gen. 28:3; 49:6; Ps. 26:5), nor even to a congregation of human beings (Ps. 89:5 NASB), though most often it does refer to the congregation of Israel.

C. The Greek Word

The Greek word *ekklesia* meant an assembly and was used in a political, not a religious, sense. It did not refer to the people but to the meeting; in other words, when the people were not assembled formally they were not referred to as an *ekklesia.* The word is used in this same secular Greek way two times in the New Testament (Acts 19:32, 41).

When the Greek word is used in the New Testament, it takes on much richer and fuller aspects to that basic secular meaning. For example, the people themselves, whether assembled or not, are the *ekklesia*. Nevertheless, the word as used in the New Testament still retains the basic meaning of an assembly and does not take on a supposed theological meaning (based on the breakup of the word into its two parts, "call" and "out of") of a "called out" people. If the word is going to be translated on the basis of etymology, then it should be translated "called together," not "called out."

II. THE USES OF THE WORD IN THE NEW TESTAMENT

If the word *church* has to do with an assembled group, then different uses of the concept in the New Testament should tell us (a) what is the character or nature of the group assembled, and (b) what are the foci and reasons that draw that particular assembly together.

A. Acts 19:39, 41

Here the group was composed of heathen people whose reason for assembling was to exercise a political privilege. The citizens of this free city had the right to meet in a legislative assembly, which they did three times a month. But this occasion was an illegal assembly on which Rome would not look kindly; hence the town clerk's urgency to dismiss the people.

B. Acts 7:38

Here the group were Israelites assembled to receive God's Law through Moses. The spiritual character of this group was mixed—some personally and individually rightly related to God and some not. Of course, all were related to Him in the sense that God had chosen the nation, but this alone did not guarantee the spiritual salvation of each person. This national calling was the reason for the gathering at the base of Mt. Sinai.

C. Ephesians 1:22–23

Here the assembly is the church, which is Christ's body. The character of this group is 100 percent regenerated, and the reason for its existence is the baptizing ministry of the Spirit, which places those who believe into this body of Christ (1 Cor. 12:13). This church is universal, including every believer in every place on earth and those who are in heaven (Heb. 12:23). Strictly speaking, the church is not invisible, for many of its members are quite visible. A better designation is the universal church.

D. Romans 16:5; 1 Corinthians 16:19; Colossians 4:15; Philemon 2

Here are groups of people very much localized—churches in houses. The nature of the people (at least in New Testament times) would have been those who professed to have accepted Christ as Savior. In some instances those who only professed but who did not possess salvation would have been associated with local churches (1 John 2:19; Rev. 3:20), but to be Christian churches, the people would have had to make a Christian profession.

What were the foci of these local churches? One was geographical. Another was that profession of faith in Christ. Another was the practice of baptism and the Lord's Supper. Another was the exercise of group responsibilities, like teaching.

III. THE NEW TESTAMENT CONCEPT OF THE CHURCH

Customarily the concept of the church has focused on the universal and local church. Sometimes, erroneously, the categories are stated as invisible and visible. But even universal and local do not seem to cover all the facets of the concept. Universal serves well as a label for the body of Christ, whether on earth or in heaven (Heb. 12:23). But local needs further defining. How local is the local church?

As we have seen, sometimes local stands for a church in a house. This is as local a unit as is pictured in the New Testament. But the church at Corinth (1 Cor. 1:2) must have included several house churches. Yet it was "local" in that it was confined to the city of Corinth and did not include other churches in Greece such as the church in Thessalonica (1 Thess. 1:1).

Yet the singular "church" is used to designate several churches in a region (Acts 9:31 NASB). Here "the church" included groups throughout all Judea and Galilee and Samaria. When Paul persecuted the church in his preconversion days, he did not confine himself to one local church (1 Cor. 15:9). So the concept of the local church can include a group in a single house, the several groups in a city, or even the many groups in a region. Even with these categories 1 Corinthians 10:32 may not fit any of them. Giving no offense to the church of God must relate to visible groups, yet not all of them even in a region. It must concern any aspect of the visible church one comes in contact with.

Apparently we need more than the customary twofold categorization of the church—universal and local. (1) There is the universal church—all believers in heaven or on earth. (2) There is the visible church—local churches in various areas, especially those I am acquainted with. (3) There is the local church—the particular assembly with which I have my primary and sustained relation. Every believer actually belongs to all these three aspects of the church, and 1 Corinthians 10:32 applies to any of them with which he has contact at any time.

IV. OTHER CONCEPTS OF THE CHURCH

A. The Roman Catholic Concept

The Roman Catholic concept of the church is that "it is a divinely constituted society consisting of members from every race and nation, all holding one faith, all using the same sacraments as means of holiness and salvation, and all governed benignly by the successor of St. Peter, the Vicar of Christ, the pope . . ."[1]

B. The Anglican Concept

The Anglican concept states that "the visible church of Christ is a congregation of faithful men, in which the pure Word of God is preached, and the Sacraments be duly ministered according to Christ's ordinance. . . ."[2] The Anglican Church is, of course, under the temporal headship of the King or Queen of England.

C. The Reformed Concept

The Westminster Confession of Faith states: "The catholic or universal church, which is invisible, consists of the whole number of the elect. . . . The visible church, which is also catholic or universal under the Gospel, consists of all those throughout the world that profess the true religion, together with their children . . ." (chap. XXV).

D. The Baptist Concept

The Baptist Confession of Faith of 1646 says that "the church is a company of visible saints, called and separated from the world by the Word and Spirit of God, to the visible profession of the faith of the Gospel; being baptized into that faith" (Article XXXIII). Some contemporary Baptists acknowledge the reality of the universal church and some do not.

NOTES

1. C. B. Pallen, "Catholic Church," in *The New Catholic Dictionary* (New York: The Universal Knowledge Foundation, 1929), 180–81.
2. Article XIX of the Thirty-Nine Articles of the Church of England.

Chapter 70
THE DISTINCTIVENESS OF THE CHURCH

The church stands unique in the purposes of God. Although God has related Himself to other groups, His activity with the church remains distinct. "I will build My church," the Lord said, and that is His special work today. Those words of Christ indicate specific distinctions about the church: (a) it was a work future to His earthly life; (b) it was not the same as the kingdom about which He also taught; (c) it must have been something different from the theocracy of Israel. These distinctions, and others, we shall now examine.

I. THE RELATION OF THE CHURCH TO THE KINGDOM

Much confusion exists because of the failure to carefully define, distinguish, and compare the church and the kingdom. Based on Augustine's *City of God,* the equation of the church and the kingdom resulted in the absolute authority of the church on earth. Postmillennialism builds the earthly kingdom on the growth and success of the church. The mistaken concept of theonomy sees the church's mission as establishing the Old Testament Law of God in the kingdoms of the world today. Reformed theology, less frontal than theonomy, builds on the concept of the lordship of Christ over all the structures of the world and sees the church as a principal agent in accomplishing this. What is the relation between the church and the kingdom?

A. The Meaning of the Kingdom

The dictionary defines kingdom as a politically organized community. It therefore involves ruler(s), ruled, and realm. To define a particular kingdom, one needs to ask several questions: Who is the ruler? Who are the ruled? When and where is the kingdom? The various kingdoms of Scripture can and need to be distinguished by asking such questions.

B. The Various Concepts of Kingdom

1. The universal kingdom. The Scriptures reveal God as Ruler of the whole world (1 Chron. 29:11; Ps. 145:13). As such He exercises jurisdiction over the nations of the world, appointing rulers of His choosing and judging the world (Ps. 96:13; Dan. 2:37). In Jewish thought this concept of the kingdom began with Adam, was disfigured when sin entered, yet continued on until Abraham, who recalled people to the kingdom with only partial success (witness the rebellion of Sodom and Gomorrah). However, when Israel accepted the Mosaic Law, this kingdom was reestablished, though rebellion erupted almost immediately (with the golden calf) and repeatedly throughout Israel's history. Only the godly remnant revived the kingdom. Only Messiah would bring the full realization of this kingdom.

Christian theology acknowledges this concept of a universal kingdom (though usually including angels in it, which Judaism did not). God is Ruler of the nations (Rev. 15:3), and ultimately they will answer to Him when He judges them (Ps. 110:6).

In summary, in the universal kingdom God is the Ruler; He rules over all; and He does it in all time and eternity.

2. The Davidic/messianic kingdom. Both Judaism and premillennial Christian theology give a major place to this concept of kingdom. It is Davidic in that the promises concerning the kingdom were made in the great covenant with David (2 Sam. 7:12–16). It is messianic since Messiah will be the Ruler. It will be realized at the second advent of Christ when He will establish His kingdom and fulfill those promises made to David. (See further discussion under eschatology, beginning with chapter 77.)

In summary, in the Davidic messianic kingdom Christ is the Ruler; He will rule over the earth and its inhabitants during the one thousand years that follow His second coming.

3. The mystery form of the kingdom. In Matthew 13 Christ revealed mysteries concerning the concept of the kingdom (v. 11). In accord with the meaning of "mystery," this means He told the disciples some things about the kingdom that were previously unknown. This idea of the kingdom, then, began when the Lord was teaching and will end at His second advent (vv. 39–40). In other words, it is the concept of kingdom used to encompass the period between the two advents of Christ. The Ruler is God. The ruled are people on the earth who have related themselves in a positive, neutral, or negative way to "Christendom" (including true believers, professing people, rejecters, and even opponents). The time is the period between His comings.

4. The spiritual kingdom. Spiritual may not be the best label,[1] but nothing seems better to characterize this concept of kingdom. It refers to the kingdom into which all believers have been placed (Col. 1:13), and it is entered by the new birth. The Ruler is Christ; in this concept of the kingdom He rules over believers only; and the relationship exists now.

C. The Relationship of the Church to These Kingdoms

1. To the universal kingdom. In the sense that the church is in the world it is part of God's universal kingdom. He designed it, brought it into being, and rules over it, as He does all aspects of His universe.

2. To the Davidic/messianic kingdom. The church is not a part of this kingdom at all. When this kingdom is established the church will have been resurrected and will reign with Christ over the millennial kingdom.

3. To the mystery form of the kingdom. Since the church is part of Christendom, she is part of this concept of the kingdom.

4. To the spiritual kingdom. The true church, the body of Christ, is equivalent to this concept of the kingdom.

If one were to try to summarize the relationship of the church to the kingdom, he would have to say that it is related but not equivalent to certain concepts of the kingdom; it is unrelated to another concept; and it is equivalent to another. The concept of the kingdom must be defined before one can determine the relationship of the church to it.

II. THE RELATION OF THE CHURCH TO ISRAEL

The church stands distinct from Israel and did not begin until the Day of Pentecost, and thus did not exist in the Old Testament period.

The distinction between Israel and the church is verified by several facts. (1) In the New Testament natural Israel and Gentiles are contrasted *after* the church was clearly established (Acts 3:12; 4:8, 10; 5:21, 31, 35; 21:19). (2) Natural Israel and the church are clearly distinguished, showing that the church is not Israel (1 Cor. 10:32). The apostle's distinction would be meaningless if Israel were the same as the church. (3) Galatians 6:16 provides no clear proof that the church is equated with Israel. Only if the *kai* is explicative would the phrase equate the Israel of God with the New Creation, the church. But the *kai* may be emphatic, emphasizing an especially important part (Jewish believers) in the benediction on the whole church (as the *kai* is in Mark 16:7 and Acts 1:14). Or it may simply connect Jewish Christians to the New Creation. The thrust of the book of Galatians argues against the explicative use (the only one that would identify the church as Israel). Since Paul had severely attacked the Jewish legalists, it would be expected that he would single out for special blessing those Jewish people who had forsaken legalism and truly followed Christ.

III. THE RELATION OF THE CHURCH TO THIS AGE

The church did not exist in Old Testament times but was constituted on the Day of Pentecost. It is distinct to this present time period. Four lines of evidence support this conclusion.

(1) Our Lord said: "I will build My church" (Matt. 16:18). He did not say that He would continue to add to something already in existence, but that He would do something not yet begun.

(2) The church could have no functioning Head until after the resurrection of Christ; therefore, it could not exist until some time after He rose from the dead (Eph. 1:20).

(3) The church could not have been an operating entity with functioning spiritual gifts until after Christ's ascension (Eph. 4:7–12).

(4) The mystery character of the one body was unknown in Old Testament times (Eph. 3:5–6; Col. 1:26). In classical Greek, *musteijon* means something hidden or secret. It designated the sacred rites of the Greek mystery religions, secrets that only the initiated shared. In the Dead Sea Scrolls the relevant words indicate not so much something unknown but wisdom far above finite understanding. In the Old Testament the equivalent word occurs only in Daniel 2:18–19, 27–30, 47; 4:9. Thus the concept of a mystery is that of a secret that only the initiated share. It also includes two ideas: (a) a time when the secret was not known followed by a time when it became known and (b) deeper or higher wisdom that is revealed to those initiated.

What is the content of the mystery in these passages? It is that Gentiles would be fellow heirs, fellow members of the body, fellow partakers of the promise in Christ by the Gospel. That Gentiles would share in God's plan of redemption was revealed in the Old Testament (Gen. 12:3; Isa. 42:6–7), so that truth is no mystery. But that there would be a joint body in which Jews and Gentiles would share was not revealed in the Old Testament. A concordance examination of the use of the word "body" will reveal quickly and conclusively that the idea of the body of Christ or of any body into which the redeemed were placed is nowhere found in the Old Testament. The first time Paul used the word "body" meaning the body of Christ was in his extended discussion of that concept in 1 Corinthians 12:12–25. The next occurrence was in Romans 12:4–5, and all the other uses appear in Ephesians and Colossians. In Ephesians 2:15 a synonym for that one body (v. 16) is "new man." Clearly, this mystery was unknown in the Old Testament, and because the body is the new man it is not a continuation or remaking of Israel.

Though there is a continuity between the redeemed of all ages (simply because they are redeemed and their common destiny is heaven), there is a discontinuity because redeemed today are placed in the body of Christ and not in some sort of Israel. Similarly the redeemed before Abraham's day (like Enoch and Noah) did not belong to Israel, yet they belonged to the family of God. So there are pre-Israel redeemed (pre-Abrahamic saints) and post-Israel saints (Christians in the body of Christ).

But does not the "as" in Ephesians 3:5 merely mean that this mystery of one body was only comparatively unknown in the Old Testament? Observe that no such idea of "lesser known/better known" exists in the parallel passage in Colossians 1:26, where the contrast is clearly unknown/known. To bring these two passages into harmony, the "as" in Ephesians 3:5 must not be comparative. Of course, *as* can have other meanings. It may introduce a clause that adds additional information (as clearly in Acts 2:15—the disciples were not simply less drunk than the crowd thought). Or with a negative preceding it the word may mean "but" (as in 1 Cor. 7:31). In other words, the new body was not known in other ages, but is now revealed. And since the church is the body of Christ, and since that body was not revealed and operative until the New Testament era, the church is distinct to this age.

IV. THE RELATION OF THE CHURCH TO JESUS CHRIST

During His earthly ministry our Lord announced that He would do a new thing in building His church (Matt. 16:18). "I will build" is clearly future tense, indicating that this was something Christ had not yet done up to that time. Actually the church did not begin as a functioning reality until the Spirit came on the Day of Pentecost. What then was the Lord's relationship to the church since during His earthly life it was not yet in operation?

In one word, He was the Founder. It is His church (Matt. 16:18). He is the Foundation (1 Cor. 3:11). (1) As Founder He chose the disciples who would also occupy a place in the foundation of the building (Eph. 2:20). (2) As Founder He taught the disciples about matters that would become effective when the church began to function. Most of that teaching is recorded in the Upper Room Discourse (John 13–17). Some of Christ's teachings related to the Mosaic Law under which He lived, some to the future millennial kingdom, and some to the future church. The Upper Room Discourse serves as a seed-plot of that which is found later in the epistles of the New Testament. Some of the new things He revealed include a new command (13:34), a new hope in the Rapture of the church (14:1–3), a new relationship (you in Me and I in you, v. 20), and a new basis for prayer (16:24).

(3) The Founder also became the Cornerstone by His death and resurrection (Acts 4:11; Eph. 2:20). He purchased the church with His own blood (Acts 20:28). His resurrection and ascension made Him the Head over the church (Eph. 1:20–23) in which capacity He, among other things, gives gifts to the members of His body (4:8).

(4) As Founder He also was the One who sent the Holy Spirit, who activated the church into a functioning entity (Acts 2:33).

What is the Rock on which the church is built? (Matt. 16:18). Some understand it to refer to Peter. If so, Christ was playing on the words *petros* (Peter) and *petra* (rock). The first word is masculine and means a stone, whereas the second is feminine and means a massive rock. Because of these differences in words and genders, it seems unlikely that the reference is to Peter. Sometimes one suspects that some are afraid that such an interpretation will lend support to the claim of the Roman Catholic church that Peter is the rock on which the church is built (as the Latin inscription around the base of the dome of St. Peter's church in Rome indicates, since in Latin the different words and genders do not show up). However, the apostles do constitute the foundation of the church (Eph. 2:20), though Peter, as prominent as he was, certainly had no papal primacy (Acts 2:14; 10:34; Gal. 2:11).

Others understand Christ to be the Rock referred to in this passage as He is in other Scriptures (1 Cor. 3:11; 1 Pet. 2:5–9). However, this seems to create a disjuncture between the two rocks contrary to their close connection in the text itself. A modification of this view sees the rock as Peter's confession of Christ (Matt. 16:16).

Perhaps the truth combines elements of both ideas; that is, the rock is Peter using the keys to the kingdom (Matt. 16:19; Isa. 22:22) in proclaiming the truth about Christ to Jews and Gentiles.

Thus Christ is the Founder of His church in that He chose the apostolic foundation, gave basic teaching concerning relationships in the church, gave His life to become the Cornerstone, and then sent the Holy Spirit on the Day of Pentecost to activate the church.

V. THE RELATION OF THE CHURCH TO THE HOLY SPIRIT

Pentecost marks the beginning of the church as a functioning body by the outpouring of the Spirit on that day. Before His ascension the Lord promised that the disciples would be baptized with the Holy Spirit soon (Acts 1:5). Though the word "baptism" does not appear in the account of Pentecost in chapter 2, it is quite clear from 11:15–16 that the baptism occurred for the first time on that day. Since, according to Paul (1 Cor. 12:13), Spirit baptism places people in the body of Christ, and since the body of Christ is the church (Eph. 1:22–23), the church, the body, began when those first individuals were baptized at Pentecost.

Several other things occurred on the Day of Pentecost. The disciples were filled with the Spirit (Acts 2:4). Three thousand were baptized with water (v. 41). The visible church began that day (vv. 42–47).

In addition to baptizing those who believe into the body, the Spirit also indwells individual Christians (1 Cor. 6:19), local churches (3:16), and the body of Christ (Eph. 2:22). The Spirit also empowers, leads, comforts, and gives gifts to the church (Acts 1:8; 9:31; 1 Cor. 12:4). In a very real sense, the Spirit is the energizing life and power of the church.

NOTE

1. I take the term from J. Oliver Buswell, *A Systematic Theologyof the Christian Religon* (Grand Rapids: Zondervan, 1962), 2:346.

Chapter 71
PRINCIPLES AND/OR PATTERN?

Before considering the biblical teaching concerning organization, order, and ordinances for local churches, a basic question should be raised. Does the New Testament give principles for these areas to be followed generally, but to be adapted to various cultures and times; or does it expect the pattern practiced in New Testament times to be followed today in all cultures? For example, does the New Testament teach principles of church government that can be adapted in a variety of ways, or does it also prescribe the particular pattern which must be followed? Many would say that flexibility in this area is permitted. The church must have leaders, but it makes little difference whether they are called elders or deacons or whether a group has both. One might even call them stewards and still follow the New Testament principle of leadership.

Or take another example. The New Testament teaches the principle of believers gathering together. But in New Testament times they gathered in homes. Are we today allowed the flexibility of building church buildings, or should we follow the pattern of meeting in homes? Most would allow for flexibility in this case.

Or another example: The principle in water baptism (whatever mode is used) is to show leaving the old life and entering into the new. Is there any way that principle can be followed without using the pattern of actual baptism? Almost all would say no. But why not erect a little closet on the church platform, have the candidate enter it in old clothes, change his clothes inside the closet, and then emerge in new clothes? Would that not illustrate the same truth as baptism does? And is it not a scriptural illustration? (Col. 3:9–12). In church government we allow some flexibility between principle and pattern. In using church buildings we permit complete flexibility between principle and pattern. In water baptism we insist on no flexibility between principle and pattern. Whatever be a person's or group's theoretical views on this question, I doubt that anyone is totally consistent in practice.

Arguments for flexibility are mostly historical and analogical. Historically, it is pointed out that since the early church was influenced by its culture and adopted its forms from that culture, we can do the same today. To be sure, elders came from the synagogue organization (though Gentile communities also had them). Whether the idea of deacons was taken over from the synagogue is much less clear. Baptism was practiced as one of the requirements for proselytes to Judaism and in the mystery religions. The Lord's Supper was new to the church, though it grew out of the Passover feast. Instruction in the Jewish synagogue and instruction in the Christian church were similar. Excommunication was practiced by both groups. Unquestionably many practices that the church used had their antecedents in Judaism. This is to be expected. But the question still remains: When the church took over these practices, did they become divinely sanctioned (to be followed today) or simply divinely exemplified (not necessarily to be followed today in every detail)? The historical argument really does not settle the matter.

Analogies are often drawn to support flexibility between principles and patterns. For example, the Gospel is an inviolable principle, but there are many patterns to follow in presenting it. Salvation is an absolute; but conversion experiences vary. Therefore, it is argued, though the church is an absolute, its forms and functions are variable. But because it is not exegetical the argument is weak.

Those who feel that church practices should conform closely to the principles and patterns of the New Testament point out that the Scriptures claim to be sufficient for every good work, including the work of the local church (2 Tim. 3:16–17). Specifically, Paul wrote 1 Timothy with all its details about church life and government so that Timothy might know how to conduct himself in the house of God and how to instruct others in those same specifics (3:15). And in the same epistle, cultural conditioning of truth is specifically ruled out (2:11–14). Furthermore, Paul expected the churches to follow the "traditions," which included both principles and practices (1 Cor. 11).

Can this matter be settled? Probably not conclusively (and no one is entirely consistent). But to conclude, much flexibility seems to ignore the detailed patterns that are revealed in the New Testament. It is one thing to acknowledge a difference of interpretation about some detail, but it is quite another to say it is unimportant. My own feeling is that we should attempt to follow as many details as possible of the patterns for church life as they are revealed in the New Testament. Otherwise, there is no satisfactory answer to the question of why the patterns are there. And since they are there, I want to use them today.

Chapter 72
TYPES OF CHURCH GOVERNMENT

What constitutes a local church? Does a church exist wherever and whenever two or three believers are gathered in the name of Christ? If so, then every Christian home would also be a Christian church. How much organization is necessary to have a local church? Some say the less the better, while others opt for a developed organization.

The New Testament does not contain a formal definition of a local church. However, it does describe the normal features of a local assembly. On the basis of these features we can formulate a definition of a local church. It is an assembly of professing believers in Christ who have been baptized and who are organized to carry out God's will. Notice the important facets of that definition. (1) Those who do not make a profession of faith are excluded. The profession may not be genuine, but it must be made. (2) Without debating the mode of baptism, it is clear that the New Testament knows nothing of unbaptized church members. (3) A church always has some kind of organization, and in the New Testament organization was instituted as soon as possible (Acts 14:23). (4) A church exists for a purpose—to do God's will. This includes a number of things: observing the ordinances, evangelizing, building up believers, worship, giving, ministering to all age groups, etc. A specialized ministry to a particular age group cannot be a church even though it may have features and activities similar to a church. Because it does not open its doors to all professing believers, it is not a church.

Though the definition may seem to some to be too rigid, notice that there is latitude in it. The mode of baptism may be debated, but the fact of baptism for church members cannot (if the New Testament example is followed). The specific type of organization may be unclear, but the fact of organization is not. Nothing is said about place of meeting, number of meetings, frequency of the ordinances, or structures for carrying out the ministry.

Because there has been and continues to be debate over the specifics of organization of the church, there exist different basic types of churches. But that the early church was organized is undebatable. At the very first (though not later), they numbered the group (Acts 2:41; 4:4). Soon they had to choose helpers for the apostles (6:1–7). Relief activities for the poor had to be organized early (4:32–37). Elders were recognized as leaders (11:30). On the return leg of the first missionary journey, Paul ordained elders in the newly established churches (14:23).

I. MINIMAL GOVERNMENT

A. Characteristics of This View

Generally those groups that endeavor to keep organization at a minimum are led by a small group of elders, emphasize the exercise of spiritual gifts by all members, downplay the concept of membership, and give prominence to the headship of Christ.

B. Some Observations

Such groups are obviously not without organization. For example, they practice church discipline more than some more highly organized groups, and that requires organized activity. They lean toward a federal system of government, though probably with even less congregational involvement in decision making. A single minister is usually not a part of the structure. We need not think of this type of government applying only to small groups; it can work well in large groups too. Some Quaker groups and the Plymouth Brethren favor minimal government.

II. NATIONAL GOVERNMENT

A. Characteristics of This View

A national church is a group of churches organized under the head of state or within the limits of the state. The implicit right of the state to be involved with and to exercise control in the churches exists within this organizational structure. How explicitly and extensively those rights may be exercised varies from state to state. The state may or may not allow the coexistence of free churches along with the national church. It may or may not convene councils or synods. It may or may not be involved in the exercise or ratification of discipline. It may or may not collect tithes and be involved in the support of individual churches. Whatever be the particulars of the relationship between the national church and the state, a formal relationship does exist, and that constitutes the basic characteristic of this form of church government. The Anglican Church in England and the Lutheran Church in Germany are national churches.

B. Some Relevant Scripture

Arguments for the separation of church and state are based on the following Scriptures. As recorded in Matthew 22:21, Christ distinguished the two spheres of responsibility (Caesar and God) and His followers' relationship to each. Other passages detail the Christian's responsibility to the state (Rom. 13:1–7; 1 Pet. 2:13–17; Titus 3:1). When a conflict arises between the two spheres in which the state seeks to contravene the law of God, there are biblical examples of civil disobedience (Dan. 3; 6; Acts 5:29). There is also at least one example of passive resistance (not illegal) to force the secular power to acknowledge an injustice (Acts 16:37).

State involvement is totally absent from all the instances of church discipline in the New Testament (Matt. 18:17; 1 Cor. 5; 2 Thess. 3:11–15). If a national church be the scriptural kind of organization, one would expect in Matthew 18:17 that the steps involved in trying to correct a problem would include as a final step taking the matter to the state authorities. However, the church is the last court to hear the matter in the New Testament.

Some difficult practical problems arise in the effort to keep church and state separate. Should churches accept tax exemptions? To what extent should churches use the legislative process to promote religious goals in society? Should the church advocate tax credit for tuition paid to Christian schools?

III. HIERARCHICAL GOVERNMENT

A. Some Examples

In a hierarchical system the ruling body of clergy is organized into orders or ranks, each of which is subordinate to the one above it. In the Methodist system the authority of the hierarchy is less absolute; in the Episcopal Church the hierarchy of authority is more pronounced; but in the Roman Catholic Church authority rests totally in the hierarchy, which is carried to its logical end in the person of the pope. The government of the Church of England combines both the hierarchical and national forms of government.

B. Alleged Support

Support for this concept is based on (a) the primacy of the apostles, especially Peter, and (b) an unbroken line of succession from the apostles to today. Although it is true that the apostles constituted the foundation on which the church was built (Eph. 2:20), and although it is also true that Peter was prominent though not primary (Gal. 2:11), the apostolate disappeared by the end of the first century and there has not been any kind of unbroken line of succession of bishops (the apostles' successors) to the present time.

Clearly the two offices of elders and deacons existed in New Testament times. But a third distinct office, that of bishops, is not seen in the New Testament, bishops and elders usually being considered as referring to the same office. The ascendancy of a single bishop over other officials began as early as the second century. But such transference of power from the apostles to the bishops is never enjoined or regulated in the New Testament. Actually, at the end of the first century, the *Didache,* a church manual, instructed each congregation to choose its own bishops and deacons (15.1), which is totally contrary to the concept of apostolic succession. To be sure, there is a legitimate facet to apostolic succession in that the doctrine of the apostles is what all succeeding generations should teach (2 Tim. 2:2), but that is a succession of doctrine, not of ordination.

IV. CONGREGATIONAL GOVERNMENT

A. Description

1. Authority. Basically the congregational form of government means that ultimate authority for governing the church rests in the members themselves.

2. Autonomy. Additionally, it also means that each individual church is an autonomous unit with no individual or organization above it, except Christ the Head.

3. Responsibility. Congregationalism does not imply that the entire congregation votes on every decision. Responsibility is delegated to officials and leaders, though, like other members, they have only one vote in the congregation.

4. Fellowship. Neither does it mean that churches are so autonomous that they have no fellowship with each other. Berkhof calls congregationalism a system of independency that denies the unity of the body of Christ,[1] but this is not so.

B. Support

1. Local autonomy. Though the apostles and their delegates did exercise authority over more than one local church, elders and deacons in New Testament times did not. Therefore, today, since apostles have passed off the scene, local churches are autonomous.

2. Discipline. The whole church was empowered to exercise discipline (Matt. 18:17; 1 Cor. 5:4–5; 2 Cor. 2:6–7; 2 Thess. 3:14–15). Since the important matter of discipline was not committed to the leaders only but to the whole congregation, this supports the concept of congregational government.

3. Leadership. The whole church was involved in choosing leaders. Certain passages clearly support this (Acts 1:23, 26; 6:3, 5; 15:22, 30; 2 Cor. 8:19). Others, like Acts 14:23 and Titus 1:5, seem to argue against congregational involvement in choosing. Acts 14:23 records the appointing of leaders on the return leg of the first missionary journey. The verb *cheirotoneo* does mean appoint, though congregationalists would prefer a more etymologically related understanding of the verb as indicating a choice by raising the hands; that is, a congregational vote. However, even congregationalist Baptist theologian A. H. Strong recognizes that the idea of a popular vote cannot be sustained by the verb. He negated the use of this verse, as well as Titus 1:5 (where Titus was instructed to appoint elders in every city), to support the federal type of government by stating that the verses "decide nothing as to the mode of choice, nor is a choice by the community thereby necessarily excluded."[2] It might be better for the congregationalist simply to acknowledge these examples as apostolic and not instructive for us today.

4. Ordinances. Several passages commit the ordinances to the whole church, not simply to the leaders or to a hierarchy (Matt. 28:19–20; 1 Cor. 11:2, 20).

5. Government. The priesthood of all believers argues for a democratic, congregational concept of government (1 Pet. 2:5, 9).

C. An Appraisal of Congregationalism

1. Authority. That ultimate authority rests in the local church under Christ's headship does seem to be clearly taught in the New Testament. This does not preclude fellowship with other congregations, but it does not allow for organizational structure above the local church.

2. Choosing leaders. That the whole church was involved in many of the affairs of the congregation also seems clear. But it was not involved in everything. In some instances leaders were clearly appointed and not voted on by everyone. The choosing of the first nonapostolic helpers in Acts 6 exemplifies a gracious harmony between the apostles, who asked the congregation to choose and the congregation, which placed their choices before the apostles for ratification. We are not told what would have happened had the congregation chosen someone the apostles did not approve of. Presumably such a person would not have been allowed to serve (which means that the congregation was not the final authority).

3. Restrictions. Sometimes there seems to be a subtle but consequential blurring of the distinction between what all believers possess equally as members of the body of Christ and what all believers can do as far as ministry within that body is concerned. Because all believers are priests does not mean that all believers can function in the same offices. The qualifications for leadership do exclude some. To cite an analogy, though all adult United States citizens can vote, not all can be members of Congress (they must have reached a certain age) and not all can be president (the president must be a natural-born citizen). Although there is a democratic base, there are restrictions that eliminate some citizens from certain activities. So it seems equally true in the church, and congregationalism may consciously or unconsciously sublimate this.

4. Plurality of leadership. In practice, congregationalism is not fully congregational. The congregation does not make all the decisions. Leaders do take authority that is not always specifically given to them. The deacons often function like elders so that in effect there is a plurality of leadership. Actually some congregational and federal churches function very similarly. This is especially true when the federally governed church is autonomous. If it is part of a denomination, then it differs clearly from the autonomous congregational church.

V. FEDERAL GOVERNMENT

A. Meaning

In relation to a governmental concept, the federal system means, according to the dictionary definition, that individual units "surrender their individual sovereignty to a central authority but retain limited residuary powers of government." In relation to church government, the federal pattern means that individual members give some of their powers to leaders, and in cases where there is also a denominational structure, it also means that individual churches give up aspects of their autonomy to a higher organizational structure. By contrast, the congregational pattern retains the authority in the hands of individual members and local, autonomous churches.

Among denominations, the Presbyterian and Reformed groups are structured along this line. But so also are a number of independent, Bible churches, except that their federalism is limited to the local church and does not involve any kind of organization that has power over a group of churches. In other words, federal-type denominations involve presbyteries, synods, and general assemblies; whereas federal-type local churches do not.

B. Support

1. Leadership. Unquestionably leaders occupy a prominent place in the picture of New Testament church government. Admittedly they seem to hold a position of responsibility that does not require them to be accountable in every matter to the members of the church. In Hebrews 13:17 members are enjoined to submit to leaders; thus the authority is given to leaders, not to members. To be sure, leadership is not dictatorship. It is leadership, and leadership to which membership is responsible.

2. Appointment. In some instances it is quite clear that leaders were appointed, not elected. This is the obvious meaning of Acts 14:23 and Titus 1:5. A congregationalist might argue that, at least in Acts 14:23, this was a practice unique to the apostles. Conceivably Titus's commission to appoint leaders might also come under the apostolic umbrella. But, even if this be so, it does not follow that congregational vote was the New Testament method of choosing leaders. No specific verse indicates this, whereas specific verses do indicate appointment.

3. Discipline. Though the whole congregation was involved ultimately in discipline problems, leaders gave instructions as to what should be done (1 Cor. 5; 1 Tim. 5:20).

4. Ordination. Federalists point out that "ordination" was signified by the laying on of the hands of the elders (1 Tim. 4:14).

Congregationalists argue that the elders simply act on behalf of the entire congregation and that the authority for ordination lies with the congregation.

C. Observations

In practice many churches are a blend of congregationalism and federalism. Too much federalism often places too much authority in some organizational structure above local churches. If doctrinal defections come into a denomination, history teaches that it is difficult, if not impossible, for a local church to call the superstructure to account; and if the local church feels it necessary to leave the denomination it can often do so only at considerable cost and sometimes even the loss of all its property.

Too much congregationalism fails to profit from the gifts of leadership. It also allows immature and carnal believers to have equal say with others.

In this debate, some things are clear. The church and the Roman government were separate. There was no national church in New Testament times. The hierarchical church was a postbiblical development. The early church did have a governmental structure. Local churches, though they fellowshiped and cooperated with each other, were not organizationally linked together. The congregation was involved in some matters. Leaders did take the reins in other matters. The New Testament picture seems to include a blend of congregational and federal government, limited to the local level.

NOTES

1. L. Berkhof, *Systematic Theology* (Grand Rapids: Eerdmans, 1941), 580.
2. A. H. Strong, *Systematic Theology* (Philadelphia: Judson, 1907), 906.

Chapter 73
QUALIFIED LEADERSHIP FOR THE CHURCH

I. THE NECESSITY OF LEADERSHIP

Whatever be a person's or organization's preferences concerning the classes of leadership, no one can deny that leadership was considered necessary in New Testament churches. Recall a few facts. (1) Early in the life of the churches, relief funds were sent from Antioch to the elders in the churches in Judea (Acts 11:29). (2) Paul appointed elders almost immediately in the churches founded on the first missionary journey (14:23). (3) The council at Jerusalem was called, conducted, and concluded by leaders (chap. 15). (4) Elders and deacons appear as part of the normal picture of the life of various churches (Acts 20:17; Phil. 1:1). (5) Paul seemed to consider leaders a necessity for the proper functioning of churches (Titus 1:5). (6) Leadership is one of the spiritual gifts (Rom. 12:8) that functions in local churches (Heb. 13:7, 17).

II. THE CLASSES OF LEADERSHIP

All agree that there existed at least two classes of leaders in New Testament churches—elders and deacons. Not all agree that both are necessary today. It has been argued, for example, that since Paul mentioned only elders in Titus 1 (though he wrote of both elders and deacons in 1 Tim. 3), deacons are optional in the organization of the church. Neither do all agree on the matter of a single versus several elders in each congregation (though probably all concur on plurality of deacons). In the Baptist-Congregational system, the single pastor of the church fills the office of elder, whereas in the Presbyterian-Federal system, the pastor serves as one of several elders.

A more basic question is whether or not there exists a third class of leaders—bishops. The word is used once of Christ (1 Pet. 2:25); otherwise it refers to human leaders of the churches. That bishops and elders referred to the same group seems clear for the following reasons. (1) Paul commissioned Titus to appoint elders in every city in Crete, and then described them immediately as bishops (Titus 1:5–7). (2) When Paul called the elders of the church of Ephesus to meet him at Miletus, he described their position as overseers (bishops) (Acts 20:17, 28). He also recognized that one of their functions was to shepherd or pastor the people (v. 28). (3) When Paul listed qualifications for the bishop and deacons (1 Tim. 3:1–13), he did not mention elders (though we know from 5:17 that the church had elders), strongly suggesting that bishops and elders referred to the same group. (4) In Philippians 1:1 Paul mentioned only bishops and deacons. Why would he omit elders if there were in fact three classes of leaders?

Some claim that bishops were a distinct third class of leaders because of James's prominence over the Jerusalem Council (Acts 15) and because they say that Timothy and Titus served as bishops over the churches in Ephesus and Crete respectively. However, Ignatius (ca. A.D. 50–ca. 115) was the first to distinguish bishops from elders and deacons as three separate classes of officials (*Ad Smyrna,* vii). The necessity for bishops was related to the need to preserve the unity of the church, to the need to guarantee the continuance of the true apostolic faith, and later to the need to have a human channel to minister divine grace.[1]

To sum up: the evidence points to only two classes of officers in the church, bishops-elders (or overseeing elders) and deacons.

III. DISTINCTIONS BETWEEN GIFTS AND OFFICES

Confusion often exists between the gifts God bestows in a Christian's life and the offices he may hold in the organization of the church. For example, pastor and pastorate are often equated rather than distinguished as they should be. Pastor is a spiritual gift, whereas pastorate (in our contemporary ecclesiology) is an office occupied by the principal leader of the church (particularly in the congregational system). Notice some important distinctions, however, between spiritual gifts and offices.

1. Gift vs. office. A person may have certain spiritual gifts but not occupy any office in the local church. In fact this is the case with the majority of believers. They have gifts (for all believers do) but are not officials in the church. However, those who do hold offices should also exercise certain spiritual gifts. Elders teach and rule, and deacons should exercise the gift of service (Rom. 12:7). Thus a gifted person may not occupy an office, but an officer must also be a gifted person.

2. Men and women. Gifts are given to both men and women, but the principal offices in the church are to be filled by men. The only gift not given to women was the gift of apostleship. But God gave the others to both men and women. Even the gift of pastor can be exercised by women if one understands correctly the gift as being the ability to shepherd. But this is not to say that a woman may occupy what is called today the pastorate. The principal offices in the New Testament churches were held by men. This is perfectly clear because both elders and deacons are expected to be "husbands of one wife." No woman could meet that qualification!

3. *In and out of church.* Spiritual gifts may be exercised in and out of the local church. The offices relate only to the local church. The gift of evangelism, for example, can and should be exercised in and out of the church. Elders and deacons, on the other hand, function only with respect to their particular local assembly.

IV. ELDERS

A. Their Number

Considerable debate exists over the question of the number of elders each church had (in New Testament times) or should have (today). Those who hold to elder rule (the federal system) believe that each congregation had several elders; while congregationalists see only a single elder (the pastor) in each congregation. Both agree that each church had more than one deacon.

The fact that the early church met in homes (Rom. 16:5; 1 Cor. 16:19; Col. 4:15) makes it more difficult to settle this debate conclusively. Clearly the church in each city (that is, the sum total of the house churches in each city) had elders (Phil. 1:1; Titus 1:5), but whether this also means that each house church had more than one elder is not certain. In other words, each house church might have had a single elder who, together with the other elders in other churches, constituted the elders of the church in that city.

Furthermore, the letters from the risen Lord to the churches in Asia Minor were sent to "the angel" of each church. If this refers to an angelic creature, then it has no relevance to the question. But if "angel" designates the human leader of each church, then obviously there was only one, which reinforces the view that each church did not have several elders.

Another intriguing argument for a single elder in each congregation is found in 1 Timothy 3. When Paul described the qualifications for the bishop, he did so consistently in the singular (vv. 1–7). But when he listed the qualifications for deacons, he switched to the plural (vv. 8–13). Does this indicate that there was one elder and several deacons in each church?

Or perhaps each church had at least one elder and often more than one. The one was a "ruling elder" (1 Tim. 5:17) who because of his place of prominence was the elder of the church (even though the church may have had other elders as well). Some would not even give consideration to this idea lest it would seem to support the concept of a single bishop ruling over elders. However, the very fact that that is exactly what developed in later centuries may mean that there was a ruling elder in each assembly in the first century.

B. Their Ministry

If elder and bishop refer to the same person, then the principal ministry of the elders consists of overseeing the work of the church in all its aspects. Elders are not responsible only for the spiritual welfare of the church while deacons care for the financial matters, as is sometimes thought. Elders have the oversight of all facets of the work. Notice that the famine offering in the early church was sent to the elders in Jerusalem for distribution (Acts 11:30). Thus the basic organizational chart for a church is not like this:

ELDERS	DEACONS
(Spiritual)	(Financial)

But like this:

ELDERS
(All aspects)
DEACONS
(Whatever is delegated to them by the elders)

1. General oversight involves ruling. This means presiding (1 Tim. 5:17) and leading (Heb. 13:17), not as lord and dictator, but nevertheless with control and authority (1 Pet. 5:3; Heb. 13:17). A presiding officer, for example, does not even have a vote, except in case of a tie, but he does have control (over the agenda, length of discussions, whom to recognize, etc.). Desirably this aspect of the elder's ministry would involve the spiritual gift of government (1 Cor. 12:28—the different word used here has the basic idea of steering, as in Acts 27:11). Thus an elder leads, guides, rules, steers his flock, piloting it skillfully through the treacherous waters of this world.

2. General oversight also includes guarding the truth (Titus 1:9). This means both the positive proclamation and explanation of doctrine as well as its defense against false teaching. This is why elders must be able to teach (1 Tim. 3:2). Certainly no one should ever be chosen an elder unless he knows well the doctrines of our faith and is able to explain and defend them accurately.

C. Their Qualifications

1. In relation to personal character. Two passages list qualifications for elders, 1 Timothy 3:1–7 and Titus 1:5–9, the largest number being related to his personal character. In 1 Timothy 3:2–4 and Titus 1:7, thirteen items are listed.

a. An elder must be blameless. That is, of such character that no accusation can be brought against him.

b. He must be the husband of one wife. Does this mean he must be married? Those who say no point out that if Paul meant that an elder must be married he would have written "husband of a wife." On the other hand, those who believe that an elder must be married observe that an elder is always described not only as having a wife but also children. Further, all these qualifications are headed by the word "must." What about Paul? Several observations are in order: he is never said to be an elder; he was clearly unmarried (either never married or a widower) when he wrote 1 Corinthians 7:8; and it is difficult to prove he was married on the grounds that he was a member of the Sanhedrin, since Acts 26:10 does not necessarily indicate membership, and it is uncertain if marriage was a requirement for membership before A.D. 70.

Does this mean an elder cannot be remarried after a divorce? Some argue that if a divorce is justified, then remarriage is permitted, and thus a divorced and remarried elder may serve. In other words, "husband of one wife" means one wife at a time.[2] However, the same phrase exactly reversed ("wife of one man") occurs in 1 Timothy 5:9 where it precludes an enrolled widow having had a second husband.[3] To conclude that a man remarried after a divorce cannot serve as an elder does not necessarily also mean that a divorced but not remarried man may not serve. That would involve the question of whether or not he was above reproach in what was involved in the divorce. Clearly this is not a prohibition against bigamy or polygamy since these were not practiced among the Greeks and Romans. They had multiple women in their lives, but only one wife. It is a question of whether Paul was prohibiting digamy (being married twice legally). Personally I see the evidence as prohibiting digamy for an elder.

Does the phrase mean that a widower who remarries cannot serve as an elder? Paul did permit (1 Cor. 7:39–40) and encourage (1 Tim. 5:14) the remarriage of widows (and presumably widowers). But some conclude nevertheless that remarried widowers cannot serve as elders. This may have been a matter of stricter discipline for elders as an example to others.[4]

c. He must be temperate. The word originally meant wineless.

d. He must be of sound and sober mind; that is, sensible.

e. He must be orderly (from the word *kosmos*).

f. He must be hospitable.

g. He must be able and willing to teach (in order to instruct others and refute error [Titus 1:9]).

h. He must not be given to wine.

i. He must not be given to physical violence.

j. He must be forbearing, not determined to have his just due.

k. He must not be contentious.

l. He must be free from the love of money. This certainly includes misusing his position for personal gain.

m. He must not be self-willed (Titus 1:7).

2. In relation to family life. The smaller, intimate circle of the home serves as the proving ground for an elder's ability to guide the church. Therefore, he must (the "must" of 1 Tim. 3:2 still governs this requirement as well) rule (lit., preside) over his family well so that his children are in a dignified subjection. Must his children be born again? The words in Titus 1:6, "who believe," might indicate that, or it may mean that they must be faithful to the family, though not necessarily born again. This qualification assumes that an elder will not only be married but also have children of sufficient age to show their voluntary allegiance to the family. Of course the very word "elder" signifies an older man.

3. In relation to spiritual maturity. An elder must not be a new convert lest he be lifted up in a cloudbank of conceit and that pride cause his downfall, as it did Satan's.

4. In relation to community life. His testimony in the community must also be good.

Obviously a man might not exhibit all of these characteristics all of his natural life, for he might have been converted from a rough background. But he certainly needs to demonstrate these qualifications when he serves as an elder. What he was before salvation need not limit his qualifying as an elder with one possible exception. By the interpretation that husband of one wife means married only once; then, of course, this is not something that can be changed by conversion. By this interpretation, then, if a man were married twice before or after he was saved, he would not meet the requirements for the eldership.

D. Their Selection

1. How are elders chosen? The term "elder" was used in Israel and in other nations to designate leaders. The Jewish synagogue had elders who were responsible for the government of the Jewish community. The Jerusalem Council apparently took over the concept of elders from the synagogue. As new churches were started, the apostles appointed elders (Acts 14:23; Titus 1:5). How they were chosen thereafter, the Scripture does not say. How they will be chosen today will probably be determined by the type of church government the congregation has. In the hierarchical arrangement, they will be appointed. In the federal setup, they will likely be chosen by the existing elders. In the congregational system, they will be elected by the congregation. Many churches use a combination of methods; e.g., the elders nominate and the congregation votes or ratifies.

2. How long should they serve? Again the New Testament is silent on this question. Certainly an elder should not continue to serve if for any reason he becomes disqualified.

3. Should they be ordained? The apostles laid their hands on the first helpers who were chosen in Acts 6:6. The church laid hands on Paul and Barnabas when they sent them on the first missionary journey (13:3). Elders laid their hands on Timothy (1 Tim. 4:14). Titus appointed elders in Crete (Titus 1:5). Paul warned against laying on hands hastily (1 Tim. 5:22). If this was a kind of ordination, it indicated public recognition, attestation of calling and ability, and association of the congregation with the ministry of the one or ones being ordained. Laying on of hands seemed to be the visible symbol of "ordination." That rite has its roots in the Old Testament where it had the ideas of (a) setting apart for office (Num. 27:23); (b) blessing (Gen. 48:14); (c) dedicating to God (Lev. 1:4); and (4) transfer and participation in the action (v. 4, the verb means to lean on).

Ordination in the New Testament was not appointment to an office, but a recognition of approval and support. Notice too that a continuing relationship existed between those who ordain and the one ordained (1 Tim. 5:22). That is why it should not be done hastily. If practiced today, it does not have to be restricted to "pastors." Elders may be ordained, deacons also, and even missionaries, according to the New Testament example.

V. DEACONS

A. Their Number

No disagreement exists over the number of deacons in an assembly. There were several. The first clear reference to an official group of deacons occurs in Philippians 1:1, where they are plural in number (as are the bishops or elders, thus not necessarily proving that there were several deacons in each congregation any more than there were several elders in each congregation). The same is true in 1 Timothy 3:8–13. Here several deacons are associated with the single elder, stronger evidence that there were several deacons in each church.

B. Their Ministry

The word means to serve and it is used most often in an unofficial sense, both before and after the office of deacon becomes clear in the New Testament (Col. 1:7; 1 Tim. 4:6). "Deaconing" was ministry in general, both officially and unofficially. What official deacons did specifically remains unclear in the New Testament. Some use Acts 6 as an indication that deacons should be involved in distributing alms. But whether the seven men chosen at that time were in fact official deacons is far from clear. Probably it would be more accurate to call them the first nonapostolic helpers. The fact that deacons were not to be double-tongued and that their wives were not to be slanderers (1 Tim. 3:8, 11) may indicate that they had some kind of personal, one-on-one, counseling ministry with individuals in the congregation, making it especially necessary that they not break confidences learned in the course of that ministry.

In Greek writings "deacon" described a waiter, a messenger, a steward, and a servant. These uses may reinforce the concept that official deacons in the church did whatever kinds of service the elders delegated to them.

C. Their Qualifications (1 Tim. 3:8–10, 12–13)

1. Personal (v. 8). Deacons should be (a) grave, dignified, serious, (b) not double-tongued (saying one thing to one person and another to another), (c) those who do not care for or pay attention to wine, and (d) those who are not greedy.

2. *Doctrinal* (v. 9). Deacons should hold to the objective body of Christian truth ("the faith") with a clean conscience, that is, with a life that is consistent with what they believe.
3. *Spiritual* (v. 10). Deacons are to be tested and approved and without reproach.
4. *Family* (v. 12). Like elders, deacons are to be husbands of one wife whose families are presided over well.

D. Their Selection

Nothing clear and definite is said about choosing deacons or their term of office. The congregation was deeply involved in choosing the helpers of Acts 6.

VI. DEACONESSES

A. An Office or a Ministry?

Two passages relate to this question: Romans 16:1–2, where Phoebe is designated as a servant (lit. "deacon") and "helper" of the church at Cenchrea; and 1 Timothy 3:11, where *gunaikas* may refer to a distinct group of women leaders or simply to the wives of the deacons. Unquestionably women performed a ministry in the early church, but it is not clear whether some of them were considered as occupying the office of deaconess.

In favor of the office are the following considerations. (1) "Helper" in Romans 16:2 is used outside the New Testament of an official in a religious society. However, this is true only of the masculine form, not the feminine form, which is what is used in verse 2. (2) In 1 Timothy 3:11, "likewise" introduces the women as it does the deacons in verse 8, possibly indicating a distinct office for these women.

Against seeing an office of deaconess are the following considerations. (1) A Greek word for deaconess does exist, but this is not used in the New Testament. (2) Although Phoebe was called a "helper" and although this title was used of an officeholder, there is no known example of its use with respect to a woman (unless Phoebe be the exception). (3) If verse 11 introduces a new office (that of deaconess), then why did not Paul finish listing the qualifications for deacons before introducing it? Instead, he continues with the list of qualifications for deacons in verses 12–13. This may indicate that he was referring to the deacons' wives in verse 11, rather than to a separate office in the church. Some liberals, feeling the force of this point, argue that verse 11 is out of order in the text and should follow verse 13.

In A.D. 112 Pliny, the Roman governor of Bithynia, wrote to Trajan and mentioned two Christian female *ministrae.* But that these were official deaconesses is far from clear, especially since no deaconesses are mentioned by that specific word (*diakonissa*) in any literature until the third-century writing called the *Didascalia.* Here deaconesses appear as a well-recognized and established order of helpers who were either to be virgins or once-married widows.[5]

B. Their Qualifications

The only biblical list of qualifications would be in verse 11 if indeed that verse refers to deaconesses. The nonbiblical list appears in the *Didascalia* where they are to be virgins or once-married widows, faithful and honorable.

C. Their Ministry

The *Didascalia* lists their duties as assisting in the baptism of women, visiting the sick, ministering to the needy and to those recovering from illness (III.16.12).

VII. TRUSTEES

Trustees are, of course, a nonbiblical, but contemporary (and not antibiblical) necessity in some societies. They hold the property in the name of the group to prevent legal complications when someone dies. If property were held in individual names, then it would not belong to the group, but the individual's portion would pass to his heirs (who might be unbelievers) upon his death. Having trustees prevents such complications.

NOTES

1. See Edwin Hatch, *The Organization of the Early Christian Churches* (London: Rivingtons, 1881), 83–112.
2. A. T. Robertson says, without elaboration or proof, that this is the meaning "clearly" in *Word Pictures in the New Testament* (New York: Harper, 1931), 4:573.
3. On this verse Robertson inconsistently concludes that "widows on this list must not be married a second time," *Word Pictures,* 4:585.
4. Alan G. Nute, *A New Testament Commentary* (Grand Rapids: Zondervan, 1969), 510.
5. For added documentation see Charles Ryrie, *The Role of Women in the Church* (Chicago: Moody, 1979), 85–91, 102–3, 131–36.

Chapter 74
ORDINANCES FOR THE CHURCH

I. THE CONCEPT OF AN ORDINANCE

Baptism and the Lord's Supper are generally referred to as ordinances today, though some groups prefer to call them sacraments. The word "sacrament" means to make sacred, to dedicate to a god or to sacred use. The Latin word was used in the Vulgate to translate the Greek *mustērion,* which gave it the idea of something mysterious or magical. Thus groups that prefer to call these rites of the church sacraments usually connect with them some mysterious power or actual conveying of grace. The Council of Trent defined a sacrament as "something presented to the sense, which has the power, by divine institution, not only of signifying, but also of efficiently conveying grace."

By contrast, "ordinance" (though a synonym of sacrament in the dictionary) does not incorporate the idea of conveying grace but only the idea of a symbol. Thus the ordinance itself has no inherent power to change those observing it, though God may use it to minister to them.

II. THE NUMBER OF ORDINANCES

Many (like Thiessen) restrict the ordinances to those ordered by Christ to be administered in the church. By this kind of definition baptism and the Lord's Supper are clearly ordinances, though foot-washing might also be.

If an ordinance may be more broadly conceived (yet within the parameters of being God-ordained and related to the church), then marriage and the rite of praying for the sick in James 5 might also be considered ordinances. Marriage was God-ordained and symbolizes the important relationship between Christ and the church, and praying for the sick involves the church through its elders. All agree, however, that baptism and the Lord's Supper qualify as ordinances of the church.

III. THE ORDINANCE OF BAPTISM

A. The Importance of Baptism

The importance of baptism is underscored by the following considerations.

1. Christ was baptized (Matt. 3:16). Though the meaning of His baptism was entirely different from the significance of Christian baptism, nevertheless there exists a sense in which we follow the Lord when we are baptized. To be sure, we can never fully imitate a sinless Person; yet we are to follow His steps, and baptism was one of them (1 Pet. 2:21).

2. The Lord approved of His disciples baptizing (John 4:1–2).

3. Christ commanded that people be baptized in this age (Matt. 28:19). Clearly this command was not only for the apostles who heard it but for His followers throughout the entire age, since He promised His presence to the end of the age.

4. The early church gave an important place to baptism (Acts 2:38, 41; 8:12–13, 36, 38; 9:18; 10:47–48; 16:15, 33; 18:8; 19:5). The early church never conceived of a believer remaining unbaptized.

5. The New Testament used the ordinance to picture or symbolize important theological truths (Rom. 6:1–10; Gal. 3:27; 1 Pet. 3:21).

6. The writer to the Hebrews termed baptism a foundational truth (6:1–2). It is no more optional or less significant than the doctrines of repentance, resurrection, and judgment.

B. The Meaning of Baptism

Biblically, baptism is associated with forgiveness (Acts 2:38; 22:16), union with Christ (Rom. 6:1–10), making disciples (Matt. 28:19), and repentance (Acts 2:38). This is not to conclude that water baptism effects forgiveness, etc., but that it is closely connected with those things that begin the Christian life.

Theologically, baptism may be defined as an act of association or identification with someone, some group, some message, or some event. Baptism into the Greek mystery religions associated the initiates with that religion. Jewish proselyte baptism associated the proselyte with Judaism. John the Baptist's baptism associated His followers with His message of righteousness (he had no group for them to join). (Incidentally, John was apparently the first person ever to baptize other people—usually baptisms were self-administered.) For James and

John to be baptized with Christ's baptism meant to be associated with His suffering (Mark 10:38–39). To be baptized with the Spirit associates one with the body of Christ (1 Cor. 12:13) and with the new life in Christ (Rom. 6:1–10). To be baptized into Moses involved identification with his leadership in bringing the Israelites out of Egypt (1 Cor. 10:2). To be baptized for the dead means to be identified with the Christian group and take the place of a believer who had died (15:29). Christian baptism means identification with the message of the Gospel, the person of the Savior, and the group of believers. Some of the baptisms listed do not involve water. Also observe how impoverished we would be without a proper understanding of the meaning and ramifications of baptism.

C. The Subjects of Baptism

The question is: Should only believers be baptized or should infants of believing parents also be baptized? Arguments in favor of infant baptism include these.

1. The circumcision argument. Colossians 2:11–12 clearly links circumcision and baptism. Since infants were circumcised under the Old Covenant, they should be baptized under the New Covenant. The argument rests on the covenant theology concept of a single covenant of grace that involved an initiatory rite into that covenant, the rite being circumcision in the Old Testament and baptism in the New. These rites indicate membership in the covenant, not necessarily personal faith.[1]

2. The historical argument. From early times the church practiced infant baptism; therefore it is permissible. The Fathers did support infant baptism, often relating it to circumcision, but the fact that the early church practiced or believed something does not in itself make it right. Some in the early church taught baptismal regeneration, which is heretical.

3. The household argument. Households were baptized in New Testament times. It would be likely that some infants at least were included in some of the households (see Acts 11:14; 16:15, 31, 33; 18:8; 1 Cor. 1:16). Some also cite the household promise of 1 Corinthians 7:14 as not only permitting but expecting the baptism of infants of a household where there is one believing parent.

The position against infant baptism and thus for believers' baptism points out (a) that the scriptural order is always believe and then be baptized (Matt. 3:2–6; 28:19; Acts 2:37–38; 16:14–15, 34); (b) that baptism is the initiatory rite into a believing community, the church; therefore it should only be done to believers. By contrast, circumcision initiated people (including infants) into a theocracy, which did have unbelievers in it. (c) The age of children is never mentioned in any passage that mentions household baptism. But it is said that all who were baptized in those households believed. This, then, would exclude infants from being included in the baptisms. (d) If 1 Corinthians 7:14 allows or requires the baptism of children in a household where there is a believing parent, then it would also allow or require the baptism of the unbelieving adult mate.

D. Rebaptism

There is only one clear example of people being baptized twice (Acts 19:1–5). These twelve men, who had been baptized by John the Baptist, were rebaptized by Paul after they believed the Christian message. This furnishes an example for counseling those who today were baptized either as unbelieving infants, adolescents, or adults and who then came to faith in Christ. It also serves as an argument against infant baptism, for why baptize an infant if later, after he personally receives Christ, he should be baptized again?

E. The Time of Baptism

The examples in the New Testament indicate that believers were baptized right after they believed. No probationary period is indicated, though such might be justified in order to attest to the genuineness of the faith.

F. The Mode of Baptism

1. The case for sprinkling. (1) Certain Old Testament rituals of cleansing involved sprinkling (Exod. 24:6–7; Lev. 14:7; Num. 19:4, 8), and these are classified as washings (lit. "baptisms") in Heb. 9:10. (2) Sprinkling best pictures the cleansing of the Spirit as in Ezekiel 36:25. (3) *Baptizo* may have a secondary meaning of "bringing under the influence," and sprinkling can readily picture this. (4) Immersion was improbable or impossible in certain instances (Acts 2:41, too many people; 8:38, too little water in a desert place; 16:33, too little water in a house). (5) The greater majority of the visible church practices nonimmersion.

2. The case for pouring (or affusion). (1) Pouring best pictures the ministry of the Spirit coming on and into the life of a believer (Joel 2:28–29; Acts 2:17–18). (2) The phrases "into the water" and "out of the water" may equally well be translated "to the water" and "away from the water." In other words, the one to be baptized went to the water, perhaps even into the water, but not under the water. (3) Drawings in the catacombs show the candidate for baptism standing about waist deep in water while the one doing the baptizing pours water over his head from a vessel he holds.

3. The case for immersion. (1) Immersion is unquestionably the primary meaning of *baptizo*. The Greek language has words for sprinkle and pour that are never used of baptism. (2) Immersion best pictures the significance of baptism, which is death to the old life and resurrection to the new (Rom. 6:1–4). (3) Immersion could have been done in every case. Sufficient pools existed in Jerusalem to permit the immersion of three thousand converts on the Day of Pentecost. The road to Gaza was deserted, but not waterless. Houses often had pools outdoors where, for example, the Philippian jailer's family could have been immersed. (4) Proselyte baptism was performed by self-immersion in a tank of water. This mode would naturally carry over to the Christian church. (5) Pouring, not sprinkling, was the first exception to immersion and was allowed in cases of sickness. This was called "clinical baptism." Cyprian (ca. A.D. 248–258) was the first to approve of sprinkling. Even nonimmersionists acknowledge that immersion was the universal practice of the apostolic church (see Calvin *Institutes* IV.XV, 19).

An observation: It seems to me that those who wish to justify sprinkling proceed this way in their thinking. If you can show that any form of nonimmersion (like pouring) was practiced early then you can legitimately practice sprinkling, even though it evidently was not practiced in the apostolic church. In other words, if pouring can be a hole in the dike of universal immersion, then sprinkling can flood in also. However, if anything, the evidence only says that pouring (if it was practiced) was considered the same as immersion, but sprinkling was not considered valid as baptism.

G. Trine Immersion

Trine immersion is the immersion of the candidate three times (usually forward) to symbolize the association with the Trine God. The *Didache* states that if immersion is not possible then water was to be poured three times on the head (chap. 7). Notice that this early work does not say to immerse three times, only pour three times. Proponents of trine immersion point out that some lexicons say that *bap-*

tizo means to dip repeatedly (but some do not). The evidence for this view is not strong.

IV. THE LORD'S SUPPER

A. Its Institution

Apparently the Lord instituted the Supper in connection with eating the Passover meal before His crucifixion even though this poses a chronological problem. Assuming a Friday crucifixion, John's Gospel seems to state that Passover was not celebrated until after Jesus' death and burial (18:28; 19:14). However, some think that the Galileans and/or the Pharisees ate the Passover on Thursday night, while the Judeans and/or the Sadducees celebrated on Friday night. (The imperfect tense, "were sacrificing," used in Mark 14:12 may indicate that priests offered the sacrifices both days.)

B. Its Order

The ordinance alone (without the meal) consisted of Christ taking unleavened bread, giving thanks, distributing it to the disciples, and doing the same with the cup.

During the early centuries the more extended service included a love feast, various prayers of thanksgiving and confession, reading and instruction from the Scriptures, the Supper itself, a collection for orphans, widows, sick, and needy, and a holy kiss. See *Didache* 7–15; Justin Martyr *Apology* C.lxvii, and C. lxv.

The first reference above from Justin Martyr states that the wine was mixed with water. The Scriptures do not use the word "wine" in connection with the Supper, only "the cup" or "the fruit of the vine." Of course it was juice from the grape, but whether fermented or not is not stated. Unfermented wine was used more in the time of Christ than most suppose. Nevertheless, if this was fermented some it was apparently diluted with water. For the sake of converted alcoholics or even to forestall anyone beginning to drink, unfermented juice is preferable in the light of today's worldwide problem with alcohol.

C. Its Significances

1. It is a remembrance of Christ (1 Cor. 11:24). It recalls His life (the bread), His death (the cup), His resurrection and living presence (the service itself).

2. It is a proclamation of His death (1 Cor. 11:26). The service itself states the Gospel message as well as the claims of the Gospel on the redeemed person. A missionary whom I knew was directed to service on the mission field when he, as a pastor presiding at a Lord's Supper in his church, was meditating on its meaning while the deacons were distributing the elements.

3. *It is an assurance of Christ's second coming* (Matt. 26:29; 1 Cor. 11:26).

4. *It is a time of fellowship with Christ and His people* (1 Cor. 10:21). In what sense is Christ present in the Supper? The Roman Catholic Church teaches that the literal body and blood of Christ are present in the bread and cup and at the time of consecration the elements are actually changed (transubstantiation). The Lutheran Church teaches that the individual partakes of the true body and blood of Christ in, with, and under the elements. The elements remain unchanged, but the prayer of consecration communicates Christ to the participants (consubstantiation). The Reformed view (Calvin) teaches that though the elements are only symbols, partaking of them involves partaking of Christ in His redemptive presence. However, Zwingli taught that the Supper was only a memorial. It is a memorial, but it is also a service in which the presence of Christ in His people effects a real communion.

D. Its Requirements

1. *Regeneration.* Only believers can experience Communion.

2. *Fellowship with a local church.* Unrepentant believers under discipline were excluded from the Supper (1 Cor. 5:11–13; 2 Thess. 3:6, 11–15).

3. *Cleansing before partaking* (1 Cor. 11:27–32).

E. Its Frequency

The Scriptures do not specify on this point. After Pentecost the believers broke bread from house to house, but this does not prove a daily observance of the Supper (Acts 2:46). For one thing it is not clear that "breaking bread" in this text meant anything other than taking a fellowship meal together. For another thing, the text does not even imply that whatever was done was done daily in each house. At Troas the believers evidently included the Supper in their first day of the week meeting (20:7). However often a church observes this ordinance, it should be given sufficient time so that it is not "tacked on" to a service.

F. Some Questions

1. *At what service of the church should the Supper be observed?* The example of the early church answers Sunday. But since it was a Supper,

it seems appropriate to observe it during an evening service on Sunday, at least sometimes.

2. *Should it only be observed in the church?* This seemed to be the normal pattern (1 Cor. 11:18, 20).

3. *Should only church members partake?* Again, this seems to be the New Testament example, since only baptized believers were clearly associated with a local assembly. Should visitors be excluded if they are believers? Not necessarily. As a courtesy they could participate. But since discipline by a local church and fellowship within a local church are related to the Supper, then normally only those who are clearly associated with that local church should partake of the Supper in that group.

V. THE LOVE FEAST

As part of the extended service that included the Lord's Supper, a full meal was also eaten in and by the church. This feast of love is mentioned specifically in 2 Peter 2:13 (in some manuscripts) and Jude 12 and implied in 1 Corinthians 11:20 (and possibly also in Acts 2:42, 46; 6:1).

Whatever the origin of the meal was (pagan feasts, Jewish common meals, Christians' desire to avoid meats offered to idols, etc.), it had fallen into abuse by the time Paul wrote 1 Corinthians. Some were making it an excuse for gluttony, taking as much as possible for themselves, and refusing to share what they had brought with others. Paul instructed that church to have the people eat at home rather than negate the ideas of fellowship and love that the *agape* stood for. During the fourth century the love feast came into increasing disfavor and is seldom practiced today. The fact that Paul could counsel its suspension in the church excludes it from being an ordinance.

VI. FOOT-WASHING

In accord with the common custom in the East because of the effect of dusty or muddy roads on sandaled feet, the Lord at the Last Supper washed and dried the disciples' feet (John 13:1–20). This act served as an example of humility (v. 15), as an exhortation to forgive one another (v. 14), and as a lesson in the need for cleansing in the Christian life (v. 10). As baptism symbolizes the cleansing of the forgiveness of sin, foot-washing symbolizes the cleansing needed for fellowship.

Those who focus on cleansing find ground for continuing the observance of this as an ordinance today. Those who emphasize the example or forgiveness aspects do not feel it is necessary to perform the ritual but rather to practice the spiritual truths the ritual illustrated. It is true that the exhortation to follow Christ's example in verses 14 and 15 related to forgiving one another in humility, rather than to God's forgiving our missteps in life. This, then, would argue against considering foot-washing as an ordinance.

NOTES

1. See J. Oliver Buswell, *A Systematic Theology of the Christian Religion* (Grand Rapids: Zondervan, 1962), 2:262.

Chapter 75
The Worship of the Church

I. THE MEANING OF WORSHIP

A. The Words Involved

1. Proskuneō. This primary word for worship is connected with the idea of kissing (as kissing the earth to honor the deities of the earth); it came to connote prostrating oneself in reverence. This showed that the worshiper considered the object worthy of whatever he was offering. Even the English word "worship" (a shortened form of "worthship") means to attribute worth to the object worshiped. Our Lord used this word in His classic statement on worship in John 4:24. In relation to the church the word occurs only in 1 Corinthians 14:25 and refers there to the worship of an unbeliever who comes into the assembly. Perhaps the use of this term was avoided to describe the worship of the early church because of its associations with heathen rites, and the idea that *proskuneō* worship was done in the visible presence of the object worshiped. That may be why most of its occurrences are in the Gospels and the Revelation (in relation to both true and false worship but in the presence of the visible object). Nevertheless, the idea of prostrating oneself in reverence of the object worshiped remains a legitimate facet of Christian worship.

2. Latreuō. This highly significant word conveys the idea that worship is priestly service. The believer's entire life should be one of service-worship (Rom. 12:1); prayer reflects this kind of worship (Acts 13:2; Rom. 1:10); the word occurs several times in relation to giving (Rom. 15:27; 2 Cor. 9:12); and then general ministry of the Gospel is service-worship (Rom. 15:16; Phil. 3:3). Perhaps the reason this word is used of the believer's worship rather than the first one is simply that since Christ is not visible today our worship is to be shown in service.

B. The Concept

The worship of the church, then, consists of individual, corporate, public, and private service for the Lord, which is generated by a reverence for and submission to Him who is totally worthy.

II. THE CHARACTER OF WORSHIP (JOHN 4:24)

Our Lord revealed two basics about true worship when He declared it must be in spirit and in truth. "In spirit" includes three things about the center of worship. (1) Worship can and should take place anywhere and everywhere since spirit is not confined to a particular place or time. (2) Worship comes from man's spirit (Heb. 4:12). It is no mere surface ritual. (3) True worship is a person-to-Person experience, honoring with our spirit God who was revealed through the Lord Jesus at all times and in all places.

"In truth" means that the character of true worship must be genuine and without pretense. God hates insincere worship (Isa. 1:10–17; Mal. 1:7–14; Matt. 15:8–9). Fake worship is that which is not in accord with the revealed Word of God. Therefore, to worship in truth necessitates a growing knowledge of the Word, which will also increase our appreciation for the worth of the God we worship.

III. THE CONTENT OF CORPORATE WORSHIP

Actually the New Testament says little about the form and content of worship in the local church. Still, there are some indications given in Acts 2; 20; 1 Corinthians 12–14, and other scattered passages.

A. The Word

From the beginning the church put prime importance on doctrine (Acts 2:42). This was used both to build up believers (v. 42; 11:26; 1 Cor. 14:26; 2 Thess. 2:5 where Paul taught eschatology to new converts; 2 Tim. 4:2) and in evangelism (Acts 4:2; 13:5; 17:2, reaching unbelievers outside the church; 1 Cor. 14:23–24, when unbelievers come into the church service). All of the epistles demonstrate the kind of teaching that must have been customary in the churches, and these include all aspects of doctrinal teaching with application.

Within the assembly the procedure for preaching and teaching seemed to be flexible. Clearly any male believer could speak if it was done in an orderly fashion and if his message passed the test of truth (1 Cor. 14:26–33). Women were restricted in public and mixed groups, though older women were commissioned to minister to younger women (v. 34; 1 Tim. 2:12; Titus 2:3–5).

B. Prayer

Prayer was practiced both individually and corporately (Acts 4:24;

6:4; 10:9; 12:5; 13:3; 1 Tim. 2:1–8). According to the last passage, men led in public prayer in the church (for the word in v. 8 is males). Whether women also prayed in public worship depends on one's interpretation of 1 Corinthians 11:5. Paul may have been allowing such a practice, or he may have only been acknowledging that it happened at Corinth without approving it.

C. Singing

The New Testament exhorts both private and public singing as a facet of worship. When one is happy he should sing (James 5:13). Paul and Silas sang hymns of praise in jail (Acts 16:25). Singing was part of corporate worship as well (1 Cor. 14:26, this was likely a solo; Col. 3:16). Though distinctions have been made between psalms, hymns, and spiritual songs, they cannot be held rigidly. Psalms possibly refers to Old Testament psalms, though perhaps with Christians' additions. Hymns may be praises directed to God (yet might include using the psalms, Acts 16:25). Spiritual songs may include a wider variety of themes. Music is an important part of worship in most churches today.

Several New Testament passages may contain parts of hymns that the early church used (Eph. 5:14; 1 Tim. 3:16). The many doxologies also underscore this important aspect of worship (Rom. 9:5; 11:33–36; 16:27; Phil. 4:20; 1 Tim. 6:16; 2 Tim. 4:18).

It is not improbable that some of these verses reflect creedal statements that were spoken without musical accompaniment. First Timothy 3:16 serves as the clearest example. Others may include 1 Corinthians 12:3; 15:3–5; 16:22. These glimpses suggest that the reciting of a church covenant (not so much practiced today as formerly) may be appropriate and helpful.

Can we glean any principles for the use of music in the church today? Singing should be encouraged on many levels: by individuals privately, together as a group in the church, solos in the church, with or without instruments. The New Testament examples, including doxologies, praise the character of God and His works with language that is rich, not thin and repetitious. The New Testament gives no indication of particular musical forms used.

D. Giving

The New Testament says more about giving than about any other single aspect of church life. Giving to others serves as clear proof of one's love for God (James 2:15–17; 1 John 3:17–18), should stem from a life that has first been given to Him (2 Cor. 8:5), and should be done voluntarily (vv. 11–12; 9:7), liberally even in poverty (8:12), cheerfully (9:7), and according to the measure of prosperity God gives to the individual (1 Cor. 16:2). As far as New Testament revelation is concerned, giving was the principal area in which there was a cooperative effort among a number of churches (Acts 11:27–30; 2 Cor. 8–9).

E. Fellowship

The early church continued in fellowship (Acts 2:42). This means they had a close relationship with each other. This closeness consisted of their common doctrinal allegiance, their willingness to share material things, the experience of Communion in the Lord's Supper, and in sharing prayers.

In other words, all the aspects of worship constitute fellowship. It is not a separate entity that exists by itself. It is the practice of corporate worship. Based on the illustration in 1 Corinthians 12, it may be called body life. But based on the illustration in Ephesians 2, it may just as well be called household life. The goal, whatever the label, is to increase the health, strength, commitment, and numbers of the body or household (Eph. 4:12–17).

IV. THE DAY FOR CORPORATE WORSHIP

The New Testament church used Sunday as their day of corporate worship. They did this in spite of the fact that it was not a weekly holiday that people had free. Undoubtedly many Christian slaves were on call all day every day; yet they made time for corporate worship.

A. The Origin of the Lord's Day

Though modern writers invariably attempt to emphasize the connection between the Lord's Day and the Sabbath, the early church and the church Fathers did not make that emphasis. They did see a moral value in applying the Ten Commandments but made an exception of the fourth one concerning the Sabbath. Notice the absence of a Sabbath-Lord's Day problem in Acts 15:29 and the clear teaching of the New Testament as to the end of the Mosaic Law, including the Ten Commandments (except as nine of them, all but the Sabbath one, are repeated in the epistles, 2 Cor. 3:7–11; Col. 2:16). The idea of a particular day for worship may have been connected with the Sabbath, but the particular day was unrelated to the Sabbath.

Neither did the concept of the Lord's Day originate from the calendar. Though the Jews observed a seven-day cycle (based on the Creation week), a weekly division of time was unknown in the Greek and Roman world till after the establishment of the church in the first century. By the third century the weekly arrangement had spread, because the Roman calendar was in shambles until Constantine. Before that time there were both four- and eight-day "market" weeks. The seven-day delineation arose from putting together the sun, moon, and the five known planets of that time. Even as late as the French Revolution in the 1800s an attempt was made to have three ten-day weeks in each month with each tenth day a day of rest plus five holidays each year to make up the 365 days in the year.

The only explanation as to why the early church established a new day of worship unrelated to the Sabbath and the existing calendar was that Sunday was the day of the Lord's resurrection. He not only arose on Sunday, but six post-Resurrection appearances were also on Sunday, and the Day of Pentecost when the body of Christ was formed fell on Sunday. Almost always the day is designated as the first day of the week (Matt. 28:1; Mark 16:2, 9; Luke 24:1; John 20:1, 19; Acts 20:7; 1 Cor. 16:2). In Revelation 1:10 it is called the Lord's Day, a term similar to the Lord's Supper (1 Cor. 11:20) and used by the believers to protest and contrast the Emperor's or Augustus's Day. The Lord's Day, then, is the first day of the week, the day of His resurrection, and the day used by believers to celebrate that greatest event in history.

B. The Distinctiveness of the Lord's Day

Clearly the early church made this day distinct, for though they went to the synagogue services on the Sabbath they went to evangelize. When they met with other believers it was on Sunday. Romans 14:5 does not mean that Christians did not distinguish the first day for worship. Rather Paul was exhorting them not to be pressured by the Jewish element in the church to observe or fast on certain days.

C. The Activities of the Lord's Day

1. *Remember and celebrate Christ's resurrection.*
2. *Gather together for corporate worship* (Heb. 10:25; 1 Cor. 3:16).
3. *Do your accounting relative to giving* (1 Cor. 16:2).
4. *Observe the Lord's Supper* (Acts 20:7).

D. The Contemporary Neglect of the Lord's Day

1. The reason. In Christianized countries the civil Sunday with its partial cessation of regular activities has become filled with other activities (special games, opportunities to shop, etc.). Believers too are caught up in these secular uses of the Lord's Day. Churches also abandon opportunities to use available hours on Sunday for their activities. The result may soon be that Sunday will be like every other day of the week, requiring normal work hours as well, and believers will be back in the first century trying to find early morning or late evening hours for worship.

2. The results. To neglect the Lord's Day is to slight Him, to blunt the testimony to His resurrection, and to miss the benefits of the ministry and protection of corporate worship.

Chapter 76
OTHER MINISTRIES OF THE CHURCH

In addition to the ministries involved in worship, the New Testament also gives examples and commands concerning other ministries. Worship is primarily directed toward the object worshiped, Christ, the Head of the church; but it also has an effect on the members of the church and reaches out to those who are not committed.

I. THE MINISTRY OF DISCIPLINE

Christ's purpose for the church is to sanctify it and present it to Himself without spot or wrinkle (Eph. 5:26–27). All the activities of a church should also aim at this goal, including discipline, for it, too, is designed to produce a holy character in the one who has to be disciplined.

A. Objectives in Discipline

Scriptures give at least four reasons discipline is necessary. (1) To remove the defilement and leavening influence that sin brings (1 Cor. 5:6–8). (2) To protect other believers from sinning and challenge them to godliness (Gal. 6:1; 1 Tim. 5:20). (3) To produce soundness in faith (Titus 1:13). (4) To reclaim and restore the erring brother (2 Cor. 2:5–11).

B. Attitudes in Discipline

Those involved in the process of disciplining should show these attitudes: (a) meekness (Gal. 6:1); (b) uncompromising stand against sin (Titus 1:13); (c) love (2 Thess. 3:9–15); (d) forgiving spirit at repentance (2 Cor. 2:5–11).

C. Principles for Discipline

The three main principles for discipline are (a) no partiality (1 Tim. 5:21), (b) not hasty, but with deliberate steps (Matt. 18:15–20), and (c) with the goal of correction and eventual restoration (2 Cor. 2:6–8).

D. People to Be Disciplined

The Scriptures mention seven kinds of people (some of these overlap) who need discipline.

1. An accused elder (1 Tim. 5:19–20). In the case of persistent sin in an elder, two or three witnesses need to be involved, and the rebuke must be public to make others fearful of sinning.

2. A sinning brother (Matt. 18:15–20). The steps include private rebuke (how often is unstated), involvement of other people (again how often is unstated), then exposure to the whole church if the person is still unrepentant. The church then must cut off both spiritual and social fellowship with the individual.

3. An overtaken brother (Gal. 6:1). This refers to someone tripped up by sin in an unguarded moment, rather than persistent sin. He needs the help of someone mature to readjust his life and make it usable again (the word "restore" is used also in Matt. 4:21, "mending"; Eph. 4:12, "building up"; and 1 Thess. 3:10, "complete").

4. An unruly brother (2 Thess. 3:6). This concerns someone who has gotten out of step with the teachings of Scripture, specifically, in this passage, of someone who refused to work, thinking that the Lord's coming was immediate. Paul's discipline was to tell them to get to work because other believers need not feel any obligation to support them.

5. False teachers (Titus 1:10–16). When false teachers make inroads within the church, they are to be rebuked severely. Hymenaeus and Philetus, who apparently taught that the resurrection was to be understood spiritually or allegorically, were to be avoided; Paul delivered Hymenaeus and Alexander over to Satan for punishment (1 Tim. 1:20; 2 Tim. 2:17–18).

Although Paul dealt severely with false teachers, he showed considerable patience with people who were misled doctrinally. He did not counsel excommunication for those in Corinth who denied the resurrection; rather he patiently taught them the truth. Presumably, if they had then rejected what he taught and in turn promoted heresy he would have disciplined them in some way.

6. Factious people (Titus 3:8–11). These include those who cause divisions over worthless and unprofitable disputes, unsettling the church. Such people are to be warned twice, then rejected or avoided. Romans 16:17 commands similar action, "turn away" which includes personal, social, and spiritual contact.

7. *The immoral brother* (1 Cor. 5). Because the sin of incest in this case was both persistent and public, the guilty party was to be delivered to Satan; that is, excommunicated from the fellowship of the church and given back to Satan's domain of the world for whatever ruin that might bring, such as sickness or death. For other sins mentioned in verse 11 that believers commit (immorality, covetousness, idolatry, abusiveness, drunkenness, swindling), the punishment was cutting off fellowship (including social—do not eat with such).

John Wesley was well known for his emphasis on sensitivity to sin and discipline. Leaders of the small home classes (the forerunner of the mini-church) were instructed to inquire each week into each member's spiritual life and behavior. Every three months those who truly lived the Gospel received a ticket attesting to that fact and those who did not were excluded from the weekly meetings.[1]

Failure of the church to exercise this ministry of discipline can only lead to weaker (though probably larger) churches.

II. THE MINISTRY TO WIDOWS

Pure religion, James declares, includes visiting (overseeing) orphans and widows (James 1:27). No detail as to what this involves with regard to orphans is found in the New Testament, but there are detailed guidelines for the church's ministry to widows.

A. The Family's Responsibility

At the time of Christ there existed a fund in the temple that was used to support widows and orphans. When many Jewish widows were converted to Christianity the church undertook their continued support. However, Paul made it crystal clear in the central passage on the subject that a widow's family has the first and primary obligation to care for the widow. This is true of both younger, unenrolled widows (1 Tim. 5:4, 8) and of any older, enrolled widows (v. 16).

B. The Church's Responsibility

If there are no relatives to support a widow, then the church must assume that obligation, regardless of the age of the widow. A "widow indeed" is not necessarily an enrolled widow but one who is destitute in that she has no family to support her (1 Tim. 5:5). Therefore, her church family must underwrite her support. Younger widows are encouraged to remarry (v. 14); widows who qualify can be put on the church roll after age sixty (vv. 9–10).

What should a church do about this responsibility in a day of social security, insurance, annuities, and other financial provisions often made for a widow? The principles seem clear: to whatever extent her own family cannot support her (whether through living relatives or through the provision of relatives who have died), the church should assume the obligation whether it means partial or full support. Needs often exist today for widows of Christian workers who are left in need through no fault of their own.

III. THE MINISTRY OF CHARITY

The church also should minister to others who are in need.

The circles of responsibility toward those in need spread out from the local church. Those whose needs we come in contact with in the church (whether believers or unbelievers) have first claim (James 2:2–3, 15–16; 1 John 3:17). The early church was also concerned with the needs of believers in other places (Acts 11:27–30). Paul spent considerable effort and time collecting money for the poor believers in Jerusalem. It involved the cooperative effort of a number of churches. The money did not pass directly from donors to recipients but was supervised by a committee chosen by the churches and apparently distributed under the direction of the leadership (2 Cor. 8:18–22).

Sometimes the early church concerned itself with the support of missionaries. Though Paul worked to support himself and his associates, he also received gifts. Apparently the Philippian church gave gifts to Paul on at least three occasions (Phil. 4:16), and he clearly defended the right of those engaged in ministry to be supported by others (1 Cor. 9:4–14).

No individual or church can possibly meet all the needs that they have knowledge of in this day of mass communication, which brings so many needs across our paths almost daily. What, then, should be our priorities? As far as people to whom we should give, the priorities should focus on the Lord's servants, the Lord's people who are in need, then others (Gal. 6:10). Normally a church or individual would give priority to those under its care and responsibility in the local area, then to those in other places.

NOTE

1. See *Works of John Wesley,* VIII.250ff.

Section XIII
THINGS TO COME

Chapter 77
INTRODUCTION TO ESCHATOLOGY

I. THE MEANING OF ESCHATOLOGY

Eschatology means the theology of last things. That study can cover all things that were future at the time of their writing, or it can include only those things that are still future from our present vantage point. It deals with the consummation of all things, both those things that relate to individuals and to the world.

Everyone has some sort of eschatology. For many moderns, eschatology is a study in despair, for all things will end in death—the death of the individual and the death of the universe. Even evolution does not promise immortality. For others the despair is modified by a vague hope in some sort of life after death. For the Christian the Bible provides clear and detailed teaching concerning the future so that he may know with certainty what lies ahead.

II. THE SCOPE OF ESCHATOLOGY

The study of last things (those that are yet future from our viewpoint) includes the biblical teaching concerning the intermediate state, the resurrections, the Rapture of the church, the second advent of Christ, and the Millennium.

III. THE DEVELOPMENT OF ESCHATOLOGY

The study could be developed in a number of ways. One would be to separate the future for the individual from the future for the world. Another would be to catalog the future for the church, the future for Israel, the future for Gentiles, and the future for the world. Another approach might study the various teachings in their chronological order. A biblical theology approach would study the eschatology of the Old Testament, the eschatology of Jesus, the eschatology of Paul, the eschatology of John, etc.

No one method is necessarily superior to another. Most writers seem to combine various approaches, and so shall I. Some of the topics, such as resurrection, will be discussed from the individual viewpoint.

Others, such as the Tribulation, will be outlined chronologically. The three basic approaches to eschatology—premillennialism, postmillennialism, and amillennialism—need to have a more systematic treatment in order to see their distinctive approaches as a whole. Because of the contemporary debate concerning the relation of the Rapture of the church to the Tribulation, this will need special attention.

IV. THE IMPORTANCE OF ESCHATOLOGY

Because there is much divergence in this area of doctrine, and because some things are not crystal clear, some assume that eschatology should be given a lesser importance than other areas of biblical truth. Is there any area of doctrine that has not been debated? Think of the Trinity, or the nature of the person of Christ, or church government, or predestination, or eternal security, or the effects of Adam's sin. And think of some of the difficult concepts to interpret in these areas, concepts like the triunity of God, Deity and humanity united in one Person, the meaning of only begotten, the concept of imputed sin, etc. Yet we do not, nor should we, shy away from a detailed study of these teachings. Similarly we must not slight what the Bible says about the future.

For the believer, the knowledge of prophecy (a) provides joy in the midst of affliction (2 Cor. 4:17), (b) cleanses and encourages holy living (1 John 3:3), (c) is profitable, like all Scripture, for a number of important needs in the Christian's life (2 Tim. 3:16–17), (d) gives facts about life after death (2 Cor. 5:8), (e) gives truth about the end of history, (f) gives proof of the reliability of all Scripture, for the number of prophecies that have come to pass precisely as predicted cannot be accounted for by chance but only by God, and (g) draws our hearts out in worship to the God who is in complete control and who will accomplish His will in history. To slight prophecy is to miss these benefits.

Chapter 78
A Survey of Postmillennialism

I am a premillennialist, and this will be the framework in which this section on eschatology will be discussed. However, before explaining the premillennial understanding of the future, I think it would be helpful to first survey the three major systems of eschatology: postmillennialism, amillennialism, and premillennialism.

I. A DEFINITION OF POSTMILLENNIALISM

Loraine Boettner gave a careful descriptive definition of postmillennialism. It is

> That view of last things which holds that the kingdom of God is now being extended in the world through the preaching of the Gospel and the saving work of the Holy Spirit in the hearts of individuals, that the world is eventually to be Christianized, and that the return of Christ is to occur at the close of a long period of righteousness and peace commonly called the "Millennium." . . . The second coming of Christ will be followed immediately by the general resurrection, the general judgment, and the introduction of heaven and hell in their fullness.[1]

A. H. Strong described the Millennium as "a period in the later days of the church militant, when, under the special influence of the Holy Spirit, the spirit of the martyrs shall appear again, true religion be greatly quickened and revived, and the members of Christ's churches become so conscious of their strength in Christ that they shall, to an extent unknown before, triumph over the power of evil both within and without."[2]

II. DOCTRINAL CHARACTERISTICS OF POSTMILLENNIALISM

A. Concerning the Bible

Biblical postmillennialists believe in the authority of the Bible. Of course, liberals who expect a Golden Age to come through human efforts have a kind of postmillennial view of history, though it is not biblically based.

B. Concerning the Power of God

Their confidence in the power of God causes them to believe that the Great Commission will be fulfilled in that most of the world will be saved. To believe otherwise makes the Commission ineffective and the power of God impotent.

C. Concerning the Church

The church, fulfilling the Great Commission, will be the instrument to bring about and promote the Millennium on earth.

D. Concerning the Return of Christ

Postmillennialists believe in the actual return of Christ at the conclusion of the Millennium. His return will be followed immediately by the general resurrection and judgment.

E. Concerning the Millennium

1. Length. The Millennium, according to postmillennialism, will be an extended period of time, not necessarily a thousand years. It may perhaps be much longer than a literal thousand years.
2. Beginning. Some understand that the Millennium will begin gradually; others see a more abrupt beginning to the spread of righteousness throughout the earth.
3. Characteristics. The Millennium will be a time of peace, material prosperity, and spiritual welfare on the earth. However, not all will be saved, nor will all sin be eradicated. But Christian principles will be the rule, not the exception, and sin will be reduced to negligible proportions.
4. Activities. Some postmillennialists allow for a brief time of apostasy at the conclusion of the Millennium just prior to the return of Christ.[3]

F. Concerning Satan

Postmillennialists understand Satan is bound at all times in that he is always under God's control. But he will be bound at the beginning of the Millennium in a special way according to Revelation 20. However, this has not yet occurred since we are not yet in the Millennium but are at this time laying the foundations for the Millennium.

III. EVIDENCE THAT THE WORLD IS GETTING BETTER

If we are not yet in the Millennium but are laying the groundwork for it, then we ought to be able to see evidence that things are getting better in the world. Postmillennialism believes we can. That evidence includes a number of things. (1) Social conditions are certainly improved in many parts of the world. As one example, the status of women has been greatly improved wherever the Gospel has been received. (2) The enormous amount of money given to Christian causes promotes better conditions in the world. (3) The Bible continues to be the world's best-seller. It is now translated into more languages than ever before in the history of the world. (4) The Gospel is disseminated in many more ways and to many more places than ever before. Radio and literature distribution are two ways this is being done.

Of course this evidence is true, and no believer can be anything but thankful for it. But whether this presages an imminent Millennium is another question that must also take into account the contemporary increase of evil before it can be answered accurately.

IV. SCRIPTURAL SUPPORT FOR POSTMILLENNIALISM

A. Passages That Tell of a Golden Age

Since the many passages that speak of a triumphant reign of Christ have not been fulfilled in history, they are yet to be fulfilled in the future but before the second advent of Christ. Many of these Scriptures are the same ones that premillennialists understand as referring to the millennial kingdom. The postmillennialist sees them fulfilled before Christ returns, while the premillennialist expects them to be fulfilled after Christ returns. Such passages include Psalms 2:8; 22:27; 47; 72; 86:9; Isaiah 2:2–4; 11:6–9; Jeremiah 31:34; Daniel 2:35, 44; and Micah 4:1–4.

B. Passages That Characterize the Gospel as Powerful and Worldwide

Because the Gospel is the power of God (Rom. 1:16), it is unthinkable, postmillennialists argue, that the world will not be converted. God wishes all men to be saved (1 Tim. 2:4), so to pray expecting this will happen is to pray in the will of God.

C. Other Passages

Christ's Parable of the Leaven affirms the universal extent of the kingdom (Matt. 13:33). Romans 11 predicts the conversion of a great number of Jews and Gentiles. Revelation 7:9–10 pictures a great multitude of redeemed people from all peoples of the world.

V. HISTORICAL SKETCH OF POSTMILLENNIALISM

A. Joachim of Fiore (ca. 1135–1202)

An early exponent of a postmillennial scheme, Joachim explained history as being trinitarian; that is, the first age was that of the Father when mankind lived under the Law of the Old Testament; the second was that of the Son, the period of grace covered in the New Testament; and the third age was to be that of the Spirit, beginning about A.D. 1260, in which the world would be converted.

B. Daniel Whitby (1638–1726)

An erudite clergyman, Whitby published thirty-nine works, including *A Treatise of the True Millennium.*[4] He taught that after the world would be converted, the Jews restored to the Holy Land, and the pope and Turks defeated, the world would enjoy a time of peace and righteousness for a thousand years. At the close of this Millennium, Christ would personally come to earth, raise the dead, and judge all people. His views were very popular and were adopted by many eighteenth- and nineteenth-century preachers and commentators.

Whitby's postmillennialism was quite Jewish-oriented. He described the Millennium as the reign of converted Jews with Gentiles "flowing in to them." All spiritual blessings in the Millennium will be conveyed from the Jews to other nations. He believed that the church will live in a revitalized state during the Millennium, though bodily resurrection will not occur till after the Millennium.

C. Other Postmillennialists

Liberals who hold to inevitable progress through natural (or evolutionary) processes may rightly be labeled postmillennial. However, they do not take the Scriptures seriously and see world improvement coming through the power of man.

Conservative postmillennialists do take the Scriptures as the Word of God and attribute improvement to the power of God. James Snowden understood the Millennium to be the entire time between the first and second advents of Christ.[5] His scheme differed from amillennialism in that he taught that the world was getting better. He interpreted the events of Revelation 20 either as already past or as describing heavenly bliss.

Charles Hodge taught that the Second Advent will be preceded by the universal diffusion of the Gospel, the national conversion of the Jews, and the coming of Antichrist. When Christ comes, there will be the general resurrection and judgment of all mankind.[6]

The postmillennialism of the post-World War II era has till recently generally been of the liberal variety. The great advancements of the twentieth century through man's achievements gave credibility to the concept. There were scarcely any biblical postmillennialists (Loraine Boettner being an exception).

But in the latter part of this century an interesting phenomena has developed. Some former amillennialists have become postmillennialists because of their belief in theonomy. Theonomy is the state of being governed by God. Theonomists promote subduing the earth by means of science, education, the arts, and all other pursuits in order to effect God's dominion over all things. For some, this means imposing the Law of the Old Testament on life today not only in moral matters but also in governmental, financial, and other areas. Now, of course, if this is done, conditions in the world will improve and we will then experience the rule of God over life in the world. Thus, many Reformed theologians who strongly support the use of the Law and who were amillennial have switched to embrace postmillennialism as the goal of their theonomistic program.

To sum up: Liberals promote a postmillennial goal through humanism. Biblical postmillennialists promote it through the church's preaching of the Gospel. Theonomists promote it through the Gospel and the imposition of Old Testament Law.

Notes

1. Loraine Boettner, *The Millennium* (Nutley, N.J.: Presbyterian and Reformed, 1957), 14.
2. A. H. Strong, *Systematic Theology* (Philadelphia: Judson Press, 1907), 1013.
3. See Boettner, *The Millennium,* 69.
4. Daniel Whitby, *A Treatise of the True Millennium* (London: W. Bowyer, 1700).
5. James Snowden, *The Coming of the Lord* (New York: Macmillan, 1919).
6. Charles Hodge, *Systematic Theology* (New York: Scribners, 1887), 3:792.

Chapter 79
A Survey of Amillennialism

I. A DEFINITION OF AMILLENNIALISM

Amillennialism is the view of last things that holds there will be no Millennium before the end of the world. Until the end there will be a parallel development of both good and evil, God's kingdom and Satan's. After the second coming of Christ at the end of the world there will be a general resurrection and general judgment of all people.

II. DOCTRINAL CHARACTERISTICS OF AMILLENNIALISM

A. Concerning the Bible

In general, amillennialists hold a high view of the inspiration and authority of the Bible. If some do not, it is not their amillennialism that causes this. One need only recall names like Oswald T. Allis, William Hendriksen, and Anthony A. Hoekema, all amillennialists, yet strong proponents of the infallibility of the Scriptures.

B. Concerning the Millennium

Among conservative amillennialists two views exist concerning the Millennium. One sees fulfillment of millennial passages to be in the present age by the church on earth (e.g., Allis and Berkhof). The other finds fulfillment by the saints in heaven now (e.g., Warfield and Floyd Hamilton). Both views agree that there will be no future earthly kingdom.

C. Concerning the Covenants

Premillennialists lean on the argument that the biblical covenants contain promises yet unfulfilled and requiring an earthly Millennium if they are fulfilled literally. Amillennialists say that those promises are fulfilled spiritually in the church, or that the promises need not be fulfilled at all since they were conditional and the conditions were not met.

D. Concerning the Church

Amillennialists see the church as fulfilling God's promises in an antitypical and spiritual way. The church is a heavenly, spiritual kingdom, whereas the Millennium of premillennialism is a carnal, earthly kingdom. (But cannot the church be described as earthly and carnal? And cannot the future kingdom be described as spiritual?) The church fulfills the promises, and the new heaven and new earth that immediately follow the Church Age consummate history.

III. THE HERMENEUTICS OF AMILLENNIALISM

Unquestionably, different millennial views result from different hermeneutics, that is, different interpretive principles. Premillennialists use literal or normal interpretation in all areas of biblical truth, whereas amillennialists employ a nonliteral or spiritual principle in the area of eschatology. All conservatives, whatever their eschatological persuasions, use literal or normal interpretation everywhere except eschatology. Floyd Hamilton, an amillennialist, acknowledges that "a literal interpretation of the Old Testament prophecies gives us just such a picture of an earthly reign of the Messiah as the premillennialist pictures."[1] The amillennialist, of course, does not accept that picture of the future because he employs a different hermeneutic in the area of prophecy.

Although writers generally do not detail their hermeneutics before detailing their commentaries or developing their theologies, Oswald T. Allis does discuss the hermeneutical principles he employs in interpreting prophecy.[2] I want to summarize his ideas about how to interpret prophecy and briefly interact with them.

(1) He first seeks to establish that both the literal and figurative methods of interpretation have their proper places and their necessary limitations. However, he seems to place all the limitation on the literal and none on the figurative.

(2) Some of those limitations on literal interpretation include: (a) the presence of figures of speech that cannot be interpreted literally allows us freedom to interpret in other ways; (b) the fact that the main theme of the Bible is spiritual gives validity to figurative or spiritual interpretation; and (c) the fact that the Old Testament is preliminary and preparatory to the New Testament causes us to expect that the New Testament will interpret the literal Old Testament prophecies in a figurative manner.

No literalist denies that the Bible contains figures of speech. But he insists that they depict very literal truths. For example, the best roses grown in the part of the country where I live are grown in Tyler, Texas. Tyler roses are famous. Now, if I see an advertisement that says, use such-and-such brand of fertilizer and you, too, can grow Tyler roses, I do not understand this to mean that I must live in the city of Tyler but that wherever I live I can grow the same kind of magnificent roses that are grown in Tyler. The figure of speech has a very literal and plain meaning about the actual roses I can grow. Tyler roses means roses, not tomatoes; but Tyler roses also stands for roses that are outstanding, whether actually grown in Tyler or not.

(3) If his first two theses be true, then the question naturally arises, how does one know whether to interpret a passage literally or figuratively? Allis's answer is, whichever gives the true meaning of the passage! Comment is unnecessary.

(4) Allis continues by saying that the only way prophecy can be understood literally is when its literal meaning is clear and obvious. Almost all prophecy is filled with figurative and parabolic language, which must be interpreted accordingly. So in reality, most prophecy will be interpreted nonliterally.

(5) To interpret and understand a prophecy correctly and fully, its fulfillment must also be known. Every prophecy ever given was given before its fulfillment was known. Otherwise it would not have been a prophecy. If we follow Allis's principle, then no prophecy could ever have been or will be understood until after the fulfillment came. No Israelite needed to have taken the prophecies about the coming Assyrian or Babylonian Captivities literally, because he could not be sure those prophecies would be fulfilled literally until the Captivities actually happened. By such a principle of interpretation, what force would those prophecies have had? But, you see, amillennialists want to be able to claim that we cannot be sure that the Old Testament prophecies concerning the millennial kingdom will be fulfilled literally because no such kind of fulfillment has yet come to pass. But since the church has some similar characteristics to the kingdom, the church must be fulfilling those Old Testament prophecies.

(6) As if to reinforce his idea that we should expect a vagueness in how to interpret prophecy, Allis, throughout his discussion of hermeneutics, characterizes prophecy as indefinite, enigmatical, even deceptive, filled with symbols, imprecise, and subject to various interpretations. These are his phrases, not mine. But, of course, those alleged charac-

teristics are true only if the interpreter abandons the principles of literal or normal interpretation.

IV. INTERPRETIVE EVIDENCES FOR AMILLENNIALISM

Amillennialists interpret certain key passages and doctrines in ways that support their system.

A. Interpretation of the Abrahamic Covenant

Premillennialists point out that if the yet unfulfilled part of that covenant is to be fulfilled literally (the promise of the land of Palestine), this will have to occur in a future Millennium, since there has been no place in past or present history for a literal fulfillment. Amillennialists say that we need not expect a future fulfillment because either (a) the promises were conditional and the conditions were never met; or (b) the land promise was fulfilled in the time of Joshua (Josh. 21:43–45); or (c) it was fulfilled by David (2 Sam. 8:3); or (d) it was fulfilled during King Solomon's reign (1 Kings 4:21); or (e) it is now being fulfilled by the church on earth; or (f) it is being fulfilled now by the church in heaven; or (g) it will be fulfilled by all the redeemed on the future new eternal earth. If any of these seven options be correct, then the other six are unnecessary. It appears that amillennialists do not really know how or when or if the Abrahamic Covenant needs to or has been or will be fulfilled. They are only certain that it will not be in a future, earthly Millennium, since there is no such period in their system.

B. Interpretation of Ephesians 3:5

To the amillennialist the mystery in this passage is that the church actually was in the Old Testament and therefore fulfills those Old Testament promises. This was discussed under the church.

C. Daniel's Seventy Weeks

Amillennialists have certain common features in their interpretation of Daniel 9:24–27. These include (a) the beginning of the seventy weeks was in 536 B.C. in the time of Cyrus, not (as premillennialists say) in 445 B.C. under Artaxerxes. This has the effect of allowing the seventy sevens to be imprecise in duration. (b) The seventieth week is the entire Church Age, not a future seven-year period of Tribulation.

These characteristic interpretations of amillennialism stem from not consistently practicing literal interpretation.

V. HISTORY OF AMILLENNIALISM

A. From the New Testament to Augustine

Up to the time of Origen (ca. 185–ca. 254), stress on a literal hermeneutic caused apologists to be premillennial. The fathers felt that they were in the last days and expected the immediate second coming of Christ to bring in the kingdom. Origen, using an allegorical method of interpretation, spiritualized the future kingdom and understood it to be the present Church Age from Adam on. This amillennial eschatology was popularized by Augustine.

B. Augustine (354–430)

By spiritualizing the concept of the kingdom, Augustine made it mean the existence of the church in this world. The Millennium is the time between the first and second comings of Christ. "During the 'thousand years' when the devil is bound, the saints also reign for a 'thousand years' and, doubtless, the two periods are identical and mean the span between Christ's first and second coming" (City of God xx.9). However, he understood the binding of Satan not to mean that Satan has no power to deceive, but that during this interadvent period he is not allowed to exercise his full powers. Just before the end, Satan will be free to deceive the nations against the church, a rebellion that God will put down. This will be followed by the general judgment and eternal state.

Augustine did understand the thousand years literally and expected that the second coming of Christ would occur within one thousand years after His ascension. When the year 1000 came and went without the Second Coming occurring, the thousand years were spiritualized to mean an indefinite period of time or the whole period between the first and second comings of Christ.

C. Reformation Eschatology

The great leaders of the Reformation were amillennial in their eschatology. They were content to follow the Roman Church's teaching, which in turn followed Augustine.

Luther saw the Great Tribulation and the bodily return of Christ. He believed he was in the midst of that Tribulation. As many did, Luther also divided history into six ages of one thousand years each, followed by the seventh age of eternal Sabbath rest. He taught that the sixth age was the age of the popes, beginning in 1076 but not lasting the full thousand years. Thus he believed that he was living in the time just before the Second Advent.

Calvin taught that Israel and the church were the same and looked for the Second Coming to usher in a general resurrection and judgment and the eternal state. He did criticize chiliasm, (belief in a millennium), describing its teachings as "fiction," "insult," "dream," and "intolerable blasphemy." He objected strenuously to a thousand-year limitation on the eternal blessedness of the saints (a misunderstanding of what premillennialism taught).

D. The Modern Era

Though Augustinian amillennialism is generally followed in this modern time (i.e., the Millennium is the interadvent period on earth), another form of amillennialism arose. B. B. Warfield (following Kliefoth who wrote in 1874) taught that the Millennium is the present state of the saints in heaven.[3] In general, Reformed creeds say little about the millennial question, focusing rather on the general resurrection and judgment and eternity. One of the popular reasons for preferring amillennialism over premillennialism contrasts the premillennial concept of fulfillment in an earthly kingdom (usually the adjective *carnal* is placed with this phrase) with the amillennial concept of fulfillment of Old Testament prophecies in the church in this age (and usually the adjective *spiritual* is put with this phrase). Thus the system that emphasizes the spiritual church rather than the carnal kingdom is to be preferred. When I hear or read this argument, I want to ask, Since when is the church only spiritual and the kingdom only carnal? The church (look around) has carnal people in it, and the kingdom will have many spiritual facets to it. Spiritual and carnal characterize both the church and the future kingdom.

Always, of course, the conclusive evidence for the truth of a doctrine is not historical but exegetical.

NOTES

1. Floyd Hamilton, *The Basis of Millennial Faith* (Grand Rapids: Eerdmans, 1942), 38.
2. Oswald T. Allis, *Prophecy and the Church* (Philadelphia: Presbyterian and Reformed, 1945), 17–30.
3. B. B. Warfield, *Biblical Doctrines* (New York: Oxford, 1929), 643–44.

Chapter 80
A SURVEY OF PREMILLENNIALISM

Though the rest of this section will be a development of premillennial eschatology, it may help to give a brief survey of it at this point.

I. A DEFINITION OF PREMILLENNIALISM

Premillennialism is the view that holds that the second coming of Christ will occur prior to the Millennium, which will see the establishment of Christ's kingdom on this earth for a literal one thousand years. It also understands that there will be several occasions when resurrections and judgments will take place. Eternity will begin after the thousand years are concluded. Within premillennialism there are those who hold differing views as to the time of the Rapture.

II. DOCTRINAL CHARACTERISTICS OF PREMILLENNIALISM

A. Concerning the Bible

Premillennialists hold a high view of Scripture. It is probably safe to say that pretribulational premillennialists believe in the inerrancy of the Bible almost without exception.

B. Concerning the Millennium

All forms of premillennialism understand that the Millennium follows the second coming of Christ. Its duration will be one thousand years; its location will be on this earth; its government will be theocratic with the personal presence of Christ reigning as King; and it will fulfill all the yet-unfulfilled promises about the earthly kingdom.

Although premillennialists generally view the coming kingdom literally, some interpret it less so. For George E. Ladd the prophecies concerning Israel are spiritualized, and the millennial kingdom is viewed more as an extension of the spiritual kingdom of God.[1] For Robert Mounce the thousand years of Revelation 20 are literal, but the coming kingdom is not "the Messianic Age foretold by the prophets of the Old Testament."[2]

C. Concerning the Covenants

Premillennialists understand that the promise of the Abrahamic Covenant giving to Abraham's descendants the land from the river of Egypt to the River Euphrates has never been fulfilled but will be fulfilled in the coming millennial kingdom (Gen. 15:18). The promises of the Davidic Covenant also necessitate the establishment of the millennial kingdom for their fulfillment (2 Sam. 7:12–16).

D. Concerning the Church

Dispensational premillennialists consistently distinguish the church from Israel. Because the church does not fulfill the yet-unfulfilled promises made to Israel, there must be a time when they will be fulfilled, and that time is in the Millennium.

The extent to which a theological system consistently distinguishes Israel and the church will reveal its eschatological position. Observe the following chart.

O.T.	**N.T.**	**MILLENNIUM**
Israel = Church	Israel = Church	No Millennium = Amillennialism
Israel = Church	Israel = Church	Israel ≠ Church = Covenant Premillennialism
Israel ≠ Church	Israel ≠ Church	Israel ≠ Church = Dispensational Premillennialism

III. THE HERMENEUTICS OF PREMILLENNIALISM

Premillennialists employ a literal or normal hermeneutic. And this, of course, gives their picture of future events.

IV. HISTORY OF PREMILLENNIALISM

A. The Ancient Period

In the earliest centuries of the church, a general premillennial scheme was widely held, though chronological details were not always clear. Descriptions of the Millennium are literalistic, the future reign of Christ in Jerusalem is a prominent theme, and that reign will follow the return of Christ. Church historian Philip Schaff summarized as follows. "The most striking point in the eschatology of the ante-Nicene Age is the prominent chiliasm, or millenarianism, that is the belief of a visible reign of Christ in glory on earth with the risen saints for a thousand years, before the general resurrection and judgment. It was indeed not the doctrine of the church embodied in any creed or form of devotion, but a widely current opinion of distinguished teachers."[3]

With the union of church and state under Constantine, the hope of Christ's coming faded some. The Alexandrian school of interpretation attacked the literal hermeneutic on which premillennialism was based, and the influence of the teachings of Augustine reinterpreted the concept and time of the Millennium.

B. The Medieval and Reformation Periods

In the medieval period most doctrines, including eschatology, were eclipsed by the darkness of those centuries. As we have seen, the reformers were generally amillennial in their eschatology, though Anabaptists and Huguenots were chiliasts.

C. The Modern Period

The modern period has witnessed the rise of premillennial teaching. A number of commentators (like J. A. Bengel and Henry Alford) wrote from this viewpoint. The spread of dispensationalism in the nineteenth and twentieth centuries brought with it a lively interest in prophetic studies.[4]

NOTES

1. George E. Ladd, *A Theology of the New Testament* (Grand Rapids: Eerdmans, 1974), 64–69, 629–32.
2. Robert Mounce, *The Book of Revelation* (Grand Rapids: Eerdmans, 1977), 359.

3. Philip Schaff, *History of the Christian Church* (New York: Scribners, 1884), 2:614. For quotes from some of those "distinguished teachers" see Ryrie, *The Basis of the Premillennial Faith* (Neptune, N.J.: Loizeaux, 1954), pp. 17–33.
4. For detailed discussions see Ernest R. Sandeen, *The Roots of Fundamentalism* (Chicago: Univ. of Chicago Press, 1970); and C. Norman Kraus, *Dispensationalism in America* (Richmond: John Knox, 1950).

Chapter 81
God's Covenant with Abraham

I. THE ESCHATOLOGICAL IMPORTANCE OF THIS COVENANT

The interpretation of the Abrahamic Covenant is a watershed between premillennialism and amillennialism. The central question concerns its fulfillment. All agree that certain aspects of it have been fulfilled. But all do not agree on the fulfillment of other aspects of it, particularly the land promise. Amillennialists, while not agreed on the time of fulfillment of the land promise, unanimously agree that it will not be fulfilled in a future earthly millennial kingdom. Premillennialists, on the other hand, insist that since there has been no literal fulfillment in the past or present, there must be one in the future, and theirs is the only system that includes a future time when it may be fulfilled on this earth.

II. THE PROMISES OF THE COVENANT

A. Personal Promises to Abraham (Gen. 12:2)

Three short clauses addressed to Abraham (using the Hebrew cohortative form of the verb) contain the personal promises God made to Abraham.

1. "I will make you a great nation." When God said this, Abraham had no heir. The promise refers, of course, to the Jewish nation, the descendants of Abraham through Isaac and Jacob.

2. "I will bless you." In fulfillment of this promise, God gave Abraham temporal blessings of land (13:14–15, 17), servants (15:7), and wealth (13:2; 24:34–35), and He gave him spiritual blessings (13:18; 21:22).

3. "I will make your name great." God promised Abraham fame, renown, and good reputation.

The last clause of 12:2 states the purpose or result of God's blessing Abraham—"so you shall be a blessing."

B. Universal Promises (Gen. 12:3)

1. The promise of divine blessing or cursing people on the basis of their treatment of Abraham. Abraham's relationship with God was so close that to bless him or curse him was, in effect, to bless or curse God (20:2–18; 21:22–34; 23).

2. The promise that all the families of the earth would be blessed. Paul made it clear that Christ fulfilled this promise (Gal. 3:16). "Seed" may be both collective and individual; that is, the seed was one line, one family, and especially one Person, Christ (v. 19). Paul's concluding point in that chapter is this: do not try to become sons of Abraham by being circumcised but by being in Christ (vv. 27, 29). Our position in Christ makes us heirs of this particular promise of the Abrahamic Covenant. Note carefully that Paul was not saying that the church fulfills the entire covenant. He focused only on this one promise concerning blessing in the seed (v. 16—the plural, "promises," is used because the covenant was repeated several times to Abraham, not because Paul wanted to indicate that the church fulfills the entire covenant).[1]

C. National Promises (Gen. 15:18–21)

1. The promise that Abraham would father a great nation was both a personal and a national promise. Abraham did have an heir miraculously by Sarah (21:2).

2. The promise to that nation of specific land as an inheritance. See Genesis 12:7; 13:15, 17; 15:7–8, 18; 17:8; 24:7; 26:3; 28:13–14; 35:12; 48:4; 50:24. Genesis 17:1–8 emphasizes that the land was to be an everlasting possession; and 15:18 describes the boundaries as from the river of Egypt to the Euphrates.

Debate continues on the identity of the river of Egypt. One view equates the river (*nahar*) of Egypt with the wadi (*nahal*) of Egypt, the modern wadi el-'Arish, which, during the rainy season, flows from the middle of the Sinai Peninsula into the Mediterranean ninety miles east of the Suez Canal (Num. 34:5; Josh. 15:4, 47; 1 Kings 8:65; 2 Kings 24:7; 2 Chron. 7:8; Isa. 27:12; Ezek. 47:19; 48:28). This is the view of Walter C. Kaiser, Jr.[2] The other view identifies the river of Egypt as the Nile, specifically its eastern channel. The word *nahar* used in Genesis 15:18 always refers to a continuously flowing river, which the Nile is and the wadi el-'Arish is not. This is the view of Bruce K. Waltke and K. A. Kitchen.[3]

To be sure, in some passages the focus is on Canaan, or some part of that larger area promised in verse 18 (17:8; 1 Kings 8:65; Ezek. 47:13–20). Israel has occupied at various times part of the larger area, but never the larger area, nor ever as an everlasting possession.

III. THE SOLEMN RATIFICATION OF THE COVENANT

The ratification ceremony described in Genesis 15:9–17 when compared with near Eastern custom indicates that God alone obligated Himself to fulfill the terms of the covenant since only He walked between the pieces of the sacrificial animals. The significance of that is striking: it means that God swore fidelity to His promises and placed the obligation of their fulfillment on Himself alone. Abraham made no such oath; he was in a deep sleep, yet aware of what God promised.[4] Clearly the Abrahamic Covenant was not conditioned on anything Abraham would or would not do; its fulfillment in all its parts depends only on God's doings.

IV. ALLEGED CONDITIONS IN THE COVENANT

The unconditionality of the Abrahamic Covenant furnishes an important support for premillennialism, since the land promise needs a future time (the Millennium) in which it will be fulfilled. Therefore, amillennialists allege that there were in fact conditions attached to the fulfillment of the covenant that make it impossible to view the covenant as unconditional.

A. Genesis 12:1

The imperative, "Go forth from your country," expresses a condition that would have invalidated the covenant if Abraham had not obeyed. However, grammatically this imperative, followed by two imperfects and a series of cohortative imperfects in verses 2–3, expresses an intention, namely what God intended to do for Abraham. Other examples of this use are found in 30:18 and 45:18.

B. Genesis 12:2

The phrase "be a blessing" is seen by some to be a condition for fulfillment of the covenant. However, grammatically this expresses a consequence that is expected to occur with certainty or an intention. The Gesenius, Kautzsch, Cowley Hebrew grammar cites this passage as an example of intention.[5]

C. Genesis 17:1

Some understand "walk before Me" as a condition for fulfillment of the covenant. However, the grammar is the same as in 12:1 and expresses intention.

D. Genesis 22:16–18; 26:5

Since the covenant had been firmly established several times before these events, it would be incongruous to view these passages as conditions imposed after the clear statements of unconditionality. Rather, in these instances God acknowledged the worthiness of Abraham to remind him and his descendants that faith and obedience were necessary for participation in the benefits of the unconditional promises of the covenant.[6]

V. VIEWPOINTS AS TO THE FULFILLMENT OF THE COVENANT

A. The Amillennial Viewpoint

Amillennialism teaches that all the provisions of the covenant have been fulfilled, including the land promise. This is done either by spiritualizing the land promise so that the church fulfills it, or by seeing it fulfilled in Israel's past history. One such supposed fulfillment occurred in the days of Joshua. In Joshua 21:43–45 we read that God told Joshua that He had now kept the promises made to Israel in giving them the land which He promised to their fathers. Of course, they did not possess the land of Canaan forever, nor had they fully conquered it at that time. But, those considerations aside, God did declare that what had happened was a fulfillment of the covenant. How could this be? In the several statements of the covenant, the land promised was both from the river of Egypt to the Euphrates (Gen. 15:18) and the land of Canaan (17:8). The former, which was greater, included the latter, which was smaller. Under Joshua the Israelites in no way occupied the larger limits of the land, but they had staked their claim to the land of Canaan. So neither promise has been fulfilled everlastingly.

In 2 Samuel 8:3, the "he" who went to restore his rule at the river is not David; "the subject of the sentence is Hadadezer."[7] Though Solomon's kingdom was extensive, he did not reign over all the territory promised to Abraham, nor did he do it eternally.

Perhaps an illustration will help. Suppose I promise to pay for a student's entire college education. This might normally mean four one-year payments. At the end of the first year I could say that I have kept my promise. And I could even say (like Gen. 26:5), "Because you have made such good grades, I am happy to pay the next year's tuition." The larger promise of paying for the total education includes the lesser promises to pay for each year's expenses.

The larger promise of the land between the two rivers includes the land of Canaan and the territory Solomon ruled, but it does not mean that the land of Canaan or Solomon's kingdom is equivalent to the larger area.

Please observe the inherent self-contradiction of the amillennial position. If the covenant is conditional, then even the amillennialist does not need to look for a fulfillment in the days of David, Joshua, or Solomon. If the covenant was fulfilled in either of those times, then it was not conditional. If it was fulfilled under Joshua or Solomon, then the church does not fulfill it. If the church fulfills it, then one need not look for a fulfillment in the days of Joshua or Solomon. It would appear that the amillennialist needs to have the spare tires of possible fulfillments under Joshua or Solomon or by the church in case the argument for conditionality goes flat!

A novel approach to the fulfillment of the land promise was proposed by Anthony Hoekema, who sees multiple fulfillments of the land promise during Israel's history but an ultimate antitypical fulfillment on the new earth. He expands the Promised Land to include the entire earth and the recipients of the promise to include all the redeemed. He clearly denies any fulfillment on the present earth during a future Millennium.[8]

B. The Premillennial Viewpoint

Premillennialism insists that all the provisions of the Abrahamic Covenant must be fulfilled since the covenant was made without conditions. Much of the covenant has already been fulfilled and fulfilled literally; therefore, what remains to be fulfilled will also be fulfilled literally. This brings the focus on the yet-unfulfilled land promise. Though the nation Israel occupied part of the territory promised in the covenant, she has never yet occupied all of it and certainly not eternally as the covenant promised. Therefore, there must be a time in the future when Israel will do so, and for the premillennialist this will be in the coming millennial kingdom. Thus the Abrahamic Covenant gives strong support for premillennial eschatology.

Notes

1. See J. B. Lightfoot, *A Commentary on St. Paul's Epistle to the Galatians* (New York: Macmillan, 1892), 142.
2. Walter C. Kaiser, Jr., "The Promised Land: A Biblical-Historical View," *Bibliotheca Sacra* 138: 311 n.6.

3. Bruce K. Waltke, *The Zondervan Pictorial Encyclopedia of the Bible* (Grand Rapids: Zondervan, 1975), 5:121; K. A. Kitchen, *The New Bible Dictionary* (Grand Rapids: Eerdmans, 1962), 353–54.
4. See Cleon L. Rogers, Jr., "The Covenant with Abraham and Its Historical Setting," *Bibliotheca Sacra,* 127:241–56.
5. William Gesenius, *Gesenius' Hebrew Grammar,* ed. E. Kautzsche and A. E. Cowley (Oxford: At the Clarendon Press, 1898), 325.
6. Walter C. Kaiser, Jr., *Toward an Old Testament Theology* (Grand Rapids: Zondervan, 1978), 93–94.
7. A. F. Kirkpatrick, "The Second Book of Samuel," in *The Cambridge Bible for Schools and Colleges* (Cambridge: Univ. Press, 1897), 106.
8. Anthony Hoekema, *The Bible and the Future* (Grand Rapids: Eerdmans, 1979), 206–12, 274–87.

Chapter 82
GOD'S COVENANT WITH DAVID

God's covenant with David, like His with Abraham, also gives strong support to premillennial eschatology.

I. THE PROVISIONS OF THE COVENANT (2 Sam. 7:12–16)

David desired to build a temple for the Lord to replace the temporary tentlike tabernacle. Since David himself lived in a house of cedar, it seemed only fitting that there be a more permanent building for the worship of God. But God revealed to Nathan the prophet that He had something far greater in mind for David, and that revelation is the Davidic Covenant.

A. Promises Related to David

1. Descendants. David would have a son who would succeed him and establish his kingdom (v. 12).
2. Kingdom. David's house, throne, and kingdom would be established forever (v. 16). However, the covenant did not guarantee uninterrupted rule by David's family, though it did promise that the right to rule would always remain with David's dynasty. The Babylonian Captivity did, of course, interrupt the Davidic rule.

B. Promises Related to Solomon

1. Temple. Solomon, rather than David, would build the temple (v. 13a).
2. Throne. The throne of Solomon's kingdom would be established forever (v. 13b).
3. Punishment. He would be chastened for his sins, but not deposed (vv. 14–15).

God did not promise specifically that the posterity of David would be through the line of Solomon. Jeconiah (or Coniah), one of Solomon's descendants, was decreed by God to be "childless" (Jer. 22:30). Actually Coniah had seven sons (perhaps adopted, 1 Chron. 3:17–18), though none occupied the throne.

Thus as far as a continuing dynasty was concerned, Coniah was "childless." His line did retain legal throne rights, which were claimed for Jesus through His legal father Joseph (Matt. 1:7, 12, 16).

Again it is important to remember that these promises were made unconditionally. Still some attempt to deny that it was unconditional, claiming that the covenant could be broken and citing the "if" (KJV) in 2 Samuel 7:14 and verses like 1 Kings 2:4; 8:25; 9:4–5; Isaiah 24:5; and Ezekiel 16:59. The resolution is simply this:

> The "breaking" or conditionality can only refer to *personal* and *individual* invalidation of the benefits of the covenant, but it cannot affect the transmission of the promise to the lineal descendants. This is why God would staunchly affirm His fidelity and the perpetuity of the covenant to David in spite of succeeding rascals who would appear in his lineage. For in that case, He "finds fault with them" but not with His Abrahamic-Davidic-New Covenant.[1]

II. OLD TESTAMENT CONFIRMATION OF THE COVENANT

Actually all Old Testament passages that describe the Messiah as King and His coming kingdom confirm the promises of the Davidic Covenant. All the royal psalms, for example, give more information about the Davidic kingdom (Pss. 2; 18; 20–21; 45; 72; 89; 101; 132; 144). Psalm 89:3–4, 19–37 provides strong confirmation of the immutability of the covenant. It seems almost as if God was anticipating the amillennial claim that the kingdom promise should be spiritualized into the church when He said that even though chastisement for sin would come, the covenant would not be broken or altered (vv. 32–34).

A number of passages in Isaiah also predict and describe the visible, earthly kingdom promised in the Davidic Covenant. Isaiah predicted the reign of Messiah "on the throne of David and over his kingdom" (9:7). In other places he described some of the characteristics of that kingdom (chaps. 11; 24–25; 54; 60–61).

Other significant Old Testament promises concerning the Davidic kingdom include Jeremiah 23:5–6; 30:8–9; 33:14–17, 20–21; Ezekiel 37:24–25; Daniel 7:13–14; Hosea 3:4–5; Amos 8:11; and Zechariah 14:4, 9.

III. NEW TESTAMENT CONFIRMATION OF THE COVENANT

The crucial question concerning the New Testament evidence about the kingdom is this: Did the teachings of Christ or the apostles in any way change or alter the Old Testament concept of an earthly kingdom? At the time of our Lord's first advent the national hope for a kingdom was exceedingly strong among the Jewish people. The terms "kingdom of God" and "kingdom of heaven" were on everyone's lips. The chief characteristics of this kingdom in the conception of the Jewish people were that it would be (a) earthly, (b) national, (c) messianic, (d) moral, and (e) future. This meant (a) on this earth, (b) specifically related to the nation Israel, (c) ruled by the personal presence of Messiah, (d) with high, God-given standards, and (e) not yet in existence. Did the teachings of the Lord or others change this conception?

A. In the Preaching of John the Baptist

His message was simplicity itself: "Repent, for the kingdom of heaven is at hand" (Matt. 3:1–2). His emphasis was on repentance and not on describing the kingdom, though his preaching confirmed the promises of the Davidic Covenant.

B. In the Preaching of Christ

Gabriel announced to Mary that God would give to her Child the throne of His father David and rulership over Israel forever (Luke 1:31–33). The magi sought the "King of the Jews" (Matt. 2:2). Our Lord proclaimed the kingdom was at hand (4:17, 23; 9:35). He insisted on righteousness for entrance into the kingdom (5:20). He also commissioned the seventy disciples with this same message (Luke 10:1–9).

However, as His message continued to be rejected by the people, and especially by their leaders, our Lord introduced the mysteries of the kingdom (Matt. 13). These described aspects of the kingdom not revealed up to that time, for they describe what form the kingdom would take between the first and second advents of Christ. Did this mean that the Davidic kingdom would take a new form with the church fulfilling the promises made to David? No, for the simple reason that the Lord continued to speak of the Davidic kingdom to the end of His earthly life (note esp. Matt. 25:34). Also, when the disciples questioned the Lord just before His ascension concerning when the kingdom promised to Israel (not to the church) would come, He did not tell them that the kingdom had been changed to the church, but only said that He could not reveal the time when the kingdom would come (Acts 1:6–8). In other words, whatever form the kingdom would take in the present age (i.e., the mysteries of the kingdom) would not change or abrogate the promises of the Davidic Covenant concerning the future, earthly kingdom.

Thus the teaching of the New Testament confirms the Davidic Covenant.

NOTE

1. Walter C. Kaiser, Jr., *Toward an Old Testament Theology* (Grand Rapids: Zondervan, 1978), 157.

Chapter 83
AN OUTLINE OF FUTURE EVENTS

This chapter will present an outline of future events according to the pretribulational premillennial understanding of the Scriptures. This will serve as a framework for further detailed discussions of selected future events.

I. EVENTS SURROUNDING THE END OF THE CHURCH AGE

A. Increasing Apostasy

The term "last days" covers the entire period from the first to the second advents of Christ (Heb. 1:2). Defection and apostasy, among other things, will characterize that entire period (2 Tim. 3:1). So the presence of apostasy is not in itself indicative of the end of the Church Age, but the increase of it is. Apostasy is both present and future, when the climactic apostasy will occur that leads to the religious reign of the man of sin during the Tribulation period (2 Thess. 2:3). We may expect apostasy to become increasingly widespread as we draw nearer to the Tribulation days.

1. The doctrinal characteristics of apostasy. These include at least three, including (a) a denial of the doctrine of the Trinity (1 John 2:22–23); (b) a denial of the doctrine of the Incarnation of Christ (1 John 2:22; 4:3; 2 John 7). In John's day this took the form of denying the true and real humanity of Christ, though it also takes the form of denying the true deity of Christ. Rejecting either the Trinity or the Incarnation denies the existence of the God-man, which is essential to our salvation. If Jesus Christ were not a man, He could not have died; but if He were not also God, that death could not atone for sins. The third point is (c) a denial of the doctrine of the return of Christ (2 Pet. 3:4).

2. The lifestyle characteristics of apostasy. Defection in doctrine always brings a decline in morals. Paul listed eighteen characteristics of such declension in 2 Timothy 3:1–5. They are love of self, love of money, a spirit of pride, blasphemy, disobedience to parents, lack of thankfulness, lack of holiness, lack of natural affection, unceasing enmity so that men cannot be persuaded to enter into treaties with each other, slander, lack of self-control, savagery, opposition to goodness, traitors, headiness (rashness or recklessness), high-mindedness, love of pleasure, a pretense of worship without godliness of life.

B. Preparation for the Ecumenical Church

During the first part of the Tribulation days, organized, ecumenical religion will have its heyday. This apostate religious system is described in Revelation 17 under the label "Mystery, Babylon" (KJV). It will be worldwide (v. 15), be unfaithful to the truth and to the Lord (the term "harlot" appears in vv. 1, 5, 15–16), have extensive political clout (vv. 12–13), have a "gold cup full of abominations," that is, be inwardly corrupt while outwardly glorious and splendid (v. 4), and will persecute the saints of the Tribulation days (v. 6).

The groundwork for such a system will apparently have to be laid before the Tribulation begins, that is, during the closing years of the Church Age. The preparation will likely include both organizational moves toward unity in Christendom as well as the ascendancy of doctrines to which diverse groups can give support.

II. THE RAPTURE OF THE CHURCH

A. The Concept of the Rapture

Our modern understanding of rapture appears to have little or no connection with the eschatological event. However, the word is properly used of that event. *Rapture* is a state or experience of being carried away. The English word comes from a Latin word, *rapio,* which means to seize or snatch in relation to an ecstasy of spirit or the actual removal from one place to another. In other words, it means to be carried away in spirit or in body. The Rapture of the church means the carrying away of the church from earth to heaven.

The Greek word from which we take the term "rapture" appears in 1 Thessalonians 4:17, translated "caught up." The Latin translation of this verse used the word *rapturo*. The Greek word it translates is *harpazō,* which means to snatch or take away. Elsewhere it is used to describe how the Spirit caught up Philip near Gaza and brought him to Caesarea (Acts 8:39) and to describe Paul's experience of being caught up into the third heaven (2 Cor. 12:2–4). Thus there can be no doubt that the word is used in 1 Thessalonians 4:17 to indicate the actual removal of people from earth to heaven.

B. The Components of the Rapture (1 Thess. 4:13–18)

1. The return of Christ (v. 16). The Lord Himself will return for His people, accompanied by all the grandeur His presence deserves. There will be a shout of command (whether uttered by the Lord or an archangel is not stated), and the trumpet of God will summon the dead in Christ to their resurrection as well as sounding a warning to those who have rejected Him and thus have missed the Rapture.

2. A resurrection (v. 16). At this time only the dead in Christ will be raised. This means believers since the Day of Pentecost, for though there were believers before then, none of them were placed "in Christ." The dead in Christ will be raised just before the living are changed. Yet both groups will experience their respective changes "in a moment, in the twinkling of an eye" (1 Cor. 15:52). The entire procedure will be instantaneous, not gradual. The word for "moment" is the word from which the word "atom" comes. When the atom was discovered it was thought to be indivisible; therefore, it was named "atom." Even though subsequently the atom was split, the word retains its meaning of indivisible. The resurrection of the dead and the translation of the living will occur in an indivisible instant of time.

3. A rapture (v. 17). Strictly speaking, only living believers are raptured (though we use the term to include all that happens at that time). This means they will be caught up into the Lord's presence without having to experience physical death.

4. A reunion (v. 17). The reunion will be with the Lord and with the loved ones who have died.

5. A reassurance (v. 18). The truth of the Rapture both comforts and encourages us (for the word does have both meanings).

Paul's descriptions of the Rapture in both 1 Corinthians 15:51–58 and 1 Thessalonians 4:13–18 give no support to the partial Rapture view, which teaches that only spiritual believers will be raptured at several times during the Tribulation period. Paul stated clearly that "we shall be changed" at that time, and he wrote those words to the Corinthians, many of whom could hardly be called spiritual.

III. EVENTS OF THE TRIBULATION PERIOD

Since the Scriptures describe so many events during the seven years of Tribulation, and since I would like to try to put them all together in as nearly a chronological sequence as possible, I think it would be best to do this in the following chapter.

IV. EVENTS AT THE SECOND COMING OF CHRIST

A. The Second Coming

At the climax of the campaign of Armageddon, the Lord will return to this earth to judge and to reign. His return is described in Zechariah 14:1–11 and Revelation 19:11–16. It is referred to in many other passages, but these two give the most detailed description of it.

B. The Judgments at the Second Coming

These will be discussed in a separate chapter.

V. THE MILLENNIUM

Since the Scriptures give many details about the future millennial kingdom of Christ, I would like to devote a separate chapter to the Millennium and to the events at the end of it.

Chapter 84
The Tribulation Period

I. ITS UNIQUENESS

In describing the period of the Great Tribulation, the Lord said it will be a time "such as has not occurred since the beginning of the world until now, nor ever shall" (Matt. 24:21). It will be a time of trouble unique in the history of the world. There have been many difficult times since the Lord spoke these words, and He Himself warned the disciples, "In the world you have tribulation" (John 16:33). What is it, then, that makes this future period different? How will the Great Tribulation be unique?

Two characteristics will distinguish the Tribulation from all other hard times that the world has seen. First, it will be worldwide, not localized, as stated in the promise of deliverance (Rev. 3:10) and as described in detail in the judgments of the Revelation. The intense local persecutions and calamities of this present day cannot be the beginning of the Tribulation, for that time will affect *the entire world.*

Then too the Tribulation will be unique because of the way men act. In one of the early judgments, men will hide themselves in the dens and caves of the mountains and say, "Fall on us and hide us from the presence of Him who sits on the throne, and from the wrath of the Lamb" (Rev. 6:16). When the Great Tribulation comes, men will act as if they think the world is coming to an end.

For years some men have been talking as if they *thought* the end were near, but at the beginning of the Tribulation, they will *realize* that the end is actually at hand. Scientists, politicians, and even church leaders warn today that the end of human history could be upon us, and even use the term "Armageddon," but people are not behaving as if they believe it. Real estate is being bought and sold, savings are being accumulated, and plans are continually being made for the future. But when the Tribulation comes, people will hide in bomb shelters and will actually seek death rather than try to preserve life. The future, in those days, will hold no attraction.

The uniqueness of the Tribulation lies in its being worldwide and in its terror, which will cause people to want to die rather than live. For a time during the Tribulation, even suicide will be impossible, forcing people to live.

II. THE BEGINNING OF THE TRIBULATION

The Tribulation does not necessarily begin the day the church is taken to meet the Lord in the air. Though I believe that the Rapture precedes the beginning of the Tribulation, nothing is said in the Scriptures as to whether or not some time (or how much time) may elapse between the Rapture and the beginning of the Tribulation.

The Tribulation actually begins with the signing of a covenant between the leader of the "Federated States of Europe" and the Jewish people. This treaty will set in motion the events of the seventieth week (or seven years) of Daniel's prophecy. There is an interval of undetermined length between the first sixty-nine weeks of seven years each and the last or seventieth week of seven years.

We are living in that interval. It is the time in which God is forming the church, the body of Christ, by saving Jews and Gentiles alike. Since God has not yet finished this present program, the last week of the seventy has not yet begun. When it does, God will once again turn His attention in a special way to His people the Jews and to His holy city Jerusalem, as outlined in Daniel 9:24.

When this last period of seven years begins, "He will make a firm covenant with the many for one week" (v. 27). Who does the "he" refer to? Grammatically it could refer either to Messiah (v. 26) or to "the prince who is to come," who will probably be related to the people who destroyed Jerusalem in A.D. 70. The latter view is better, because usually the antecedent nearer to a pronoun is preferred and in this case it is the prince, not Messiah. Then too nothing in the record of Christ's life in any way connects Him with the making (and later breaking) of a seven-year covenant with the Jewish people.

This man is the "little horn" (Dan. 7:8, 24–25) who heads the coalition of Western nations in the Tribulation days. He is also called the "man of lawlessness" (2 Thess. 2:3) and is referred to as the beast (Rev. 11:7; 13:1; 17:11; 19:20). At the beginning of the Tribulation he will make a covenant, or enter a league, with Israel. This treaty will align the West with the Jewish nation and will guarantee protection to Israel so that she may reestablish the ancient rituals of Judaism. It appears that this provision will also assure protection while Israel rebuilds the temple in Jerusalem as the center of her religious observances. Since we know that the covenant will be broken and the man of sin will be worshiped in the temple of God, obviously a temple will have been already built during the first part of the Tribulation (2 Thess. 2:4).

The alignment of western Europe with Israel is interesting in the light of current events. It seems to indicate that Israel will not of herself be sufficiently strong to feel secure in the face of the hostile states around her. She will not be able to "go it alone" at this point, and so will form an alliance with the Western nations. Then the outlook for Israel will seem bright. She will feel secure in her land, she will be worshiping according to the Old Testament pattern, she will have a temple again in Jerusalem, and she will be important among the nations of the world. But this is only the beginning.

III. THE JUDGMENTS OF THE SEALS, TRUMPETS, AND BOWLS

A. The Sequence

Revelation 6–19 describes the Tribulation in detail. We read here about three series of judgments. The first series is related to the opening of the seven seals of a scroll, the second to the blowing of seven trumpets, and the third to the pouring out of the contents of seven bowls.

Do these three series of judgments follow each other in succession, or do the trumpets and the bowls recapitulate the judgments of the seals with greater intensity? In other words, do the trumpet and bowl judgments follow the seals as different and distinct judgments, or do they picture the same judgments?

I believe the three series follow one another in chronological sequence and that there is no recapitulation. Either way, however, the seal judgments are the first judgments of the Tribulation days and will probably occur during the first year of that period.

B. The Seals

1. The first seal judgment (Rev. 6:1–2). The opening of the first seal revealed to John a white horse ridden by one who went forth conquering. In interpreting the Revelation, always begin with what is the clearest. Here, it is quite obvious that the opening months of the Tribulation will see nations conquered by the rider on the horse. Some think this rider is the man of sin, the head of the Western coalition of nations. His method of conquest, however, we would call "cold" war. Clearly, this description coincides exactly with the picture of the beginning of the Tribulation given in 1 Thessalonians 5:3—it will be a day when men are talking about peace and safety. This may indicate that we are living in the days immediately preceding the Tribulation—but, on the other hand, there is nothing in the Word of God that would indicate that there could not be another world war in this present age, then *another* time of peace before the Lord comes. Other evangelical scholars agree that the first rider simply represents the spirit of conquest—an attitude that has characterized the nations throughout human history. Doubtless this spirit will be intensified as the end approaches.

2. *The second seal judgment* (Rev. 6:3–4). In the judgment of the second seal, peace will be removed from the earth and men will war with each other. The phrase, "a great sword was given him," confirms this interpretation. The red color of the second horse suggests bloodshed. War has always followed the spirit of conquest.

3. *The third seal judgment* (Rev. 6:5–6). The third judgment (still probably in the first year of the Tribulation) brings famine to the world. A black horse pictures this event, and the pair of scales carried by his rider bespeaks a careful rationing of food. The Roman denarius (v. 6) was a day's wages in Palestine in Jesus' day (Matt. 20:2). Normally it would buy ten quarts of wheat or thirty of barley. Under the famine conditions of these coming days, a day's wage will buy only one measure of wheat or three of barley—one tenth the normal supply of food. However, there is an ironic twist to this famine. Oil and wine, the very things a majority of people cannot afford, will not be in short supply. The scarcity of basic foods and the availability of luxury items will taunt the common people in their impoverished state.

4. *The fourth seal judgment* (Rev. 6:7–8). This horse will be, literally, a yellowish green. He is the only horseman who is named, and he is called Death. Death, of course, claims the physical part of man, and it is accompanied by Hades, the place of the dead (v. 8), which claims the immaterial part. The effect of this judgment will be devastating—one fourth of earth's population will be killed by the sword (war), by hunger (the famine that often accompanies war), by death (perhaps by the plagues and diseases that follow war), and by wild beasts of the earth, which apparently will be unrestrained at this time and will roam about freely, killing men. Man's cleverly devised schemes for bringing in peace, plenty, and longevity will be overturned in the short space of time this judgment will take.

5. *The fifth seal judgment* (Rev. 6:9–11). Though the action of the fifth

seal is in heaven, it presupposes that certain events have happened on earth. The group of martyrs in heaven (v. 9) implies that these people have already been killed on earth, early in the Tribulation. These people will be witnessing for Christ early in the Tribulation. They will be slain because of their testimony.

6. The sixth seal judgment (Rev. 6:12–17). This judgment unleashes universal havoc on the earth. It will include six catastrophic events: (1) A single great earthquake will take place. (2) The sun will be darkened so that it becomes black as sackcloth. The text does not say that the sun will be turned into sackcloth, but that it will be blackened as sackcloth. (3) The moon will become as red as blood. (4) There will be a meteor shower, with all the natural devastating consequences that follow. (5) Apparently heaven will be opened for a moment so that the men on earth can have a glimpse of that awesome scene, with God on His throne. (6) Every mountain and island will be moved.

These judgments will produce terror in the hearts of all living men. Their hearts will be filled with fear—not primarily because of the physical disturbances or the awful wars and pestilences, but because they will see God on His throne. Men will plead to be hidden "from the presence of Him who sits on the throne, and from the wrath of the Lamb" (v. 16). They will go to any length to avoid facing their Creator and Judge, even to seeking death under the rocks and mountains in which they will try to hide. All classes of people (v. 15) will be affected. As has been true throughout history, there will be no *general* or mass turning to God in repentance, but only a turning *from* God's face.

These will be the first judgments of the Tribulation. But these will be only the beginning—the worst is yet to come.

IV. THE REDEEMED OF THE TRIBULATION

By the time of the fifth seal a number of true believers will have been martyred. In other words, during the first years of the Tribulation there will be a true witness to the Gospel, and this will be opposed by the ecumenical church, which will be "drunk with the blood of the saints, and with the blood of the witnesses of Jesus" (17:6). In the name of religion, the organized church of the first part of the Tribulation will kill true believers for their faith.

How will these true believers have been converted in the first place? With the Rapture of the church, all Christians will have been removed from earth, so none will be alive immediately after the Rapture. If there are to be martyrs, there must first be believers. How will men be saved? In Revelation 7:1–8, we are introduced to a sort of parenthesis in judgment. Even the wind does not blow. (Incidentally, can you imagine the effect on climate of the cessation of the wind even for a short time? Add the disturbance in the topography of the earth, with the shifting of islands and mountains, and you can begin to grasp the increased chaos during these early years of the Tribulation.)

The purpose of this suspension of judgment is that a certain group of people may be "sealed" (v. 3). These people are called "the bond-servants of our God." Who they are is described in detail in verses 4–8. They are Jews from each of the twelve tribes, and they do some particular service for God. Whether the seal placed on them is a visible mark or characteristic of some kind is neither stated nor implied in the text. A seal need not be visible to be real (Eph. 4:30). It is principally a guarantee of ownership and security. Both these ideas are involved in the sealing of this group. These people are owned by God, which means that they are redeemed. They are kept secure by God, which may mean He protects them from their enemies on earth while they complete their service for Him.

But how were these people saved? Even though there will be no Christians on earth immediately after the Rapture, there will be Bibles and books about the Christian faith. In other words, information will be available to give people the facts on which to find saving faith.

What will be the important work for which God will protect these people supernaturally? Actually, this passage does not specify, but we have hints as to the answer in Revelation 14, where the same group is described as in heaven after their work has been completed. They are said to be the redeemed followers of the Lamb, which may indicate that they are a group of special witnesses to the Gospel in the Tribulation days. They will not be the only ones witnessing, but they will be the only group given special protection from their enemies.

The first judgments of the Tribulation and the religious situation in the first part of that period are repeated, in summary form, in the Lord's Olivet discourse (Matt. 24). Verses 4–14 cover the events of the first half of the Tribulation, for at verse 15 we read about an event that occurs exactly halfway through the seven-year period. Notice how the seal judgments are summarized: "And you will be hearing of wars and rumors of wars. . . . For nation will rise against nation, and kingdom against kingdom, and in various places there will be famines and earthquakes" (vv. 6–7). Notice the reference to the martyrs of the fifth seal: "Then they will deliver you to tribulation, and will kill you"

(v. 9). Look at the false religion: "And many false prophets will arise, and will mislead many" (v. 11). The ministry of the 144,000 sealed ones, and other witnesses, will account for the fact that "this gospel of the kingdom shall be preached in the whole world for a witness to all the nations" (v. 14). Here are all the major events of the first half of the Tribulation, in capsule form, from Christ's lips before the Crucifixion.

V. EGYPT AND RUSSIA IN THE TRIBULATION

So far we have focused our attention chiefly on the Western federation of nations, headed by the man of sin. But during the first part of the Tribulation other powerful alliances will exist or be in the making. Egypt, to the south of Palestine, will continue to be a strong and threatening nation until the man of sin conquers her. This defeat is predicted in Daniel 11:40–43, and though scholars do not agree as to when this will occur, it seems to be no later than the middle of the Tribulation.

So we can expect to see Egypt remain a power to be reckoned with until about three years of the Tribulation have elapsed. Then, she will be defeated and looted by Antichrist and his army. Egypt does not figure in any of the power blocs or wars of the last half of the Tribulation.

The nations of the East will be forming some sort of coalition and will not actively take part in any of the events involving Palestine until the very end of the Tribulation. All trends among Eastern nations toward independence and detachment from Western influence are significant. They may be preparatory to the alliance that those nations will form.

By far the most important bloc, besides the Western confederation of nations, is that of Gog and Magog. The names listed in Ezekiel 38–39 are identified in Genesis 10:2 as sons of Japheth. The Japhethites migrated, after the Flood, from Asia Minor to the north, beyond the Caspian and Black Seas. They settled in the area occupied today by Russia, Ukraine, and Kazakhstan. "Gog" and "Magog," therefore, may refer to the people who live in the area north of Palestine. She will have with her as allies Persia (modern Iran), Ethiopia (northern Sudan), Put (Libya), Gomer (probably the eastern part of Turkey and the Ukraine), and Togarmah (the part of Turkey near the Syrian border) (Ezek. 38:5–6). The West will lodge a protest (v. 13), but to no avail, and this invading army from the north will cover Israel like a cloud (v. 16). These soldiers will go to rob and plunder the land that thought it was safe under the protection of the West.

At this point God will step in and utterly destroy the forces of Russia and her allies (Ezek. 38:21–39:7). The seemingly invincible troops will be supernaturally defeated and completely routed. The Russian army will be buried in Israel (v. 11), and only then will Russian influence in the Middle East be ended—by the direct intervention of God.

VI. THE PROGRAM OF ANTICHRIST

The Scriptures often divide the seven years of the Tribulation into two equal parts. The last of Daniel's seventy "weeks" of seven years is divided in the middle by a significant event (Dan. 9:27). In Revelation the two halves of the Tribulation are designated either by "time and times and half a time" (Rev. 12:14), or "forty-two months" (11:2; 13:5), or 1,260 days (11:3; 12:6), each of which works out to three and one half years.

With the invasion of Palestine from the north by Gog and Magog, it may seem for a time that the plans of the man of sin (Antichrist) are almost crushed. But supernatural intervention by God and the destruction of the Russian hordes will clear the way for the beast to resume his scheming.

A. Slaying the Two Witnesses

First, Antichrist must eliminate opposition from two individuals (Rev. 11:3–13) who have been plaguing him. The killing of these "two witnesses" will be the beast's first great feat at the middle of the Tribulation.

The two witnesses will have a spectacular ministry during the first part of the Tribulation. They will have power to kill their enemies with fire, to prevent rain, to turn water to blood, and to bring plagues on the earth as often as they wish. Their frequent use of these powers will add to the general devastation. Think, for instance, what will happen when they use their power to prevent rain. Along with the climatic and topographical changes that will occur on earth, unimaginable disaster will result.

Though the witnesses will be invincible for three and a half years, God will permit the beast to kill them after they have finished their work (Rev. 11:7). Making martyrs of the witnesses will win Antichrist wide support among the people of the world. But he will not be satisfied with merely killing them; he will display their bodies in the streets of Jerusalem. People, seeing the witnesses dead, will rejoice that they will no longer have to hear their warnings.

Merely to look on the decaying bodies of these two men will not satisfy people. They will make a great holiday of the occasion and will send gifts to each other. Interestingly enough, this is the only occasion, during the entire Tribulation period, in which rejoicing is mentioned. People will be so overjoyed that the witnesses are dead that this will be a happy holiday for them. If they had believed the witnesses' preaching, their deaths would have been a sad occasion instead of a holiday.

But God will intervene. After three and a half days, the bodies of the two witnesses will be resurrected and translated into heaven in a cloud of glory. Imagine the scene. Long lines will be waiting to view the corpses. Perhaps TV cameras will be focusing on them at the very moment of their resurrection. People in Europe and America will be watching via satellite transmission. The calm, matter-of-fact announcer will suddenly become nearly hysterical as he sees a resurrection in process and realizes that millions of people are depending on him for an explanation. How will the interpreters of the news manage this one? Even the voice from heaven (v. 12) will be heard in millions of homes.

But even before the newspapers can report the story or the commentators write their analyses, there will be another great event for them to cover, an earthquake that will center in Jerusalem and that will destroy a tenth part of the city, killing seven thousand people.

At this time, apparently, the 144,000 witnesses (Rev. 7) will also be killed, and the beast will destroy the ecumenical church (17:16) to clear away opposition to his next great act.

B. Demanding Worship

Having rid himself of all religious opposition, the beast will issue an edict: "Worship me." To enforce his command he will have to break his treaty with the Jews, which allowed them to restore Jewish worship in their rebuilt temple at Jerusalem. This he will do (Dan. 9:27), demanding that he be the object of all worship (Matt. 24:15; 2 Thess. 2:4).

How will he accomplish this?

First of all, he will have superhuman help. Satan, we are told, will give him his power and throne and great authority (Rev. 13:2). The devil will work furiously, from this point on, to do everything in his power to thwart God's plans. He will make war with Michael and his angels—and lose. This will result in his being cast out of heaven. Then

God will warn the inhabitants of the earth, "Woe . . . because the devil has come down to you, having great wrath, knowing that he has only a short time" (12:12). The power of Satan will be behind the acts of the beast, Antichrist, and he will use him to the full.

Another reason for the beast's greatness involves his being wounded unto death. His deadly wound will be healed (Rev. 13:3), so that all the world will wonder. The phrase, "wounded to death" (KJV), literally means, "as having been slain to death," and it is exactly the same phrase as is used in 5:6 in reference to the death of Christ.

Since Christ actually died, perhaps the beast also will actually die and then be restored to life. He is said to rise out of the abyss (Rev. 11:7), which seems to confirm the idea that he experiences a resurrection. If not, the text at least means he will have some kind of spectacular restoration so that the world will wonder after him. His miraculous resurrection or restoration will make all men acknowledge his uniqueness ("Who is like the beast?") and his might ("Who is able to wage war with him?") (13:4).

The beast's program will include blasphemy and war (Rev. 13:5–7). He will speak insolently against God (Dan. 7:25). Objects of his blasphemy will include the name of God, the dwelling place of God, and those who dwell in heaven. He will be allowed (notice that God is still in control) to make war with the saints (Rev. 12:17) and to kill them. But his power will be limited by God to forty-two months.

Here is an example of the interweaving of the many forces behind events: God will control all, but Satan will empower the beast, who in turn will act on his own in blaspheming God. Men who join his army and fight for him will do so voluntarily, and they in turn will make martyrs of God's people who, though they are killed, will still be within God's protecting care!

In order to promote his program more efficiently, Antichrist will have an important lieutenant. He is the "second beast" (Rev. 13:11–18), and his sole duty is to promote the purposes and expedite the worship of the first beast, the man of sin. At no time in his career does the second beast promote himself, but his concerns are always centered in the first beast. His power will be as great as that of the man of sin, but he will use it in the interests of his superior, not for himself (v. 12).

This lieutenant will be able to make fire come down on the earth, duplicating the power of the two witnesses in order to show the world that he is as great as they were (v. 13). He will be able to work other miracles (vv. 13–14). He will order men to make an image of the first beast (v. 14), and apparently they will do it willingly and quickly. His next step will be to give life to the image they have made. The word for "breath" (v. 15) is *pneuma,* and this could indicate a supernatural miracle (empowered by Satan) that will actually give life to the image. Of course, the word may be translated "wind," which may indicate some magical sleight of hand, on the part of the lieutenant, to give the image the appearance of real life. The speech and movement of an image could easily be artificial, but they could with equal ease be the work of Satan.

C. Controlling Commerce

However, the greatest feat of the second beast, who is sometimes called "the false prophet" (Rev. 16:13; 19:20; 20:10), will be a squeeze play on men to force them to worship the man of sin. It will be a simple scheme, cleverly devised: "And he causes all, the small and the great, and the rich and the poor, and the free men and the slaves, to be given a mark on their right hand, or on their forehead, and he provides that no one should be able to buy or to sell, except the one who has the mark, either the name of the beast or the number of his name" (13:16–17). In other words: bow or starve.

A "mark" is an impression made by a stamp, such as a brand used on slaves and animals. Men will become slaves of the man of sin and will have to bear the identifying mark of their slavery. Perhaps timid slaves will have the mark placed in their right hands. To avoid embarrassment, they may try to avoid shaking hands with people in order to conceal the mark. Bold followers of Antichrist may have the mark placed in the middle of their foreheads.

What will this mark be like? Verse 17 indicates that it will be either the name of the beast or his number, and the number is further explained as 666, the number of the man of sin, *not* of his lieutenant. This number has been linked to so many personages as to make them all unreliable coincidences. When this great ruler comes to power, however, there will be no mistake as to who he is. In some way unknown to us now, the number 666 will play a principal part in his identification (16:1–3; 19:20; 20:10).

This will be a grim time in the history of the world. I suppose that Antichrist would succeed completely in bringing the entire world to his feet were it not for the presence of the godly remnant, who will refuse to bow, and for the shortness of the time available to him.

VII. THE TRUMPET AND BOWL JUDGMENTS

A. The Trumpets

In the meantime, God will continue to pour out the judgments of His wrath on the earth. The first series of judgments will be unleashed as the seals of a book are opened. We have already seen what will happen as the first six seals are broken. With the opening of the seventh seal (Rev. 8:1), one would expect a holocaust to let loose. Instead, there is silence—the still silence of expectancy and foreboding. The silence will last for half an hour and will be awesome. The opening of this seventh seal introduces another series of judgments, which are announced by the blowing of seven trumpets (8:7–9:21; 11:15–19). The last three of the seven trumpet judgments are distinguished from the first four by being specially designated as "woes," which seems to imply that they are of harsher character.

Where is the middle (three-and-a-half-year) point of the Tribulation in relation to these judgments? The Scriptures do not specifically say, but many feel that the middle point comes either with the first trumpet judgment or with the first woe judgment (which is the fifth trumpet judgment). If this is so, the first trumpet judgment comes when Antichrist kills the two witnesses and sets himself up to be worshiped. The trumpet judgments seem to continue on into the last year of the period. They are followed by a final rapid series of further judgments in the last months of the seventh year.

1. The first trumpet judgment (Rev. 8:7). There will be hail and fire, mingled with blood, on the earth so that a third part of the earth, trees, and grass will be burned. Fire and blood, here, are not symbols of something else. We are to take them literally. They will devastate vegetation on the earth and further add to the climatic disruptions.

2. The second trumpet judgment (Rev. 8:8–9). This is explained with a figure of speech—"something like a great mountain burning with fire." Probably nothing in the realm of our present experience corresponds to this. It will likely be something about which we do not yet know anything, but its effect is clear—a third part of the sea will become blood, and a third part of the world's shipping will be destroyed. Think of how this judgment will affect the headlines in the papers and the hearts of the people.

3. The third trumpet judgment (Rev. 8:10–11). This judgment will affect the supply of fresh water, making it bitter to the taste and polluting to the system. As a result, many will die from the contamination and pollution.

4. The fourth trumpet judgment (Rev. 8:12–13). This judgment will affect the sun, moon, stars, and the uniformity of the day-night cycle. Since one third of the heavenly bodies will be smitten, perhaps the twenty-four hour cycle of day and night will be shortened to sixteen hours. The Lord Jesus predicted, in His Olivet discourse, "signs in sun and moon and stars" (Luke 21:25).

5. The first woe—the fifth trumpet judgment (Rev. 9:1–12). Like arrows from a bow, the locusts of this first woe judgment will be discharged on the earth. They originate from the bottomless pit—literally, from the "shaft of the abyss." This pit, entered by a shaft, is under lock and key. Incidentally, chapter 9 contains more occurrences of the words "as" and "like" than any other chapter in the Bible. It was difficult for John to describe what he saw in the vision. Nevertheless, the horror of the judgment is clear.

From the shaft will come "locusts" (Rev. 9:3–11) that are no ordinary insects. They will come straight from Satan's domain. They seem to be animal creatures *like* locusts, but they are demonic in nature. Perhaps they are demons who take on the form of these unique locusts and who are directed by the king of the shaft of the abyss (v. 11).

These locusts inflict a sting like a scorpion's. "The pain from the sting of a scorpion, though not generally fatal, is perhaps, the most intense that any animal can inflict upon the human body. The insect itself is the most irascible and malignant that lives, and its poison is like itself. . . . It is also difficult to guard against them [the locusts], if they can be warded off at all, because they fly where they please, dart through the air, and dwell in darkness."[1] Unlike ordinary locusts, these creatures will not attack vegetation, but only men. They will be released for five months, during which time men will be unable to commit suicide. This seems impossible, but somehow it will be so.

It is difficult for us to imagine such creatures, but this is no reason for thinking they are mere symbols. Remember that the power of Satan and his demons is great—and these ferocious locusts are demonic. Little wonder that this is called the first *woe*. Since men do not believe in or accept the existence and activity of demons, people then alive will probably try to give some natural explanation for these creatures and will try to destroy them with a hastily concocted pesticide. But they will find no explanation, and their antidotes will not work.

6. The second woe—the sixth trumpet judgment (Rev. 9:13–21). Under the fourth seal judgment, one fourth of the earth's population will be killed; under the sixth trumpet judgment, an additional one third will die. This means that these two judgments alone will reduce the population of the earth by one half. Add to this all those who will be killed through war, famine, and disease, and it is not difficult to see how common death will be during this awful time.

The means of this judgment will be an army of horsemen numbering 200 million. Many understand these troops to be the armies of the Orient as they march to invade Palestine. Others see them as a horde of demons, for Scriptures give other examples of supernatural armies (2 Kings 2:11; 6:13–17; Rev. 19:14). The weapons of destruction here will be fire, smoke, and brimstone (Rev. 9:17). Since these are weapons of hell, they perhaps indicate that this army is made up of demons, the inhabitants of hell.

One would think that the long obituary columns in the newspapers would startle men into facing their responsibility toward God. Instead of repenting and turning to Him for mercy, however, those who are not killed by this army will harden their hearts. The religion of unsaved men during the Tribulation will be the worship of demons and idols, and murder, sorcery, fornication, and stealing will be common (vv. 20–21). Sorcery may include the misuse of drugs, for we derive the word *pharmacy* from the Greek term. It is interesting to notice that three of these four practices are direct violations of the Ten Commandments. Man's ethics will be a reflection of his religion, and during those days vice, rather than virtue, will reign triumphant.

7. The third woe—the seventh trumpet judgment (Rev. 11:15–19). With the sounding of the seventh trumpet will come the announcement that the end is at hand, though seven other judgments must be poured on the earth before all will be finished. These judgments will be the bowls of the wrath of God (16:1–21). These last plagues will come in the closing months, or possibly even weeks, of the last year of the Tribulation, without interruption or pause. The seven angels that have to do with these last judgments will all be told to pour out their judgments at one time. All this will be happening at the same time that Antichrist demands that men worship him. Men will be pressured from every side. Most will decide to cast their lot with Antichrist.

B. The Bowls

1. The first bowl judgment (Rev. 16:2). This will bring on men a grievous sore described as "loathsome and malignant." These words could indicate some sort of cancer. This affliction will come only on those who worship the beast, believers being exempt. But apparently the beast will be able to do nothing for his followers, for they will continue to curse God for these sores even after the fifth bowl has been poured out (v. 11).

2. The second bowl judgment (Rev. 16:3). The waters will turn into blood during this judgment. Every living thing in the sea will die. The rather vivid phrase pictures ships wallowing in blood. Under the second trumpet judgment, a third of the sea creatures die (8:9); now the destruction of marine life will be total. Can you imagine the stench and disease this will bring to people who live along the seashores of the world? Seventy-two percent of earth's surface is water.

3. The third bowl judgment (Rev. 16:4–7). At this time, as in the third trumpet judgment, the fresh-water supply is affected. Now, instead of wormwood, it turns to blood. The victims of this plague will experience inexorable retribution. They will have shed the blood of the saints and prophets, so now they will have to drink blood. They will deserve what they receive. It is not easy for us to conceive of God dealing with people in this manner. For thousands of years He has been long-suffering and gracious, not dispensing the kind of judgment the world deserves.

4. The fourth bowl judgment (Rev. 16:8–9). During this time the strength of the sun will be so heightened that it will scorch men with intense heat. Once again, men will harden their hearts instead of turning to God in repentance.

5. The fifth bowl judgment (Rev. 16:10–11). The throne of the beast will be affected, and his capital will be darkened. This will likely slow down his attempt to force all men to worship him. The result will be that men will gnaw their tongues and blaspheme God for their pains and sores, for pain always seems worse in darkness than in the light.

6. The sixth bowl judgment (Rev. 16:12–16). The Euphrates River will dry up (it was previously turned into blood). This will facilitate the crossing of the river by the armies of the kings of the East (Dan. 11:44) as they rush to the war of Armageddon.

7. The seventh bowl judgment (Rev. 16:17–21). Widespread destruction and havoc will occur, and with it will be heard the cry, "It is done!" Many physical disturbances will follow. An earthquake will divide Jerusalem and cause other cities to fall. Islands and mountains will disappear, and there will be an unheard-of storm in which single hailstones will weigh one hundred pounds. But in spite of the severity and universality of these last judgments, men who survive them will persist in blaspheming God rather than turning to Him for mercy. Everything that man has built in this world will literally collapse before his very eyes, yet he will think he is still the master of his fate and that he has no need for God.

The conclusion of this judgment will bring men to the end of the Tribulation and to the second coming of Christ to begin His reign over earth. Only one more part of the picture remains to be completed.

VIII. ARMAGEDDON

To review: Before the middle of the Tribulation, the Western ruler, Antichrist (the man of sin), keeping his treaty with Israel, will invade and conquer Egypt. At that point the Russian armies from the north will invade and overrun Palestine, and when all appears hopeless for both Antichrist and Israel, God will step in and supernaturally destroy Russia's northern armies. This will give the man of sin a free hand to break his covenant with Israel, set himself up to be worshiped, and try to conquer the world.

As he proceeds with his program, however, the nations of the Orient will unite and attempt to stop him. To do this, they will march west into Palestine. The sixth bowl judgment will dry up the Euphrates River, speeding their entry into the Promised Land. In the meantime, Antichrist will have planted himself firmly in Palestine as a religious and political ruler.

The battlefield in which the armies from East and West will meet will be the Plain of Esdraelon, the area around the mountains of Megiddo. That's why the battle is called Armageddon—*Ar* meaning mountain. This plain is about twenty miles south-southeast of Haifa, and the valley today is about twenty miles by fourteen.

Another battlefield will focus on Jerusalem, where there will be house-to-house fighting and temporary success for the enemies of the Lord. But the Lord will send a plague and then stand on the Mount of Olives and "destroy all the nations that come against Jerusalem" (Zech. 12:9; 14:12; 14:4; 12:9).

At the second coming of Christ still another area of conflict will center in Bozra in Edom, which is about twenty miles southeast of the southern tip of the Dead Sea (Isa. 63:1–6). Viewing these three areas of the war together, we see a gruesome picture of unbelievable carnage encompassing the entire land from Megiddo in the north, Jerusalem in the center, and Edom in the southeast (about 140 miles).

In the midst of the battle, the Lord Jesus Christ will return, and the armies of heaven will conquer the armies of earth (Rev. 19:11–21). The carnage will be unbelievable (14:20; 19:17–18).

But the outcome is certain—the beast will be defeated and his armies captured. He and his false prophet-lieutenant will be thrown into the lake of fire to be tormented forever. Thus the Tribulation will close.

Why must there be such a time as this? There are at least two reasons: First, the wickedness of man must be punished. God may seem to be doing nothing about evil now, but someday He will act. A second reason is that man must, by one means or another, be prostrated before the King of kings and Lord of lords. He may do so voluntarily now by coming to Christ in faith and receiving salvation. Later he will *have* to do so, receiving only condemnation.

NOTE

1. J. A. Seiss, *The Apocalypse* (New York: Cook, 1865), 83.

Chapter 85
The Rapture of the Church

I. DEFINITION AND DESCRIPTION OF THE RAPTURE

As explained in chapter 83, the word "rapture" comes from the Latin translation of the Greek for "caught up" in 1 Thessalonians 4:17. Strictly speaking, in this text it relates only to the change in living believers at the time of Christ's return. However, the label, Rapture, usually refers both to the translation of living believers from earthly mortality to heavenly immortality and to the resurrection of the corrupted bodies of believers to heavenly incorruption.

Three passages describe the Rapture: John 14:1–3; 1 Corinthians 15:50–58; and 1 Thessalonians 4:13–18. The facets of the Rapture have been discussed in chapter 83.

II. VARIOUS VIEWS

In the nineteenth century, teaching concerning the Rapture of the church began to be widely disseminated. This raised such questions as whether the second coming of Christ involves several stages, the relation of those stages to the Tribulation period, and the distinctiveness of the church from Israel in God's program. In the twentieth century one of the most debated questions in eschatology concerns the time of the Rapture.

To that question premillennialists have given four answers. (Amillennialists regard the coming of Christ as a single event to be followed by the general resurrection and judgment. For postmillennialists there is also no distinct Rapture.)

The four premillennial views of the Rapture are partial rapture (that is, only certain believers will be raptured), pretribulational rapture, midtribulational rapture, and posttribulational rapture. Partial rapture concerns the extent of the Rapture, whereas the other three views focus on the time of the Rapture.

III. THE EXTENT OF THE RAPTURE—PARTIAL OR TOTAL?

A. Definition of the Partial Rapture

Partial rapture teaches that only those believers who are "watching" and "waiting" for the Lord's return will be found worthy to escape the terrors of the Tribulation by being taken in the Rapture.

B. Supporters of This View

Apparently this view originated with Robert Govett in 1835 in his book *Entrance into the Kingdom: The Apocalypse Expounded by Scripture.* It was also taught by J. A. Seiss, G. H. Pember, G. H. Lang, and the Local Church Movement.[1]

C. Theological Framework of This View

1. Salvation. Advocates hold to salvation by grace and eternal security of the believer, but they interpret debated passages on security as Arminians do with this important exception: the danger facing the believer who fails is not perdition but millennial disinheritance. Every believer has the right to inherit the kingdom, but this can be forfeited through disobedience.

2. Sanctification. Often partial rapturists give strong emphasis to sanctification and holiness. They may teach that the baptism of the Holy Spirit is connected with power for witnessing and that the filling and indwelling of the Spirit are for some believers only, rather than for all. This emphasis carries over into their view of the Rapture; namely, that only spiritual believers will be raptured to escape the Tribulation.

3. First resurrection. The first resurrection is viewed as a resurrection for reward for spiritual believers, rather than for all. Believers who are not overcomers will be raised after the Millennium. Therefore, that second resurrection (usually seen as involving only unbelievers) will include both believers and unbelievers.

D. Outline of This View

Partial rapturists teach that there will be several times for the Rapture and resurrection of overcomers.

1. Before. Just before the beginning of the Tribulation mature living saints will be translated and mature dead saints will be raised.

PRETRIBULATIONISM

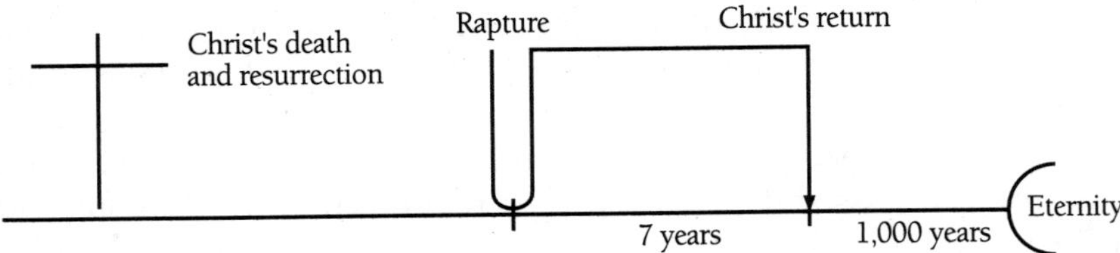

MIDTRIBULATIONISM

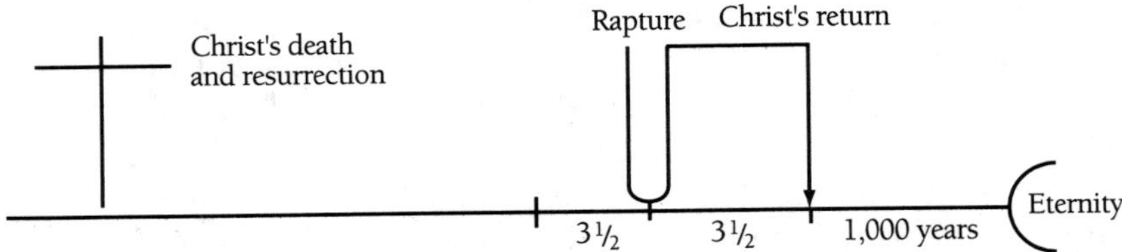

POSTTRIBULATIONISM

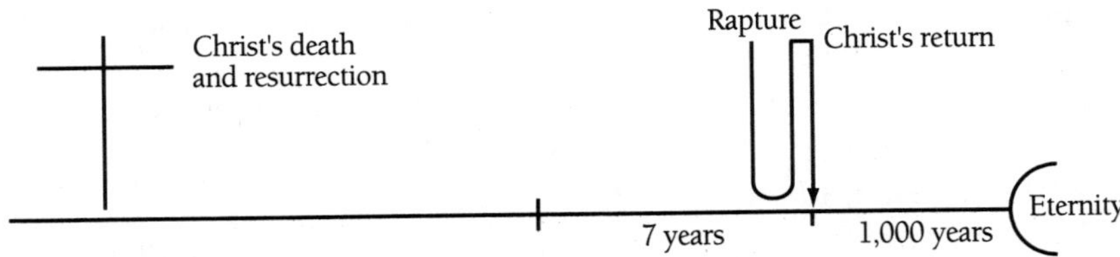

PARTIAL RAPTURE

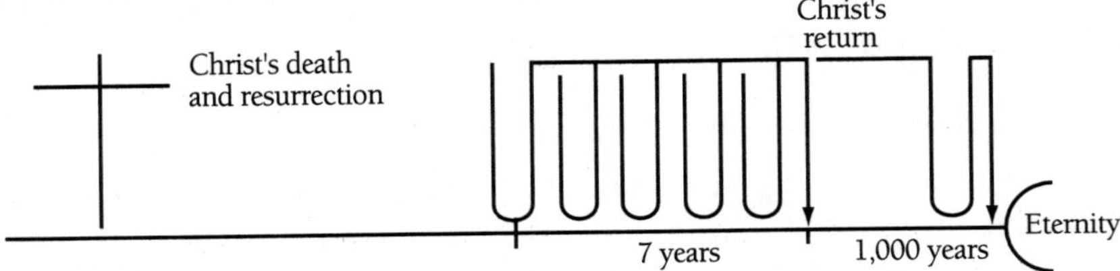

2. During. Then during the seven years of Tribulation other Church Age saints who were unprepared for the initial Rapture will be raptured at various intervals. These are seen in Revelation 7:9, 14; 11:2; 12:5 (the male child includes believers); 16:15 (a Rapture to deliver watching believers from the war of Armageddon); and a final Rapture at the end.
3. After. At the close of the Millennium, there will be a resurrection of believers who missed these earlier resurrections of rewards along with the resurrection of unbelievers. The believers will enter the everlasting kingdom, though they will have missed the millennial kingdom.

E. Biblical Support Cited for This View

1. Suffering. Many passages teach that believers must endure suffering before they can reign with Christ. Therefore, believers must either suffer now or in the Tribulation period (Luke 22:18–30; Acts 14:22; Rom. 8:16–17; Col. 3:24; 2 Thess. 1:4–5). Some identify the fire in 1 Corinthians 3:12–15 as the Tribulation. Revelation 3:5, it is said, may refer to a temporary blotting out of the Book of Life for carnal believers during the period of rewards that overcomers will enjoy.
2. What is the first resurrection? Since the Scriptures view the first resurrection as a prize to be gained, this means not all believers will gain it, only overcomers (Matt. 19:28–29; Luke 9:62; 20:35; Phil. 3:11–14; Rev. 2:11; 3:5).
3. Birthright. A believer, it is said, may lose his birthright and thus forfeit his chance to be raptured before the Tribulation (1 Cor. 6:9–10; Gal. 5:19–21; Heb. 12:14).
4. Baptism of the Spirit. Since the baptism of the Spirit is seen as empowerment for witnessing, not all believers are in the body of Christ and therefore not all are necessarily raptured.
5. Reward. The Rapture is viewed as a reward that not all believers will attain (Matt. 24:40–41; 25:1–13; 1 Cor. 9:27; 2 Tim. 4:8; Titus 2:13; Heb. 9:24–28; Rev. 3:10).

F. Some Problems with This View

1. Exclusiveness. First Corinthians 15:51–52 plainly states that all will be changed, not some.
2. Baptism of the Spirit. The baptism of the Spirit does place all believers in the body of Christ (1 Cor. 12:13), thus all will experience the promise of the Rapture.

3. *Who will be punished?* The Tribulation period is never spoken of as a time of chastening for the church or part of the church. It is the time of *Jacob's* trouble.
4. *Reward?* The Rapture is not a reward for godly living; godly living will be rewarded with crowns, not Rapture (2 Tim. 4:8, and other passages on crowns).

IV. THE TIME OF THE RAPTURE

Basically there are three answers to the question of when the Rapture will occur in relation to the seven years of Tribulation. Pretribulationism says it will precede the beginning of the entire period. Midtribulationism teaches it will occur at the midpoint of the seven years; that is, the church will be on earth during the first three and one-half years but will be taken to heaven at that point, thus escaping the last half of the Tribulation. Posttribulationism understands that the church will continue on the earth during the entire period, but that there will be a Rapture as described in 1 Thessalonians 4:13–18 at the end, followed immediately by the Second Coming. Each of these views will be examined in the next chapters.

NOTE

1. J. A. Seiss, *The Apocalypse* (New York: Cook, 1865); G. H. Pember, *The Great Prophecies of the Centuries Concerning the Church* (London: Hodder & Stoughton, 1895); G. H. Lang, *The Revelation of Jesus Christ* (London: Paternoster, 1948); and *The Local Church Movement* (Witness Lee, *Revelation*, Recovery Version [Anaheim, Calif.: Living Stream Ministry, 1976]).

Chapter 86
THE PRETRIBULATIONAL RAPTURE VIEW

I. DEFINITION OF THIS VIEW

Pretribulationism teaches that the Rapture of the church (both dead and living saints) will occur before the seven-year Tribulation period, that is, before the beginning of the seventieth week of Daniel 9:24–27. It is necessary to say "before the seven-year Tribulation period" because some who hold to midtribulation Rapture state that the Rapture is pretribulational, because they understand the Tribulation to refer only to the last three and one-half years of the seven-year period.

II. SUPPORTERS OF THIS VIEW

John Nelson Darby (1800–1882) gave the greatest initial impetus to the systematizing of pretribulationism. This is because he saw the church as a special work of God, distinct from His program for Israel. This, integrated into his premillennialism, led him to the position that the church would be raptured before the Tribulation period when God would again deal specially with Israel.

In the twentieth century the view has been expounded and defended through *The Scofield Reference Bible; Is the Rapture Next?,* by Leon Wood; *The Rapture Question,* by John F. Walvoord; *Things to Come,* by J. Dwight Pentecost; *A Revelation of Jesus Christ,* by J. B. Smith; and *What You Should Know About the Rapture,* by Charles C. Ryrie.[1]

III. SUPPORT FOR THIS VIEW

A. Revelation 3:10

The promise is based on keeping the word of His patience, a reference to all believers (see similar Johannine designations in John 8:51; 14:23–24; and 1 John 2:3). It was made to all the churches, not just the one in Philadelphia in the first century (note Rev. 3:13 and the similar close to each of the letters to these representative churches). It relates to the coming hour of testing on the earth; that is, to the tribulations prophesied later on in the Revelation. It states that believers will be kept from that hour (*tereso ek tes horas*). Those who oppose pretribulationism understand the phrase to mean "I will guard"; that is, believers will be guarded throughout the seven years and then emerge from it at the second coming of Christ.

The pretribulationist's understanding of *ek* is supported by a number of verses that have nothing to do with the Rapture and therefore do not beg the question. "He who guards his mouth and his tongue, guards his soul from troubles" (Prov. 21:23). Guarding your mouth and tongue is not the means of protecting yourself in the time of trouble; rather, it is the means of escaping trouble you are not presently in. In the Septuagint *ek* indicates an external, not internal, preservation. *Ek* also is used in the same way of external protection in Joshua 2:13 and Psalms 33:19; 56:13. Likewise in the New Testament, *ek* clearly has the same meaning. In Acts 15:29 Gentile believers were asked to keep themselves *from* certain practices that were offensive to Jewish believers. The only way they could do that would be by abstaining entirely from the practices. They must withdraw, not somehow protect themselves while practicing those things. In James 5:20 we are told that if a sinning Christian can be turned away from his backslidden state he will be saved *from* physical death. There is no way *ek* could mean he will be protected in the midst of physical death and then emerge from it in some kind of resurrection. He will escape a premature death by being exempt from it.[2]

The same phrase *keep from,* occurs in John 17:15: "I do not ask Thee to take them out of the world, but to keep them from the evil one." Posttribulationists point out that this promise is fulfilled not by removing believers from the world but by protecting them from Satan while they live on the earth. Then they assert that, similarly, believers will live during the Tribulation but be kept from its wrath.

Such an analogy fails to answer the basic question, How are believers kept from Satan's power? True, it is not by removing them from this world, but a removal is involved. Paul described it this way: "For He delivered us from the domain of darkness, and transferred us to the kingdom of His beloved Son" (Col. 1:13). John said the same thing when he wrote that "the evil one does not touch [cling to] him [the believer]" (1 John 5:18). Believers have been transferred from one domain (Satan's) to another (Christ's), and that is how we are kept from the evil one.

However, the promise of Revelation 3:10 not only guarantees being kept from the trials of the Tribulation period but being kept from the time period of the Tribulation. The promise is not, "I will keep you from the trials." It is, "I will also keep you from the *hour* of trial" (NIV). Posttribulationists have to resort to finding means to "undercut stress on the term 'hour'"[3] by insisting that "hour" means the experiences of a time period but not the time itself. In other words, the church will live through the time but will not experience (some of) the events. But if the events of the Tribulation are worldwide and directly and indirectly affect everybody, how can the church be on the earth and escape the experiences? If our Lord had been saved from the hour of His atoning sacrifice (John 12:27) by living through that time but not experiencing the events of His passion, there would have been no atonement.

Granted, it is possible to live through a time and miss some of the events (like being present at a social function but missing some of the activities), but it is not possible to miss the time without also missing the events.

To summarize, posttribulationists teach unclearly the meaning of the promise of Revelation 3:10. (1) Some seem to say that it means protection (for some believers who escape martyrdom throughout the Tribulation) and then Rapture at the end. (2) Some seem to say that it means protection from the last crisis (which includes Armageddon and the "lull" of peace and safety that supposedly precedes it) by Rapture just before that last crisis. (3) Some seem to say that it means the church will live through Armageddon, be guarded during that time, and emerge (all believers unscathed?) in the Rapture-Second Coming. One thing is clear to posttribulationists: it cannot mean deliverance before the Tribulation begins.

But how clear and plain the promise is: "I . . . will keep you from the hour of testing." Not from just any persecution, but the coming time that will affect the whole earth. The only way to escape worldwide trouble is not to be on the earth. And the only way to escape the time when events take place is not to be in a place where time ticks on. The only place that meets those qualifications is heaven.

Perhaps an illustration will help keep the promise in its clear, uncomplicated form. As a teacher I frequently have to give exams. Let us suppose that I announce to a class that I am going to give an exam on such-and-such a day at the regular classtime. Then suppose I say, "I want to make a promise to students whose grade average for the semester so far is A. The promise is: I will keep you from the exam." If I said nothing more by way of explanation, I expect that the A students would puzzle over that promise. "Does it mean we have to take the exam or not?" they would ask. And just to be safe, I would expect, they would show up at the appointed time because they would not have understood clearly what I meant.

Now I could keep my promise to those A students this way: I could pass out the exam to everyone and give to the A students a sheet containing the answers. They would take the exam and yet in reality be kept from the exam. They would live through the time but not suffer the trial. This is posttribulationism. Protection while enduring.

But if I said to the class, "I am giving an exam next week. I want to make a promise to all the A students. I will keep you from the *hour* of the exam," I very seriously doubt if the A students in that class would spend any time debating what I meant or whether or not they had to show up at the time of the exam. They would understand clearly that to be kept from the hour of the test exempts them from being present during that hour. This is pretribulationism, and this is the meaning of the promise of Revelation 3:10. And the promise came from the risen Savior who Himself is the Deliverer from the wrath to come (1 Thess. 1:10).

B. 1 Thessalonians 5:1–11

In 1 Thessalonians 4:13–18 Paul tried to allay the fears of some who thought that deceased believers might not share in the kingdom. His explanation in that paragraph was something about which they were uninformed. But, in contrast, they were well informed about the beginning of the Day of the Lord as he explained in 5:1–11.

The beginning of that day will come unexpectedly in a time of peace and safety (v. 2), with pain (v. 3) and wrath (v. 9). In the meantime, believers are to live with alertness and sobriety. The exhortations of verses 6, 8, 10 are not to watch for signs during the Tribulation in preparation for the Day of the Lord at the end of the Tribulation, but to live godly lives in view of the coming Tribulation that believers will escape. Of this teaching Paul said they were fully aware (v. 2). How? Partly from Paul's own teaching to them, but also from their knowledge of the Old Testament.

In the Old Testament, the Day of the Lord is referred to by that phrase about twenty times, often with eschatological implications. In addition, a parallel term, "the last days," occurs fourteen times, always eschatological. Furthermore, the phrase "in that day" occurs more than one hundred times and is generally eschatological. In Isaiah 2:2, 11–12 (KJV), the three phrases appear, referring to the same eschatological time. So there was ample reason for Paul to say that his readers knew about the Day of the Lord from the Old Testament itself.

But concerning the Rapture there is no Old Testament revelation. This omission from more than a hundred passages seems hard to understand if the Rapture is the first event of the Day of the Lord, as posttribulationism teaches. But if the Rapture is a mystery, unrevealed in the Old Testament, and if it precedes the actual beginning of the Day of the Lord, as pretribulationism teaches, then it is not strange that Paul had to inform them about the Rapture but needed only to remind them what they already knew about the Day of the Lord.

Posttribulationists, then, want to make a very close connection between 1 Thessalonians 4:13–18 and 5:1–11, whereas pretribulationists are better served by seeing a contrast of subjects between the two paragraphs.

Thus the posttribulational scenario runs like this: Paul moved with ease from his discussion of the Rapture in 4:13–18 to the discussion of the *parousia* in 5:1–11 because he was talking about events that occur at the same time and not events separated by seven years. Paul's choice of *de* (the first Greek word in 5:1), a simple connective with only a slight contrastive sense, indicates this close connection. And since the Day of the Lord will not begin until the Second Coming, the Rapture will occur then also.

Pretribulationists point out that the contrast between the subjects of the two chapters is sharpened by the fact that Paul did not simply use a *de* to begin verse 1 but a phrase, *peri de*. This is very significant, because elsewhere in his writings Paul used *peri de* to denote a new and contrasting subject. Notice 1 Corinthians 7:1, 25; 8:1; 12:1; 16:1, 12; and 1 Thessalonians 4:9 and 5:1. Granted, the posttribulationists' contention that the same subject is being discussed in 4:13–18 and 5:1–11 might be supported by the use of *de* alone, but it is completely nullified by the use of *peri de*. So the pretribulationists' use of the passage is strongly supported exegetically. The Rapture is not a part of the Day of the Lord and therefore cannot be posttribulational.

To summarize: The question of the beginning of the Day of the Lord is a watershed between pre- and posttribulationism. Pretribulationism sees the Day of the Lord beginning at the start of the Tribulation for the following reasons:

(1) The very first judgments (by whatever chronology one uses) include war, famine, and the death of one-fourth of the population of the earth.

(2) The one time the Scriptures mention peace and safety during the Tribulation period is at its very beginning. This time will be followed immediately by war, destruction, and upheavals that will continue unabated until Christ comes. Thus the Day of the Lord must begin at the beginning of the Tribulation, and the Rapture must be before.

(3) The revelation of the man of sin will occur at the beginning of the Tribulation when he makes a pact with the Jewish people.

(4) The much more normal understanding of the verb in Revelation 6:17 conveys the idea that the wrath has already come and continues.

(5) Paul's use of *peri de,* not simply *de,* in 1 Thessalonians 5:1 indicates contrasting subjects.

(6) The removal of peace from the earth just after the Tribulation begins fits only pretribulationism.

If posttribulationism is correct, then it must provide much more satisfactory answers than it has to the following questions:

(1) How can the Day of the Lord not begin with the Tribulation or any part of it and yet begin with the judgments of Armageddon?

(2) How can the final conflict at the end of the Tribulation be shrunk into a single battle of short enough duration so that the church can be raptured before it starts (in order to escape the wrath) and yet turn right around and accompany Christ on His return to earth at the conclusion of what would have to be a very brief battle?

(3) Does protection from wrath poured out on unbelievers really include exemption from the fallout effects of the actions of those unbelievers on whom the wrath is poured? It does not today. Why should it in the future?

(4) How does bunching the wrath judgments at the end of the Tribulation take care of the problem that equally severe judgments seem to take place earlier in the Tribulation and fall on believers as well as unbelievers?

(5) What is the more normal interpretation of the aorist in Revelation 6:17? Does it not indicate that the wrath has already been poured out, that it did not begin with the sixth seal?

(6) Does not the use of the phrase *peri de* in 1 Thessalonians 5:1 indicate that the Rapture is really not a part of the Day of the Lord at the end of the Tribulation?

Only pretribulationism fits harmoniously with all the scriptural evidence and answers those questions satisfactorily.

C. The Church

Other arguments for the pretribulation Rapture include the absence of the church in Revelation 4–19 where the Tribulation is described in great detail; the removal of the Restrainer before the Day of the Lord and the revelation of the man of sin (2 Thess. 2:1–9); and the need to have some human beings survive the Tribulation in their earthly bodies in order to become the parents of the millennial population. This last argument we shall examine in detail in the next chapter.

NOTES

1. Leon Wood, *Is the Rapture Next?* (Grand Rapids: Zondervan, 1956); John F. Walvoord, *The Rapture Question* (Grand Rapids: Zondervan, 1970); J. Dwight Pentecost, *Things to Come* (Findlay, Ohio: Dunham, 1958); J. B. Smith, *A Revelation of Jesus Christ* (Scottdale, Pa.: Herald Press, 1961); and Charles C. Ryrie, *What You Should Know About the Rapture* (Chicago: Moody, 1981).
2. For an excellent discussion of these and other points related to Revelation 3:10, see Jeffrey L. Townsend, "The Rapture in Revelation 3:10," *Bibliotheca Sacra* (July 1980): 252–66.
3. Robert H. Gundry, *The Church and the Tribulation* (Grand Rapids: Zondervan, 1973), 59.

Chapter 87
POPULATING THE MILLENNIAL KINGDOM

I. THE PROBLEM

When the Millennium begins, some people have to be alive in unresurrected bodies, who can beget children and populate that kingdom. All premillennialists agree with this.

The Millennium not only involves the reign of Christ with His people, who will then have resurrected bodies, but also the reign of Christ over people on this earth who will not have resurrected bodies. If there were only resurrected saints in the kingdom, then there would be no death, no increase in population, and no differences in the ages of millennial citizens (all of which are indicated as characterizing the kingdom—Isa. 65:20; Zech. 8:5; Rev. 20:12). Since resurrected people do not propagate, there would be no way to populate the kingdom unless some unresurrected people enter the Millennium. Thus all premillennialists see the need to have some adults who survive the Tribulation who are not taken to heaven at the end of the Tribulation but who enter the Millennium in unresurrected bodies to become the first parents of the millennial population.

II. THE PRETRIBULATIONAL SOLUTION

The pretribulational understanding of future events satisfies this need easily. The Rapture will occur before the Tribulation, removing all the redeemed who are living on the earth at that time. But many people will be saved during the Tribulation (Rev. 7:9, 14) including a specific group of 144,000 Jewish people (v. 4). Of those saved during that horrible time, many will be martyred (6:11; 13:15), but some will survive to enter the Millennium (Matt. 25:34; Zech. 14:11). The initial group who will enter the Millennium will not only enter with natural bodies but will also be redeemed people who willingly submit to the rule of the King. In due time, babies will be born and grow up. Some will receive Christ into their hearts; others will not. But all will have to give allegiance to the King's government or suffer the consequences. By the end of the Millennium, there will be innumerable rebels who will have given outward obedience to the King, but who, when given the opportunity by Satan after his release, will join his revolution against Christ (Rev. 20:7–9).

Thus in the pretribulational understanding of these future events, the original parents of the millennial kingdom will come from the redeemed (but unresurrected) survivors of the Tribulation, the "sheep" of Matthew 25:32–34 and the faithful Jewish survivors of Ezekiel 20:38.

III. THE POSTTRIBULATIONAL SOLUTION

In contrast stands the posttribulational picture. The church, of course, will live through the Tribulation. Though some will be martyred, many will be protected and survive. The 144,000 Jews and the great multitude of Revelation 7 are included in the church. At the end of the Tribulation, all living believers will be raptured, given resurrection bodies, and return immediately to earth in the single event of the Rapture and Second Coming. This would seem to eliminate all redeemed, unresurrected people from the earth at that point in time so that there will be no one left to begin to populate the kingdom. If the wicked survivors are either killed or consigned to hades at the end of the Tribulation, then there will be no one left in an unresurrected body to enter the Millennium.

So, either the posttribulationist must find some people who will not be saved when the Rapture begins but will be saved by the time that single, instantaneous event of the Rapture-Second Coming concludes (how much time is there?), or he must allow the initial parents of the Millennium to be unsaved people who somehow are not killed or judged at or after Armageddon. Those are the only options open to the posttribulationist to find millennial parents.

We need to be reminded of another detail at this point. The millennial population includes both Jewish and Gentile people (Isa. 19:24–25). So the first generation must be made up of both races. But a posttribulational Rapture will remove all the candidates for redeemed millennial parents of every race. And the judgments of the Second Coming will remove all the candidates for unredeemed millennial parents of every race. Where will those parents come from?

Most posttribulationists do not attempt to give an answer to this question. This may be because posttribulationists do not usually put the details of their system together in an orderly way. Their picture of the future is painted with broad strokes, not fine detail. Posttribulationists do not sponsor prophecy conferences in which their speakers are expected to describe rather specifically the system they promote. Some posttribulationists may never have seen this question as a question, simply because they have not spelled out systematically and in detail their outline of future events. But whatever the reason, most do not address this question.

Robert Gundry is an exception.[1] His answer is twofold. The Jewish progenitors of the millennial population will come from the 144,000 who will not be saved at any time during the Tribulation but only at the end.[2] The Gentile parents will come from the wicked who will somehow escape death and/or judgment at the end of the Tribulation. Those wicked are the ones left in Matthew 24:40–41 (in contrast to the ones taken in the posttribulational Rapture). He says, "A partial destruction would leave the remaining unsaved to populate the millennial earth."[3]

Furthermore, an adjustment has to be made in the time of the judgment of the sheep and goats in Matthew 25:31–46 if the posttribulational picture be correct. The reason is simple: If the Rapture is after the Tribulation, then all the sheep (redeemed) will have been removed from the earth, and there would be no sheep to be part of that judgment if it occurs at the Second Coming, which is a single event with the Rapture. There is no way the Rapture can remove the sheep and yet have sheep present on the earth to be judged immediately following the Rapture. So either the Rapture cannot be posttribulational or the judgment of the sheep and goats must be after the Second Coming (Gundry places it after the Millennium).

We need to examine three things that are necessary to the posttribulational answer: (a) the conversion of the 144,000, (b) the identification of the groups in Matthew 24:40–41, and (c) the time of the judgment of the sheep and goats in 25:31–46.

IV. THE 144,000 JEWS

Some posttribulationists consider the 144,000 Jews to be "spiritual Israel—the church."[4] If so, then their sealing is at the beginning of the Tribulation and relates to their spiritual salvation as well as physical protection. Gundry acknowledges that the 144,000 might belong to the church (and therefore be saved at the beginning); he prefers to regard them as unsaved throughout the Tribulation and identical with the group that will look on Christ when He returns and believe (Zech. 12:10) and with the Israel who will be saved at the Second Coming (Rom. 11:26–27). The reason for his preference is logical. If the 144,000 were saved any time during the Tribulation years—at the beginning, in the middle, or even during the last year—they would be raptured in the posttribulation Rapture, given resurrection bodies at that time, then return at the same time to reign with Christ in the kingdom. But having been given resurrection bodies would preclude their being the parents of anybody in the kingdom. On the other hand, if they were not saved until the very end of the Second Coming, they would "escape" the Rapture, yet be converted, but remain in unresurrected bodies and thus be able to become parents of millennial children.

Actually, pretribulationists understand that there will be a group of Jewish people converted at the conclusion of the Tribulation who will become the parents of the Jewish portion of the millennial population. They will come from among the Jewish people who survive the Tribulation even though they were unsaved throughout it. When the Lord returns they will be gathered and judged, the rebels (possibly two thirds, Zech. 13:8) to be excluded from the kingdom and those who turn in faith when they see Him to enter the kingdom (Ezek. 20:33–44). Those believing survivors constitute the "all" of all Israel that will be saved at the Second Coming (Rom. 11:26). But they will not be given resurrection bodies at that time; rather they will enter the kingdom in material bodies with the ability to propagate.

Why cannot the posttribulationist also let this group be the millennial parents? Because that group will believe when they see the Lord coming, which would be at the posttribulational Rapture. So they also would be raptured, taken to heaven, given resurrection bodies, and eliminated from parenting. The Rapture, whenever it occurs, will be the greatest separation of believers from unbelievers imaginable, so if there is to be a group of Jewish people who will believe when they see the Lord coming, and if that coming is the posttribulational Rapture-Second Coming, then they will be raptured because at that moment they will become believers. So the posttribulationist needs to have a group that is sealed in an unsaved state long enough to miss the Rapture but not long enough to miss entering the Millennium in material bodies. Thus, as one would expect, Gundry says of Ezekiel 20 that "that passage may not portray a formal judgment at all."[5] Actually, it cannot in the posttribulational system.

Can the 144,000 be considered unconverted throughout the Tribulation years? The answer is yes. One can hold any interpretation one wishes. The question is not, Is it possible to interpret that way? The question is, Is it reasonable to do so? What does the text of Revelation 7:1–8 say?

It states two very significant facts: the 144,000 have "the seal of the living God" (v. 2) and they are "the bond-servants of our God" (v. 3). The text does not specifically say *what* their service is, but it does say *whom* they serve. They serve God, not Antichrist. Are we to imagine here a group of 144,000 unsaved people designated as God's bond-servants? Posttribulationists weakly explain that the designation is anticipatory of their millennial service when they will have been converted. Any explanation is possible, but is it the most likely meaning of the text? Certainly not.

But even granting that their designation as God's servants does not apply to the 144,000 in the Tribulation period but only in the Millennium, the statement in verse 2 is very difficult to harmonize with the posttribulational system. The group is said to be sealed *before* the judgments of the Tribulation begin (v. 3). Try to fit this into posttribulationism. Here would be a distinct group of unconverted Jewish people on whose foreheads God has placed His seal. As unsaved people, they (or surely some of them) will follow Antichrist, who also will place his mark on their foreheads or hands. And the destiny of Antichrist's followers *has already been predetermined:* they will be tormented forever with fire and brimstone (14:9–11). None of his followers will be saved, not even 144,000 of them.

To sum up: Posttribulationism needs to have an unconverted group of Jews who will survive the Tribulation, but who, because they are unconverted, will not be raptured at the end, but will be converted by the time the Millennium begins so they can enter the Millennium in their unresurrected bodies and beget children. The only group that can qualify is the 144,000, assuming they can be described as unconverted servants of God who have on their foreheads God's seal before the Tribulation begins and who do not follow Antichrist so they will not have his mark. Is all this possible?

V. MATTHEW 24:40–41

Not only must the 144,000 be identified in a particular way, but the groups distinguished in verses 40–41 must also be identified in a certain way to come up with the posttribulational picture.

According to the posttribulational understanding, these verses say the following: "Then [at the posttribulational Rapture-Second Coming] there shall be two men in the field; one [saved, representing the church] will be taken [in the posttribulational Rapture], and one [unsaved, representing the wicked] will be left [for judgment, though not all will be judged, so some will be left to be parents of the Gentile population of the Millennium]." And the same for verse 41—the one taken is raptured, and the one left is judged.

By contrast, the pretribulationist sees the verses as a general statement of the results of the specific judgments on surviving Jews and Gentiles at the Second Coming. Those who are taken are taken into the judgments and condemned, and those who are left successfully pass the judgments and are left for blessing in the kingdom.

Notice that the posttribulationist must add the stipulation that not all who are left are judged and condemned so that there will be some left to populate the earth. But therein lies an inconsistency: the Rapture will take all the redeemed, but the judgment will not include all the unredeemed. Only part of the wicked will be judged.

Pretribulationists support their view by pointing out that according to verse 39 the Flood took the people of Noah's day into judgment; therefore, those taken at the Second Coming will also be taken into judgment.

Posttribulationists observe that a different word is used in verse 39 for "took away" than in verses 40–41, indicating two different kinds of taking away—verse 39 into judgment but verses 40–41 into heaven at the Rapture. They reinforce this argument by pointing out that the word in verses 40–41 is the same word used to describe the Rapture in John 14:3, "receive you to Myself."

The two interpretations look like this:

	PRETRIBULATIONAL INTERPRETATION	POSTTRIBULATIONAL INTERPRETATION
"Taken"	Into judgment	Into heaven in the posttribulational Rapture
"Left"	For blessing in the kingdom (in unresurrected bodies to propagate)	For judgment (but only a part will be judged so the rest can enter the kingdom in unresurrected bodies)

Pretribulationists note that in John 19:16 the same word used in Matthew 24:40–41 (supposedly of the Rapture according to posttribulationists) is used of taking the Lord into judgment, so obviously it could mean judgment in verses 40–41, as pretribulationism teaches.

Back and forth the discussion of the words goes. What can we conclude? Simply that the words themselves are inconclusive.

But the debate is not without resolution. It can easily be settled by looking at the parallel passage in Luke 17:34–37, where the same warning about one being taken and one left is given by the Lord. However, Luke adds a question that the disciples asked: "Where, Lord?" They asked Him where those taken would be taken. They did not inquire where those left would be left. If the Lord intended us to understand that those taken would be taken in the Rapture (as posttribulationism teaches), He would have answered the question by saying heaven, or the Father's house, or some similar expression. But His answer conveyed that they would be taken somewhere quite opposite to a blissful heaven. His answer was, "Where the body is, there also will the vultures be gathered." Christ's answer is a proverb about vultures appearing out of nowhere when an animal dies. Where will they be taken? Where there is death and corruption, not life and immortality. The reference is not to heaven, but to judgment. Thus the pretribulationist's understanding of the identity of the one taken and the one left is the correct one according to Luke 17:37. A posttribulational Rapture is nowhere indicated in these verses.

VI. THE TIME OF THE SHEEP AND THE GOATS JUDGMENT

This judgment of the sheep and goats, placed at the Second Coming by pretribulationists, has to be moved to a later time if posttribulationism be consistent. The reason is that if the Rapture occurs at the end of the Tribulation, that is, at the Second Coming and if all the sheep are taken to heaven in that Rapture, how will there be any left to be assembled before Christ when He comes? They will already have gone. Or to put it another way: the Rapture-Second Coming will separate the redeemed from the wicked; yet this judgment at the Second Coming will do the same, only there will not be any righteous on the earth to separate since they will just have been raptured.

Moving this judgment also provides for unsaved survivors of the Tribulation and Second Coming to enter the Millennium in unresurrected bodies. Gundry admits, "We are therefore forced to put the judgment of the nations after the Millennium."[6] Forced? Why? Because the condemnation of the goats cannot be of only a part of them, since the text says "all" will be judged. In his interpretation of those left in Matthew 24:40–41, Gundry says that represented only "a partial destruction,"[7] but here all are specifically said to be involved (25:32).

No text requires that there be *unsaved* entering the Millennium. After a few years have passed there will be people, born during the early days of the Millennium, who will grow to adulthood rejecting the Savior-King in their hearts (though outwardly obeying Him). But no text requires that there be unsaved people among the survivors of the Tribulation who enter the Millennium. Zechariah 14:16 (sometimes used to support this idea) refers to the first generation of millennial citizens who came through the judgments as redeemed, not rebels, and who will voluntarily go to Jerusalem to worship the King. But verses 17–21 move on to describe conditions throughout the Millennium, not just at the beginning. As time goes on, some will not obey the King and will have to be punished.

Perhaps the more compelling reason for the posttribulationists' moving this judgment to the end of the Millennium is not to get goats into the Millennium as much as it is to get sheep into the judgment itself. Let me press the point again: if the judgment occurs at the Second Coming, and if the Rapture has just occurred as part of the Second Coming, and if the Rapture has removed the sheep (as it would), then where will the sheep come from to be present in this judgment?

If, however, the judgment can be moved to the close of the Millennium, then, of course, there will be both righteous and wicked people living at the conclusion of the Millennium to be present. But how, then, does one reconcile the rather diverse characteristics of Matthew 25:31–46 with those that describe what would supposedly be the same judgment at the Great White Throne in Revelation 20:11–15? Notice some of the contrasts between the judgment of the sheep and goats and the judgment at the Great White Throne.

Gundry calls the judgment of the sheep and goats a "pattern for the general judgment at the end of time."[8] If it is a pattern, it is rather inexact! To be sure, passages describing the same event do not each have to contain all the same details, but these two passages seem to be entirely dissimilar in their details.

If the judgment of the sheep and goats is to be moved to the end of the Millennium then, of course, Matthew 25:31 must be understood as referring to the Second Coming and verse 32 to the end of the Millennium, one thousand years later. In other words, the gap of the one-thousand-year Millennium must come between verses 31 and 32. Premillennialists recognize that such gaps occur in Scripture (Isa. 9:6 and John 5:28–29, for example), so this is not an impossible idea. But is it the likely interpretation?

SHEEP AND GOATS	GREAT WHITE THRONE
No resurrection (though OT saints may be raised at the Second Coming, they will not be a part of the judgment)	Resurrection of the dead
No books opened	Books opened
The word "nations" used (and the word is never used of the dead)	The word "dead" used
Sheep present	Righteous not mentioned as present
Three groups mentioned: sheep, goats, brethren	Only one group mentioned: the dead
Reward is the kingdom and eternal life	No mention of reward, only condemnation
Occurs at the place Christ comes to, i.e., the earth	Earth has fled away

Matthew 25:35–40 gives the answer. Do these verses describe millennial conditions? They have to if this judgment will occur after the conclusion of the Millennium. If they do, then the Millennium will have to be a time when Christ and His brothers (i.e., Jewish believers) are hungry, thirsty, naked, sick, and in prison. Those who disobey the King during the Millennium may be imprisoned, but the text says that during the period preceding the judgment Christ's brothers will be in prison. As certainly as this will not be true during the Millennium, it *will* be true during the Tribulation. Christ's brothers will be hungry, thirsty, naked, sick, and imprisoned during the Tribulation years, but not during the Millennium when Christ will be ruling in righteousness.

Clearly then, verses 35–40 preclude inserting a gap of one thousand years between verses 31 and 32. The judgment will immediately follow the coming of Christ and will test people on the basis of their heart reactions to conditions that will exist during the Tribulation—

conditions that will not be present during the Millennium for Christ's followers.

VII. CONCLUSION

Where has our discussion led? To the conclusion that posttribulationism cannot provide an answer to the question, Who will be the parents of the millennial population? To be sure, posttribulationism offers some wishful thinking on the subject. They wish the 144,000 would be the Jewish parents, but in order to qualify they will have to remain unconverted throughout the Tribulation as well as through the Rapture-Second Coming, and then be converted. They wish that some of the ones left in the separation of 24:40–41 would be the Gentile parents (others will be condemned to hell). But this twists the meaning of "taken" and "left," making the taking to heaven in the Rapture contrary to the clear meaning of "taken" in Luke 17:36. And to make these suggestions consistent, the judgment of the sheep and goats must be placed at the conclusion of the Millennium, and Matthew 25:35–40 must describe millennial conditions.

How much simpler *not* to have to place the Rapture at the conclusion of the Tribulation. That allows for people to accept or reject Christ during the Tribulation, some of whom will survive that time (none of whom will be raptured, because the Rapture will already have occurred) to be judged at the Second Coming (both living Jews and Gentiles), and those who pass those judgments successfully as redeemed people to go into the kingdom in earthly bodies to be the first generation of the millennial population and the parents of the next generation.

NOTES

1. Robert H. Gundry, *The Church and the Tribulation* (Grand Rapids: Zondervan, 1973), 81–83, 134–39, 163–71.
2. Ibid., 83.
3. Ibid., 137.
4. George E. Ladd, *A Commentary on the Revelation of John* (Grand Rapids: Eerdmans, 1971), 114.
5. Gundry, *The Church and the Tribulation,* 168.
6. Ibid., 166.
7. Ibid., 137.
8. Ibid., 167.

Chapter 88
THE MIDTRIBULATIONAL RAPTURE VIEW

I. DEFINITION OF THIS VIEW

The midtribulational Rapture view holds that the Rapture of the church will occur at the midpoint of the seven years of Tribulation; that is, after three and one-half years have elapsed. In this view, only the last half of Daniel's seventieth week is Tribulation. That is why midtribulationalism is sometimes described as a form of pretribulationalism, since it teaches that the Rapture occurs before the tribulations of the last half of the seven years.

II. SUPPORTERS OF THIS VIEW

J. Oliver Buswell, Jr. taught the midtribulation view.[1] Gleason L. Archer, well-known scholar, also holds this view.[2]

III. ARGUMENTS FOR THIS VIEW

A. The Emphasis on the Time Period of Three and One-Half Years

Prophetic passages emphasize the last three and one-half years of the seventieth week of Daniel as the time of intense judgments on the earth and a time that begins with some great event. It seems reasonable to conclude that that event is the Rapture of the church. Put these two concepts together (intense judgments in the last half of the seven years and some important event occurring at the midpoint of the seven years) and you must conclude a midtribulation rapture of the church. Scriptural support for this includes Daniel 7:25; 9:27; 12:7, 11; Revelation 11:2; 12:6, 14.

Unquestionably, the prophetic passages do distinguish the two halves of the seven years of Tribulation. But this does not mean that the intense judgments will only occur during the last half. Nor do any of these passages cited speak, even by implication, of the Rapture. But some of them do indicate specific events that will occur at the midpoint of the seven years. For example, Daniel 9:27 states that in the middle of the week Antichrist will cause sacrifice and oblation to cease. Daniel 12:11 mentions the same event. Revelation 12:6 and 14 relate how Israel will flee to a wilderness place of refuge at the midpoint. No Rapture is indicated, for the believing remnant will flee to a place on this earth, and will not be taken to heaven as will occur at the Rapture. The fact that some of these passages do mention great events that will happen at the midpoint but nowhere state that the Rapture is one of those great events is most significant.

Midtribulationists do believe that there will be trials and judgments during the first half of the Tribulation, but these are due to the wrath of men, whereas the judgments of the second half come from the wrath of God. However, notice that Revelation 6:16–17 states that the wrath of the Lamb "has come." That indicates that the wrath of God will begin before the sixth seal is opened. To fit the midtribulation scheme one would have to place the beginning judgments of the seals in the second half of the Tribulation.

B. The Olivet Discourse

Midtribulationists find support for their view in the Olivet Discourse. The argument goes like this. Matthew 24:27 indicates the Rapture because the word *parousia* used there is also used of the Rapture in 1 Thessalonians 4:15. Also Matthew 24:31 and 2 Thessalonians 2:1 use words from the same root word (*episynago*). To me the argument so far seems to support a posttribulational chronology, since these comparisons seem to conclude that the Rapture and the Second Coming are the same event, or at least, that they occur at the same time (the end of the Tribulation). But the midtribulationist avoids that conclusion by arguing that the Rapture in the Olivet Discourse is preceded by signs that should alert believers to the nearness of the Rapture. These signs include the spread of the Gospel (Matt. 24:14), the rise of the beast (v. 15), and general persecution (vv. 10–27). Because these signs will appear during the first half of the week, the Rapture must occur at the midpoint. But frankly, if this is a good argument for midtribulationism, it would seem to be a better argument for posttribulationism.

What about the use of some of the same words for the Rapture and the Second Coming? Does this indicate that they are the same event? (This, of course, is an argument used to support posttribulationism as well.) Of course not. One would expect to find similar vocabulary used to describe events that have some similarity. But similarity does not make sameness.

C. The Last Trumpet

Midtribulationism argues that the seventh trumpet of Revelation 10:7 corresponds to the last trumpet of 1 Corinthians 15:52. If this be true, then the Rapture (described in 1 Corinthians) will occur at the midpoint of the Tribulation (the time when the seventh trumpet sounds). This is a somewhat simplistic argument that assumes that all blowing of trumpets must indicate the same kind of event. This is not true. In Jewish apocalyptic literature, trumpets signaled a variety of great eschatological events, including judgments, the gathering of the elect, and resurrection. The seventh trumpet is a trumpet of judgment, whereas the trumpet in 1 Corinthians is one of resurrection and deliverance. That they indicate the same event is a gratuitous assumption.

NOTES

1. J. Oliver Buswell, *A Systematic Theology of the Christian Religion* (Grand Rapids: Zondervan, 1962), 2:450, 462.
2. Reiter, Feinberg, Archer, Moo, *The Rapture* (Grand Rapids: Zondervan, 1983), 115–45.

Chapter 89
THE POSTTRIBULATIONAL RAPTURE VIEW

I. DEFINITION OF THIS VIEW

Posttribulationism teaches that the Rapture and the Second Coming are facets of a single event that will occur at the end of the Tribulation when Christ returns. The church will be on earth during the Tribulation to experience the events of that period.

II. PROPONENTS OF THIS VIEW

Though a number of writers have held and do hold this view throughout church history, three works have been especially influential: *The Approaching Advent of Christ,* by Alexander Reese; *The Blessed Hope,* by George E. Ladd; and *The Church and the Tribulation,* by Robert H. Gundry.[1]

III. PRE- AND POSTTRIBULATIONISM CONTRASTED

Since pretribulationism and posttribulationism are the two Rapture views most debated today, let me contrast their principal differences.

PRETRIBULATIONISM

1. Rapture occurs before the Tribulation.
2. Church experiences Revelation 3:10 before the Tribulation.
3. Day of the Lord begins with the Tribulation.
4. 1 Thessalonians 5:2–3 occurs at beginning of Tribulation.
5. 144,000 redeemed at start of Tribulation.
6. Rapture and Second Coming separated by seven years.
7. Living Israelites judged at Second Coming.
8. Living Gentiles judged at Second Coming.
9. Parents of millennial population come from survivors of judgments on living Jews and Gentiles.
10. Believers of Church Age judged in heaven between Rapture and Second Coming.

IV. ARGUMENTS FOR POSTTRIBULATIONISM

A. The Vocabulary for the Second Coming

Briefly stated the argument is this. Since New Testament writers use several words to describe the Second Coming, if the Rapture and the Second Coming are different events separated by seven years, why did they not reserve one word for the Rapture and another for the Second Coming instead of seeming to use them interchangeably?

For example, *parousia,* meaning "coming," "arrival," or "presence," is used in relation to the Rapture in 1 Thessalonians 4:15. It also describes the second coming of Christ in Matthew 24:27. Two different conclusions are possible from this evidence. (1) *Parousia* describes the same, single event, meaning that the Rapture and the Second Coming are a single event at the end of the Tribulation. (2) *Parousia* describes two separate events, both characterized by the presence of the Lord, but events that will not happen at the same time. Either conclusion is valid.

Consider an illustration. Suppose proud grandparents should say to their friends. "We are looking forward to enjoying the presence (*parousia*) of our grandchildren next week"; then later in the conversation add, "Yes, we expect our grandchildren to be present at our golden wedding celebration." If you heard those statements you could draw one of two conclusions. (1) The grandchildren are coming next week for the golden wedding anniversary. In other words, the grandparents were speaking of the coming and the anniversary as a single

POSTTRIBULATIONISM

1. Rapture occurs after the Tribulation.
2. Church experiences Revelation 3:10 at end of Tribulation.
3. Day of the Lord begins at close of Tribulation.
4. 1 Thessalonians 5:2–3 occurs near end of Tribulation.
5. 144,000 redeemed at conclusion of Tribulation.
6. Rapture and Second Coming are a single event.
7. No such judgment.
8. Living Gentiles judged after Millennium.
9. Parents of millennial population come from 144,000 Jews.
10. Believers of Church Age judged after Second Coming or at conclusion of Millennium.

event, occurring at the same time. Or (2) the grandchildren will be making two trips to see their grandparents—one next week (perhaps as part of their vacation) and another later to help celebrate the golden wedding anniversary.

Likewise, since the Lord's presence (*parousia*) will characterize both the Rapture and the Second Coming, the word itself does not indicate whether these are a single event or separate events. In other words, the vocabulary used does not necessarily prove either pre- or posttribulationism.

A second word used for the Lord's coming is *apokalupsis,* meaning "revelation." It occurs in Rapture passages like 1 Corinthians 1:7 and 1 Peter 1:7; 4:13, because when Christ comes for the church He will reveal Himself to her. At His coming we shall see Him as He is. The word also appears in passages that describe His coming to the earth at the close of the Tribulation (2 Thess. 1:7), because that event also will reveal Christ to the world.

Two conclusions are possible. (1) The Rapture and the Second Coming are the same single event. Since both are called a revelation of Christ, they must occur at the same time and be part of the same event at the end of the Tribulation. (2) Both the Rapture and the Second Coming will reveal Christ, but not at the same time or under the same circumstances. Therefore, the Rapture and the Second Coming can be separated as pretribulationism teaches.

Notice that the first conclusion used the word *revelation* as a *cataloging* word; that is, it catalogs whatever event is referred to in all the passages where the word is used as the same, single event. The second conclusion sees the word *revelation* as a *characterizing* word; that is, it is used to characterize different events in the same way, as a revelation.

It becomes more obvious, then, that the vocabulary used in the New Testament does not seem to prove either pre- or posttribulationism. The third principal word for the Second Coming is *epiphaneia,* meaning "manifestation." At the Second Coming, Christ will destroy Antichrist by the sheer manifestation of His coming (2 Thess. 2:8). The word is also used in reference to the hope of the believer when he will see the Lord (2 Tim. 4:8; Titus 2:13). Are we to conclude that the word is cataloging those references to refer them to the same single event? Or can we conclude that it is characterizing two different events as both involving a manifestation of Christ but not occurring at the same time? The answer is either (but not both!).

Clearly, then, the vocabulary does not prove either a pre- or posttribulational Rapture of the church.

Why, then, does this argument continue to be used? Simply because posttribulationists continue to believe that it is a valid support for their view, even claiming that it "substantiates" their view.[2]

But the posttribulationist's underlying assumption in continuing to use this argument is that these words catalog rather than characterize. To be sure, vocabulary might do that; but to be equally sure, it might not.

Take the word "motor." My automobile has a motor. My wife's washing machine has a motor. My moped has a motor. Our furnace fan has a motor. My camera has a motor that automatically advances the film. Is the term "motor" a characterizing feature of these rather diverse machines? Or is it a means of cataloging them that would force us to conclude that everything that has a motor is the same thing? The answer is obvious.

Do presence, revelation, and manifestation characterize different events or catalog the same event? The pretribulationist says the former; the posttribulationist concludes the latter.

B. The Church Is Not Said to Be in Heaven but on Earth During the Tribulation According to Revelation 4–18

Pretribulationists point out that though the word "church" occurs nineteen times in Revelation 1–3 and once in chapter 22, it does not appear even once in chapters 4–18, which describe the Tribulation period. Therefore, they conclude, the church is not on earth during the Tribulation but in heaven.

In response, posttribulationists say the church (that is, the last generation of the church) will be on earth during the Tribulation according to Revelation 4–18 for these reasons. (1) Nowhere in these chapters is the church said to be in heaven, something we would expect the text to say if it were true. (2) The occurrence of the word "saints" in 13:7, 10; 16:6; 17:6; and 18:24 shows that the church is in fact on the earth during the Tribulation. (3) Other descriptions of believers in the Tribulation aptly apply to Church Age believers, indicating that Tribulation believers will be the last generation of Church Age believers and that they will go through the Tribulation. Let's examine and critique each of these arguments in more detail.

(1) Is the church in heaven during the Tribulation? To this question pretribulationists reply along either or both of two lines. Most identify

the twenty-four elders as representing the church, and since they are seen in heaven in 4:4 and 5:8–10, the church is mentioned as in heaven. Some think this argument is nullified since the critical text of verses 9–10 has the elders singing of redemption in the third person as if redemption were not their own experience (thus they could not represent the church, which has been redeemed). But this is really not a strong argument. Notice that Moses sang of redemption that he experienced in the third person (Exod. 15:13, 16–17).

Pretribulationists also point out that the background of Hebrew marriage customs argues for the church's already being in heaven before the coming of Christ at the end of the Tribulation. Jewish marriage included a number of steps: first, betrothal, which involved the prospective groom traveling from his father's house to the home of the prospective bride, paying the purchase price, and thus establishing the marriage covenant; second, the groom returning to his father's house and remaining separate from his bride for twelve months, during which time he prepared the living accommodations for his wife in his father's house; third, the groom's coming for his bride at a time not known exactly to her; fourth, his return with her to the groom's father's house to consummate the marriage and to celebrate the wedding feast for the next seven days (during which the bride remained closeted in her bridal chamber).

In Revelation 19:7–9 the wedding feast is announced, which, if the analogy of the Hebrew marriage customs means anything, assumes that the wedding has previously taken place in the father's house. Today the church is described as a virgin waiting for her bridegroom's coming (2 Cor. 11:2); in Revelation 21 she is designated as the wife of the Lamb, indicating that previously she has been taken to the groom's father's house. Pretribulationists say that this requires an interval of time between the Rapture and the Second Coming. Granted, it does not say seven years' time, but it certainly argues against posttribulationism, which has no time between the Rapture and Second Coming.

(2) Does the word "saints" refer to Church Age saints? Actually the appearance of the word "saints" in chapters 4–18 does not prove anything until you know what saints they are. There were saints (godly ones) in the Old Testament (Ps. 16:3); there are saints today (1 Cor. 1:2); there will be saints in the Tribulation years (Rev. 13:7, etc.). The question is: Are the saints of this Church Age distinct from saints of the Tribulation period (pretribulationism) or not (posttribulationism)? The uses of the word will not answer the question.

(3) Do other phrases identify Tribulation believers with Church Age saints to indicate the church will go through the Tribulation? Such phrases include "die in the Lord" (Rev. 14:13; cf. "dead in Christ" of 1 Thes. 4:16–18), "who keep the commandments of God" (Rev. 12:17; 14:12; cf. 1:9). To use these similarities to prove that the church will be present in the Tribulation requires that similarity means sameness (a major assumption). On the other hand, one would expect distinct groups of saints (i.e., church saints and Tribulation saints) to be described in similar ways since they are all saints.

The same holds true for the use of the word "elect" or "chosen." Some have concluded that since the elect are mentioned as being in the Tribulation in Matthew 24:22, 24, and 31, the church will go through the Tribulation. But what elect people are meant? The heathen king Cyrus was called God's anointed (Isa. 45:1). So was Christ (Ps. 2:2). Israel was called God's chosen one (Isa. 45:4) even though the nation was a mixture of redeemed and unredeemed people. Christ is also God's chosen One (42:1). So is the church (Col. 3:12). So are some angels (1 Tim. 5:21). All elect are not the same, and the chosen ones of the Tribulation days do not have to be the same as the elect of the church simply because the same term is used of both groups.

C. Second Thessalonians 1:5–10 Is Best Interpreted as Teaching Posttribulationism

Posttribulationists understand this passage to say that "Paul places the release of Christians from persecution at the posttribulational return of Christ to judge unbelievers, whereas according to pretribulationism this release will occur seven years earlier."[3] In other words, since release comes at the Second Coming and release is connected with the Rapture, the Rapture must be at the same time as the Second Coming.

Let us examine the posttribulationist's answers to three questions about this passage.

(1) What is the subject of Paul's discussion in these verses? The posttribulational answer is release for Christians from persecution.

(2) When will this release occur? At the posttribulational return of Christ.

(3) What group of people will experience this release? Obviously, just those Christians who survive the Tribulation and are alive at the posttribulational Rapture.

First of all, observe the posttribulational answer to question 3. The passage only addresses the release of Christians living at the conclusion of the Tribulation. If that is true, why did Paul seemingly ignore the Thessalonians, who had suffered persecution and who had already died? Death was the means of release for them. Indeed, why did he not mention that avenue of release, which some of those to whom he was writing might yet experience? To be sure, the rapture of the living will bring release from persecution, but only a relatively small percentage of believers will ever experience that means of release, since most will have died prior to the Rapture. If release was Paul's chief concern here, and if that release will come at the posttribulational Rapture, then Paul was offering that hope of release to a very small group of believers.

Viewing this passage from a posttribulational slant, one must conclude that the release for Christians is connected with flaming judgment on unbelievers. It is not described in terms of meeting the Lord and forever being with Him, nor in terms of a resurrection for those who have died, as other Rapture passages describe it. Obviously if one's enemies are punished, then there will be release from their persecution. But the point is this: where is the Rapture described in this passage at all? The judgmental aspect of the Second Coming is given the prominence, and though, according to posttribulationism, the Rapture is the initial part of the Second Coming, that initial part is *entirely absent* from this discussion.

If Paul so clearly believed in a posttribulational Rapture, then why did he not at least mention that Rapture in passing since it is the moment of Rapture that brings release, not the following judgment on the enemies of God? Christians who live through the Tribulation (if posttribulationism be correct) will be released from persecution the instant they are raptured, *whether or not* Christ judges their enemies at that same time.

Notice some of the words in this passage that emphasize God's judging of His enemies: "righteous judgment" (2 Thess. 1:5), "just" (v. 6), "repay" (v. 6), "affliction" (v. 6), "flaming fire" (v. 7), and "retribution" (v. 8). This vocabulary is strangely absent from the Rapture passages of John 14:1–3; 1 Corinthians 15:51–58; and 1 Thessalonians 4:13–18. Actually the Rapture can be found in this passage only if one's eschatological scheme superimposes it there. Exegesis does not produce the Rapture from this passage.

Why is the posttribulationists' use of this passage so jumbled? Simply because they have answered the first question wrongly. That question was, What is the subject of Paul's discussion here? And the answer is not, as posttribulationists say, the release of Christians from persecution.

The subject of the passage is not release but vindication. Paul did not focus on when or how the persecuted Thessalonians will be relieved of persecution; rather, he assured them that God will judge His enemies and thereby vindicate those who have suffered.

One of the most spectacular displays of God's judging will occur at the second coming of Christ when the armies of the world arrayed at Armageddon are defeated by Him and when all living people will have to appear before Him (Ezek. 20:33–44; Matt. 25:31–46). It is on those people living at that time that vengeance will fall. Dead rejectors of Christ will not be judged until after the Millennium at the Great White Throne. Looking back, we know for a fact that none of the unsaved who actually persecuted the Thessalonians will be judged at the Second Coming but at the Great White Throne.

Since vindication is the subject, that explains why Paul did not mention that Rapture in this passage, for the Rapture is not a time of vindication of God's righteousness by judging the world. It is a time of release, of hope, of meeting the Lord. Some Thessalonians had found release through death even before Paul wrote. Eventually all of them found it that way. Since the first century, many persecuted Christians have found the same release through death. Some will find it at the pretribulational Rapture. But only those believers living at the end of the Tribulation will find it then, not because a Rapture takes place then, but because they successfully pass the judgments and see their enemies condemned.

But if vindication at the Second Coming falls on a relatively small group of Christ's enemies (think, by comparison, of the many who have opposed Him through the centuries), why should this particular time of vindication be given such prominence? Simply because the end of the Tribulation brings to a climax the long rebellion of mankind, a rebellion that will be halted by the personal intervention of the Lord. Not all of the Lord's enemies will be judged then, but those who will be are the epitome of rebellion. Awful as the persecution of the Thessalonians may have been, horrible as subsequent persecutions of believers have been and are, those in the past or present do not compare with that which will transpire during the Tribulation period.

Think of an analogy. Antichrists were present in the first century (1 John 2:18). Antichrists have come and gone throughout the centuries. But one great Antichrist is yet to appear on the scene of history, and he will be the epitome of opposition to God. Other antichrists are now in hades awaiting the judgment at the end of the Millennium that will cast them into the lake of fire forever. But the coming great Antichrist will be judged at the Second Coming, and when he is, God will be vindicated over all antichrists, though their particular judgment will occur much later.

All persecutors of believers will be judged later, as well. The judgment of those living at the Second Coming will vindicate God's righteousness with respect to them and to all persecutors who died before them.

If death or the Rapture brings release from personal persecution, why should believers be concerned with this future vindication? Because the case against persecutors cannot be closed until Christ is vindicated and righteousness prevails. Persecution may cease when death occurs, but the case against the persecutors is not closed until they are judged. And believers are concerned not only about relief but about vindication.

Notice a biblical example of that principle. Hear the Tribulation martyrs in heaven, before the end of the Tribulation, crying out to God for vindication (Rev. 6:9–11). "When will You settle the score against those who killed us?" they ask. Of course, they have already obtained release through physical death and are in heaven; yet they are concerned about vindication. And the Lord replies that they will have to wait a little longer for that vindication until others are also martyred on earth.

In 1 Thessalonians 1:10 and 5:9, Paul extended the hope and assurance of escape from wrath by means of a pretribulational Rapture. In 2 Thessalonians 1, he assured his readers that the enemies of the Lord will be judged.

In summary, chapter 1 does not teach that release from persecution will necessarily occur at the same time as the Second Coming. It does not picture the Rapture at all but focuses on the judgment on the wicked and the vindication of Christ that will occur at the Second Coming. That vindication gives assurance to saints of all ages that righteousness will prevail.

NOTES

1. Alexander Reese, *The Approaching Advent of Christ* (Grand Rapids: Kregel, 1975); George E. Ladd, *The Blessed Hope* (Grand Rapids: Eerdmans, 1956); and Robert H. Gundry, *The Church and the Tribulation* (Grand Rapids: Zondervan, 1973).
2. Ladd, *The Blessed Hope,* 70.
3. Gundry, *The Church and the Tribulation,* 113.

Chapter 90
THE MILLENNIUM

To build the kingdom on the first coming of Christ produces a theological error with many serious ramifications. By kingdom, I mean the rule of Messiah on earth as promised to David (2 Sam. 7:12–16). To claim that Christ established this Davidic kingdom at His first advent requires a deliteralizing of the promises made to David and results in confusion between the church and the kingdom. Among other things, church ethics and kingdom ethics are intermixed, usually with the result that kingdom ethics are promoted more than church ethics. Thus Christians are urged to live the kingdom here and now.

That mistake was made by some during the earthly life of Christ (Luke 19:11). The truth is that the messianic kingdom will be inaugurated at the second coming of Christ. At that time the land promise made to Abraham and his descendants will be fulfilled (Gen. 15:18–21). Then the promise made to David that his descendant (Messiah) will sit on the throne of the kingdom forever will be fulfilled. Without a Millennium in which all these promises can be fulfilled, the promises have to be canceled for some reason or be fulfilled in Israel's past or in the present nonliterally.

I. THE LENGTH OF THE MILLENNIUM

Six times in Revelation 20:2–7 the length of the Millennium is stated to be 1,000 years. The repetition of this figure underscores both its literalness and its importance. George E. Ladd, a premillennialist who denies the literalness of the figure, says: "It is difficult to understand the thousand years for which he [Satan] was bound with strict literalness in view of the obvious symbolic use of numbers in Revelation. A thousand equals the third power of 10—an ideal time."[1] Apparently Augustine first conceived of 1,000, the cube of 10, as representing the perfection or fullness of time.[2] Amillennialists usually interpret the number in this same manner. One may properly ask why 10 raised to the third power is ideal instead of 10 raised to the tenth power, or some other power? Furthermore, to deny the literalness of the number because Revelation is a symbolic book is to ignore that not everything in the book is symbolic, and therefore it would be necessary to give reasons why any given passage is symbolic. There is no reason to reject the literal meaning of 1,000 as indicating the length of the millennial reign of Christ.[3]

II. THE GOVERNMENT OF THE MILLENNIUM

A. The Type of Government

The government of the messianic, millennial kingdom will be a theocracy. This is the same form of government God used for Israel in Old Testament times; only in the Millennium the Lord Jesus Christ will personally and visibly reign over the affairs of all mankind (Dan. 7:14). His rule will be as a benevolent despot (Rev. 19:15). As a result, there will be perfect and complete justice for all, and sin will be immediately punished (Isa. 11:4; 65:20).

B. The Center of Government

The topography of the earth will be changed by the time the kingdom begins to function, and the city of Jerusalem will be the center of government (Isa. 2:3). That city will be exalted (Zech. 14:10); it will be a place of great glory (Isa. 24:23); it will be the site of the temple (33:20) and the joy of the whole earth (Ps. 48:2). Jerusalem, scene of so much war and turmoil both in the past and present and victim of future judgments during the Tribulation, will never again need to fear for her safety (Isa. 26:1–4).

C. The Rulers in the Government

David will apparently be a regent in the millennial kingdom. A number of prophecies speak of David's important place in the kingdom (Jer. 30:9; Ezek. 37:24–25). Apparently David, who with other Old Testament believers will be resurrected at the second coming of Christ, will act as a prince under the authority of Christ, the King.

Authority over the twelve tribes of Israel will be vested in the hands of the Twelve Apostles (Matt. 19:28). Other princes and nobles will likewise share in governmental duties (Isa. 32:1; Jer. 30:21). It seems too that many others of lesser rank will have responsibilities in various departments of the kingdom government. The Parable of the Minas (Luke 19:11–27) indicates that those who have proved their faithfulness will be given much authority. The church, too, will have a part in governing the earth (Rev. 5:10). Though many of the normal procedures of government will be carried out by subordinates, Christ will be King over all.

D. The Subjects of the Government

The first subjects of the rule of Christ during the kingdom will be the Jews and Gentiles who survive the Tribulation and enter the kingdom in earthly bodies. At the very beginning of the Millennium all the people on earth will be redeemed, for all unredeemed will have been judged at Christ's return. Of course, babies will be born right away so that in a few years there will be many who will be of age to decide for themselves their own spiritual relation to the King. They will have to be subject to Him at least outwardly, but whether they give heart allegiance will be a matter of personal choice. All will have to accept Him as King; some will also accept Him as personal Savior. All of these people will be living in mortal bodies. Resurrected saints will, of course, have resurrection bodies, not subject to physical limitations. This also means they will not contribute to space, food, or governmental problems during the Millennium.

III. THE CHARACTERISTICS OF THE MILLENNIUM

A. Spiritual

Some allege that the millennial kingdom cannot be a spiritual one if it is earthly. But "earthly" and "spiritual" are not necessarily mutually exclusive. If the two concepts were incompatible, Christians today could not be expected to live spiritual lives in earthly bodies. During the Millennium, God will join the spiritual and the earthly in a full display of His glory on this earth. The earthly kingdom will manifest the highest standards of spirituality.

B. Righteous

Our Lord will be a King who reigns in righteousness (Isa. 32:1). Righteousness will be the belt of His loins (11:5). With righteousness He shall judge the poor (11:4; 16:5). Zion shall be called the city of righteousness (1:26). Only the righteous shall enter the kingdom at its inauguration (Matt. 25:37), and those who thirst after righteousness shall be filled (5:6).

C. Peaceful

As a consequence of righteousness, the Millennium will be an era of peace. Former enemies, like Egypt, Israel, and Assyria, will be at peace with each other (Isa. 19:23–25). Jerusalem, site of many conflicts throughout the centuries, will be at peace (Zech. 8:4–5). Indeed, the whole earth will be at peace (Isa. 2:4). One ramification of this will be the elimination of defense budgets, which will release resources for other purposes.

D. Prosperous

The earth will be increasingly productive throughout the Millennium as wilderness and desert places become useful (Isa. 35:1–7). One harvest will be followed by another (Amos 9:13–14). Social needs and injustices will be eliminated (Ps. 72:12–13). The curse to which the earth was subjected when Adam sinned will be reversed, though not completely lifted until the end of the Millennium when death will be finally conquered.

E. Religious

Full knowledge of the Lord will cover the earth during the Millennium (Isa. 2:2–3). Apparently sacrifices will again be offered in a temple which will be built and in operation during the Millennium (Ezek. 40–48). Premillennialists understand these sacrifices as a means of memorializing the death of Christ. Religious holidays will also be observed during the Millennium (46:1–15; Zech. 14:16).[4]

IV. WHAT THE MILLENNIUM WILL MEAN TO CHRIST

In premillennial eschatology much is made of what the Millennium will mean to the world, to Jerusalem, to Palestine, to Israel, to the nations, etc., and rightly so, for it will affect many changes for good in the entire earth. But there is another perspective perhaps more important to consider: What will the Millennial Age mean to our Lord?

In Psalm 2:7–8 King Jesus was promised authority to rule the earth in righteousness. Certainly He did not see that promise fulfilled during His first advent, though He paid the price of His own life for it. In Revelation 5 He is proclaimed worthy to take the sealed book, open it, and receive the inheritance that is rightfully His. This will be fulfilled when He comes again (11:15).

Why is an earthly kingdom necessary? Did He not receive His inheritance when He was raised and exalted in heaven? Is not His present rule His inheritance? Why does there need to be an earthly kingdom? Because He must be triumphant *in the same arena* where He was seemingly defeated. His rejection by the rulers of this world was on this earth (1 Cor. 2:8). His exaltation must also be on this earth. And so it shall be when He comes again to rule this world in righteousness. He has waited long for His inheritance; soon He shall receive it.

NOTES

1. George E. Ladd, *A Commentary on the Revelation of John* (Grand Rapids: Eerdmans, 1971), 262.
2. Augustine, *The City of God* 20.7.
3. See Jack S. Deere, "Premillennialism in Revelation 20:4–6," *Bibliotheca Sacra* 135, (January–March 1978): 58–73.
4. For a detailed discussion of these matters see J. Dwight Pentecost, *Things to Come* (Grand Rapids: Zondervan, 1958), 512–31.

Chapter 91
FUTURE JUDGMENTS

In the program of God, there are several judgments yet in the future. It is not accurate to speak of one great Judgment Day to come, for these future judgments will occur at different times.

I. JUDGMENT OF BELIEVERS' WORKS

A. The Scriptures Involved

Two principal passages recount the fact and details of this judgment (1 Cor. 3:10–15; 2 Cor. 5:10). Other relevant passages include Romans 14:10; 1 Corinthians 4:1–5; 9:24–27; 1 Thessalonians 2:19; 2 Timothy 4:8; James 1:12; 1 Peter 5:4; and Revelation 2:10; 3:11; 4:4, 10.

B. The Judgment Itself

Though not specifically stated, this judgment will apparently take place immediately after the Rapture of the church, since the twenty-four elders who likely represent believers have their crowns in the scene in heaven at the beginning of the Tribulation (Rev. 4:4, 10). Further, when the bride returns with Christ at His second coming, she is clothed with the righteous deeds that have survived the examination of this judgment (19:8).

The site of this judgment is the bema of Christ. Earthly bemas were raised, thronelike platforms on which rulers or judges sat when making speeches (Acts 12:21) or hearing and deciding cases (18:12–17).

Only believers will stand in this judgment, for Paul made clear that it relates to those who have built on the Foundation, Jesus Christ (1 Cor. 3:11–12).

The nature of the believer's works will be examined in this judgment to distinguish worthy works from worthless ones. These works are the deeds done by the believer during his Christian life. All will be reviewed and examined. Some will pass the test because they were good; others will fail because they were worthless. Both good and bad motives will be exposed; then every believer will receive praise from God (1 Cor. 4:5). What grace!

C. The Outcome of Judgment

The outcome will be either reward or deprivation of reward. Salvation is not in question, for those deprived of reward "shall be saved, yet so as through fire" (1 Cor. 3:15). Yet, as mentioned above, apparently every believer will have done some things that God can praise.

Nevertheless, the deprivation is real and may involve forfeiture and shame. Certainly it means forfeiting rewards that otherwise might have been received. The word *zemioo* in 1 Cor. 3:15 carries no idea of suffering in the sense of physical or mental suffering. Its basic idea is loss in the sense of forfeiture of reward that could have been received.[1]

John clearly taught that rewards may be lost because of unfaithfulness during one's lifetime (2 John 8). His concern was that his readers would receive a full reward, that is, receive all that could be theirs through continued faithfulness. This same idea of loss is part of Paul's analogy of the Judgment Seat with running a race (1 Cor. 9:24–27). His concern was that he not be disapproved, that is, do nothing that would make him unworthy to receive rewards. Perhaps even more vividly John wrote about the possibility of a believer being ashamed at Christ's coming (1 John 2:28). "The passive voice coupled with the expression *autou* suggests that a believer withdraws in shame. It suggests a shrinking back from Christ, perhaps from a sense of guilt, with the believer producing the action [rather than Christ putting the believer to shame]."[2]

Summarizing in a very balanced way, Hoyt concluded as follows:

> The Judgment Seat of Christ might be compared to a commencement ceremony. At graduation there is some measure of disappointment and remorse that one did not do better and work harder. However, at such an event the overwhelming emotion is joy, not remorse. The graduates do not leave the auditorium weeping because they did not earn better grades. Rather, they are thankful that they have been graduated, and they are grateful for what they did achieve. To overdo the sorrow aspect of the Judgment Seat of Christ is to make heaven hell. To underdo the sorrow aspect is to make faithfulness inconsequential.[3]

II. JUDGMENT OF OLD TESTAMENT SAINTS

Daniel 12:1–3 speaks of the Tribulation period (v. 1), resurrections of the righteous and the wicked (v. 2), and rewards for the righteous (v. 3). Many understand the resurrection and reward of the righteous to refer to the resurrection and judgment of believers of the Old Testament at the conclusion of the Tribulation. New Testament revelation places the resurrection and judgment of the wicked of all time at the conclusion of the Millennium (Rev. 20:11–15). Of course it is not unusual for Old Testament prophets to place side by side events that later revelation separates by some period of time.

It is possible that Daniel 12:1–3 refers only to the resurrection and rewarding of Jewish believers of the Tribulation days. They will be rewarded for having insight for seeing through Antichrist's deception and for leading others to faith during the Tribulation days.

III. JUDGMENT OF SAINTS OF THE TRIBULATION PERIOD

Revelation 20:4–6 relates the resurrection of saints of the Tribulation period who died during that time. Because of their opposition to Antichrist's program, they were martyred, but God raises them from the dead just before the Millennium begins. No specific mention is made of a judging and rewarding; it can only be assumed to take place at the time of resurrection. (The phrase "judgment was given to them" in v. 4 refers not to being judged but to the activity of saints judging people in the millennial government.)

IV. JUDGMENT OF JEWISH SURVIVORS OF THE TRIBULATION

Before the inauguration of the millennial kingdom, the survivors of the Tribulation, both Jewish and Gentile, must be judged in order to ensure that only believers will enter the kingdom.

The judgment of Jewish survivors is described in Ezekiel 20:34–38 and illustrated in Matthew 25:1–30. Ezekiel states that it will occur after all surviving Israelites have been regathered from the ends of the earth to the land of Palestine. Christ will cause them to "pass under the rod" (see Lev. 27:32) to purge out the rebels. As a result, those rebels (unsaved) will not enter the land of Israel (Ezek. 20:38) but will be cast into the outer darkness (Matt. 25:30). In contrast, those who successfully pass through this judgment will enter the millennial kingdom to enjoy the blessings of the New Covenant (Ezek. 20:37). This group will not be given resurrection bodies at this time, but will go into the kingdom in their earthly bodies and will become the parents of the first millennial Jewish babies.

V. JUDGMENT OF GENTILE SURVIVORS OF THE TRIBULATION

Also at the second advent of Christ, Gentile survivors of the Tribulation will be judged by Him. Matthew 25:31–46 describes this in detail. Joel predicted that it would take place in the "valley of Jehoshaphat" (Joel 3:2), which may refer to the Kidron Valley on the east side of Jerusalem. Jehoshaphat simply means "Yahweh judges."

Both passages say that these Gentiles will be judged for their treatment of Israel during the Tribulation period. Christ is the Judge; the Gentiles are being judged; by all rapture schemes the church has already been raptured to heaven; the "brethren," the treatment of whom becomes the basis for the judgment, can only refer to Christ's natural brethren, other Jewish people (Rom. 9:3). For a Gentile to treat any Jewish person with kindness during the Tribulation will place his life in jeopardy. No one will do this merely out of a beneficent attitude, but only out of a redeemed heart. Therefore, this is not a judgment of works, but of genuine faith that produced such selfless works (or the lack of it which produced no such works).

Those who lack saving faith and demonstrate that lack by not doing good works will be sent to the lake of fire. Those whose good deeds prove the presence of saving faith will enter the kingdom. Like the Jewish survivors of the preceding judgment, they will enter in earthly bodies and become parents of the first millennial Gentile babies.

You will notice that I have understood this judgment to concern individual Gentiles, and not, as some translations imply, national groups of people. The word used in the passage is translated in the New Testament by "people" two times, "heathen" five times, "nation" sixty-four times, and "Gentiles" ninety-three times. Other references to a judgment at the second advent of Christ depict a judgment of individuals (Matt. 13:30, 47–50).

VI. JUDGMENT OF SATAN AND FALLEN ANGELS

Satan and his angels will also be judged, evidently at the conclusion of the millennial kingdom. To be sure, Satan has had other sentences passed on him, but this will be his final one that confines him forever in the lake of fire (Matt. 25:41; Rev. 20:10). The angels who are judged at this time also will experience the same fate (Jude 6–7). Believers will apparently be associated with the Lord in judging (1 Cor. 6:3).

VII. JUDGMENT OF THE UNSAVED DEAD

At the conclusion of the millennial reign of Christ, unbelievers of all time will be raised and judged. Their resurrection is the resurrection of judgment spoken of by the Lord in John 5:29. Their judgment will take place before a Great White Throne (Rev. 20:11–15). Their Judge is the Lord Christ (see John 5:22, 27).

Those judged are simply called "the dead"—unbelievers (in contrast to "the dead in Christ," which refers to believers). This judgment will not separate believers from unbelievers, for all who will experience it will have made the choice during their lifetimes to reject God. The Book of Life that will be opened at the Great White Throne judgment will not contain the name of anyone who will be in that judgment. The books of works that will also be opened will prove that all who are being judged deserve eternal condemnation (and may be used to determine degrees of punishment). It is not that all their works were evil, but all were dead works, done by spiritually dead people. It is as if the Judge will say, "I will show you by the record of your own deeds that you deserve condemnation." So everyone who will appear in this judgment will be cast into the lake of fire forever.

NOTES

1. See A. T. Robertson and Alfred Plummer, *A Critical and Exegetical Commentary on the First Epistle of St. Paul to the Corinthians* (Edinburgh: T. & T. Clark, 1914), 65.
2. Samuel L. Hoyt, "The Negative Aspects of the Christian's Judgment," *Bibliotheca Sacra* 137 (April–June 1980): 129–30.
3. Ibid., 131.

JUDGMENT	TIME	PLACE	PERSONS	BASIS	RESULTS	SCRIPTURE
Believers' Works	Between Rapture and Second Coming	*Bema* of Christ	Believers in Christ	Works and walk of the Christian life	Rewards or loss of rewards	1 Cor. 3:10–15; 2 Cor. 5:10
Old Testament Saints	End of Tribulation/ Second Coming		Believers in Old Testament times	Faith in God	Rewards	Dan. 12:1–3
Tribulation Saints	End of Tribulation/ Second Coming		Believers of Tribulation period	Faith in and faithfulness to Christ	Reign with Christ in the Millennium	Rev. 20:4–6
Living Jews	End of Tribulation/ Second Coming	Wilderness	Jews who survive the Tribulation	Faith in Christ	Believers enter kingdom; rebels are purged	Ezek. 20:34–38
Living Gentiles	End of Tribulation/ Second Coming	Valley of Jehoshaphat	Gentiles who survive the Tribulation	Faith in Christ as proved by works	Believers enter the kingdom; others go to lake of fire	Joel 3:1–2; Matt. 25:31–46
Satan and Fallen Angels	End of Millennium		Satan and those angels who follow him	Allegiance to Satan's counterfeit system	Lake of fire	Matt. 25:41; 2 Peter 2:4; Jude 6; Rev. 20:10
Unsaved People	End of Millennium	Before the Great White Throne	Unbelievers of all time	Rejection of God	Lake of fire	Rev. 20:11–15

Chapter 92
RESURRECTION AND ETERNAL DESTINY

I. THE FACT OF RESURRECTION

The Bible teaches clearly and in many places the truth of resurrection of the body. Bodily resurrection is primarily a biblical revelation, for Greek philosophy, which saw the body as a hindrance, taught only the immortality of the soul.

A. In the Old Testament

1. Job 19:25–27. During his affliction Job longed for death as a way of relief and wished that he could know there was some sort of hope beyond the grave that would make his present suffering tolerable (14:13–14). He expressed that hope in 19:25–27, a hope in a living God who would vindicate his case even after his death. He is sure that even after his body is decayed, he will see God from his flesh (v. 26). When the Hebrew preposition, *min,* is used with the verb "to see," it indicates the vantage point from which a person sees; i.e., Job expected to be in a body in his resurrected state.

2. Exodus 3:6. In His debate with the Sadducees, the Lord cited this verse as proof of the fact of resurrection (Matt. 22:31–32). The argument is based on the fact that when God identified Himself to Moses at the burning bush He did so by associating Himself with Abraham, Isaac, and Jacob in a living relationship that did not cease when those patriarchs died.

3. Psalm 16:8–11. In these verses David was writing of his own future resurrection. These verses were cited by Peter in Acts 2:25–28 and 31 as finding their ultimate fulfillment in the resurrection of Jesus Christ on the first Easter.

4. Psalm 49:14. Here the psalmist asserts that the righteous will ultimately triumph over the wicked, either in this life or in the life to come ("in the morning").

5. Isaiah 26:19. Here the prophet explicitly teaches the bodily resurrection of the redeemed.

6. Daniel 12:2. Here both the resurrection of the righteous and the resurrection of the wicked are taught. The New Testament reaffirms these two resurrections (John 5:28–29) but reveals they will not occur at the same time (Rev. 20:4–5).
7. Zechariah 14:5. If "holy ones" refers to believers, then this prophecy assures their resurrection, for they come with Christ at His second coming. Some, however, think it refers to angels, though possibly to both resurrected believers and angels.

B. In the New Testament

1. Matthew 16:21; 17:23; 20:19. Christ predicted His own resurrection on the third day after His death.
2. Matthew 22:31–32; John 2:19–22; 5:28–29; 11:25–26. Christ taught the truth of resurrection.
3. 1 Corinthians 15:20–24, 35–50; 2 Corinthians 5:1–4; Philippians 3:21; 1 Thessalonians 4:13–18. Paul not only taught bodily resurrection but also gave added details about the resurrection body.

II. THE ORDER OF RESURRECTIONS

As already noted, all bodily resurrections fall into two categories: the resurrection of life or the first resurrection, and the resurrection of condemnation or the second resurrection (Luke 14:13–14; John 5:28–29). These resurrections will not occur at the same time, so time is not the distinguishing feature; life or eternal death is.

A. The Resurrection of Christ

First in the order of resurrections was the resurrection of Christ. Though others had been raised from the dead before Christ, He was the first to rise from the grave with a body that was no longer subject to death (Rom. 6:9; Rev. 1:18). This is why Paul called Him the Firstborn from the dead (Col. 1:18). His resurrection is the first of many to come (1 Cor. 15:23).

B. The Resurrection of Those Who Are Christ's at His Coming

This resurrection will include several groups: the dead saints of this Church Age (1 Thess. 4:16), the dead saints of Old Testament times (Dan. 12:2), and martyrs of the Tribulation period (Rev. 20:4). These resurrections of the saints of all ages constitute the first resurrection (Rev. 20:6), the resurrection of life (John 5:29), or the resurrection of the righteous (Luke 14:14).

C. The Resurrection of Unsaved Dead at the End

The last group to be raised will include the unredeemed dead of all time, and they will be raised at the end of the millennial kingdom to stand before the Great White Throne in a judgment that will sentence all of them to the lake of fire (Rev. 20:11–14).

III. BETWEEN DEATH AND RESURRECTION

Strictly speaking, death is the separation of the material from the immaterial (James 2:26). In the case of every death, the body is disposed of, usually by placing it in a grave. But the immaterial facet of a person continues to exist for all eternity. The question before us now is, What is the state of the immaterial part between physical death and bodily resurrection?

A. For the Unredeemed Person in Old Testament Times

When such a person died, his soul, spirit, or immaterial nature went to sheol to wait for the resurrection of the body at the end of the Millennium. But the body is also said to be in sheol, for about half the times the word for sheol is used in the Old Testament it refers to the grave (see Num. 16:30, 33). Other times it refers to the place of departed spirits, of both the righteous (Gen. 37:35) and the wicked (Prov. 9:18). This is the place of darkness where the unredeemed dead are confined until death (which claims the body) and hades (the Greek equivalent of sheol, which claims the soul) give up their dead at the Great White Throne (Rev. 20:13).

B. For the Unredeemed Person in New Testament Times

The body goes to the grave, and the spirit goes to hades to wait for the resurrection of the body at the close of the Millennium (as with Old Testament unredeemed people) (Luke 16:23). Hades stands in contrast to heaven (Matt. 11:23; Luke 10:15) as a fiery place where there is weeping and gnashing of teeth (Matt. 13:40–42), a place of eternal torment (Mark 9:43–48), and a place of outer darkness where there is no light at all (Matt. 22:13).

C. For the Redeemed Person in Old Testament Times

In the case of the Old Testament saint, the debated question is, Where did his soul (spirit or immaterial nature) go at the time of death? Was he taken immediately into the presence of the Lord, or did he go to the saved compartment of sheol/hades from where he was taken into heaven when Christ descended into hades between His death and resurrection?

Hoyt expressed this latter option this way: "As a result of the resurrection and ascension of Christ, a reorganization took place in the intermediate state. There was a removal of all the righteous from the upper part of sheol-hades, and its gates were barred to entrance by any saved soul thereafter. From this time on paradise is above where Christ is, and the spirits of all the saved go to be with Christ at the moment of physical death."[1]

Several passages are cited in favor of this viewpoint. In Ephesians 4:9, Paul wrote that Christ "descended into the lower parts of the earth." Some understand this to mean that our Lord descended into hades between His death and resurrection to take those in the "saved compartment" of hades into heaven. However, the phrase "of the earth" may be an appositional phrase, meaning that Christ descended (at His Incarnation) into the lower parts (of the universe), namely the earth.

Also cited is the account of the rich man and Lazarus, which supposedly shows that both men went to hades, the rich man to punishment in one compartment of hades and Lazarus to bliss in the other compartment (which is labeled "Abraham's bosom" [Luke 16:22] in the story). Clearly the account teaches some important facts about death and hell: (a) there is conscious existence after death; (b) hell is a real place of torment; (c) there is no second chance after death; and (d) the dead cannot communicate with the living. But does it teach two compartments in hades? Not really, for Abraham's bosom is not said to be in hades but rather "far away" (v. 23) from it. Abraham's bosom is a figurative phrase for paradise, or the presence of God. It was paradise that was promised to the repentant thief by the Lord (Luke 23:43), not a blissful compartment of hades.

First Peter 3:18 is also linked with the supposed descent of Christ into sheol/hades. While there between His death and resurrection He announced His victory over sin and removed those in the paradise compartment to heaven. More likely, however, the verse means that the preincarnate Christ preached through Noah to those who, because they rejected that preaching, are now spirits in prison.

According to Harry Buis, the two-compartment theory was a development of the intertestamental period. "The main development of the doctrine of eternal punishment in this period comes from the fact that sheol is now divided into two compartments: one for the good, called paradise; the other for the evil, called gehenna."[2]

I believe that the Old Testament saint at death went immediately into the presence of the Lord. The repentant thief was promised he would be in paradise the day of his death (Luke 23:43), and paradise was the presence of the Lord (2 Cor. 12:4). At Christ's transfiguration Moses and Elijah appeared in His presence talking with Him.

Are we to understand that this conversation between Christ, Moses, and Elijah took place in the upper compartment of hades where Moses at least would have been until after the death of Christ? Are we to understand then that the transfiguration of Christ took place in paradise-hades? Are we to understand that Elijah was taken at his translation to sheol/hades and not heaven? I think not; rather, the Old Testament saint went immediately to heaven to wait for the resurrection of his body at the second coming of Christ.

IV. UNIVERSALISM

Simply stated, universalism states that sooner or later all will be saved. The older form of universalism, which originated in the second century, taught that salvation would come after a temporary period of punishment. The new universalism of our day declares that all men are now saved, though all do not realize it. Therefore the job of the preacher and the missionary is to tell people that they are already saved. Though Karl Barth denied that he taught the universal reconciliation of all men, he clearly did teach the universal election of all in Christ. Others plainly state, for example, that God's radical love pursues men until all are saved.

A. Biblical Evidence

Verses that universalists appeal to are John 12:32, "will draw all men to Myself"; 1 Corinthians 15:22, "in Christ all shall be made alive"; Philippians 2:11, "every tongue should confess"; and 1 Timothy 2:4, "who desires all men to be saved." But these verses do not teach that all people will ultimately be saved. John 12:32 says that the Cross of Christ makes possible the salvation of both Jews and Gentiles. Notice that the Lord in the same passage warned of judgment on rejecters (v. 48). First Corinthians 15:22 states that all who are in Christ will be raised, not that everybody will. Philippians 2:10–11 assures us that someday all people will acknowledge Jesus as Lord, but not necessarily as Savior. First Timothy 2:4 expresses God's desire that all be saved, but does not promise that all will be.

Universalists conveniently overlook other verses. Consider, for example, some of the Lord's own words. "He who does not obey the Son shall not see life, but the wrath of God abides on him" (John 3:36). "These will go away into eternal punishment, but the righteous into eternal life" (Matt. 25:46). Because the same word is used it is impossible to argue that eternal punishment is not unending in the same way that eternal life is.

Other New Testament passages that teach eternal damnation include 2 Thessalonians 1:8–9, "will pay the penalty of eternal destruction, away from the presence of the Lord"; 1 Corinthians 1:18; 4:3; and Hebrews 2:3. Everyone is either saved or lost, and anyone who dies without receiving Christ as personal Savior will be eternally condemned.

B. Theological Evidence

Some universalists prefer to argue theologically. They appeal to the nature of God as being totally love. How, then, they ask, could such a God condemn anyone either in this life or the life to come? God is too good to reject anyone. However, God's character involves not only love and goodness but also righteousness, holiness, and wrath. Universalists sacrifice God's righteousness to His love, which results in a god different from the God of the Bible.

Others argue that a just God would not give infinite punishment for finite sin. But this ignores that important principle that crime depends on the object against whom it is committed (an infinite God) as well as on the subject who commits it (finite man). Striking a post is not a culpable act as striking a human being is. All sin is ultimately against an infinite God and deserves infinite punishment.

V. CONDITIONALISM

Conditionalism or conditional immortality defines everlasting punishment as utter extinction into oblivion forever.

A. Biblical Arguments

Eternal destruction in such a passage as 2 Thessalonians 1:9 means, for the conditionalist, a quality of destruction, namely, extinction. "Eternal" is also understood to be a qualitative word mainly; thus, eternal fire means a fire that neither begins nor ends with the present age, which gives us no clue as to what happens to those thrown into it. Concerning the parallelism between eternal punishment and eternal life in Matthew 25:41 and 46, one conditionalist says that "we must be careful in pressing the parallel between 'eternal' life and 'eternal' punishment that we do not fall into any spirit of vindictiveness or ungodly joy at the fate of the wicked."[3] No further exegesis of that passage is offered. The same author states that there is "no clear exegetical basis in Luke 16 for any conclusion concerning the end of the wicked."[4]

This sample shows the kind of artificial exegesis conditionalists must resort to in order to substantiate their position.

B. Theological Arguments

Traditionalists usually understand death as separation. Conditionalists define it as nonlife, that is, eventual extinction. Of course, such a definition will not work in the case of the death of Christ, or of physical death, or of death to self.

Conditionalists insist that God alone has immortality (1 Tim. 6:16) and human beings, therefore, do not. However, a number of other attributes are predicated of God alone that do have correspondence in man (e.g., wisdom, Rom. 16:27).

The unanswerable question for the conditionalist is this: If the wicked are to suffer an unspecified length of punishment before being annihilated, could we not expect that such a climactic event as that annihilation be stated somewhere in the many eschatological passages in the Bible?

Will it be possible for believers to be without tears in heaven when some they knew on earth will be in hell? Apparently so, and only because the believer's own perspective will be so changed to realize the serious consequences of sin (Isa. 66:24).

Of course no one takes any delight in the eternal punishment of the wicked. That doctrine should serve to compel even more to persuade people to come to Christ to receive eternal life.

Notes

1. Herman A. Hoyt, *The End Times* (Chicago: Moody, 1969), 45.
2. Harry Buis, *The Doctrine of Eternal Punishment* (Philadelphia: Presbyterian and Reformed, 1957), 18. The following pages give proof from the apocalyptic literature of that period.
3. Edward William Fudge, *The Fire That Consumes* (Houston: Providential Press, 1983), 195.
4. Ibid., 208.

Section XIV
CENTRAL PASSAGES

Chapter 93
SOME CENTRAL PASSAGES FOR THE STUDY OF THEOLOGY

For the Christian, theology must be built on the Bible. We recognize that it is Scripture that gives us the doctrines of our faith. It does this not only by providing clear proof texts, but also by giving clear principles and by offering the data from which we can make deductions or inductions or logical conclusions. But the basis of all our theology, however derived, must be the Scripture.

Through the years of teaching I have tried to insist that students know not only how to state a doctrine correctly but also what are the principal biblical passages from which it is formulated.

In this chapter I want to list useful central passages with a brief description of their contribution to theology. If a person could use this list in both directions, he or she would have a great grasp of the Bible and theology. By "both directions" I mean: (a) if one were given a passage, he could describe its major doctrinal content; and (b) if one were asked where a doctrine is taught in the Bible, he could cite the most important references.

If this is "proof-texting" so be it. What is wrong with that?

> Both liberalism and neo-orthodoxy have strongly castigated the orthodox use of proof texts, and not with good reason. There is no doubt that the Scriptures quoted closely yield the doctrines of orthodoxy, not liberalism nor neo-orthodoxy. . . . The conservative insists the citation of Scripture is nothing more than a special application of "footnoting" which is standard scholarly procedure. . . . The liberal and neo-orthodox objection to the use of proof texts reflects a deep theological prejudice . . . rather than a rebuttal of a false method of scholarship. . . . The mere listing of proof texts is of no value unless each verse is underwritten by sound exegetical work. . . . Many of the older theologians were guilty of citing a verse in the Old Testament to prove something with reference to salvation and justification, and treating it as if it were as clear and lucid as something in Romans and Galatians. This is one of the most unhappy features of the older theologies which has been happily corrected by a much better sense of historical and progressive revelation, nor can the beneficial influence of dispensationalism be gainsayed at this point.[1]

AREA OF THEOLOGY	CENTRAL PASSAGES	THEMES IN THOSE PASSAGES
PROLEGOMENA		
	1 Cor. 2:10–16	Need for the Spirit's teaching
GENERAL REVELATION		
	Ps. 19:1–6	Revelation is world-wide and continuous
	Rom. 1:18–32	Revelation of the wrath of God
	Acts 14:17	The providence of God
	Matt. 5:45	The goodness of God
	Acts 17:28–29	God is intelligent and living
THE LIVING AND TRUE GOD		
His attributes	Ps. 90:2	Eternality
	James 1:17	Immutability
	Ps. 99	Holiness
	Ps. 139:7–11	Omnipresence
	1 John 1:5	God is light
	1 John 4:8	God is love
	John 4:24	God is spirit
His names	Gen. 1:1	Elohim
	Exod. 3:14	Yahweh
His triunity	Deut. 6:4	The unity and uniqueness of God
	Isa. 48:16	Suggestion of Trinity
	Matt. 28:18–20	Oneness (name) and threeness
	2 Cor. 13:14	Trinitarian benediction
THE BIBLE		
Its Inspiration	2 Tim. 3:16	Bible is God-breathed
	2 Pet. 1:21	Spirit moved human authors
	1 Tim. 5:18	Deut. 25:4 and Luke 10:7 linked together as "Scripture"

AREA OF THEOLOGY	CENTRAL PASSAGES	THEMES IN THOSE PASSAGES
	2 Pet. 3:16	Paul's writings called "Scripture"
	1 Cor. 2:13	Words of Bible are inspired
Its Inerrancy	Matt. 4:4	Every word came from God
	Matt. 5:17–18	Jot and tittle (KJV)
	Matt. 22:23–33	Tense of verb is accurate
	Matt. 22:41–46	Letters of words are accurate
	Gal. 3:16	Singular is accurate
Its Canonicity	Luke 11:51	The limits of the OT canon
Its Illumination	John 16:12–15; 1 Cor. 2:9–3:2	The Spirit's ministry in understanding the Bible
ANGELS		
	Eph. 3:10	Their ranking and organization
	Gen. 3:24	Cherubim
	Isa. 6:2	Seraphim
	Luke 1:26	Gabriel
	Jude 9	Michael the archangel
	Exod. 3	Angel of Yahweh
	Heb. 1:14	Their service
SATAN		
	Ezek. 28:11–19	His creation and sin
	Isa. 14:12–17	Details of his rebellion
	Matt. 4:1–11	His temptation of Christ
	John 12:31	Ruler of the world
	Rev. 12:10	Accuser of the brethren
	2 Cor. 4:4	Blinding unbelievers
	Eph. 6:11–18	Armor for believers

AREA OF THEOLOGY	CENTRAL PASSAGES	THEMES IN THOSE PASSAGES
DEMONS		
	Matt. 17:18; cf. Mark 9:25	Demons are unclean spirits
	Eph. 6:12	Their ranking and organization
	1 Tim. 4:1	Doctrines of demons
	Matt. 25:41	Destiny in lake of fire
MAN		
	Gen. 1:26–27	His creation by God
	Exod. 20:11	The days of Creation
	Matt. 19:4–5	Christ and creation of man
	1 Thess. 5:23; Heb. 4:12; James 2:26	Aspects of the immaterial nature of man
	Gen. 3:1–7	Original sin
	Gen. 3:8–24	Penalties for sin
SIN		
	Rom. 3:23; 1 John 3:4	The meaning of sin
	Eph. 2:3	Inherited sin
	Rom. 5:12–21	Imputation of sin
	Heb. 7:9–10	An example of imputation
	Rom. 3:9–18	Personal sins
JESUS CHRIST		
	John 8:58	His eternality
	Matt. 1:23; Luke 1:35	His Virgin Birth
	John 1:14	His Incarnation
	John 1:1; 10:30	His Deity
	Luke 2:52; Gal. 4:4	His humanity
	Phil. 2:7	His kenosis
	John 8:29; 1 Pet. 2:21–22	His sinlessness
	Heb. 4:15	His impeccability

AREA OF THEOLOGY	CENTRAL PASSAGES	THEMES IN THOSE PASSAGES
	Matt. 28:6	His resurrection
	Acts 1:9–11	His ascension
SALVATION		
	Eph. 1:4	Pretemporal
Election	Rom. 8:29–30	Predestination
	1 Pet. 2:8	Preterition
The Death of Christ	Mark 10:45	Substitution
	1 Pet. 1:18	Redemption
	2 Cor. 5:18–21	Reconciliation
	1 John 2:2	Propitiation
The Plan of God	Matt. 11:28	General call in Salvation
	Rom. 8:30	Effective call
	John 16:8–11	Conviction of the Spirit
	Acts 16:31	Faith
	Rom. 3:24	Justification
	Titus 3:5	Regeneration
	Gal. 4:5	Adoption
	2 Cor. 3:7–11	End of the Law
	Rom. 6:1–4	Union with Christ
Assurance/Security	1 John 5:10–13	Based on the Scripture
	Rom. 8:31–39	Because of the love of God
	Eph. 4:30	Because of the Spirit's seal
Extent of the Atonement	2 Pet. 2:1	Ransom paid for all people
	2 Cor. 5:19	Reconciliation for the world
	1 John 2:2	Propitiation for all
THE HOLY SPIRIT		
	John 16:13–14; 1 Cor. 2:10–11	His personality
	Acts 5:3–4	His Deity
	John 14:17	Contrast between OT and NT ministry of the Spirit

AREA OF THEOLOGY	CENTRAL PASSAGES	THEMES IN THOSE PASSAGES
	Matt. 12:22–37	Blasphemy against the Spirit
	Rom. 8:1; 1 Cor. 6:19	Indwelling
	1 John 2:20, 27	Anointing
	Eph. 4:30	Sealing
	1 Cor. 12:13	Baptism into the body
	1 Cor. 12:7–11	Gifts of the Spirit
	Eph. 5:18	Filling
	John 16:12–15	Teaching
	Gal. 5:22–23	Fruit of the Spirit
THE CHURCH		
	Acts 19:39, 41	A nonreligious assembly
	Acts 7:38	Israel as an assembly
	Eph. 1:22–23	Church, the body of Christ
	Rom. 16:5	Church in a house
	1 Cor. 1:2	Church in a city
	Acts 9:31; 1 Cor. 15:9	Church in a region
	1 Tim. 3:1–13	Qualifications for elders and deacons
	Titus 1:7–9	Qualifications for elders
	Acts 2:42; 1 Cor. 12–14	Activities of the church
	Matt. 18:15–20; 1 Cor. 5:6–8	Discipline by the church
THE FUTURE		
Postmillennialism	Dan. 2:35, 44	Stone fills the whole earth
Amillennialism	Gal. 6:16	Israel-church
Premillennialism	Rev. 20:1–7	1,000 years mentioned six times

AREA OF THEOLOGY	CENTRAL PASSAGES	THEMES IN THOSE PASSAGES
	Gen. 15:9–17	Ratification of unconditional covenant with Abraham
	2 Sam. 7:12–16	Covenant with David
	1 Thess. 4:13–18	The Rapture
Pretribulationalism	Rev. 3:10	Kept from the hour
	1 Thess. 5:1–11	Kept from the wrath
Against Partial Rapture	1 Cor. 15:51–52	All will be changed
The Millennium	Rev. 19:15	Christ the Ruler
	Isa. 2:1–4	Jerusalem the capital
	Isa. 11:4	Righteousness
	Isa. 35	Productivity
	Isa. 19:24–25	Peace
The Judgments	1 Cor. 3:10–15	Of believers
	Ezek. 20:34–38	Of Jewish survivors of the Tribulation
	Matt. 25:31–46	Of Gentile survivors of the Tribulation
	Rev. 20:11–15	Of unbelievers at the Great White Throne
	Matt. 25:46; 2 Thess. 1:8–9	Punishment is eternal

NOTE

1. Bernard Ramm, *Protestant Biblical Interpretation* (Boston: Wilde, 1950), 175–78.

Section XV
DEFINITIONS

Chapter 94
SOME DEFINITIONS FOR THE STUDY OF THEOLOGY

Precise definitions are the sign of careful theological thinking. Every definition must be an accurate reflection and summation of the biblical truth involved.

When insisting on good definitions from students, and especially when challenging a word that a student used because it was not the most precise one, I often received this retort: "It's only a matter of semantics. One word is as good as another." That retort is totally without merit. Definitions are very much a matter of semantics; therefore, one word is not necessarily as good as another. Accurate definitions have to be constructed with carefully chosen words. Sloppy formulation is never acceptable.

I have tried to generously sprinkle this work with accurate and concise definitions of various doctrines. In this section I have culled many of these definitions from the pages of this book and listed them in alphabetical order. After each definition I have placed the chapter number so that you can locate that subject in the body of the work for further study.

Adoption

Placing the believer in God's family as an adult son (52).

Aseity of God

His self-existence (6).

Amillennialism

View that holds that there will be no Millennium before the end of the world and that teaches a parallel development of good and evil until the end (79).

Anthropological argument for the existence of God

The several facets of man, and all of them together, demand some explanation as to their origin and argue for a being who is moral, intelligent, and living who could have produced man (5).

Arianism

Taught that the Son was generated by the Father and thus had a beginning (8, 68).

Arminianism

Teaches that Adam was created innocent, that we inherit from him pollution but not guilt or a sin nature, and that man has the ability to do good (36, 57).

Assurance

The realization that the believer does possess eternal life (57).

Attributes

Qualities that inhere in a subject (6).

Baptism of the Spirit

The Spirit's activity that joins the believer to the body of Christ at the time of salvation (64).

Barthianism

System of theology taught by Karl Barth (1886–1968). Emphasizes God sovereignly revealing Himself through the Word, which is ultimately Christ, the Bible being a fallible pointer to Christ (11, 68).

Biblical theology

Deals systematically with the historically conditioned progress of the self-revelation of God in the Bible (1).

Canon of Scripture

The collection of books that met certain tests and thus were considered authoritative, and are our rule of life (15).

Carnality

To exhibit the characteristics of an unsaved life either because one is an unbeliever or because, though a believer, one is living as an unsaved person (67).

Chalcedon

Church council (in 451) that formulated a definitive statement concerning the two natures of Christ and gave a clear affirmation of the deity of the Holy Spirit (68).

Church

An assembly of people who have been called together (69).

Church, local

An assembly of professing believers in Christ who have been baptized and who are organized to carry out God's will (72).

Conditionalism or conditional immortality

Everlasting punishment is utter extinction into oblivion (92).

Constantinople, Council of (381)

Produced a statement that affirmed the Holy Spirit's deity (8, 68).

Conviction

Ministry of the Holy Spirit that gives proof of the truth of the Christian message (56).

Cosmological argument for the existence of God

The universe around us is an effect that connotes an adequate cause to account for it (5).

Cosmos

That organized system headed by Satan that leaves God out and is a rival to Him (25).

Creationism

A view of the transmission of the immaterial aspect of man that teaches that God creates the soul at the moment of conception or birth and immediately unites it with the body (31).

Creationism, progressive

The same as threshold evolution (29).

Cultural mandate

Mankind is to bring all this world's structures under the lordship of Christ, demolishing all opposition against God (33).

Depravity, total

The unmeritoriousness of man in the sight of God (36).

Dichotomy

Man is viewed as a bipartite unity of material and nonmaterial entities (32).

Election

God's pretemporal choice of those who would be saved (54).

Elohim

Name of God that means the strong One, the mighty Leader, the supreme Deity (7).

Eternality of God

God's endless existence (6).

Evolution

The process of organization and development of all things from lower, simpler, or worse to higher, more complex, or better through natural means (29).

Evolution, theistic

God directed, used, and controlled the processes of naturalistic evolution to "create" the world and all that is in it (29).

Evolution, threshold

God stepped in to create at the major steps of history, but otherwise allowed the naturalistic processes of evolution throughout the long period of geologic time (29).

Faith

Giving credence, confidence, trust or holding something or someone as true (56).

Heart

The center and seat of life, both physical and psychical, including intellectual, emotional, volitional, and spiritual life (32).

Hermeneutics

The study of the principles of interpretation (16).

Holiness of God

God is separate from all that is unclean and evil, and He is positively pure and thus distinct from all others (6).

Impeccability

The inability of Jesus Christ to sin (45).

Inerrancy

The Bible tells the truth, which may include approximations, free quotations, the language of appearances, and different accounts of the same event as long as these do not contradict (12).

Inspiration

God superintended (or carried along) the human authors of the Bible so that they composed and recorded without error His message to mankind in the words of their original writings (10).

Justification

To announce a favorable verdict, to declare righteous (52).

Kenosis

Christ's emptying Himself of retaining and exploiting His status in the Godhead and taking on Himself humanity in order to die (44).

Kingdom, Davidic or messianic

The millennial kingdom on earth ruled by Messiah (70).

Kingdom, mystery form

Christendom during the time between the first and second comings of Christ (70).

Kingdom, spiritual

That into which all believers are placed in the Church Age (70).

Kingdom, universal

God's rule over the entire world (70).

Last days

The entire period from the first to the second coming of Christ (83).

Limited atonement or particular redemption

The effect of Christ's death for sin was limited to a particular group known as the elect (55).

Lordship salvation

The teaching that to be saved a person must not only trust Jesus as Savior but also the Lord of his or her life, submitting (or at least being willing to submit) his or her life to His sovereign authority (58).

Love of God

God's seeking the highest good and glory of His perfections (6).

Monarchianism, dynamic (adoptionism)

Belief that Jesus was a man endowed with special power by the Spirit at His baptism (8).

Monarchianism, modalistic (Sabellianism, Patripassianism)

The Persons of the Godhead were modes in which God manifested Himself (8).

Montanism

A movement around A.D. 170 that taught God was giving new revelation to people (68).

Omnipotence of God

He is all-powerful; He can do anything consistent with His own nature (6).

Omnipresence of God

God is everywhere present with His whole Being always (6).

Omniscience of God

God knows everything, things actual and things possible, effortlessly and equally well (6).

Ontological argument for the existence of God

Since the idea of a most perfect Being exists, it must come from a most perfect Being (5).

Ordinance

A God-ordained rite or symbol administered in the church (74).

Ordo salutis

The attempt to arrange in logical (not temporal) order the activities involved in applying salvation to the individual (56).

Pantheism

God is the mind or soul of the universe. Process theology teaches that His Being penetrates the whole universe, yet is not exhausted by it (6).

Pelagianism

Man was created neither sinful nor holy and with the capacity and will to choose freely to sin or to do good (36, 68).

Perseverance

The Calvinistic belief that a believer cannot fall away from grace but will continue (persevere) in good works to the end of his life (57).

Postmillennialism

The kingdom is now being extended in the world by preaching the Gospel so that the world will be Christianized for a millennial time after which Christ will return (78).

Predestination

God's pretemporal planning of the destiny of His children, the elect (54).

Premillennialism

The second coming of Christ will be followed by the establishing of His kingdom on earth for 1,000 years (80).

Preterition

The passing over of those not chosen to salvation (54).

Prolegomena

Prefatory remarks (1).

Propitiation

The turning away of the wrath of God because of the offering of Christ (51).

Rapture

The catching away of the church from earth to heaven (83).

Regeneration

The work of God that gives new life to the one who believes (56).

Repentance

A genuine, not superficial, change of mind about something, which is followed by some change (58).

Revelation, general

All that God has revealed in the world around us, including man (5).

Revelation, special

God's message in what was codified in the Bible as communicated by various means (5).

Salvation

Rescue, deliverance, remedy, especially from sin (49).

Sanctification

God setting the believer apart for Himself: positionally at salvation, progressively throughout life, and ultimately when the believer arrives in His presence in heaven (67).

Satan

Means adversary or opposer (22–25).

Security, eternal

The work of God that guarantees that the gift of salvation, once received, is forever and cannot be lost (57).

Semi-Pelagianism

Teaches that man retains a measure of freedom by which he can cooperate with the grace of God (36).

Simplicity of God

God is not a composite or compounded being (6).

Sin

Any defection from God's standards; missing the mark (34).

Socinianism

Denies the deity of Christ, predestination, original sin, and penal substitution (8, 36).

Soul

Can refer to the whole person, alive or after death; can designate the immaterial part of a person with its many feelings and emotions; an important focus of spiritual redemption and growth (32).

Spirit

Indicates the immaterial part of a person, not the whole, with its various functions and feelings; in Paul's thought it assumes prominence in relation to the spiritual life (32).

Systematic theology

The correlation of the data of biblical revelation as a whole in order to exhibit systematically the total picture of God's self-revelation (1).

Teleological argument for the existence of God

The organization of the world requires that someone planned it (5).

Toledo, Synod of

In 589 declared that the Holy Spirit proceeded from the Father and the Son (*filioque*) (8).

Traducianism

The view that holds that the transmission of the immaterial aspect of man is transmitted along with the body through the process of natural generation (31).

Trichotomy

View that man is composed of three parts: body, soul, and spirit (32).

Trinity

In the one living and true God there are three coeternal and coequal Persons, the same in substance but distinct in existence (8).

Vicarious

Someone taking the place of another (51).

Worship

The individual, corporate, public, or private service for the Lord, which is motivated by a reverence for and submission to Him who is totally worthy (75).

Yahweh

The active, self-existent God (7).

Index of Scripture

INDEX OF SUBJECTS

Moody Press, a ministry of the Moody Bible Institute,
is designed for education, evangelization, and edification.
If we may assist you in knowing more about Christ
and the Christian life, please write us without obligation:
Moody Press, c/o MLM, Chicago, Illinois 60610.